MOTOCOURSE

THE WORLD'S LEADING GRAND PRIX ANNUAL

HAZLETON PUBLISHING

CONTENTS

ACKNOWLEDGEMENTS

The Editor and staff of *Motocourse* wish to thank the following for their assistance in compiling the 1992-93 edition:
Henny Ray Abrams *(additional Grand Prix research, Brazil)*, Anne-Marie Gerber and Marc Pétrier (FIM), Paul Butler (IRTA), Carlo Pernat, Garry Taylor, Ian Mackay, Charlie Hennekam, Kay Edge, Dennis Noyes (Dorna), Stefano Zaragoni and Yves Jamotte (IRPA), Vic Monllau, Waldemar De Rin, Gunther Wiesinger, Hans van Loozenoord, Colleen Dooley, Dawn Lemon and many others.

Photographs published in *Motocourse 1992-93* have been contributed by:
Chief Photographer: **Malcolm Bryan**; Clive Challinor, David Collister, Adam Duckworth, Kel Edge, *Flick of the Wrist*, David Goldman, Patrick Gosling, Paul Kearney, *Kenny P*, Henk Keulemans, Nigel Kinrade, John McKenzie, Phil Masters, Hidenobu Takeuchi, *Two Plus Two*, Mark Wernham and James Wright.

The dust-jacket photograph shows Wayne Rainey in Australia on the Team Roberts Marlboro Yamaha he rode to a historic third title in succession.

The title page picture shows Michael Doohan riding his Rothmans Honda *en route* to his fourth straight win of the year at Jerez.

Pictured left: the great Eddie Lawson, who rode the Cagiva to a famous victory in the Hungarian Grand Prix.

Photos: Malcolm Bryan

PUBLISHER
Richard Poulter

EDITOR
Michael Scott

TECHNICAL EDITOR
Peter Clifford

EXECUTIVE PUBLISHER
Elizabeth Le Breton

ART EDITOR
Steve Small

PRODUCTION MANAGER
George Greenfield

PRODUCTION CONTROLLER
Peter Lovering

ADVERTISING CO-ORDINATOR
Jocelyne Bia

RESULTS AND STATISTICS
Kay Edge

CHIEF PHOTOGRAPHER
Malcolm Bryan

Motocourse is published by Hazleton Publishing, 3 Richmond Hill, Richmond, Surrey TW10 6RE.

Colour reproduction by Barrett Berkeley Ltd, London.

Printed in England by Richard Clay Ltd, Bungay, Suffolk.

ISBN: 0-905138-97-X

DISTRIBUTORS

UNITED KINGDOM
Reed Illustrated Books
Michelin House
81 Fulham Road
London SW3 6RB

NORTH AMERICA
Motorbooks International
PO Box 2
729 Prospect Ave.
Osceola
Wisconsin 54020, USA

AUSTRALIA
Technical Book and Magazine Co. Pty
289-299 Swanston Street
Melbourne
Victoria 3000
Universal Motor Publications
c/o Automoto Motoring Bookshop
152-154 Clarence Street
Sydney 2000
New South Wales

NEW ZEALAND
David Bateman Ltd
'Golden Heights'
32-34 View Road
Glenfield
Auckland 10

SOUTH AFRICA
Motorbooks
341 Jan Smuts Avenue
Craighall Park
Johannesburg

MOËT & CHANDON

FOREWORD
by WAYNE RAINEY

Photo: Malcolm Bryan

If anyone had said to me half way through the year that I'd be writing this Foreword for the third year in succession as World Champion, I'd have said they were nuts.

I guess the way things panned out was tough on Mick Doohan, and I really respect him and his efforts. But I know he also understands that things were tough on me earlier in the year. I started the season hurt, then it seemed to keep happening again.

By the mid-point I could have sworn that this just wasn't meant to be my year. But the one thing you learn in racing is that you should never give up, because anything can happen.

In fact, you can get tired of hearing that. But it's true, and it worked for me.

I need to thank all my sponsors, and Kenny Roberts and all the guys on my team. Together with Michelin and Yamaha they worked real hard to make us strong when we needed it most, at the end of the year.

I need to thank my wife Shae as well, who has been such a support in all my World Championships.

It's an honour to write the Foreword to *Motocourse*, because it's the book people will turn to again and again in the future to remember all the ups and downs of 1992.

I look forward to doing the same myself – but first I'll be putting all my efforts into getting ready for 1993. Now I want to make it four in a row.

'When I won in 1991, I vowed to
Kenny Roberts. And
one better with a fourth

Why

For next season Wayne will be riding the new improved '93 version of our all conquering YZR 50

EDITOR'S INTRODUCTION

BRAVE NEW WORLD CHAMPIONSHIP

LAST year, Grand Prix racing survived the biggest upheaval since its inception in 1949. At the end of 1991, the constant muttering within the ranks had hardened to open rebellion against FIM control. This was not the first attempted coup, but this one had been meticulously planned. And this time it was successful.

By the time the new season started, the FIM were effectively ousted and the architects of the brave new World Championship had handed control to Bernie Ecclestone. The sport had finally changed to become a coherent commercial entity first and foremost, and a sport only secondarily.

To the outside world, the change of emphasis was unnoticeable. The brave new TWP/Dorna/FIM World Championship began on time, and ran through to what was, in two out of the three solo classes, a riveting conclusion. The only change was that perhaps more people knew about GP racing – television coverage was more readily available worldwide, considerably helped in Britain by the increased accessibility of cable TV to augment the undersubscribed satellite stations.

Inside racing, in the final analysis, things weren't that much different either, at least for those at the sharp end. Familiar heroes on familiar bikes absorbed themselves and everybody watching with their game of I-can-go-faster-than-you-can.

Just as well, too, and just as well also that they were joined in the 500 class by privateers on a brave new breed of works bike replica, the Roc and Harris Yamaha V4s. The first truly competitive production racers in the class since the Suzuki RGs of one-and-a-half decades ago restored dwindling numbers at a stroke, and Yamaha are to be wholeheartedly thanked.

Sadly, not all their riders were brave, or new, or even fast; but even the slowest served a purpose by demonstrating the new financial viability of a privateer GP assault, a message certain to be heeded next year by better riders who this year were too cautious to abandon successful national careers for the deeper waters of the World Championships.

The racing, by and large, was excellent. A clean year, with no major organisational hiccups beyond the perennial and let us hope now terminal problems in Brazil, and no ghastly accidents. Even so, injury created an extraordinary start and finish to the 500 class, with Rainey hurting and luckless at the beginning, and Doohan ditto at the end. The crown went to Rainey and was well deserved; the same would have been true if Doohan had won it.

The biggest change came in both the style and substance of racing management. It is big business now, quite rightly, and as a result paddock life has changed for ever. It remains to be seen how quickly the crescendo of rules and restrictions will convert the once relaxed bike racing paddocks into the caviare concentration camps of Mr Ecclestone's other piece of racing property – F1 cars.

The year marked the finish of three careers that illuminated the closing of the FIM-dominated era.

Kyalami was the last race of quicksilver Carlos Lavado, the Venezuelan 250 star whose mercurial career included two World Championships and some of the most inspired 250 riding ever seen.

It was also a swansong for Wayne Gardner, a leading light of the rough, tough breed of daredevil riders, always going for it, throttle to the stop. Gardner was an acerbic presence in racing, and inspiring to watch as time and again he cast caution to the winds, never accepting defeat even when the bike or the tyres weren't up to victory. His last season was flawed by crashes but brilliantly finished.

And Eddie Lawson, a man of often incomprehensible but never hidden inner anger, who displayed a dedication to racing perfection that has carved his name in stone in GP history. Lawson – always smooth, always fast and always there – won three world titles on a Yamaha, one more on a Honda, and concluded his giant career as the central cog of Cagiva's final achievement of competitive status, with their first GP win, his 31st. He may miss racing more than he expects – and vice versa.

This Italian revival was echoed in the 250 and 125 classes, with Aprilia taking a clear technical lead over Honda, while Suzuki and newcomers Gilera added to the works bike contingent. The national success was celebrated by hordes of Italian riders, who dominated both classes. This upsurge, rivalled by that of the Spanish, was a welcome counterpoint to the American and Australian domination of the 500 class, and yet more proof that, no matter who was pulling the strings, GP racing is alive and very well.

Long may it continue.

Michael Scott
October 1992

Photo: Malcolm Bryan

Phalanx of 500s at Montmelo – once the racing began, it was obvious that the new regime did have some things very right.

A colourful, exciting record of Nigel Mansell's heroic progress to win the coveted 1992 Formula 1 World Championship for Drivers. One of the most popular sporting heroes Britain has ever produced, he achieved an almost unprecedented stranglehold on Formula 1 racing, winning five of the first eleven races of the season to take the title with five rounds remaining.
96 pages, over 90 colour photographs
ISBN: 1 874557 00 4 Price: £9.99

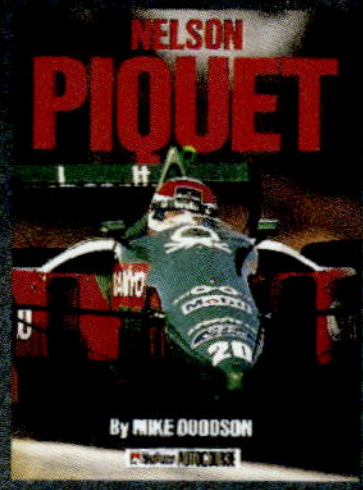

His long career in Formula 1 brought two World Championships with Brabham, followed by a third in a Williams four years later in 1987.
ISBN: 0 905138 81 3
112 pages Price: £12.95

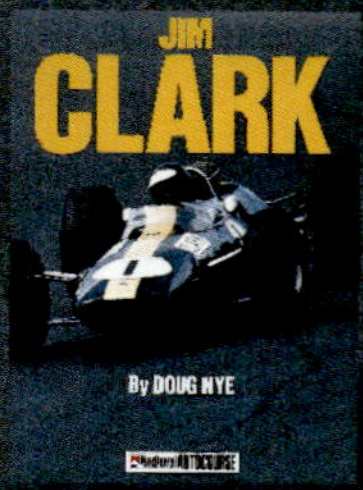

From 1962 until his tragic fatal accident at Hockenheim in 1968 he was absolutely the standard-setter of his time, twice winning the World Championship.
ISBN: 0 905138 77 5
112 pages Price: £12.95

AUTOCOURSE DRIVER PROFILES

Each volume contains approximately 20 colour and 80 black and white photographs.

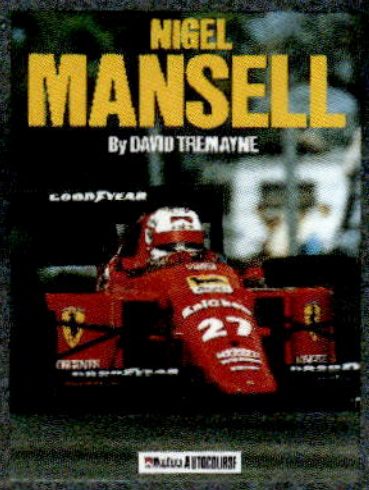

The remarkable career story of the 1992 World Champion up to the end of the 1989 season describing the fierce ambition which was eventually rewarded with Grand Prix victory and universal recognition.
ISBN: 0 905138 67 8
112 pages Price: £11.95

Hailed as the greatest Formula 1 driver of all time, his single-minded approach to racing has produced three World Championships in four years.
ISBN: 0 905138 92 9
112 pages Price: £12.95

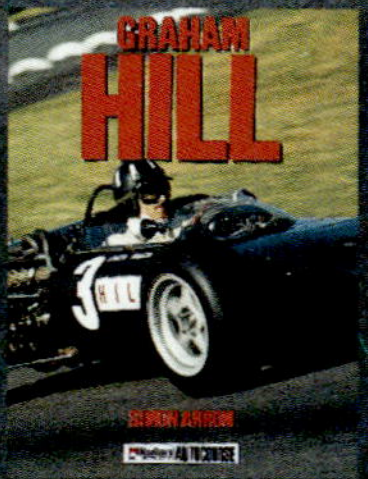

During a Grand Prix career that spanned 17 seasons he twice became World Champion and also won the Indianapolis 500 and the Le Mans 24 Hours.
ISBN: 0 905138 86 4
96 pages Price: £12.95

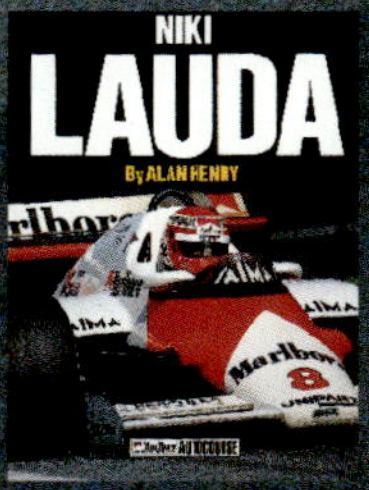

One of the most pragmatic men ever to drive a racing car, this volume reflects the shrewd mind, iron determination and wry sense of humour of this three-times World Champion.
ISBN: 0 905138 68 6
112 pages Price: £11.95

Winner of three World Championships in a McLaren, Alain Prost holds the record for the greatest number of Grand Prix wins.
ISBN: 0 905138 69 4
112 pages Price: £11.95

His pure genius for driving, with no apparent sense of fear, inspired the adulation which has made him a legend.
ISBN: 0 905138 70 8
112 pages Price: £11.95

The youngest World Champion in history at 25, he won a second title in 1974 before deciding to build and race his own Formula 1 cars. Still a major force in Indy cars.
ISBN: 0 905138 78 3
112 pages Price: £12.95

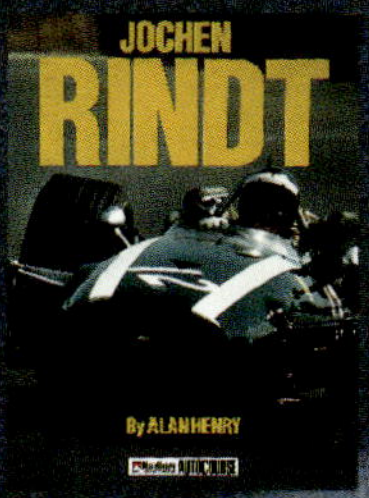

His tempestuous career ended in tragedy when he was killed during practice for the Italian Grand Prix in 1970, thus becoming the only posthumous winner of the World Championship.
ISBN: 0 905138 79 1
112 pages Price: £12.95

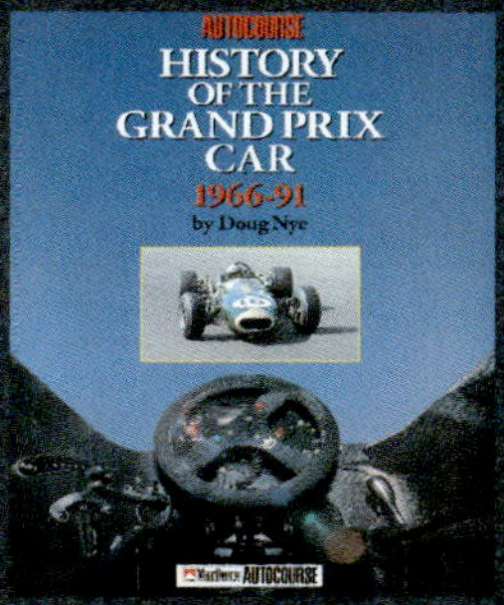

In the 25 years since the introduction of the 3-litre Formula 1, Grand Prix cars have changed beyond recognition. This detailed, illustrated history spans the era from the 350 horsepower tube-framed cars to the 650 horsepower, computer designed, carbon composite cars of 1991.
352 pages, approx. 32 colour and 200 black and white photographs
ISBN: 0 905138 94 5 Price: £40.00

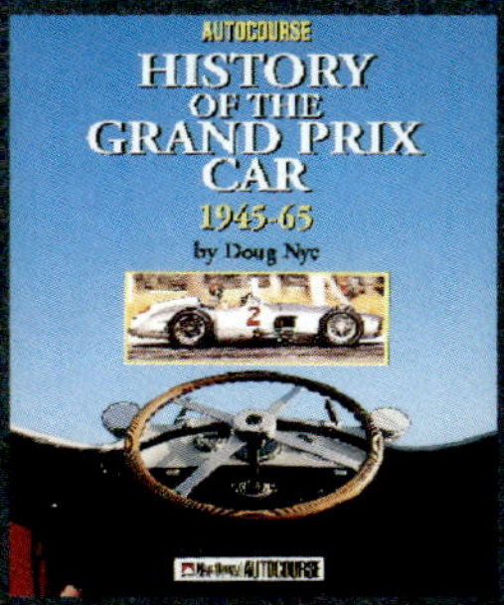

Beginning with the post-war racing revival and the new regulations establishing the Formula 1 and Formula 2 categories, it describes all the cars of the era including the many legendary cars and engines of the 2½ litre formula, followed by the multi-cylinder rear engines and monocoque chassis of the 1960s.
Approx. 272 pages, 40 colour and 200 black and white photographs
ISBN: 0 905138 93 7 Price: £40.00

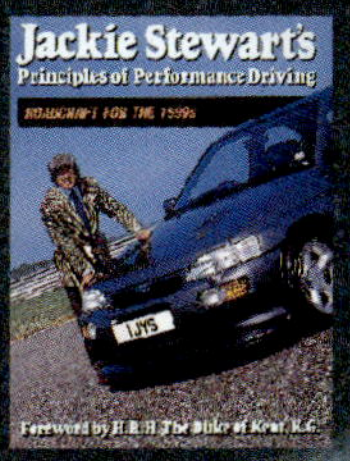

This best-selling title has now been extensively revised and updated by three-times World Champion Jackie Stewart whose ability to analyse driving skills and car performance gives him an unrivalled authority in describing the techniques of car control.
240 pages, 36 colour and 119 black and white photographs
ISBN: 0 905138 91 0 Price: £16.99

This eleventh edition once again combines the writing talents of Editor David Williams with the exciting and evocative photography of Reinhard Klein to provide the definitive record of the 1992 World Rally Championship. Top journalists contribute a range of interesting and informed features on the technical advances, the drivers and the future of the sport. This luxury book is completed by comprehensive results and stage times, plus colour coverage of the European, British and National Championships.
176 pages, over 140 colour photos
ISBN: 0 905138 98 8 Price: £25.00

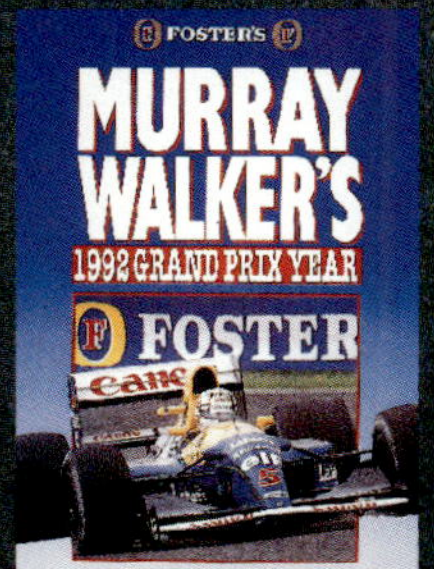

In its sixth year of publication and dramatically illustrated by John Townsend's colour photographs of the race action and personalities, this popular annual captures all the excitement, incidents and emotion of Nigel Mansell's championship-winning season. Murray Walker writes with infectious enthusiasm on every round of the Grand Prix season, supported by his own profile of the new Champion and detailed results.
160 pages, over 160 colour photos
ISBN: 0 905138 99 6 Price: £9.99

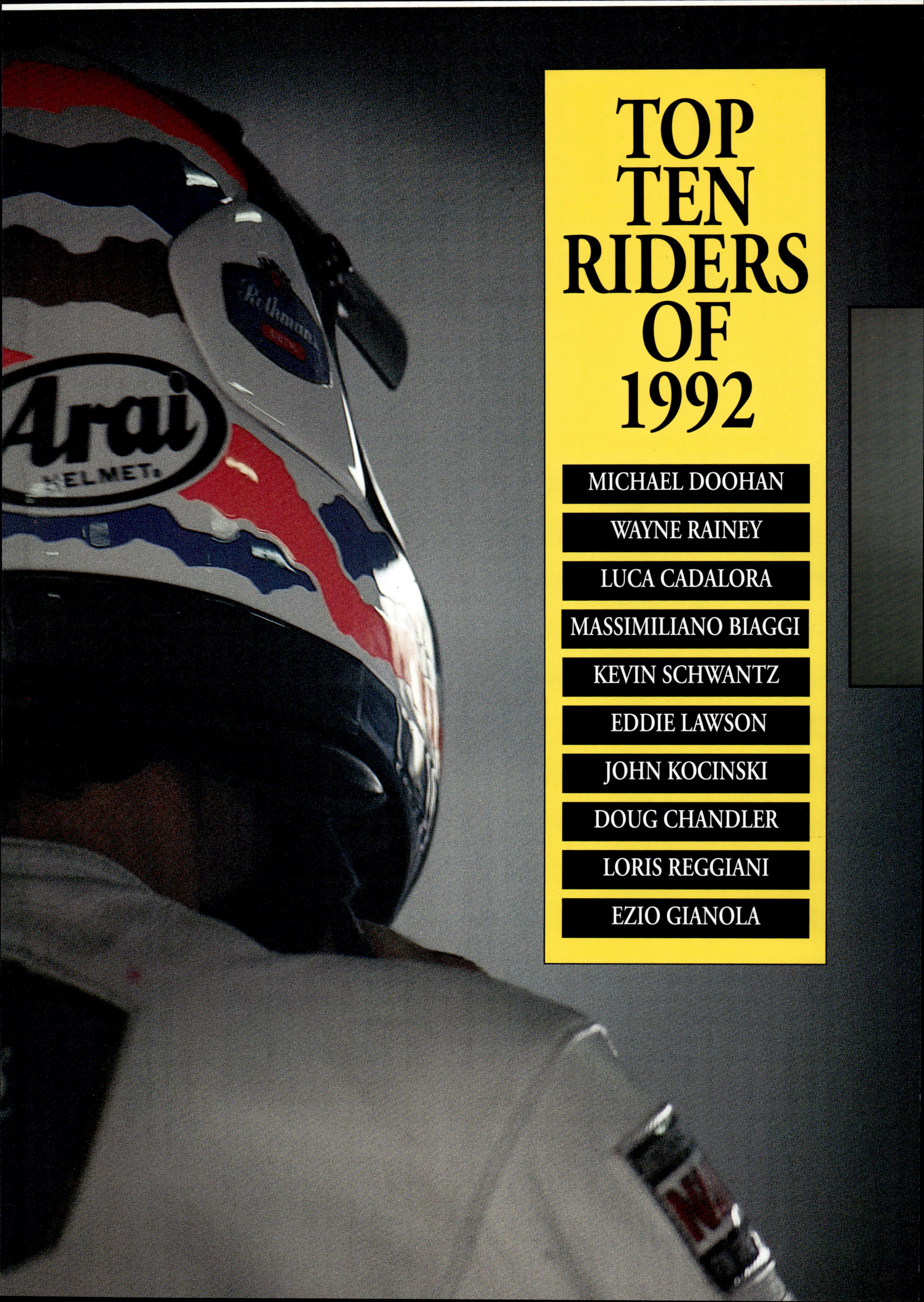

TOP TEN RIDERS OF 1992

- MICHAEL DOOHAN
- WAYNE RAINEY
- LUCA CADALORA
- MASSIMILIANO BIAGGI
- KEVIN SCHWANTZ
- EDDIE LAWSON
- JOHN KOCINSKI
- DOUG CHANDLER
- LORIS REGGIANI
- EZIO GIANOLA

1 MICHAEL DOOHAN

TEAM ROTHMANS HONDA
1992 World Championship position – 2nd
Race wins – 5 (JPN, AUS, MAL, SPA, GER)
Pole positions – 6
Born: 4 June 1965, Brisbane, Australia

David Goldman

Until he crashed, the World Championship belonged to Michael Doohan – and that impression lingered indelibly even when complications to his injury effectively ruled him out.

It was a matter of the combination.

At the start of the year, he and Honda were not merely ready, but so superior as to set the opposition reeling. By the end, all the rival manufacturers had hastily imitated the new drone NSR, but if other things had remained equal it would by then have been far too late.

This paragon of a bike still had to be ridden, and Doohan was just the man to do it. HRC's fruitful winter had honed the bike to his particular skills, and vice versa.

The year before, reluctant steering and a propensity to run wide mid-corner had left him scrabbling for grip on the exit. Now the chassis had been altered to suit his style, making his corner entries more assured, while the altered power-on characteristics gave him such an advantage on the way out of the corners that he was visibly gaining yards, and making his first upshift while his rivals were still trying to tame wheelspin and remain in control.

The combination utterly dominated the first four races, won the seventh and was second in the intervening pair. Although he was by now no longer unbeatable, his points lead was such that he didn't need to win again to be sure of defeating early injury victims Schwantz and Rainey.

It was simple bad luck when he broke his leg in a crash that might as easily have proved harmless, and a major medical misfortune that turned the injury into an eight-week nightmare. When he did return, for the penultimate race, he was a tragic spectacle. Looking like death he strove desperately to score a few points and, after he failed, he broke down for the first time anyone had seen.

Hard facts gave the title to another but, for those who followed the whole season, 1992 will remain Doohan's year.

2 WAYNE RAINEY

TEAM MARLBORO ROBERTS YAMAHA
1992 World Championship position – 1st
Race wins – 3 (EUR, FRA, BRA)
Pole positions – 0
Born: 23 October 1960, Los Angeles, California, USA

Nobody can say that Wayne Rainey didn't earn his third successive title. He'd finished the previous year with an injury that left him painfully short of testing time, then he fell again when he did get a chance to try the 1992 bike.

He crashed in the first race in Japan, then smouldered unhappily as he found himself condemned to a pursuit role in the next three. He was challenging for the lead at Mugello when he crashed again, but once more he fought back against the odds and, at the next race, he finally managed to beat Doohan. Although by now painfully far behind, at least he was back on course.

Even this turned sour when yet another debilitating crash in Germany left his earlier reputation of dogged consistency in tatters, and when he withdrew in practice from the next round at Assen it seemed tacit acceptance that his title defence was in the same state.

The crashes were symptomatic of something other than a loss of ability – that his Yamaha had been left lagging by the new Honda, while the Marlboro Roberts switch from Dunlop to Michelin put them all at sea for most of the year as they tried and tried again to adapt the bike's handling and regain the initial steering bite he needed to exploit his aggressive riding style.

Then the title race opened up again with Doohan's crash, and yet again Rainey's determination was put to the test. It passed, and he redoubled his efforts, so that by the year's end he'd tamed the bike somewhat to be clearly the strongest of the survivors.

It was unfortunate for the first triple champion since Kenny Roberts that his win was tainted by Doohan's bad luck. In the end, however, it was the points tally that mattered, and Rainey had, by hook or by crook, accumulated more of them. This made him the embodiment of the sporting cliché that you make your own luck, and proof that never giving up is a vital part of getting there in the end.

David Goldman

3 LUCA CADALORA

TEAM ROTHMANS KANEMOTO HONDA
1992 World Championship position – 1st
Race wins – 7 (JPN, AUS, MAL, ITA, EUR, HUN, BRA)
Pole positions – 2
Born: 17 May 1963, Modena, Italy

Luca produced a second successive season of domination in the 250 class, winning seven out of the 13 races, and seldom faltering.

But things were different this year for the Kanemoto teamster. Where last year his main job had been to beat other NSR riders, now he also had to beat the rising home country challenge from the strongest ever Aprilia attack.

His efforts carried him far clear of the other Hondas, and his talents made it possible for him to transcend what was at times a clear machine disadvantage to claim not only the lion's share of wins, but also to be the only rider in the class to score points in every race.

Luca is a thinking rider who specialises both in fluent and stylish riding and also in demoralising his rivals whenever possible. His stalk-and-pounce technique was as devastatingly effective in 1992 even when he wasn't going for first place.

He is also a private person who doesn't give much away, though it was obvious by the end of the year that he was no longer on good terms with either HRC or Rothmans. His extraordinary ability blossomed with Honda and Erv Kanemoto, and it seems a waste that he was obliged to look elsewhere for his planned move to the 500 class in 1993.

Malcolm Bryan

4 MASSIMILIANO BIAGGI

TEAM TELKOR VALESI APRILIA
1992 World Championship position – 5th
Race wins – 1 (ZA)
Pole positions – 4
Born: 26 June 1971, Rome, Italy

Malcolm Bryan

Max Biaggi burst into GP racing after dominating the European Championship the year before – a young man on an express train to the top.

It is this exceptional potential that puts him higher on the list than his single GP win would suggest. It is not even his four pole positions and five rostrum finishes that elevate him, but the way he rode to achieve them.

At 21, Biaggi is entitled to ride like a hot-head. The fact that he was up with the leaders while doing so is what matters. Imagine how fast he will be when maturity refines his abilities.

As it is, he displayed an ability to venture further into the accident than any other 250 rider. His Aprilia was almost constantly wobbling and flicking, and he spent more time bouncing off or over kerbs than anyone has a right to. Even when he did win, he almost threw it away with an over-exuberant last lap.

Max's ultimate goal is an F1 car drive. His next step is to replace Cadalora at the Rothmans Kanemoto Honda team.

Just watch him go.

5 KEVIN SCHWANTZ

TEAM LUCKY STRIKE SUZUKI
1992 World Championship position – 4th
Race wins – 1 (ITA)
Pole positions – 0
Born: 19 June 1964, Paige, Texas, USA

Kevin Schwantz has long been one of the most naturally gifted 500 riders. In the past two years he has added a depth to his approach that makes him a worthy elder of the class.

It is a measure of his maturity that he was able to accept that sometimes his new team-mate, Doug Chandler, was faster than he was, and calmly to set about improving his own efforts to match.

His year started solidly, only to be interrupted by injury in the third race. After that he race-crashed three more times, the first being the extraordinary T-boning by Eddie Lawson at Assen. The second crash was attributable to weakness through resultant injuries – he came back extraordinarily quickly – and the third was on spilled oil or coolant. But for these mishaps, he would have made it a two-man challenge to Doohan.

Some thought his new approach meant that he was already past his best, and he added only one victory to his previous total of 18. But it was a typically swashbuckling ride at Mugello which proved he still had his old race-winning ability as well as the new-found consistency that, with a bit more good luck, might have brought him his first long-awaited World Championship.

David Goldman

6 EDDIE LAWSON

TEAM CAGIVA
1992 World Championship position – 9th
Race wins – 1 (HUN)
Pole positions – 2
Born: 11 March 1958, Upland, California, USA

Malcolm Bryan

Almost an honorary member, Lawson concluded an historic career as the dominant force in racing by bringing Cagiva their first GP win in 12 years of trying.

It was a tactical victory, involving the right guess on drying conditions in Hungary – and his rivals were not slow to point out that Lawson could afford to take a tyre gamble since he had no championship position to protect.

No matter. The victory was a symbolic reward for two years during which the four-times World Champion transformed the by now rather comical Italian also-rans into something very closely resembling a fully competitive factory GP team.

It was his austere and commanding presence as much as his technical ability that forged Cagiva into an effective entity, and they will do well if they can survive his departure without serious damage.

More than this, Lawson was still riding as hard at the end of his career as he had in his glory years, and his pole position laps at Assen and Donington Park were a joy to watch.

The supreme craftsman had matured into a past-master who remained at the height of his powers until the end – then walked out of racing without a backward glance.

7 JOHN KOCINSKI

TEAM MARLBORO ROBERTS YAMAHA
1992 World Championship position – 3rd
Race wins – 1 (ZA)
Pole positions – 2
Born: 20 March 1968, Little Rock, Arkansas, USA

Ever the enigma, Kocinski at least finished his second 500 class season well.

A man who views second place as bitter failure, he had been growing increasingly disillusioned as the season wore on and he failed to take up where he had left off at the end of 1991, when he'd won the Malaysian GP.

Like Rainey, he found the Yamaha all at odds with Michelin tyres, and he expressed his frustration in tirades against Yamaha and his team. The inevitable result was a mutual split with his mentor Kenny Roberts at the end of the year.

By then he was even seriously contemplating moving back to the 250 class so as to rebuild his confidence – a typically unexpected reaction to his problems.

Kocinski is a hard man to understand. Some of that may be deliberate, but a lot is because he was himself bemused by a year in which he found himself butting up against everything and everyone.

Two things that remained clear were his riding talent and his determination to be the best. It makes for a formidable combination.

Malcolm Bryan

8 DOUG CHANDLER

TEAM LUCKY STRIKE SUZUKI
1992 World Championship position – 5th
Race wins – 0
Pole positions – 2
Born: 27 September 1965, Salinas, California, USA

Malcolm Bryan

The quiet Californian never did win a GP in the end, but his overall performance so far exceeded all expectations that he must rate as one of the discoveries of the 500 class.

From his first race on the Suzuki, in only his second GP season, he showed himself one of the fastest – and he made few mistakes from then on.

When he did err, it was costly: he twice asked too much of cold front tyres (in Holland and France) and paid the price. His championship position was damaged, too, when he was another victim of Kocinski's Donington spillage.

But if he lacked top five consistency, he also managed a string of good finishes and was four times on the rostrum.

Again it is his approach that marks him out as championship material – calm and reasonable, a thinking rider who can maximise his performance without taking excessive risks.

In this as well as in some elements of his smooth style he is reminiscent of Lawson, though he lacks the latter's stern personality. It will be interesting to see if he is man enough to continue the improvement wrought at Cagiva by his predecessor.

9 LORIS REGGIANI

TEAM APRILIA UNLIMITED JEANS
1992 World Championship position – 2nd
Race wins – 2 (SPA, FRA)
Pole positions – 0
Born: 7 October 1959, Forli, Italy

Malcolm Bryan

Who to choose out of the Aprilia elders – Chili or Reggiani? The latter finished higher in the championship in spite of starting the season injured; the former won three races and took four pole positions and was also immensely entertaining, his inadvertent clownery peaking when he finished the Spanish GP one lap too soon.

Somehow, this sort of thing makes him less of a racer – and this could never be said of Reggiani, still a serious contender for the championship, and likely to be so again.

Reggiani's own evergreen riding skill has also played a crucial part in bringing the Aprilia to its current Honda-beating state. He was the factory's first development rider and gave them their first win in 1987; and (after a brief and fruitless interruption to ride a works Honda) he still fills the same role.

A tendency to get involved in other people's crashes gave Loris the 'Luckless' tag. He races with the number 13, but in his 13th GP season seemed to have shaken off at least some of the bad luck.

Loris finished 11 out of 13 races and was on the rostrum 10 times, more often even than Cadalora. At 33, he is a major figure of the 250 class.

10 EZIO GIANOLA

TEAM SEMPRUCCI HONDA
1992 World Championship position – 4th
Race wins – 4 (ITA, EUR, NED, FRA)
Pole positions – 5
Born: 13 June 1960, Lecco, Italy

The wiry little 125 class veteran had no particular advantage at the start of the season. His best years seemed long past, and his mount was a relatively undistinguished B-kitted Honda that should have consigned him to the middle of the top ten pack.

Instead, riding with all the tucked-in style and verve of his youth, and backed by a most effective machine development programme, he emerged with the most race wins in a year when even a top five finish deserved a medal.

When things went right he won with profound assurance, and seemed certain to take a fifth win in Hungary before suspension problems dropped him out of the points. Other little problems (one bafflingly described by his team as 'a fastidious jumping of the limber') as well as uncertain performance by his Bridgestone tyres proved costly in the end, and he dropped to fourth overall.

Gianola has been an exciting rider for years. He was fourth on a Garelli twin in 1984, a giant-killing sixth in 1987 on a Honda single against the twins, and second and third in 1988 and 1989. He wasted the next two years enduring the death-throes of Derbi; 1992 was a last chance.

In his maturity, he recaptured all the excitement of his youth, and he deserves to win a World Championship.

Malcolm Bryan

Shell

THE STATE OF RACING

Photos: Malcolm Bryan

RACING'S new regime swaggered onto the world stage wearing a fancy top hat and a ringmaster's confident bluster. It failed to distract attention from the fact that stage-hands were still banging nails into the set.

Born out of dissent, beset by rapacious winners and vengeful losers, fuelled by millions of dollars, sealed with a Judas kiss, the transition from total FIM control to that of the new TWP/Dorna/FIM triumvirate had been sudden and far from smooth and was, it transpired, far from settled.

The calendar had been late and was two races short of the promised 15, the sidecars remained in limbo while inconveniently declining to fade away gracefully, and the first three races were set about with teething troubles.

As the year wore on, the new brooms swept clean in the paddocks and among the sponsors' tents, with a stream of often pettifogging and always restrictive new decrees. As a counterpoint, simmering resentment at an erosion of power and privilege in several quarters led to the foundation of new power groups, giving rise to yet more sets of initials for the race fans to memorise – or more likely forget.

But no matter how many noses were put out of joint, nobody could deny that the scheduled races all proceeded more or less smoothly and on time, with rather fewer hiccups than in the preceding two or three seasons. All solo classes had provided good racing, and the 500s – which earlier had seemed to be dying on their wheels – had seen full grids and a completely revitalised midfield group of privateers.

The increased wealth of racing and the fairer distribution of that wealth created a financial climate that made it at least viable for new riders to join top level racing without first having to win one of the handful of works rides, while the availability of the new Harris and Roc Yamahas gave them the bikes to show whether or not they really had any talent. It was certain that 1993 would see even more (and better) riders prepared to take the risk of a self-propelled step into GP racing.

The revolution was over, the evolution had begun.

The takeover had been swift and deadly; the manoeuvrings of IRTA, TWP and turncoats Dorna were mapped in full in last year's *Motocourse.* By then, the FIM had clearly lost control, and racing was firmly in Bernie Ecclestone's hands. The F1 mogul had struck a deal with IRTA whereby the latter agreed to contract and pay all the teams, while Ecclestone himself arranged the calendar and effectively promoted the races; he – or his organisation, TWP – in turn had an agreement with Dorna whereby the Spanish concern was in charge of all matters relating to TV, from production to international marketing of the rights.

The FIM retained 'sporting control', a rather nebulous privilege that gave them a formal role in actual race stewardship, although TWP had appointed a full-time race director, Pierpaolo Gardella, whose powers seemed to overlap those of the FIM. However, tradition maintained a foothold on real power, with FIM President Jos Vaessen appointed the third member of the all-powerful Permanent Bureau, which had total control over any changes in rules and contracts. The other two members were Richard Golding, representing Dorna, and Ecclestone himself. This triumvirate had one tricky requirement: all their decisions must be unanimous.

On the surface, it appeared that the above arrangements had reduced IRTA to the role of mere contract brokers. They had gone to all the trouble of getting GP racing into a neat and marketable package, and then meekly handed it over to Ecclestone. This may yet turn out to be true, but for the present (and for

By MICHAEL SCOTT

Left: **Grab him while you can – sidecar association chief Lee van Dam *(right)* snatches an impromptu meeting with rare paddock visitor Bernie Ecclestone.**

Motorhomes and trucks all in line, no washing hanging out, satellite dishes synchronised, garbage cans all matching. Right – now we can go racing. Randy Mamola *(centre)* can remember when racing paddocks were very different from this well-ordered display at the Hungaroring.

the future of the current five-year contract) it overlooks their active and major part in almost every sphere of race management, as well as their apparently cordial relationship with Ecclestone. Of course relationships can change, but it is worth remembering that, without an Ecclestone waiting in the wings to take over, their revolution might have failed for a lack of direction and muscle power.

Ecclestone personally kept a low profile, dropping in once or twice but staying for only one race, the British GP. He hardly needed to throw his weight around, with such willing lieutenants: Dorna exercised plenty of muscle in matters great and small, while IRTA were similarly zealous in keeping everything shipshape and Bernie fashion. The preparations for his first GP visit (to Jerez practice) included a careful check that all the trucks and motorhomes were arranged in perfectly straight lines, and more than one privateer was reprimanded for failing to have a sufficiently spick-and-span awning.

Yet the signs of Ecclestone's iron fist were everywhere, which was especially welcome when one or another of the continual skirmishes between IRTA and the FIM threatened to become too public or drawn out, as happened both with the sidecars and the ghost riders. In one case Bernie stepped in, in the other he loomed, the ground rules changed almost overnight, and the problems were shuffled off-stage amid wreaths of embarrassed smiles.

He wasted no time in showing who was in charge, and what that meant. The first problem to be settled was the calendar and, considering just how much everything had changed, there was obviously going to be a lot of negotiating before dates could be fixed. Set against that was the obvious need for sponsors, and riders still seeking sponsors, to have some sort of a programme of events. The clamouring for at least a provisional calendar grew louder as Christmas passed into New Year, and the days grew longer. Ecclestone remained obdurate, declining to make any comment or any promises beyond the long-standing pledge that the season would be 15 races long. At one point, he galvanised journalists at a meeting by saying: 'Okay then, I'll give you next year's calendar – get your notebooks ready. January, February, March, April...'

The calendar was eventually announced with barely six weeks to go before the first race. It turned out to have 13 events, not the promised 15, and even two months later tracks had not been confirmed for the French and Brazilian GPs. Spain had two races, the second at Montmelo in Barcelona dubbed at first the Andorran GP, and later the GP of Europe, effectively taking over from Italy's usual privilege of hosting two events. The Yugoslavian GP was out for obvious reasons, Spa-Francorchamps remained off, while three more of last year's events went missing – the Austrian, Czechoslovakian and (most worryingly) the USA GPs had dropped off the list, with Laguna Seca reportedly quite uninterested in even discussing the rigid TWP terms of contract. In their place, Hungary was back, and Brazil back again, in spite of having been cancelled for the last two years in succession.

The delay in assembling this curtailed list was the inevitable result of the problems of changing the entire *modus operandi* of running and especially financing each race. The new contract terms basically meant that individual circuit owners and GP promoters now had to pay a flat fee of $1 million to Ecclestone, while at the same time forfeiting (or buying back) rights to trackside advertising.

Not all promoters were entirely happy with these conditions although, on the other side, Eastern Creek in Australia were said to be so keen to secure the race that they actually paid Ecclestone $2 million to be first on the list for the brave new world. The last to sign were the Dutch, who obviously felt that Assen was a special case. And rightly so – the Dutch TT is not only the oldest race on the calendar, it is one of the best attended (although now overtaken by Jerez in sheer weight of numbers). Traditionally it comes as the climax of 'Speed Week', where European Championship and a panoply of other races make a popular bike racing binge at the sole bikes-only circuit.

Assen was still in doubt long after the season had started, and it was rumoured that the obstinacy of its organisers won them major financial concessions, *inter alia*. Unofficially, they were said to have paid only $400,000 of the $1 million asking fee, to be topped up by a $2 royalty on every race-day ticket sold (bringing the total to less than three-quarters of the supposed set fee). They also bucked the system by being the only race all year to be held on Saturday rather than Sunday, another long-standing tradition that triumphed over the otherwise rigid timings of the TV-oriented TWP; and it was the only race where four-stroke classic racers, with all their potential for oil spillage, shared the track with the GP brigade. By year's end, dark mutterings within IRTA suggested that Ecclestone would sooner or later extract a price for the Dutchmen's unwillingness to toe the line.

The next hurdle coincided with the very first race, and what had started as an unexpected confrontation of IRTA by the Japanese factories soon became a predictably acrimonious direct stand-off between IRTA and the FIM. It was the notorious affair of the Ghost Riders of Suzuka

This extraordinary sequence of events was triggered by the so-called 'wild card' system, itself part of IRTA's inevitably team-based racing structure. Under the new rules, teams were contracted for the full season, with their nominated riders, 30 per class, subsequently expanded to 36, including 6 'B-list' riders. Teams were not obliged to field a replacement for an injured rider, but this was the only legal chance for a non-contracted rider to gain a race

Ironically, even as they faced extinction, the sidecars put on a season of the closest racing for years.

entry (and for privateers to keep the income rolling in). The new GP racing was always meant to be a closed shop.

The FIM opposed these restrictions, feeling that a true World Championship should at least nominally be open to anyone good enough to take part. IRTA made another concession, introducing the wild cards. Two places would be open on the grid in each class at each race, for riders nominated by the national federation of the home country.

The Japanese GP, meanwhile, had always been rather special. Home heroes were not merely top level national riders, as elsewhere, but factory pets on full works bikes. For the rest of the year they contest the All Japan series, with a high level of sponsorship. Suzuka had always given these men an annual chance to play against the world's best, with the considerable advantage of top machinery on their home track, while big-hitting sponsors like Kirin Mets, Nescafé and Cup Noodle had always been able to assume that a GP outing, with associated TV coverage, would be part of the deal.

The request that the rules should be relaxed for the Japanese GP, to allow eight local works or works-backed riders into each class, came via the Japanese federation, but it was immediately clear that once again it was the factories that were pulling the strings. And, amid all the polite language and bowing, it was also clear that they meant business, and that there was a very real threat that they would pull out of the new GP series if they were denied. 'Nobody actually made arrangements to take bikes back from the teams,' said IRTA chief executive Paul Butler. 'But it was made clear, in so many words, that the factories would withdraw their support if they didn't get what they wanted.'

Backed against the wall, IRTA might have called the factories' bluff, but they dared not take the risk. Instead, they grasped at the chance to show themselves flexible and reasonable, as well as grateful for the crucial support of the factories in the earlier stages of their hijack of racing. In other words they caved in, but with a good grace. They said that the extra riders could start – and it only remained for the Japanese federation to nominate which two of the eight in each class were official points-scoring wild card riders, in accordance with the system. The remainder would officially not be there at all, an obvious absurdity that IRTA never had any trouble in defending as being right, proper and entirely sensible.

Now the cracks in the racing management structure started to show, as well as the shortcomings in the rule book, which had failed to anticipate this admittedly unexpected turn of events. IRTA made a formal pre-race application to the FIM stewards for a ruling on which six of the 24 riders were wild cards. The FIM, doubtless scenting at least a moral victory over the architects of their downfall, ignored it. This, they insisted, was a sporting matter, and therefore entirely in their jurisdiction, without reference to IRTA, or the race director, or anybody else. As FIM President Jos Vaessen later said: 'I advised IRTA against allowing the eight riders into the race – but once they had been allowed to start, they must all be treated as full participants in the race.'

Common sense, however, must always give way to the rules, and it was to niceties of the rules that IRTA and race director Gardella turned after the race, declaring that in the absence of any response from the FIM to their earlier request, *none* of the ghost riders would be eligible for points, which would instead go to the top ten IRTA finishers. In the case of the 500s, there *were* only ten IRTA finishers. Corrado Catalano actually came 16th and last, two laps behind the leaders, but was adjudged by IRTA to have come tenth.

IRTA's position was not enviable. Blackmailed by the factories, they were now forced into a position that made them look increasingly foolish. They justified it by saying they were acting as they were obliged to do by their own charter – in the interest of their members.

Well – yes, and no. It depended which members they meant. For example, Luca Cadalora won the 250 race, and was very properly awarded 20 points for his efforts. Helmut Bradl only came fourth – but was none the less given 15 points, as though he had come second. This was certainly in Bradl's interests, but the message to Cadalora seemed to be that he was foolish for taking the risks involved in winning, when he could have had the same money and points for a safe third, behind the top two Japanese ghost riders. (Luca's reaction to this was that of a genuine racer – he didn't care how many points they gave Bradl, because he knew he could beat him anyway.)

The FIM, meanwhile, firmly placed on the moral high ground, published their own rival set of points to include all finishers – and thoroughly enjoyed the discomfiture of their rivals. Over the next two races the atmosphere grew rather nasty, with Dorna heavies patrolling the press room and punishing anyone who didn't follow the IRTA line. Copies of Marlboro's normal preview for the Australian GP were temporarily confiscated by Dorna press officer Denis Noyes because they showed FIM and not IRTA points. In Malaysia, journalists (including the writer) were reminded none too subtly that Ecclestone had provided the extensive facilities for the press, the implication being that the expression of non-aligned views endangered one's right to use them. IRTA, meanwhile, was accusing the FIM of duplicity, in having changed their position after it was too late for any alterations, and of exploiting the situation for their own ends. Then FIM President Vaessen arrived in Kuala Lumpur in bullish mood, telling me: 'They will take points away from those riders over my dead body.'

The bickering descended into a rather menacing farce – but one man's opinion was conspicuously missing. Nobody knew how Ecclestone felt, for he was totally aloof, though most people assumed he would be obliged to back up IRTA and his race director, Gardella.

They were wrong.

The affair was eventually settled at a meeting of the Permanent Bureau before the Spanish GP, and after taking legal advice, the Ecclestone/Vaessen/Golding triumvirate deciding unanimously that the FIM were right, and that all those who start a race must share in its rewards. The ghost riders were made flesh, and they kept the points they had won.

Thus IRTA was confounded, and obliged to apologise at a packed Jerez press conference. Paul Butler earned some respect by doing so manfully, and may have reflected that while it is no fun getting egg all over your face, at least it can be washed off again.

But the resolution of this problem coincided exactly with the start of

Malcolm Bryan

the next one – the still unresolved question of the sidecars.

The three-wheelers have been part of GP racing from its inception in 1949. This was natural – they were, after all, motor cycles with an extra wheel, closely related to the then relatively popular road-going sidecars of the post-war pre-Mini generation. Since then, sidecars have all but vanished from the roads, while their racing counterparts have changed beyond all recognition. Apart from engine and gearbox (a choice more or less dictated by the 500 cc capacity rule), they have nothing else in common with bikes, borrowing their monocoque chassis design, wheels, brakes and tyres from racing cars and glorying in a literally and figuratively eccentric suspension technology entirely irrelevant to anybody except themselves. No motor cycle factory takes any interest, reinforcing the taint of mindless hedonism that infects all racing ... if sidecar racers are indeed improving the breed, it is not a breed that matters much.

Unique also in all circuit racing in carrying a two-man crew, sidecars do have a hard core of passionate support, both from participants (Switzerland, Britain and Holland being particularly well represented) and from the fans from these countries. But their isolation from the mainstream had left them as the underfinanced Cinderella class of GP racing, and they were already out on a limb when IRTA started to gather strength for the putsch of 1991.

It gradually became clear to the sidecar competitors that even though they had originally been IRTA members, their days there were numbered. The split, towards the end of 1991, was mutual, and the class turned towards the International Sidecar Riders' Association, headed by Lee van Dam, a Dutch businessman with a long-standing involvement with the class. ISRA had been formed mainly to make travel and other arrangements for their previous foreign trips to the US GP. Now it became a power group, fighting for survival, for it was abundantly clear that IRTA's new series had no place for them.

Bereft of friends, status, support, influence and power, the chairmen were by now mere pawns in the game. The FIM's pawns – and, for a time, it seemed that they had a valuable friend. Without FIM insistence, they would not even have been included in the calendar for the eight scheduled races. IRTA accepted this provision, though very grudgingly, and when the three-wheelers turned up for their first race, at Jerez, they were given paddock space in a distant car park, well away from the IRTA area, and a fair distance also from the track. Crews making their way to the pits for practice and races had to show passes to get there.

They also found they had no place within the strict practice or race schedules, and van Dam had to fight every inch of the way just to get the three-wheelers out on the track.

And then it turned out that nobody had any intention of paying them – not IRTA (they had known that all along); not the organisers, who were only running sidecars under sufferance; and now they also discovered the promises they thought they had from the FIM fell short on the delivery of hard cash.

A less robust group might by now have taken the hint and quietly faded away, but the last GP amateurs are made of sterner stuff, and they simply refused to disappear. In so doing, they saved their skins, at least for the moment. Unpaid, they raced at Jerez, and they arrived at Hockenheim still without having received any money. Now came the first payment from the FIM – $100,000 to ISRA, with the second instalment to be paid at the next race. But that, said the FIM, was the end; they must look elsewhere for the rest. Divided among 24 crews, this was less than $10,000 apiece, barely covering running expenses. And by the time they arrived at Assen for the third race, there was a real chance that they would be forced to give up.

Now came what seemed like a rather sudden change of heart from IRTA, prompting rumours that Ecclestone had started to crack the whip. Not so, said IRTA: it came as the culmination of weeks of discussions because they were themselves anxious to put a stop to this embarrassingly public display of poverty-stricken social disgrace.

The beleaguered sidecar competitors seized on the new initiative with glee, but IRTA's statement about what they admitted had been 'a shotgun wedding' was considerably more guarded. From henceforth, it said, the sidecars were incorporated into the new World Championships with the specific approval of IRTA, in a contract that envisaged ten years of continued participation. But they also warned that the sidecar class would not survive as a credible part of the World Championships if they did not address their own 'commercial problems'. In other words, rather than insisting on racing at places like Jerez by right, they should concentrate on becoming viable by holding more races in countries like Britain, Holland and Germany, where at least they had some support.

The main details of the deal concentrated first on tidying up the rest of the season and arranging a further payment of $400,000, to be shared between IRTA and TWP. (At the time of writing, this had not yet been paid.) Furthermore, they were given a confirmed if lowly status in proposals for 1993 – where they were expected to run four rounds at GPs in Europe and at one foreign round, and another four rounds under the aegis of the FIM, at Superbike or European Championship rounds, or indeed with any

Ashen-faced IRTA chief Paul Butler leaves the riders' meeting in Brazil. The race was saved by lack of accord among the riders.

Bottom left: Spectator power at Jerez, now the best attended race of the year.

other series that would have them.

But they were not yet out of the woods. There remained the final two rounds of 1992. They were scheduled to race in Brazil and South Africa but, given their current financial state and declining general morale, the likelihood of them ever getting there was laughably remote. Now van Dam put together a package through ISRA that would make Brazil at least a financial possibility, and he put it to the riders at Donington Park. With two weeks to go, and after having been repeatedly let down by everybody else in racing, however, they were in no mood to trust anybody's promises, and they declined. Van Dam, the unifying force in what success ISRA had so far achieved, promptly resigned from the association, and the sidecars were again left in a parlous state, not knowing when or indeed if they would ever get any more money, or if they were to have any more races this year.

In the end, they did have one more round, at a World Superbike meeting at the Assen short circuit, and they ended the year much as they had started it, broke, and wondering if they had any friends left at all.

Still, knowing who your friends were was becoming a scarce commodity in the highly politicised atmosphere of the new World Championship; and there were a number of attempts at formalising relationships by the strengthening of old associations or the formation of new ones.

Certainly the sponsors' association found themselves drawn closer together by the various strictures of the Ecclestone regime. Where before they had enjoyed extensive freedom, they were now fenced in on all sides and in matters large and small. One problem was the track signage, which had previously been available through negotiation with individual tracks or organisers. Now it was directly under the control of TWP, and it had leapt in price. Another matter concerned exactly what they could and couldn't do in the paddock and press room, circumscribed by all sorts of minor but often high-handed rules that seemed to be added to race by race. Clearly, things were being steered in the direction of F1 racing, where corporate entertainment is only allowed in Ecclestone's own Paddock Club, and sponsors are not allowed to use their own letterhead stationery for their own press releases and public statements.

It is likely that the ghost riders affair was the trigger for the formation of a new manufacturers' association, dubbed GPMA, which was announced at Donington. Hitherto, the Japanese factories have had trouble speaking with one voice and have expressed themselves through their domestic federation, the MFJ. But the events of the past year had thrown them together more and, in any case, it was politically embarrassing to be thus tied in with the FIM. Cagiva were also founder-members of the new association, but not Aprilia or Gilera from the 250 and 125 classes.

Then there was the case of the riders, whose status within IRTA had melted away over the past few years and who, in the new system, didn't even get paid prize money. At the start of the year they had been willing to fall in with the new contract terms, whereby they had to negotiate their own rewards with their teams. But many of them liked it less and less as the season wore on, and it was combined with a number of other minor losses of privilege including access to paddock passes for pals and (believe it or not) a rule which banned the hanging out of washing in the paddock not only on the three days of practice and the race, but also on the preceding Thursday as well.

As a result, the International Motorcycle Racers' Association (IMRA) was born, but unfortunately promptly scored an own goal with the debacle over passing the obviously dangerous Brazilian GP track at Interlagos fit for racing (q.v.). This troublesome venue also damaged the credibility of the FIM and IRTA men who had approved the track in company with the riders' representative, however, and it is certain to be dropped from the calendar anyway, luckily without loss of blood.

It now remains only for the spectators to form an association to protect their position, which was also significantly eroded during 1992, with rocketing prices at many tracks. As is well known, Ecclestone cares little for race-day attendance: his empire is built largely on TV revenue, and empty grandstands are neither here nor there.

There were many signs that bike racing will eventually go the same way as F1, which is seen among the two-wheel fraternity as a humourless affair, run as an Ecclestone dictatorship, dominated by ridiculously large amounts of money and the sort of people that attracts, and having created a breed of sullen superstar drivers who are absurdly overpaid and barely seem to enjoy racing at all.

Of course, there are many who think that bike racing had already gone a long way down the same road even before the new commercial era of TWP; but there are many others who are thankful that most of the riders are still accessible: they talk to one another, they clearly enjoy themselves, and they were all able, at the end of the year, to get together for a massive party after the South African GP. There is plenty of residual camaraderie, even if it is only a fraction of that of the 'good old' impecunious days.

One must reach a similar judgement over the first year of the new World Championship. Much has changed, and much has been lost in the transition. But the gains include such important matters as prosperity for (almost) all, and a long-overdue degree of professionalism in the way the sport is organised.

While GP racing in general is in a much stronger overall position than a year ago, that's not enough to secure the future. Tobacco sponsors have been a good friend to bike racing, but now the dependency on nicotine is becoming embarrassing as legislation closes in around cigarette advertising and sponsorship.

If racing is to survive without being displaced to Third World tracks, it is imperative that other sponsors should be attracted, not so much to oust the existing cigarette sponsors, but to add a degree of respectability and independence to the sport which would inevitably then reflect a better light on the smoky stalwarts like Marlboro, Lucky Strike, Rothmans, Ducados, Coronas and others.

The new series has turned GP racing into an attractive professional commercial package. It is now urgent that it should find funds and friends in the broader commercial world.

Photos: Malcolm Bryan

Sometimes, pushing the rev counter into the **Red Zone** means pushing forward the very limits of performance.
It's certainly true of these two machines.
And to keep their Countach securely on the tarmac, Lamborghini fit **Pirelli** as standard.
On two wheels, Bimota's **Tesi** is an equally formidable projectile. No prizes for guessing whose tyres are fitted to this Bimota.
For the ultimate superbikes we developed the ultimate superbike tyre: The MP7 Sports Radial.
To make this tyre almost as rapid in the wet as it is in the dry, we spent hundreds of computer hours comparing tread patterns.
While for the carcass elements we used Kevlar. Stronger yet lighter than steel, Kevlar withstands the forces that cause high speed tyre distortion, so maintaining stability like no other material.
On the track, the 1991 British Supercup Supersport 600 and European Superbike Championship were both won for the second year running on MP7 radial technology.
So if you're a regular visitor to the **Red Zone,** don't go without **Pirelli**.
Talk to your local dealer or phone
Pirelli Information Line on 0788 540606.

MP7
SPORT
RADIAL
ZR RATED

PIRELLI

Grips right into the Red Zone

Pirelli Motorcycle Tyres, Gladiator Way, Glebe Farm Estate, Rugby, Warwickshire CV21 1PX.

Vehicles kindly supplied by Kinetic Art Limited Tel: 0403 752644

MICHAEL DOOHAN THE MAN WHO NEARLY WAS

MICHAEL Doohan has in the past made light of the World Championship. 'It's just a number one you put on your bike, then the next year it starts all over again. What I like is to win races.'

When he said that, he was leading the 1991 championship, and looking towards the completion of his three-year GP plan: one year to learn, one to consolidate, one to win. The philosophy was to serve him well when he was forced to reconcile himself to second place.

Losing the points lead was a lot harder to bear in 1992. For one thing, it happened in the last race, following an epic fight back to fitness after that fateful Assen practice crash. And it came after a year that, in its early stages, Michael Doohan had simply claimed as his own.

By the time the name at the top of the points list changed, the Australian was more or less resigned to it. He'd watched powerless from his Italian hospital bed as Rainey drew closer race by race – but when Dr Claudio Costa, the man who saved his leg, finally got him strong enough to ride a bike (just barely), he was still ahead and still theoretically able to stay there. The real emotional shock came at the penultimate round in Brazil, after he had failed to score points in the race he had fought eight long weeks to be ready for. All that time in hospital, in surgery, in physiotherapy ... even in a damned decompression chamber, to try and restore circulation to his damaged leg – and he might as well have stayed home after all.

The reserved Brisbane boy, who turned 27 three weeks before the Assen accident, was able to take it on the chin by the time the Damoclean thread finally dropped the sword at Kyalami. He took refuge in cliché ('I always said it wasn't over until the end') and determined threats ('I'll be back stronger than ever next year'). And if the disappointment had been momentarily acute, he wasn't about to let it spoil his summer Down Under, with the important task of restoring his depleted reserves of strength and fitness. After all, aside from the obvious kudos and earning potential of the championship – and Doohan has long since outstripped all his expectations in both those directions – it doesn't really mean much. As predecessor Kenny Roberts once famously said: 'Ten cents and the World Championship won't buy you a cup of coffee.'

Doohan is not given to aphorisms, though he does tend to be pithy. His speciality at turning away unwelcome questions (which is most of them), and in just keeping himself to himself, is deadpan drollery. He pretends to be obtuse, and turns aside too subtle examinations of attitudes or events with patient explanations of the blindingly obvious. Asked what had happened after a crash a year or two back, instead of the expected explanation about front wheel wash-out or a too cool rear tyre he grins and says: 'I went one way, and the bike went the other.' Again, after another mishap, he was asked if he'd gone into the corner too fast. 'I think so,' he replied. And try to press him into revealing details of his unique riding style, and he stops investigation short with: 'I don't really know what I'm doing – just what feels right.'

Yet a conversational reserve and a tendency towards solitary brooding don't mean the second Australian to challenge for the title is unfriendly or difficult to like. In fact, his basic down-to-earth character leaves him refreshingly unaffected by the superstar syndrome. He knows very well that what he can do on a motor cycle makes him very special indeed ... but only while he is actually on the motor cycle.

Thus while he's pleasant company in a friendly group, he doesn't relish the public appearances, TV interviews and press conferences that his tenure with a top sponsored team require of him. He tends to freeze up, to glower somewhat and appear sullen, his face increasingly gaunt and bony as he moves into his late twenties.

Doohan, a slight figure, set off by very broad shoulders and an athletic mien, had every reason to be sullen this year.

The consequences of what should have been a fairly straightforward double fracture to his leg at Assen were out of all proportion to the original injury. Questions still remain to be answered as to just why successful surgery was followed by post-operative disaster, though Doohan points his finger firmly at an inexplicable delay in treating complications that arose the morning after the operation. It was another 36 hours before he was returned to the operating table.

For reasons he was unable to understand, they sliced his skin from ankle to knee at the back, and also on the top of his foot, wounds that would stay open for weeks as the nightmare worsened and that have left him terribly scarred. Doohan was suffering from 'compartment syndrome', a circulation problem which seems to have been allowed to take hold due to the delay in action, and which condemned him to more surgery, skin grafts, and eventually the daily visit to the decompression chamber before he was able to get out of bed and hobble almost directly to his devastating disappointment in Brazil.

If 1992 took him from the heights of achievement to the depths of defeat, Doohan is philosophical enough to consign the year to the past and get on with the future. His four GP years have also given him ample material recompense, including a pair of Porsches and an enormous speedboat.

At the tracks, he prefers his motorhome to hotels, driven between the circuits by his stepfather, Ken Johnstone, and his mother, Colleen. There he keeps company with girlfriend Kelly, a blonde Brisbane girl whose own matter-of-fact nature is the perfect foil for his personal quest to demystify his stardom.

The other close relationship that is of vital importance is with his crew chief from the start, fellow-Australian Jeremy Burgess, whom he acknowledges as an important part of his success. The pair form a partnership with every sign of potential greatness, having long since achieved the almost wordless understanding that is essential to rapid progress at getting the best out of a motor cycle for each new race. Of course, Doohan isn't quite so reticent with Burgess in matters of riding technique and the appreciation of how to make the machine work with his style, and vice versa. Jeremy grins at Mick's chosen image as an innocent just doing what comes naturally, and confirms that in truth he is as analytical as anybody. 'He's spoken about things to me that I've never heard from any other rider.'

Doohan's riding skills and knowledge have been acquired over many years. Like most of the best GP rid-

By MICHAEL SCOTT

Photos: Malcolm Bryan

Left: **Michael Doohan in Brazil – his reserves stretched to the limit.**

Opposite page: **In his first GP year, Doohan showed no fear in making a 500 cc GP bike behave like a motocrosser on dirt.**

ers, he was motor cycling as soon as he could reach the controls, and pretty soon he wanted to be in front of everyone else doing the same. His first contests were informal and rough and ready: riding the bush trails outside Brisbane with his two older brothers on minibikes provided by his late father, who had a Honda dealership. Since both his siblings became successful racers in their own right, the littlest Doohan was hard pushed from the start.

Doohan's rise in road racing was astonishingly quick, even by the standards of the 500 class, the inevitable ultimate destination for meteors with sufficient momentum. It took him less than five years from his first amateur road race at the age of 18 to conquer the rough school of Australian racing and break directly into the ranks of the top level works riders in his first GP year. Mind you, he had a wealth of competitive experience. His father, worried about the dangers of unsupervised sibling rivalry out in the bush, decided they'd be better off doing it where there was a first aid team on hand, so the whole family went racing regularly at the unromantically named Nudgee Dump, with the local minibike club.

That was in 1974, a year when Colin, Scott and Michael Doohan turned 15, 11 and nine. History records that Mick's best year was at 11, when he came second in the Queensland 10-to-12 championship, and photographs from that time show the skinny Doohan on a yellow Suzuki, wheelieing and powersliding impressively.

Doohan recalls that the main aim was just to have fun, a family having a good time together. Always game for a laugh, he even raced an off-road sidecar outfit for a spell. But something much more important was happening. Not only was he learning how to become a racer, in the sense of developing the determination and a few handy tricks to get in front of the next man; he was also taking on board all sorts of lessons on how a motor cycle behaves when you push it over the limit. All the nuances of tyre feel, steering reaction, braking response and the knowledge of how to stay in control even though both tyres are no longer gripping and your machine isn't even pointing in the direction you want to go.

What happened next is a fine example of what is, by now, a typically Australian rake's progress. (Wayne Gardner had to pay lots of dues before he got his works ride, but Doohan was on the fast track to GPs laid out by Kevin Magee, and since followed by Daryl Beattie and now Mat Mladin.) It started almost by chance, when a Brisbane bike wrecker agreed to fix Mick's damaged RZ350 (RD350LC) road bike on condition that the obviously quick young rider would have a go at road racing – an offer no impecunious late teenager could refuse.

Race-track novice Doohan treated his production Yamaha in the way he'd learned on dirt tracks: 'I pushed it down in the corner and waited for it to slide.' This prowess at the precise skill required to ride a GP 500 was soon noticed, and it was a short step to a dealer-backed ride in 1985 on a fearsome RZ500, Yamaha's road-going V4 rough replica of the YZR500 GP bike.

Doohan was one of the only riders in the world to achieve racing success on this mongrel of a bike. He went on winning race after race in 1986 also, on a four-stroke FZR750 Yamaha.

It was still all for fun, so to speak; but it got a mite more serious in 1987, when he was fully backed by the Queensland Yamaha distributors for a season on an RZ250 in one of the fiercest production racing classes anywhere in the world. He usually won, no mean achievement in the unseemly brawl that was week-in week-out Aussie production racing, and raced abroad for the first time in Japan. By the end of what was to be his last amateur year, his career score sheet was an impressive 26 wins out of 57 starts in production and Superbike races.

The express train was now well under way as he was offered the Australian equivalent of a works ride for 1988, the second Marlboro Yamaha Superbike alongside Dow-

MICHAEL DOOHAN

THE MAN WHO NEARLY WAS

Doohan at Hockenheim – World Champion elect, but not for long.

son. At the time, in only his fourth full season of road racing, it seemed way too soon to consider making a living out of what was admittedly by now a lot more than a hobby – but then chucking up swimming pool installation was hardly a major career sacrifice.

This team was something of a finishing school for Australian shooting stars – Doohan was taking Magee's place as the older rider took his own step into GP racing. He pretty much blitzed the Australian Superbike Championship, and with the help of then team manager Warren Willing (now in GP racing with Team Roberts), he rode for the Yamaha factory in Japan, taking the chequered flag at the Sugo World Superbike race among other wins there. He also won both legs of the Australian World Superbike round, and improved his average by scoring 16 wins out of 33 starts.

With Gardner having won the World Championship, and Magee winning a race in his first GP year, Australia was already the flavour of the moment as far as Grand Prix talent scouts were concerned. Doohan was simply too good to miss. He had also made overtures on his own account, visiting Assen in 1988 with new Queensland resident Barry Sheene, to see and be seen. By the end of 1988 he was in the enviable position of being able to take his pick of works GP rides from all three major Japanese factories.

He chose Honda, and moved straight into the core HRC Rothmans-backed team, to ride alongside Gardner in the World Championships. It was a big step from production 250s, in just two years.

His first year was marred by injury – first the gruesome finger that was trapped beneath a handlebar at Phillip Island, second race of the year, then mangled again at the Suzuka Eight Hour race; finally a post-season broken arm in factory tests in Japan. He finished up ninth overall, missing only three races, but he was in pain for all of them except the first and the last.

1990 was rather better, with Doohan picking his own pace and steadily improving until, by year's end, he'd won his first GP in Hungary and almost won another at Phillip Island. He was everybody's favourite for 1991.

Sure enough, by the halfway point he was well on target. He was leading Rainey on points after a performance of remarkable consistency, on the rostrum at every one of the first eight races, and winner of three of them. Even when he fell at Assen, when making a bid for a breakaway win, he retained the points lead under the curious system of last year where riders dropped their worst two scores. But he had lost one of his lives, and he knew the truth was that his Honda, although fast, was reluctant to attack the corners in his preferred style, running visibly wider lines than Rainey's Yamaha and Schwantz's Suzuki. Gradually Rainey racked up the points, and Doohan had to be content with second.

The first race of 1992 seemed to have reversed all that. Rainey was starting the season injured, and Schwantz soon followed suit. Far more important was the machine equation. The performance advantage wrought by HRC in adopting the 'big bang' firing order was the revelation of the year. More importantly for Mick, he was now clearly the top man in the Honda team, having quickly supplanted the crash-prone Gardner, and the bike had been tailored closely to his style. He had everything right. The year was his to command.

How and why he again lost the title to the same formidable rival is analysed elsewhere in *Motocourse*. It is more important here to examine why he got into the position to do so.

The first question is one that has vexed a number of disgruntled European riders, and continues to do so: just what is it about Australian and American riders that means they get all the best jobs?

The short answer is 'lap times'. But there is a lot more to it than that, and the full reply includes a peroration on the fashion for things Australian (soap operas, beer and wine, films, comedians and pop singers included), as well as a passing look at the national characteristics of young countries where a brashly competitive spirit can be nurtured without Old World angst about offending good taste.

But the single most important common American/Australian ingredient is a matter of being able, first, to race on loose surfaces from a very early age.

Yet every rider is an individual, with his own complex pattern of techniques and responses that he has developed over the course of his early years. Doohan's riding style is very distinctive. He likes to ride the front wheel, putting his broad shoulders right over the steering axis and working away at that front tyre contact patch, while controlling the bike's attitude with the spinning rear. He likes to break the tyres loose, the front as well as the rear, using incipient front slide to supplement the front brake to scrub off excess speed as well as to initiate the turn. By the same token he uses the rear brake extensively in the early and middle part of the corner, to apply fine adjustments to line. And, all the while, he is juggling his weight on the footrests, loading the inside peg to promote more slide and the outside to reduce it. He wears out a pair of boots in a race meeting.

Though he pretends that he doesn't really understand exactly what it is he does, he does admit the value of his early influences. 'My style comes from a dirt bike ... get over on top of it, and push it down. That's why I sit over the front. That's how I feel comfortable. My brothers ride the same style – it may be something in the family. I've never been influenced by other riders' techniques. I guess you learn things all the time from other riders, but I've never actually watched anyone to see how they do it.'

But crew chief Burgess does allow there is an element of truth in Doohan's disingenuity. Jeremy previously worked with Freddie Spencer in his good years, and later with Wayne Gardner in his championship year; and it is the former who comes to his mind when he considers his current charge. 'He has a lot more natural ability than anyone I've seen since Freddie. He is the same sort of rider – if there is some sort of problem with suspension or handling, he will compensate for it with his riding. Unless things are really bad, he can disguise the bike's failings with his own performance. His throttle control is exceptional. He spins the rear tyre a lot, but it seldom looks like it.' The new bike, with its more easily modulated power, was a real godsend to Doohan. It didn't change the way he rode, but it made it a lot easier for him to do it.

Doohan had to swallow a big and bitter pill in 1992. It would be serendipity if 1993 presented him with the same opportunity – of a bike demonstrably better than those of his rivals. Either way, he'll be trying to win races. And maybe just hoping a little secretly that this time it will be his turn to put the number one on the front of the bike.

Five good reasons for buying a Honda.

1ST

On Wednesday 10th June 1992, Honda's CBR600F dominated the Isle of Man Supersport 600 by taking the first 5 places.

Truly the leader in its class.

CASTROL HONDA BRITAIN TEAM RESULTS

TT FORMULA ONE

Phillip McCallen's first TT win. Honda achieve 11 consecutive TT F1 wins and secure Manufacturers Award.

1st – P McCallen (VFR750R)
3rd – J Dunlop (VFR750R)
4th – N Jefferies (VFR750R)

SUPERSPORT 600

Fastest race average 115.04mph P. McCallen.
Honda win Manufacturers Award.
Steve Hislop sets a new lap record of 117.01mph.

1st – P McCallen
2nd – S Hislop
3rd – S Ward
4th – N Jefferies
5th – B Jackson
(All CBR600Fs)

SUPERSPORT 400

2nd – P McCallen (VFR400)
4th – N Jefferies (VFR 400)

125 TT

Joey Dunlop takes first place equalling Mike Hailwood's all time record of 14 TT wins.

All entrants rode Honda RS125s – Honda win Manufacturers Award.

SIDECAR A & B

M Boddice and D Wells (CBR600F) achieve 2nd overall.

And, of course, for the 17th year in succession, the TT travelling marshals were Honda mounted – this year on VFR750Fs.

Racing with Castrol

HONDA
COME RIDE WITH US

LIVING IN THE SHADOW OF THE NSR

FROM the moment that it burbled down the pit lane for the first time at Suzuka, the NSR500 Honda had the attention of the racing world. And interest deepened as Mick Doohan added total dominance at the Australian Grand Prix to his Japanese Grand Prix victory.

Long before another two straight wins were added to Doohan's points total, the opposition had realised that they could not beat the NSR without joining Honda's switch to a 'Big Bang' or close firing order engine.

Suzuki got their act together fastest and raced their version for the first time at the Hockenheimring. At least Doug Chandler did, while Kevin Schwantz stuck to the older powerplant, saying that he hoped to slipstream the NSR and that the older engine's over-rev potential would be needed. He was optimistic, but never picked up the Honda's slipstream.

Cagiva fielded their version at the next round in Holland. Yamaha were slowest and got theirs into action two weeks later, in Hungary. They all suffered from reliability problems, however, the Yamahas splitting crankcases and the Suzukis breaking crankshafts. The Cagivas seemed to have fewest problems and, all in all, it was the Italian marque's best season ever.

Some of their success may well be down to engineer Ricardo Rosa, new to motor cycles after two years with Ferrari. He took overall charge of the race effort, co-ordinating the work of the talented engineers who were already there, Andrea Goggi in charge of engine development and chassis designer Ramano Albesiano.

It seems that Cagiva made the biggest improvement when they built their close firing order engine. It was unveiled at Assen where Lawson took Cagiva's first-ever pole position and was battling for the lead when he collided with Schwantz.

Doohan was already injured when Lawson seized pole, but he had still bettered Schwantz's time on the Suzuki. 'You have to forget the fact that the engine feels slow. It doesn't seem to be going anywhere,' said Lawson. 'You just have to believe the lap times. If you didn't have those you'd park the new engine straight away because it sure doesn't feel fast.'

Cagiva engineer Andrea Goggi naturally did not want to give too much away about the revised engine, but he admitted that they had followed what they believed was Honda's lead. 'We have an idea about the firing interval that they use, about 60 to 80 degrees. We tested our ideas on the bench and, of course, had to do some different balance calculations.'

After the controversial Lawson–Schwantz crash at Assen, Cagiva won the next round in Hungary. It was a race won in peculiar circumstances, because Lawson was one of the few who picked intermediate tyres, but there's no denying the Cagiva had come far enough to win a Grand Prix in '92.

They'd overcome the very limiting front tyre problems of '91, swapping from Michelin to Dunlop and from Ohlins to Showa. At the start of the year the changes seemed to have given them a disadvantage: the team struggled to get the bike to work and produced dismal results. By the European Grand Prix, however, the bike was quick enough for Lawson to race with the leaders for a few early laps.

Lawson had recommended Showa suspension after his experience racing the Honda in 1990. During the season Showa developed their answer to the Ohlins CES rear suspension unit, an electronic logic control for the damping. Showa offered Honda the same system but, although it was used on the older model '91 NSR being raced by Shinichi Itoh in Japan, the electronic Showa unit was never used at the Grands Prix. As HRC chief engineer Mr Shigeru Hattori explained: 'While it seems to be an advantage on the 1991 NSR it offers no advantage on the '92 bike. This year's machine just doesn't seem to need it.'

Honda's 'Big Bang' engine has improved the handling of the machine so much that far less experimentation has been required all round. 'It seems that the bike is right and there is no need for adjustment,' continued Hattori. 'We have found the same thing with the front geometry. The standard head angle is 67.5° (22.5°) and we have inserts that can alter that up to +1° and move the head forward or back up to 10 mm, but Mick Doohan does not use them. It seems that the bike is right the way it is.'

The NSR made great strides in handling but the chassis and suspension remained virtually unchanged from the '91 model. Though there have been some internal changes, the forks are the same 43 mm diameter Showa units used last year, with carbon inner tubes and steel outers. This gives an exceptional degree of stiffness from the carbon tube while retaining the low friction and good wear properties of the coated steel outers. The Showa rear suspension unit was similarly improved.

Though the engine is completely new it retains the 36 mm carburettors Doohan used in '91 and while previously Gardner has preferred the 38s, this year only the 36 mm carbs have been employed. Hattori also put that down to the characteristics of the new engine. 'It just seems that this engine has the right characteristics with the 36 mm carbs and there is no advantage in using the bigger carbs.'

One of the few differences between the NSRs ridden by Doohan and Gardner are the rim sizes. Gardner uses wider rims, preferring a 3.75-in. front and 6.25-in. rear while Doohan goes for the 3.5-in. front and 6.00-in. rear. 'It is because of riding style,' explained Hattori. 'Mr Gardner likes to brake very late, turn sharply and accelerate hard. Mr Doohan uses a higher bank angle and higher corner speed. That also causes them to use a different engine position. Wayne Gardner has his engine much lower in the frame. If he has his engine as high as Mick Doohan he has a lot of problems with the bike pitching forward and back because of his rapid deceleration and acceleration. Mr Doohan does not have that problem and prefers the higher engine position because of the feeling and control that it gives him.'

Honda started the season with their NSR in a different class from the rest of the field, but they know it will not last forever. 'We realise that the other manufacturers were catching up towards the end of the season,' admitted Hattori. 'We think that we still have the edge in two areas, reliability and power. Vibration causes loss of power and we worked hard to limit that in our design. We have yet to decide exactly what to do for next year, it might be a big change or just details, we are still considering it. We had six items under consideration for this year's engine and we did not use all of them. We will be testing those items again for next year's engine but there is not much time for experimentation.'

Mr Yoichi Oguma, vice-president of HRC, has already said that they will be seriously considering electronic fuel injection for next season and Hattori said that it would be something a little special. 'We prefer not to copy other manufacturers. We have a single crank engine instead of a twin and we will probably have a different sort of fuel injection system.'

Honda have already experimented with fuel injection on NSR250s raced in the Japanese championship and they are well advanced with the electronic measurement required for the engine management system – things like the detonation detectors, the airflow measurement and various engine temperature recordings have been seen on the NSR already.

The airflow sensors were mounted in the handlebar level air intakes this year, whereas last year they were hidden in the lower level air intakes. This year's airbox is a beautiful design that certainly looks as though it provides a mass of cool air for the engine. 'The airbox design is very important,' Hattori confirmed. 'We did a lot of wind tunnel work on it and it contributes both to the power output and the engine characteristics. We have improved the radiators, which are not greatly different in shape or size, but we have found considerable improvements through more detailed changes, things like fin thickness and number.'

Engine cooling continues to be an important consideration. Radiator designs improve all the time but, as power outputs increase, higher heat outputs go hand in hand and races in hot countries are always an extra concern. HRC tried extra-wide radiators at Eastern Creek during practice but used the narrower, more aerodynamic originals for the race. In Malaysia they were featured on Doohan and Beattie's machines. The small triangular radiator in the bottom of the fairing was also retained.

The Marlboro Yamaha squad received new fairings in Australia,

By PETER CLIFFORD

Honda's NSR appeared at Suzuka, and cast its shadow over the year. This is Doohan's race bike. Neat new fairing-nose intakes concealed electronic sensors behind the grill – oddly the shapely carbon-fibre air ducts behind weren't also used to provide support.

Inset: Honda riders had a neatly finished handlebar module that would have done credit to a production model. Red slide switch is the engine kill button; yellow three-way to select alternative ignition/exhaust curves to change the shape of the power curve.

Cagiva didn't use the Ferrari-designed carbon-fibre frame, but did use a similar swing arm. This is Barros at Hockenheim before the advent of the drone-clone engine. The bike lacked top speed, possibly because of poor aerodynamics.

which were not built to run extra cool but rather for improved aerodynamics. The engine air intakes had been moved from the leading edge of the side panels and placed inside. They are near rectangular holes in the inside of the fairing, in front of the radiator and above the front wheel. They feed the carbs via ducts in the sides of the fairing in the same way as the old versions. The fairing is much cleaner with the new system.

At the Malaysian Grand Prix one of the neatest cooling modifications was sported by Jochen Schmid, who had mesh panels moulded into the fairing of his 250 Yamaha. Panels either side of the front number plate let air onto the rider's arms and chest while panels in the side of the fairing let air out from the radiator. 'It is probably about two degrees better for the rider and the engine,' quipped Schmid.

Aprilia's chief engineer Jan Witteveen said that it was very hard to keep the engines running cool in Malaysia. 'We have a bigger radiator here but it hardly makes any difference at all. The problem is that the outside air temperature is 35 to 38 degrees and is so warm that you could have a radiator the size of a truck and the bike would still not get cool, no matter how much water you pumped through it.

'You can certainly lose a lot of power if you let the temperature get too high. The power loss curve is not a straight line either. If you let the engine temperature rise from 50 to 55°C then you might lose 1.5 horsepower with the 250, half that with the 125. The next five degrees loses you 2.5 horsepower on the 250 and the next five degrees another 4 or 5 horsepower.'

Hockenheim is the place where engineers hope that the ambient temperature will not be too high so that they can concentrate on aerodynamics rather than cooling. Schmid was using some very interesting detail fairing changes in the form of a small letterbox slot in the nose beneath the number plate taking air into a flat chamber created by a double skin over the number plate area. The air flowed upwards behind the number plate to three-quarters of the way up the nose where it exited out onto the number plate again through a long horizontal row of tiny holes, less than a millimetre in diameter.

The theory is that this creates a special boundary layer that cuts skin friction. Similar ducting either side of the top of the front mudguard fed rows of holes down either side of the tiny front fork fairings.

Hockenheim saw Honda debut special nose extensions for their NSR500s. These took advantage of the new rule for this season that allows the nose to extend up to 100 mm in front of the wheel spindle.

The extension clipped onto the standard fairing and just covered the front number plate and air intakes. Starting from the base of the screen it sloped out at a greater angle to the vertical, giving the fairing a more aggressive look and presumably helping penetration and/or downforce for stability.

The Yamaha France team continued to experiment with the Honda-style noses they tried at Catalunya, i.e. with air intakes either side of the front number plate. Mackenzie and DuHamel raced with the new fairings which were also available to some of the Roc Yamaha riders (but not used by Goddard).

Unofficial Hockenheim speeds

Rider	*Machine*	*Session*	*Speed (mph)*
Mick Doohan	Honda	Sessions 1 & 2	192
Wayne Gardner	Honda	Sessions 1 & 2	192
Doug Chandler	Suzuki	Session 4	191
Wayne Rainey	Yamaha	Sessions 1, 2 & 3	190
John Kocinski	Yamaha	Sessions 3 & 4	190
Kevin Schwantz	Suzuki	Session 3	189
Alex Criville	Honda	Sessions 1, 2 & 4	189
Alexandre Barros	Cagiva	Session 3	188
Juan Garriga	Yamaha	Sessions 1, 2 & 4	187
Eddie Lawson	Cagiva	Session 4	187
Miguel DuHamel	Yamaha	Session 3	186
Peter Goddard	Roc Yamaha	Session 4	185
Niall Mackenzie	Yamaha	Session 3	184

From the trap speed at Hockenheim it looked as though the Cagiva needed help either from improved aerodynamics or engine power. That was before their 'Big Bang' engine, but while the Cagiva was more competitive in the second half of the year, perhaps it would benefit from better aerodynamics.

Cagiva have access to the very best technology through their association with Ferrari. It was the Italian automotive legend that produced Cagiva's carbon swing arm and carbon front wheel. Ferrari were working on a full carbon frame, an updated version of the one that Randy Mamola tried at the end of his last season with Cagiva in 1990, but it never appeared.

Carbon frames may seem less essential with the current weight rule of 130 kg minimum but there is a school of thought which says that even the current huge section aluminium frames are not stiff enough. That is the view of Lars Isaksson of Ohlins.

'Stiffness is still a big problem. I think any chassis today is too weak, any bike. Maybe not the Honda, that looks pretty good. From 125 to 500 there are problems, both swing arm and chassis. With stiffer construction we would have fewer problems,' explained the Swede during the European Grand Prix at Barcelona's Circuit de Catalunya.

'On this track you have a high speed chicane and if you go and look there you can see the wheels moving out of line because the chassis is twisting. The riders can really feel it also. If you ask me, our choice for the future would be to stiffen the chassis. I am sure the future is in carbon-fibre chassis, things like that. It has got to be, because it is the best material for this kind of thing, light and strong.

'We can do big changes on suspension now and it doesn't change very much because suspension isn't the problem. There is no point in trying to control the suspension when the chassis is a spring over which you have no control. You just make it worse if you try to control it. If you make the suspension harder you make it worse because you are giving the chassis more load, and it flexes more.

'Achieving a stiff chassis is the first thing, to feel the differences resulting from the changes that we are able to make. We can change anything, not only suspensionwise but also geometry, in terms of offsets, steering angles, ride heights, swing-arm heights and so on, but I don't think they have such a big effect so long as we don't have a stiff chassis. That is true from 125 to 500, all bikes, both front and rear, they both affect each other and both are affected by the stiffness of the chassis and swing arm.'

For the World Championship-winning Marlboro Yamahas, Ohlins produced some new lower triple clamps to improve stiffness and these made their debut at Donington. They clamped the outer fork tubes over a greater length and left less unsupported. The fork tubes had been increased in diameter from 42 to 46 mm for the '92 season.

The Ohlins CES system became a permanent fixture. 'The CES works really good right now,' explained Isaksson. 'It took us a couple of

Malcolm Bryan

months to sort it out but right now it is very good, we use it all the time and both Wayne and John are very, very happy with it. We don't have it entirely sorted out for wet conditions and Wayne still uses the standard unit then, though John uses the CES.' Isaksson admitted that they hoped to produce a CES front fork for the '93 season.

White Power were also working on electronically controlled suspension, their efforts being conducted with Aprilia's Loris Reggiani and the team's electronics expert, Nino Bandiera, who explained why they had come to look at a system that relies on an electronically controlled motor to alter damping in real time. 'The problem on the bike is that when the rider is on the brakes, all the weight tips forward and the rear wheel has little or no traction. In this instance it is better to have softer compression damping on the rear shock. But when the rider is accelerating out of the corner then you need harder suspension, more compression damping.

'Because of this we thought about something that could alter this while the bike is being ridden. We came up with the idea of an electric motor to alter the damping under electronic logic control. We take three pieces of information, one is the shock position, two the speed of the bike and the third is the acceleration of the bike. With this information the logic chip decides what to do.

'There is an electric motor outside the shock that then turns and alters the compression damping of the shock. The valving is inside, connected to the motor by a shaft.

'We use this system all the time, only on Reggiani's bike. Loris has eight positions available to him but normally he will only change one or two clicks more or less. He will probably just use it to compensate as the tyre gets worn: one click less as the tyre wears.

'At the moment we are only working with the rear suspension but everything we are doing here is also applicable to the front. We just prefer to do things step by step. There are a lot of problems with anything new, you never know quite when you are going to be ready to race with it, so we prefer to solve one problem at a time.'

Bandiera went on to explain that this is only the beginning. 'We could alter the pre-load of the spring and everything else, the rebound damping, for example, by electronic means. Certainly if you could control all facets of the shock performance electronically you could improve the bike's performance greatly. It would help stability and acceleration.

'We started to test the adjustable pre-load in the middle of the year but it was not really possible to do the work we wanted to during the season. That will have to wait till the winter. The problem is that the power required to drive this system is significant, the batteries are heavy. The damping system changes are not such a problem because the power requirement is much lower.

Pretty new production Aprilias were popular in the 125 class, and an effective alternative to the dominant Hondas. Here Alessandro Gramigni's victorious works bike (39) makes for the track with the production Aprilias of Bruno Casanova (15), Carlos Giro (31) and Maik Stief (40).

Malcolm Bryan

'The time taken to alter the suspension unit is critical and obviously that is a major consideration with the pre-load pump, a real problem because it demands such a powerful pump. The pump in a Formula One car takes power from the engine but our pump is electrical. The pump system uses the same input signals and we change the pre-load and damping at the same time, for the same reason. We will try to have everything working, rebound, compression and pre-load adjustment, ready for the start of next season.'

In the respect that it uses an electronic logic system, the factory Aprilia's suspension is more advanced than the engine and there is a good reason for this, as Jan Witteveen explained. 'My programme is to develop the engine mechanically to the point where we believe it is operating at 90 to 95 per cent of the potential of the mechanical parts before looking to electronics. Honda already do this but on our engine the only electronic thing is the ignition. We have a pneumatic powervalve rather than an electronic one. Our concept is inexpensive and easy to alter.'

Aprilia had a very impressive season. Even though their 125 effort is a spin-off from their 250 development, they still won the 125 championship and almost took the 250 manufacturers' title from Honda. Witteveen claimed that Aprilia had made no dramatic developments for the 1992 season, only detail changes. 'The whole bike is better,' he explained. 'The cycle parts and engine are both improved slightly. The bike handles a bit better, steers a bit easier and is more stable under braking. We eliminated a lot of the problems we had last year. The main thing was the change in engine position and making everything more rigid, the frame, swing arm, updating the suspension and so on. Another important thing is the Dunlop tyres. They are very good.

'The engine changes are only very fine detail modifications, and we are surprised that the small changes we made produced enough of an improvement. They have, though, because the lap times show the improvement. I think that is due a little bit to the tyres, the frame and probably least of all the engine.

'Perhaps the most important thing on the engine side is not the changes that we made but the fact that we have more information now, more experience. We set up the team last year, the two teams, the Valesi team and the Unlimited team. The same teams are in their second year and can set up the bike a little better.

'We haven't made such a revolutionary change that we can say we have 2, 3 or 4 horsepower more because we've changed this or that. The main area we worked on was to reduce internal friction and we looked at all the components in this respect. We looked at the control of the water temperature as this can have a significant effect.

'Working in this careful way is effective, but it is also expedient. We don't have huge resources, we are a very small company and have a small budget. I prefer to go step by step because I see that with the concept we have now we can make a lot of progress. We are not finished. There is a lot still to be gained.'

If there really is a great deal still for Aprilia to gain, then the opposition will have to watch out. Honda won the techno war in the 500 class by fundamentally changing the way we think about power requirements while Aprilia took the conservative path.

Both were right.

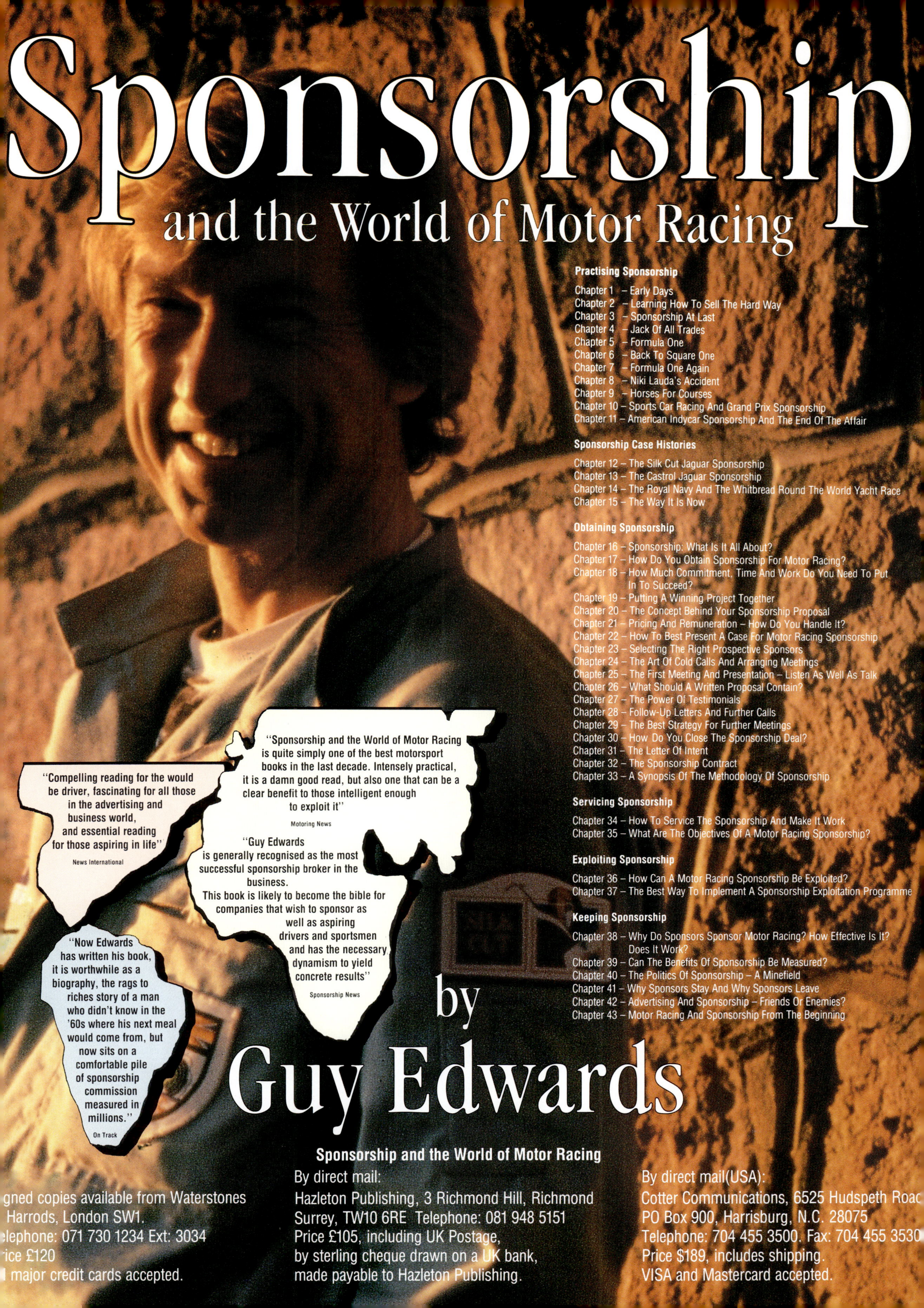
Sponsorship
and the World of Motor Racing
Practising Sponsorship
Chapter 1 – Early Days
Chapter 2 – Learning How To Sell The Hard Way
Chapter 3 – Sponsorship At Last
Chapter 4 – Jack Of All Trades
Chapter 5 – Formula One
Chapter 6 – Back To Square One
Chapter 7 – Formula One Again
Chapter 8 – Niki Lauda's Accident
Chapter 9 – Horses For Courses
Chapter 10 – Sports Car Racing And Grand Prix Sponsorship
Chapter 11 – American Indycar Sponsorship And The End Of The Affair
Sponsorship Case Histories
Chapter 12 – The Silk Cut Jaguar Sponsorship
Chapter 13 – The Castrol Jaguar Sponsorship
Chapter 14 – The Royal Navy And The Whitbread Round The World Yacht Race
Chapter 15 – The Way It Is Now
Obtaining Sponsorship
Chapter 16 – Sponsorship: What Is It All About?
Chapter 17 – How Do You Obtain Sponsorship For Motor Racing?
Chapter 18 – How Much Commitment, Time And Work Do You Need To Put In To Succeed?
Chapter 19 – Putting A Winning Project Together
Chapter 20 – The Concept Behind Your Sponsorship Proposal
Chapter 21 – Pricing And Remuneration – How Do You Handle It?
Chapter 22 – How To Best Present A Case For Motor Racing Sponsorship
Chapter 23 – Selecting The Right Prospective Sponsors
Chapter 24 – The Art Of Cold Calls And Arranging Meetings
Chapter 25 – The First Meeting And Presentation – Listen As Well As Talk
Chapter 26 – What Should A Written Proposal Contain?
Chapter 27 – The Power Of Testimonials
Chapter 28 – Follow-Up Letters And Further Calls
Chapter 29 – The Best Strategy For Further Meetings
Chapter 30 – How Do You Close The Sponsorship Deal?
Chapter 31 – The Letter Of Intent
Chapter 32 – The Sponsorship Contract
Chapter 33 – A Synopsis Of The Methodology Of Sponsorship
Servicing Sponsorship
Chapter 34 – How To Service The Sponsorship And Make It Work
Chapter 35 – What Are The Objectives Of A Motor Racing Sponsorship?
Exploiting Sponsorship
Chapter 36 – How Can A Motor Racing Sponsorship Be Exploited?
Chapter 37 – The Best Way To Implement A Sponsorship Exploitation Programme
Keeping Sponsorship
Chapter 38 – Why Do Sponsors Sponsor Motor Racing? How Effective Is It? Does It Work?
Chapter 39 – Can The Benefits Of Sponsorship Be Measured?
Chapter 40 – The Politics Of Sponsorship – A Minefield
Chapter 41 – Why Sponsors Stay And Why Sponsors Leave
Chapter 42 – Advertising And Sponsorship – Friends Or Enemies?
Chapter 43 – Motor Racing And Sponsorship From The Beginning
"Compelling reading for the would be driver, fascinating for all those in the advertising and business world, and essential reading for those aspiring in life"
News International
"Sponsorship and the World of Motor Racing is quite simply one of the best motorsport books in the last decade. Intensely practical, it is a damn good read, but also one that can be a clear benefit to those intelligent enough to exploit it"
Motoring News
"Guy Edwards is generally recognised as the most successful sponsorship broker in the business. This book is likely to become the bible for companies that wish to sponsor as well as aspiring drivers and sportsmen and has the necessary dynamism to yield concrete results"
Sponsorship News
"Now Edwards has written his book, it is worthwhile as a biography, the rags to riches story of a man who didn't know in the '60s where his next meal would come from, but now sits on a comfortable pile of sponsorship commission measured in millions."
On Track
by
Guy Edwards
Sponsorship and the World of Motor Racing
gned copies available from Waterstones
Harrods, London SW1.
elephone: 071 730 1234 Ext: 3034
rice £120
major credit cards accepted.
By direct mail:
Hazleton Publishing, 3 Richmond Hill, Richmond
Surrey, TW10 6RE Telephone: 081 948 5151
Price £105, including UK Postage,
by sterling cheque drawn on a UK bank,
made payable to Hazleton Publishing.
By direct mail(USA):
Cotter Communications, 6525 Hudspeth Roac
PO Box 900, Harrisburg, N.C. 28075
Telephone: 704 455 3500. Fax: 704 455 3530
Price $189, includes shipping.
VISA and Mastercard accepted.

THE REMARKABLE HISTORY OF THE NSR HONDA

By KEVIN CAMERON

RACE bike design is meaningless considered apart from the rider. At a given factory, the trend of design follows the needs of its lead rider's style, and may in time become its prisoner. That style, in turn, is the joint creation of the rider's nature, and of the strengths and weaknesses of the machines he rode as he developed that style. Eventually the rider, too, becomes a prisoner of his own style. It resists change because it is security, the sum of what he has found to be both fast and safe.

Before Freddie Spencer met tuner Erv Kanemoto in 1977, he preferred a tractor-like torque curve, but Erv's creations made explosive power in a narrow range. Freddie, marvellously adaptable, not only learned to use this but made a virtue of it, utilising the sudden torque to snap the rear wheel loose as an aid to steering.

Lucky for Honda. When Honda failed to win GPs with its four-stroke NR500, it sent in HRC's two-stroke group, ably motivated by the get-it-done-today engineer Miyakoshi. By a curious accident of history, their creation, the NS3, fitted Spencer's style perfectly.

It's commonly supposed that the NS, with its reed valves, had the wide power of the MX machines that inspired it. It did not. In fact, the early engines gave power only from 9800-11,000 rpm, and little of it – 108 bhp in early races. For Freddie, this machine was like a peaky 250 with double power. His style was to enter corners fast enough to lose the front end, then recover front grip with instant throttle, transferring weight from the overloaded and sliding front tyre on to the underused rear. To onlookers, the effect of this instant-on throttle looked like bottom-end grunt, but in fact it was simply Spencer recovering the front end.

Engineers, too, find security in their accustomed ways. Previously, Miyakoshi had seen a simple, well-executed single-cylinder prototype engine outperform a twin of equal displacement. Why should this be, when conventional wisdom expects more power from a twin's larger port area and higher potential rpm? Miyakoshi's answer was that the single had less friction, because of its fewer bearings and other moving parts. The concept would influence all future road racing designs from Honda.

Despite this engine fundamentalism, a strong element in Honda's Grand Prix fortunes is the company's penchant for technological gambling, as we shall see.

The NS3 was a distillation of simplicity: reed valves, three MX-like cylinders in a dense package, a single crank. It wouldn't have worked in hands other than Spencer's. Yet his unique success on the triple confirmed Honda engineers in their method. Spencer and Kanemoto knew how lucky they had been to take the title from more powerful opposition, and pressed Honda to build its own horsepower machine. It was produced for 1984 as the first NSR500, its engine designed in familiar simple style: a single, five-

Henk Keulemans

Photos: Malcolm Bryan

bearing crank, four cylinders in a compact V, with reed induction entering the crankcases from the rear.

With this minimalist engine was combined risky chassis pioneering. Like the French Elf prototype bikes Honda had cautiously supported, the new NSR500 carried its fuel beneath the engine, with the four exhaust pipes looped up and over, insulated beneath a dummy fuel tank. A taste for radical solutions had created the complex NR500; the NSR chassis proved the appetite still existed.

In the drawing office, far from trackside reality, engineers focus on the simple fact that rate of acceleration equals thrust, divided by weight. The relationship is true, but much mischief is committed in its name. In pre-season testing at Surfers' Paradise, Australia, Freddie consistently chose the heaviest combinations of chassis and swing arm. Those stiffer parts gave the stability needed for fast laps. The lightweight

Opposite page: **A penchant for technological gambling: an HRC technician plays hunt the sparking plugs, cunningly hidden beneath a tangle of hot exhausts on the original 1984 'inverted' NSR** ***(top)*****; more high-risk technology added a carbon-fibre rear wheel, which broke in practice for the first GP** ***(centre)*****. Detail** ***(bottom)*** **shows horrendous inaccessibility of complex new engine, with wacky underslung fuel tank, and the rough-and-ready look of a developing prototype.**

By the German GP, fifth race of 1984, Spencer was so desperate that he asked for his old NS three-cylinder back. Honda succumbed and he won the race. Four races later, at Spa-Francorchamps, the same switch yielded the same result. Here in the Belgian pits ***(below left)*** **the NSR is on the left.**

components, designed with such faith in numbers, were hopeless wobblers.

The final design pushed its front end, the result of too little weight up front. Acceleration was good, but top speed was no better than the NS3's – 175 mph. As the season developed, Freddie noted that the NSR was slower to change direction than the NS. Back-to-back tests were made through an artificial chicane. The NS shot through neatly, but the NSR knocked down the cones. When they retested with the NSR's fuel tank nearly empty, with 35 pounds of ballast up among the pipes, versus an NS with full fuel, the two bikes flicked through with equal ease. The underslung fuel tank, which increased roll polar moment, had been a mistake.

As they had done with the famous RC-166 'six' and the NR500 before, Honda gave the NSR very light flywheels. With its 130 bhp, it tached-out the instant the rear tyre broke traction. It pulled from 9500-12,000, but lacked the explosive torque Spencer now liked to use for rear-steering. New porting boosted power over 140 but Spencer might willingly have traded much of it away for a wider band. The gamble on novelty had been too big. Despite Freddie's skills and Honda's hard work, the title went to Yamaha.

Everything was again new for 1985, but this time the changes were refinement, not revolution. The fuel returned to its traditional position above the engine. The many tubes of the 1984 chassis coalesced into the much stiffer twin beams of a pure Cobas-inspired design. The swing arm became a simple twin-beam cantilever structure.

Yamaha had by now adopted Honda's reed intake system, and its twin-crank OW bikes were fast. They also changed direction quickly: a single spinning crank resists being twisted out of its plane of rotation; paired cranks, counter-rotating like Yamaha's, less so. To make the NSR manoeuvre with the Yamaha, yet adhere to its single-crank philosophy, Honda were forced to adopt steeper steering geometry. Steep geometry made this very fast bike buck and weave, but Freddie was able to cover its shortcomings by further amazing extensions of his own performance. The 1985 season looked perfect as Spencer won both 500 and 250 titles – but it had consumed him, eventually putting him out of GP racing.

The 1985 bike ***(top)*** **was utterly conventional in layout, and swept Spencer to his second 500 class title.**

In 1986, HRC allowed Moriwaki to build a mildly unconventional chassis for the bike ***(middle)*****. Note the four low-level exhaust expansion chambers, fighting for space within the fairing belly-pan.**

Above: **Gardner perforce took over from the mysteriously ailing Spencer in 1986, the bike's last year with four low-level exhausts and the haphazard air intake by the rider's knee for the rear-mounted carburettors.**

Anticipating his return, Honda developed a new bike for 1986. Every time more rear tyre grip, more power or more sudden power is given to a race bike, it lifts weight off the front wheel during off-corner acceleration, making it 'push', or run wide. To compensate, Honda moved the NSR engine forward. Its torque curve was adjusted for a sharper onset, but with considerable over-rev capability. Over-rev is not gratuitous abuse imposed by the rider, but is the engine's ability to give usable power for hundreds of rpm beyond the power peak – an ability as desirable as a seventh gearbox speed.

Wayne Gardner now became the *de facto* lead rider. His style had evolved on large production-based four-strokes, whose wide, flat torque was completely different from the new NSR's violent power. Gardner gamely rode in bronc-busting style, accepting the machine's slip-and-grip corner-exit performances. Many windscreens were broken in his efforts to remain on the machine as it went its own way. Yamaha took the title, and Gardner made it clear that he expected the 1987 machine reconfigured to suit his, and not Spencer's, preferences.

Engine concerns continued to dominate. The intake system was now moved from behind the engine to a position in the cylinder V. One pair of exhaust pipes now ran straight back through the seat, while the others ran under the engine to emerge on the right. After comparative testing, Honda set aside its ATAC system of variable exhaust pipe volume, and adopted a Yamaha-like but improved variable exhaust port height control in its place. The direction of crankshaft rotation was also reversed, to reduce front wheel lift

A major redesign for 1987 saw the enclosed cylinder angle widened from 90 degrees to 112 to accommodate carburettors between the V, and lead the upper cylinder exhausts directly out through the seat *(right)*. Crankshaft rotation was also reversed to reduce torque-induced wheelstands.

The result was a bike fit to win the World Championship for Wayne Gardner *(below)*.

Henk Keulemans

Malcolm Bryan

under acceleration.

Through his own absolute determination and mental toughness, together with the Honda's now tremendous top speed, Gardner over-rode handling difficulties to become World Champion in 1987. Honda's strategy had been to counter Yamaha's handling with speed, balancing points lost on slower courses with those gained on tracks with 'Honda lanes' – long straights on which the Hondas could simply pull out of other bikes' slipstreams and disappear.

Yamaha's development aim was different, pursuing high torque over a range beginning low down, with little over-rev. The goal was to use power to steer. Smooth, high torque made it possible for Yamaha riders to hold the back tyre loose in long, controlled slides. The Honda, making power more from revs than from torque, could not yet match this ability. The Yamaha could now change direction more quickly than the Honda. While a Yamaha would snap smartly upright after corners, the NSR would overshoot the vertical and oscillate briefly. These effects appeared to arise from the single-crank concept.

For 1988, HRC chassis engineer Tsunoda addressed this problem by radically lowering the whole machine. With most of the droop thus taken out of its swing arm, the Honda now fell prey to unusual changes of attitude during braking and acceleration.

Fashion is powerful. Yamaha had one success in improving its half-hearted 250's handling – by reducing chassis stiffness. They had removed a major chassis cross-member and had hung the engine from thin, bolted-on flex plates at the front. Had chassis at last become too stiff? Some handling dynamics specialists were saying yes, and Yamaha's experience seemed to prove it. Honda desperately needed something that might improve the NSR's handling; they, too, now tried the 'tuned flex' concept. It was a disaster for handling, yielding a machine that was only notionally under its rider's control.

Like warhead counts in the arms race, NSR horsepower ballooned upward, while Honda engineers worked to manage what they had created. In 1988 they tried to smooth acceleration with a system that interconnected throttle angle with exhaust-gate position. They also produced programmable ignition curves, allowing the power curve to be switched instantly from one characteristic to another – softer in lower gears, full power in higher ones. Development of these systems was promising.

As bikes become faster, conventional iron brake technology needs more disc mass to keep brake temperatures at non-destructive levels. A switch to temperature-tolerant carbon allows some escape from this relationship, but carbon brakes needed more development. Honda engineers fiddled endlessly with brake details that were supposed to allow light iron-based discs to handle ever more energy. The real world result was blackened, distorted discs and brake levers that came to the bar – as they did after the 1988 US GP at Laguna Seca. The 1988 NSR, with its odd, pro-squat swing-arm angle, its reduced chassis stiffness and with Gardner's peculiar suspension set-up, was exhausting even to watch, much less to ride. Even the impressive 160 bhp of the more compact, narrower 1988 engine could not compensate. The title returned to Yamaha.

Now Lawson joined Honda. It was not Lawson's style simply to cope, as Gardner had done so frighteningly. He would require the bike to be altered so it could be ridden in his style. So 1989 became the year of

Malcolm Bryan

Eddie Lawson *(left)* brought the number one plate to Honda in 1989, added his craftsmanlike touch to development, and won the NSR's third title.

Lawson complained about chassis flex; HRC responded with an effective second guess, with an extra section welded onto the top of the main frame *(below)*.

maximum development. All problems were attacked simultaneously, and testing was constant. After the failed experiments of 1988, Honda now stiffened everything definitively. Showa's 1989 male-slider fork development would increase front-end stiffness by almost 50 per cent. Ventilated brake rotors improved stopping power. To counter the opposition's faster direction-changing, lighter 16-in. front wheels were again used, sometimes in carbon material. Despite this, the machine remained, in Lawson's words, 'the ponderous Honda'. Kenny Roberts expressed the view that Honda would not get any single-crank machine to handle properly.

Just as predicted by English motor cycle dynamics researcher Geoff Rowe, the greatly stiffened Honda now displayed magnified sensitivity to small bumps. Previously absorbed through slight frame deflections, these were now passed on to dampers that couldn't even 'see' them. On balance, however, the stiffer chassis was a success, handling the engine's massive power far better than before, and settling down more quickly after upsets. Intensive development plus Lawson's craftsmanlike riding won the 1989 title.

At season's end, Tsunoda confirmed to the press that Honda had indeed built and tested a twin-crank engine. Performance was good – an improvement. No, the machine would not be used now. Why not? The single crank was now immutable; it had become Honda's Way.

For 1990, the engine torque controls that had been in development for more than a year reached maturity. They made a tremendous improvement, transforming the sliding, near-high-siding performances of previous seasons into relatively smooth, fast corner exits. But Yamaha and Suzuki now had similar systems.

Careful design integration now took the place of the 'tacked-on-bits look' that is the natural state of a fast-developing GP bike. Internal airflow was managed with ducts, supplying carburettors with cool, fresh air, while handling radiator intake and exhaust flows as well. Honda GP motor cycles now defined the state of the art in execution. Visual parts quality had become flawless. Nevertheless, 1990 brought only three wins against the Yamaha/Roberts/Rainey success train.

Fuel injection was now a major development programme, but technologies that succeed on cars simply make a GP motor cycle, with its limited traction, very touchy to ride. Further in the future lay direct cylinder fuel injection, with its ability to stop all loss of unburned fuel from the exhaust ports. This would be an advantage simply in reducing the weight of fuel carried. But progress was deliberate rather than revolutionary.

Mick Doohan, riding in a defensive style akin to that of Wayne Gardner, won three GPs in 1991 to come second in the 500 championship – a

Henk Keulemans

Left: **Michael Doohan in 1990 – a new riding style that made fresh demands and revealed long-standing weaknesses in Honda's hallowed single-crankshaft design.**

Bottom: **The 1992 NSR was kept under wraps – but the innovation was in any case out of sight behind the plumbing: a revised firing order and internal changes to improve the engine's strength in the face of the new vibration.**

The 1991 NSR displays its deep frame *(below)*, the top of the carburettor still-air box, the linked exhaust powervalves of the upper cylinders, and an all-of-a-piece appearance that comes with lengthy development and refinement of an established racing bike.

Henk Keulemans

tremendous accomplishment.

Desperate pressure now existed within Honda to overcome the handling advantages enjoyed by Yamaha and Suzuki, both of whom were now using twin, contra-rotating crankshafts. Further, Soichiro Honda, the revered figure who had started it all, now passed from the scene. Perhaps this event inspired even more dogmatic adherence to the single-crank concept.

Desperation can lead men to consider ideas that they would otherwise reject. Tests in 1989 had shown improved off-corner acceleration with a 180 degree paired firing order, instead of the previously used equally spaced 90 degree order. But how can one cylinder 'know' when its mates are firing? Isn't a four-cylinder engine just four singles, working together? Still, the track test was suggestive. What might other firing orders do? Of course, the dyno showed no differences: adding the power curves of four cylinders gives the same total no matter how you stack them. Could the track differences have to do with the manner, rather than the amount, of power delivery?

Honda must now have tested even closer firing orders, firing one pair of cylinders together, then the other pair soon after. The resulting engine sounded more like a big, droning single than a 13,000 rpm road race engine.

Some engineers surely objected. Lumping the engine's four torque impulses together in big bangs would break things – gears, clutch, even chassis or crankcase. Reinforcement – and more weight – would be necessary. Performance would suffer.

But it didn't. The test bike accelerated off corners magnificently. But why, if the dyno saw no significant change? The great scourge of recent seasons had been the corner-exit, high-side crash, in which the rear tyre, pushed to its limit by engine torque, loses grip, slides briefly and then abruptly regains grip, the impact tossing the rider over the high side. Knowing that this hectic process is the reward for pushing the traction limit, riders back away; better to err on the side of safety and championship points than on the other (high) side.

With the Big Bang firing order, the rear tyre receives its torque not as a smooth twisting force, but as a series of concentrated pulses – especially so with the multiplication of lower gears. These pulses would do the work of breaking the tyre's grip – ten times per revolution – so the rider would not have to do it in one big risky slide. It would soften the breakaway. As the rider opened the throttle, the period of slip at each torque bang would grow wider, and the corresponding period of non-slip would shrink. As it slipped a bit at each pulse, it would also slide outward slightly. That would add up to hanging the back end of the bike out in familiar dirt-track style, telling the rider how close to the edge he was. Knowing that, he could confidently run much closer to the limit. That is just what Mick Doohan did.

In early 1992 season races, he would already be in second gear while Wayne Rainey struggled with the ill effects of first. Using the new Big Bang engine, Doohan won the first four GPs straight. Previous to this, Yamaha had acceleration and handling, and could let Honda go on fast tracks yet still win titles. Now Honda had it all – acceleration, off-corner smoothness and top speed. The durability problem was dealt with by using stronger components, and by taking power from the centre of the crank rather than from the end. Big Bang was a gamble that worked.

Honda's competitors began to field narrow firing angle engines of their own at mid-season – only after Doohan had accumulated a vast points lead. Suzuki were first with a 'sound-alike', with a deep, flat exhaust note like the new NSR's. Cagiva were next, and Lawson used the Italian banger to set pole in Holland, then win Cagiva's first-ever GP – in Hungary.

Honda's marriage to the single-crank concept was strong enough to make the company's engineers willing to try crazy means of preserving it – and it had worked. In the long run, though, this success can hurt development. It would be only human for Honda management now to feel they were right all along in clinging to the single crank. What happens next season, when all competitors have Big Bangers? Only Honda will be limited by a single-crank engine, with its congealing effect on direction-changing.

HONDA POWER IN 92

McCALLEN AND DUNLOP ONCE AGAIN THIS SEASON PROVED THAT THE TOP ROAD RACERS RIDE THE TOP MACHINES

27 ROAD RACE WINS IN ONE SEASON INCLUDING 5 AT THE NORTH WEST 200 - ALL ON HONDA POWERED MACHINERY

14TH T.T. WIN AND LAP RECORD HOLDER JOEY DUNLOP EQUALLED THE ALL TIME RECORD OF MIKE HAILWOOD. HONDA AGAIN SHOWED THEIR RELIABILITY

Castrol

Photographs taken using professional riders. Do not try to emulate or copy on public roads.

HONDA
COME RIDE WITH US

500 cc SPECIFICATIONS

Rider's name Machine	Michael Doohan 494.6 cc NSR500 Honda	Wayne Rainey 498 cc YZR500 Yamaha	Kevin Schwantz 498 cc RGV500 Suzuki	Eddie Lawson 498 cc C592 Cagiva
ENGINE **Type/no. cylinders**	Water-cooled four-cylinder two-stroke, single pressed crank, five roller bearings.	Water-cooled four-cylinder two-stroke, twin pressed cranks, four roller bearings each.	Water-cooled four-cylinder two-stroke, twin pressed cranks, four ball bearings each.	Water-cooled four-cylinder two-stroke, twin cranks, four roller bearings each.
Bore & stroke	54 x 54.5 mm.	56 x 50.6 mm.	56 x 50.7 mm.	56 x 50.6 mm.
Induction	Two twin-choke 36 mm Keihins, crankcase reed-valve induction.	Two twin-choke 35 mm electronic power jet flat-slide Mikunis, crankcase reed-valve induction.	Two twin-choke 36 mm electronic power jet flat-slide Mikunis, crankcase reed-valve induction.	Two twin-choke 35 mm electronic power jet flat-slide Mikunis, crankcase reed-valve induction.
Porting	Five transfer, two exhaust.	Seven transfer, three exhaust.	Six transfer, three exhaust.	Five transfer, three exhaust.
Exhaust valve	Electronically controlled draw bridge.	Electronically controlled cylindrical.	Electronically controlled guillotine.	Electronically controlled cylindrical.
Ignition	Electronic with programmable advance curve linked to exhaust powervalve and throttle opening. NGK sparking plugs.	Electronic with programmable advance curve linked to exhaust powervalve and carburettor power jet. NGK sparking plugs.	Electronic with programmable advance curve linked to exhaust powervalve and carburettor power jet. NGK sparking plugs.	Electronic with programmable advance curve linked to exhaust powervalve and carburettor power jet. NGK sparking plugs.
Oil	Elf fuel, engine and gearbox oil.	Castrol engine and gearbox.	Motul engine and gearbox.	Agip engine and gearbox.
Other details	Single plain piston ring, needle-roller small and big end bearings.	Single plain piston ring, needle-roller small end and roller big end bearings.	Single plain piston ring, needle-roller small and big end bearings.	Single plain piston ring, needle-roller small end and roller big end bearings.
TRANSMISSION **Primary drive**	Straight cut gear to clutch via cross shaft from centre of crank.	Straight cut gear to clutch from right-hand end of lower crank.	Straight cut gear to clutch from right-hand end of lower crank.	Straight cut gear to clutch from right-hand end of lower crank.
Clutch	Dry multi-plate, seven friction and seven steel plates, six springs.	Dry multi-plate, five sintered, two organic and six steel plates, six springs.	Dry multi-plate, nine friction and ten steel plates, six springs.	Dry multi-plate, seven friction and eight steel plates, six springs.
Gearbox	Six-speed, alternative ratios for all gears. Drum selection.	Six speed, nine possible ratios for first, seven for second, six for third and fourth, four for fifth and five for sixth. Drum selection.	Six-speed, five possible ratios for first, seven for second, fourteen for third and fourth, seven for fifth and sixth, five different primary ratios giving a total of 200 possibilities. Drum selection.	Six-speed, alternative ratios for all gears. Drum selection. Ten possible ratios for first and fourth, seven for second and fifth, nine for third and sixth.
RUNNING GEAR **Frame**	Twin-spar extruded section aluminium, taper roller head bearings.	Twin-spar fabricated box-section aluminium, taper roller head bearings with inserts for adjusting head angle.	Twin-spar fabricated box-section aluminium with rear section machined from solid, ball and roller head bearings with inserts for adjusting head angle.	Twin-spar fabricated box-section aluminium, taper roller head bearings.
Front suspension	Showa telescopic forks, coil springs, oil damped, externally adjustable.	Ohlins OUT telescopic forks, coil springs, oil damped, adjustable.	Kayaba OUT telescopic forks, coil springs, oil damped, externally adjustable for both high and low speed (compression) and high speed (rebound).	Showa OUT telescopic forks, coil springs, oil damped, adjustable.
Rear suspension	Triangulated box-section aluminium swing arm, needle-roller bearings. One Showa unit, coil spring, nitrogen pressure, oil damped, adjustable with lower end linkage.	Triangulated box-section aluminium swing arm, needle-roller bearings. One Ohlins unit, coil spring, nitrogen pressure, oil damped, either manually adjustable with lower end linkage or CES (automatic electronic) adjustment, direct mounting.	Triangulated box-section aluminium swing arm, needle-roller bearings and shims. One Kayaba unit, coil spring, oil damped, externally adjustable for both high and low speed (compression) and high speed (rebound) with lower end linkage.	Triangulated box-section carbon swing arm, needle-roller bearings. One Showa unit, coil spring, nitrogen pressure, oil damped, manually adjustable with lower end linkage and optional electronic control of compression damping.
Wheels	Honda cast magnesium: 3.50 (occasionally 3.75) in. x 17 in. front and 5.50, 5.75, 6.00, 6.125 and 6.25 in. x 17 in. rear.	Marchesini cast magnesium: 3.75 or 3.50 in. x 17 in. front and 6.00 in. x 17 in. rear (5.50 in. x 18 in. or 6.25 in. x 17 in. for rain tyres).	Suzuki-Marchesini cast magnesium: 3.50 in. x 17 in. front and 6.00 in. x 17 in. rear.	Marchesini cast magnesium: 3.75 in. x 17 in. front and 6.25 in. x 17 in. or 6.25 in. x 16 in. rear.
Tyres	Michelin.	Michelin.	Michelin.	Dunlop.
Brakes	Front: two Brembo supplied carbon-carbon (320 or 290 mm) or cast steel (320 mm) discs. Brembo four piston calipers. Brembo pads. Rear: one Honda ventilated steel (190 mm) disc. HRC two piston caliper. HRC pads.	Front: two Brembo carbon-carbon (290 or 320 mm) or cast iron (270 or 230 mm) discs. Brembo four piston calipers. Brembo pads. Rear: one Yamaha steel (210 mm) disc. Nissin two piston caliper. Yamaha pads.	Front: two AP carbon-carbon (290 or 310 mm) discs. AP six piston calipers. AP pads. Rear: one Suzuki iron (210 mm) disc. Two piston caliper.	Front: two Brembo carbon-carbon (290 or 320 mm) discs. Brembo four piston calipers. Brembo pads. Rear: one Brembo steel (190 mm) disc. Brembo two piston caliper. Brembo pads.

Above: **Honda's all-conquering NSR; frame little changed, engine crucially different.**

Top right: **Honda's neat fairing-nose air intakes led to a substantial still-air box. Note ignition/exhaust control box and servo motor for cable-operated exhaust valves.**

Right: **Cagiva: note sensors on gear linkage: one for computer diagnostics, the other to trigger the ignition cut-out for the 'kill-shift' gearchange system.**

Far right: **Spot the difference:** *centre:* **works 1992 YZR500 Yamaha (Mackenzie's bike) compared with Harris Yamaha** ***(bottom)*****. Works bike has adjustable swing-arm pivot, and extra lower frame cross-brace.**

Below: **Schwantz's Suzuki had a revised frame, and was later first to acquire Honda-copy engine.**

Photos: Henk Keulemans

250 cc SPECIFICATIONS

Rider's name Machine	Luca Cadalora 247.3 cc NSR250 Honda	Loris Reggiani 249.6 cc AFI 92 Aprilia	Wilco Zeelenberg 249 cc RGV250 Suzuki	Jochen Schmid 249 cc YZR250 Yamaha	Jean-Philippe Ruggia 249 cc Gilera
ENGINE **Type/no. cylinders**	Water-cooled twin-cylinder two-stroke, single pressed crank, three ball bearings.	Water-cooled twin-cylinder two-stroke, twin pressed cranks, three ball bearings each.	Water-cooled twin-cylinder two-stroke, single pressed crank, three ball bearings.	Water-cooled twin-cylinder two-stroke, single pressed crank, two ball and two roller bearings.	Water-cooled twin-cylinder two-stroke, single pressed crank, three ball bearings.
Bore & stroke	54 x 54.5 mm.	54 x 54.5 mm.	56 x 50.7 mm.	56 x 50.7 mm.	56 x 50.7 mm.
Induction	Two 38 mm Keihins, crankcase reed-valve induction.	Two 35 x 42 mm oval bore flat-slide Dell'Ortos, disc-valve induction.	Two 39 mm flat-slide Mikunis, crankcase reed-valve induction.	Two 39 mm flat-slide Mikunis, crankcase reed-valve induction.	Two 38 or 40 mm Dell'Ortos, crankcase reed-valve induction.
Porting	Five transfer, two exhaust.	Five transfer, three exhaust.	Six transfer, three exhaust.	Seven transfer, three exhaust.	Seven transfer, three exhaust.
Exhaust valve	Electronically controlled draw bridge.	Vacuum controlled guillotine.	Electronically controlled guillotine.	Electronically controlled cylindrical.	Electronically controlled guillotine.
Ignition	Electronic with programmable advance curve linked to exhaust powervalve. NGK sparking plugs.	Electronic with programmable advance curve linked to exhaust powervalve. NGK sparking plugs.	Electronic with programmable advance curve linked to exhaust powervalve. NGK sparking plugs.	Electronic with programmable advance curve linked to exhaust powervalve. NGK sparking plugs.	Electronic linked to exhaust powervalve. NGK sparking plugs.
Oil	Castrol engine and gearbox.	Mobil engine and gearbox.	Motul engine and gearbox.	Castrol engine and gearbox.	Agip engine and gearbox.
Other details	Single plain piston ring, needle-roller small and big end bearings.	Single plain piston ring, needle-roller small and big end bearings.	Single plain piston ring, needle-roller small and big end bearings.	Single plain piston ring, needle-roller small and roller big end bearings.	Single plain piston ring, needle-roller small and big end bearings.
TRANSMISSION **Primary drive**	Straight cut gear.	Straight cut gear.	Straight cut gear.	Straight cut gear.	Straight cut gear.
Clutch	Dry multi-plate, six friction and six steel plates, five springs.	Dry multi-plate, five friction and six steel plates, six springs.	Dry multi-plate, seven friction and eight steel plates, six springs.	Dry multi-plate, five friction and six steel plates, six springs.	Dry multi-plate, six friction and six steel plates, six springs.
Gearbox	Six-speed, five possible ratios for first four gears, six for fifth and seven for sixth. Drum selection.	Six-speed, nine possible ratios for first, eight for second, four for third, three for fourth and five for fifth and sixth. Drum selection.	Six-speed, seven possible ratios for first, second and fourth gears, fourteen for third and nine for fifth and sixth. Three different primary drive ratios. Drum selection.	Six-speed, drum selection, alternative ratios for all gears.	Six-speed, eight possible ratios for each gear, two possible primary ratios. Drum selection.
RUNNING GEAR **Frame**	Twin-spar extruded section aluminium, with machined section in addition, ball head bearings.	Twin-spar fabricated aluminium, taper roller head bearings with spherical seating.	Twin-spar fabricated box-section aluminium, ball and roller head bearings with inserts for adjusting head angle.	Twin-spar fabricated box-section aluminium, taper roller head bearings with inserts for adjusting head angle.	Twin-spar fabricated aluminium, taper roller head bearings.
Front suspension	Showa telescopic forks, coil springs, oil damped, adjustable.	White Power OUT telescopic forks, coil springs, oil damped, adjustable.	Kayaba OUT telescopic forks, coil springs, oil damped, adjustable.	Ohlins OUT telescopic forks, coil springs, oil damped, adjustable.	Kayaba OUT telescopic forks, coil springs, oil damped, adjustable.
Rear suspension	Triangulated box-section aluminium swing arm, needle-roller bearings. One Showa unit, coil spring, oil damped, adjustable with lower end linkage.	Triangulated box-section aluminium swing arm, roller bearings. One White Power unit, coil spring, oil damped, adjustable with lower end linkage.	Triangulated box-section aluminium swing arm, needle-roller bearings. One Kayaba unit, coil spring, oil damped, adjustable with lower end linkage.	Triangulated box-section aluminium swing arm, needle-roller bearings. One Ohlins unit, coil spring, oil damped, adjustable with lower end linkage.	Triangulated box-section aluminium swing arm, needle-roller bearings. One White Power unit, coil spring, oil damped, adjustable with lower end linkage.
Wheels	Honda cast magnesium: 3.5, 3.65, 3.75, 3.85, 3.95 or 4.00 in. x 17 in. front and 5.10, 5.25, 5.35 or 5.50 in. x 17 in. rear.	Marchesini cast magnesium: 3.50 in. x 17 in. front and 4.50 or 5.00 in. x 17 in. rear.	Marchesini cast magnesium: 3.75 in. x 17 in. front and 5.50 in. x 17 in. rear.	PVM cast magnesium: 3.50 in. x 17 in. front and 5.00 in. x 17 in. rear.	Marchesini cast magnesium: 3.75 or 3.50 in. x 17 in. front and 4.50, 5.25 or 5.50 in. x 17 in. rear.
Tyres	Michelin.	Dunlop.	Michelin.	Dunlop.	Michelin.
Brakes	Front: two Brembo cast steel (290 mm) or one 290 mm steel and one 255 mm carbon-carbon discs. Brembo four piston calipers. Brembo pads. Rear: one Nissin cast steel (180 mm) disc. Nissin two piston caliper. Nissin pads.	Front: two Brembo cast steel (300 mm) or one 300 mm steel and one 273 mm carbon-carbon discs. Brembo four piston calipers. Brembo pads. Rear: one Brembo aluminium (184 mm) disc. Brembo two piston caliper. Brembo pads.	Front: two AP carbon-carbon (270 mm) or cast steel (305 mm) discs. AP four piston calipers. AP pads. Rear: one Suzuki cast steel (210 mm) disc. Two piston caliper. AP pads.	Front: two Brembo cast steel (290 mm) discs. Brembo four piston calipers. Brembo pads. Rear: one Yamaha cast steel (220 mm) disc. Nissin two piston caliper. Nissin pads.	Front: two Brembo cast steel (285 mm) discs. Brembo four piston calipers. Brembo pads. Rear: one steel (190 mm) disc. Brembo two piston caliper. Brembo pads.

Right: **Yamaha's works-bike comeback was only for Jochen Schmid; it was a workmanlike effort that improved steadily throughout the year.**

Photos: Henk Keulemans

Left: **NSR250 Honda was all-new, but not a major improvement on the previous model.** ***Below:*** **Space is tight in compact new design; no room for adjustment of rear suspension pivot.**

Top: **Smooth Aprilia AF1, with shapely carbon-fibre seat/subframe. Reggiani's works bike exploited electronics to the full – note sensors on front fork leg. Here it downloads data in the pits. Reggiani uses a rare right-foot gearchange because of an old injury.**

Centre: **Suzuki's RGV250, in its second year of development, had many echoes of the RGV500 in its frame, and a wider-angle V for its single-crankshaft motor.**

Gilera ***(above)*** **was the newest works bike, brought little design innovation, but was close to the top standards in the class.**

125 cc / Sidecar
SPECIFICATIONS

Rider's name Machine	Alessandro Gramigni 124.8 cc Aprilia	Ralf Waldmann 124 cc Honda	Fausto Gresini 124 cc Honda	Rolf Biland 498 cc LCR-Krauser	Steve Webster 498 cc LCR-Krauser-Yamaha
ENGINE **Type/no. cylinders**	Water-cooled single-cylinder two-stroke, single pressed crank, two ball bearings.	Water-cooled single-cylinder two-stroke, single pressed crank, two ball bearings.	Water-cooled single-cylinder two-stroke, single pressed crank, two ball bearings.	Water-cooled four-cylinder two-stroke, twin pressed cranks, four needle-roller bearings each.	Water-cooled four-cylinder two-stroke, twin pressed cranks, four needle-roller bearings each.
Bore & stroke	54 x 54.5 mm.	54 x 54.5 mm.	54 x 54.5 mm.	56 x 50.6 mm.	56 x 50.6 mm.
Induction	One 39 mm cylindrical-slide Dell'Orto, disc-valve induction.	One 38 mm cylindrical-slide Keihin, crankcase reed-valve induction.	One 38 mm cylindrical-slide Keihin, crankcase reed-valve induction.	Four 39 mm cylindrical-slide Dell'Ortos, crankcase reed-valve induction.	Four 39 mm cylindrical-slide Dell'Ortos, crankcase reed-valve induction.
Porting	Six transfer, three exhaust.	Five transfer, three exhaust.	Five transfer, three exhaust.	Five transfer, two exhaust.	Five transfer, two exhaust.
Exhaust valve	Vacuum controlled guillotine.	Electronically controlled draw bridge.	Electronically controlled draw bridge.	—	—
Ignition	Electronic. NGK sparking plugs.	Electronic. NGK sparking plugs.	Electronic. NGK sparking plugs.	Electronic programmable ignition. NGK sparking plugs.	Electronic. NGK sparking plugs.
Oil	Mobil engine and gearbox.	Elf engine and gearbox.	Elf engine and gearbox.	Wintershall engine and gearbox.	Silkolene engine and gearbox.
Other details	Single plain piston ring, needle-roller small and big end bearings.	Single plain piston ring, needle-roller small and big end bearings.	Single plain piston ring, needle-roller small and big end bearings.	Single plain piston ring, needle-roller small and roller big end bearings.	Single plain piston ring, needle-roller small and roller big end bearings.
TRANSMISSION **Primary drive**	Straight cut gear.	Straight cut gear.	Straight cut gear.	Straight cut gear.	Straight cut gear.
Clutch	Dry multi-plate, five friction and five steel plates, six springs.	Dry multi-plate, six friction and five steel plates, five springs.	Dry multi-plate, five friction and five steel plates, six springs.	Dry multi-plate, seven friction and seven steel plates, six springs.	Dry multi-plate, nine carbon plates, one diaphragm, six springs.
Gearbox	Six-speed, seven possible ratios for first, second and third, three for fourth, fifth and sixth. Drum selection.	Six-speed, four possible ratios for first and second, three for third, fourth and fifth and two for sixth. Drum selection.	Six-speed, four possible ratios for first and second, three for third, fourth and fifth and two for sixth. Drum selection.	Six-speed, three possible ratios for first three gears. Drum selection.	Six-speed, three possible ratios for first four gears, two for sixth. Drum selection.
RUNNING GEAR **Frame**	Twin-spar extruded section aluminium, taper roller head bearings.	Twin-spar extruded section aluminium, taper roller head bearings.	Twin-spar extruded section aluminium, taper roller head bearings.	Sheet aluminium monocoque, riveted and araldited.	Sheet aluminium monocoque, riveted and araldited.
Front suspension	White Power OUT telescopic forks, coil springs, oil damped, adjustable.	White Power OUT telescopic forks, coil springs, oil damped, adjustable.	White Power OUT telescopic forks, coil springs, oil damped, adjustable.	Parallelogram front suspension, Ohlins unit, coil spring, oil damped, adjustable.	Parallelogram front suspension, Koni unit, coil spring, oil damped, adjustable.
Rear suspension	Triangulated extruded section aluminium swing arm, taper roller bearings. One White Power unit, coil spring, oil damped, adjustable with lower end linkage.	Triangulated extruded section aluminium swing arm, plain bearings. One White Power unit, coil spring, oil damped, adjustable.	Triangulated extruded section aluminium swing arm, plain bearings. One White Power unit, coil spring, oil damped, adjustable.	Wishbone rear suspension, Ohlins unit, coil spring, oil damped, adjustable. No sidecar suspension.	Wishbone rear suspension, Koni unit, coil spring, oil damped, adjustable. No sidecar suspension.
Wheels	Marchesini cast magnesium: 2.50 in. x 17 in. front and 3.00 in. x 17 in. rear.	PVM cast magnesium: 2.50 in. x 17 in. front and 3.00 in. (Mugello only) x 17 in. rear.	PVM cast magnesium: 2.50 in. x 17 in. front and 3.00 in. x 17 in. rear.	BBS cast magnesium: 13 in. diameter front and side, 14 in. rear; 9 in. wide front, 12 in. rear, 10 in. side.	OZ cast magnesium: 13 in. diameter front, 14 in. rear and side; 8.2 in. wide front, 10 in. rear, 9 in. side.
Tyres	Dunlop.	Dunlop.	Dunlop.	Yokohama.	Avon.
Brakes	Front: one Brembo cast steel (280 or 300 mm) disc. Brembo four piston caliper. Brembo pads. Rear: one Brembo cast steel (180 mm) disc. Brembo two piston caliper. Brembo pads.	Front: one PVM cast steel (296 mm) disc. Brembo four piston caliper. Brembo pads. Rear: one Honda cast steel (190 mm) disc. Nissin two piston caliper. Nissin pads.	Front: one PVM cast steel (296 mm) disc. Brembo four piston caliper. Brembo pads. Rear: one Honda cast steel (190 mm) disc. Nissin two piston caliper. Nissin pads.	Front: one cast iron (290 mm) disc. AP four piston caliper. Mintex pads. Rear: one cast iron (240 mm) disc. AP four piston caliper. Mintex pads. Side: one cast iron (240 mm) disc. AP four piston caliper. Mintex pads.	Front: one AP carbon-carbon (240 mm) disc. AP four piston caliper. AP pads. Rear: one AP carbon-carbon (240 mm) disc. AP four piston caliper. AP pads. Side: one cast steel (240 mm) disc. AP four piston caliper. Ferodo pads.

Photos: Henk Keulemans

Left: **Aprilia's straight-line 125 frame was simpler than the 250's; carbon subframe ultra-chic. With rising-rate rear suspension, it was good enough to win the title. This is Gramigni's victorious bike.**

Below: **Rolf Biland's outfit used Honda cylinders on Krauser crankcases. Note neat extension carrying gear pedal.**

Left: **Honda's RS came in one size, but various mechanical guises. This is Waldmann's A-kit bike, with exhaust powervalve, but without his experimental rising-rate rear suspension link. Carbon-fibre shroud on rear suspension was not structural.**

Above: **Steve Webster used an AP carbon-fibre clutch with some success.**
Photo: John McKenzie

THE NEW K1100LT. THE ONLY WAY TO ROAM.

WHO WAS WHO *in* '92

Photos: Malcolm Bryan

By MICHAEL SCOTT

ANYONE seeking confirmation that things were different under the new regime had only to count the works-replica V4 500s on the starting grid. First, of course, he must be sure of what he was counting: another of the changes in 1992 was the dropping of colour-coded number plates that had, until now, made the different classes distinguishable at a glance, without having to count exhaust pipes or examine the location of air intakes.

The pointlessness of this particular change – inspired through a desire to allow sponsors to colour-code their full fairing designs – was illustrated by Michael Doohan's spare Honda at Hockenheim, which carried a dayglo red figure two on a yellow background, making it effectively invisible in strong sunlight. Future historians sorting through pictures should be advised that when no number is visible in a head-on shot, it is Doohan in practice in Germany. Probably.

Many other changes appeared to be pointless, and one in particular affected the racing – the move to copy F1 cars by timing only two of the four practice sessions, instead of the last three as before. Morning runs were 'untimed'; only the afternoons would count towards grid positions. This was not only generally unpopular, but not even widely known about. The faces in the Team Roberts pit and that of Doug Chandler were a picture when they discovered the fast times they'd set at Suzuka on Saturday morning didn't actually count. Sadly, in spite of widespread discontent, other political influences prevailed in preventing this clanger from being rectified.

Not so the equally fatuous decision to abandon the traditional engine-capacity nomenclature for the classes. Instead, the three categories were to be known as GP1, GP2 and GP3. When the sidecars arrived, unkind observers dubbed them GP4. These titles were quietly pushed into the background as the season progressed and, by year's end, it was safe to talk again of 500s, 250s, 125s and sidecars without fear of retribution from IRTA's thought-police.

A more significant change was in the allotting of points. First, last year's experiment of dropping the worst two scores was abandoned. Then, instead of the first fifteen, only the top ten would get points, a system last used in 1987. This was another step towards F1 rules, where only the first six are rewarded.

The spread of points was also more widely spaced at the front: the top three finishers would gain 20–15–12 points instead of the previous 20–17–15. This gave a significant advantage to the winner, now claiming five more points than the next man instead of three. The intention was to put the soft option of cruising to second further out of reach for anyone who built up an early advantage. But the more things change... A computation at the end of the year showed that, in fact, either 1991's or 1992's systems would have given the same top three, although last year Chandler would have beaten Schwantz to fourth overall, and the more consistent Garriga would have displaced race winner and lengthy absentee Gardner from sixth.

There was one other significant change, which came as something of a comfort to those who had been accepted for IRTA contracts. They now took part in what had effectively become a closed shop (or, as some preferred, a glorified club championship). Except for the rigid limits of the wild card system, allowing two nominated riders per class in each country, local heroes and talented shooting stars were ruled out of the GPs, substantially reducing their chances of breaking into the big time. Instant success stories like Kevin Magee, John Kocinski and Noboru Ueda weren't welcome any more.

Daryl Beattie *(right)* **– here today, here tomorrow. Without a full-time GP ride for 1992, he was ready to replace the injured Gardner.**

Juan Garriga and returnee Randy Mamola both rode Yamahas *(middle row)*.

Bottom: **Sito Pons** *(left)* **quit riding to head his own team, hired 125 star Alex Criville to ride the new NSR500 Honda, and may have regretted it.**

500 cc – GP1

All three participating Japanese factories had pledged more support to the top class in the form of more machines – but only Yamaha had come up with the hardware. Their co-operation with and supply of engines to Harris Performance Products and Roc Engineering had unleashed 13 new V4s onto the grid, as near as dammit the technical equivalent of last year's works YZRs (although, in the case of the Roc, with some extra built-in adjustability to geometry).

This added enough new names and revitalised enough old ones to elevate the whole level of the game for the better privateers. But it made little difference to the power struggle for the major prizes – apart from the predictable fact that the slow privateers could now get in the way much more effectively, since they could run almost as fast in a straight line as the top works bikes.

Almost as fast, thanks to six months or more on this year's works bikes, designed specifically to make last year's bikes yesterday's heroes. All the new works bikes had gained straightline speed – and a whole lot of other things besides.

The most significant leap in technology came from Honda, whose new NSR500 used virtually the same frame as last year's bike, but had undergone a major character transformation due to the reworking of its V4 engine. The new bike looked different, with its shovel-nose screen and nasal air intakes, and it certainly sounded different, with a flat and deceptively understressed droning exhaust.

There were just three of these scheduled to make the startlines of the new closed shop World Championship. The most senior was, as usual, the Rothmans team, fielding the same rider line-up as for the past three years.

In that time, Michael Doohan had become the top rider, while Wayne Gardner remained with the team after prolonged speculation that he was looking for a ride elsewhere. In the end, the older Australian stayed put, on the 'best-yet' financial terms he had ever negotiated.

Doohan and Gardner ran in essentially separate teams, each free to pursue their own lines of development under direct factory supervision. Doohan chose to stick with his existing crew chief, Jeremy Burgess; Gardner was happy to be back with Erv Kanemoto, long-serving Honda racing guru.

The third new droning Honda went to Spanish sponsors Campsa, where ill-starred former 250 champ Sito Pons switched from rider to team owner (a move that he might have regretted, considering the amenable and highly effective nature of the new NSR compared with last year's wild beast), and 22-year-old Alex Criville took over the controls. Criville was a dazzling surprise 125 World Champion in 1989, had since then made little impact in the 250 class on a Cobas Honda, and was very much an unknown quantity on a full 500.

Suzuki's promised extra racers were also conspicuously absent – just the usual pair of factory bikes, dressed again by Lucky Strike. There had been the usual mechanical revision to the motor cycle, too, but an unprecedented programme of winter testing and a significant change not only to the number two rider, but also within the team. Kevin Schwantz remained as team stalwart – his fifth year on the RGV. This year he was joined by former US Superbike champion Doug Chandler, in his second GP year after an unsponsored Yamaha ride in the Kenny Roberts B-team in 1991.

Admittedly, Schwantz was recovering from hand injuries sustained before the end of the 1991 season, but test sessions had suggested that Chandler was rather too fast to be considered a number two rider, while his different riding style promised an interesting dynamic to development of a machine where Schwantz had hitherto been the main guiding force. A human dynamic was to be found in the garage, where Schwantz's long-time crew chief, Simon Tonge, was now wrenching for Chandler, while former Kawasaki (Ballington) and Honda (Gardner et al.) spannerman Stuart Shenton was taking over Schwantz's bike. Tonge's tenure at the team dated back to the days of Barry Sheene, but his alliance with Schwantz had been troubled. He, for one, would be pleased to see Chandler defeat his illustrious team-mate.

Yamaha's effort was diversified but not diffused: the main repository of talent and technology remained with the dominant Team Marlboro Roberts. One question concerned the fitness of defending double champion Wayne Rainey, whose leg was badly injured in tests for last year's Malaysian GP, and who hurt his right hand (losing part of a finger) in another pre-season crash. His notable determination would surely be put to the test. His team-mate, John Kocinski, buoyed up by his first class win at the end of last season, seemed set once again to play the role of precocious upstart.

Roberts again fielded a B-team rider – none other than Randy Mamola, returning somewhat sobered by a fallow year after losing his Cagiva job, and sponsored (for the full season, he hoped) by Budweiser. Randy's bike was a '91-spec factory machine rather than one of the European replicas, but would not receive the same direct factory input as official Marlboro works bikes.

There were other already well-established works teams operating the lease-lend system, one being the Ducados-backed Juan Garriga, in his third year of trying to recapture

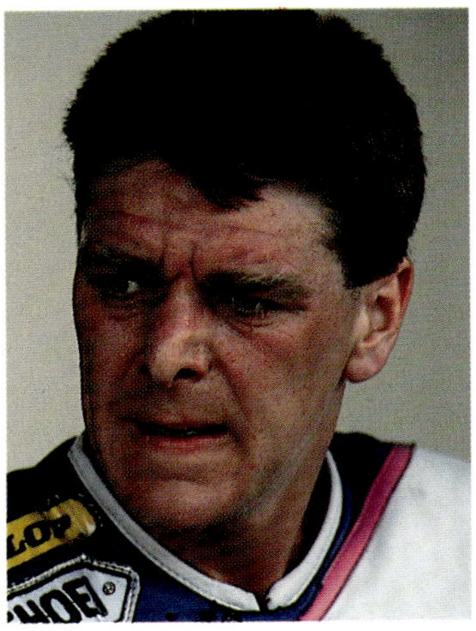

the glittering form of his 250 days.

Two more wore the French (and one-time Gauloises) racing blue of the Sonauto team, backed now by Yamaha France and state lottery Banco. Team manager Serge Rosset had retained last year's part-timer Niall Mackenzie (now nicknamed 'Jean-Pierre' Mackenzie by the British contingent), and had recruited the fast-rising French Canadian star Miguel DuHamel, son of Yvon DuHamel, who'd earned infamy as a win-or-crash hero of the American road racing renaissance of the Sixties and Seventies.

Rosset is also head of Roc Engineering, the French firm who supplied eight of the new works-replica Yamahas; and he fielded one of them himself, for Banco-sponsored Dominique Sarron. The remaining seven went to a selection of new and old privateers, the most notable of whom was All Japan title winner Peter Goddard from Australia, backed by noted long-time American sponsor (of Mike Baldwin, among others), Bob Maclean. Other newcomers taking advantage of the opportunity to go GP racing on a sensible financial basis were Toshiyuki Arakaki from Japan, Swiss former motocrosser Serge David, French endurance racer Thierry Crine and Italian Corrado Catalano, moving up from the 250 class. Existing privateers Niggi Schmassman and Sepp Doppler both replaced their outdated machinery with Rocs.

Harris Yamahas filled a similar role, with 1991 privateers Cees Doorakkers and Michael Rudroff as well as former class-runner Simon Buckmaster upgrading to the new V4s, the Briton sponsored by Padgetts Yamaha; Kevin Mitchell moved up from the 250s, and Peter Graves rejoined the class after some years of European Championship racing. Venezuelan Larry Moreno was also on the original entry lists, but he was a late arrival and an early departure.

Finally, yet another class of Yamaha was represented by Irish rider Eddie Laycock, racing his leased 1991 YZR for a second year.

The only change at Cagiva came at the top – Giacomo Agostini was brought in to head the all-Italian team, a return from the wilderness for the 17-times World Champion after he lost the Marlboro Yamaha team to Kenny Roberts. This meant he was again team boss to Eddie Lawson, in his second year on the red bikes, and his last year as a GP

Photos: Malcolm Bryan

racer (or so he insisted). This unlikely alliance was expected to lead to some fireworks, as the pair had fallen out during their time and three world titles together in the works Yamaha team. Lawson's team-mate was again the quick but accident-prone Brazilian, Alexandre Barros.

Librenti's proposed customer racer made an appearance, ridden by Italian Marco Papa, who deserved much better; the Paton V4 was passed on to another Italian, Lucio Pedercini; and long-serving back-marker Andreas Leuthe was down to ride the German-backed VRP, yet another very slow home-brewed V4.

The last remaining issue concerned tyres – and it was of major importance. The scene had been set at the end of 1990, when the dominant Michelin announced that they were to quit racing. As it transpired, this was not strictly true; they had a much-reduced presence in 1991, serving Honda and Cagiva, while the other significant works teams all switched to Dunlop.

For 1992, Michelin planned a complete comeback, although on rather different financial terms. All the 500 class Honda teams already used them, and they found willing new (or rather returned) customers elsewhere. First their old allies Lucky Strike Suzuki rejoined, hoping (as Schwantz later explained, taking much of the blame for the slap in the face to Dunlop) to steal a march on Team Roberts. In this they failed, for the Marlboro Yamaha men promptly followed suit, after Kocinski rode back-to-back comparison tests. The French Yamahas were also on Michelin; Garriga began the season with Dunlop and finished it on the French rubber.

Just to be different, Cagiva switched to Dunlop after similar back-to-back tests, largely at the instigation of Lawson, and as a result of the better grip of their front tyres. Their battle throughout the season to find tyres that would go the distance was to find a counterpart in the fight by the Michelin returnees to find tyres that would restore their lost confidence in steering bite and the facility to ride aggressively.

250 cc – GP2

The profile of the 250 class had changed in several ways. Honda's dominance had been under threat, and they responded with a new motor cycle, while Aprilia came back

Opposite page: **Alex Barros** ***(top left)*** **rode a Cagiva for a third year; Miguel DuHamel** ***(top centre)*** **a Yamaha for a first. Kevin Mitchell** ***(top right)*** **was a worthy privateer recruit to 500s on his MBM-backed Harris Yamaha.**

Australian Peter Goddard ***(below left)*** **got a long-awaited GP ride on the Valvoline Roc Yamaha after winning the All Japan title last year.**

Niall Mackenzie ***(bottom left)*** **and new wife Jan went French again.**

Pier Francesco Chili ***(main picture)*** **was again set to be a leading light in the 250 class.**

Mixed faces heading for mixed fortunes ***(clockwise from top left)*****: Carlos Cardus had a works Honda, Doriano Romboni nearly did, Masahiro Shimizu definitely did; while Alberto Puig switched from Yamaha to Aprilia to go fast again.**

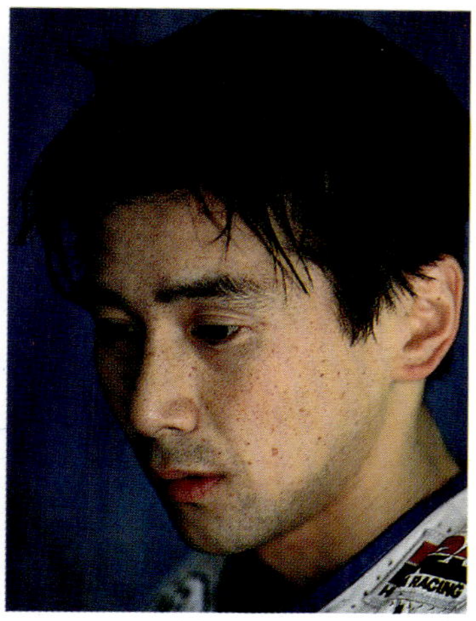

with refinement and an increased presence. Suzuki's works bike was in its second year, and was due to make its presence felt; Yamaha were embarking on a fresh works initiative after semi-withdrawal; and Gilera returned to the class to bring the number of factory works teams to five.

The new Honda NSR replaced the machine of the same name that had served faithfully and successfully since 1985, when it took Spencer to victory in its debut year. The 1992 machine was a more compact V-twin with a revised twin-beam chassis that successfully addressed the problem of the old machine's sluggish steering. The major outward change was the so-called 'single-sided swing arm' first seen on the Elf, and later on HRC's endurance racers. The new machine was reputedly fast as well – but would it be fast enough?

There were four of the new bikes. The first was for Luca Cadalora, defending his title, again in Rothmans colours, the machine prepared by Kanemoto. Another was for 1991 runner-up Helmut Bradl, again HB backed and prepared by his brother; and the third (after many shenanigans) went to Carlos Cardus, whose Repsol-financed team included the redoubtable Kel Carruthers as crew chief. The fourth bike again went to Masahiro Shimizu.

There was more to HRC's challenge, with a selection of power-up kits for the production RS. In fact, all the RS machines at GPs were thus equipped, making them into RS Specials (or Spls in HRC-speak); but this only approximated to a B-kit bike. There was another level of specialness, which added NSR-type ignition and associated paraphernalia to the special crankshaft, carburettors, cylinders and exhaust pipes of the Spls. These A-kit bikes were dubbed Spl/Spls by HRC, and double-specials by most other people.

Three riders were awarded these almost-works bikes. Two went to the pair of Italian coming men, HB-backed Doriano Romboni and class newcomer Loris Capirossi. The double 125 champion was still only 19 at the start of the season, and was running in Marlboro colours. A third went to Euromoto-backed French rider, Jean-Pierre Jeandat, for at least the first part of the year. Riders of mere single-specials included Germans Stefan Prein and Adi Stadler, both ex-125 racers and the former in his second year; Japan's Katsuyoshi Kozono, again on Bridgestone tyres; and class newcomers Luis D'Antin and Antonio Sanchez from Spain, Yves Briguet and Adrian Bosshard from Switzerland, and Bernard Cazade from France.

Aprilia responded with a refinement of their own twin-crank Rotax-based rotary disc-valve induction AF-1, with the factory effort backed by a new system of factory-lease development engines as well as a new privateer machine.

The sole official works rider in the Aprilia Unlimited Jeans team was again Loris Reggiani, a vital part of the Italian factory's racing effort from the start. The veteran, now 32 years old and commencing his 13th GP season, was also the official factory tester, and was the first and frequently the only rider to benefit from mid-season improvements.

Only slightly lower in status came former rider Alex Valesi's team, backed by South African communications company Telkor, and fielding not only Pier Francesco Chili again, but also GP newcomer Massimiliano Biaggi. Aged 20 at the start of the season, Max was on an express train to the top, having stomped all over the European Championship the previous year.

Privateers favoured with deals for updated engine parts included last year's top privateer, Andy Preining from Austria, and ex-Yamaha rider, Alberto Puig. The latter's career had been troubled by injuries and bad luck, and also by Yamaha's half-hearted approach in recent years. Now he had taken his Ducados backing to Aprilia, with his team to be run as an offshoot of the Dutch-based Exact Software outfit that had formerly been Sharp-Samson sponsored. Puig's nominal team-mate (although they operated quite separately) was Patrick van den Goorbergh; his younger brother Jurgen was another GP recruit, riding an independent Yokohama-shod Aprilia. Other Aprilia-mounted privateers included the veteran Harald Eckl, Swiss Marlboro-backed riders Bernard Hänggeli and ex-motocrosser Eskil Suter, Bernd Kassner in the Martin Wimmer-backed Rallye Sport Munich team, Finn Erkka Korpiaho and Frenchman Frédéric Protat.

Yamaha had only four bikes to pit against these armies. Three were lowly privateer TZ models ridden by Gallina/Compagnucci pair Paolo Casoli and Stefano Caracchi (later to be replaced by Roberto Gallina's son,

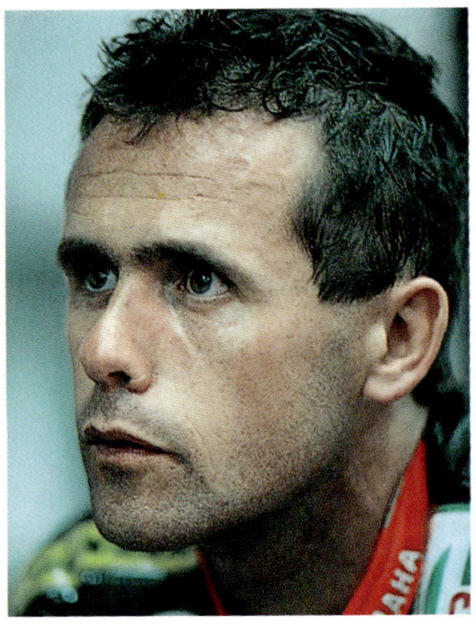

Herri Torrontegui and Jochen Schmid ***(far left and left)*****: the former ran his first 250 season with Suzuki; the latter switched to Yamaha after years with Honda.**

Alessandro Gramigni ***(below)*** **gave Aprilia their first 125 class GP win last year. Could he do better as sole works rider this year?**

Dirk Raudies and Ralf Waldmann ***(bottom left and right)*** **led the 125 Honda hordes for Germany.**

Photos: Malcolm Bryan

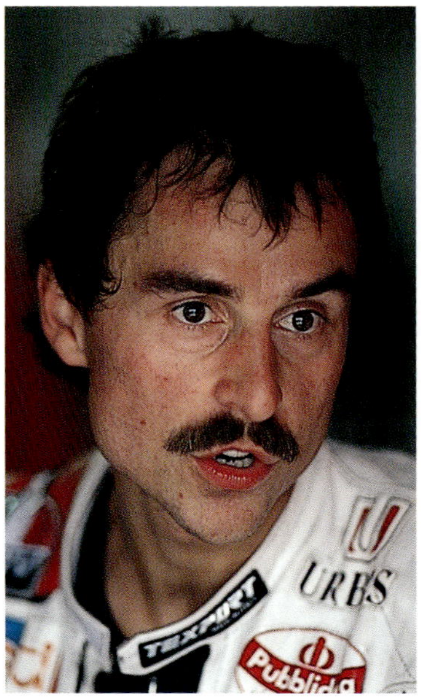

Michele), and Renzo Colleoni. The fourth, however, was a full scale works bike a long way ahead of the TZ-M (for modified) machines fielded last year, although sharing the same name. Jochen Schmid's bike was a works machine in every way, with an all-new engine and the backing of German Yamaha importer Mitsui. This represented an improvement in circumstances for Schmid, after he'd spent several years as chief on-track tester for Honda's privateer effort without getting the long-awaited rewards of a full works NSR.

Suzuki's second year in the class, in Lucky Strike colours again, brought a two-rider team to replace development rider Wimmer, with operations moving from Munich to the south of France. Dutchman Wilco Zeelenberg had come from the works Honda ranks, and much was expected of this former GP winner. His team-mate was Herri Torrontegui, the Basque former tiddler star's first full year on a 250.

The works newcomers were Gilera, now part of the Piaggi group and undergoing a revival of a name that was famous in the Sixties. Their all-new disc-valve V-twin, designed by ex-Bimota engineer Federico Martini and fettled by veteran freelance tuner Harald Bartol, was ridden by Carlos Lavado, in what was to be the mercurial Venezuelan double World Champion's last year; and by one-time Yamaha-mounted elbow-scraper Jean-Philippe Ruggia, a refugee from an unsuccessful attempt to move up to the 500 class.

125 cc – GP3

Honda deliberately avoid direct works involvement in the smallest class, not least because the majority of the field consists of their customers, who would not take kindly to being soundly thrashed by the people who had taken their money. Nor did 1992 yield any significant new entries from other manufacturers – Cagiva had lost interest completely, the pair of MX-based Yamahas that pitched up weren't even in the same race, while the crop of backyard specials that once enlivened the single-cylinder 80 cc class failed to show.

Only Aprilia fielded an official works bike. Their customers must be presumed not to mind so much, since seven people had purchased examples of the newly available and rather gorgeous production Aprilias, whose curvaceous carbon-fibre subframe and rising-rate rear suspension provided a sharp contrast to the workaday monoshock production Hondas.

Even the top Hondas lacked a rising-rate rear end, the bike still clearly showing its humble production racing and MX roots; but the machines fitted with HRC kits were still good enough to win most of the races.

There are two levels of factory support, ending up as A-kit and B-kit modifications to the stock RS machine. Both comprise different crankshafts, cylinders, exhausts and carburettors, but the A-kit version adds an exhaust valve and a more sophisticated ignition to go with it, as well as a number of gearing options, all of which should add up to a significant difference.

There were just four favoured recipients of these coveted power-up options. Two went to the Marlboro-backed Team Pileri, who had won for the last two years with Capirossi. They retained former two-times champion Fausto Gresini, and replaced Capirossi with last year's find of the class, Noboru Ueda. A third bike went to multi-champion Jorge Martinez, still struggling to make as big a mark on the opposition as when he rode the all-conquering 80 cc and 125 cc Derbis. The fourth went to Ralf Waldmann, riding for Team Zwafink, also in Marlboro colours.

Then there were the B-kit machines, allotted on a country-by-country basis by the local distributors, with the delineation becoming rather loose as they filtered down among the teams. Principal users included the new Semprucci Honda squad, fielding class veteran Ezio Gianola (after two fallow years with Derbi in their death-throes) and last year's number two Aprilia rider, Gabriele Debbia. There was also German Dirk Raudies, and Waldmann's Swiss Zwafink team-mate, Oliver Petrucciani.

This was still only the start of a horde of Hondas, at different levels of development, with or without the tacit help and approval of HRC. Prominent among these were the Japanese riders, always a force in this class. Notable among them were Nobuyuki Wakai on the evocatively named Moto Bum Honda and frequent crasher Kazuto Sakata, ably backed in this enterprise by class veteran Hisashi Unemoto, Kinya Wada (riding alongside Briton Robin

Photos: Malcolm Bryan

A grid of 125 talent *(clockwise from top left)*: Bruno Casanova, Carlos Giro, Jorge Martinez, Oliver Petrucciani, Hans Spaan and Nobuyuki Wakai.

Rolf Biland *(below)* won his first sidecar title 14 years ago, and was now trying for his fifth.

Photos: Malcolm Bryan

Appleyard in a two-man team) and newcomer Takao Shimizu.

Add the Europeans: Swiss Heinz Lüthi; Germans Alfred Waibel, Hubert Abold and newcomer Oliver Koch; Spaniard Julian Miralles; promising new Dutchman Loek Bodelier; Frenchman Alain Bronec and Briton Steve Patrickson; and Australian Peter Galvin – and you have a total of 23 Hondas out of the original 36-strong IRTA entry list.

Aprilia's opposition was concentrated principally on their sole works bike, in the same Unlimited Jeans colours as their 250, and ridden by Alex Gramigni for a second successive year after a single GP victory (at Brno) in 1991.

The seven customer teams were ostensibly all equal, though Scot Racing – who fielded Bruno Casanova and youngster Emilio Cuppini – would be obliged to deny that they had a hot line to the factory for parts for the Rotax-based engine during the course of the year. Other recruits to the Aprilia order-book were Hans Spaan and Exact Software team-mate Arie Molenaar from Holland, Spaniard Carlos Giro (son of the noted Ossa race engineer and tuner), his countryman Manuel Hernandez and German charger Maik Stief.

Two more bikes ran Rotax engines, the now conventionally suspended Gazzanigas ridden by veteran Maurizio Vitali and Giovanni Palmieri.

The numbers were made up by the fast but misfortunate Peter Öttl, riding a Bakker-framed Rotax backed by the Austrian factory; and the two low-grade Yamahas, entered under the aegis of former champion rider Eugenio Lazzarini, and ridden fitfully by Giuseppe Fiorillo and Fausto Ricci.

SIDECARS

In spite of all their problems, the sidecars managed to muster 24 crews for their first race of the season, including all the top men from the previous year except Alain Michel, who had retired.

Free from direct factory involvement, the sidecars plough their own lonely furrow, all using LCR (or LCR-derived) chassis and fitted with a rag-tag of engines ranging from the original in-line four TZ Yamahas with Hummel cylinders to the basically identical but newer Krauser and ADM motors fitted with their own cylinders or, in some cases, Honda cylinders.

For better or worse, they are also relatively free from sponsorship on the scale of the solo classes, with only one tobacco-backed team, comprising two outfits out of the top three – Rolf Biland/Kurt Waltisperg and Egbert Streuer/Peter Brown – racing in Hollywood livery. These two were quite independent, with Biland racing an LCR-Krauser fitted with Honda cylinders, and Streuer an LCR fitted with a hybrid but generally Yamaha-based engine (he threatened but never raced his own flat-four unit).

The apex of the eternal triangle was defending champions Steve Webster/Gavin Simmons, the Britons again sporting Silkolene colours. Their LCR had ADM crankcases, and Webster was to join the move to Honda cylinders.

There were other notables among the challengers. Ralph Bohnhorst/Bruno Hiller had shown well last year (their version of the straight-four engine was dubbed the BRM); the Swiss Güdel brothers, Paul and Charly, had been knocking on the door of the big time; tough Britons Steve Abbott/Shaun Smith were also a threat.

Plus the newer arrivals who were likely to be stronger this year than last, prominent among them Briton Darren Dixon, now with Andy Hetherington replacing brother Sean Dixon in the chair; and the hard-charging Austrian youngsters Klaus Klaffenböck/Christian Parzer.

Britain, Switzerland and the Netherlands continued to provide the majority of entries. Yoshi Kumagaya may only be a nominal Englishman, but the Brindley family provided two outfits, ridden by Barry and Derek, while Mark Reddington, Tony Baker, Robert Fisher and Eddie Wright were all the genuine article. Swiss contenders included the veteran Egloff brothers, Markus and Urs, another brotherly outfit ridden by Tony and Kilian Wyssen, as well as Markus Bösiger, Hans Hügli and Reiner Koster.

With a full field, all that was lacking at the start of the year was a full calendar. They're still waiting for that.

actual reality

At Suzuki, we're turning tomorrow's dreams into today's reality. We've developed a fresh approach to design, backed by innovative refinements in performance and reliability, creating a range of quality motorcycles. With precision engineering and over 70 years experience, we're establishing a new era of total motorcycling enjoyment. That's no idle boast. It's actual reality.

FOR INFORMATION

FREEPHONE

0800 526263

Heron Suzuki PLC, 46-62 Gatwick Road, Crawley, West Sussex RH10 2XF

HERON A Heron International Company

SUZUKI

1992
GRANDS PRIX

500 cc	DOOHAN
250 cc	CADALORA
125 cc	WALDMANN

JAPANESE GRAND PRIX

As I was going up the stair
I met a man who wasn't there
He wasn't there again today –
Oh! How I wish he'd go away!

The anonymous author of the well-known doggerel would have loved the Japanese GP. Especially when he discovered that his ever-present absentee now had some 24 descendants, all Japanese motor cycle racers. Some of them were rather good – filling five of the top ten places in the 500 cc class, for instance, and second and third in the 250 cc race.

The ghost riders were local Japanese heroes, eight per class and mostly on full works or works-backed bikes. They had been nominated by the national federation, backed by the FIM, and accepted by IRTA under threat of blackmail from the factories. There is a wealth of political intrigue within the above sentence, and the Japanese entries cast a long and most unspectral political shadow. For the purposes of the race this weekend, the puzzle was to divine their sporting role.

Photos: Malcolm Bryan

Aoki shifts spray on his works Honda. Nowhere else all year were there so many of the new bikes with the distinctive single-sided rear suspension.

Opposite page: Domestic works Yamaha riders Fujiwara (52) and Honma (56) had a hard battle for eighth place. Or was it eighth place? That depended on whether you believed in ghosts.

For some Japanese fans, coming to Suzuka in the rain *(below)* was almost as good as staying at home and watching on TV.

Although they were undeniably present on the track, IRTA officials had told all their members before the race that the Japanese competitors did not count in terms of the World Championship, and could officially be ignored. Much later, they turned out to be wrong but, at the time, the instructions imposed a whole new set of variables on the riders. And it was rather a tall order, for it is hard to ignore another rider when his back wheel is tantalisingly and frustratingly present a few feet ahead of you.

Thankfully, most of the GP competitors are racers first and businessmen second, and decided to ignore IRTA. Almost all of them said afterwards they had ridden for the best possible result with or without the ghost riders, bearing in mind that the usual pre-cherry blossom showers and the unusual track surface were both treacherous, and there was a full season ahead. (In previous years, without any of the controversy over points, local one-race heroes have been given their heads, and often a wide berth too.) Thus the major effect of the strong Japanese contingent was much as usual – to interfere with the race results without having much effect on the championship, and to reinforce the existing principle that the first race of the season is seldom much of a pointer to the year ahead.

This has often been so in the 500 class – Schwantz has won here three times, and has never gone on to take the title. This year, however, Suzuka saw the arrival of a potent new force in racing, with Michael Doohan's victory giving early warning of crushing machine superiority from the new Honda.

The new NSR was so good in all conditions that the improvement over last year's fast but ill-tempered beast left Yamaha and Suzuki stunned. The bike looked much the same as before, but sounded weird, with a deep-throated drone that triggered intense speculation about the secret innards of the new V4. The change from the high-rev warble of all previous NSRs made it clear that the timing had been significantly altered, with all four cylinders now firing very close together, and perhaps even simultaneously. Other evidence was more suggestive still – pressure and temperature sensors in the air intake, and a three-position switch on the left handlebar.

The sensors clearly had something to do with some form of fuel injection or electronic carburation, but were not currently being used, said Doohan. The latter suggested switchable ignition management maps, but when questioned the Australian deployed his legendary laconic wit. 'It works the indicators,' he told a press conference, adding: 'No, actually it's our new kill switch. One position is on, the next off, and the third really off.' But he told the unadorned truth about the machine's performance. 'Last year's bike really suffered from wheelspin – this year's doesn't have that problem at all. It's much more user-friendly.' As anyone could see from the smooth and rapid way it drove out of slippery corners at a wet Suzuka, so well hooked up that the front wheel hoisted into the air before the rear stepped sideways.

At least Honda's unfair advantage couldn't be laid at the door of Bernie Ecclestone and/or IRTA – although the opposite was almost true, and the Honda came close to missing the race. For some inexplicable reason the new regime had decided to follow the F1 car practice format. There were still two sessions on Friday and two on Saturday, but this year only the afternoon sessions would count towards grid positions. There turned out to be shortcomings either in IRTA's communications or in the ability of the member teams to process and understand the information, for a lot of people didn't know about the new system, including the boss of the biggest team of all, Kenny Roberts, and also Doug Chandler, who put up a strong effort on Saturday morning to move up to third overall only to discover that his time didn't count.

Luckily nobody crashed trying to go for a ghost time; a different side-effect almost did for Doohan, though. Both timed afternoons were wet, but the second one began dry, for the first couple of laps anyway. Most team managers had already observed that the barometer was falling, in the words of Suzuki boss Garry Taylor, 'as though the spring had broken', and the wise riders went out with the knowledge that if they didn't go fast in the first lap or two, they might not get another chance. Schwantz was even the subject of complaints because he pushed past the flagman out of the pits to gain another few seconds of dry time. It earned him pole position, and even then his second (fast) lap was completed with rain already falling.

Doohan, meanwhile, was cruising – breaking in pistons, gambling on getting up to speed before it rained. No such luck, and as it kept on getting wetter he was in and out of the pits striving to beat the conditions and go fast enough to qualify. He only just managed it.

The start of the season marked the return of Randy Mamola, a genuine ghost rider last year, but now back with Team Roberts. He was also caught in the non-qualification bind, but managed to squeeze onto the grid. His role as a joker would remain suppressed, he said, until he had shaken off some of the rust of a year's inactivity – though many chuckled unkindly when he fell off on the sighting lap, a jape he has perpetrated before while riding for Cagiva.

Present but even ghostlier was Kevin Magee, now a factory Yamaha rider in Japan and entered for a one-off outing in this GP. But the misfortunate Australian had crashed in practice for a Japanese championship race (which was subsequently rained off anyway) and had broken his hand. Rather than spoil what would have been his third GP comeback by riding below par, he elected to stay on the sidelines.

Almost all the riders of the new generation works-replica Yamahas also missed the race – not voluntarily, but because they were caught out by the conditions. Works riders had pre-warmed tyres and good advice to go fast quickly; the privateers didn't, and missed the pole-plus-ten-per cent cut. Because of the unusual conditions, IRTA agreed to pay them qualifying money anyway, so that the race would not be a complete loss. Which was indubitably big-hearted, but rather ironic, since they refused to pay the non-IRTA riders who did race.

But here we are talking politics again, when there is a race about to begin. Which just goes to underline the disappointment many people felt. Most had hoped the start of the season would bring the political wrangles of the previous months to a halt. Instead, one merely overlapped the other.

500 cc PRACTICE

Wet practice is a Suzuka tradition, and the untimed Saturday morning session was almost the only chance for riders to test dry tyres and settings. Except for the first four minutes in the afternoon – the crucial

The lead is about to change hands as Doohan's remarkable new Honda gets a better corner drive than Chandler's Suzuki.

The return to racing after a year of smelling the roses found self-appointed court jester Randy Mamola *(below)* in sombre mood.

qualifying window, when Schwantz made his premature charge onto the track. He was closely followed by Rainey and Chandler, among a small pack of similarly wised-up riders.

Schwantz was fastest when it mattered, but almost ten seconds slower than the time Doohan had set to lead the 'untimed' morning session. Alongside him, domestic works Yamaha rider Toshihiko Honma showed that even ghost riders can read the barometer, while Chandler embarked on an impressive first Suzuki ride by placing third.

The front row was completed by Gardner's Honda, a mightily impressive time achieved towards the end of the session on rain tyres on a drying track. But the Australian's start to the season had not been entirely happy after he'd crashed and bruised an ankle painfully in the wet on Friday.

The track's lack of wet grip compounded Doohan's problem of trying to match dry times. His was a highly fraught 40 minutes, during which it seemed possible that the race favourite might, for the first time in his life, fail to qualify. He tried wets and he tried intermediates, and only just managed to stay calm throughout the risky business. He was just four minutes away from missing the race when it dried enough for him to slot into fifth behind Gardner.

'It was like grease out there,' he said. 'I had to tell myself to settle down and hope that if I couldn't make it there would be a realistic solution, and I'd be allowed to start from the back of the grid.' Maybe so, but luckily the resultant arguments were avoided.

Photos: Malcolm Bryan

Mamola's comeback was also threated with instant abort, until he managed to jump up among the qualifiers. His success, with some 13 minutes remaining, was greeted with cheers all along pit lane, where a large proportion of already qualified riders were sitting out the rest of the session; Doohan's was met with silence.

Honda's one-race entry Daryl Beattie ended up seventh after an impressive first 500 class showing, riding a shrieking 1991 model NSR; Dunlop-shod Juan Garriga completed the second row.

The third row was led by Rainey, the defending champion far from full strength as he showed off a still-swollen left-hand little finger missing the final joint. ('My stump is bigger than yours,' crowed Barry Sheene, comparing his similar injury for Australian TV viewers.) This was the American's first ride since crashing at Barcelona, and he was not brimming with confidence. 'I can manage one or two fast laps,' he said. 'But 22 might be a different matter. I crashed in Spain because though my mind was 100 per cent, my body was only 80 per cent' (from his broken leg last year), 'and I won't make the same mistake again.'

His enigmatic team-mate Kocinski was at the other end of row three, clearly not getting on well with the latest Yamaha. In between the two came Peter Goddard, another opportunistic early effort that put him top of the Roc/Harris Yamaha semi-works riders, and ahead also of Shinichi Itoh's domestic Honda, another '91 bike.

Mackenzie led row four. He'd also found himself unqualified and obliged to stick his neck out to get a start; next came Criville in his first 500 class outing, and showing well in spite of crashing his 1992 NSR on Friday. Newcomer Miguel DuHamel was next, with Kenichiro Iwahashi alongside, both on Yamahas.

Lawson's steady but unexciting Cagiva led row five from Fujiwara's Yamaha, Cagiva team-mate Barros (the Brazilian having been seventh overall in the dry in the morning), and German Harris Yamaha-mounted Michael Rudroff ahead of a three-strong sixth row, making a 23-strong 500 grid, similar to last year's figures. But if it had not dried enough for seven lucky riders to squeeze in at the end of the session, there would have been just 16 starters out of the 37 original entrants. And lots of arguments.

500 cc RACE – 22 LAPS

All that wet practice came in handy, with the race taking place in steady rain on a streaming wet track. Conditions were unpleasant, and things started going wrong even before the start, with Mamola slipping off on the sighting lap, though rapidly remounting, and out-of-luck Beattie pitting and retiring with a persistent misfire. In the first two laps there were four more crashes, with some illustrious victims.

Schwantz and Chandler took off up front on the Suzukis; Doohan, Kocinski and Gardner were pushing hard behind; the remainder disappeared in their spray.

Well down the pack, Goddard was the first to fall foul of the conditions, losing his Roc on the exit from the second corner. 'It had some water in the works, then it suddenly came in on all four and spun out,' he explained. Criville also failed to finish the first half-lap. He was trailing Kocinski into the looping and difficult Spoon Curve before the main straight when his front wheel tucked under and he slid into the gravel.

By the end of the lap, the Suzukis seemed to be making an early break, with Schwantz on target for a typical win. Gardner was ahead of Doohan, but only stayed there until the Esses, when he too fell. He jumped up, ripped off the remaining shreds of windscreen, and set off on an epic but doomed pursuit at the back of the field.

One corner later, it was Rainey's turn. 'The rear end stepped out as I came over the hill. I was close to saving it, but it had just gone too far,' he said, nursing a sore left wrist. A lap more and GP debutant DuHamel was down, after losing the front while chasing Kocinski after an excellent start.

Schwantz stayed ahead for almost four laps, but Chandler was right on his back wheel, and as Doohan started to close up he took his chance and outbraked his team-mate at the end of the straight, much to everybody's surprise. Two days before, he had ridden the Suzuki for the first time ever in the rain – now he led his first GP. 'I've never even been in the top five before,' he said later.

One lap later, with Chandler moving almost one-and-a-half seconds ahead, Doohan also outbraked Schwantz into turn one. The American had run into problems with front-wheel grip.

Now the Honda showed what it could do. Doohan caught Chandler quickly, passed him on lap eight, and just kept drawing away. 'I

Malcolm Bryan

Fairing broken and filthy, screen missing, Gardner hurries to keep his appointment with the guard rail.

NSR
RACING

Ralf Waldmann *(opposite)* started the strongest of Honda's 125 hordes with his works-kitted German-prepared bike.

Battered, sore and now wet as well, Loris Reggiani *(below right)* gazes anxiously at the in-pit TV monitor during rain-hit practice to see if his 17th-fastest time will be good enough to keep him qualified.

thought they would come back at me, so I kept going,' said the Australian. Not much chance, with the new NSR displaying an unbeatable combination of iron hand and velvet glove. 'It works so well in the rain now – it hardly wheelspins,' confirmed Doohan.

Chandler was safe in second, but now Schwantz was forced to submit to Kocinski. He only had to look at the Yamaha's rear for a lap, however, for Kocinski was trying too hard, and fell at the entrance to the hairpin. 'Too much front brake,' he said.

Schwantz managed to miss him, and decided then and there to settle for third. 'I didn't want to end my race in the same way and get no points at all,' he said. Asked how it felt to be beaten for the first time by a team-mate, he replied cheerfully: 'It's great! And it stinks! But I'm sure Doug's going so well will raise the standard of the whole team.' Unexpectedly, he seemed better able to deal with this defeat than one by a rider on a different bike.

The many crashes left Itoh's Honda in a lonely fourth with Mamola some way behind. The American had taken a risk with a front Michelin he had never used before, but 'I've never pushed the front so often in a race before,' he said.

The interest in the latter half of the race came from Gardner's stirring charge. Breathing fire, his battered bike snaking and weaving, he charged through the field. At his best under pressure, and with the back-markers flattering his speed, he gave a bravura performance, close to crashing as he carved through a four-bike group in the space of a lap and a half. Now he had Mamola in his sights, and was closing at more than three seconds a lap. He would soon have been in a position to pass, but he didn't want to wait, and kept right on charging. There was a sense of inevitability as he lost the front wheel on the way out of the last left-handed Ess. It's a bad place to crash, with the Armco close to the trackside. Gardner slid feet first beneath the ineffective foam rubber protection, breaking his lower right leg badly. At the time it seemed highly likely he would never race again.

Just behind him, Mackenzie took it as an object lesson. After a bad start, he had also been moving up steadily, riding well within himself. 'I'd decided to ride at 90 per cent, and be sure of finishing,' he said. 'I reckon that Gardner was at about 105 per cent.'

Niall should have been sixth, but in the last laps his rear wheel started to vibrate, and he was obliged to back off, to be passed by the leader of the three-strong Japanese group he had earlier defeated, Keiji Ohishi (Suzuki). Honma (Yamaha) was eighth, ahead of Fujiwara's similar YZR.

Tsujimoto's Honda in tenth was the last rider on the same lap as the leaders – 11th-placed Barros (Cagiva) and team-mate Lawson (14th) both had tyre trouble, Garriga faded backwards to 12th, with Iwahashi's Honda 13th.

There were 16 finishers, six of them ghosts. Now all that remained was for them to be exorcised from the results. Resolution of that conflict took far longer than the race itself, and it wasn't until the first European round that anybody knew for sure that IRTA's ghosts had been as real as you or I.

250 cc PRACTICE

The changing conditions through practice affected the 250s slightly differently. Their best times also came on Saturday morning, when Tadayuki Okada led Bradl (both on Hondas) from Chili's Aprilia. It didn't really matter; grid positions were decided that afternoon, mostly in the closing minutes as the track gradually dried.

The Olivetti-Longines timing monitors were just a blur as first one, then the next rider found his particular tyres suited the changing conditions. Early leader Zeelenberg dropped away to 16th when he stayed on a wet front and an intermediate rear, while the fast times came from cut slicks and getting a clear run. A little local knowledge also seemed to help.

Thus ghost rider Nobuatsu Aoki (Honda) took a canny pole, with Tetsuya Harada's TZ-M Yamaha slotting into second, Romboni's kitted RS Honda third, and another Japanese Honda rider, Sadanori Hikita, completing row one. Locals dominated row two as well: Osamu Miyazaki (Yamaha) heading Okada, Puig's Aprilia and Katsuyoshi Kozono's Bridgestone-shod Honda.

Only then came the European stars – Bradl's Honda heading Jochen Schmid's Yamaha, Loris Capirossi's Honda and Andy Preining's Aprilia.

Cardus (Honda) and Zeelenberg (Suzuki) were on opposite ends of row four after this highly chancy business, while row five saw some classy company – Reggiani's Aprilia leading Ruggia's new Gilera, defending champion Cadalora's Honda and Torrontegui's Suzuki.

There had been a positive spate of crashes during the two days of mostly wet riding, including Cadalora (twice), Capirossi (also twice), Chili, Zeelenberg, Lavado, Biaggi and a number of Japanese riders. Luckily, there were no serious injuries. Or not until morning warm-up when Cardus embarked on a dismal season by breaking his collarbone, flying straight home for surgery.

There were 40 qualifiers for the especially enlarged grid.

250 cc RACE – 20 LAPS

IRTA instructions notwithstanding, it was hard to ignore Aoki and Kozono as they took off in the lead, rapidly drawing away, with Cadalora coming through from the middle to take a distant third by the end of lap one. Kozono promptly moved ahead, but both leaders were right on the ragged edge and on lap three he slid off, one of many to do so.

Aoki was well ahead of Cadalora still, but there was a long way to go, and gradually the Italian closed up, catching him before half-distance. It didn't take long for him to find his way past. From then on, it was a foregone conclusion, and Luca gradually pulled away to win his third successive Suzuka GP by almost ten seconds.

Okada took advantage of this kindly light, following Luca past Aoki one lap later. He also gradually drew away, but it was more dramatic than the telling, because they were both slithering about on the puddles, and might easily have joined the ever-growing number of crashers.

Bradl had led morning warm-up before crashing, and had been delayed in the pack before gradually moving through to fourth, riding too cautiously to close up. 'I had crashed in the morning, and I knew that Cardus and Gardner were in hospital – so I just wanted to be sure of finishing.'

Chili was fifth after starting badly and slipping his clutch; Puig was sixth, some eight seconds adrift in what was now a rather tedious race; and Zeelenberg seventh after stalling on the line with a dragging clutch. 'I had to pull back off the line and push-start, and when I looked up the green light was already showing,' he said.

With Nanba (Yamaha) moving through to eighth, Capirossi began his 250 career in the points in ninth, narrowly holding off Jeandat's similar kitted RS over the line. New Suzuki rider Herri Torrontegui was close behind – he had been in the top ten after a strong start, but had slipped off and remounted to charge back on a battered bike. Schmid's works Yamaha was 12th.

There were a number of crashers, including Reggiani from ninth place just three laps from the end, and fellow-Aprilia man, Biaggi.

The Gileras had been third and fourth in warm-up, but Ruggia pitted early on with water in the works, while Lavado retired after moving up towards the points when a plug lead came adrift.

125 cc RACE – 18 LAPS

Last year, the plain-and-simple monoshock Honda was the only choice for privateers; this year Aprilias are also on the menu, and it was one of the Italian bikes on pole position, ridden by class veteran Bruno Casanova. In the Honda heartland, with a strong local contingent, this was a fine debut, Casanova leading row one from the Hondas of Hinokio, Waldmann and Debbia.

This first race was wet, and set the pattern for a crash-happy day. None of the others quite managed to match the 125s, however, with almost half the 42-strong field eliminated.

Gramigni's works Aprilia led into the first corner, but was soon displaced by the hard-charging GP regular Kazuto Sakata (Honda) and Martinez (Honda). The crashes started almost at once, with Ueda falling on lap two, closely followed by others including Hans Spaan (in his first Aprilia race) on lap two, Peter Öttl (who broke his arm), Gresini, Vitali and Unemoto.

Leader Gramigni also left the track twice, both times at the Spoon Curve, and both times without actually falling off. He lost ground, but went on to finish an eventual sixth.

This left the race as a tense three-way battle between Casanova, Waldmann and Wakai (Honda), with Waldmann biding his time before pouncing with two laps to go, to win by less than 1.5 seconds. Casanova was second, with Wakai outdistanced in the closing stages. Ezio Gianola (Honda) was fourth, unable to stay in touch.

There were just 22 finishers.

Marlboro
elf
3
Müllermilch
SHOEI
Ráctiv
DUNLOP
HONDA
Marlboro
schuh
DUNLOP
elf
PVM

13
aprilia
UNLIMITED
Mobil 1
13

Japanese Grand Prix, 29 March/statistics

Suzuka Circuit, 3.644-mile/5.864-km circuit

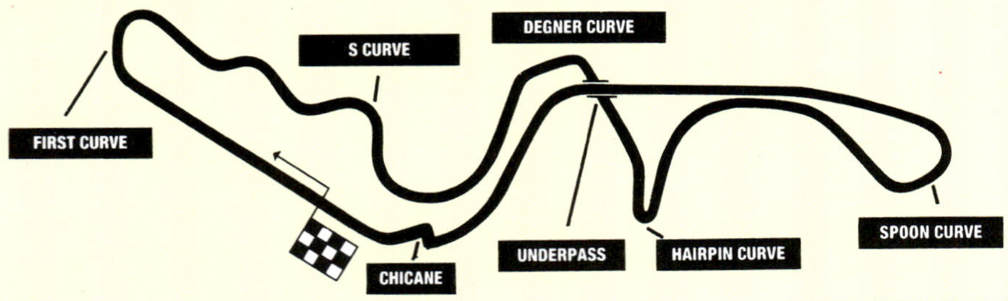

500 cc

22 laps, 80.168 miles/129.008 km

Place	Rider	Nat.	Machine	Laps	Time & speed	Fastest lap	Lap
1	**Michael Doohan**	AUS	Honda	22	56m 21.831s 85.334 mph/ 137.331 km/h	2m 32.090s	11
2	**Doug Chandler**	USA	Suzuki	22	56m 50.129s	2m 32.86s	5
3	**Kevin Schwantz**	USA	Suzuki	22	57m 17.623s	2m 33.154s	8
4	**Shinichi Itoh**	J	Honda	22	58m 09.633s	2m 33.692s	4
5	**Randy Mamola**	USA	Yamaha	22	58m 22.815s	2m 36.245s	4
6	**Keiji Ohishi**	J	Suzuki	22	58m 35.539s	2m 37.202s	21
7	**Niall Mackenzie**	GB	Yamaha	22	58m 36.836s	2m 37.932s	7
8	**Toshihiko Honma**	J	Yamaha	22	58m 37.322s	2m 38.203s	22
9	**Norihiko Fujiwara**	J	Yamaha	22	58m 38.422s	2m 38.466s	11
10	**Satoshi Tsujimoto**	J	Honda	22	58m 49.096s	2m 38.578s	5
11	Alexandre Barros	BR	Cagiva	21	56m 36.365s	2m 39.439s	21
12	Juan Garriga	E	Yamaha	21	56m 37.271s	2m 39.840s	21
13	Kenichiro Iwahashi	J	Honda	21	56m 40.094s	2m 39.702s	21
14	Eddie Lawson	USA	Cagiva	21	56m 53.775s	2m 40.444s	14
15	Michael Rudroff	D	Yamaha	20	57m 09.212s	2m 47.169s	15
16	Corrado Catalano	I	Yamaha	20	57m 34.859s	2m 45.391s	10
	Wayne Gardner	AUS	Honda	18	DNF	2m 34.266s	18
	John Kocinski	USA	Yamaha	6	DNF	2m 33.189s	6
	Miguel DuHamel	CAN	Yamaha	3	DNF	2m 34.927s	2
	Wayne Rainey	USA	Yamaha	1	DNF	2m 46.975s	1
	Alex Criville	E	Honda	1	DNF	3m 40.133s	1
	Peter Goddard	AUS	Yamaha	0	DNF		
	Daryl Beattie	AUS	Honda	0	DNF		
	Thierry Crine	F	Yamaha		DNQ		
	Toshiyuki Arakaki	J	Yamaha		DNQ		
	Serge David	CH	Yamaha		DNQ		
	Eddie Laycock	IRL	Yamaha		DNQ		
	Cees Doorakkers	NL	Yamaha		DNQ		
	Dominique Sarron	F	Yamaha		DNQ		
	Sepp Doppler	A	Yamaha		DNQ		
	Kevin Mitchell	GB	Yamaha		DNQ		
	Niggi Schmassman	CH	Yamaha		DNQ		
	Peter Graves	GB	Yamaha		DNQ		
	Simon Buckmaster	GB	Yamaha		DNQ		
	Marco Papa	I	Librenti		DNQ		
	Lucio Pedercini	I	Paton		DNQ		
	Andreas Leuthe	D	VRP		DNQ		

Fastest lap: Doohan, 2m 32.090s, 86.248 mph/138.802 km/h.
Lap record: John Kocinski, USA (Yamaha), 2m 11.149s, 99.934 mph/160.828 km/h (1991).

Practice leaderboard: 1 Schwantz, 2m 20.324s; **2** Honma, 2m 21.082s; **3** Chandler, 2m 22.023s; **4** Gardner, 2m 24.413s; **5** Doohan, 2m 24.413s; **6** Mamola, 2m 27.000s; **7** Beattie, 2m 27.641s; **8** Garriga, 2m 27.684s; **9** Rainey, 2m 27.979s; **10** Goddard, 2m 28.683s; **11** Itoh, 2m 28.706s; **12** Kocinski, 2m 29.013s; **13** Mackenzie, 2m 29.175s; **14** Criville, 2m 30.390s; **15** DuHamel, 2m 30.410s.

World Championship: 1 Doohan, 20; **2** Chandler, 15; **3** Schwantz, 12; **4** Itoh, 10; **5** Mamola, 8; **6** Ohishi, 6; **7** Mackenzie, 4; **8** Honma, 3; **9** Fujiwara, 2; **10** Tsujimoto, 1.

Photos: Malcolm Bryan

Chasing spectres. Cadalora seizes the lead from Aoki; Okada (51) will soon follow him past for a Honda clean sweep.

Inset: **Schwantz was beaten by new team-mate Chandler – a novel experience.**

250 cc

20 laps, 72.874 miles/117.280 km

Place	Rider	Nat.	Machine	Laps	Time & speed	Fastest lap	Lap
1	**Luca Cadalora**	I	Honda	20	52m 50.357s 82.750 mph/ 117.280 km/h	2m 35.862s	16
2	**Tadayuki Okada**	J	Honda	20	53m 00.326s	2m 37.276s	15
3	**Nobuatsu Aoki**	J	Honda	20	53m 14.000s	2m 37.639s	13
4	**Helmut Bradl**	D	Honda	20	53m 41.626s	2m 39.038s	18
5	**Pier Francesco Chili**	I	Aprilia	20	54m 06.693s	2m 39.631s	16
6	**Alberto Puig**	E	Aprilia	20	54m 14.602s	2m 40.439s	14
7	**Wilco Zeelenberg**	NL	Suzuki	20	54m 21.934s	2m 39.567s	8
8	**Kyoji Nanba**	J	Yamaha	20	54m 37.309s	2m 41.686s	7
9	**Loris Capirossi**	I	Honda	20	54m 44.510s	2m 40.744s	17
10	**Jean-Pierre Jeandat**	F	Honda	20	54m 44.911s	2m 40.068s	17
11	Herri Torrontegui	E	Suzuki	20	54m 46.168s	2m 39.631s	19
12	Jochen Schmid	D	Yamaha	20	54m 48.637s	2m 40.148s	17
13	Sadanori Hikita	J	Honda	20	55m 26.806s	2m 41.835s	15
14	Eskil Suter	CH	Aprilia	20	55m 29.039s	2m 43.274s	8
15	Stefano Caracchi	I	Yamaha	20	55m 29.502s	2m 43.058s	20
16	Adrian Bosshard	CH	Honda	20	55m 32.075s	2m 43.393s	16
17	Stefan Prein	D	Honda	20	55m 32.840s	2m 43.117s	14
18	Yves Briguet	CH	Honda	20	55m 37.411s	2m 43.611s	19
19	Bernard Cazade	F	Honda	19	52m 58.906s	2m 44.126s	18
20	Jurgen van den Goorbergh	NL	Aprilia	19	53m 20.285s	2m 45.252s	10
21	Renzo Colleoni	I	Yamaha	19	53m 44.160s	2m 44.819s	19
22	Bernard Hänggeli	CH	Aprilia	19	53m 59.081s	2m 47.304s	17
23	Bernd Kassner	D	Aprilia	19	53m 59.081s	2m 47.304s	17
24	Osamu Miyazaki	J	Yamaha	18	54m 09.037s	2m 43.777s	18
	Loris Reggiani	I	Aprilia	17	DNF	2m 41.932s	12
	Tetsuya Harada	J	Yamaha	15	DNF	2m 40.424s	14
	Doriano Romboni	I	Honda	15	DNF	2m 44.557s	10
	Carlos Lavado	YV	Gilera	10	DNF	2m 43.023s	8
	Masahiro Shimizu	J	Honda	7	DNF	2m 44.474s	7
	Adi Stadler	D	Honda	7	DNF	2m 50.431s	5
	Luis D'Antin	E	Honda	6	DNF	2m 45.394s	6
	Frédéric Protat	F	Aprilia	6	DNF	2m 54.350s	2
	Yoshiaki Kato	J	Yamaha	5	DNF	2m 40.970s	5
	Massimiliano Biaggi	I	Aprilia	3	DNF	2m 48.314s	3
	Katsuyoshi Kozono	J	Honda	3	DNF	2m 37.289s	3
	Tsutomu Udagawa	J	Honda	1	DNF	2m 56.952s	1
	Paolo Casoli	I	Yamaha	1	DNF	3m 02.725s	1
	Jean-Philippe Ruggia	F	Gilera	1	DNF	3m 17.131s	1
	Andy Preining	A	Aprilia	1	DNF	3m 18.575s	1
	Carlos Cardus	E	Honda	0	DNS		
	Patrick van den Goorbergh	NL	Aprilia		DNQ		
	Erkka Korpiaho	SF	Aprilia		DNQ		
	Harald Eckl	D	Aprilia		DNQ		

Fastest lap: Cadalora, 2m 35.862s, 84.160 mph/135.443 km/h.
Lap record: Luca Cadalora, I (Honda), 2m 15.075s, 97.029 mph/156.153 km/h (1991).

Practice leaderboard: **1** Aoki, 2m 18.696s; **2** Harada, 2m 18.857s; **3** Romboni, 2m 20.213s; **4** Hikita, 2m 20.362s; **5** Miyazaki, 2m 20.532s; **6** Okada, 2m 20.593s; **7** Puig, 2m 20.668s; **8** Kozono, 2m 20.881s; **9** Bradl, 2m 21.395s; **10** Schmid, 2m 21.478s; **11** Capirossi, 2m 22.004s; **12** Preining, 2m 22.294s; **13** Cardus, 2m 22.669s; **14** Kato, 2m 22.797s; **15** Shimizu, 2m 22.882s.

World Championship: **1** Cadalora, 20; **2** Okada, 15; **3** Aoki, 12; **4** Bradl, 10; **5** Chili, 8; **6** Puig, 6; **7** Zeelenberg, 4; **8** Nanba, 3; **9** Capirossi, 2; **10** Jeandat, 1.

125 cc

18 laps, 65.592 miles/105.552 km

Place	Rider	Nat.	Machine	Laps	Time & speed	Fastest lap	Lap
1	**Ralf Waldmann**	D	Honda	18	48m 49.661s 80.594 mph/ 129.703 km/h	2m 29.888s	18
2	**Bruno Casanova**	I	Aprilia	18	48m 51.120s	2m 40.980s	18
3	**Nobuyuki Wakai**	J	Honda	18	48m 57.031s	2m 41.462s	11
4	**Ezio Gianola**	I	Honda	18	49m 10.355s	2m 41.585s	18
5	**Akiro Saito**	J	Honda	18	49m 16.362s	2m 42.033s	17
6	**Alessandro Gramigni**	I	Aprilia	18	49m 16.488s	2m 40.081s	17
7	**Yutaka Fujihara**	J	Honda	18	49m 16.569s	2m 41.527s	11
8	**Kinya Wada**	J	Honda	18	49m 16.917s	2m 42.094s	15
9	**Dirk Raudies**	D	Honda	18	49m 26.941s	2m 41.736s	12
10	**Oliver Petrucciani**	CH	Honda	18	50m 01.019s	2m 43.412s	12
11	Robin Appleyard	GB	Honda	18	50m 06.457s	2m 43.313s	13
12	Alfred Waibel	D	Honda	18	50m 06.534s	2m 43.435s	13
13	Oliver Koch	D	Honda	18	50m 24.642s	2m 44.181s	12
14	Peter Galvin	AUS	Honda	18	50m 26.396s	2m 45.194s	8
15	Heinz Lüthi	CH	Honda	18	50m 41.649s	2m 46.650s	17
16	Alain Bronec	F	Honda	18	50m 46.626s	2m 46.391s	14
17	Manuel Hernandez	E	Aprilia	18	50m 52.269s	2m 46.268s	10
18	Emilio Cuppini	I	Aprilia	17	49m 12.359s	2m 49.706s	14
19	Steve Patrickson	GB	Honda	17	49m 57.805s	2m 49.111s	12
20	Tomoko Igata	J	Honda	17	50m 52.416s	2m 45.287s	2
21	Hubert Abold	D	Honda	17	51m 13.097s	2m 53.929s	5
22	Takao Shimizu	J	Honda	14	49m 38.714s	2m 51.740s	7
	Julian Miralles	E	Honda	14	DNF	2m 45.854s	7
	Hisashi Unemoto	J	Honda	7	DNF	2m 46.474s	7
	Maurizio Vitali	I	Gazzaniga	7	DNF	2m 48.243s	7
	Hideyuki Nakajyo	J	Honda	7	DNF	2m 42.159s	4
	Masato Shima	J	Honda	6	DNF	2m 44.718s	6
	Giovanni Palmieri	I	Gazzaniga	6	DNF	2m 55.412s	5
	Maik Stief	D	Aprilia	5	DNF	2m 48.763s	5
	Soichiro Sato	J	Honda	5	DNF	2m 45.135s	3
	Fausto Gresini	I	Honda	3	DNF	2m 43.184s	2
	Gabriele Debbia	I	Honda	3	DNF	2m 44.137s	3
	Masafumi Ono	J	Honda	3	DNF	2m 45.730s	2
	Peter Öttl	D	Rotax	3	DNF	2m 45.505s	3
	Loek Bodelier	NL	Honda	3	DNF	2m 46.899s	3
	Yukiho Hinokio	J	Honda	2	DNF	2m 43.767s	2
	Hans Spaan	NL	Aprilia	2	DNF	2m 59.023s	1
	Kazuto Sakata	J	Honda	2	DNF	2m 48.241s	1
	Jorge Martinez	E	Honda	1	DNF	2m 50.903s	1
	Carlos Giro	E	Aprilia	1	DNF	2m 57.817s	1
	Arie Molenaar	NL	Aprilia	1	DNF	3m 07.731s	1
	Noboru Ueda	J	Honda	1	DNF	3m 27.417s	1

Fastest lap: Waldmann, 2m 39.888s, 82.041 mph/132.032 km/h.
Lap record: Noboru Ueda, J (Honda), 2m 22.264s, 92.126 mph/148.262 km/h (1991).

Practice leaderboard: **1** Casanova, 2m 23.630s; **2** Hinokio, 2m 23.805s; **3** Waldmann, 2m 23.825s; **4** Debbia, 2m 23.833s; **5** Sakata, 2m 23.871s; **6** Martinez, 2m 24.082s; **7** Gramigni, 2m 24.109s; **8** Saito, 2m 24.281s; **9** Gianola, 2m 24.340s; **10** Wakai, 2m 24.484s; **11** Ueda, 2m 24.533s; **12** Ono, 2m 24.582s; **13** Ikata, 2m 24.857s; **14** Sato, 2m 24.931s; **15** Wada, 2m 25.066s.

World Championship: **1** Waldmann, 20; **2** Casanova, 15; **3** Wakai, 12; **4** Gianola, 10; **5** Saito, 8; **6** Gramigni, 6; **7** Fujihara, 4; **8** Wada, 3; **9** Raudies, 2; **10** Petrucciani, 1.

AUSTRALIAN GRAND PRIX

Away from the spirituality of Suzuka, it was possible to see just how racing's New Deal for privateers had swelled their numbers in the 500 class, and given them raceworthy tackle in the shape of works-replica Roc and Harris Yamahas. The other items of race-winning equipment – that combination of technical support and inbred riding ability – they would have to supply for themselves.

Given the level of performance and competition, even the most talented riders should be given a race or two to settle in, but a respectable handful were already showing a willingness to twist the throttle. When it came to matters technical, it was a different story. Team Roberts had around 12 technicians plus an army of ancillary technical support combining many years of sharp-edge experience, all devoted to serving the needs of just two riders. Each privateer had one, maybe two people helping out, and all as much in the dark as one another about the manifold subtleties of the fastest racing bikes in the world.

Photos: Malcolm Bryan

500 cc	DOOHAN
250 cc	CADALORA
125 cc	WALDMANN

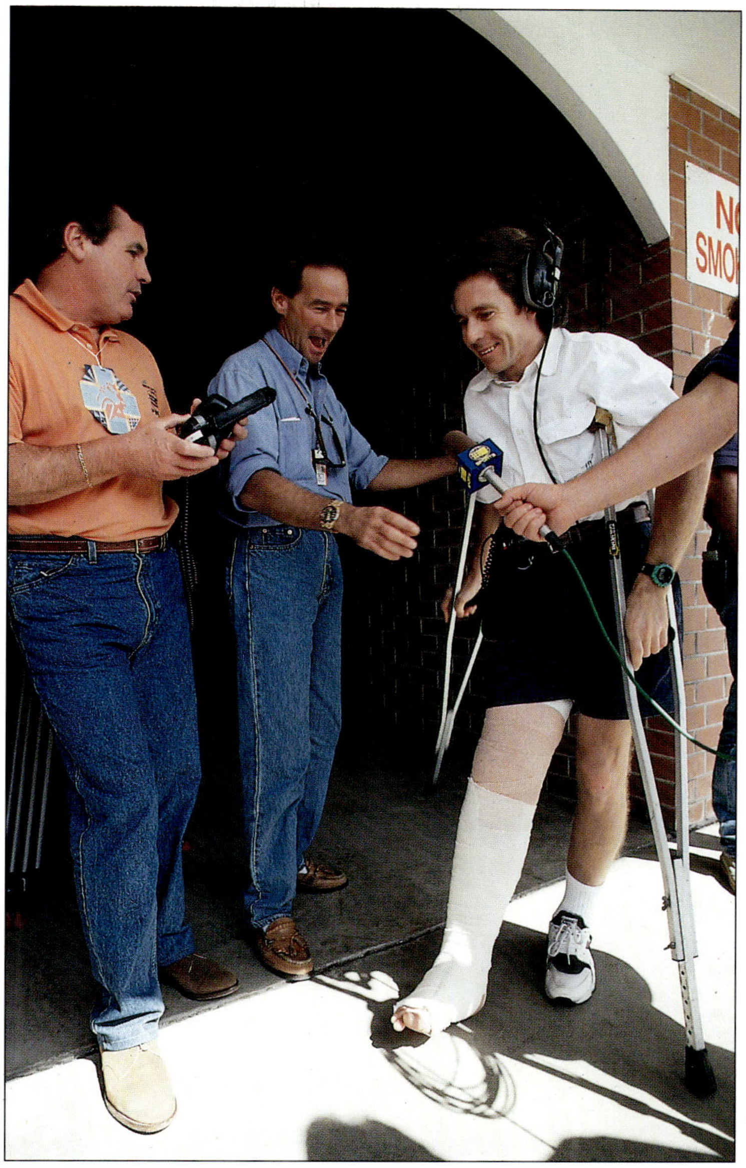

Opposite page: **Power tightens the top chain run as Randy sprints to the next too tight corner – for him, the race was one lap too short.**

Inset opposite: **Doohan faced an Ocker anthem at the Creek, but failed to show much emotion in response.**

Right: **Gardner's broken leg consigned him to the TV commentary team. Ex-World Champions Alan Jones and Barry Sheene help him to adjust his antennae.**

The YZR Yamaha has a reputation for being user-friendly, but this is only in comparison with the delicately balanced Suzuki, the erratic Cagiva and the hitherto wilful and flawed NSR Honda. Compared with the Superbikes or three-cylinder Hondas that most of the privateers had ridden until now, it was a monster – with an over-powerful engine, finicky carburation and a baffling range of gearing possibilities in a chassis offering a bewildering range of adjustment. All to be learned while adapting their riding to a style that allowed them to make use of the excess of power.

Not surprisingly, they and their bikes were still way off the standard of the works machines. Even those who weren't still floundering had only just stepped onto the bottom of the learning curve. Yet there was already a band of fast men emerging to mix it in the midfield: like endurance champion Thierry Crine from France, Dutch veteran all-rounder Cees Doorakkers, French ditto Dominique Sarron, the improving German Michael Rudroff and hair-raising Japanese GP wild man from nowhere, Toshiyuki Arakaki.

And among them was Briton Kevin Mitchell, whose switch from 250s to a Harris Yamaha had brought with it a spur to his enthusiasm and an impressive revitalisation of his press-on riding style. (Fellow-Britons Simon Buckmaster and Peter Graves were having trouble with obsolete Metzeler tyres and deep-end nerves respectively.) Mitchell was still trying to drop his hard-leaning 250 style so he could use the wheelspin to turn the bike more, but old habits die hard. He leaned so far over at Eastern Creek that he wore through his second-hand knee-sliders and his leathers to the skin beneath.

He should have been picking the bike up and sliding the rear rather than ear-holing, but he still qualified 20th, which was perfectly fine in the context of the B-group battle. But the flip side was that even Mitchell and his cohorts were five seconds a lap slower than pole qualifier Doohan, and he would catch up to lap their midfield scrap at only some half-distance of the race. By then, he would also have had to dispose of the stragglers – there were 29 starters.

Nothing too unusual in that, perhaps. But something had changed this year. In the old days of the three-cylinder Hondas, the works riders could simply jet past on the straights. Now the privateer bikes were potentially as fast in a straight line.

Eastern Creek is a modern twisty sort of track, with strictly limited overtaking opportunities, particularly compared with the many subtleties of Suzuka. In qualifying the works riders encountered the new mobile chicanes for the first time this year, and many dark imprecations were muttered. 'It's so dangerous,' said Rainey. 'They're going so slow that they can change their line any old how – but when you're going fast and overtaking them, you're committed to one safe line. I've been avoiding overtaking them in corners because you have no idea of where they're going to go next, but now they're as quick as we are down the straights.' Team-mate Kocinski chimed in, while Doohan wondered why the slow men hadn't stayed at home to win their national championships before coming GP racing. A perennial problem, and it is hard to imagine any solution beyond an improvement in race track design, away from the current trend to continuous looping low gear single-file corners.

Doohan in any case needed to say something, if only to claim some of the attention being lavished on Wayne Gardner. The former was merely winning races. The latter was in the popular and well-practised role of injured hero and, as the media made a circus of his musings on possible retirement and regrets at not being able to race, Gardner enraged Doohan by telling Australia how much it hurt watching him (Doohan) having such fun on the brilliant new NSR that he (Gardner) had developed.

This is at best only partly true, and it stung to see it splashed across the Sydney newspapers. But it probably only helped Doohan to concentrate on the job in hand, and he set about proving that he was certainly far from unfamiliar with the new NSR, and that it was as devastatingly effective on a slow corner track as it had been at Suzuka. He qualified on pole by a big margin, and then ran away with his second successive race.

At this stage, the opposition were still somewhat bemused by the efficacy of the droning new Honda, and were hoping beyond hope that another race would reveal some chink in its armour. It was whispered that the high torque and concentration of four power strokes within a few degrees of crankshaft rotation were wreaking havoc with over-stressed gears, and everyone waited in vain for a failure.

Yamaha had a knee-jerk response of two new chassis for Team Roberts, specifically for Rainey. He liked them. Or was he just trying to convince himself when he said: 'It slides easier, and moves around a lot more, but it means I can feel the tyre better.'

For Suzuki, the Creek has always been a problem track, with the unbanked low gear bends bringing out the worst in its too delicate cornering balance. The acquisition of a prototype digital dashboard like those used in F1, and capable of showing not only revs and water temperature but also lap times and more or less anything else you might care to programme in, merely confused matters, causing the existing electronics to play up. Schwantz, meanwhile, was troubled by a numbness in one leg that he blamed in public on too tight new leathers – although he knew it was the result of a pinched nerve in his spine which he blamed on an over-enthusiastic exercise routine in the preceding week. A worrying problem.

Thus the controversial Sydney track proved a second successive Honda playground, not only for Doohan but also for erstwhile team-mate Daryl Beattie, drafted in to fill Gardner's saddle in a lull in his All-Japan Championship commitments. The 21-year-old Queenslander made no secret of how much he hated racing in Japan, where he was being held on ice by Honda for a second successive year, but was rather more coy in revealing all the details of how he was using a 1991 chassis for the new engine in preference to Gardner's set-up, with a lower engine height for better corner entry. And he certainly was fast, qualifying on the front row and finishing strongly on the rostrum in his first 500 class GP start. (He retired on the warm-up lap in Japan.)

A star is born – but Kocinski gave a cautionary demonstration of how things get harder for instant heroes when they try to get dug in to the top positions. Trying to match the Hondas in practice he lost the front wheel on the tricky approach to the last corner set, where the track bends right under hard braking for a pair of tight lefts. He skinned his right-hand little finger badly enough to require a skin graft, which put him out of this race and the next one too, effectively spoiling his year and certainly denying him the chance of the repeat victory he had been promising in Malaysia. 'I have to think of my whole career, and not take risks riding injured for the sake of one race,' he said manfully.

Mechanical new stars have no easier a time of it than humans, so

Photos: Malcolm Bryan

Beattie failed to start at Suzuka, so this was effectively his first GP. He finished it on the rostrum.

Gilera's first championship points for 35 years was an impressive achievement in only their second modern era GP, especially in the brawling 250 class. Success was achieved without particular accord in the Arcore team, where team engineer Harald Bartol, a long-time two-stroke luminary, was at loggerheads with factory designer Federico Martini. One bone of contention was the need for an intake airbox, upstream of the carburettor bellmouths. Such plenum chambers are considered essential by all except Martini, and he decreed that the Gilera would do without them. Bartol monitored carburettor float-bowl temperatures, and found to his dismay that they were rising by five degrees as the engine heated up.

The race was run amid growing local controversy over the always troublesome Sydneyside circuit. Since the first GP visit here last year promoter Bob Barnard's company had gone bust, and Dovigo, the syndicate which owned the new track, had needed a costly government rescue. The New South Wales state government (which had underwritten the project to the tune of some $A25 million with loans from the state bank) had to swallow their losses, and had taken over ownership. Australia's top permanent racing facility had always been a political hot potato for state premier Nick Greiner, who was at the race, and the whole affair contributed substantially to his downfall and resignation less than four months later.

Purely in the short term, after all the delays in sorting out the calendar, there had been a serious shortage of time to promote the event thoroughly, although the organisers later claimed 'a small profit' on the crowd of 60,000.

Barnard, who could justifiably claim to be the father of the event both at Phillip Island and at the new track he had personally developed, was also present, and was both puzzled and hurt that he'd not been enlisted to help out in one way or another. He was now working as a civil engineer, but later in the year found a job back in bike racing, with Team Roberts.

Teething troubles still bedevilled the series. The argument about the Japanese ghost riders was hotting up nicely, accompanied by some heavy-handed tactics from the new regime as they tried to make IRTA's view stick. Marlboro released their usual printed preview in the press room, whereupon Dorna's new press officer, Denis Noyes, promptly confiscated all of them because they showed FIM points (including Japanese riders) and not IRTA's. At first, Marlboro seemed cravenly ready to destroy all 500 brochures, before agreeing to staple a corrected sheet of IRTA points to them instead.

There were also complaints about the rather arbitrary imposition of only two timed practice sessions. Almost everybody would have preferred to return to the 1991 system, with the Saturday morning session once again counting – which would have solved the problems of changing weather in Japan. However, already making a stand on principle, IRTA decided to leave things as they were, on the grounds that the rules should not be alterable willy-nilly.

There was also another glitch in the results, caused this time by the colourful Australian flagman, whose enthusiasm led him to show the chequered flag to the wrong Honda. Subsequent protests delayed the results by five hours as the FIM stewards decided to extrapolate, and IRTA began to wonder if they were operating under some sort of a jinx.

500 cc PRACTICE

A greening of grass and the addition of some strategic sand traps and straw bales improved the appearance and the safety of the track a little, but the short lap, low gear turns and some extra bumps on the straight (which had been used as a drag strip since the last meeting) kept the grumbles going.

Mercifully, this year nobody tested the safety provisions, with only one significant crash, when Kocinski fell with his hand trapped under the clip-on. 'He got in too hot and lost the front,' said crash spectator Kenny Roberts, while John added: 'I got mauled.' But nobody could blame the circuit.

Kocinski was fifth at the time, just one of the fancied runners finding it rather hard work to keep Doohan's Honda in view. The new NSR revelled in the dry Australian weather, as it had the rain in Japan, and the combination of the flat-sounding torque and plentiful traction out of the slow corners meant Doohan dominated throughout – a performance we were already getting used to. He was able to spend much of practice carrying out tyre endurance tests, to update the considerable data the Rothmans Honda team had already gathered here and at Phillip Island, in far more punishing heat than this mild autumn sunshine. It left Mick well prepared, and able to contemplate such matters as the wisdom of putting the pole-starter on the inside of the track, condemning him to the wrong line for the crucial Turn One, which is followed by a long one-line stretch with few passing opportunities for the rest of the lap. 'I'd prefer to be in the middle,' he said.

After his spill at Suzuka, defending champion Rainey was in a feisty mood, although still less than completely fit. His new chassis meant he could again use elements of his favoured riding style, wiggling and sliding aggressively around the constant twists, although it all looked rather hard work.

It was fast enough for him to secure second in both timed practice sessions, ending up a fraction slower than his own pole of last year, but less than half a second down on Doohan. 'We're developing two new bikes here,' he said. 'But I'm happy. The new chassis are different from each other. Both are less stable than before, but at least I can feel the tyres better.'

Michelin boss Pierre Dupasquier did not approve, however, when asked if it meant that the new generation French tyres were more sympathetic than the old, and easier to slide, like the less grippy Dunlops. 'It is not anything different about our new tyres. He should not be sliding. It tears the tyres up,' he opined. 'But this is the first chance we've had since the season started with dry weather, and we are still testing a lot of different tyres.'

Beattie made the most of his holiday from Japan and unexpected second chance in a GP. After switching to a combination that put Gardner's new engine in a 1991-style chassis the same as Doohan's, his local track knowledge and a year of 500 class experience were enough to win him an impressive third on the grid. The youngster's style was smooth and calm, and he didn't look as though he was taking risks. Even Doohan might have been feeling his fellow-Queenslander's hot breath down the back of his neck. 'I don't expect to beat Mick or the other top guys,' said Beattie. 'They're really fast, and when they break away from the start you never get it back.'

The youngster had displaced Schwantz from third, but the Texan's front row position meant that the Suzuki was a great deal closer than a year ago to being competitive at one of its worst tracks. 'The bike's improved a whole lot since then, and even since our tests here before the season,' he said. 'It's not a whole way off, though we're still short of rear traction.' Being ahead of Chandler this time helped Kevin's spirits, while he had run comfortably with Doohan in Saturday morning's free practice, the Suzuki holding tight lines while the Honda was jumping around rather. In fact, as Schwantz realised, Doohan was on well-used tyres while his were new – but it was still encouraging.

Lawson took over in sixth to head the depleted row two, missing Kocinski. The Cagiva had a new carbon fibre swing arm, part of a package of minor improvements that helped the American cut almost one-and-a-half seconds off his first session time. This put him narrowly ahead of Mamola's Yamaha, the returned veteran admitting to finding the highly technical and slow circuit difficult to learn after a year off GP bikes. 'You try and figure out places to go faster, but it's just going back and forth all the time and I'm still getting my mind back into race mode.'

Chandler was rather dispirited to be only eighth. One drawback was

Chandler looked neater on the Suzuki than Schwantz, turning similar times with a different riding style.

that his team spent much of the first day of practice chasing an elusive engine problem before discovering that the exhaust power valve mechanism on the lower pair of cylinders was snagging on the extra lower radiator used in hot conditions. After that he was simply behindhand and, at the end of practice, was getting increasingly desperate about the problems (very familiar to Schwantz last year) of getting the bike balanced. 'I get the front to stick and the back goes loose, so I fix that then the front moves around,' he said. 'I'm almost tearing my hair out.'

'Jean-Pierre' Mackenzie was next, now with a British mechanic to lend him moral and mechanical support in his French team. He was within hundredths of Chandler, with the pair of them more than two seconds slower than Doohan. But the Scotsman was happy enough. 'This is the first time we've had the bike in the dry, so there's basic testing to do. We've made a lot of progress,' he said.

Criville's NSR was less than a tenth slower, followed by Garriga's Yamaha. Fierce rivalry was building up as Criville began to take team manager Pons's place as the other would-be hero from Barcelona.

Then came Peter Goddard's Roc, by far the top privateer. Racing at home meant he was trying especially hard, and he crashed on Friday. His 500 cc experience in Japan, as well as close ties with Serge Rosset, whose firm built his bike, had already lifted the Australian above the common herd of privateers.

Row four was led by Barros, charging hard without much effect, followed by the '91 works Yamahas of Laycock and DuHamel. The GP new boy was acquiring a reputation for crashing as he adapted from US Superbikes, but did not accept any blame for a last session spill, instead blaming Arakaki for knocking him off.

The privateers were spread out from Crine in 16th place, and more than four seconds slower than pole-man Doohan, via Serge David in 17th, then Arakaki, Sarron and Mitchell, all the way down to Graves in 27th, Pedercini (Paton) 28th and Sepp Doppler (Roc Yamaha) in 29th. These latter were obviously the main targets of the works riders' criticism, but all made the qualifying cut, in Doppler's case by just half a second.

Rothmans
HONDA
elf
NGK
Malcolm Bryan

All alone, Doohan kept his NSR on the ragged edge to preserve his concentration.

500 cc RACE – 30 LAPS

Doohan's grumble about his starting position proved justified. Rainey out-dragged him to Turn One, and pulled the train from then on, with Doohan second, Schwantz third and Beattie fourth.

By the end of lap one Beattie had moved past Schwantz into the first turn, and the first three positions were all but settled. It only remained to see how long Doohan would wait, because the Honda was leaning on the Yamaha all the way round, and Rainey's fitness was still in question.

It took longer than Doohan would have preferred. 'He gave me a hard time – I just couldn't get past,' he said. 'Every place I had an advantage he'd get me somewhere else. I wondered if I'd ever get by.'

Well, of course he did eventually, with the favourite manoeuvre of slipstreaming past the pits then out-braking Rainey into the first corner. But his misgivings gained credence when he didn't run away from the Marlboro Yamaha. It was only when they came upon a group of back-markers, which Doohan judged perfectly, that he was able to open a decisive gap.

He kept pressing on, slipping around close to the edge and on one occasion over it – on the inside of the corner for a change. He gouged turf and scattered stones with his knee-slider, but he is accustomed to exceeding his own limits and his only real moment came when he passed a back-marker to then find yet another, much slower bike in front of that. 'I had no choice but to go off line to pass both of them,' he said. But he recovered to wheelie across the line to tumultuous applause, triggering a crowd invasion of the track that is in danger of becoming a tradition.

Rainey had settled for second after losing touch with the Honda, and finished almost seven seconds adrift, nursing his painful left hand. 'Mick was towing me along a bit until we got into those back-markers,' he admitted. But he rode like a champion, and threatened Doohan for far longer than had been expected. 'If he's like that when he's only 70 per cent fit, it's going to be tough,' grinned the Australian.

For Beattie, the race was a lonely triumph, equalling Kocinski's record of a rostrum finish in his first GP start (a result from the 1989 Belgian race that was later disallowed on a technicality). Schwantz's expected counter-attack hadn't come, and the youngster could concentrate on being fast and smooth and keeping out of trouble, finishing 18 seconds behind Doohan and easily outpacing the pursuit.

Schwantz had problems of his own, once again from team-mate Chandler, who gradually closed up from his fifth place start, moving past Kevin into the first corner just after half-distance. For the next six laps it seemed that the Suzuki new boy would beat the team's top man in the dry, as he had done in the wet at Suzuka. Then Schwantz got going again, gritting his teeth to conquer both pogo-stick rear suspension and numbness in his leg to push firmly past and secure fourth by five seconds. Chandler was having problems with the opposite end of the bike, not for the last time, as the different riding styles of the new team-mates demonstrated the Suzuki's knife-edge balance. But Doug was 'real happy, considering the problems in practice. The bike still wasn't right – the front was diving too fast and when Kevin went by there was nothing I could do.'

Some distance behind, Lawson was riding to a lonely sixth, the Cagiva ever an unknown quantity. 'The Dunlops were real good, and though my bike lacked bottom end it is good at the top. I spent too long early in the race stuck with Randy. If I'd woken up earlier, I might have been able to run with the Suzukis,' he said.

Behind him, Criville had been moving through gradually from a 17th place start, and had overcome and broken free from an almost race-long battle between Garriga and Mamola. But it took a special stewards' meeting to decide their finishing order, and in fact the trio – the last riders on the same lap as Doohan – nearly didn't qualify as finishers. As Criville, Mamola and Garriga crossed the line at the end of lap 29, the flagman greeted them with a waving signal meant for Doohan, coming up behind. They all slowed and prepared to pull in to take the short link back to the paddock, but were frantically waved back onto the track by commendably alert marshals.

Mamola and Garriga got the message at once, but Criville tarried and was left behind as the others gassed up and sprinted off. He finally crossed the line 16 seconds behind them. His Campsa team manager

All arms and elbows – and knees, thighs, back, bottom, shoulders, head .... Nobuyuki Wakai was much too big for his 125, and he meant to make it suffer.

Sito Pons protested successfully, and five hours after the race fresh results were issued (without race finishing times) restoring Criville to seventh.

It may have seemed fairer simply to take results from the lap before, but this would have affected some other finishers – notably DuHamel, who finished tenth to take his first World Championship point. He passed both the Cagiva of Alex Barros and Peter Goddard's Roc Yamaha on the last gallop to the flag, much to Goddard's chagrin. The Australian had planned a last lap move on Barros, but hadn't seen the pit signals warning of the coming threat from DuHamel. The team promptly promised to get a bigger pit board.

Crine's Roc Yamaha was 13th, with Catalano's similar bike another 20 seconds adrift. Behind him, Sarron's Roc triumphed over a race-long dice with Arakaki's Roc and Doorakkers's Harris. Mackenzie was among six non-finishers, after his carburettor main jets fell out!

250 cc PRACTICE

Both Cadalora and his team owner Erv Kanemoto were down with 'flu in Australia, and another kind of chill wind was blowing through their pit. It came from a growing awareness that not only was the new NSR Honda in many ways inferior to last year's bike (especially in top speed), but that this year's Aprilias had developed in the opposite direction. They were very fast, and would soon pose a real threat.

The Hondas held on to the high ground in practice, with Bradl displacing Cadalora from pole by three-tenths to become the only rider to break 1m 34s. His big improvement came after an enforced access of logic. 'I have four mechanics now, and I was getting very confused with all the different suggestions. In the end, I told them to set both bikes exactly the same with the same tyres and gearing.'

Cadalora was one of only two riders who didn't improve on Saturday afternoon, but he held second, saying that he'd run out of time after doing extensive tyre tests. 'At the end I went out to make a couple of fast laps. Unfortunately I only had time to make one. But I don't care so much. My 'flu makes me feel not so good, but during the race I expect to forget it.'

Chili rode the first Aprilia, qualifying his red and white factory-backed Telkor Aprilia third, less than a quarter of a second adrift. But he'd had to work for it on this track of slow turns, where the disc-valve bike's endemic sensitivity to part-throttle corner exit work made life difficult. 'The Hondas can do their lap time more easily than me. I think it will be a hard race,' he said.

Cardus was back, patched up after his morning warm-up spill in Japan with his collarbone freshly plated in the interim, and having more trouble getting his bike right than his fellow-NSR riders. He claimed the last front row position by two-tenths from charging privateer Andy Preining on his lease-engine Aprilia, the Austrian apparently ready to fulfil the promise he had shown last year.

Zeelenberg was alongside, with his team growing increasingly baffled at the gap between the Suzuki's impressive speed gun figures and its lap times, which were less so. Zeelenberg blamed a lack of mid-range, which cost him dear here. 'The chassis is really good, but if you make a mistake or anyone is in your way, you lose a second, and it is very hard to make it up again,' he said.

Shimizu's NSR Honda was seventh, with Capirossi continuing his strong class debut in eighth on his kitted RS, on the tail of the factory bikes and hoping that his performance would persuade Dunlop to come up with something better than his stock tyres for the race.

Biaggi led row three from Schmid's Yamaha and Reggiani's Aprilia – the official factory rider was still not fully fit. On the end of the row was Ruggia on the Gilera, in only its second race and getting well on the pace earlier in practice, though rather left behind as the pace hotted up at the end. Ruggia fell heavily in race morning warm-up, however, although without injury.

Romboni led row four, and all 37 entrants qualified.

250 cc RACE – 28 LAPS

Cadalora and Cardus started battling at the first bend, where the injured Spaniard got the better of the ailing Italian, and they kept on scrapping for the full race distance.

Cadalora always seemed to have the better of it, though, and Cardus actually only led across the line for six laps, including the first two, while under extreme pressure. But even after he'd been passed he refused to let go, remaining close enough to threaten a last lap shoot-out that might put both of them in jeopardy.

With five laps to go, Cadalora took control of the situation, waving Cardus past into the lead again. The Spaniard jumped at the chance, but he'd been sold a dummy. As he pushed himself and his tyres to the outer limits trying to break away, the pitiless Cadalora latched close on behind, to apply his well-tested cat-and-mouse strategy.

Having seen just where his rival was fast and just where he could hold him off, he pounced going into the first corner of the last lap, and then dashed for the line while also making himself wide enough to foil all of Cardus's increasingly desperate counter-attacks to win by less than a quarter of a second.

Last year Bradl had been the victim of a similarly humiliating drubbing, and it was the German who Cadalora had feared most this year. 'When I got the message he was way down, I was surprised to see Carlos right on my tail. He didn't seem to get tired and slow down as I'd expected. He forced me to ride a lot harder than I had planned.'

Cardus set fastest lap, although slower than Cadalora's 1991 record, and said he might have put up a harder fight but for some pain from his post-operative collarbone. 'My bike was going well at last,' he said. In fact, it was his best ride for the next few months, as his effort continued to disintegrate.

Bradl missed all the fun after spiking his own threat at the start, wasting pole position by bogging the engine, and dropping right to the back as it failed to pick up again instantly. He took all sorts of chances to carve through the backmarkers, but still ended the first lap in 13th place and out of touch with the battle for the lead. He gradually picked his way forwards, taking third on lap nine, and settling for a safe rostrum finish comfortably ahead of a big brawl for fourth.

The remarkable Capirossi led the pursuit pack for the first four laps, until his over-stretched RS Honda blew up. Then Chili moved ahead of the impressive Preining, only to crash in full view of his own on-bike camera one lap later.

By half-distance the group comprised the Aprilias of Biaggi, Preining and Reggiani, Zeelenberg's Suzuki and Romboni's Honda RS, with Ruggia closing up fast on the Gilera. This sextet frequently crossed the line three or even four abreast, with Preining mainly getting the best of it, but Zeelenberg well placed to size up the opposition, and Reggiani another seasoned joker in the pack.

Their experience paid off, and with two laps to go Zeelenberg and Reggiani started to stretch away from their erstwhile companions, with the Dutchman outbraking the Italian in the last lap. 'I frightened the hell out of him,' he said. 'He thought I was running straight. My Suzuki wasn't as fast as the others, but it was better under brakes and in the corners.'

He secured a fine fighting fourth, with Reggiani fifth, then Romboni, Preining, Biaggi and Ruggia, who just managed to save ninth place from Casoli's Yamaha, the Italian claiming the last point.

Nine seconds back, Schmid's works Yamaha stayed clear of the second Suzuki of Torrontegui, who was one of several riders delayed by a first lap melee which put four riders out.

Malcolm Bryan

It was triggered when French privateer Fred Protat fell, taking out Australian wild-card rider Stephen Whitehouse, Italian Renzo Colleoni and Spaniard Luis D'Antin. Ironically, Whitehouse and Colleoni were eliminated in a first lap crash in the 1990 GP.

125 cc RACE – 26 LAPS

Much-feared Japanese charger Kazuto Sakata qualified on pole, but lived up to his reputation by running wide into the first turn, then crashing on the fourth lap as he tried too hard to make up lost ground.

He missed an educational experience as the front-runners fought all the way to the usual closest finish of the day in a stirring battle between the emergent Aprilias and the top dog Hondas.

Gramigni's works Aprilia led from the start; Waldmann's Honda and Casanova's semi-works Aprilia soon tucked in behind, then Gresini's A-kitted Honda shot through to take a short-lived second place before he faded with his tyres shot.

This interference let Gramigni open up a gap of almost two seconds – but it was not enough, and by one-third distance Casanova and Waldmann were back with him, taking up where they left off for a breathtaking three-bike battle.

Martinez might have been among them, but his Honda had nipped up on lap two, dropping him to 14th. He fought his way back, but engine damage meant his performance was below par, and he never could catch Gresini. Young Charlie Giro's Aprilia was also coming up into the frame when he dropped back – a footrest had become detached, and he fell away to next to last.

Up front, Waldmann at first looked strongest, but he was taking wider and wider lines as the race wore on, while Casanova seemed to be holding something in reserve for a last lap attack.

Instead it was Gramigni who forced past both of them to try for a breakaway, only to be repassed by the determined Waldmann. The Italian waited and attacked again on the exit from the last corner.

It was a pure sprint to the line, and the Aprilia seemed certain to win, with Waldmann weaving in vain as he tried to block the apparently faster bike. Then, incredibly, Waldmann came back in the final yards, brilliantly exploiting the Aprilia's draft and his own slight top speed advantage to cross the line half a wheel ahead, with the time interval measured at 0.011 seconds. Another two-tenths back came Casanova, after a truly epic race.

Gramigni needed some convincing that he had in fact been beaten, but was thrilled anyway at the potential of his Aprilia; Casanova revealed that he had been battling with a sliding rear tyre, and was happy to have finished where he did.

With Ueda a dispirited 16th, Wakai again showed himself the strongest of the Japanese contingent, taking fourth after a determined ride, one second ahead of Gresini, with Martinez sixth. Little Dirk Raudies was seventh, well out of touch, while impressive German newcomer Oliver Koch was eighth. The Semprucci Hondas of Ezio Gianola and Gabriele Debbia, later to come to the fore of the class, took the last two points-scoring positions.

But the hero of the crowd was young Australian GP novice Garry McCoy, who replaced the injured Peter Öttl on the Rotax. It was only the cheery 19-year-old former speedway rider's eighth road race, after being put forward as a last minute replacement by new Australian Barry Sheene. He was completely undaunted by Europe's finest, however, battling back and forth between 10th and 12th places with his eye on the points until he was forced to retire with a fractured exhaust.

Foster's Australian Grand Prix, 12 April/statistics

Eastern Creek, 2.442-mile/3.3930-km circuit

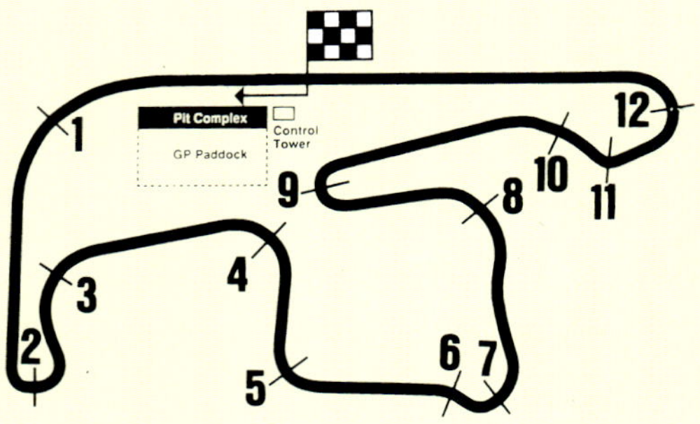

500 cc

30 laps, 73.26 miles/117.900 km

Place	Rider	Nat.	Machine	Laps	Time & speed	Fastest lap	Lap
1	**Michael Doohan**	**AUS**	**Honda**	**30**	**46m 04.276s 95.408 mph/ 153.545 km/h**	**1m 31.411s**	**22**
2	**Wayne Rainey**	**USA**	**Yamaha**	**30**	**46m 11.098s**	**1m 31.664s**	**16**
3	**Daryl Beattie**	**AUS**	**Honda**	**30**	**46m 22.701s**	**1m 31.919s**	**5**
4	**Kevin Schwantz**	**USA**	**Suzuki**	**30**	**46m 35.338s**	**1m 32.319s**	**6**
5	**Doug Chandler**	**USA**	**Suzuki**	**30**	**46m 40.295s**	**1m 32.333s**	**7**
6	**Eddie Lawson**	**USA**	**Cagiva**	**30**	**47m 07.929s**	**1m 33.397s**	**13**
7	**Alex Criville**	**E**	**Honda**	**30**	**47m 56.115s***	**1m 33.330s**	**12**
8	**Randy Mamola**	**USA**	**Yamaha**	**30**	**47m 40.227s***	**1m 33.982s**	**29**
9	**Juan Garriga**	**E**	**Yamaha**	**30**	**47m 40.526s***	**1m 33.923s**	**10**
10	**Miguel DuHamel**	**CAN**	**Yamaha**	**29**	**46m 07.097s**	**1m 34.387s**	**26**
11	Peter Goddard	AUS	Yamaha	29	46m 07.190s	1m 34.412s	10
12	Alexandre Barros	BR	Cagiva	29	46m 07.711s	1m 34.211s	7
13	Thierry Crine	F	Yamaha	29	46m 14.856s	1m 34.541s	21
14	Corrado Catalano	I	Yamaha	29	46m 35.045s	1m 34.970s	6
15	Dominique Sarron	F	Yamaha	29	46m 46.291s	1m 35.593s	27
16	Toshiyuki Arakaki	J	Yamaha	29	46m 48.038s	1m 35.363s	24
17	Cees Doorakkers	NL	Yamaha	29	46m 48.748s	1m 35.953s	27
18	Michael Rudroff	D	Yamaha	29	46m 55.180s	1m 35.717s	11
19	Serge David	CH	Yamaha	29	46m 55.569s	1m 35.993s	11
20	Kevin Mitchell	GB	Yamaha	29	47m 45.062s	1m 36.438s	7
21	Simon Buckmaster	GB	Yamaha	28	46m 22.826s	1m 38.361s	11
22	Niggi Schmassman	CH	Yamaha	28	46m 40.332s	1m 38.888s	22
	Sepp Doppler	A	Yamaha	24	DNF	1m 38.588s	23
	Eddie Laycock	IRL	Yamaha	12	DNF	1m 35.579s	9
	Niall Mackenzie	GB	Yamaha	11	DNF	1m 34.487s	2
	Lucio Pedercini	I	Paton	9	DNF	1m 36.513s	9
	Marco Papa	I	Librenti	4	DNF	1m 39.154s	2
	Peter Graves	GB	Yamaha	3	DNF	1m 40.992s	3
	John Kocinski	USA	Yamaha		DNS		

*Times set aside following stewards' enquiry.

Fastest lap: Doohan, 1m 31.411s, 96.171 mph/154.773 km/h (record).
Previous record: Wayne Rainey, USA (Yamaha), 1m 31.455s, 96.126 mph/154.699 km/h (1991).

Practice leaderboard: **1** Doohan, 1m 30.756s; **2** Rainey, 1m 31.193s; **3** Beattie, 1m 31.518s; **4** Schwantz, 1m 31.767s; **5** Kocinski, 1m 32.399s; **6** Lawson, 1m 32.432s; **7** Mamola, 1m 32.496s; **8** Chandler, 1m 32.955s; **9** Mackenzie, 1m 32.990s; **10** Criville, 1m 33.300s; **11** Garriga, 1m 33.502s; **12** Goddard, 1m 33.914s; **13** Barros, 1m 33.970s; **14** Laycock, 1m 34.266s; **15** DuHamel, 1m 34.660s.

World Championship: **1** Doohan, 40; **2** Chandler, 23; **3** Schwantz, 22; **4** Rainey, 15; **5** Beattie, 12; **6** Mamola, 11; **7** Itoh, 10; **8** Lawson and Ohishi, 6; **10** Criville and Mackenzie, 4; **12** Honma, 3; **13** Fujiwara and Garriga, 2; **15** DuHamel and Tsujimoto, 1.

Malcolm Bryan

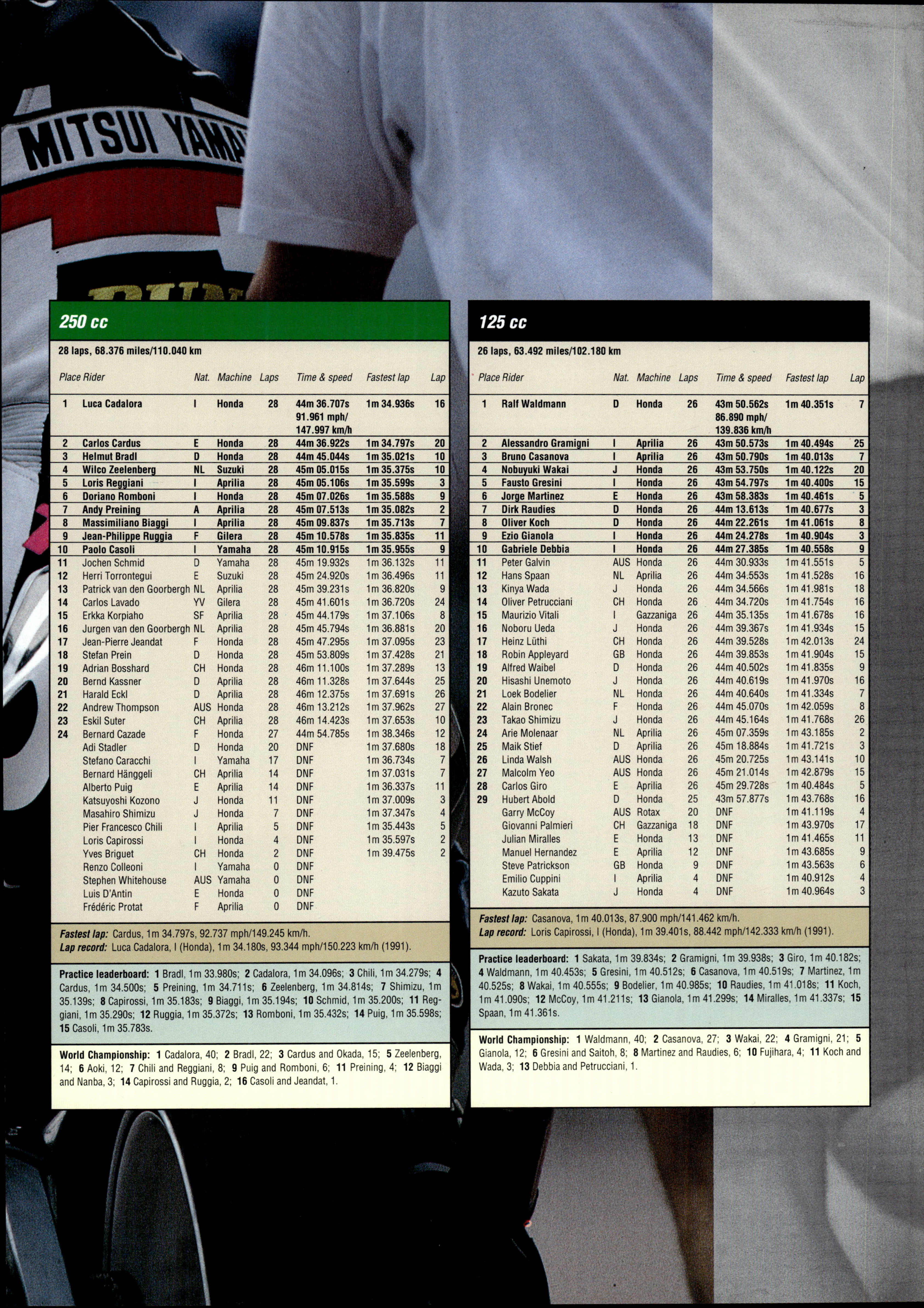

250 cc

28 laps, 68.376 miles/110.040 km

Place	Rider	Nat.	Machine	Laps	Time & speed	Fastest lap	Lap
1	**Luca Cadalora**	**I**	**Honda**	**28**	**44m 36.707s 91.961 mph/ 147.997 km/h**	**1m 34.936s**	**16**
2	**Carlos Cardus**	**E**	**Honda**	**28**	**44m 36.922s**	**1m 34.797s**	**20**
3	**Helmut Bradl**	**D**	**Honda**	**28**	**44m 45.044s**	**1m 35.021s**	**10**
4	**Wilco Zeelenberg**	**NL**	**Suzuki**	**28**	**45m 05.015s**	**1m 35.375s**	**10**
5	**Loris Reggiani**	**I**	**Aprilia**	**28**	**45m 05.106s**	**1m 35.599s**	**3**
6	**Doriano Romboni**	**I**	**Honda**	**28**	**45m 07.026s**	**1m 35.588s**	**9**
7	**Andy Preining**	**A**	**Aprilia**	**28**	**45m 07.513s**	**1m 35.082s**	**2**
8	**Massimiliano Biaggi**	**I**	**Aprilia**	**28**	**45m 09.837s**	**1m 35.713s**	**7**
9	**Jean-Philippe Ruggia**	**F**	**Gilera**	**28**	**45m 10.578s**	**1m 35.835s**	**11**
10	**Paolo Casoli**	**I**	**Yamaha**	**28**	**45m 10.915s**	**1m 35.955s**	**9**
11	Jochen Schmid	D	Yamaha	28	45m 19.932s	1m 36.132s	11
12	Herri Torrontegui	E	Suzuki	28	45m 24.920s	1m 36.496s	11
13	Patrick van den Goorbergh	NL	Aprilia	28	45m 39.231s	1m 36.820s	9
14	Carlos Lavado	YV	Gilera	28	45m 41.601s	1m 36.720s	24
15	Erkka Korpiaho	SF	Aprilia	28	45m 44.179s	1m 37.106s	8
16	Jurgen van den Goorbergh	NL	Aprilia	28	45m 45.794s	1m 36.881s	20
17	Jean-Pierre Jeandat	F	Honda	28	45m 47.295s	1m 37.095s	23
18	Stefan Prein	D	Honda	28	45m 53.809s	1m 37.428s	21
19	Adrian Bosshard	CH	Honda	28	46m 11.100s	1m 37.289s	13
20	Bernd Kassner	D	Aprilia	28	46m 11.328s	1m 37.644s	25
21	Harald Eckl	D	Aprilia	28	46m 12.375s	1m 37.691s	26
22	Andrew Thompson	AUS	Honda	28	46m 13.212s	1m 37.962s	27
23	Eskil Suter	CH	Aprilia	28	46m 14.423s	1m 37.653s	10
24	Bernard Cazade	F	Honda	27	44m 54.785s	1m 38.346s	12
	Adi Stadler	D	Honda	20	DNF	1m 37.680s	18
	Stefano Caracchi	I	Yamaha	17	DNF	1m 36.734s	7
	Bernard Hänggeli	CH	Aprilia	14	DNF	1m 37.031s	7
	Alberto Puig	E	Aprilia	14	DNF	1m 36.337s	11
	Katsuyoshi Kozono	J	Honda	11	DNF	1m 37.009s	3
	Masahiro Shimizu	J	Honda	7	DNF	1m 37.347s	4
	Pier Francesco Chili	I	Aprilia	5	DNF	1m 35.443s	5
	Loris Capirossi	I	Honda	4	DNF	1m 35.597s	2
	Yves Briguet	CH	Honda	2	DNF	1m 39.475s	2
	Renzo Colleoni	I	Yamaha	0	DNF		
	Stephen Whitehouse	AUS	Yamaha	0	DNF		
	Luis D'Antin	E	Honda	0	DNF		
	Frédéric Protat	F	Aprilia	0	DNF		

Fastest lap: Cardus, 1m 34.797s, 92.737 mph/149.245 km/h.
Lap record: Luca Cadalora, I (Honda), 1m 34.180s, 93.344 mph/150.223 km/h (1991).

Practice leaderboard: 1 Bradl, 1m 33.980s; **2** Cadalora, 1m 34.096s; **3** Chili, 1m 34.279s; **4** Cardus, 1m 34.500s; **5** Preining, 1m 34.711s; **6** Zeelenberg, 1m 34.814s; **7** Shimizu, 1m 35.139s; **8** Capirossi, 1m 35.183s; **9** Biaggi, 1m 35.194s; **10** Schmid, 1m 35.200s; **11** Reggiani, 1m 35.290s; **12** Ruggia, 1m 35.372s; **13** Romboni, 1m 35.432s; **14** Puig, 1m 35.598s; **15** Casoli, 1m 35.783s.

World Championship: 1 Cadalora, 40; **2** Bradl, 22; **3** Cardus and Okada, 15; **5** Zeelenberg, 14; **6** Aoki, 12; **7** Chili and Reggiani, 8; **9** Puig and Romboni, 6; **11** Preining, 4; **12** Biaggi and Nanba, 3; **14** Capirossi and Ruggia, 2; **16** Casoli and Jeandat, 1.

125 cc

26 laps, 63.492 miles/102.180 km

Place	Rider	Nat.	Machine	Laps	Time & speed	Fastest lap	Lap
1	**Ralf Waldmann**	**D**	**Honda**	**26**	**43m 50.562s 86.890 mph/ 139.836 km/h**	**1m 40.351s**	**7**
2	**Alessandro Gramigni**	**I**	**Aprilia**	**26**	**43m 50.573s**	**1m 40.494s**	**25**
3	**Bruno Casanova**	**I**	**Aprilia**	**26**	**43m 50.790s**	**1m 40.013s**	**7**
4	**Nobuyuki Wakai**	**J**	**Honda**	**26**	**43m 53.750s**	**1m 40.122s**	**20**
5	**Fausto Gresini**	**I**	**Honda**	**26**	**43m 54.797s**	**1m 40.400s**	**15**
6	**Jorge Martinez**	**E**	**Honda**	**26**	**43m 58.383s**	**1m 40.461s**	**5**
7	**Dirk Raudies**	**D**	**Honda**	**26**	**44m 13.613s**	**1m 40.677s**	**3**
8	**Oliver Koch**	**D**	**Honda**	**26**	**44m 22.261s**	**1m 41.061s**	**8**
9	**Ezio Gianola**	**I**	**Honda**	**26**	**44m 24.278s**	**1m 40.904s**	**3**
10	**Gabriele Debbia**	**I**	**Honda**	**26**	**44m 27.385s**	**1m 40.558s**	**9**
11	Peter Galvin	AUS	Honda	26	44m 30.933s	1m 41.551s	5
12	Hans Spaan	NL	Aprilia	26	44m 34.553s	1m 41.528s	16
13	Kinya Wada	J	Honda	26	44m 34.566s	1m 41.981s	18
14	Oliver Petrucciani	CH	Honda	26	44m 34.720s	1m 41.754s	16
15	Maurizio Vitali	I	Gazzaniga	26	44m 35.135s	1m 41.678s	16
16	Noboru Ueda	J	Honda	26	44m 39.367s	1m 41.934s	15
17	Heinz Lüthi	CH	Honda	26	44m 39.528s	1m 42.013s	24
18	Robin Appleyard	GB	Honda	26	44m 39.853s	1m 41.904s	15
19	Alfred Waibel	D	Honda	26	44m 40.502s	1m 41.835s	9
20	Hisashi Unemoto	J	Honda	26	44m 40.619s	1m 41.970s	16
21	Loek Bodelier	NL	Honda	26	44m 40.640s	1m 41.334s	7
22	Alain Bronec	F	Honda	26	44m 45.070s	1m 42.059s	8
23	Takao Shimizu	J	Honda	26	44m 45.164s	1m 41.768s	26
24	Arie Molenaar	NL	Aprilia	26	45m 07.359s	1m 43.185s	2
25	Maik Stief	D	Aprilia	26	45m 18.884s	1m 41.721s	3
26	Linda Walsh	AUS	Honda	26	45m 20.725s	1m 43.141s	10
27	Malcolm Yeo	AUS	Honda	26	45m 21.014s	1m 42.879s	15
28	Carlos Giro	E	Aprilia	26	45m 29.728s	1m 40.484s	5
29	Hubert Abold	D	Honda	25	43m 57.877s	1m 43.768s	16
	Garry McCoy	AUS	Rotax	20	DNF	1m 41.119s	4
	Giovanni Palmieri	CH	Gazzaniga	18	DNF	1m 43.970s	17
	Julian Miralles	E	Honda	13	DNF	1m 41.465s	11
	Manuel Hernandez	E	Aprilia	12	DNF	1m 43.685s	9
	Steve Patrickson	GB	Honda	9	DNF	1m 43.563s	6
	Emilio Cuppini	I	Aprilia	4	DNF	1m 40.912s	4
	Kazuto Sakata	J	Honda	4	DNF	1m 40.964s	3

Fastest lap: Casanova, 1m 40.013s, 87.900 mph/141.462 km/h.
Lap record: Loris Capirossi, I (Honda), 1m 39.401s, 88.442 mph/142.333 km/h (1991).

Practice leaderboard: 1 Sakata, 1m 39.834s; **2** Gramigni, 1m 39.938s; **3** Giro, 1m 40.182s; **4** Waldmann, 1m 40.453s; **5** Gresini, 1m 40.512s; **6** Casanova, 1m 40.519s; **7** Martinez, 1m 40.525s; **8** Wakai, 1m 40.555s; **9** Bodelier, 1m 40.985s; **10** Raudies, 1m 41.018s; **11** Koch, 1m 41.090s; **12** McCoy, 1m 41.211s; **13** Gianola, 1m 41.299s; **14** Miralles, 1m 41.337s; **15** Spaan, 1m 41.361s.

World Championship: 1 Waldmann, 40; **2** Casanova, 27; **3** Wakai, 22; **4** Gramigni, 21; **5** Gianola, 12; **6** Gresini and Saitoh, 8; **8** Martinez and Raudies, 6; **10** Fujihara, 4; **11** Koch and Wada, 3; **13** Debbia and Petrucciani, 1.

MALAYSIAN GRAND PRIX

One seldom looks twice at the recording equipment used at the trackside by the hordes of Japanese technicians sent by the factory race departments – like Honda's 'Ice Station Zebra', a portable weather station measuring among other things wind speed, direction, temperature and humidity, used in conjunction with the radar gun to gather data on top speed. Thus nobody noticed that the unobtrusive Suzuki and Yamaha boffins had something different here – high quality tape recorders, with the microphones aimed surreptitiously at the passing NSR Hondas.

Flabbergasted at first by the sheer effectiveness of Honda's drone-engine firing order change, the Japanese engineers (joined by those from Cagiva) were now using technology to discover the secrets of the new engine. Almost before the engines had cooled down, the tapes were away to be analysed in high-tech laboratories. Oscilloscopes dissected the pulse of the Honda's engine, and thence its crankshaft timing; sound spectrum analysis revealed much else about port timing and techniques; and within days the rivals had all started to make droners of their own.

The heat of battle had shifted from the race track, where already Doohan was romping away, to the factory race R & D facilities, where a different kind of race was on. Let the ground troops keep on firing, while the technicians moved on to the next weapon.

Visitors to the Shah Alam Motor Sports Paradise had to settle for the shadow rather than the substance, with the heavily hyped Kevin Schwantz missing a second Malaysian GP in succession.

'Get this straight, Wayne. There are no poisonous snakes out there any more.' Mike Sinclair and a sombre Wayne Rainey *(below)* discuss practice problems in the jungle heat.

WORLD CHAMPIONSHIP • ROUND 3

500 cc	DOOHAN
250 cc	CADALORA
125 cc	GRAMIGNI

Below: **Criville leads Goddard, Rainey and Mackenzie in practice.**

Photos: Malcolm Bryan

The return to the steamy 'Shah Alam Motor Sports Paradise' outside Kuala Lumpur, barely six months after the last visit, had one major similarity with last year's final race here: two of the top 500 runners were out before it began.

In 1991 Rainey and Schwantz were injured in pre-practice tests at Shah Alam, letting Kocinski in to take his first 500 class victory. This year, the young maverick had been mouthy about repeating the feat with the all-stars present, just to prove it was no fluke. Instead, it was his turn to be sidelined by injury.

Rainey was still weak, although fit to race – but Schwantz became another absentee, after a crash on Friday morning, adding to an almost perfect dump record at a track where he could justifiably claim a jinx. He crashed here in 1990 pre-season tests, after colliding with then team-mate Kevin Magee; and he broke his left hand testing before the last GP. Now he described a loss of concentration on a second gear corner after another rider fell and a marshal ran across the track. Off-line when he opened the throttle, he was spat over the Suzuki's high-side, landing painfully on his left hand again, dislocating a finger and breaking bones in four places.

There were two interesting aspects to this crash. The first concerned just how much Schwantz's chosen Michelins were to blame for what was after all a typically Michelin slip-grip-flick high-sider. Dunlops are known to be more sympathetic at the limit, and Schwantz did permit himself a wry grin when tackled on the topic. 'Michelins hook up better, and break loose real quick – but you can't blame the tyres for the crash. As riders, we have to adjust to their characteristics. That's one of the bad things about switching as we did this season. But it's not a defect in the Michelins.' The pay-off was supposed to be that the Michelins yield faster lap times. But the stopwatches did not seem to bear this out, as we shall see.

The second aspect concerned what effect the withdrawal of the heavily hyped Lucky Strike superstar might have on the crowds. Schwantz did promise he'd come back on Saturday and try to qualify, but the feeling that this was a charade on behalf of the organisers was reinforced by a rogue press statement on Friday evening, quoting a track doctor, that Schwantz was definitely out. The doctor and the over-zealous author of the statement were both reprimanded ... for being right. Nobody could know the effect on the crowds, with once again a cruelly reduced cast for the Malaysian GP hardly compensated for by the inclusion of Beattie on Gardner's bike. (Even then, with an admission price of just 15 Malaysian dollars, the effect of losing a few thousand would signify little next to the total cost of the event.)

The controversy over championship points was simmering nicely, with IRTA increasingly uncomfortable in the position they had adopted. FIM chief Jos Vaessen turned up in Malaysia, perhaps not to gloat, though he was certainly happy to exploit the moral strength of the FIM's position of points for all-comers, and said (at a lavish come-all reception hosted by the local Raja): 'The points will be taken away from those riders over my dead body.'

At Gilera, there was more bickering between engineer Martini and technical boffin Harald Bartol, with the latter vouchsafing that Ruggia's bike had lost half a second a lap from morning to afternoon because he'd been obliged to run with Martini's unorthodox ideas for chassis settings. But the Gileras had sprouted conspicuous combined air-intakes/screen-supports to direct fresh air at the carburettors after Bartol's Australian experiences with elevated float-bowl temperatures. They had also acquired an under-belly 'keel', after wind tunnel tests.

Heat was likely to be a problem for everybody here, not to mention the sapping humidity. Apart from the obvious difficulties of human and mechanical fatigue, the more exotic question was raised of the effects of riders' heads becoming overheated inside their full face helmets. This theory is little understood and much decried, but it was cited as the cause of a heavy practice crash suffered by little Kinya Wada in the 125 class. Wada had been reeling and wobbling in his pit before insisting on going out again, only to fall. On a lighter note, Bruno Casanova came in complaining that the routing of the exhaust under his Aprilia's seat made it intolerably hot. Other Aprilia riders smiled – his discomfort came courtesy of a special flat sided expansion chamber: no gain without pain.

It was decided that race distances would be cut in the interests of safety if race day temperatures exceeded 35 degrees – but in the end tropical storms kept ambient temperatures down. They also played havoc with people's carefully considered race plans. Even then, in two out of three classes, the same people won as in Japan and Australia. As the saying goes, in racing, you make your own luck.

Malcolm Bryan

Ride the monsters. Criville (nearest the camera), Beattie, Rainey and Doohan set off for start number one.

500 cc PRACTICE

For a second successive race, on a directly comparable track, on supposedly new and improved machinery, lap times were slower than last year's. Since there was a general reluctance to accept the simple theory that perhaps last year's Dunlops were better than this year's Michelins, people were casting around for other explanations. Was it the extra heat and humidity (35 degrees and 70 per cent on Saturday)? Or a layer of dust left on the track after the gravel traps were remade?

Either way, Doohan's pole was more than half a second off Kocinski's 1991 time, and slower than his own qualifying time as well. 'I guess we're all struggling for grip,' said the Australian, whose Honda once again looked by far the best bike out there. 'Last year we were consistently quicker. I want to get on the gas, but I can't.'

This statement drew a wry grin from most of his rivals, because his second pole in a row simply seemed to underline the likelihood of a third win in a row, and whatever problems he had, they had worse.

In fact, Rainey had been ahead of the Honda after the first day of qualifying, but failed to improve on day two and was consigned to second. He had a face of thunder as he contemplated the unequal struggle ahead in his slow starting title defence. 'We just can't get the bike dialled in to the Michelins,' he said. 'We've been searching through the tyres, and while you're doing that it's hard to make chassis adjustments.'

Beattie had never seen the track before, and steadfastly denied that he was taking extra risks because he didn't have the pressure of a full GP season ahead. But he was on the crest of a wave, and looked calm, confident and fast as he slotted into third on the grid. 'They told me it was an easy track to learn, and I guess I proved it.'

More proof of the new NSR's strength was the unexpected arrival up front of former 125 World Champion, but rather lacklustre 250 rider, Alex Criville, on the front row of the grid in his third 500 cc GP. The Spaniard achieved his single fast lap by following Rainey, a technique that earned opprobrium for Pier Francesco Chili last year, but is none the less effective, both in practice and in the race.

Mackenzie was starting to get on top of his new Yamaha, and clearly enjoying it, adding impressive corner exits to his already good braking and mid-corner speeds. He ran a string of consistent laps just outside Criville's time, promising much for the race. 'Now we've got some dry time with it, the chassis just keeps on getting better and better,' he said.

Chandler alongside was less cheerful, after butting up against the balance problem that plagued Schwantz last year. 'The biggest thing is getting the rear wheel stuck – it keeps trying to come around on me,' he said. 'When we do find something that makes it better, then the front's loose.' A familiar Suzuki refrain.

He ended up just a hundredth ahead of Mamola, who continued to regain form as he tried to get his Yamaha to steer quicker. 'We changed engine position and lots of other stuff,' he said. But he was already frustrated by the problem of only having one bike with which to experiment, ruling out major mid-session setting changes.

The last man on row two was Garriga, spurred on by the arrival of speedy fellow-Spaniard Criville, but who like Rainey did not improve from day one to day two.

Goddard was top privateer, leading row three and reporting an improvement from a change to front chassis geometry as he got to grips with his Roc Yamaha; then Barros stole tenth by over a tenth from Cagiva team-mate Lawson. DuHamel completed row three – the Canadian charger had crashed his Yamaha hard in untimed practice on Saturday morning, at least his sixth crash of the season, counting test sessions.

The privateers were sorting out their pecking order, Laycock heading Catalano, Sarron and Crine on row four; David, Mitchell, Doorakkers and Rudroff were on row five. Less than three-quarters of a second covered all eight, with Buckmaster tucked in behind, his confidence suffering with his second-rate Metzeler tyres.

There were 26 entries, all of whom qualified, with the slowest being Briton Peter Graves. But Dominique Sarron (15th) did not start following a freak crash at the end of practice. He had already done a plug chop and was freewheeling to a stop in neutral when his bike kicked back into gear and threw him. He dislocated his shoulder, an injury that was to spoil his whole year. Pedercini (like Schwantz) was already out of the race after crashing his Paton in the first free training session.

500 cc RACE – 16 PLUS 14 LAPS

In hazy sunshine and baking heat, Doohan charged straight into the lead, with Criville and Rainey tagged on behind. If Criville had only qualified so well because he'd been able to follow faster riders, he was now able to do so again, and very convincingly, pulling up alongside Doohan from time to time at the big right-hand sweeper at the end of the straight that leads into tricky hard braking and a breathtaking plunge into a tight left-hand loop.

This sight was painfully frustrating to Rainey, who was probing and pushing behind the Hondas, but seemed outgunned in this crucial gallop up to one of the few passing places on the tight track. Then he did manage to get a better run onto the straight, and finally passed Criville to start working on Doohan, just over a second ahead. The gap wavered between half a second and one second as Criville gradually dropped back, and the two were shaping up for a sustained battle when the first fat drops of tepid rain blotched the track.

The red flags came out for the first time after 16 laps. The gap was still just over half a second, and Rainey said: 'I was feeling him out. My front tyre was really hot, and I was trying to look after that, but I found I could charge right back on him.' But the race stoppage meant he never could test whether he could actually pass the Australian.

The leading trio had rapidly drawn away from Beattie, Mackenzie and Garriga, with Mackenzie's Yamaha leaning on the Australian's Honda. His outbraking move at the end of the back straight finally succeeded at the third attempt on the tenth lap – whereupon the Scotsman started to pull away, though not closing significantly on Criville.

A little way back Barros and Garriga battled back and forth, with Lawson dropping back, soon to retire with front tyre trouble. Then came DuHamel, Mamola, Goddard and Chandler, the last-named becoming accustomed to yet another chassis change made after morning warm-up and ahead of the group by lap six. He quickly passed Garriga and Barros, and was even closing on Beattie when the rain set in and everyone

Malcolm Bryan

ran for cover.

The restart half an hour later was designated a Wet Race, which meant there would be no further stoppage except on safety grounds. But the track was drying rapidly, and there were many frantic tyre changes before the warm-up lap, with all the front-runners except Barros (on full wets) choosing intermediate fronts and cut slick rears. Then Chandler's crew elected to change from steel to carbon brakes, but the Suzuki was still without a front wheel as the others took off for the warm-up lap. He was pushed off the track, to start from pit lane at the back of the field.

With the track still wet, Barros made the early running. Then as it quickly dried Garriga charged ahead, using a slightly more heavily patterned front Dunlop than the Michelin intermediate.

By lap three Doohan was second, Criville third and Rainey sixth. Doohan was on the move once more, and went cleanly past Garriga to lead on lap nine. By then, Rainey had passed Goddard and Criville to take third, but was about seven seconds adrift of his major rival. Although he closed the gap to around five seconds, this had in any case to be added to the half-second he was already missing from the first race, and it was a losing battle. Unless...

Because the rain had started again, and lap 12 presented a very different picture. The track was awash, and now it all depended on who could tiptoe the fastest and (as the lower orders started to tumble about) stay wheels down. It was easier said than done.

As the deluge strengthened, lap times soared. Doohan wished they had stopped the race. 'I was lucky to stay on. I was on the footpegs at one stage – the biggest moment I had all weekend.'

Rainey pushed on to attack Garriga. 'Then I had a big tank-slapper when I hit a puddle out the back that lost me everything I'd gained,' he said. 'It wasn't nice out there. We were on quarter-throttle on the straights, and couldn't even lean it on the turns.' He settled for a safe third on the road, second overall.

Garriga then closed right up on Doohan again on lap 14, at which point results were eventually taken (after protests), for the red flag was out on the 15th lap. And not a moment too soon, considering the drama behind the leaders.

Chandler had stormed out of pit lane and carved through the field to take fourth on the road ahead of Criville and Beattie by lap eight. Goddard, meanwhile, was closing up to the back of this group, with Mamola, DuHamel and Mackenzie behind him.

There was a bit of a reshuffle after the rain started, with Criville and Beattie both passing Chandler, whose carbon brakes now proved a drawback. And then people started to fall off.

Of the notable riders, the first to go was Mackenzie, who was closing on Mamola when he was high-sided, badly bruising his ankle. Then Goddard slithered off at low speed, hurriedly remounting to rejoin the sodden throng.

The crash that caused the race to be stopped happened on lap 14, and it was DuHamel yet again, bringing his repair bill for the meeting to close on $100,000. And it was a big one, after he ran out of brakes on the back straight and took off for the jungle. He managed to leap off the bike and slide in among the shrubbery, very lucky not to be hurt. But his bike hacked a path deep into the undergrowth and wasn't found for some 30 minutes after the race.

All rather a shambles, made worse when results were declared after a total of 29 laps. This gave DuHamel a finish, and left Catalano out of the points. He protested, and this was upheld, so after a lengthy delay another lap was added to the total, DuHamel becoming a non-finisher, and Catalano moving to ninth.

In the final final analysis, Doohan defeated Rainey by 10 seconds. Criville was third, with Garriga's strong second race ride moving him up to fourth, four seconds ahead of Chandler.

Beattie was sixth, after a careful ride nursing some suspension problems. 'I wasn't able to use full power, and when Mackenzie went by I

Opposite: **It took Rainey several laps to find his way past Criville and set his sights on Doohan.**

Alberto Puig held off Chili's similar Aprilia for second – an effort that proved his long spell in the doldrums hadn't dimmed the former trials champion's talent.

decided not to end my short spell in GPs by falling over.'

Mamola was seventh, Goddard eighth after his brief off, with Laycock claiming the last point after an encouraging midfield privateers' battle including 11th-placed Mitchell, Doorakkers, Arakaki and Rudroff.

250 cc PRACTICE

The new afternoons-only timed practice system came close to causing another shambles, with the first official session cut short by rain before many people had run fast times. Luckily the afternoon downpour held off on Saturday, leading to a hectic session.

By the end it was business almost as usual – Aprilias versus Honda, with Chili taking his first pole of the season. The speed and sweet handling of the Italian bike helped here, with the longish back straight interrupted and concluded by fast sweeping corners. Chili had solved early tyre and suspension problems to emerge looking like a strong threat. 'I will go on a drip before the race tomorrow to reduce dehydration,' he said.

Cadalora tried hard to take pole again, but never did get the clear lap he needed. His 'flu was just about better, but he was worried about the speed of the Aprilias, both here and in the races to come. 'They say it is not as fast as the Honda, but I think different.'

Schmid worked hard in the closing minutes to put his sole works Yamaha onto the front row, three-tenths slower than Cadalora, and pushing Cardus's Honda to the far end.

The 250 class seemed more competitive than ever, with times packed up close, and ten bikes within the first second behind Chili. Puig's factory-lease Aprilia led row two from Bradl, Romboni and Biaggi. Bradl was suffering from the heat, and said: 'This is the hardest and most difficult race of the year.' He was looking forward to Europe, when he felt the war with Cadalora could begin in earnest.

Ruggia's Gilera led row three – another impressive showing from the newest bike on the grid, with Capirossi's Honda alongside, then Lavado's Gilera and Shimizu's works Honda.

The close times saw some fancied runners further back on the grid than they would have chosen – Reggiani's Aprilia 14th, with Zeelenberg's works Suzuki 15th and Andy Preining 19th. All 36 entries were well inside the qualifying time.

250 cc RACE – 31 LAPS

The 500 class shenanigans delayed the last race of the day; but by then the weather had settled again. The track was damp but drying, leading to the almost universal choice of intermediate front and cut slick rear.

Biaggi charged off to get his first taste of running up front at a GP, but was displaced before the lap was out by Puig, with Chili and Cadalora soon following him past the perennially out of shape youngster. Puig stayed ahead for four more laps, while Biaggi soon had his hands full

Malcolm Bryan

Photos: Malcolm Bryan

with Cardus, eventually crashing before half-distance after a collision when he lapped German Adi Stadler, who had pitted for a tyre change.

All the while, Capirossi was watching as the leaders sorted each other out. Now he embarked on an epic charge, setting fastest lap as he rapidly closed on the leaders, joining the group on lap 11. Who knows what the double 125 champion might have done had he not run onto the grass on the 13th lap, dropping back to the midfield from whence he'd come. He twisted his foot and rather messed up his tyres, and his brief but glorious challenge was over.

Bradl had ridden carefully early on, then thrown caution to the winds to get the leaders in sight. He was sixth behind Cardus when he lost the front wheel and crashed, remounting to tour into the pits with no front brakes.

By lap 20, Schmid had lost touch with the leading trio, and Puig was back in front, narrowly, from Chili. But Cadalora was waiting to pounce, and decided to make a run for home in the last ten laps, pulling out a convincing lead of five seconds at the flag. 'I was really surprised by how easy it was to increase the pace on intermediate tyres,' he said. 'The bike was sliding, but it was really fun.'

Puig was a fine second, signalling the start of a revival in the talented but luckless Spaniard's career. 'I was scared for the last six or seven laps, because the front tyre was really sliding,' said the former trials champion. He was just two-tenths ahead of the identically mounted Chili.

Chili was happy with his close third. 'I said yesterday that any podium position would be good, and so it is,' he said. 'I started to feel bad in the race, and I had to take my face mask down to get more air' – adding, with a grin, 'I don't like breathing in the smoke coming from Luca's bike. I hope to be in front next time.'

Cardus rode a solid race to close to within eight seconds of Chili at the end, passing Schmid on the way. Doriano Romboni was sixth, after a mostly lonely ride.

There was a torrid battle for seventh, won in the end by Zeelenberg, obliged for a second race in succession to deploy all his skill and trackcraft to overcome a poor starting position, and to defeat some high class opposition on a Suzuki that lacks mid-range power. He picked his way through the group to finish half a second ahead of Shimizu, Capirossi and Casoli, with Preining's Aprilia just out of the points.

Neither of the Gileras finished. Ruggia succumbed to ignition both-

Left: **125 Aprilias at play: Casanova leads Gramigni and Giro, with Honda riders Martinez (6) and fast-starting Dutch new boy Loek Bodelier (35) behind. Raudies is obscured, Waldmann is number three, Sakata (13) is just coming out of the previous bend.**

Gramigni ***(below)*** **celebrates his and Aprilia's second win in the 125 class.**

ers after an ill-advised software change before the race, and Lavado to mysterious engine trouble.

Reggiani was another victim, taken out by a crashing Hänggeli's Aprilia on the second lap.

125 cc RACE – 29 LAPS

As always, the opening race of the day proved a hard act to follow, with the lead changing hands sometimes twice in one corner, let alone one lap. And, refreshingly, there was a different winner, with Aprilia star Alessandro Gramigni finally outfoxing Bruno Casanova and Ralf Waldmann on the last lap.

Less than a quarter of a second covered the trio across the line, after a battle for the lead that had earlier included eight riders. Fourth-placed Jorge Martinez had been among them, along with the very impressive newcomer Charlie Giro – but the older Spaniard was delayed when the younger crashed on the last lap.

Gramigni started from pole, and at first led from Casanova and Giro, with Casanova slipping his Aprilia through on lap two. But Waldmann and Martinez were both on the way up, and the German, winner of the first two races of the season, picked his way through to take the lead for the first time on the tenth lap.

Casanova pushed back in front, but it was impossible to say who was really in control, while Kazuto Sakata and Dirk Raudies also joined on the back of the group, to make a close-coupled freight train weaving through the Malaysian heat.

The pace increased with six laps to go. Raudies and Sakata couldn't match it, but the leading pack continued the brawl, with Waldmann under extreme pressure.

Casanova led lap 27, Gramigni lap 28, and then there was just one to go. And the pair of Italians successfully blocked Waldmann to keep him in third.

Giro was in fourth when he crashed in the tight loop at the end of the back straight, and Martinez was lucky not to be brought down as well.

Debbia was a relatively distant seventh, then came a lonely Fausto Gresini, with Hans Spaan ninth and Heinz Lüthi tenth, opening their championship scores. Noboru Ueda had an undistinguished weekend, finishing 11th, just two seconds short of scoring points.

There was the usual midfield drama, with Wakai forcing through to try to join the leaders, only to crash.

There were 21 finishers.

Malaysian Grand Prix, 19 April/statistics

Shah Alam Racing Circuit, 2.178-mile/ 3.505-km circuit

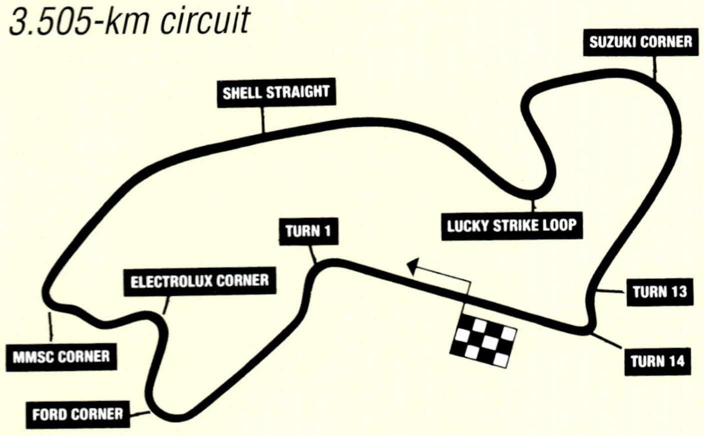

500 cc

30 laps, 65.337 miles/105.150 km

Place	Rider	Nat.	Machine	Laps	Time & speed	Fastest lap	Lap
1	**Michael Doohan**	AUS	Honda	30	45m 45.608s 85.669 mph/ 137.871 km/h	1m 26.107s	10
2	**Wayne Rainey**	USA	Yamaha	30	45m 56.041s	1m 26.074s	11
3	**Alex Criville**	E	Honda	30	45m 59.915s	1m 26.134s	9
4	**Juan Garriga**	E	Yamaha	30	46m 13.301s	1m 27.442s	2
5	**Doug Chandler**	USA	Suzuki	30	46m 17.037s	1m 26.701s	12
6	**Daryl Beattie**	AUS	Honda	30	46m 17.887s	1m 26.896s	2
7	**Randy Mamola**	USA	Yamaha	30	46m 49.105s	1m 27.311s	12
8	**Peter Goddard**	AUS	Yamaha	30	47m 48.232s	1m 28.382s	13
9	**Corrado Catalano**	I	Yamaha	30	47m 52.518s	1m 29.806s	2
10	**Eddie Laycock**	IRL	Yamaha	30	47m 57.540s	1m 29.808s	4
11	Kevin Mitchell	GB	Yamaha	30	48m 12.945s	1m 29.847s	2
12	Cees Doorakkers	NL	Yamaha	30	48m 16.901s	1m 29.044s	3
13	Toshiyuki Arakaki	J	Yamaha	29	46m 53.579s	1m 29.303s	12
14	Michael Rudroff	D	Yamaha	29	47m 30.779s	1m 30.705s	2
15	Serge David	CH	Yamaha	28	46m 20.659s	1m 29.592s	5
16	Niggi Schmassman	CH	Yamaha	28	47m 23.684s	1m 31.244s	10
	Miguel DuHamel	CAN	Yamaha	29	DNF	1m 28.345s	13
	Thierry Crine	F	Yamaha	29	DNF	1m 28.738s	2
	Niall Mackenzie	GB	Yamaha	27	DNF	1m 26.814s	3
	Alexandre Barros	BR	Cagiva	20	DNF	1m 27.413s	2
	Eddie Lawson	USA	Cagiva	10	DNF	1m 28.553s	2
	Sepp Doppler	A	Yamaha	7	DNF	1m 31.516s	4
	Peter Graves	GB	Yamaha	7	DNF	1m 34.107s	3
	Simon Buckmaster	GB	Yamaha	4	DNF	1m 31.241s	3
	Marco Papa	I	Librenti	3	DNF	1m 34.051s	2
	Dominique Sarron	F	Yamaha		DNS		

Fastest lap: Rainey, 1m 26.074s, 91.089 mph/146.595 km/h.
Lap record: John Kocinski, USA (Yamaha), 1m 25.100s, 92.133 mph/148.273 km/h (1991).

Practice leaderboard: **1** Doohan, 1m 25.513s; **2** Rainey, 1m 25.764s; **3** Beattie, 1m 26.312s; **4** Criville, 1m 26.406s; **5** Mackenzie, 1m 26.654s; **6** Chandler, 1m 26.816s; **7** Mamola, 1m 26.826s; **8** Garriga, 1m 26.989s; **9** Goddard, 1m 27.361s; **10** Barros, 1m 27.506s; **11** Lawson, 1m 27.639s; **12** DuHamel, 1m 27.786s; **13** Laycock, 1m 28.455s; **14** Catalano, 1m 28.606s; **15** Sarron, 1m 28.641s.

World Championship: **1** Doohan, 60; **2** Chandler, 31; **3** Rainey, 30; **4** Schwantz, 22; **5** Beattie, 18; **6** Criville, 16; **7** Mamola, 15; **8** Garriga, 12; **9** Itoh, 10; **10** Lawson and Ohishi, 6; **12** Mackenzie, 4; **13** Goddard and Honma, 3; **15** Catalano and Fujiwara, 2; **17** DuHamel, Laycock and Tsujimoto, 1.

250 cc

31 laps, 67.515 miles/108.655 km

Place	Rider	Nat.	Machine	Laps	Time & speed	Fastest lap	Lap
1	**Luca Cadalora**	I	Honda	31	47m 49.876s 84.692 mph/ 136.298 km/h	1m 29.278s	25
2	**Alberto Puig**	E	Aprilia	31	47m 54.582s	1m 29.738s	23
3	**Pier Francesco Chili**	I	Aprilia	31	47m 54.826s	1m 29.778s	23
4	**Carlos Cardus**	E	Honda	31	48m 02.660s	1m 29.899s	18
5	**Jochen Schmid**	D	Yamaha	31	48m 11.998s	1m 30.507s	12
6	**Doriano Romboni**	I	Honda	31	48m 16.632s	1m 30.275s	17
7	**Wilco Zeelenberg**	NL	Suzuki	31	48m 18.591s	1m 30.158s	19
8	**Masahiro Shimizu**	J	Honda	31	48m 19.086s	1m 29.461s	18
9	**Loris Capirossi**	I	Honda	31	48m 21.580s	1m 30.260s	26
10	**Paolo Casoli**	I	Yamaha	31	48m 21.750s	1m 30.069s	26
11	Andy Preining	A	Aprilia	31	48m 31.310s	1m 30.202s	15
12	Patrick van den Goorbergh	NL	Aprilia	31	48m 49.510s	1m 31.232s	14
13	Jurgen van den Goorbergh	NL	Aprilia	31	48m 55.745s	1m 31.348s	19
14	Herri Torrontegui	E	Suzuki	31	49m 01.439s	1m 30.872s	29
15	Stefan Prein	D	Honda	31	49m 02.374s	1m 32.008s	29
16	Katsuyoshi Kozono	J	Honda	30	48m 11.748s	1m 31.359s	22
17	Adi Stadler	D	Honda	30	48m 40.278s	1m 32.962s	26
18	Harald Eckl	D	Aprilia	29	48m 53.617s	1m 37.236s	19
19	Eskil Suter	CH	Aprilia	29	49m 00.657s	1m 32.130s	16
20	Luis D'Antin	E	Honda	28	48m 59.508s	1m 32.848s	18
	Erkka Korpiaho	SF	Aprilia	23	DNF	1m 30.789s	19
	Helmut Bradl	D	Honda	20	DNF	1m 29.676s	16
	Massimiliano Biaggi	I	Aprilia	19	DNF	1m 29.705s	18
	Frédéric Protat	F	Aprilia	16	DNF	1m 45.858s	8
	M. Heng Kuan	MAL	Yamaha	13	DNF	1m 39.871s	6
	Bernard Cazade	F	Honda	12	DNF	1m 41.654s	8
	Jean-Philippe Ruggia	F	Gilera	11	DNF	1m 33.220s	10
	Carlos Lavado	YV	Gilera	10	DNF	1m 36.176s	9
	Bernd Kassner	D	Aprilia	9	DNF	1m 40.425s	5
	Stefano Caracchi	I	Yamaha	7	DNF	1m 40.949s	5
	Jean-Pierre Jeandat	F	Honda	5	DNF	1m 43.426s	4
	Loris Reggiani	I	Aprilia	1	DNF	1m 54.114s	1
	Bernard Hänggeli	CH	Aprilia	1	DNF	1m 55.158s	1
	Adrian Bosshard	CH	Honda	1	DNF	1m 55.309s	1
	Renzo Colleoni	I	Yamaha	0	DNF		
	Yves Briguet	CH	Honda	0	DNF		

Fastest lap: Cadalora, 1m 29.278s, 87.821 mph/141.334 km/h.
Lap record: Luca Cadalora, I (Honda), 1m 27.826s, 89.272 mph/143.670 km/h (1991).

Practice leaderboard: **1** Chili, 1m 27.838s; **2** Cadalora, 1m 28.032s; **3** Schmid, 1m 28.300s; **4** Cardus, 1m 28.325s; **5** Puig, 1m 28.561s; **6** Bradl, 1m 28.571s; **7** Romboni, 1m 28.646s; **8** Biaggi, 1m 28.833s; **9** Ruggia, 1m 28.872s; **10** Capirossi, 1m 28.877s; **11** Lavado, 1m 28.934s; **12** Shimizu, 1m 29.108s; **13** Casoli, 1m 29.224s; **14** Reggiani, 1m 29.266s; **15** Zeelenberg, 1m 29.320s.

World Championship: **1** Cadalora, 60; **2** Cardus, 25; **3** Bradl, 22; **4** Puig, 21; **5** Chili, 20; **6** Zeelenberg, 18; **7** Okada, 15; **8** Aoki and Romboni, 12; **10** Reggiani and Schmid, 8; **12** Capirossi and Preining, 4; **14** Biaggi, Nanba and Shimizu, 3; **17** Casoli and Ruggia, 2; **19** Jeandat, 1.

Malcolm Bryan

125 cc

29 laps, 63.160 miles/101.645 km

Place	Rider	Nat.	Machine	Laps	Time & speed	Fastest lap	Lap
1	**Alessandro Gramigni**	**I**	**Aprilia**	**29**	**45m 45.290s 82.823 mph/ 133.291 km/h**	**1m 33.624s**	**28**
2	**Bruno Casanova**	**I**	**Aprilia**	**29**	**45m 45.442s**	**1m 33.864s**	**29**
3	**Ralf Waldmann**	**D**	**Honda**	**29**	**45m 45.523s**	**1m 33.587s**	**4**
4	**Jorge Martinez**	**E**	**Honda**	**29**	**45m 47.704s**	**1m 33.886s**	**27**
5	**Dirk Raudies**	**D**	**Honda**	**29**	**45m 51.536s**	**1m 34.109s**	**9**
6	**Kazuto Sakata**	**J**	**Honda**	**29**	**45m 56.950s**	**1m 34.060s**	**6**
7	**Gabriele Debbia**	**I**	**Honda**	**29**	**46m 00.301s**	**1m 33.962s**	**14**
8	**Fausto Gresini**	**I**	**Honda**	**29**	**46m 09.058s**	**1m 34.294s**	**11**
9	**Hans Spaan**	**NL**	**Aprilia**	**29**	**46m 14.098s**	**1m 34.325s**	**9**
10	**Heinz Lüthi**	**CH**	**Honda**	**29**	**46m 21.088s**	**1m 34.385s**	**4**
11	Noboru Ueda	J	Honda	29	46m 23.104s	1m 34.984s	18
12	Takao Shimizu	J	Honda	29	46m 24.913s	1m 34.696s	12
13	Maurizio Vitali	I	Gazzaniga	29	46m 25.115s	1m 34.745s	12
14	Peter Galvin	AUS	Honda	29	46m 25.286s	1m 34.792s	12
15	Oliver Koch	D	Honda	29	46m 39.200s	1m 34.921s	9
16	Julian Miralles	E	Honda	29	46m 45.074s	1m 35.259s	3
17	Arie Molenaar	NL	Aprilia	29	46m 48.496s	1m 35.084s	13
18	Ezio Gianola	I	Honda	29	46m 55.043s	1m 35.173s	5
19	Giovanni Palmieri	I	Gazzaniga	29	47m 09.407s	1m 35.911s	5
20	Hisashi Unemoto	J	Honda	29	47m 09.603s	1m 36.170s	3
21	Steve Patrickson	GB	Honda	29	47m 18.102s	1m 36.723s	23
	Carlos Giro	E	Aprilia	28	DNF	1m 33.904s	27
	Nobuyuki Wakai	J	Honda	26	DNF	1m 34.111s	11
	Loek Bodelier	NL	Honda	26	DNF	1m 34.373s	4
	Robin Appleyard	GB	Honda	25	DNF	1m 36.602s	4
	Alain Bronec	F	Honda	18	DNF	1m 34.203s	9
	Garry McCoy	AUS	Rotax	15	DNF	1m 34.951s	13
	Kinya Wada	J	Honda	8	DNF	1m 35.601s	5
	Emilio Cuppini	I	Aprilia	7	DNF	1m 36.055s	5
	Hubert Abold	D	Honda	5	DNF	1m 39.135s	2
	Oliver Petrucciani	CH	Honda	4	DNF	1m 34.475s	4
	Alfred Waibel	D	Honda	3	DNF	1m 39.230s	2
	Maik Stief	D	Aprilia	0	DNF		
	Manuel Hernandez	E	Aprilia	0	DNF		

Fastest lap: Waldmann, 1m 33.587s, 83.777 mph/134.826 km/h.
Lap record: Nobuyuki Wakai, J (Honda), 1m 33.172s, 84.150 mph/135.427 km/h (1991).

Practice leaderboard: **1** Gramigni, 1m 33.155s; **2** Sakata, 1m 33.285s; **3** Casanova, 1m 33.342s; **4** Giro, 1m 33.629s; **5** Martinez, 1m 33.677s; **6** Debbia, 1m 33.823s; **7** Wakai, 1m 33.959s; **8** Waldmann, 1m 34.013s; **9** Raudies, 1m 34.225s; **10** Koch, 1m 34.241s; **11** Cuppini, 1m 34.482s; **12** Bodelier, 1m 34.582s; **13** Lüthi, 1m 34.679s; **14** Molenaar, 1m 34.716s; **15** Petrucciani, 1m 34.760s.

World Championship: **1** Waldmann, 52; **2** Casanova, 42; **3** Gramigni, 41; **4** Wakai, 22; **5** Martinez, 16; **6** Raudies, 14; **7** Gianola, 12; **8** Gresini, 11; **9** Saitoh, 8; **10** Sakata, 6; **11** Debbia, 5; **12** Fujihara, 4; **13** Koch and Wada, 3; **15** Spaan, 2; **16** Lüthi and Petrucciani, 1.

500 cc	DOOHAN
250 cc	REGGIANI
125 cc	WALDMANN
SIDECARS	WEBSTER

SPANISH GRAND PRIX

'Compromise never works,' said the small man standing outside the IRTA bus surrounded by a host of journalists. He was pronouncing on the final and timely solution of the problem of the ghost riders, but the principle he articulated serves as well in racing as such more earthy exhortations as: 'When the flag drops, the bullshit stops.'

The speaker was Bernie Ecclestone, the new overlord of racing, paying his first fleeting visit to a bike GP since his takeover. He didn't stay for the race (in case you wondered) but, as usual, his visit made a big impact ... most of the time. When Kevin Schwantz was approached and addressed mid-practice session by the proprietorial but otherwise nondescript Ecclestone, he gave a perfunctory reply, then turned to his pit crew and asked: 'Who the f* is that?'**

The 125 Express: Waldmann, Casanova and Gresini pull the train, Debbia, Martinez, Sakata, Wakai and Giro make the freight.

Photos: Malcolm Bryan

Right: **Luckless no more – this was Reggiani's third 250 win, all achieved on Aprilias.**

Below: **The man who mistook his wife for a chequered flag – Chili ponders his fate.**

Ecclestone's visit to Jerez was more than a matter of the convenient proximity of the first European track of the year. He was there to oversee the final exorcism of the ghost riders of Suzuka. The compromise had been IRTA's, who had let extra riders start in the Japanese GP, and had ever since been at loggerheads with the FIM over whether these ghost riders should be given championship points. Their respective posturing and shouting from adjacent hilltops had been entertaining for all, but without doubt embarrassing for Ecclestone's TWP outfit. And so the all-powerful Permanent Bureau had met in the lull before the start of the European season – Ecclestone for TWP, Richard Golding for Dorna and Jos Vaessen for the FIM – and on legal advice decided to back the FIM and award points to all-comers in Japan, rather than only to IRTA members.

This was a major squelch for the men who sold racing to Bernie and had counted him as an ally. IRTA president Michel Metraux was still wriggling and blaming the FIM, but chief executive Paul Butler proved himself man enough to take it on the chin, announcing to a packed press conference: 'We screwed up, and we're here to apologise to everybody.' Most people were just glad the foolishness was over and that natural justice had prevailed. 'Once they had been allowed to take part, I guess they deserve to take points off whoever they beat,' said Eddie Lawson, who lost three points in the new deal. Team owner Kenny Roberts also welcomed the decision. 'I always argued the Yamaha factory's case that the guys should be allowed to race. I don't want to see the same old cronies going round and round together every weekend. As for the points – it's like a bunch of kids taking candy away from each other.'

Another saying that held truths beyond the current situation. Now the big candyfight had come home to Europe, to start the week-in week-out campaign, and there were no more excuses for those who were slow to start scoring.

And an end also to all the prevarication about the sidecar men, who turned up for their first race of the year to be treated (as Steve Webster later said) like lepers. Their status in the paddock was unmistakable. They were consigned to a distant car park, far out of sight of the main paddock, and were obliged to show passes as they wheeled their vehicles to the track (and in one case to go to the rostrum after the race!). In spite of vociferous complaints, they were given only two practice sessions. Most crucially, there was no money for them – no prize money, no travel money. No money. IRTA had always ruled them out of their new World Championship, and now the FIM were back-pedalling after giving the impression that they would foot the bill. They raced unpaid.

So it was not surprising that the first questions to Webster after he'd won the race did not concern his choice of tyres or his championship hopes, but the political situation. He summed it up neatly. 'I tried to get involved with the politics last season, and they were so far over my head that I decided I should stick to riding. The important thing is that we were here and we raced. We have a calendar, and we have riders. I am sure the problems will be sorted out; I hope in time for our next race at Hockenheim.' Well, it took a bit longer than that. But by refusing to go away and die the sidecars in the end saved themselves.

Jerez was traffic gridlocked as usual, swamped with crowds (230,000 on race day) butting up against the overflow from Expo 92 at nearby Seville, and all encountering hotel prices double or more the usual rate. Never mind that there was to be a second GP in Spain, at Barcelona, in five weeks; absolutely everybody went to Jerez.

They saw Doohan make a little bit of history, becoming not only the first man to win four 500 races in a row since Lawson in 1986, but also the first rider to win the four opening rounds since Agostini in 1972. They also saw a better GP than usual, on a much improved circuit. The Andalucians had demonstrated how minor alterations can transform a too slow one-line modern circuit into something closely resembling the real thing.

The change was confined to one stretch of the circuit, leading up to the tight 'Dry Sack' corner. Two near-90 degree corners were opened out into a single sweep, the faster approach to which also eased the fourth gear exit from the previous corner and created a new passing place. The zig-zag chicane a little further along was also removed, creating a second straight almost as long as pit straight.

With the length increased by almost 200 metres to 4.423 km, lap times were not directly comparable; but average race speed and lap record speed were up by around 10 km/h. 'It's made it a fun track to ride around, where before it seemed to be full of first and second gear corners,' said Kevin Schwantz, back racing, but wearing a special glove on his injured left hand with his second and third fingers still bound together.

Kocinski was also back, somewhat subdued but insisting his injury was no problem, even if the Yamaha was. The increased pace dictated by the Honda saw all the works Yamaha riders chasing a positive feel from the front end while Mackenzie, who was given an example of the latest frame here, ran into similar problems with it. (Team-mate DuHamel, having destroyed two '91-spec frames in Malaysia, also had full '92-spec frames, perforce, with team owner Serge Rosset saying quite implausibly: 'I really don't know who pays for the new frames. That is between Sonauto and Yamaha.')

Bernie's visit was preceded by a

Malcolm Bryan

flurry of tidying up and lining up of trailers by IRTA's men, and paddock security was well manned if not particularly zealous. With track signage under tight control, and home-based Dorna TV folk getting highly twitchy about their first real-time live broadcast to Europe, the presence of Ecclestone was felt everywhere long before he arrived and long after he left.

There was just one thing he didn't own – the sky above Jerez. And there patrolled a single light aircraft towing one Lucky Strike banner, a lonely symbol of just how hard it is to grab any slice of GP action these days if you don't buy it off Ecclestone first.

There was one other example of supreme bathos, as clear an illustration as you could require of yet another racing dictum: 'It ain't stopped until the chequered flag's dropped.' Or whatever that might be in Italian. The exemplar was Pier Francesco Chili, who came within a lap of winning a fierce battle for second place, to make it an Aprilia one-two behind Loris Reggiani. He surged over the line at the head of his group, then rose triumphantly from behind the fairing to punch the air in exultation, which rapidly turned to confusion and shame as his so recently defeated rivals kept their heads down and came charging past him again. By the time he realised there was still a lap to go, a broken Chili had dropped back to sixth. 'I have no words,' he said later, understandably dismayed by his error.

Aprilia had a less amusing turn of misfortune in the 125 class, with their works rider and Malaysia winner Alessandro Gramigni injured in a road bike crash near Mugello in the lull before the start of the European season. He broke his leg, and was out for this race and severely hampered for two or three more after that.

Former Dunlop and Pirelli tyre technician Peter Ingley was at Jerez wearing Yokohama gear. Ingley, from Birmingham, worked in F1 car racing last year before Pirelli withdrew, and is now back in motor cycling with the Japanese firm, who support 250 rider Jurgen van den Goorbergh, among others.

Yamaha also made a return – to the 125 class. Although apparently with factory blessing the Italian team were a low key effort, none the less rewarded by a perfect finish record. Giuseppe Fiorillo was 23rd and Fausto Ricci 26th out of 27 finishers on machines entered under the auspices of former class champion Eugenio Lazzarini.

Mackenzie rode the race of his life, coming from the back to claim his sixth rostrum finish, achieved on three different makes of machine.

500 cc PRACTICE

Michelin tyre users had been testing at Hockenheim the week before, and the sessions had ended in a grudge match between Rainey and Doohan, with the latter falling unhurt as the climax. Thus a scrap of comfort for the Honda's rivals – the combination was vulnerable.

They needed all the hope they could muster, for the three-times winner was in dominant form, leading free training on Thursday (to learn the new track), and every other session to claim his third successive pole from Rainey by more than half a second. The laconic Queenslander was chasing his own phantoms. 'I never feel confident. I reckon it's always best to feel like there's some strong opposition so I have to push myself.' On the smooth and slickish new surface, he was visibly able to open the throttle earlier in the corner than the rest of them.

Not that the opposition was conspicuously weak – just slower, with a formidable array of talent packed up seven-strong within the same second.

Schwantz had been second in Saturday morning's free training, and for much of the final timed session. Then a flurry of activity in the closing minutes saw Rainey move back ahead. Still complaining vociferously about the Yamaha/Michelin mismatch, his comments were blistering. 'I've never ridden a motor cycle as bad as this one.' (He must have been lucky.) 'I've no feeling from the front – no feedback. We've made so many changes – tyres, rim widths, wheel sizes, suspension geometry, springs ... it doesn't make any difference.'

Third place at least saw a cheery face – Chandler also elbowed past Schwantz in the closing minutes. Already he was showing growing strength, and crucial familiarity with the Suzuki. This was the first time he'd finished practice without a parcel full of changes to test in morning warm-up. 'We expected that. I didn't expect to be so high up after running in eighth for most of the last session.'

Less than a tenth down, Schwantz again seemed incongruously cheerful at having been pipped by his new team-mate. 'Being on the front row is what matters, and I prefer to be where I am because I'm on the outside for the first bend, and I can close the door on all of them,' he grinned. After the tight tracks of the last two races, the Suzuki was working well on the faster corners, but he felt the lack of torque and mid-range acceleration compared with the Honda. 'It should be close for second,' he grimaced.

The close-packed bravadoes on row two were led by the narrowest of margins by Mackenzie, also a late arrival up front after wasting time on Friday with his new Mark 2 chassis, then deciding: 'I don't think it's possible to set up a new bike at a GP,' and switching to his old faithful.

Lawson was alongside, aggrieved at rumours that he was just cruising through his retirement year. Justly so: by his conspicuous on-track efforts he was riding as hard as ever he had, though to little avail, until the Italian squad in desperation decided to break all the rules. 'We're down on the speed trap and we have some chatter. We had to go in at the deep end,' said Lawson. 'We changed just about everything we could ... gearbox, cylinder head compression, timing, jetting, tyres. It'll either work or it'll be worse.' He was right all down the line, and at one point was fourth fastest.

Next came Criville, responding to the heat of racing at home by boiling over, the only notable rider to crash in practice, losing the front and sliding off unhurt in a cloud of dust at the new 'Sito Pons' right-hander.

The last rider in the 1m 46s bracket was Kocinski, back after two lost races to resume his struggle with his 'understeering' Yamaha which had already slipped away from him once. Another, like Rainey, to miss the bite of the Dunlop front tyres, he said he was fit, but felt compelled to be cautious. 'I've lost a lot of riding time, but I'm trying to come back as soon as I can without getting into trouble,' he said.

Ninth fastest, Goddard led row three. The top works-replica Yamaha rider, having been as high as fifth on Friday, was clearly benefiting from his year of YZR experience in Japan in 1991. 'Yesterday I started to feel really comfortable on the bike,' he said. 'But I'm a bit confused because it didn't feel so good today.'

Mamola was next, painfully short of practice time after an ignition problem kept him in the pits for much of Friday. Garriga's Yamaha was alongside, then came Barros, with DuHamel leading the next row and the last rider in the 1m 47s band.

The privateers were more spaced out, with Catalano leading Arakaki, Laycock, Sarron, Mitchell, Crine, David and newcomer Juan Lopez Mella. There were 31 qualifiers, the slowest being Andreas Leuthe, riding the Italian-made VRP V4 in its GP debut. He was half a second down on the other newcomer, Claude Arciero, whose stately progress on the Roc Yamaha made even the likes of Peter Graves's Yamaha and Marco Papa's leisurely Librenti look as though they were racing.

500 cc RACE – 28 LAPS

For Doohan, the action in the race came from his encounters with backmarkers. He led from the first bend, and was able to draw away from the dogged Rainey as he liked – at almost a second a lap for the first five. Having thus easily disposed of his main worry, he kept pressing on to keep his concentration until, with better than 20 seconds in hand, he backed off to save his tyres.

His first anxious moment saw him almost tangle with a crashing backmarker; his second was ten laps from the end, following Catalano, awaiting a chance to overtake, when the Italian slewed sideways and narrowly survived an out-of-the-saddle moment. Two near-misses impelled

Right: **Helmut Bradl low-flying to second – at last a satisfactory start to his championship campaign.**

Carlos Lavado *(bottom)* enjoyed his works team revival on the Gilera ... as long as it kept going.

him to further caution, and he had all the time in the world to employ it.

Rainey was second into the first bend, and also held his position throughout, powerless to prevent Doohan's escape, but drawing away from his pursuers at almost the same rate. He'd finally found some better chassis settings in morning warm-up, which cheered him up a bit.

All the real racing happened behind this pair.

At first Schwantz was third, trying in vain to keep Rainey in sight. He soon had trouble from Chandler, whose identical Suzuki had burned off Kocinski's Yamaha before closing up. Chandler's style is reminiscent of Lawson's, but he has still to achieve the latter's consistency. He slowed briefly, blaming a brake knock-off problem ('That got my attention for a while,' he said drily), then came back on Schwantz by concentrating on smoother corner entries. But by lap 11 he was dropping back again, his unwise choice of rear tyre having let him down so badly that he gradually faded to tenth.

Simultaneously, and to the delight of the crowd, Criville was moving up on Schwantz, and by lap ten was attacking fiercely. But the American was not for giving way, and eventually Criville decided to bide his time. Already Kevin was suffering from a lack of rear grip, but he made up for it with his fast corner entries.

By now, however, Mackenzie was charging up from behind, after a typically poor start. He'd despatched the other works bikes without wasting any time, with Kocinski the last to be defeated. Well on the warpath, he quickly caught Schwantz and Criville, got in between them one lap later, and then promptly outbraked Schwantz to move into third place on lap 16. Criville followed him through, and then the battle was on, with Schwantz unable to match their drive out of the corners, condemned to the role of front row spectator, ready to seize his chance should one or both of them get into trouble.

This seemed highly likely as they niggled at each other, with Criville making a decisive move past under brakes into Turn One on the 25th lap. But Mackenzie was having the ride of his life, and kept on pressing hard until the last lap, when he got a better drive out of the final fast left after the Dry Sack hairpin (Criville later said he'd missed a gear) and outbraked the Spaniard into the ensuing slow rights.

There follows a short straight, a pair of fast rights and a left hairpin before the finish line. Usually the hairpin is the place where battles are finally decided, but Criville couldn't wait. As Mackenzie braked at the last possible moment for the first right-hander the Spaniard kept the power on and swept past magnificently. And much, much too fast. He had hardly even leaned the bike over when the front wheel tucked under and he was down.

'I just kept out of the way,' said Mackenzie, who might have been skittled had the Spaniard been going only a few mph slower. And while Schwantz was able to close up to within a tenth over the line, the Yamaha rider was still in front, to claim his sixth rostrum finish in six years of GP racing. Said Niall: 'That was probably my best ride ever – because I got a bad start and came through, and all the top riders were there.'

Schwantz had to be satisfied with fourth, but wasn't about to blame his still-bandaged left hand. 'That wasn't the problem,' he said. 'I just couldn't get the drive.'

Kocinski was fifth in his comeback ride, and admitted to feeling 'a bit rusty'. He hadn't been able to sustain his pace after a strong start, but held off an attack from an on-form Peter Goddard. The Australian had already beaten off Garriga's works Yamaha, and was obliged to kick again when the Spaniard came back in the final laps. He was not only the top Yamaha-replica finisher, but also the best on Dunlop tyres. 'They've done a great job,' he said after his best ever GP finish.

Garriga was seventh, under pressure from Mamola. The American had had trouble early in the race when his bike handled badly on a full tank, but he'd won a good battle with Lawson's Cagiva and also managed to hold off the strong finishing DuHamel by six-tenths.

Chandler took the final point for tenth place, with a disillusioned Lawson 11th another five seconds back and Cagiva team-mate Barros 12th. 'If I rode any faster, I'd kill myself,' said Lawson.

Thierry Crine was the next best privateer in 13th, with Kevin Mitchell a lap down in 14th. Then came Sarron, Rudroff, Doorakkers, Arakaki and Lopez Mella: 24 finishers, including Papa's Librenti, three laps down.

Doohan, not surprisingly, also took the lap record, and stretched his championship lead to a massive 35 points over Rainey. The season was taking an uncomfortable shape for anyone not riding a Honda NSR.

250 cc PRACTICE

On paper, the Hondas looked strong again. Bradl and Cadalora had dominated Saturday's 'untimed' morning session, the fastest of all of them, and Luca put himself on pole position for the first time this year. But it had been far from easy, and the Italian stylistic master only displaced Reggiani's Aprilia in the closing minutes of practice, and by an effort that had him still juddering on the brakes past the apex of the last hairpin.

He'd beaten the Aprilia by two-hundredths, and when you recalled that Reggiani was only just fully fit after crashing heavily at Jerez in pre-season tests, the figures looked more ominous. 'My bike is going like a rocket,' grinned Loris, clearly confident about his prospects for the race.

Earlier, Shimizu had been fastest, making one wonder if at last the long-time favourite of the Honda factory was going to fulfil his promise instead of only going fast at the end of the year. He ended up four-tenths down on Reggiani, but less than a tenth ahead of Chili.

The front-runners had stretched the times somewhat, making the spread of figures more like those in the 500 class. Here again was an impressive second row: Cardus from Puig, Romboni and Schmid.

Photos: Malcolm Bryan

Cardus, butting up against engine seizure problems and facing the imminent disintegration of his team, was lucky to escape unhurt from a heavy high-side crash in the last minutes of the final session. At the other end of the row, Schmid pulled out all the stops to put his works-backed Yamaha well up, after losing time earlier on testing a new crankcase that proved a backward step.

Bradl ended up leading row three, after suffering a major engine blow-up at the start of the second timed session – a sparking plug shed a ceramic scrap, destroying a piston before passing into the cases and damaging the crankshaft as well. Riding his slower spare, he was one of only three riders out of 36 not to improve on his Friday time; but with a low first gear fitted to ensure a good start from his lowly position, he was likely to be a big threat.

Both Gileras were alongside him, but with Lavado more than half a second down on his team-mate Ruggia. Capirossi was 12th to finish row three.

Both works Suzukis were in trouble, qualifying 15th and 17th, with Wilco Zeelenberg just faster than Herri Torrontegui, and both battling with wayward handling on the fast bends. The real puzzle was that the bikes always showed up well on the speed guns – so why was Zeelenberg also complaining of a lack of acceleration?

250 cc RACE – 26 LAPS

Chili burst through from row two to lead lap one, Shimizu took the lead on lap two, then Cadalora took over and for the next three laps it looked as though things would be much the same as for the previous three races.

But it soon became clear that he couldn't make any sort of break, nor could he wait and attack at the finish, for both he and his bike were, as he discreetly put it, not 100 per cent today. In fact, his problem was his Michelins. The same tyre that had worked in practice didn't work in the race, suggesting a bad batch of rubber; and he just didn't have the bite he needed to fend off the sweet-handling and definitely fast Aprilias.

Reggiani was ready and moved into the lead on lap six, gradually pulling away from a fierce battle for second. He was riding immaculately, two-wheel drifting his Aprilia, and while on some laps he was only able to open the gap by fractions, it was still inexorable, and by half-distance he had an advantage of better than three seconds which he stretched to more than five at the finish. Luckless Loris, the soulful-looking GP veteran, had claimed his third 250 class victory and opened the scoring for Aprilia.

The group behind were slowing each other down as a high class brawl drew in six of the current top 250 riders: Shimizu, Cadalora, Chili and Puig were locked together and

Photos: Malcolm Bryan

shuffling back and forth as they sought advantage here and there. Puig was the first to drop off the back. Cardus was also unable to hold the pace towards the end. But Bradl was on the charge and with two laps to go he was in second with Chili, Cadalora and Shimizu lined up virtually wheel to wheel.

Now came Chili's mortifying mistake. He led the group over the line next time round, but in the heat of the battle he missed his own pit signal, miscounted the laps and thought he saw the chequered flag. Delighted, he closed the throttle and punched the air as they ran into the first turn.

Bradl was lucky not to run into his back wheel, and the remaining trio swerved past to continue battle into the first corner. They kept their heads down and kept racing, of course, leaving Chili flabbergasted as he realised what he'd done. The real race for second was over less than two minutes later, with Bradl holding on from Shimizu and Cadalora, and all three covered by less than half a second.

Cardus was fifth, Chili a woebegone sixth, returning tearfully to his pit where he was ushered away behind closed doors. Puig was seventh; Jochen Schmid's Yamaha was a lonely eighth, while Stefan Prein's HB Honda, fitted for the first time with an Spl engine kit, won a close battle for the last points, with Biaggi tenth.

Capirossi was less than a tenth adrift, then came Romboni and Torrontegui's Suzuki, after a fierce battle. Zeelenberg's Suzuki was 14th but well out of touch, with the Dutchman bitterly disappointed after choosing a too hard rear tyre after seeing his 500 class teammates struggling with softer rubber. Both Gileras retired with ignition trouble, and there were 27 finishers.

So Cadalora's ambition of winning every race of the year was denied him, and the championship looked a little less cut and dried. But he still had a 33-point lead, the same as he thought he had in Malaysia, before the reinstatement of the Japanese ghosts knocked five points off second-placed Bradl's total.

125 cc RACE – 24 LAPS

Ten little 125 riders, sitting in a row. And amazingly hardly anyone in this leading pack ever did fall off, although it had dwindled to six at the finish – a tribute to the quality of riding in a class where all tracks are fast tracks and close racing is almost inevitable.

The six were covered by three seconds, and the one at the front was Ralf Waldmann, for the third time this season, the 25-year-old one-time plumber showing maturity in producing the right combination of aggression and tactics. The little German Honda rider had made most of the running, and deserved to win. Especially since he was fighting too soft tyres and some lurid slides, relying on horsepower to fight off his challengers on the straights.

Ezio Gianola's Semprucci Honda had led early on, but dropped to tenth after losing power. Then Casanova had put up a strong chal-

Left: **Surrounded by so great a cloud of witnesses – Casanova, Waldmann, Gresini, Debbia and the rest are dwarfed by the record race-day crowd of 230,000.**

Below right: **Winner Webster gives sidecar veteran but rostrum first-timer Barry Brindley some tips on comportment.**

Darren Dixon and new passenger Andy Hetherington were in fine form at Jerez, but out of luck. Here they fend off Klaffenböck *(bottom)*.

lenge, his Aprilia upping the pace before sputtering to a stop with ignition failure when there were nine laps to go.

At the finish, home hero in the making Charlie Giro came through the group to stretch it out, and Gresini and Kazuto Sakata followed him. But neither could get ahead of Waldmann for long enough to matter, and at the end Gresini was second, Giro third and Sakata fourth. Nobuyuki Wakai had also closed up in the last lap to take fifth.

Gabriele Debbia hung on to sixth from Dirk Raudies and newcomer Oliver Koch, Hondas all the way; Jorge Martinez's challenge for the lead didn't last after he ran onto the dirt, and he was lucky to finish ninth.

And the one who fell? Ueda again, as his dismal season got worse. At least he was unhurt.

SIDECAR RACE – 23 LAPS

A race full of incident started with Darren Dixon moving into the lead from pole position while Steve Webster and Klaus Klaffenböck battled over second place. Webster was past by lap three, and then started a fierce battle with Dixon. 'We banged fairings once or twice – it reminded me of my club racing days,' said Webster later.

The World Champion, racing for the first time with Honda cylinders, eventually prevailed and moved away in a safe lead, while Dixon and Klaffenböck battled it out, with Steve Abbott moving up to make a challenge that was spiked by engine trouble. Then Dixon was forced to retire: wheelspin had started his rear tyre chunking, which in turn caused the gearbox to fail.

This left Barry Brindley to take third, his first GP rostrum position in ten years of sidecar racing, with Yoshi Kumagaya fourth and the Güdel brothers fifth.

Some big names were out of luck. Egbert Streuer and passenger Peter Brown had overturned in practice, and had tyre trouble in the race, with their Yokohama first blistering and then finally going flat. Luckily by then the race was almost over, and the Hollywood-sponsored driver limped home to take ninth.

Rolf Biland also had trouble with his tyres, and was contemplating pitting to change them when his engine failed.

And so the season began, with a strong race to counter the gloom and despondency. And no prize money at all.

Gran Premio Ducados de España, 10 May/statistics

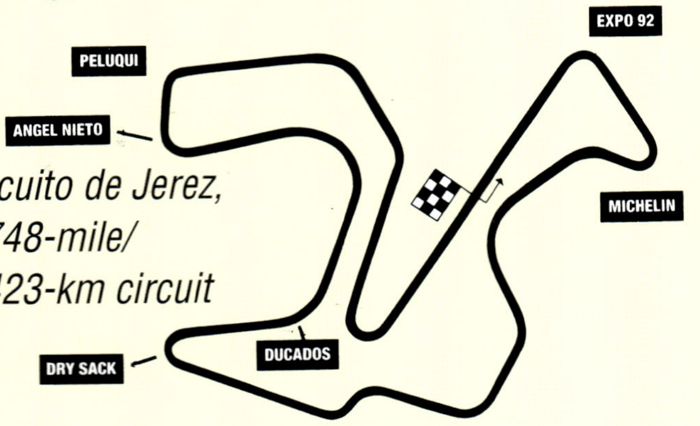

Circuito de Jerez, 2.748-mile/ 4.423-km circuit

500 cc

28 laps, 76.944 miles/123.844 km

Place	Rider	Nat.	Machine	Laps	Time & speed	Fastest lap	Lap
1	**Michael Doohan**	**AUS**	**Honda**	**28**	**49m 42.940s 92.872 mph/ 149.463 km/h**	**1m 45.356s**	**5**
2	**Wayne Rainey**	**USA**	**Yamaha**	**28**	**50m 01.931s**	**1m 45.968s**	**6**
3	**Niall Mackenzie**	**GB**	**Yamaha**	**28**	**50m 11.313s**	**1m 46.336s**	**12**
4	**Kevin Schwantz**	**USA**	**Suzuki**	**28**	**50m 11.421s**	**1m 46.545s**	**3**
5	**John Kocinski**	**USA**	**Yamaha**	**28**	**50m 22.297s**	**1m 46.887s**	**7**
6	**Peter Goddard**	**AUS**	**Yamaha**	**28**	**50m 31.741s**	**1m 47.290s**	**4**
7	**Juan Garriga**	**E**	**Yamaha**	**28**	**50m 35.422s**	**1m 46.987s**	**4**
8	**Randy Mamola**	**USA**	**Yamaha**	**28**	**50m 36.628s**	**1m 47.518s**	**24**
9	**Miguel DuHamel**	**CAN**	**Yamaha**	**28**	**50m 36.872s**	**1m 47.637s**	**28**
10	**Doug Chandler**	**USA**	**Suzuki**	**28**	**50m 41.732s**	**1m 46.396s**	**5**
11	Eddie Lawson	USA	Cagiva	28	50m 46.417s	1m 47.875s	19
12	Alexandre Barros	BR	Cagiva	28	51m 04.400s	1m 48.073s	4
13	Thierry Crine	F	Yamaha	28	51m 29.765s	1m 48.295s	3
14	Kevin Mitchell	GB	Yamaha	27	49m 51.285s	1m 48.994s	6
15	Dominique Sarron	F	Yamaha	27	49m 59.983s	1m 49.811s	23
16	Michael Rudroff	D	Yamaha	27	50m 01.977s	1m 50.054s	14
17	Cees Doorakkers	NL	Yamaha	27	50m 05.110s	1m 50.006s	25
18	Toshiyuki Arakaki	J	Yamaha	27	50m 08.380s	1m 48.897s	6
19	Juan Lopez Mella	E	Yamaha	27	50m 09.506s	1m 49.663s	20
20	Corrado Catalano	I	Yamaha	27	50m 18.234s	1m 49.514s	15
21	Serge David	CH	Yamaha	27	50m 29.338s	1m 50.047s	9
22	Niggi Schmassman	CH	Yamaha	27	51m 11.499s	1m 52.230s	27
23	Sepp Doppler	A	Yamaha	27	51m 12.615s	1m 52.250s	10
24	Marco Papa	I	Librenti	25	50m 47.290s	1m 51.626s	3
	Alex Criville	E	Honda	27	DNF	1m 46.827s	9
	Lucio Pedercini	I	Paton	9	DNF	1m 53.564s	3
	Andreas Leuthe	D	VRP	5	DNF	1m 54.685s	4
	Eddie Laycock	IRL	Yamaha	3	DNF	1m 50.612s	2
	Simon Buckmaster	GB	Yamaha	2	DNF	1m 55.202s	2
	Peter Graves	GB	Yamaha	0	DNF		
	Claude Arciero	F	Yamaha	0	DNF		

Fastest lap: Doohan, 1m 45.356s, 93.910 mph/151.133 km/h (record).
Previous circuit record: Wayne Rainey, USA (Yamaha), 1m 47.615s, 87.677 mph/141.103 km/h (1991).

Practice leaderboard: 1 Doohan, 1m 45.480s; **2** Rainey, 1m 46.165s; **3** Chandler, 1m 46.310s; **4** Schwantz, 1m 46.403s; **5** Mackenzie, 1m 46.501s; **6** Lawson, 1m 46.738s; **7** Criville, 1m 46.876s; **8** Kocinski, 1m 46.879s; **9** Goddard, 1m 47.268s; **10** Mamola, 1m 47.289s; **11** Garriga, 1m 47.322s; **12** Barros, 1m 47.398s; **13** DuHamel, 1m 47.456s; **14** Catalano, 1m 48.100s; **15** Arakaki, 1m 48.560s.

World Championship: 1 Doohan, 80; **2** Rainey, 45; **3** Chandler and Schwantz, 32; **5** Beattie and Mamola, 18; **7** Criville, Garriga and Mackenzie, 16; **10** Itoh, 10; **11** Goddard, 9; **12** Kocinski, 8; **13** Lawson and Ohishi, 6; **15** DuHamel and Honma, 3; **17** Catalano and Fujiwara, 2; **19** Laycock and Tsujimoto, 1.

250 cc

26 laps, 71.448 miles/114.998 km

Place	Rider	Nat.	Machine	Laps	Time & speed	Fastest lap	Lap
1	**Loris Reggiani**	**I**	**Aprilia**	**26**	**47m 24.923s 90.421 mph/ 145.520 km/h**	**1m 48.283s**	**17**
2	**Helmut Bradl**	**D**	**Honda**	**26**	**47m 30.006s**	**1m 48.538s**	**16**
3	**Masahiro Shimizu**	**J**	**Honda**	**26**	**47m 30.296s**	**1m 48.722s**	**16**
4	**Luca Cadalora**	**I**	**Honda**	**26**	**47m 30.419s**	**1m 48.597s**	**11**
5	**Carlos Cardus**	**E**	**Honda**	**26**	**47m 36.375s**	**1m 48.856s**	**5**
6	**Pier Francesco Chili**	**I**	**Aprilia**	**26**	**47m 38.946s**	**1m 48.465s**	**23**
7	**Alberto Puig**	**E**	**Aprilia**	**26**	**47m 49.541s**	**1m 48.788s**	**7**
8	**Jochen Schmid**	**D**	**Yamaha**	**26**	**47m 50.964s**	**1m 49.626s**	**13**
9	**Stefan Prein**	**D**	**Honda**	**26**	**47m 59.044s**	**1m 49.920s**	**25**
10	**Massimiliano Biaggi**	**I**	**Aprilia**	**26**	**48m 00.628s**	**1m 49.597s**	**22**
11	Loris Capirossi	I	Honda	26	48m 00.756s	1m 49.916s	7
12	Doriano Romboni	I	Honda	26	48m 03.216s	1m 50.081s	11
13	Herri Torrontegui	E	Suzuki	26	48m 04.963s	1m 49.942s	6
14	Wilco Zeelenberg	NL	Suzuki	26	48m 15.150s	1m 50.401s	10
15	Paolo Casoli	I	Yamaha	26	48m 20.272s	1m 50.136s	26
16	Frédéric Protat	F	Aprilia	26	48m 20.326s	1m 49.973s	26
17	Bernd Kassner	D	Aprilia	26	48m 21.242s	1m 49.777s	26
18	Bernard Hänggeli	CH	Aprilia	26	48m 24.752s	1m 50.767s	19
19	Erkka Korpiaho	SF	Aprilia	26	48m 30.430s	1m 50.368s	24
20	Luis D'Antin	E	Honda	26	48m 30.441s	1m 50.843s	12
21	Adrian Bosshard	CH	Honda	26	48m 34.609s	1m 50.832s	10
22	Katsuyoshi Kozono	J	Honda	26	48m 34.858s	1m 50.845s	9
23	Jean-Pierre Jeandat	F	Honda	26	48m 46.385s	1m 51.002s	12
24	Jurgen van den Goorbergh	NL	Aprilia	26	48m 53.942s	1m 51.562s	24
25	Yves Briguet	CH	Honda	26	48m 55.194s	1m 51.422s	11
26	Bernard Cazade	F	Honda	25	47m 37.011s	1m 52.524s	9
27	Manuel Gibernau	E	Yamaha	25	48m 12.949s	1m 53.212s	5
	Adi Stadler	D	Honda	22	DNF	1m 51.228s	14
	Jean-Philippe Ruggia	F	Gilera	20	DNF	1m 49.199s	11
	Renzo Colleoni	I	Yamaha	18	DNF	1m 53.232s	5
	Stefano Caracchi	I	Yamaha	16	DNF	1m 50.957s	14
	Harald Eckl	D	Aprilia	14	DNF	1m 52.535s	9
	David Sanchez	E	Honda	11	DNF	1m 52.140s	9
	Carlos Lavado	YV	Gilera	9	DNF	1m 50.894s	7
	Andy Preining	A	Aprilia	4	DNF	1m 50.599s	2
	Eskil Suter	CH	Aprilia	3	DNF	1m 53.865s	3
	Patrick van den Goorbergh	NL	Aprilia		DNS		

Fastest lap: Reggiani, 1m 48.283s, 91.371 mph/147.048 km/h (record).
Previous circuit record: Helmut Bradl, D (Honda), 1m 50.002s, 85.775 mph/138.041 km/h (1991).

Practice leaderboard: 1 Cadalora, 1m 47.725s; **2** Reggiani, 1m 47.743s; **3** Shimizu, 1m 48.140s; **4** Chili, 1m 48.223s; **5** Cardus, 1m 48.267s; **6** Puig, 1m 48.308s; **7** Romboni, 1m 48.406s; **8** Schmid, 1m 48.629s; **9** Bradl, 1m 48.650s; **10** Ruggia, 1m 48.650s; **11** Lavado, 1m 49.274s; **12** Capirossi, 1m 49.319s; **13** Biaggi, 1m 49.357s; **14** Korpiaho, 1m 49.692s; **15** Zeelenberg, 1m 49.697s.

World Championship: 1 Cadalora, 70; **2** Bradl, 37; **3** Cardus, 33; **4** Reggiani, 28; **5** Chili, 26; **6** Puig, 25; **7** Zeelenberg, 18; **8** Okada and Shimizu, 15; **10** Aoki and Romboni, 12; **12** Schmid, 11; **13** Biaggi, Capirossi and Preining, 4; **16** Nanba, 3; **17** Casoli, Prein and Ruggia, 2; **20** Jeandat, 1.

Malcolm Bryan

125 cc

24 laps, 65.952 miles/106.152 km

Place	Rider	Nat.	Machine	Laps	Time & speed	Fastest lap	Lap
1	**Ralf Waldmann**	D	Honda	24	45m 57.309s 86.118 mph/ 138.594 km/h	1m 53.786s	24
2	**Fausto Gresini**	I	Honda	24	45m 57.389s	1m 53.559s	24
3	**Carlos Giro**	E	Aprilia	24	45m 58.409s	1m 53.813s	14
4	**Kazuto Sakata**	J	Honda	24	45m 58.880s	1m 53.713s	22
5	**Nobuyuki Wakai**	J	Honda	24	45m 59.077s	1m 53.671s	22
6	**Gabriele Debbia**	I	Honda	24	46m 00.458s	1m 53.509s	5
7	**Dirk Raudies**	D	Honda	24	46m 02.040s	1m 53.989s	24
8	**Oliver Koch**	D	Honda	24	46m 02.929s	1m 54.077s	24
9	**Jorge Martinez**	E	Honda	24	46m 04.551s	1m 54.117s	17
10	**Ezio Gianola**	I	Honda	24	46m 18.941s	1m 54.429s	9
11	Loek Bodelier	NL	Honda	24	46m 31.724s	1m 54.219s	6
12	Emilio Cuppini	I	Aprilia	24	46m 33.499s	1m 54.692s	7
13	Hans Spaan	NL	Aprilia	24	46m 35.577s	1m 55.210s	7
14	Kinya Wada	J	Honda	24	46m 35.598s	1m 55.479s	7
15	Peter Öttl	D	Rotax	24	46m 40.949s	1m 55.483s	7
16	Takao Shimizu	J	Honda	24	46m 41.671s	1m 55.402s	24
17	Peter Galvin	AUS	Honda	24	46m 41.998s	1m 55.461s	23
18	Alain Bronec	F	Honda	24	47m 01.602s	1m 56.011s	17
19	Maik Stief	D	Aprilia	24	47m 02.264s	1m 55.827s	22
20	Heinz Lüthi	CH	Honda	24	47m 02.337s	1m 55.894s	24
21	Arie Molenaar	NL	Aprilia	24	47m 04.442s	1m 56.402s	14
22	Giovanni Palmieri	I	Gazzaniga	24	47m 17.295s	1m 56.372s	15
23	Giuseppe Fiorillo	I	Yamaha	24	47m 25.673s	1m 56.369s	10
24	Hisashi Unemoto	J	Honda	24	47m 32.183s	1m 57.273s	8
25	Manuel Luque	E	Cobas	24	47m 32.324s	1m 57.647s	20
26	Fausto Ricci	I	Yamaha	23	48m 14.556s	2m 00.281s	3
27	Maurizio Vitali	I	Gazzaniga	20	46m 08.083s	1m 55.355s	18
	Noboru Ueda	J	Honda	20	DNF	1m 54.013s	17
	Alfred Waibel	D	Honda	18	DNF	1m 56.259s	17
	Julian Miralles	E	Honda	17	DNF	1m 54.950s	4
	Bruno Casanova	I	Aprilia	15	DNF	1m 54.251s	12
	Hubert Abold	D	Honda	8	DNF	1m 59.115s	6
	Oliver Petrucciani	CH	Honda	6	DNF	1m 56.905s	3
	Manuel Hernandez	E	Aprilia	5	DNF	1m 57.221s	3
	Robin Appleyard	GB	Honda	5	DNF	1m 58.326s	3
	Steve Patrickson	GB	Honda	4	DNF	1m 59.087s	3
	Luis Alvaro	E	Cobas	3	DNF	1m 59.752s	2

Fastest lap: Debbia, 1m 53.509s, 87.165 mph/140.278 km/h (record).
Previous circuit record: Ezio Gianola, I (Derbi), 1m 54.038s, 82.740 mph/133.156 km/h (1991).

Practice leaderboard: **1** Sakata, 1m 53.790s; **2** Waldmann, 1m 53.915s; **3** Gresini, 1m 53.977s; **4** Wakai, 1m 54.053s; **5** Giro, 1m 54.319s; **6** Casanova, 1m 54.362s; **7** Gianola, 1m 54.426s; **8** Martinez, 1m 54.485s; **9** Miralles, 1m 54.561s; **10** Debbia, 1m 54.663s; **11** Ueda, 1m 54.800s; **12** Cuppini, 1m 54.824s; **13** Raudies, 1m 55.110s; **14** Shimizu, 1m 55.275s; **15** Wada, 1m 55.354s.

World Championship: **1** Waldmann, 72; **2** Casanova, 42; **3** Gramigni, 41; **4** Wakai, 30; **5** Gresini, 26; **6** Martinez and Raudies, 18; **8** Sakata, 16; **9** Gianola, 13; **10** Giro, 12; **11** Debbia, 11; **12** Saitoh, 8; **13** Koch, 6; **14** Fujihara, 4; **15** Wada, 3; **16** Spaan, 2; **17** Lüthi and Petrucciani, 1.

Sidecars

23 laps, 63.204 miles/101.729 km

Place	Driver & passenger	Nat.	Machine	Laps	Time & speed	Fastest lap	Lap
1	**Steve Webster/ Gavin Simmons**	GB GB	LCR- ADM	23	42m 38.606s 88.940 mph/ 143.134 km/h	1m 49.517s	7
2	**Klaus Klaffenböck/ Christian Parzer**	A A	LCR- ADM	23	42m 55.849s	1m 50.586s	12
3	**Barry Brindley/ Scott Whiteside**	GB GB	LCR- Yamaha	23	43m 18.276s	1m 51.432s	12
4	**Yoshisada Kumagaya/ Bryan Houghton**	J GB	LCR- Krauser	23	43m 24.126s	1m 51.071s	10
5	**Paul Güdel/ Charly Güdel**	CH CH	LCR- Yamaha	23	43m 42.195s	1m 50.958s	3
6	**Markus Bösiger/ Beat Leibundgut**	CH CH	LCR- ADM	23	43m 49.039s	1m 52.655s	21
7	**Tony Wyssen/ Kilian Wyssen**	CH CH	LCR- Yamaha	23	44m 04.854s	1m 53.188s	5
8	**Markus Egloff/ Urs Egloff**	CH CH	LCR- Yamaha	23	44m 21.487s	1m 52.931s	5
9	**Egbert Streuer/ Peter Brown**	NL GB	LCR- Stredor	23	44m 26.922s	1m 53.074s	4
10	**Tony Baker/ Simon Prior**	GB GB	LCR- Krauser	23	44m 31.160s	1m 54.089s	12
11	Theo van Kempen/ Geral de Haas	NL NL	LCR- Krauser	22	42m 46.034s	1m 54.319s	16
12	Billy Gällros/ Peter Berglund	S S	LCR- Streuer	22	42m 48.242s	1m 54.127s	4
13	Reiner Koster/ Jurg Egli	CH CH	LCR- Yamaha	22	43m 47.811s	1m 56.343s	6
	Derek Brindley/ Nick Roche	GB GB	LCR- Krauser	20	DNF	1m 52.420s	5
	Darren Dixon/ Andy Hetherington	GB GB	LCR- Krauser	18	DNF	1m 50.424s	10
	Steve Abbott/ Shaun Smith	GB GB	YK1- Krauser	17	DNF	1m 51.352s	7
	Eddie Wright/ Peter Hill	GB GB	LCR- Krauser	16	DNF	1m 55.256s	4
	Hans Hügli/ Adolf Hänni	CH CH	LCR- ADM	16	DNF	1m 57.654s	7
	Mark Reddington/ Robert Parker	GB GB	Krauser	11	DNF	1m 55.936s	4
	André Bosman/ Dave Kellett	AUS AUS	LCR- Krauser	9	DNF	1m 57.634s	6
	Rolf Biland/ Kurt Waltisperg	CH CH	LCR- Krauser	8	DNF	1m 51.369s	5
	Robert Fisher/ Trevor Crone	GB GB	LCR- Krauser	7	DNF	1m 56.814s	5
	Ralph Bohnhorst/ Bruno Hiller	D D	BRM	3	DNF	1m 53.132s	3
	Peter Lemstra/ Jan Kuyt	NL NL	LCR- Krauser		DNQ		

Fastest lap: Webster, 1m 49.517s, 90.342 mph/145.391 km/h (record).
Previous circuit record: Steve Webster/Gavin Simmons, GB/GB (LCR-Krauser-Yamaha), 1m 52.237s, 84.067 mph/135.292 km/h (1991).

Practice leaderboard: **1** Dixon, 1m 48.465s; **2** Webster, 1m 48.718s; **3** Güdel, 1m 49.132s; **4** Biland, 1m 49.262s; **5** Klaffenböck, 1m 49.573s; **6** Abbott, 1m 50.108s; **7** Bösiger, 1m 50.489s; **8** D. Brindley, 1m 50.566s; **9** Streuer, 1m 50.628s; **10** Bohnhorst, 1m 50.689s; **11** Egloff, 1m 50.813s; **12** B. Brindley, 1m 51.717s; **13** Kumagaya, 1m 51.804s; **14** Baker, 1m 53.647s; **15** Wyssen, 1m 53.743s.

World Championship: **1** Webster, 20; **2** Klaffenböck, 15; **3** B. Brindley, 12; **4** Kumagaya, 10; **5** Güdel, 8; **6** Bösiger, 6; **7** Wyssen, 4; **8** Egloff, 3; **9** Streuer, 2; **10** Baker, 1.

500 cc	SCHWANTZ
250 cc	CADALORA
125 cc	GIANOLA

ITALIAN GRAND PRIX

The riddle of the Italian GP – indeed, of the whole season – was why times on the new generation works bikes continued to be slower than last year.

There'd been all sorts of get-out clauses at the previous races: rain at Suzuka, dirt and new bumps at Eastern Creek, more dirt at Shah Alam and an altered race track at Jerez. Now there were no excuses, only the pitiless information from the stopwatch that revealed slower practice times in all classes and, by the end of the weekend, no new lap records.

Photos: Malcolm Bryan

Left: To cut a long story short – Erv Kanemoto and team manager Little George Vukmanovich ponder yet another victory for Cadalora *(above)*; yet another crash for Gardner. 'I feel underemployed,' said Erv, in Gardner's extended absence.

Below left: **Doohan rode close to the limit, as he had done all year. This time, it wasn't enough to fend off the streaking Schwantz.**

There were various attempts at explanation here at Mugello – Ferrari tests had brought up new ripple-bumps, or laid down too much rubber; Friday's rain had washed the rubber off; and so on – but these were getting rather lame. The most cogent reason did little credit to any of the tyre manufacturers: not to Michelin, whose front tyres were causing disquiet to all their runners, but particularly those who had run Dunlops here last year; nor indeed to Dunlop, whose depleted army of 1992 could not match last year's achievements either; nor to the newcomers from Yokohama and Bridgestone.

Dunlop's shrunken 1992 squad had been further depleted for this race, for works Yamaha-mounted Juan Garriga had spat the dummy and abruptly decamped to Michelin. This left Dunlop with Cagiva as their only factory team, along with several privateers, including Goddard.

Garriga's case is a curious one. The lean and wiry Catalan earned the nickname 'Archangel' as counterpoint to 'Architect' Sito Pons when the kids from opposite ends of the Barcelona social spectrum fought an epic battle for the 250 title in 1988. But their subsequent simultaneous switch to the 500 class in 1990 had turned them both from tooth-and-nail heroes into nothing more than midfield men. Indeed, the difficulties of such good riders in adapting to the top class posed a fresh conundrum to which Kocinski has made his own contribution, as to why a fast 250 rider should not automatically also be a fast 500 rider.

Garriga had been satisfied at first, willing to learn the new disciplines of 500 racing gradually, and he produced some strong and consistent rides. But he'd so far failed to take the crucial final step that would put him on an equal footing with the dominant Americans and Australians. And this year another Barcelona bright boy, Alex Criville, had turned up to make Garriga's best efforts look second rate. His sponsors, Ducados, had proved faithful to their man, but a late switch to Michelin carried under the circumstances the smack of desperation.

Dunlop chief Jeremy Ferguson, asked about the abrupt desertion of his sole remaining works Yamaha customer, was regretful but not ashamed. 'If he thinks just changing equipment will make him faster, why didn't he buy a Honda?' Garriga reacted with a grin, saying: 'It's easier to change the tyres than the motor cycle'; but then he grew angrier. 'I don't want a war with Dunlop, but think of my side. I used Dunlops in 1990 and finished sixth in the world. The next year Team Roberts and Suzuki joined Dunlop, and they got the best tyres before me. Before the start of this season Team Roberts tested 1992 tyres before they went to Michelin instead. I wasn't given that chance, but I stayed with Dunlop. And we are still having the same old problems. Now I am tired of hearing the same story from them. After every race they say to me: "I'm sorry. I'm sorry." So from now on I will use Michelins like the other riders.'

Mugello wasn't a good circuit to make this shift. Beautifully situated in the Apennine foothills of Tuscany, it is a classic track in that it is relatively long and predominantly fast, and has no low gear hairpins or artificial chicanes. Instead, several sets of third and fourth gear ess-bends loop up and down the valley sides, with a frequency of delicate downhill corner entries that demands total fidelity from the front wheel. And, as everybody knew by now, last year's (or any year's) Dunlop fronts were better than any of Michelin's.

But Michelin had another problem, and a very unexpected one – inconsistency from one batch to the next of ostensibly identical tyres, something more often associated with Dunlop in the past. The first duds showed at Jerez, to Cadalora's cost. At Mugello, Doohan, Criville, Mackenzie and others were stricken by the same problem while Schwantz, among others using exactly the same type of rear Michelin but from a different batch, had no trouble.

At Mugello, it proved crucial – for the deterioration of his rear tyre was surely a major factor in the first ever GP defeat of Doohan's NSR Honda.

The GP circus came to Mugello fresh from tests at Barcelona, with some minor changes in personnel. Wayne Gardner was back, having recovered quicker than expected from his leg breakage in Japan (although still wearing a light plaster cast), and itching to get racing. You're obviously a brave man, said a Rothmans sidekick in private. 'Yeah – a brave idiot,' he grinned. Too brave, for in the final practice session, while vaulting up the leaderboard (as high as fifth at one point) and still speeding up, he ran out of body-strength to muscle the bike round a left, went wide on the next fast right and into the gravel trap, where the bike flipped and he landed right on his injured leg. Back to the clinic. Do not pass go. Miss two races.

Fellow-Australian Peter Goddard also withdrew after running just three 'untimed' laps. He'd broken a little finger and torn thumb ligaments in a high speed crash in the Barcelona tests. 'I'd just been clocked at 283 km/h,' he said. 'That's the fastest crash I've ever had.' His Valvoline Roc Yamaha was virtually destroyed, with broken frame, forks, swing arm, front wheel, discs, tank, seat, fairing, ignition and a considerable list of smaller parts. Luckily, the YZR engine wasn't damaged.

John Kocinski had been in hospital in the interim, suffering from a virus infection that expressed itself by making him dizzy and affecting his vision. He was typically cagy about it, and when asked to describe the problem at a press conference answered as though the question had been about his choice of tyres. This led to all sorts of speculation, much centred on his known eye problem which had required surgery in 1989.

There was another Spanish surprise in the 250 class. Cardus, getting more than desperate after his downhill slump since his second place in Australia, had suddenly and unexpectedly dispensed with the services of Kel Carruthers as crew chief for his Campsa Honda NSR. The Australian former World Champion and long-time paddock guru (who took Roberts and Lawson to a

Doohan leads the first charge up the hill. By the end of the lap, Chandler (10) will be second, from Rainey (1), Schwantz (obscured) and Criville (28).

string of titles) had been in the second year of a three-year contract with Carlos Cardus's Repsol Honda team. Now the wheels had come off, and though Cardus's team manager (and wife) Sylvie insisted that the bust-up had been amicable on both sides, word filtered back from Carruthers's home in California that the matter was now in the hands of lawyers.

There was another can of worms here, for those who sought it. Cardus's problem was simple. He was in trouble in the championship, and this meant trouble with his own sponsor, Repsol – his key to getting a full works bike. Replacing Carruthers was a typically dramatic act by a volatile man under extreme pressure. But this was a mere subplot to the case of Carruthers, whose recent history made rewarding political study. His glory years had been abruptly ended when Lawson left Team Marlboro Agostini for Honda in 1989. The Spencer debacle in turn consigned the one-time official factory team to history, and in 1990 the otherwise redundant long-time Yamaha employee Carruthers spent a year 'co-ordinating' for the factory, a nebulous and unsatisfying role. When the chance came for hands-on work with Cardus's factory Honda in 1991, he leapt at it.

Carruthers's own preferences had had to take a back seat for many years. He wanted to work with Kevin Schwantz, and had twice tried to recruit him to ride Yamahas for Agostini. On each occasion the Yamaha factory had blocked the move, probably because they didn't want to be seen to be poaching Suzuki's major asset. Now, after one not altogether happy year with Cardus, the chance came for Carruthers to join Suzuki as Schwantz's crew chief. His dream team was within his reach, for at first the Spaniard was willing to release him from his contract. Then suddenly the door slammed shut. Carruthers had to stay with Honda.

The question now involved Cardus's double change of heart. Having seemed willing to release Carruthers, why had he then insisted that he stay? Word was that this was a condition laid down by Honda if Cardus was to get an NSR. Now, after four races, he was getting rid of him. Conspiracy theorists had a field day, but it was easy to wonder whether the hand of Honda hadn't moved to block a man who knew their bike so intimately from taking his knowledge to Suzuki.

With or without Carruthers and the other absentees, the Italian GP was one of the best races so far this season, in all classes – not least because it augured well for the rest of the championship.

Doohan was on target to break all sorts of records had he won again at Mugello, and his practice performance seemed to make his fifth victory of the season a matter of course. Then the race began, and for the first time the Honda was getting beaten. Rainey may have had his second race crash of the year (the third in his career) trying to do it, but Schwantz and his Lucky Strike Suzuki truly broke the Honda's spell.

500 cc PRACTICE

Day one of Mugello practice was wet and slippery, losing valuable set-up time for everybody. The Suzukis were fastest in these conditions, but on Friday afternoon it didn't really matter that much, and even less when Saturday and Sunday were dry and warm.

Doohan got straight on top, crushingly so in the last five minutes of practice, when he calmly carved half a second off his previous best to open up a gap of more than a second. Already, though, he was worried about tyres. 'They all push the front a little. You want the one that does it the least.'

Second place went to Schwantz, who had been ahead of Doohan several times during both morning and afternoon sessions, but whose earlier assertion that the Suzuki might challenge the Honda at this highly technical track of fast esses and few gearchanges looked rather second hand after the Honda man's final charge. 'It's kinda frustrating when you've already done your plug chop and he goes out and goes half a second faster,' said Kevin. But he was still hopeful. 'Our advantage here is that the Suzuki is easy to flick. But not as easy as last year on the Dunlops. We were faster last year, and I'm not quite sure why.'

Rainey was alongside, another two-tenths adrift and continuing his frustration with the wayward front Michelins. 'You need to be aggressive here, and that's how I like to ride. But I just can't flick it without it feels vague, so I have to do everything a lot slower. At Jerez I ran a soft rear and a hard front to take the pressure off the front – that's a heck of a way to fix a problem.'

Chandler ended up fourth, his third front row of a fine debut year on the Suzuki. Row two was led by Alex Criville, who crashed in the rain on Friday before again proving himself very handy with the Honda. Barros was alongside, taking his turn to prove that Cagiva really do make a special effort to do well when they race in Italy, and that sometimes it works. In this case, the crucial bits were new cylinders that improved power throughout the range, although Lawson – who qualified ninth – said he was still struggling with too sudden a step onto too narrow a power band.

The off-colour Kocinski was alongside Barros, with Gardner in eighth to complete the row, but a non-starter.

Lawson led row three from Mackenzie, who failed to recapture his front row form here of last year. 'We saved up a lot of brilliant ideas we wanted to use in the dry, and then when the rain stopped they didn't work,' he said. He too complained about the vagueness of the front Michelins.

Garriga was alongside him, keeping quiet about any tyre problems; then came Corrado Catalano, the

Malcolm Bryan

fastest privateer for the first time, completing row three.

Row four saw DuHamel leading Mamola, Rudroff and the ever spectacular Arakaki, with Mamola again losing virtually a full practice session while his mechanics hunted down a pesky powervalve problem. Along with losing the first two sessions to rain, it left him still guessing about race settings. 'It's just a gamble,' he said.

Thierry Crine led row five from Laycock, Sarron and Mitchell, with 29 qualifiers out of 32 entries, and Leuthe's VRP again out of luck after yet another massive seizure.

500 cc RACE – 24 LAPS

It started with all the hallmarks of another Doohan walkover. The Australian swept straight into the lead and immediately started drawing away from his pursuers, strung out line astern through the one-line swoops and swerves. By the end of the first lap, the blue and white Honda was almost 1.5 seconds ahead of Chandler, Rainey and Schwantz.

But both Schwantz and Rainey had other ideas, and piled past into second under braking for the first and tightest corner of the second lap. Almost side by side, Schwantz narrowly ahead, they steadily if gradually closed the gap on the leader.

On lap three it was less than a second, and it continued to shrink by tenths, with the Suzuki right on the ragged edge (and over it once as Schwantz ran over a corner kerb and kicked up dust after his sliding rear tyre unexpectedly found some grip). Then he was in the Honda's slipstream, and ready to mount his attack.

All the overtaking at a track of mainly one-line corners took place into Turn One and it was here, under brakes, that Schwantz moved alongside and past Doohan to take the lead for the first time this year. Rainey was with him to make a sandwich of the Honda, and the trio circulated for another two laps before both of them dived past Schwantz again, at the same spot. The race was on.

Now Rainey was in front, and he pulled away impressively, leading by more than a second as Schwantz tried to find a way back past Doohan. He eventually succeeded just before half-distance, and was slowly closing on Rainey again.

Then the orange works Yamaha was sliding, running wide, and

Photos: Malcolm Bryan

down, with Rainey skidding in the dust as his erstwhile pursuers flashed past. The front wheel had tucked under in a classic understeering low-sider on the way into the second esses. Though unhurt, he was fuming. 'I've been saying that when I try to be aggressive, I get the message from the front that I'm gonna crash unless I back off. This time I didn't back off – so I guess that proves the point.'

The pleasure of being the first to beat Doohan was left to Schwantz, who gradually drew away, the Suzuki making the Honda for once look lumbering and clumsy. Schwantz and his crew had taken a second guess at improving front traction during the Barcelona tests. 'It works,' he said, after spraying the winner's champagne for the first time since Le Mans last year. 'It's too soon to say that we've turned the tide in the championship. It's gonna be a big fight to close up on Mick. But we've proved he's not unbeatable, and that's a big mental boost.'

Doohan accepted defeat manfully. 'I got some good lap times in practice, but I couldn't string 24 of them together. I had no tyre trouble. The front was perfect, and though the rear was spinning a bit at the end that was no problem.' Typically, he made light of a major wobble when the bike flicked into a tank-slapper that put him out of the seat and forced him to back off. 'It was a moment, but not real scary.' But his manly comments, especially about tyres, reflected more tact and modesty than unadorned truth – for it was clear that his rear Michelin hadn't come up to expectations; and similar problems awaiting Criville and Mackenzie underlined the point.

The leaders had substantially outdistanced Chandler, who soon had his hands full not only with the eager Criville's Honda but also with problems of his own. 'The engine wouldn't rev past 12,000, and I was worried it might tie up. The other thing was that I'd gone the other way from Jerez, and chosen tyres that were too hard. The front never did get up to temperature, and I had a couple of scary slides. At the end it looked brand new.'

He was able to dice with Criville when the Spaniard went past, then to pass him again once and for all when the Honda had a big wobble. 'My rear tyre started to slide badly,' said Criville; confirmed by Chandler: 'I could see it getting real feathery at the edges, and I thought I'd better get by him.'

As Criville slowed, there was some hard fighting behind, with slow starter Kocinski getting back on terms with Barros's Cagiva, the American later expressing somewhat awestruck admiration for his late braking. Another close group was coming up behind – DuHamel, Garriga and Mackenzie, who had outdistanced Mamola and left Lawson behind.

Kocinski, speeding up all the way, outpaced them and rapidly overhauled Chandler in the closing laps, the Suzuki running wide after another front end slide as he tried to fend off the Yamaha.

Thus Kocinski found his way to the rostrum, half a minute behind the leaders, and surprised to be there. 'At the start of the week I was in hospital with fever and such pressure in my head that I couldn't see. Kenny came to me on the line and said if I didn't feel right I should just pull off the track right there, and in the first few laps I almost did because I couldn't see well. Then I started to feel better, and I decided to go for it.'

Chandler was fourth, Barros fifth, just one-hundredth ahead of Garriga, with DuHamel less than a tenth behind, the trio crossing the line almost three abreast. Criville was eighth, with Mackenzie losing touch at the finish to end up ninth, some way back. 'The rear tyre is the one thing we haven't had any trouble with all weekend,' he said. 'Then in the race it was awful, coming round on me everywhere.'

Mamola was tenth, able to take the last point despite losing power mid-race. Lawson was another two seconds back; and Catalano won the privateer race handsomely from Crine, Laycock and Arakaki.

250 cc PRACTICE

Cadalora led wet practice, but his warnings about the speed and good handling of the Aprilias came home to roost on a track with smooth transitions and a minimum of off-and-on throttle work. The Italian bikes were clearly faster than the Hondas on the straight, and apparently into, round and out of the corners as well. How else can you explain Chili's pole time, set (he said) 'smoothly and easily', and a full second faster than the best Honda?

Chili's 'lease-Aprilia' was only half a second ahead of Reggiani's full factory machine, now with the ill-named 'semi-active' suspension working well, though he was looking for more engine power.

Cardus was third and top Honda, mere tenths ahead of Cadalora, in a close-packed bunch of times that continued at least halfway down the tight grid. Ex-Suzuki 250 crew chief Lucas Schmidt had been promoted to fill Carruthers's shoes, while Cardus was still wondering where the Honda's top end advantage had gone.

Cadalora had been experimenting a lot and again waited until the end before going fast. 'My bike's not perfect yet, and I have more things to try tomorrow,' he said, not yet having abandoned hope.

His late charge pushed Puig's Aprilia onto row two, which he led by half a second from Bradl's Honda. Alongside him, Zeelenberg demonstrated a return to form on the works Suzuki, ahead of Doriano Romboni's kitted RS Honda. The Dutchman had a psychological rocket up his rear when Schwantz had tried his bike at the Barcelona IRTA tests. The Texan called into the pits just once to adjust front pre-load, then ran lap after fast lap with Cardus to share fastest time in the session with him. This added weight to the Lucky Strike Suzuki team's belief that it is the riders not the bikes that are having trouble getting to the front of the class.

Schmid's works Yamaha led row three, from Biaggi's Aprilia,

Left: **Early in the race, Cardus ran with the three Italians; here with Cadalora at the rear.**

'Calling me a what!' After the race, Reggiani *(left)* dubbed Cadalora 'bastard' after yet another demoralising last-lap pounce.

Capirossi's RS/Spl and Ruggia on the faster Gilera; Shimizu's works Honda led the fourth row.

Mugello is composed almost entirely of fairly fast one-line corners, and offers few opportunities to pass and many to slipstream. With privateers packed up close to the works bikes, a tight and exciting race seemed certain.

250 cc RACE – 22 LAPS

The winner's name may have been the same as usual, but this was a splendid 250 race. It had all the right dramatic ingredients, including 'Max' Biaggi starring as the impetuous youth, Reggiani as the seasoned veteran, Chili as the fall guy and Cadalora as the dastardly villain who waits until the last scene before unleashing his master-plan.

All of the above performed remarkably in one way or another. Biaggi was simply inspired, skittering over the crests and bouncing off the kerbs as he substituted raw speed for experience and tactics; ditto Reggiani, who came from nowhere to overtake the leading six bikes in the space of two laps. Cadalora – well, the stylish tactician didn't do anything he hadn't done often before.

The race started well, and got better. Cardus was first to lead, Cadalora on his tail, the pair swapping back and forth for several laps. Chili had watched and waited, and he took a run up front on lap seven; Biaggi was also in the group, but looked set to go one wobble too far at any moment.

For the first couple of laps Capirossi held fifth and was delaying the pursuit. Then Bradl burst past, with Zeelenberg on his tail, and very gradually the pair closed on the leaders. By half-distance they had caught up, making a hectic sextet – though Cardus was about to fall away behind, his tyres shot. And all the while, slow starter Reggiani was closing.

Zeelenberg, still complaining of a lack of punch out of the corners, could only hang on, using his better braking handling to regain ground lost on the front straight, but unable to get into an overtaking position. But Bradl was on fine form in spite of a dose of 'flu. In the course of one slipstreaming move he had passed five riders and led into the first turn. He stayed in front for three laps, then had a big front wheel slide and dropped back. Zeelenberg got stuck behind him again, and they gradually lost touch.

By now, Reggiani was up among the front-runners, and making a big impression. He picked his way through quickly, leading for the first time on lap 13 as the front quartet, now comprising him, Chili, Cadalora and Biaggi, continued a duel that had the 70,000-strong crowd on their feet.

Biaggi had another run up front, then it was Loris first across the line on the penultimate lap. All he had to do was to maintain his position in the hard braking into the first turn, and he could then keep the door shut for the rest of the lap.

Nobody understood this better than Cadalora, who made a supreme effort of late braking to seize control into Turn One, and to keep charging so as to secure a gap big enough for victory. Only Reggiani was fit enough to keep chasing, but with his engine off song he just didn't have the wherewithal to do it.

Biaggi, meantime, had a big slide, and in recovering swerved in front of Chili, just tipping his front wheel. The youngster survived to finish third, but Chili, who might yet have had another crack at second or even first place, was in the hay bales.

Cadalora admitted it had been one of his hardest ever races; ditto Reggiani who said, only half-jokingly: 'Cadalora is a bastard. He waits until the very last lap then runs away.' Exciting GP newcomer Biaggi (just 20) was overjoyed with his first GP rostrum, in only his fourth year of racing.

Bradl was fourth, almost five seconds back, with Zeelenberg ultimately beaten into fifth. Cardus had now fallen back into the clutches of Puig, who defeated him by less than half a second in the run to the line; Shimizu was eighth after defeating Capirossi; Romboni was tenth.

Schmid's Yamaha was 11th, and Lavado's Gilera 12th (team-mate Ruggia retired after three laps with a catastrophic power loss); then came a marvellous midfield battle that in the end comprised five bikes within the space of a second: Torrontegui's Suzuki leading Jurgen van den Goorbergh, Eskil Suter and Patrick van den Goorbergh (Aprilias) and Stefan Prein's kitted RS Honda.

125 cc RACE – 20 LAPS

Gramigni was back, obviously still in great pain and way off form, qualifying 28th, although racing bravely to 11th. Aprilia's standard-bearer was again Casanova, who performed superbly only to be struck by cruel injustice for a second race.

The first leader was Dirk Raudies, whose private Honda showed a remarkable turn of speed: even when other riders piled past in the

Less power makes for closer racing. At the start, Gresini gets the jump from Martinez and Casanova, with Hans Spaan and Waldmann just nosing into view.

corners he could get it all back again on the straight. Then it was the turn of Gianola, an enduring Italian hero climbing back to prominence on a Honda after two down years with Derbi.

Then old hand Martinez's Honda took control, and towards the end he and Casanova opened up a slight gap as they circulated in close formation. It looked as though Casanova was biding his time, waiting for a last corner dash. He never got that far.

With only a few corners left, Martinez ran too fast into a right-hand bend, almost high-sided, then ran off into the gravel trap. He just managed to stay wheels down. Casanova had been outside him, and had no choice but to hit the brakes. Inevitably he also went off, and fell in a flurry of sand. Both rejoined, Martinez to finish sixth, but Casanova had lost more time and was an angry and tearful eighth, in the middle of the gap behind the leading group.

This was serendipity for Gianola, who had dropped away and was now closing the gap again ... not fast enough to have more than an outside chance of victory. Now he was the clear winner, and didn't really mind how it had happened.

Raudies was second, narrowly the victor in the last lap dash over Ueda, who had always been in touch and had put in a strong charge in the closing stages – looking fast and scary. Just like old times, in fact.

Peter Öttl's Rotax was fourth, another two seconds down; Gresini's Honda fifth, less than a tenth ahead of Martinez. Gianola's Semprucci Honda team-mate Gabriele Debbia was seventh, with his team later blaming 'a fastidious jumping of the limber' as preventing him from achieving greater things. (Don't even ask what it means, just hope it never happens to you.)

The dusty Casanova was eighth, Koch a distant ninth, with Wakai emerging victor of a large and hectic group to take the last point from Gramigni by three-tenths. Tenth to 14th places were covered by just over half a second in this mad scramble.

Points leader Waldmann had a disastrous race. He'd been with the leading group before slowing dramatically at half-distance, and coasting into the pit, his gearbox dry of oil. The reason? None had been put in since before race morning warm-up!

6
DUNLOP
CORONAS
15
aprilia
SCOT
aprilia

Gran Premio d'Italia, 24 May/statistics

Autodromo Internazionale del Mugello, 3.259-mile/5.245-km circuit

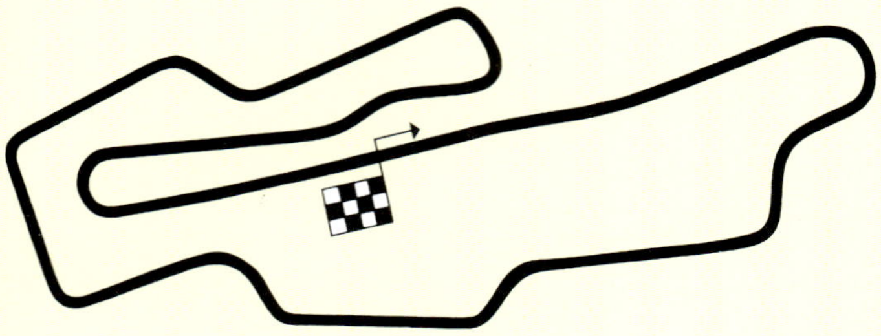

500 cc

24 laps, 78.216 miles/125.880 km

Place	Rider	Nat.	Machine	Laps	Time & speed	Fastest lap	Lap
1	**Kevin Schwantz**	USA	Suzuki	24	46m 26.225s 101.064 mph/ 162.646 km/h	1m 54.590s	5
2	**Michael Doohan**	AUS	Honda	24	46m 31.293s	1m 54.945s	5
3	**John Kocinski**	USA	Yamaha	24	46m 58.767s	1m 55.641s	23
4	**Doug Chandler**	USA	Suzuki	24	47m 02.309s	1m 56.199s	3
5	**Alexandre Barros**	BR	Cagiva	24	47m 09.831s	1m 56.808s	13
6	**Juan Garriga**	E	Yamaha	24	47m 09.842s	1m 56.887s	20
7	**Miguel DuHamel**	CAN	Yamaha	24	47m 09.936s	1m 56.829s	4
8	**Alex Criville**	E	Honda	24	47m 11.364s	1m 55.931s	3
9	**Niall Mackenzie**	GB	Yamaha	24	47m 17.119s	1m 56.409s	11
10	**Randy Mamola**	USA	Yamaha	24	47m 24.093s	1m 57.250s	7
11	Eddie Lawson	USA	Cagiva	24	47m 26.462s	1m 57.561s	7
12	Corrado Catalano	I	Yamaha	24	47m 51.985s	1m 58.183s	3
13	Thierry Crine	F	Yamaha	24	48m 03.398s	1m 58.651s	6
14	Eddie Laycock	IRL	Yamaha	24	48m 17.946s	1m 59.644s	7
15	Toshiyuki Arakaki	J	Yamaha	24	48m 18.493s	1m 58.743s	3
16	Michael Rudroff	D	Yamaha	24	48m 30.713s	1m 59.468s	6
17	Dominique Sarron	F	Yamaha	23	46m 34.002s	2m 00.082s	3
18	Juan Lopez Mella	E	Yamaha	23	46m 52.104s	2m 00.769s	14
19	Cees Doorakkers	NL	Yamaha	23	46m 52.843s	2m 00.980s	10
20	Simon Buckmaster	GB	Yamaha	23	46m 52.923s	2m 01.208s	19
21	Niggi Schmassman	CH	Yamaha	23	47m 48.617s	2m 02.842s	13
22	Peter Graves	GB	Yamaha	23	47m 59.949s	2m 03.073s	6
	Wayne Rainey	USA	Yamaha	11	DNF	1m 54.721s	10
	Serge David	CH	Yamaha	8	DNF	1m 59.625s	6
	Marco Papa	I	Librenti	7	DNF	1m 59.823s	3
	Sepp Doppler	A	Yamaha	7	DNF	2m 02.774s	3
	Lucio Pedercini	I	Paton	6	DNF	2m 05.375s	3
	Kevin Mitchell	GB	Yamaha	1	DNF	2m 10.645s	1
	Wayne Gardner	AUS	Honda		DNS		
	Claude Arciero	F	Yamaha		DNQ		
	Andreas Leuthe	D	VRP		DNQ		
	Larry Moreno	YV	Yamaha		DNQ		

Fastest lap: Schwantz, 1m 54.590s, 102.389 mph/164.779 km/h.
Lap record: Kevin Schwantz, USA (Suzuki), 1m 54.461s, 102.504 mph/164.964 km/h (1991).

Practice leaderboard: **1** Doohan, 1m 54.048s; **2** Schwantz, 1m 55.130s; **3** Rainey, 1m 55.343s; **4** Chandler, 1m 55.668s; **5** Criville, 1m 56.450s; **6** Barros, 1m 56.525s; **7** Kocinski, 1m 56.849s; **8** Gardner, 1m 56.996s; **9** Lawson, 1m 57.193s; **10** Mackenzie, 1m 57.345s; **11** Garriga, 1m 57.543s; **12** Catalano, 1m 57.561s; **13** DuHamel, 1m 57.659s; **14** Mamola, 1m 57.778s; **15** Rudroff, 1m 58.397s.

World Championship: **1** Doohan, 95; **2** Schwantz, 52; **3** Rainey, 45; **4** Chandler, 42; **5** Garriga, 22; **6** Kocinski, 20; **7** Criville and Mamola, 19; **9** Beattie and Mackenzie, 18; **11** Itoh, 10; **12** Goddard, 9; **13** Barros, 8; **14** DuHamel, 7; **15** Lawson and Ohishi, 6; **17** Honma, 3; **18** Catalano and Fujiwara, 2; **20** Laycock and Tsujimoto, 1.

250 cc

22 laps, 71.698 miles/115.390 km

Place	Rider	Nat.	Machine	Laps	Time & speed	Fastest lap	Lap
1	**Luca Cadalora**	I	Honda	22	43m 52.313s 98.058 mph/ 157.809 km/h	1m 58.062s	22
2	**Loris Reggiani**	I	Aprilia	22	43m 52.481s	1m 58.364s	22
3	**Massimiliano Biaggi**	I	Aprilia	22	43m 55.173s	1m 58.313s	21
4	**Helmut Bradl**	D	Honda	22	43m 56.904s	1m 58.714s	6
5	**Wilco Zeelenberg**	NL	Suzuki	22	43m 59.188s	1m 58.744s	7
6	**Alberto Puig**	E	Aprilia	22	44m 06.821s	1m 59.172s	17
7	**Carlos Cardus**	E	Honda	22	44m 07.209s	1m 59.208s	7
8	**Masahiro Shimizu**	J	Honda	22	44m 15.727s	1m 59.698s	17
9	**Loris Capirossi**	I	Honda	22	44m 19.616s	1m 59.936s	14
10	**Doriano Romboni**	I	Honda	22	44m 22.514s	2m 00.358s	4
11	Jochen Schmid	D	Yamaha	22	44m 28.502s	2m 00.132s	21
12	Carlos Lavado	YV	Gilera	22	44m 29.951s	1m 59.590s	17
13	Herri Torrontegui	E	Suzuki	22	44m 35.052s	2m 00.416s	14
14	Jurgen van den Goorbergh	NL	Aprilia	22	44m 35.069s	2m 00.440s	14
15	Eskil Suter	CH	Aprilia	22	44m 35.422s	2m 00.098s	16
16	Patrick van den Goorbergh	NL	Aprilia	22	44m 35.551s	2m 00.199s	17
17	Stefan Prein	D	Honda	22	44m 35.841s	2m 00.497s	3
18	Adi Stadler	D	Honda	22	44m 40.677s	2m 00.073s	16
19	Frédéric Protat	F	Aprilia	22	44m 40.693s	2m 00.487s	14
20	Andy Preining	A	Aprilia	22	44m 44.343s	2m 00.520s	15
21	Bernard Hänggeli	CH	Aprilia	22	44m 57.822s	2m 01.462s	20
22	Bernd Kassner	D	Aprilia	22	44m 57.868s	2m 01.225s	21
23	Luis D'Antin	E	Honda	22	44m 58.164s	2m 01.385s	20
24	Adrian Bosshard	CH	Honda	22	45m 30.234s	2m 02.307s	9
25	Erkka Korpiaho	SF	Aprilia	22	45m 47.630s	2m 03.187s	6
26	Jean-Pierre Jeandat	F	Honda	22	45m 53.106s	2m 03.570s	7
	Pier Francesco Chili	I	Aprilia	21	DNF	1m 58.572s	21
	Paolo Casoli	I	Yamaha	20	DNF	2m 00.434s	15
	Katsuyoshi Kozono	J	Honda	18	DNF	2m 00.465s	17
	Harald Eckl	D	Aprilia	12	DNF	2m 02.737s	9
	Renzo Colleoni	I	Yamaha	8	DNF	2m 03.456s	7
	Stefano Caracchi	I	Yamaha	5	DNF	2m 03.455s	3
	Jean-Philippe Ruggia	F	Gilera	3	DNF	2m 02.013s	2
	Yves Briguet	CH	Honda	2	DNF	2m 08.146s	2
	Bernard Cazade	F	Honda	0	DNF		

Fastest lap: Cadalora, 1m 58.062s, 99.378 mph/159.933 km/h.
Lap record: Luca Cadalora, I (Honda), 1m 57.865s, 99.544 mph/160.200 km/h (1991).

Practice leaderboard: **1** Chili, 1m 57.880s; **2** Reggiani, 1m 58.452s; **3** Cardus, 1m 58.816s; **4** Cadalora, 1m 58.867s; **5** Puig, 1m 58.970s; **6** Bradl, 1m 59.326s; **7** Zeelenberg, 1m 59.520s; **8** Romboni, 1m 59.533s; **9** Schmid, 1m 59.563s; **10** Biaggi, 1m 59.757s; **11** Capirossi, 1m 59.876s; **12** Ruggia, 2m 00.002s; **13** Shimizu, 2m 00.063s; **14** Torrontegui, 2m 00.172s; **15** Lavado, 2m 00.326s.

World Championship: **1** Cadalora, 90; **2** Bradl, 47; **3** Reggiani, 43; **4** Cardus, 37; **5** Puig, 31; **6** Chili and Zeelenberg, 26; **8** Shimizu, 18; **9** Biaggi, 16; **10** Okada, 15; **11** Romboni, 13; **12** Aoki, 12; **13** Schmid, 11; **14** Capirossi, 6; **15** Preining, 4; **16** Nanba, 3; **17** Casoli, Prein and Ruggia, 2; **20** Jeandat, 1.

Malcolm Bryan

Reggiani closes on the leading pack, topped by Cardus and tailed by Zeelenberg (4).

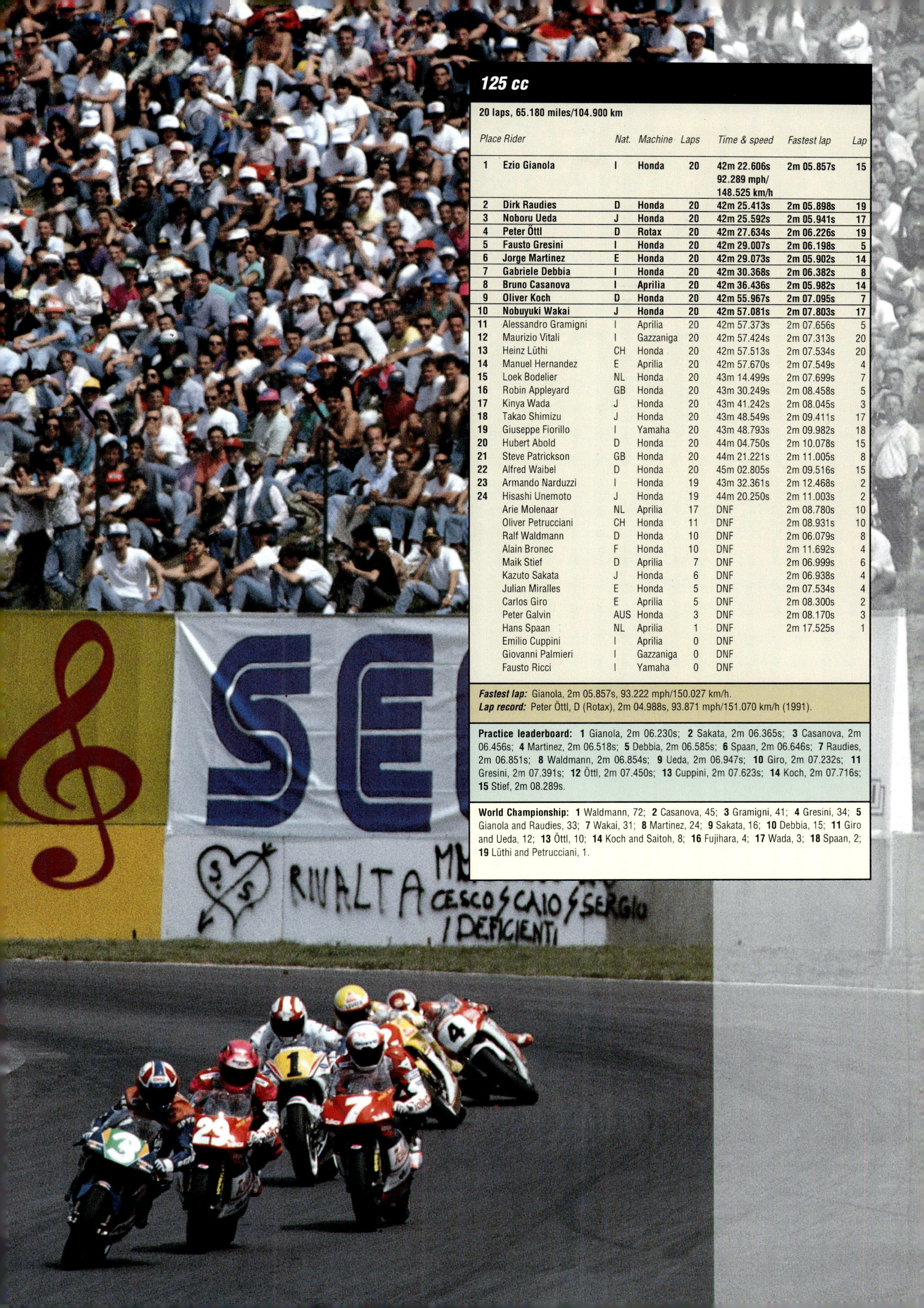

125 cc

20 laps, 65.180 miles/104.900 km

Place	Rider	Nat.	Machine	Laps	Time & speed	Fastest lap	Lap
1	**Ezio Gianola**	**I**	**Honda**	**20**	**42m 22.606s 92.289 mph/ 148.525 km/h**	**2m 05.857s**	**15**
2	**Dirk Raudies**	**D**	**Honda**	**20**	**42m 25.413s**	**2m 05.898s**	**19**
3	**Noboru Ueda**	**J**	**Honda**	**20**	**42m 25.592s**	**2m 05.941s**	**17**
4	**Peter Öttl**	**D**	**Rotax**	**20**	**42m 27.634s**	**2m 06.226s**	**19**
5	**Fausto Gresini**	**I**	**Honda**	**20**	**42m 29.007s**	**2m 06.198s**	**5**
6	**Jorge Martinez**	**E**	**Honda**	**20**	**42m 29.073s**	**2m 05.902s**	**14**
7	**Gabriele Debbia**	**I**	**Honda**	**20**	**42m 30.368s**	**2m 06.382s**	**8**
8	**Bruno Casanova**	**I**	**Aprilia**	**20**	**42m 36.436s**	**2m 05.982s**	**14**
9	**Oliver Koch**	**D**	**Honda**	**20**	**42m 55.967s**	**2m 07.095s**	**7**
10	**Nobuyuki Wakai**	**J**	**Honda**	**20**	**42m 57.081s**	**2m 07.803s**	**17**
11	Alessandro Gramigni	I	Aprilia	20	42m 57.373s	2m 07.656s	5
12	Maurizio Vitali	I	Gazzaniga	20	42m 57.424s	2m 07.313s	20
13	Heinz Lüthi	CH	Honda	20	42m 57.513s	2m 07.534s	20
14	Manuel Hernandez	E	Aprilia	20	42m 57.670s	2m 07.549s	4
15	Loek Bodelier	NL	Honda	20	43m 14.499s	2m 07.699s	7
16	Robin Appleyard	GB	Honda	20	43m 30.249s	2m 08.458s	5
17	Kinya Wada	J	Honda	20	43m 41.242s	2m 08.045s	3
18	Takao Shimizu	J	Honda	20	43m 48.549s	2m 09.411s	17
19	Giuseppe Fiorillo	I	Yamaha	20	43m 48.793s	2m 09.982s	18
20	Hubert Abold	D	Honda	20	44m 04.750s	2m 10.078s	15
21	Steve Patrickson	GB	Honda	20	44m 21.221s	2m 11.005s	8
22	Alfred Waibel	D	Honda	20	45m 02.805s	2m 09.516s	15
23	Armando Narduzzi	I	Honda	19	43m 32.361s	2m 12.468s	2
24	Hisashi Unemoto	J	Honda	19	44m 20.250s	2m 11.003s	2
	Arie Molenaar	NL	Aprilia	17	DNF	2m 08.780s	10
	Oliver Petrucciani	CH	Honda	11	DNF	2m 08.931s	10
	Ralf Waldmann	D	Honda	10	DNF	2m 06.079s	8
	Alain Bronec	F	Honda	10	DNF	2m 11.692s	4
	Maik Stief	D	Aprilia	7	DNF	2m 06.999s	6
	Kazuto Sakata	J	Honda	6	DNF	2m 06.938s	4
	Julian Miralles	E	Honda	5	DNF	2m 07.534s	4
	Carlos Giro	E	Aprilia	5	DNF	2m 08.300s	2
	Peter Galvin	AUS	Honda	3	DNF	2m 08.170s	3
	Hans Spaan	NL	Aprilia	1	DNF	2m 17.525s	1
	Emilio Cuppini	I	Aprilia	0	DNF		
	Giovanni Palmieri	I	Gazzaniga	0	DNF		
	Fausto Ricci	I	Yamaha	0	DNF		

Fastest lap: Gianola, 2m 05.857s, 93.222 mph/150.027 km/h.
Lap record: Peter Öttl, D (Rotax), 2m 04.988s, 93.871 mph/151.070 km/h (1991).

Practice leaderboard: **1** Gianola, 2m 06.230s; **2** Sakata, 2m 06.365s; **3** Casanova, 2m 06.456s; **4** Martinez, 2m 06.518s; **5** Debbia, 2m 06.585s; **6** Spaan, 2m 06.646s; **7** Raudies, 2m 06.851s; **8** Waldmann, 2m 06.854s; **9** Ueda, 2m 06.947s; **10** Giro, 2m 07.232s; **11** Gresini, 2m 07.391s; **12** Öttl, 2m 07.450s; **13** Cuppini, 2m 07.623s; **14** Koch, 2m 07.716s; **15** Stief, 2m 08.289s.

World Championship: **1** Waldmann, 72; **2** Casanova, 45; **3** Gramigni, 41; **4** Gresini, 34; **5** Gianola and Raudies, 33; **7** Wakai, 31; **8** Martinez, 24; **9** Sakata, 16; **10** Debbia, 15; **11** Giro and Ueda, 12; **13** Öttl, 10; **14** Koch and Saitoh, 8; **16** Fujihara, 4; **17** Wada, 3; **18** Spaan, 2; **19** Lüthi and Petrucciani, 1.

500 cc	RAINEY
250 cc	CADALORA
125 cc	GIANOLA

GRAND PRIX OF EUROPE

Photos: Malcolm Bryan

It was dark inside the motorhome, and the sound of racing engines came from the TV loudspeaker. Inside sat Michael Doohan and Niall Mackenzie, consoling one another for their race difficulties, and watching Nigel Mansell cruise to what seemed certain to be another tediously predictable victory in the Monaco GP.

'See how boring it gets when the same person wins all the time,' suggested an attendant on this scene. 'Yeah, well,' said Doohan, grinning ruefully. 'I bet he doesn't think it's boring.'

In fact, Mansell didn't win the race, foiled by tyre failure. Doohan hadn't won either, taking his second defeat in a row after earlier appearing to be invincible, this time at the hands of Rainey's Yamaha. Ironically, his whisper-close second place had been enough to continue to stretch his title lead, and the mathematics of the championship entered a new phase, because from now on the Australian didn't need to win any more races: he had amassed enough points to be safe even if he only came second.

Opposite page: **A to-and-fro track offered few passing places. This is where Doohan (here leading) failed to repass Rainey on the last lap. Lawson is still third, then Schwantz, Kocinski and Chandler.**

Lawson's lead was short-lived but served warning of better things to come. Behind him Rainey, Kocinski, Doohan, Schwantz and Chandler jostle into the first chicane. Fast-starting DuHamel and Japanese privateer Arakaki are behind.

The strange thing about the new 6000-million-peseta race track of Catalunya, sprawling impressively in hilly country just outside Barcelona, was the bumps. A new track should surely be free from the wave-bumps that have appeared in the last decade or so at established GP circuits – Montmelo proved this not to be so.

Of course tracks *should* be smooth, but while Montmelo was new to bikes, there had already been two car GPs there, and the bumps were symptomatic of the fact that modern F1 cars, with fat tyres and down-force bodywork, develop so much traction – especially under braking – that there is apparently no surface that can resist distortion. The result was to be found almost all the way round the fine new track – rolling whoops that upset equilibrium on the way into and through the otherwise finely flowing bends. 'On the long corners', said Schwantz, 'it feels like your tyres are out of round.'

Another hazard of using tracks where cars are the first consideration also came to the fore at Catalunya: the differing safety requirements. Thus Montmelo has generous gravel pit run-off in the early part of the corners, but in too many places exit run-off has been compromised by the terrain, and concrete walls are much too close to the track.

Since corner exits are the favourite place for racing bike crashes, you may imagine there were a string of complaints from the riders. These had been voiced at the IRTA test session there two weeks before, and the organisers had responded promptly by installing 300 metres of air-fencing – a new type of progressive collapse barrier developed in Australia, and now used for the first time in bike GP racing at three particularly hazardous sites.

In the event, nobody tested its efficacy. Instead, Ralf Waldmann slid head first at speed into a tyre wall during practice, happily bouncing almost straight onto his feet and running directly back to the pits to fetch his spare bike. In the fickle way of things, the only bad accident had nothing to do with track safety. On lap two of the 250 race, Shimizu was flipped off in the leading bunch, and Wilco Zeelenberg, on his tail, was unable to avoid the Honda sliding beneath his front wheel. Running fast in fourth gear, he was launched high into the air, landing safely in the sand trap, though heavily enough to break his left ankle badly, as well as his collarbone.

Wave-bumps aside, the track was popular – offering an interesting combination of corners and a reasonably fast straight. It comprised two loops up and off the hillside – the first incorporating some fast right-handers and a distinctly interesting downhill off-camber left-hand hairpin. Most overtaking took place at the chicane at the end of the start-finish straight, or at a slow left-hander on the second loop; but there was room for opportunistic riding elsewhere, and a variety of challenges to man and machine.

Particularly tyres. Michelin had been under pressure to produce a better front, notably for Rainey's Yamaha, so he could return to the aggressive corner entry style that is his forte, but which had caused him to crash at Mugello the week before. Here they had a new profile, dubbed 'the triangular tyre', which all the works riders tried and most used for the race. (Not Schwantz and Chandler, however, and the former's pit crew blamed time wasted with the new tyre in practice for his defeat by his team-mate.)

Yamaha, meanwhile, had knocked up and tested a revised chassis – to Team Roberts's specifications – for Magee in Japan. Tests had been encouraging, but instead of building it themselves, Yamaha commissioned Serge Rosset's Roc outfit to modify an existing frame in France, thereby saving two weeks on delivery time.

The last piece of the defending champion's victory jigsaw was simpler. Rainey blamed his Mugello crash on a lack of strength and the inability to bend his still stiff right leg fully on the preceding right-hander. Now his team lowered the right footrest so he could get his toes hard on the peg, to use his weight more effectively. And thus came his first victory of the season.

There was a small renaissance over at Cagiva as well. The team had stayed on to test at Mugello, and what Lawson described as a radical experiment in bike set-up had resulted in an equally radical improvement of better than two seconds in lap times. Eddie managed to bring this with him, to achieve a moment of glory by leading the first lap. His charge into the chicane, from the third row of the grid, gave all the other riders a lesson in how to leave the line.

One rider who is having unexpected difficulty learning is Kocinski, whose progress to race-winning form remained maddeningly slow. Now he spoke more about the illness that has plagued his whole season, admitting that he'd been troubled by it for far longer than he'd said before and that doctors were baffled by what had better be called a mystery virus. He was wearing glasses off the bike, fuelling speculation about vision problems, which he denied. 'The way I've been feeling has meant that I haven't been able to race or even to test to the maximum all year long, and that's been holding me back,' he explained. 'We're developing the chassis along different lines from Rainey, but I haven't been strong enough to push development ahead.' While the others were now settled into their motorhomes, Kocinski was still staying in hotels and had a tiny rented caravan as his paddock home. 'It's only for changing in,' he said – changing outside the door as usual. Abandonment of his huge motorhome was part of his sports psychologist's therapy – the obsessive young American was prone to stay up late at night cleaning it, instead of getting a good night's sleep before the race.

A marvellously Machiavellian story concerning the finest hams in Italy amused watchers of the 125 class imbroglio. The bone of contention arose from the fact that the Semprucci Hondas of Ezio Gianola and Gabriele Debbia seemed to be faster than the Marlboro Team Pileri bikes of Fausto Gresini and Noboru Ueda. This should not have been possible, since the latter team had top level Honda 'A' kit engines while the Semprucci mob had to rely on their own development. Pileri's men suspected dirty work, since their 'A' kits had arrived unaccountably late via Honda Italy. Enter the ham – a prize gourmet dish from Lecco, home to some of the finest hams in Italy. Gianola also happens to hail from there, and the suggestion was that the delay in delivery of the kits happened when somebody in Honda Italy enjoyed a ham sent by Gianola, while Semprucci spies were able to copy HRC's finest 125 engineering.

There was a restrained atmosphere in the paddock – the result of an IRTA ban on fireworks, with the threat that at the first explosion they would immediately impose a $1000 fine on Mamola, on the assumption that he would inevitably be the guilty party. This was the result of a post-race dust-up with the police late after the Italian GP, when Schwantz had been briefly arrested by over-zealous *carabinieri*, before matters had been smoothed over. In Spain, however, big bangs are a way of life, and the crowd was under no such restrictions.

There was another kind of atmosphere as well, that everybody wished could somehow be restrained. With its spick-and-span pits and brand new access roads, the circuit was a showpiece. But it had been built uncomfortably close to a large abattoir. Saturday morning practice was marked by a pervasive stench in pit lane, as though there was a 60-ft dead rat somewhere nearby. Luckily the wind changed for race day. At last, a rival in Europe for the open paddock drains of Malaysia.

500 cc PRACTICE

The morning sessions were slowed by rain and Doohan dominated when it mattered, in the afternoons. His fifth successive pole in six races came by almost a full second after he'd raised overall gearing to compensate for the bike's unwillingness to over-rev in some corner entries. He was using an alternative engine combination for the first time, intended to rev more quickly than the earlier sluggish-feeling engine.

All the usual stuff obtained – he would like to get a good start; tyres would be important (particularly piquant after his Mugello problems); the race was more important than practice and there were no foregone conclusions. He's a guarded personality, and being so superior once again didn't change that – even though the breakdown of lap times showed that Doohan was able to run consistent fast laps and his rivals only managed the odd one that was

Malcolm Bryan

still short of the Honda. But the Australian was prepared to be more outspoken in his criticism of fellow-Honda rider, Alex Criville, who had qualified third fastest on the strength of a time set on the first day of practice when he'd been following close on Doohan's wheel-tracks. 'I don't want to fall off and have him run over me,' said Doohan.

Criville was deposed from second in the last minutes by Kocinski, with a flash time. 'That was my best qualifying this year,' he said. 'I just put some tyres on and went for it.'

With Criville third, Rainey took the final first-row position, electing to stick with the bike he knew. Although the new chassis solved some of his problems, he needed more time than two dry qualifying sessions. 'The weather really hurt us,' he said.

Doohan was the only one below 1m 49s; the rest of the front row were below 1m 50s. Then came last weekend's winner, Kevin Schwantz, three-tenths behind Rainey. 'We're still chasing tyres – the bike's going well and seems fast, but it's a matter of getting the power down,' the Suzuki rider said. He'd shown well in the wet, but while he tried to convince himself the track was enough like Mugello for him to challenge Doohan again, a gap of 1.5 seconds yawned in his face and he would need more than blind optimism.

Mackenzie's Yamaha was barely three-thousandths slower, but seemed less threatening because he was another one to set a flash time in the closing minutes. He had a new fairing designed by team (and Roc) boss Rosset, shipping more air both for induction and cooling, but he was suffering from a shortage of the latest Michelin rubber. 'It's been a matter of forcing tyres out of them,' he said.

Chandler was next after cutting almost a second off his first day's time. He was, as ever, searching for ways to put more weight on the front, and could be seen leaning his rangy frame all over the handlebars. This time, though, he hadn't finished his experiments by the end of practice.

Alex Barros was the last man on the second row, slotting the Cagiva three-tenths behind Chandler on the strength of a first day time. Garriga led row three, saying: 'I'm still getting used to the Michelins. You have to change the bike completely, but they give a better feeling of tyre grip and suspension working than the Dunlops.' He had Lawson alongside, then Mamola and DuHamel.

Peter Goddard led row four, the Australian back as top privateer in spite of still riding tentatively because of the right hand injuries he'd sustained here two weeks ago in his fastest-ever accident. He led Arakaki, Crine and Catalano at the head of a pack of works-replica Yamahas. There were 30 qualifiers out of 32 entrants.

Different strokes – Chandler leans heavily on the front, Schwantz looks more agile as the Suzuki team-mates fight it out ahead of Kocinski.

500 cc RACE – 26 LAPS

A warning of things to come from Lawson's Red Rocket: while the riders from the front two rows fanned this way and that to try and seize an advantage after the sprint to the chicane, the ex-World Champion arrowed through from the second row, head down, and stole the first corner. He was to lead for the first full lap – a sight for sore eyes – even though he gradually dropped back to sixth. Later he praised the straight-line speed of his Cagiva. 'In high gears it was the fastest bike here – but I got left on pick-up, and I had a problem with chewing up the front tyre,' he said.

Doohan was first past the American, slipstreaming as they flashed by the pits, and outbraking him into the chicane. Rainey was also ahead by lap three, and the battle for the race was on.

The lap chart read like most races so far. Doohan was always in front, until the very end. But Rainey was always behind, and always close. The gap was never more than a second, often half that, and Rainey proved able to match every move.

Doohan kept pushing the pace, and grew increasingly nonplussed. 'I was surprised that he could stay with me when we were going more than half a second faster than he qualified,' said Doohan. But he'd raced here at last year's post-season Superprestigio, and added: 'I figured from that race it would be hard to lose anyone here, and though I tried I couldn't shake him off.'

Rainey was indeed tenacious, and more – for with three laps left he drafted past Doohan at the end of the pit straight, and set about making a break for himself. The same rules applied to him, however, and matters were further complicated because they were running into some of the faster back-markers. Although, by and large, the luck was even, the interruptions meant Doohan couldn't put up a sustained overtaking bid.

On the penultimate lap, Rainey got past Michael Rudroff into the downhill hairpin, while Doohan had to wait for two more corners. This meant that, instead of lining himself up to pounce, he had to work hard to get back in touch. He arrived at the last left-hander just too late, his outbraking move falling inches short, and appraising Rainey of what to expect on the next and final time around. 'I was usually quicker through there, but I just wasn't close enough,' said Doohan. Nor did Rainey give him another chance.

Doohan tried one last time, with a fine sweeping exit from the final turn. But it was a doomed attempt, as he knew.

Rainey was jubilant to be back on top after some eight months. 'It's been a long time,' he said. 'I feel I've held the team back with my physical problems because of my accident last year. This race, for the first time I could go round right-handers without feeling like a duck.' Later that evening, at the team's riotous first victory dinner, somewhat inebriated, he embarrassed himself and the Japanese attendants by saying: 'I want to thank Yamaha. For nothing.' *In vino veritas*, and the moment passed.

The new profile Michelin played a crucial part in the race, and especially in the battle for third, which by the finish was some 15 seconds behind. For the first half of the race Kocinski had been part of it, but he'd taken Michelin's advice to go triangular against his own preference, saying later that he knew he was in trouble from the first turn. 'I kept losing the front at the apex, and I couldn't use the lines I liked or get my rhythm. In some turns I was running first gear where I had been using second.' Even so, he had battled back and forth with the two Suzukis of Schwantz and Chandler, until eventually he ran so wide in one turn that they broke free as he struggled to regain momentum.

Schwantz did most of the leading, with Chandler lurking and awaiting the chance of an end-of-race attack – and taking an object lesson. 'Whenever I was behind Kevin and Kocinski they were going into the corners much faster than me and pulling me with them, then I'd be pushing the front. When I pulled back and decided to do it my own way, braking harder then accelerating through, I could get somewhere.' That somewhere was ahead of his team-mate, and Chandler secured third under the fiercest pressure, swapping back and forth with Schwantz over and over again, to take his first dry weather rostrum. Kevin had given everything, and came back to his pit with grass trapped in his knee-slider. His reaction to being beaten for the first time in the dry by another Suzuki? 'He was just another guy out there that I was trying to race.'

With Schwantz fourth, Kocinski fifth and Lawson sixth, there was another big battle for seventh, won eventually by Mackenzie. He'd been obliged to battle through the traffic from 15th on lap one. 'I'd have been satisfied with my normal bad start,' he said later. 'But Criville whacked into me.' (Criville had pulled a big wheelie on the front row, and when he landed he ran across into the Yamaha.)

By the end, Mackenzie had pulled up to duke it out with team-mate DuHamel, whose bike was faster. 'He was holding me up on the twists, otherwise we might have closed on Lawson,' said Mackenzie. They finished less than eight seconds behind the Cagiva and less than a second apart, with Mamola right on DuHamel's tail. He'd also taken a chance and used the triangular front tyre. 'I could brake good, but I couldn't get past them,' he said.

This trio had outdistanced Garriga, the Spaniard taking the last point; Barros was 11th, just a tenth ahead of Goddard's Roc.

There were 24 finishers, Criville retiring with 17 laps left after dropping back to 13th place from his bodged start. He complained of a lack of top-end power and a reluctance to rev; cynical rivals said that he didn't have anyone fast to follow.

For a second race in succession Doohan increased his championship lead without winning, because Rainey displaced Schwantz from second place in the points table.

Right: Max Biaggi's second rostrum finish in as many races confirmed the birth of a new star.

Pole-starter Gianola is already breaking from Raudies, Casanova and the rest of the 125 pack. Team-mate Debbia (4) will catch up and lead for most of the race – but not the last lap.

Photos: Malcolm Bryan

Ruggia shows the Gilera's air-intake/fairing supports on his way to his second points of the year.

250 cc PRACTICE

Biaggi marked another milestone in his brilliant year with his first pole. The 20-year-old slotted his Aprilia in by almost two-tenths in the very last lap of practice, displacing Cadalora, also after a last-minute charge. Biaggi had been suffering all week from stomach problems, and had visited Dr Costa again that morning; his Aprilia, however, was perfect and needed no medical attention.

Cadalora was still experimenting in the last practice session, as usual, but went back to his earlier gearbox and suspension settings to secure his front-row start. His only worry was the chance of race day rain. He had been second fastest in the wet, but felt the track was dangerously slippery.

Bradl, fastest in the wet, was third overall after missing the first 'untimed' practice session altogether ... his specially chartered private aircraft was delayed. He'd made up for lost time, though, and said: 'It's about time I made a good start. I'm tired of being in tenth after the first lap and then using up my tyres catching up.'

Fellow-countryman Schmid completed row one on the ever-improving factory Yamaha. For a second race he was using a prototype of what the same people who called electronic rear suspension adjustment 'active suspension' were calling a 'semi-automatic gearbox'. Nothing of the sort, of course, but rather incorporating elements of the drag racing air shifters, as well as a control mechanism reminiscent of the dreaded Triumph 'slick-shift' of the Fifties. The modern version, prompted by gear pedal pressure in the direction of upshifts only, momentarily cuts the ignition, allowing clutchless full throttle upward changes.

Reggiani led row two, technicians still fine-tuning his electronic suspension, which he said was better, but should by rights have helped him more over the Montmelo mounds. Chili, alongside, was complaining of unpredictable performance from his front suspension.

Then came the Suzuki of Zeelenberg, continuing his improvement in form, well up in a close batch of times which put the first nine within the same second. Puig's Aprilia completed row two; Cardus led row three, but he fell heavily in the final session, and was to retire from the race as a result.

Gilera had added former Ohlins suspension guru Lars Osth to their team, and Ruggia was a strong tenth fastest, with team-mate Lavado 12th, and Romboni's Honda RS/Spl in between them, after yet another dose of special parts from Japan.

250 cc RACE – 24 LAPS

The last race of the day started promptly, Biaggi taking an immediate lead from Reggiani, with Cadalora in third place. The big crash with Zeelenberg and Shimizu happened just behind the front-runners as they crested the hill on the second lap, with Bradl and Romboni lucky to escape involvement. Not so Capirossi and a few yards further on the promising young Dutchman, Jurgen van den Goorbergh, both unhurt.

The race soon settled into a pattern almost identical to the previous weekend's, with the leading quartet comprising the Aprilias of Biaggi and Reggiani and the Hondas of Cadalora and Bradl, and not much in it. The Aprilias shared the honours for leading past the flag, but Cadalora was in front several times, and the positions were changing several times a lap.

Bradl was the only one who couldn't get to the front, saying later: 'My problem was that my third gear was too short, so I would lose the draft onto the straights. I could make it up again under braking, but I was never close enough to pass.'

So it would inevitably come down to the familiar last-lap battle. Cadalora led across the line for the second to last time, then he and the Aprilias moved three abreast into the first chicane, a major passing point. It looked as though Reggiani had the inside line, but when they came out the other side the amazing Cadalora was still in front.

Biaggi also had a stab at passing the Honda, but once again Cadalora proved to have enough in reserve, and he led his fellow-Italians Reggiani and Biaggi across the line by less than half a second, with Bradl a similar distance behind.

'I don't know where he hides his reserves,' said Bradl afterwards; while Reggiani remarked: 'Any one of the three of us could have won, but Luca had more chances, and they have got a lot more power out of the Honda.'

Luca was reserved, as usual, and said: 'The secret lay in the trials we did in Italy where we discovered a problem with the engine. Now I have an engine fit for an Aprilia.' Privately, he told his team: 'I could have passed them anywhere.' But he must have been at least as sincere when he told the press: 'I hope the next races are a bit calmer.'

Schmid was fifth on the Yamaha, ten seconds adrift in a race depleted by the crash and the withdrawal of Cardus. A similar distance back was Chili's Aprilia, a lone sixth. He had been tussling with an on-form Herri Torrontegui on the surviving Suzuki, but the Spaniard took an excursion off the track and was forced to retire with dirt in his engine. Romboni was seventh; Puig narrowly defeated Ruggia for eighth, with Casoli's Yamaha taking the last point.

Reggiani claimed the lap record, but Cadalora the major prize. His championship total equalled Doohan's on 110, and his lead was even larger.

125 cc RACE – 22 LAPS

The first race of the day started in patchy sunlight, with Italian winner Gianola leading from the start. He and Semprucci Honda team-mate Debbia both had a new rising rate rear suspension rather than the stock monoshock, and it obviously worked, because they pulled away from the tenth lap, with Gianola letting Debbia take the lead at that point.

Gianola shadowed his team-mate for the rest of the race, then forced past him at the start of the final lap to take his second win in succession. Had they merely been following team orders, he was asked? 'Our orders were to go out there and gas it,' the wiry class veteran replied.

In their wake they left a five-bike battle, which was won after much to-and-fro by Gresini, angry at being outpowered. He was three-tenths ahead of Gramigni, who was a similar distance ahead of Raudies, with Charlie Giro's Aprilia just another half-second back. In the final sprint they had left Casanova trailing.

Ueda was eighth, having survived a late attack from Peter Öttl when the German broke his gear linkage; Nobuyuki Wakai defeated Jorge Martinez for ninth after a race-long Honda battle.

Points leader Ralf Waldmann finished a distant 12th, unable to get on terms after his rear tyre started sliding when he was closing on the leaders early in the race. He still led on points, but Gianola was closing fast, and Gramigni and Casanova were close behind. What a championship.

Grand Prix of Europe, 31 May/statistics

Circuit de Catalunya, Barcelona, 2.949-mile/4.747-km circuit

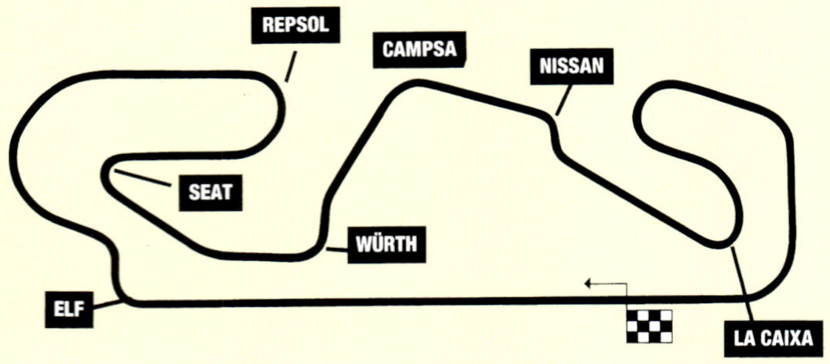

500 cc

26 laps, 76.674 miles/123.422 km

Place	Rider	Nat.	Machine	Laps	Time & speed	Fastest lap	Lap
1	**Wayne Rainey**	**USA**	**Yamaha**	**26**	**47m 31.348s 96.827 mph/ 155.828 km/h**	**1m 48.807s**	**26**
2	**Michael Doohan**	**AUS**	**Honda**	**26**	**47m 31.405s**	**1m 48.583s**	**26**
3	**Doug Chandler**	**USA**	**Suzuki**	**26**	**47m 46.110s**	**1m 48.780s**	**26**
4	**Kevin Schwantz**	**USA**	**Suzuki**	**26**	**47m 47.681s**	**1m 49.085s**	**22**
5	**John Kocinski**	**USA**	**Yamaha**	**26**	**47m 59.495s**	**1m 49.794s**	**18**
6	**Eddie Lawson**	**USA**	**Cagiva**	**26**	**48m 06.922s**	**1m 50.263s**	**10**
7	**Niall Mackenzie**	**GB**	**Yamaha**	**26**	**48m 14.161s**	**1m 49.828s**	**11**
8	**Miguel DuHamel**	**CAN**	**Yamaha**	**26**	**48m 15.153s**	**1m 50.136s**	**23**
9	**Randy Mamola**	**USA**	**Yamaha**	**26**	**48m 15.500s**	**1m 50.471s**	**17**
10	**Juan Garriga**	**E**	**Yamaha**	**26**	**48m 20.736s**	**1m 50.543s**	**18**
11	Alexandre Barros	BR	Cagiva	26	48m 42.567s	1m 50.944s	7
12	Peter Goddard	AUS	Yamaha	26	48m 42.649s	1m 51.684s	16
13	Thierry Crine	F	Yamaha	26	48m 59.944s	1m 51.851s	25
14	Toshiyuki Arakaki	J	Yamaha	26	48m 59.993s	1m 51.447s	23
15	Juan Lopez Mella	E	Yamaha	26	49m 11.690s	1m 52.526s	15
16	Kevin Mitchell	GB	Yamaha	26	49m 13.165s	1m 52.633s	10
17	Dominique Sarron	F	Yamaha	25	47m 37.256s	1m 53.246s	6
18	Michael Rudroff	D	Yamaha	25	47m 39.033s	1m 53.191s	18
19	Eddie Laycock	IRL	Yamaha	25	47m 41.399s	1m 53.292s	9
20	Serge David	CH	Yamaha	25	48m 11.211s	1m 53.507s	6
21	Niggi Schmassman	CH	Yamaha	25	48m 59.784s	1m 55.381s	4
22	Marco Papa	I	Librenti	25	49m 06.077s	1m 56.021s	3
23	Lucio Pedercini	I	Paton	24	47m 37.104s	1m 57.333s	9
24	Sepp Doppler	A	Yamaha	24	47m 43.472s	1m 57.637s	10
	Cees Doorakkers	NL	Yamaha	24	DNF	1m 53.824s	8
	Simon Buckmaster	GB	Yamaha	24	DNF	1m 54.511s	23
	Claude Arciero	F	Yamaha	11	DNF	1m 58.035s	8
	Alex Criville	E	Honda	9	DNF	1m 51.073s	4
	Corrado Catalano	I	Yamaha	8	DNF	1m 53.200s	3
	Peter Graves	GB	Yamaha	0	DNF		
	Andreas Leuthe	D	VRP		DNQ		
	Larry Moreno	YV	Yamaha		DNQ		

Fastest lap: Doohan, 1m 48.583s, 97.794 mph/157.384 km/h (record).
Previous record: none.

Practice leaderboard: **1** Doohan, 1m 48.549s; **2** Kocinski, 1m 49.492s; **3** Criville, 1m 49.533s; **4** Rainey, 1m 49.814s; **5** Schwantz, 1m 50.167s; **6** Mackenzie, 1m 50.170s; **7** Chandler, 1m 50.235s; **8** Barros, 1m 50.581s; **9** Garriga, 1m 50.652s; **10** Lawson, 1m 50.674s; **11** Mamola, 1m 50.744s; **12** DuHamel, 1m 50.940s; **13** Goddard, 1m 51.454s; **14** Arakaki, 1m 51.627s; **15** Crine, 1m 51.956s.

World Championship: **1** Doohan, 110; **2** Rainey, 65; **3** Schwantz, 62; **4** Chandler, 54; **5** Kocinski, 28; **6** Garriga, 23; **7** Mackenzie, 22; **8** Mamola, 21; **9** Criville, 19; **10** Beattie, 18; **11** Lawson, 12; **12** DuHamel and Itoh, 10; **14** Goddard, 9; **15** Barros, 8; **16** Ohishi, 6; **17** Honma, 3; **18** Catalano and Fujiwara, 2; **20** Laycock and Tsujimoto, 1.

250 cc

24 laps, 70.776 miles/113.928 km

Place	Rider	Nat.	Machine	Laps	Time & speed	Fastest lap	Lap
1	**Luca Cadalora**	I	Honda	24	45m 03.411s 94.270 mph/ 151.712 km/h	1m 51.488s	24
2	**Loris Reggiani**	I	Aprilia	24	45m 03.651s	1m 51.304s	24
3	**Massimiliano Biaggi**	I	Aprilia	24	45m 03.834s	1m 51.592s	23
4	**Helmut Bradl**	D	Honda	24	45m 04.314s	1m 51.362s	2
5	**Jochen Schmid**	D	Yamaha	24	45m 13.863s	1m 52.010s	19
6	**Pier Francesco Chili**	I	Aprilia	24	45m 21.506s	1m 52.150s	18
7	**Doriano Romboni**	I	Honda	24	45m 28.587s	1m 52.679s	6
8	**Alberto Puig**	E	Aprilia	24	45m 35.639s	1m 52.467s	8
9	**Jean-Philippe Ruggia**	F	Gilera	24	45m 37.702s	1m 52.657s	22
10	**Paolo Casoli**	I	Yamaha	24	45m 52.551s	1m 53.444s	3
11	Andy Preining	A	Aprilia	24	46m 08.808s	1m 54.008s	10
12	Frédéric Protat	F	Aprilia	24	46m 22.953s	1m 54.536s	16
13	Eskil Suter	CH	Aprilia	24	46m 26.640s	1m 54.805s	5
14	Bernard Hänggeli	CH	Aprilia	24	46m 27.449s	1m 54.369s	24
15	Luis D'Antin	E	Honda	24	46m 28.258s	1m 54.966s	17
16	Erkka Korpiaho	SF	Aprilia	24	46m 28.516s	1m 55.027s	11
17	Stefan Prein	D	Honda	24	46m 30.552s	1m 54.601s	10
18	Adi Stadler	D	Honda	24	46m 41.914s	1m 55.245s	2
19	Jean-Pierre Jeandat	F	Honda	24	46m 42.900s	1m 55.586s	3
20	Michele Gallina	I	Yamaha	24	46m 43.155s	1m 55.560s	17
21	Yves Briguet	CH	Honda	23	45m 06.735s	1m 55.545s	11
22	Javier Rodriguez	E	Honda	23	45m 35.065s	1m 57.698s	2
	Bernard Cazade	F	Honda	19	DNF	1m 57.978s	16
	Herri Torrontegui	E	Suzuki	15	DNF	1m 52.628s	4
	Harald Eckl	D	Aprilia	10	DNF	1m 55.473s	10
	Carlos Lavado	YV	Gilera	8	DNF	1m 54.560s	7
	Patrick van den Goorbergh	NL	Aprilia	8	DNF	1m 59.729s	7
	Carlos Cardus	E	Honda	5	DNF	1m 54.856s	4
	Katsuyoshi Kozono	J	Honda	3	DNF	1m 55.915s	3
	Masahiro Shimizu	J	Honda	1	DNF	1m 59.689s	1
	Wilco Zeelenberg	NL	Suzuki	1	DNF	2m 00.215s	1
	Loris Capirossi	I	Honda	1	DNF	2m 00.899s	1
	Jurgen van den Goorbergh	NL	Aprilia	1	DNF	2m 01.898s	1
	Bernd Kassner	D	Aprilia	0	DNF		
	Adrian Bosshard	CH	Honda	0	DNF		

Fastest lap: Reggiani, 1m 51.304s, 95.403 mph/153.536 km/h (record).
Previous record: none.

Practice leaderboard: 1 Biaggi, 1m 50.819s; **2** Cadalora, 1m 50.998s; **3** Bradl, 1m 51.314s; **4** Schmid, 1m 51.471s; **5** Reggiani, 1m 51.560s; **6** Chili, 1m 51.614s; **7** Zeelenberg, 1m 51.765s; **8** Puig, 1m 51.775s; **9** Cardus, 1m 51.813s; **10** Ruggia, 1m 52.314s; **11** Romboni, 1m 52.444s; **12** Lavado, 1m 52.448s; **13** Capirossi, 1m 52.640s; **14** Shimizu, 1m 52.757s; **15** Preining, 1m 52.830s.

World Championship: 1 Cadalora, 110; **2** Reggiani, 58; **3** Bradl, 57; **4** Cardus, 37; **5** Puig, 34; **6** Chili, 32; **7** Biaggi, 28; **8** Zeelenberg, 26; **9** Schmid, 19; **10** Shimizu, 18; **11** Romboni, 17; **12** Okada, 15; **13** Aoki, 12; **14** Capirossi, 6; **15** Preining and Ruggia, 4; **17** Casoli and Nanba, 3; **19** Prein, 2; **20** Jeandat, 1.

125 cc

22 laps, 64.878 miles/104.434 km

Place	Rider	Nat.	Machine	Laps	Time & speed	Fastest lap	Lap
1	**Ezio Gianola**	I	Honda	22	43m 35.994s 89.302 mph/ 143.717 km/h	1m 58.090s	4
2	**Gabriele Debbia**	I	Honda	22	43m 36.068s	1m 57.909s	6
3	**Fausto Gresini**	I	Honda	22	43m 42.622s	1m 58.224s	6
4	**Alessandro Gramigni**	I	Aprilia	22	43m 42.950s	1m 58.006s	5
5	**Dirk Raudies**	D	Honda	22	43m 43.174s	1m 58.318s	5
6	**Carlos Giro**	E	Aprilia	22	43m 43.620s	1m 57.836s	7
7	**Bruno Casanova**	I	Aprilia	22	43m 47.232s	1m 58.295s	9
8	**Noboru Ueda**	J	Honda	22	44m 02.125s	1m 58.924s	4
9	**Nobuyuki Wakai**	J	Honda	22	44m 04.495s	1m 59.251s	12
10	**Jorge Martinez**	E	Honda	22	44m 04.723s	1m 59.025s	7
11	Hans Spaan	NL	Aprilia	22	44m 10.735s	1m 59.140s	12
12	Ralf Waldmann	D	Honda	22	44m 21.368s	1m 58.854s	5
13	Maik Stief	D	Aprilia	22	44m 34.461s	1m 59.572s	5
14	Juan Borja	E	Honda	22	44m 37.349s	1m 59.856s	8
15	Manuel Hernandez	E	Aprilia	22	44m 37.472s	2m 00.445s	3
16	Alain Bronec	F	Honda	22	44m 41.602s	2m 00.617s	13
17	Julian Miralles	E	Honda	22	44m 45.130s	2m 00.158s	6
18	Hisashi Unemoto	J	Honda	22	44m 45.136s	2m 00.769s	7
19	Oliver Petrucciani	CH	Honda	22	44m 56.699s	1m 59.954s	14
20	Giovanni Palmieri	CH	Gazzaniga	22	45m 21.624s	2m 01.563s	4
21	Giuseppe Fiorillo	I	Yamaha	21	43m 37.113s	2m 02.459s	2
	Peter Öttl	D	Rotax	17	DNF	1m 59.000s	7
	Loek Bodelier	NL	Honda	17	DNF	1m 59.310s	8
	Robin Appleyard	GB	Honda	15	DNF	2m 01.544s	5
	Steve Patrickson	GB	Honda	15	DNF	2m 04.089s	13
	Oliver Koch	D	Honda	11	DNF	1m 58.783s	6
	Hubert Abold	D	Honda	8	DNF	2m 02.632s	5
	Kinya Wada	J	Honda	6	DNF	1m 59.931s	6
	Heinz Lüthi	CH	Honda	5	DNF	2m 00.817s	5
	Alfred Waibel	D	Honda	3	DNF	2m 09.314s	2
	Arie Molenaar	NL	Aprilia	0	DNF		
	Takao Shimizu	J	Honda	0	DNF		
	Luis Alvaro	E	Aprilia	0	DNF		
	Fausto Ricci	I	Yamaha		DNS		
	Kazuto Sakata	J	Honda		DNS		
	Peter Galvin	AUS	Honda		DNS		
	Maurizio Vitali	I	Gazzaniga		DNS		

Fastest lap: Giro, 1m 57.836s, 90.114 mph/145.025 km/h (record).
Previous record: none.

Practice leaderboard: 1 Gianola, 1m 58.091s; **2** Casanova, 1m 58.425s; **3** Raudies, 1m 58.702s; **4** Gresini, 1m 58.718s; **5** Debbia, 1m 58.832s; **6** Waldmann, 1m 58.951s; **7** Spaan, 1m 59.170s; **8** Giro, 1m 59.344s; **9** Martinez, 1m 59.518s; **10** Wakai, 1m 59.524s; **11** Lüthi, 1m 59.538s; **12** Ueda, 1m 59.637s; **13** Gramigni, 1m 59.747s; **14** Petrucciani, 1m 59.749s; **15** Molenaar, 1m 59.960s.

World Championship: 1 Waldmann, 72; **2** Gianola, 53; **3** Gramigni, 51; **4** Casanova, 49; **5** Gresini, 46; **6** Raudies, 41; **7** Wakai, 33; **8** Debbia, 30; **9** Martinez, 25; **10** Giro, 18; **11** Sakata, 16; **12** Ueda, 15; **13** Öttl, 10; **14** Koch and Saitoh, 8; **16** Fujihara, 4; **17** Wada, 3; **18** Spaan, 2; **19** Lüthi and Petrucciani, 1.

Malcolm Bryan

500 cc	DOOHAN
250 cc	CHILI
125 cc	CASANOVA
SIDECARS	WEBSTER

WORLD CHAMPIONSHIP • ROUND 7

GERMAN GRAND PRIX

The Hockenheimring is an extraordinary and fascinating circuit. Extraordinarily fast – Doohan's new record is approaching a 130 mph *average*. Fascinatingly perverse – because instead of leading to automatic victory for the fastest bike, it often favours incredibly close racing, where the slipstream of a quick bike ahead and some daring into the fast chicanes can make up for all sorts of other deficits.

So it was this year, with superb close-matched battles for the lead in all but the 500 class, where Doohan's ultra-speedy Honda did manage the breakaway, and the back-and-forth stuff was reserved for a bitter battle covering (at one point) third to tenth places.

The old-timers who built the Hockenheimring knew one thing that has been cast aside by modern circuit designers: that sustained high speed is an important part of racing; the relatively recent installation of a couple of fast second-gear flick-flack-flick chicanes two-thirds of the way along the two flat-out runs through the forest had, however, reduced risks without blunting the track's challenge or extinguishing its austere character. (The absence of spectators on the long runs through the forest and the stark contrast of the massed ranks in the stadium section give Hockenheim its unique atmosphere.)

Photos: Malcolm Bryan

Right: **Gardner came back – not fighting fit, just fighting.**

Below: **Gardner, Criville and Kocinski finished this close after 76 miles of typical Hockenheim racing. The atmospheric stadium section makes a contrast to the fast but lonely work in the forest** ***(opposite)*****, where Bradl is pictured at top speed.**

Unfortunately, not only the history was historic this year. The surface was showing serious damage from the passage of time and F1 cars, and a patchy repaving effort merely seemed to have been laid over the top of the old bumps, while introducing new seams and surface changes in awkward places – like the entrance to the distant Ostkurve, a daunting third-gear 150 mph loop that links the two gallops. It is approached in sixth gear, nudging 200 mph, the bike already leaning to the right when the rider commences the delicate task of braking and scrubbing off 50 mph. Right here, a jounce onto new tarmac set off a weaving wobble just where it was least welcome. 'If they did so much of the track, I can't figure out why they didn't do it all,' mused Doug Chandler.

There was one improvement since he and the other top Michelin runners had tested here in May. Then, and for the subsequent World Superbike race, the first chicane had been tightened by reprofiling the entry corner into a much sharper flick. This proved more dangerous rather than safer, with harder braking from flat out in sixth down to first rather than second gear, followed by steeper lean angles and harder acceleration: particularly scary on the flick to the underworked left-hand side of the tyres in the middle of the chicane, where the spectre of the high-side was very close. Now, in response to riders' complaints and crashes in the Superbike round, the old second-gear entry was restored, more or less as before.

Last year, high speed tyre failures proved crucial. Both Dunlops and Michelins shed chunks, the latter in the race, robbing Doohan of victory, which ultimately went to the heroic late-braking Schwantz. This year there was convincing evidence of improved tyre endurance, with nobody resorting to hand-cutting the left side in an effort to build up heat during the long periods it is out of contact with the track on the fast right-tending first long 'straight' and subsequent Ostkurve. Michelin had a new generation rear that all the top riders chose, both for endurance and grip. Rather too much grip, as Rainey ultimately discovered to his cost. 'Coming out of the Ostkurve, I was following Eddie [Lawson, on the Dunlop-shod Cagiva] and where his wheel was spinning I could just ride round the outside of him still gripping. I said to the Michelin guys

To describe Schwantz's efforts as 'dogged pursuit' is somewhat understating the case.

that if this thing ever lets go, it'll spit me into the trees. I guess I proved myself right.'

He had been chasing Doohan in the last practice session, and was close behind him into the long, looping first-gear Sachskurve bend in the stadium section. It is a well-banked left-hander and, as he put the power on, the bike stepped out of the envelope, flicked once, then hurled Rainey in a leisurely high-sider. He fell on his back, and was clobbered again by the bike as he slid. He limped away, with a hatful of minor injuries to add to a painful spine, including a chipped bone in his hurt hand. Full of painkillers, he rode bravely in the race, but had to be lifted off the bike after retiring in agony, his title defence stricken by a fresh blow.

The same bend also claimed Mamola in race morning warm-up; Randy tore ligaments in his left hand and made his Budweiser Yamaha a non-starter. It was a measure of the strength of the 500 class that the race was still exciting even without these leading lights.

The mid-point of the season brought the first of the new Honda copy drone-clone engines, with Suzuki winning the workshop race with a quick six-week turnaround from concept to race track. Cagiva and Yamaha were to follow over the next two races as all three scrabbled to match Honda's astonishing NSR. This frenzied activity back at the factories counted as a double success for HRC, for it delayed development (particularly in Yamaha's case) on new machines for next season.

Suzuki's revised RGV engine had arrived the Monday before the race. Schwantz had cut short his trip home, missing his high school reunion to join Chandler for tests at Donington Park. Opinions were mixed, with Schwantz enjoying the torquier, smoother power, and saying: 'It seems to come off the corners twice as fast, because you're less on a knife-edge. You can control the slide real good.' Chandler, who has a smoother style, felt it worsened his wheelspin problems. Ironically enough, engine trouble with his 'old' bike meant Doug raced the new engine, while Schwantz chose the old one for its better over-rev potential, which he felt might be more valuable should Hockenheim produce its usual slipstreaming battle.

The new engine droned just like the Honda, having adapted the NSR's firing order to the twin-crank RGV motor. As before, two cylinders fired simultaneously, one in each cylinder pair. But where the base engine fired the second pair 180 degrees later, the new one had them following after an estimated 20 degrees.

The rumour-mill was getting into gear, with the name Freddie Spencer cropping up again and again as the one-time genius of the 500 class started to make noises about a GP return. Closer to home was a link between Rainey and Honda, via the big money Campsa team run by his close friend, Sito Pons. Rainey was certainly on bleak terms with Yamaha, as his team cast around for the right frame formula to match their switch to Michelin tyres.

Tyres were also involved in an increasingly undignified display by Carlos Cardus in the 250 class, the volatile Spaniard flailing around in his desperation to get back to a race-winning position. His scapegoat this time was Dunlop, with whom Cardus abruptly severed a three-year relationship to follow his countryman Garriga over to Michelin. This seems to have been a sad misjudgement, with Dunlop taking five of the top six places in the 250 race, including the top three. And poor Cardus fell in practice with a typically Michelin front-wheel slither, and was out of the race with fresh hand injuries. Dunlop accepted the 'divorce' with good grace, saying: 'In racing there's not much point in trying to stop people doing what they want to do. It's always difficult to enforce contracts legally from either side.'

Cardus missed his chance to interfere with a great day for Italy. The Aprilias were quite simply too fast for the Hondas (Cadalora qualified fifth and said, deadpan: 'The reason is because I cannot go as fast as the four riders in front of me'). Bradl also fell victim to the Sachskurve, one of three practice crashes as he strove in vain to recapture his dominance here last year. A fourth crash in the race left the Aprilias unchallenged, and the race went to the first all-Italian bike/rider combination in the class since 1977, when Franco Uncini's and Walter Villa's (Aermacchi) Harley-Davidsons finished ahead of Mario Lega's Morbidelli at the old Brno road circuit. Italian fervour had already been rewarded with Bruno Casanova's long-awaited first GP win after a superlative 125 race in the morning.

The 250 class also yielded a new potential hero, after an impressive debut by Nobuyuki 'Wacky' Wakai, already highly visible in the 125 class – he is unusually tall, and all knees and elbows as he applies his ebulliently aggressive style to force his Moto Bum Honda to battle with the factory-kitted bikes in the top ten. Wakai had been recruited by the Lucky Strike Suzuki team to take over the injured Wilco Zeelenberg's bike – the Dutchman, leg in plaster and wired in to a mobile electronic massage machine, was a wistful spectator as the cheerful Japanese rider took to the works 250 like a natural. His task was made harder since he was obliged, by a twist in the new rules, to race his Honda 125 as well (he was not injured, so therefore could not legally be substituted), which was on Dunlops while the Suzuki wore Michelins. Not surprisingly, he also fell victim to the Michelin front-slide syndrome, tumbling on Friday at one of the chicanes, and remounting to return with a flapping fairing to change to his other bike. This rule was amended in time for the next race; here Wakai exploited it to become the first rider to score points in two classes on the same day since Jorge Martinez in 1990.

500 cc PRACTICE

The question of racing fuel had been brewing all season – indeed, for many years. Marlboro Yamaha patronise specialist suppliers in the USA; Honda have a hot line to Elf's R & D department, while most of the rest run Elf's 'Blue Gas', or variations thereof. All of it is specially shipped to the paddock, and there is a conspiracy of silence – a Code of Thieves – whereby nobody ever complains or protests for fear of the same happening to them.

Things came close to breaking point here, though, when Elf turned up with a new special brew for Doohan's Honda, and his existing technical advantage increased that little bit more.

Crucially, as it proved – for the vital move at Hockenheim is to win the drag into the first bend, then drive out of it and all the next ones so fast that nobody can get close enough to use your slipstream. Such was Doohan's plan, after setting his sixth steamroller pole by almost one-and-a-half seconds. 'Trouble is, everyone else will be trying to do the same thing.'

Dominating every session, he was able to work throughout towards improving corner exit, and endurance testing the new rear Michelin. Having lost two races, he would obviously be a tough nut to crack. So tough, in fact, that Rainey himself cracked in the attempt. He'd been passed by Doohan, and was chasing him hard for a couple of laps thereafter in the final session when he crashed.

Shortly before, Wayne had secured second by three-tenths from Schwantz, who'd spent the first day not only testing the new Suzuki engine but also making up for time lost when he missed the Michelin tyre tests (he was still hurt). In the end he decided to stay with the old free-revving screamer: 'Those few hundred rpm could be what you need for drafting here, and they could come in handy if it comes down to a last lap battle,' he said. With his braking and handling superiority, he obviously relished the

Malcolm Bryan

prospect. But first he had to be sure that Doohan didn't break away in the first lap, and to that end he practised running quickly on cold tyres all through training, to prepare an all-out first lap effort.

Kocinski had been home to the States meanwhile, and pronounced himself fully fit after finally shaking off the virus that had dogged him since Italy. He put his Yamaha on the front row, and was surely another candidate for any close battles. He spent most of practice working on his confidence and race set-up endurance, then ran fast at the end, to place three-tenths behind Schwantz.

Just over a tenth covered the next three: Chandler, Gardner and Barros. Chandler was obliged to use the new Suzuki engine for the simple reason that the old engine, in his other bike, had developed a mysterious lingering complaint with its exhaust powervalve system, and hadn't run right since Mugello. He'd have preferred the old one, but planned to compensate for the lack of over-rev by gearing up for the draft. And if he missed it? 'The engine will still pull that gearing.'

This was Gardner's second return after his broken leg in Japan, and this time he stayed cool. 'The Honda's so fast it flatters me,' he said. 'It's put me about five places higher than I should be – you don't have to ride much here, just open and close the throttle. My leg still hurts, but I expect a respectable result tomorrow.'

Barros had beaten team-mate Lawson by better than half a second, and the American was not confident for the race. The Cagiva was too slow, and he also had a rear suspension problem. 'It's okay for two laps, then it's gone. We don't know if it's tyres, or the rear unit is overheating from a repositioned exhaust, or shrouded by the carbon swing arm,' he said. At the time, he expressed a lack of confidence in the huge 16-in. rear Dunlop they were testing again – but in the end he used it for the race.

Garriga led row three from young rival Criville, a satisfying experience given the speed of the latter's Honda; Mackenzie was alongside, 11th fastest, the gap behind Doohan now more than three seconds. Said the Scot: 'We can't seem to get the bike stable at high speed.' Guarded words that concealed a growing rift with his French team in matters technical, particularly related to front suspension settings, where he felt Christian Sarron and Serge Rosset between them ignored his opinions and went their own sweet (wrong) way.

Mamola completed the row, again feeling the pinch of only having one bike, unable to engage in the usual leapfrog development. In Saturday morning's untimed practice he only managed two laps, with the small crowd cheering him all the way. Then he fell heavily in race morning warm-up, and was out.

Goddard led row four, half a tenth behind Randy on his Roc Yamaha, with crasher Thierry Crine next on his similar bike, then DuHamel's works Yamaha and Catalano 16th on another Roc. The Roc riders seemed better off at this stage than the men on Harris-Yamahas, the best of whom, local hero Michael Rudroff, was 21st and leading row six. Their advantage is that Roc boss Rosset has a lot of Yamaha experience, while Harris has started from scratch.

There were 31 qualifiers, with Andy Leuthe's too slow home-made VRP again failing to make the cut.

500 cc RACE – 18 LAPS

The close clutch of drafting dodgers that riders and fans alike had been hoping for didn't materialise. Instead, victory was decided by the second corner of this awe-inspiring circuit.

Malcolm Bryan

Kocinski made the best start and led into the first corner, but he lacked the necessary confidence in his front tyre to resist Doohan's out-braking move into the first chicane, and the Honda was in front once and – as it transpired – for all.

Schwantz was poised and pounced on the way out of the chicane, but he'd been behind Kocinski on the way through, and that cushion had been enough to give Doohan a few extra vital yards at the start of the flat-out run to the Ostkurve. He was just too far ahead for Schwantz – tucked in and trying his utmost – to catch his slipstream. Using his superior drive out of the corners to the maximum, the Australian spent the rest of the lap eking out the tenths at every corner exit, and by the time he crossed the line at the end of the first lap, a gap of one full second meant that he had effectively broken the tow. He was in a commanding position for the rest of the race.

Of course, he was still under extreme pressure. One little slip and Schwantz would be on him – and the Texan was putting on a fine display of lap-after-lap brinkmanship in steadfast pursuit. Doohan in turn was skittering the front into the chicanes, puffing dust and kicking the kerbs as he continued to give his utmost. Last year's tyre failure was fresh in his mind. 'I kept pressing on hard, both to keep my concentration but also so that if anything did happen at the end I'd have as big a cushion as possible,' he said. His fastest lap was his fourth, a new record on the repaved track.

Behind him, Schwantz sustained his pressure and persistence for five long laps of dogged pursuit. But Doohan never made the error he needed, and inched frustratingly away. 'When I came out of the chicane on the sixth lap and I couldn't see him ahead of me any more, then I thought I'd be better off settling for second,' said Schwantz.

By now the pack engaged in a fine battle for third would also just have lost sight of him at the same place. At first, Chandler's droning new Suzuki took over from Kocinski, but he was always under pressure, with Criville's Honda coming through fast, Rainey doing his best to beat the pain, Gardner ever-present along with Lawson and Barros, and Garriga close behind.

The Cagivas simply didn't have the speed to use the draft, although Barros, having the ride of his young life, nosed ahead now and then, exploiting his particularly heroic late braking. Lawson never got that close, but nor was he ever far away, scoring third-fastest lap in the process. Criville led the group several times, and Chandler came back to the front towards the end of the race.

Then Gardner took over firmly in the stadium section, with four laps to go, and defended the position staunchly until the finish, fending off not only Kocinski but also a very determined attack from Criville in the final bends, with the pair clashing fairings and jostling handlebars and legs in the last few turns.

At the finish, three-tenths of a second covered Gardner, Criville and Kocinski; old dog Lawson was half a second back, just ahead of Barros,

Left: **Biaggi at 20 – a formidable combination of raw courage and sheer nerve.**

and both Cagivas were ahead of Chandler, another two-tenths behind.

Hero again, the remarkable Gardner expressed surprise at finding himself on the rostrum in his comeback ride. 'I just wanted to finish in one piece, and to stay with the group so I could learn from them, and remotivate myself. Some of the younger guys, like Criville and Barros, surprised me earlier on. They're fast, but they use their tyres really hard, and about three-quarters of the way through I noticed they were slowing a bit. That's when I thought I might be able to do it.'

Kocinski had enjoyed the race, but not the result. 'I messed up the last chicane,' he said. 'Everything felt perfect but I got too close to Gardner and Criville so I couldn't get a run on them out of the corner. Then in the stadium those two guys were going pretty crazy.'

Lawson and Barros both complained afterwards simply about a shortage of speed, the former laconically and the latter in tears; Chandler, icy calm as ever, was dryly disappointed to have been consigned to the back of the group. 'My bike was fast, but I was losing traction mid-corner. I was using a lot of track picking the bike up early to get the power on just to stay with them.'

Garriga had caught up, then lost touch in the closing stages, finishing some four seconds adrift in ninth; Goddard's Roc took tenth and the last point, also racing the 16-in. rear Dunlop, and still in pain from his injured hand. His progress had been hindered after a fluffed start by DuHamel in his slipstream, but at least the Canadian didn't pip him for the last point this time, finishing some five seconds adrift and rather puzzlingly saying he'd found this simplest of tracks hard to learn.

Another 20 seconds back Spaniard Lopez Mella triumphed over a close group of privateers, including Sarron, Rudroff and Laycock within the space of three seconds. There were 22 finishers, with Pedercini's Paton last, one lap adrift.

Mackenzie would probably have been in the big battle for third as well but he got another poor start and, while he was closing up, he crashed at the first chicane, sliding heavily into the barrier and breaking a bone in his right foot. The bone was pinned in an operation that evening, but his confidence suffered lasting damage. He'd complained, to no avail, about the way the forks bottomed out. They did it again while he was late braking for the chicane, and he finally lost control while trying to make the reverse-direction flick for the second part of the corner.

250 cc PRACTICE

The Honda riders have said all year that the Aprilias were too fast to be dealt with. Here the Italian bikes clearly proved it, filling three out of four front-row places – in spite of some new Honda cylinders that seemed to have closed the gap.

For a second race in succession it was the newcomer, Max Biaggi, who took pole, the 20-year-old European champion displacing fellow-Aprilia rider Loris Reggiani by three-tenths. He didn't believe his eyes at first, and called into the pits to confirm it. But he'd done the time twice, and was left to contemplate a struggle of the slipstreams for what might lead to his first race win.

Loris had been complaining bitterly about the bumps caused by partial resurfacing work ('It's like motocross out there – it's the worst track this year'). But he had his semi-active suspension working by the end of practice, not by fiddling with the back-box but by the more tried-and-tested remedy of changing the spring to one that was more progressive.

Bradl was third, but crashed three times in contrast to his utter dominance here last year. The first was on Friday, the second on Saturday morning, both in the relatively slow stadium section, and he was not hurt. But the third crash was a high-sider in one of the fast chicanes. 'I bruised both my wrists. I shall have to see how they feel tomorrow,' the dented German would-be hero said.

Chili's Aprilia completed row one. Cadalora was more than half a second slower to lead row two – and not only was he still short of speed compared with the Aprilias, but he was also complaining of the bumps and the difficulties of getting the chassis right. 'The main problem is the front end, and I hope Erv [Kanemoto] and the team will be able to make things better tonight. Even so, this will be a very hard race to win,' the title leader said.

He had Capirossi's kitted RS Honda alongside, the 125 champion's best qualifying position yet, achieved by judicious use of works bikes' slipstreams, a tactic he hoped to repeat in the race.

Then came class debutant Wakai, placing seventh in his first attempt on the works Suzuki. Alongside him another class newcomer, this year at least, in the shape of the Gilera. It was former champion Carlos Lavado's bike, scoring the Gilera's best qualifying position so far, even though the Venezuelan veteran felt he was still short of top speed.

Torrontegui's Suzuki led row three from Shimizu's works Honda, Schmid's works Yamaha and Puig's private Aprilia; Ruggia's Gilera led row four from Prein (Honda), Bernd Kassner (Aprilia) and Doriano Romboni (Honda). Ruggia had a lucky escape after attempting his own fast lap in a works bike tow. Unfortunately he'd chosen to follow Bradl, who promptly crashed, and the Frenchman was almost involved.

There were 37 qualifiers, but Cardus would not start, after placing 20th. He crashed early in the final session, and once again went home early.

250 cc RACE – 16 LAPS

The austere and awe-inspiring stadium provided an operatic setting for the Italian triumph. Biaggi leapt into the lead from pole position, Reggiani took over a lap later, then Chili had his turn, and stayed ahead – but for the odd lap or two – until the finish. The three Aprilias simply pulled away from the field, claiming the track as their own.

Chili had not been optimistic until his team fixed a speed problem with his bike overnight, and he knew

Sharing the laurels. Biaggi, Chili and Reggiani clown happily after three Italian riders on three Italian bikes made history at Hockenheim.

Right: **Gianola (16) and Raudies (8) tried their utmost, but nothing was going to stop Bruno Casanova from claiming a long overdue first GP win.**

Bottom right: **Hard-charging Austrian Klaus Klaffenböck (19) takes centre stage among the jostling outfits, but missed his first win by a quarter of a second.**

from the morning warm-up that he was in with a chance. 'My team gave me a bike with perfect settings and I saw that everything was right,' he said. All that remained was to choose the right tactics. 'I tried to do my best before the stadium section, and once we were there it was impossible to pass me.'

Biaggi attempted the impossible anyway. His progress had been the usual over-the-limit series of whoops and wobbles; now he outbraked Reggiani into the stadium and was trying too hard to find a way past Chili when he almost crashed on the quick direction-change flick after the Sachskurve. Yet another miraculous recovery saw him take his first second-place finish by half a second.

Reggiani was a similar distance behind the pair of Telkor 'factory-lease' Aprilias on his works bike, and said happily: 'I prefer to come third to two Italians on Italian bikes than second to a Honda.'

After the first lap sorting out, the main pursuit came from Bradl, but it was short-lived. The German crashed at the end of the third lap on the run onto the start-finish straight, in full view of the stadium, banging his head as the bike landed on top of him, then standing up to stomp back to the pits, the picture of disgruntlement.

The Honda's honour was down to Cadalora, who managed to draw slowly ahead of the pursuing Shimizu, but not to make any impression on the Aprilias. 'I was held up early on by Shimizu and Puig, and lost contact with the leaders. It was impossible to make up ground.'

Fifth place saw a good battle between Shimizu and the Aprilias of Puig and Andy Preining (before the latter's bike went off song), with the Japanese rider moving ahead in the closing stages.

Seventh saw much drama before being won by Wakai. The Japanese rider personally had a steady race, while the Yamaha of erstwhile companion Schmid dropped back, and Capirossi also faded with fuel starvation problems.

Wakai's Suzuki team-mate, Torrontegui, was having a frenzied race. He'd been up to seventh earlier when he'd tangled with Shimizu on the entrance to the first chicane. The contact applied his front brake, and though he managed to avoid crashing he ran straight through the chicane. Held back by the flag marshal, he rejoined in 20th to embark on a marvellous charge on the fast Suzuki. Among his victims was Schmid, the German forced to give way in a clash at the first chicane, rejoining out of touch.

Wakai also succumbed to the vengeful Spaniard, but hung on to pass him again on the last lap. It was the first time that two Suzukis have scored points in the 250 class since the factory comeback.

Capirossi was ninth and Kassner tenth, taking his first championship point. It should really have gone to Carlos Lavado, had he not outbraked himself on the way into the stadium section for the last time. Perhaps that was poetic justice, though, for the Gilera rider was blamed for having knocked Stefan Prein off in a spectacular crash at the second chicane earlier in the race. (The other Gilera, ridden by Ruggia, retired after two laps; by then Romboni's Honda was also out.)

Cadalora's championship lead was cut, and the performance of the Aprilias was an ominous sign that the rest of the season might not be cut and dried for the Rothmans rider.

125 cc RACE – 15 LAPS

The wide open spaces may dwarf the speed of the littlest GP machines, but not the talent of their riders. There were seven of them in the leading group this time, and all of them made it to the finish line, covered by just over one second.

It hardly mattered who led when and where – the last lap decided matters – but for the record it was Bruno Casanova's Aprilia in front from the start, with Dirk Raudies's fast Honda taking the lead on the run back to the stadium to control lap one.

Casanova was in front next time round, but Peter Öttl's Rotax had crashed out of the leading group at the Sachskurve. He delayed Ueda, who tried too hard to regain the front bunch and fell himself four corners later.

The remainder put up a brilliant display of TV racing, drafting on the straights, splitting three abreast into the bends – and all looking for every chance to take control and break free.

It looked as though last year's winner, Ralf Waldmann, might do so after he led for the first time on the sixth lap. But whatever inches he managed to gain here or there soon disappeared again, with Raudies getting back in front. Gramigni's Aprilia also took a turn at leading; while Gresini had a go (inadvertently, no doubt) at knocking Gianola off in the stadium section, dropping the double race winner to the back of the group with four laps left.

So it all came down to a mad scramble at the finish, bikes ducking and weaving on the last run home.

Gresini's charge won him the lead as they ran through the last chicane. But Casanova would not be denied his long-awaited first GP win, and outbraked his countryman into the stadium section to lead to the flag. Gresini was second, Waldmann third, then came team-mates Debbia and Gianola, Raudies and Gramigni. And the crowd stopped holding its breath.

Wild card rider Stefan Kurfiss was eighth, and Wakai ninth, showing he hadn't slacked off his 125 effort in favour of the forthcoming 250 race.

SIDECAR RACE – 16 LAPS

The sidecar teams arrived at Hockenheim for their second race still without having been paid for their previous GP at Jerez and still racing on faith – though there were dark threats circulating about open rebellion. Instead they pitched up and raced, their only remaining survival tactic being simply to survive – and on the day before the race the FIM handed over an interim payment of $50,000 to Lee van Dam, secretary of ISRA, the three-wheel equivalent of IRTA.

This was enough to give the crews $2000 apiece, at least covering running costs, but the situation was a long way from resolution, with the FIM joining IRTA in washing their hands of the whole business.

Given these circumstances, they produced a polished and highly professional race, which deserved better support from the crowd, only a few of whom stayed to watch Webster and Simmons pursue a desperate start-to-finish battle with Klaus Klaffenböck/Christian Parzer that was only resolved in the final sprint to the flag. Webster took his second win of the year by less than three-tenths of a second, and both outfits ended the race well marked up by each other's paint.

Biland had qualified on pole, starting tongues wagging about special brew fuel to account for his sudden improvement in engine power. This turned out to be an embarrassment. He held second for most of the race, but then his chain started to stretch and jump on the sprockets, and he was forced to back off to finish eighth.

This left a close battle for the last rostrum place between Darren Dixon and Yoshi Kumagaya, with the Englishman taking third by a second.

Ralph Bohnhorst, winner here last year, defeated the Güdel brothers by a similar margin for fifth.

There was good scrapping down the field, with 16 finishers, all but two on the same lap as the leader. But leading light Egbert Streuer retired at the end of the first lap with crankshaft problems.

ER - SA
16
NOLAN
8
agv
15
Arai

uvex
uvex
19
weingartner
PPY - DATA - LAND

Grosser Preis von Deutschland, 14 June/statistics

Hockenheimring, 4.218-mile/6.788-km circuit

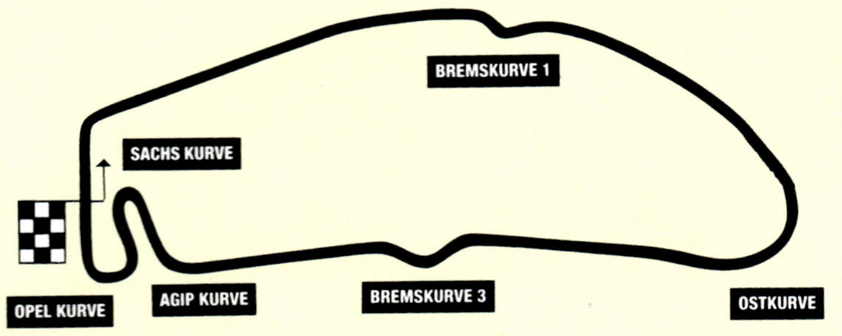

500 cc

18 laps, 75.924 miles/122.256 km

Place	Rider	Nat.	Machine	Laps	Time & speed	Fastest lap	Lap
1	**Michael Doohan**	AUS	Honda	18	35m 57.895s 126.734 mph/ 203.959 km/h	1m 58.956s	4
2	**Kevin Schwantz**	USA	Suzuki	18	36m 22.521s	1m 59.353s	4
3	**Wayne Gardner**	AUS	Honda	18	36m 33.660s	2m 00.619s	18
4	**Alex Criville**	E	Honda	18	36m 33.838s	2m 00.637s	18
5	**John Kocinski**	USA	Yamaha	18	36m 33.960s	2m 00.618s	15
6	**Eddie Lawson**	USA	Cagiva	18	36m 34.541s	2m 00.437s	16
7	**Alexandre Barros**	BR	Cagiva	18	36m 35.815s	2m 01.062s	17
8	**Doug Chandler**	USA	Suzuki	18	36m 36.099s	2m 00.904s	16
9	**Juan Garriga**	E	Yamaha	18	36m 40.158s	2m 01.182s	15
10	**Peter Goddard**	AUS	Yamaha	18	37m 08.080s	2m 02.648s	8
11	Miguel DuHamel	CAN	Yamaha	18	37m 13.171s	2m 03.010s	6
12	Juan Lopez Mella	E	Yamaha	18	37m 34.388s	2m 03.944s	17
13	Dominique Sarron	F	Yamaha	18	37m 35.352s	2m 04.145s	17
14	Michael Rudroff	D	Yamaha	18	37m 35.697s	2m 04.015s	18
15	Eddie Laycock	IRL	Yamaha	18	37m 36.835s	2m 04.210s	17
16	Kevin Mitchell	GB	Yamaha	18	37m 48.477s	2m 04.874s	15
17	Simon Buckmaster	GB	Yamaha	17	35m 59.051s	2m 05.848s	8
18	Niggi Schmassman	CH	Yamaha	17	36m 21.551s	2m 06.565s	17
19	Cees Doorakkers	NL	Yamaha	17	36m 23.555s	2m 06.776s	16
20	Sepp Doppler	A	Yamaha	17	36m 48.800s	2m 08.584s	5
21	Peter Graves	GB	Yamaha	17	36m 52.028s	2m 08.741s	14
22	Lucio Pedercini	I	Paton	17	37m 03.231s	2m 07.052s	6
	Serge David	CH	Yamaha	16	DNF	2m 04.863s	11
	Wayne Rainey	USA	Yamaha	11	DNF	2m 01.235s	4
	Niall Mackenzie	GB	Yamaha	3	DNF	2m 01.801s	3
	Marco Papa	I	Librenti	3	DNF	2m 13.157s	2
	Corrado Catalano	I	Yamaha	3	DNF	2m 21.997s	1
	Thierry Crine	F	Yamaha	2	DNF	2m 14.431s	1
	Toshiyuki Arakaki	J	Yamaha	1	DNF	2m 14.089s	1
	Claude Arciero	F	Yamaha	0	DNF		
	Randy Mamola	USA	Yamaha		DNS		
	Andreas Leuthe	D	VRP		DNQ		

Fastest lap: Doohan, 1m 58.956s, 127.721 mph/205.548 km/h (record).
Previous record: Kevin Schwantz, USA (Suzuki), 1m 59.846s, 126.773 mph/202.022 km/h (1991).

Practice leaderboard: **1** Doohan, 1m 58.325s; **2** Rainey, 1m 59.731s; **3** Schwantz, 2m 00.064s; **4** Kocinski, 2m 00.310s; **5** Chandler, 2m 00.572s; **6** Gardner, 2m 00.677s; **7** Barros, 2m 00.686s; **8** Lawson, 2m 01.200s; **9** Garriga, 2m 01.393s; **10** Criville, 2m 01.571s; **11** Mackenzie, 2m 01.703s; **12** Mamola, 2m 02.664s; **13** Goddard, 2m 02.710s; **14** Crine, 2m 03.042s; **15** DuHamel, 2m 03.162s.

World Championship: **1** Doohan, 130; **2** Schwantz, 77; **3** Rainey, 65; **4** Chandler, 57; **5** Kocinski, 36; **6** Criville, 29; **7** Garriga, 25; **8** Mackenzie, 22; **9** Mamola, 21; **10** Beattie and Lawson, 18; **12** Barros and Gardner, 12; **14** DuHamel, Goddard and Itoh, 10; **17** Ohishi, 6; **18** Honma, 3; **19** Catalano and Fujiwara, 2; **21** Laycock and Tsujimoto, 1.

250 cc

16 laps, 67.488 miles/108.672 km

Place	Rider	Nat.	Machine	Laps	Time & speed	Fastest lap	Lap
1	**Pier Francesco Chili**	I	Aprilia	16	34m 00.719s 119.121 mph/ 191.707 km/h	2m 06.681s	14
2	**Massimiliano Biaggi**	I	Aprilia	16	34m 01.224s	2m 06.579s	16
3	**Loris Reggiani**	I	Aprilia	16	34m 01.736s	2m 06.499s	15
4	**Luca Cadalora**	I	Honda	16	34m 22.168s	2m 07.797s	3
5	**Masahiro Shimizu**	J	Honda	16	34m 27.166s	2m 08.052s	7
6	**Alberto Puig**	E	Aprilia	16	34m 36.538s	2m 08.290s	7
7	**Nobuyuki Wakai**	J	Suzuki	16	34m 43.697s	2m 09.085s	14
8	**Herri Torrontegui**	E	Suzuki	16	34m 43.884s	2m 08.556s	2
9	**Loris Capirossi**	I	Honda	16	34m 47.074s	2m 08.627s	11
10	**Bernd Kassner**	D	Aprilia	16	34m 47.466s	2m 08.821s	12
11	Andy Preining	A	Aprilia	16	34m 51.700s	2m 07.735s	7
12	Jochen Schmid	D	Yamaha	16	34m 59.209s	2m 09.348s	2
13	Carlos Lavado	YV	Gilera	16	35m 10.421s	2m 08.954s	8
14	Patrick van den Goorbergh	NL	Aprilia	16	35m 12.648s	2m 10.814s	2
15	Harald Eckl	D	Aprilia	16	35m 12.903s	2m 10.244s	6
16	Katsuyoshi Kozono	J	Honda	16	35m 13.159s	2m 10.779s	8
17	Adi Stadler	D	Honda	16	35m 13.857s	2m 11.044s	8
18	Bernard Hänggeli	CH	Aprilia	16	35m 13.913s	2m 10.888s	8
19	Frédéric Protat	F	Aprilia	16	35m 20.611s	2m 11.560s	8
20	Luis D'Antin	E	Honda	16	35m 20.736s	2m 11.487s	10
21	Yves Briguet	CH	Honda	16	35m 21.251s	2m 11.650s	11
22	Jean-Pierre Jeandat	F	Honda	16	35m 21.974s	2m 11.475s	6
23	Erkka Korpiaho	SF	Aprilia	16	35m 50.543s	2m 12.629s	2
24	Evren Bischoff	D	Aprilia	16	35m 54.599s	2m 13.044s	3
25	Volker Baehr	D	Honda	16	35m 54.941s	2m 12.846s	13
26	Michele Gallina	I	Yamaha	16	35m 54.994s	2m 13.041s	12
27	Bernard Cazade	F	Honda	16	35m 55.041s	2m 13.492s	12
28	Renzo Colleoni	I	Yamaha	15	34m 22.426s	2m 14.086s	3
	Jurgen van den Goorbergh	NL	Aprilia	8	DNF	2m 11.857s	7
	Adrian Bosshard	CH	Honda	8	DNF	2m 13.778s	2
	Stefan Prein	D	Honda	6	DNF	2m 09.789s	4
	Eskil Suter	CH	Aprilia	3	DNF	2m 10.444s	2
	Paolo Casoli	I	Yamaha	3	DNF	2m 11.017s	3
	Helmut Bradl	D	Honda	2	DNF	2m 08.206s	2
	Jean-Philippe Ruggia	F	Gilera	2	DNF	2m 23.215s	1
	Doriano Romboni	I	Honda	1	DNF	2m 46.377s	1
	Carlos Cardus	E	Honda		DNS		

Fastest lap: Reggiani, 2m 06.499s, 120.106 mph/193.292 km/h (record).
Previous record: Helmut Bradl, D (Honda), 2m 06.725s, 119.892 mph/192.947 km/h (1991).

Practice leaderboard: **1** Biaggi, 2m 06.630s; **2** Reggiani, 2m 06.927s; **3** Bradl, 2m 07.134s; **4** Chili, 2m 07.205s; **5** Cadalora, 2m 07.979s; **6** Capirossi, 2m 08.488s; **7** Wakai, 2m 08.549s; **8** Lavado, 2m 08.849s; **9** Torrontegui, 2m 08.902s; **10** Shimizu, 2m 09.063s; **11** Schmid, 2m 09.284s; **12** Puig, 2m 09.424s; **13** Ruggia, 2m 09.483s; **14** Prein, 2m 09.619s; **15** Kassner, 2m 09.762s.

World Championship: **1** Cadalora, 120; **2** Reggiani, 70; **3** Bradl, 57; **4** Chili, 52; **5** Biaggi, 43; **6** Puig, 40; **7** Cardus, 37; **8** Shimizu and Zeelenberg, 26; **10** Schmid, 19; **11** Romboni, 17; **12** Okada, 15; **13** Aoki, 12; **14** Capirossi, 8; **15** Preining, Ruggia and Wakai, 4; **18** Casoli, Nanba and Torrontegui, 3; **21** Prein, 2; **22** Jeandat and Kassner, 1.

Malcolm Bryan

Another Sunday afternoon with the fans for Michael Doohan.

125 cc

15 laps, 63.270 miles/101.880 km

Place	Rider	Nat.	Machine	Laps	Time & speed	Fastest lap	Lap
1	**Bruno Casanova**	**I**	**Aprilia**	**15**	**35m 10.817s 107.967 mph/ 173.756 km/h**	**2m 19.511s**	**7**
2	**Fausto Gresini**	**I**	**Honda**	**15**	**35m 10.906s**	**2m 19.475s**	**13**
3	**Ralf Waldmann**	**D**	**Honda**	**15**	**35m 11.125s**	**2m 19.798s**	**3**
4	**Gabriele Debbia**	**I**	**Honda**	**15**	**35m 11.247s**	**2m 19.398s**	**7**
5	**Ezio Gianola**	**I**	**Honda**	**15**	**35m 11.460s**	**2m 19.065s**	**13**
6	**Dirk Raudies**	**D**	**Honda**	**15**	**35m 11.700s**	**2m 19.597s**	**13**
7	**Alessandro Gramigni**	**I**	**Aprilia**	**15**	**35m 11.994s**	**2m 19.640s**	**12**
8	**Stefan Kurfiss**	**D**	**Honda**	**15**	**35m 35.476s**	**2m 21.137s**	**7**
9	**Nobuyuki Wakai**	**J**	**Honda**	**15**	**35m 35.548s**	**2m 21.108s**	**5**
10	**Carlos Giro**	**E**	**Aprilia**	**15**	**35m 36.014s**	**2m 21.201s**	**4**
11	Hisashi Unemoto	J	Honda	15	35m 36.257s	2m 21.300s	12
12	Hans Spaan	NL	Aprilia	15	36m 01.558s	2m 22.319s	12
13	Julian Miralles	E	Honda	15	36m 01.646s	2m 22.751s	4
14	Alfred Waibel	D	Honda	15	36m 02.236s	2m 22.874s	7
15	Giovanni Palmieri	CH	Gazzaniga	15	36m 02.348s	2m 22.643s	6
16	Kinya Wada	J	Honda	15	36m 02.479s	2m 22.645s	5
17	Luis Alvaro	E	Aprilia	15	36m 02.740s	2m 22.615s	14
18	Maurizio Vitali	I	Gazzaniga	15	36m 02.897s	2m 22.352s	4
19	Takao Shimizu	J	Honda	15	36m 03.058s	2m 22.995s	13
20	Manuel Hernandez	E	Aprilia	15	36m 03.181s	2m 22.584s	13
21	Loek Bodelier	NL	Honda	15	36m 03.579s	2m 22.817s	13
22	Steve Patrickson	GB	Honda	15	36m 26.445s	2m 24.706s	3
23	Robin Appleyard	GB	Honda	15	36m 27.206s	2m 24.466s	6
24	Oliver Kohlinger	D	Honda	15	36m 27.578s	2m 24.454s	6
25	Arie Molenaar	NL	Aprilia	15	37m 07.781s	2m 26.098s	4
	Oliver Koch	D	Honda	14	DNF	2m 21.258s	2
	Oliver Petrucciani	CH	Honda	13	DNF	2m 22.703s	7
	Maik Stief	D	Aprilia	7	DNF	2m 23.148s	5
	Kazuto Sakata	J	Honda	7	DNF	2m 23.122s	4
	Peter Galvin	AUS	Honda	6	DNF	2m 25.166s	3
	Hubert Abold	D	Honda	3	DNF	2m 24.687s	3
	Alain Bronec	F	Honda	3	DNF	2m 24.963s	2
	Jorge Martinez	E	Honda	2	DNF	2m 21.093s	2
	Noboru Ueda	J	Honda	1	DNF	2m 27.335s	1
	Peter Öttl	D	Rotax	1	DNF	2m 27.506s	1
	Heinz Lüthi	CH	Honda		DNS		

Fastest lap: Gianola, 2m 19.065s, 109.253 mph/175.826 km/h (record).
Previous record: Loris Capirossi, I (Honda), 2m 20.257s, 108.324 mph/174.331 km/h (1991).

Practice leaderboard: **1** Waldmann, 2m 18.346s; **2** Gianola, 2m 18.606s; **3** Casanova, 2m 18.744s; **4** Debbia, 2m 19.894s; **5** Raudies, 2m 20.007s; **6** Öttl, 2m 20.182s; **7** Petrucciani, 2m 20.213s; **8** Gramigni, 2m 20.433s; **9** Martinez, 2m 20.517s; **10** Ueda, 2m 20.693s; **11** Gresini, 2m 20.762s; **12** Wakai, 2m 20.930s; **13** Koch, 2m 21.021s; **14** Sakata, 2m 21.607s; **15** Giro, 2m 21.672s.

World Championship: **1** Waldmann, 84; **2** Casanova, 69; **3** Gianola and Gresini, 61; **5** Gramigni, 55; **6** Raudies, 47; **7** Debbia, 40; **8** Wakai, 35; **9** Martinez, 25; **10** Giro, 19; **11** Sakata, 16; **12** Ueda, 15; **13** Öttl, 10; **14** Koch and Saitoh, 8; **16** Fujihara, 4; **17** Kurfiss and Wada, 3; **19** Spaan, 2; **20** Lüthi and Petrucciani, 1.

Sidecars

16 laps, 67.488 miles/108.672 km

Place	Driver & passenger	Nat.	Machine	Laps	Time & speed	Fastest lap	Lap
1	**Steve Webster/ Gavin Simmons**	**GB GB**	**LCR- ADM**	**16**	**34m 54.377s 116.069 mph/ 186.795 km/h**	**2m 09.785s**	**9**
2	**Klaus Klaffenböck/ Christian Parzer**	**A A**	**LCR- ADM**	**16**	**34m 54.658s**	**2m 10.082s**	**11**
3	**Darren Dixon/ Andy Hetherington**	**GB GB**	**LCR- Krauser**	**16**	**35m 20.596s**	**2m 10.953s**	**10**
4	**Yoshisada Kumagaya/ Bryan Houghton**	**J GB**	**LCR- Krauser**	**16**	**35m 21.627s**	**2m 10.909s**	**11**
5	**Ralph Bohnhorst/ Bruno Hiller**	**D D**	**BRM**	**16**	**35m 45.065s**	**2m 11.782s**	**6**
6	**Paul Güdel/ Charly Güdel**	**CH CH**	**LCR- Yamaha**	**16**	**35m 46.477s**	**2m 12.082s**	**8**
7	**Markus Bösiger/ Beat Leibundgut**	**CH CH**	**LCR- ADM**	**16**	**35m 46.990s**	**2m 12.263s**	**10**
8	**Rolf Biland/ Kurt Waltisperg**	**CH CH**	**LCR- Krauser**	**16**	**35m 47.187s**	**2m 10.668s**	**6**
9	**Barry Brindley/ Scott Whiteside**	**GB GB**	**LCR- Yamaha**	**16**	**36m 18.241s**	**2m 15.034s**	**13**
10	**Derek Brindley/ Nick Roche**	**GB GB**	**LCR- Krauser**	**16**	**36m 30.991s**	**2m 15.450s**	**11**
11	Theo van Kempen/ Geral de Haas	NL NL	LCR- Krauser	16	36m 31.804s	2m 15.603s	10
12	Tony Baker/ Simon Prior	GB GB	LCR- Krauser	16	36m 32.350s	2m 15.588s	6
13	Robert Fisher/ Trevor Crone	GB GB	LCR- Krauser	16	36m 35.253s	2m 14.816s	11
14	Hans Hügli/ Adolf Hänni	CH CH	LCR- Krauser	16	36m 51.631s	2m 15.702s	7
15	Peter Lemstra/ Jan Kuyt	NL NL	LCR- Krauser	15	35m 37.519s	2m 21.500s	2
16	André Bosman/ Dave Kellett	AUS AUS	LCR- Krauser	14	34m 59.249s	2m 17.567s	5
	Steve Abbott/ Shaun Smith	GB GB	YK1- Krauser	5	DNF	2m 12.083s	5
	Markus Egloff/ Urs Egloff	CH CH	LCR- Yamaha	3	DNF	2m 19.363s	2
	Billy Gällros/ Peter Berglund	S S	LCR- Streuer	2	DNF	2m 15.754s	2
	Reiner Koster/ Jurg Egli	CH CH	LCR- Yamaha	2	DNF	2m 20.088s	2
	Jukka Lauslehto/ Jurgen Levinsen	SF DK	LCR- ADM	1	DNF	2m 33.449s	1
	Egbert Streuer/ Peter Brown	NL GB	LCR- Stredor	0	DNF		
	Mark Reddington/ Kim Andreasen	GB DK	LCR- Krauser	0	DNF		

Fastest lap: Webster, 2m 09.785s, 117.065 mph/188.398 km/h (record).
Previous record: Egbert Streuer/Peter Essaff, NL/GB (LCR-Yamaha), 2m 10.444s, 116.474 mph/187.446 km/h (1991).

Practice leaderboard: **1** Biland, 2m 09.960s; **2** Webster, 2m 10.222s; **3** Streuer, 2m 10.566s; **4** Klaffenböck, 2m 10.628s; **5** Güdel, 2m 11.195s; **6** Bösiger, 2m 11.500s; **7** Bohnhorst, 2m 11.987s; **8** Abbott, 2m 12.325s; **9** Kumagaya, 2m 12.386s; **10** Dixon, 2m 12.812s; **11** B. Brindley, 2m 13.009s; **12** Egloff, 2m 14.327s; **13** van Kempen, 2m 14.637s; **14** Lauslehto, 2m 14.645s; **15** Fisher, 2m 15.676s.

World Championship: **1** Webster, 40; **2** Klaffenböck, 30; **3** Kumagaya, 20; **4** B. Brindley and Güdel, 14; **6** Dixon, 12; **7** Bösiger, 10; **8** Bohnhorst, 8; **9** Wyssen, 4; **10** Biland and Egloff, 3; **12** Streuer, 2; **13** Baker and D. Brindley, 1.

500 cc	CRIVILLE
250 cc	CHILI
125 cc	GIANOLA
SIDECARS	BILAND

WORLD CHAMPIONSHIP • ROUND 8

DUTCH TT

'If it wasn't for bad luck, wouldn't have no luck at all.' The Assen refrain was not that of a lone voice to a twangy guitar, but a massed choir of top level 500 class riders – a chorale by the Dr Costa Singers, direct from the intensive care ward, with accompaniment by bedpans, X-ray hum and percussive crutches.

The rest of the lyrics told an extraordinary and (in true C & W style) barely plausible tale of wreck after wreck, misfortune piled upon misfortune, with the pendulum of fate swinging wildly back and forth, favouring one only to dash him to the ground and then falsely favour another.

The list of those who crashed was long and included illustrious names. More surprising is that some of these, including Doohan and Schwantz, sustained their injuries in their second tumbles of a bizarre weekend. Others counted themselves lucky only to have fallen off once.

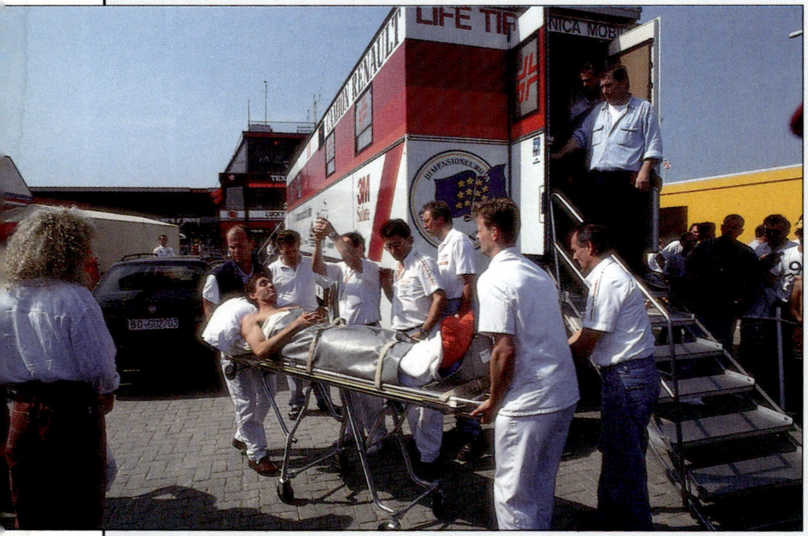

Above: **Doohan's girlfriend Kelly looks on as the points leader is stretchered out of racing – and for far longer than he expected at the time.**

Right: **Chili's second successive Assen win didn't rely on other people's errors this time.**

Photos: Malcolm Bryan.

Right: **Former 125 champion Alex Criville – no one would have predicted it.**

Below: **Early in an extraordinary race, Schwantz flicks the bitch to avoid Assen's pit-lane garden; Lawson and Chandler follow.**

Now crashes are part and parcel of racing, but given normal conditions they are usually limited to only a few at each GP, especially in the 500 class. Bikes-only Assen, with the reputation for a smooth, grippy surface and good safety provisions, now strangely showed a different side to its character. Or was there another reason for this spate of crash-happy antics?

In the end, nobody came up with a convincing explanation. To be fair, Schwantz's second crash was a collision with Lawson that was in itself highly controversial. But his first crash happened all alone at the second-gear Stekkenwal bend at the end of the back straight, and was impossible to explain for any of the usual reasons, since his tyres were warm and he wasn't going particularly fast. 'I wondered if I hit something slick,' he said later. 'Or if the tyre I had used in the morning wasn't good. Sometimes if they heat up and go cold again they change their grip.'

He bounced straight back, the major problem being that he'd damaged the bike with the new droner engine, and rather than lose more time patching up a spare with the new motor he went back to the familiar high-revver instead. Disappointing, but not (as it turned out) of any lasting significance.

Loads of other 500 riders crashed during the weekend – Lawson, Mackenzie, Gardner, Goddard, Barros, Criville, Mamola, Lopez Mella. ... The most significant was Doohan. The title leader had participated in the Assen puzzle by losing the front on the right flick taken under braking for the famous horseshoe Strubben bend. He came straight back from that. The event that changed the season, however, happened early in the final session, after three slow laps to bed in new pistons. Mick had just begun his first flying lap and was hard on the power on the fast but delicate exit from the first turn when the rear wheel spun and the bike flicked him out of the saddle and onto the ground. Later he was puzzled that it had happened so late in the corner, when he was already almost upright. The consequences of this unexpected location were that instead of sliding gently along Assen's lovely soft grass, he was still on the tarmac and trapped under his bike. Sliding at 100 mph, he felt the heat build up from friction, and tried to twist out from under the bike. At that precise moment he hit the kerb. 'I think that's when my leg broke,' he said later.

Both tibia and fibula of his right leg had snapped, but at the time it was not thought to be a complex injury. The bones were set and metal-plated at the local Assen hospital, and though most predictions were that he would miss one or two races, Doohan expressed the hope that he might be fit enough to ride in Hungary in two weeks. Instead, circulation problems ('compartment syndrome') in his leg triggered off a bizarre medical drama, with Dr Costa, not legally allowed to practise in Holland, sneaking into the hospital to try and treat the developing complications only to be interrupted and chased out by the Dutch doctors, who have since faced heavy criticism. In the end, with Doohan's foot black from a lack of circulation, and the flesh dying off round his wound, he was spirited away to Italy in a Lear Jet ambulance chartered by Costa (fellow-passenger: Kevin Schwantz) to begin the long and debilitating treatment and recuperation to recover a leg that had at one stage been in danger of amputation. He was out for eight weeks and four races, and the World Championship that had seemed his by rights slipped beyond his reach.

There's no time even for crocodile tears in racing. Doohan's downfall was, of course, the chink of championship opportunity for the only others to win a race this year, Rainey and Schwantz.

Well, it would have been an opportunity for Rainey, but he had already gone home. In a lot of pain from his experiences in Germany, Rainey had essayed a few stiff untimed laps before saying: 'It's time I listened to my body.' When he arrived home he was greeted by a fax. 'It said Lawson was on pole and that Doohan was out, and also that all those guys had fallen down. I could hardly believe it.' It was by then too late for regrets, but he was obliged to live with the knowledge that in the extraordinary race that came to pass he could probably have picked up some useful points riding his paddock bike.

Schwantz was all present and correct. He excels at the subtleties of Assen, and not only won the last two races here but also achieved a moral victory (terminated by mechanical failure) the year before that. With Doohan, Gardner and Rainey out, a win was a distinct possibility, and a

Mackenzie came back hurt, and wished he'd been strong enough to fight.

valuable top three finish a certainty, with or without the help of the new engine. His only problem, at the end of practice, was Lawson, who had put his new droner Cagiva on its first-ever pole position. The old master was back on duty at the cathedral of racing, and would also have liked to benefit from circumstances to achieve the marque's first win. As it turned out, Lawson not only stopped Schwantz from scoring any points, but also himself.

Well, that was the point of view in the Schwantz camp, who maintain to this day that the collision between the red Cagiva and the red-and-white Lucky Strike Suzuki, while disputing the lead well before half-distance, was entirely Lawson's fault. His outbraking move foiled (said Schwantz), he'd obviously got into the corner too hot and lost control before he banged into the leaned-over Suzuki's seat and exhausts. 'I was on the same line I'd been on all race – the only line for that bend at that speed. I'd seen him come alongside on the approach, but I'd held off my braking and as far as I was concerned he was beaten for the corner. I couldn't see him or hear him backshifting. The line was mine,' maintained Schwantz, adding rancorously: 'I guess he's not used to racing at the front any more. It's been a long time since he's been up there.'

Lawson saw it quite differently. 'I was past him already when he let off the brakes, then just slammed the door on me,' said Eddie. 'How did he think I was going to get round the corner?'

Endless analysis of TV footage of the crash showed that both viewpoints had merit, although it has to be said that Lawson was behind and was thus obliged to find a safe way past, which he had signally failed to do. The consensus was that the pair should share the blame, with Eddie taking the heavier load. And that it had been a surprising and rather amateurish display from two of the world's top racers, more suited to the novice race at a club meeting.

Lawson was not hurt, but the awkward fall cost Schwantz dear, fracturing his left forearm and dislocating his hip. This painful and potentially disastrous injury proved less of a problem than expected ('It just popped straight back in,' smiled the doctors), and while he and Doohan were fellow-inmates of the intensive care ward of the Wilhelmina Hospital, he was to be the easy winner of the race to get fit.

The spate of crashes also threw Assen's safety into sharper focus. Mostly, it passed, since the big star injuries both reflected specific risks inseparable from the act of riding motor cycles at high speed. Assen's run-off is ample, and in most of the other cases injuries were avoided (though Peter Goddard suffered concussion and a broken left wrist, while luckless Spanish privateer Juan Lopez Mella broke his arm after taking to the Stekkenwal escape road and hitting a photographer, who suffered a similar injury). But one unpleasant incident suggested that perhaps there might be, paradoxically, a little too much run-off, allowing crashing bikes to run unchecked.

It happened after Barros lost control of his Cagiva on one of the fast to-and-fro sections that make Assen such a delight, and although he was flicked off unhurt, the bike continued at speed before crashing explosively into a dyke, mowing down a woman marshal. She was badly hurt and later lost a leg, while the young Brazilian was visibly shaken by the affair.

As well as fresh accidents, there was the usual mid-season Assen crop of walking wounded. One such was Niall Mackenzie, who had two pins and other metalwork in his right foot after crashing in Germany, and was told he would be out of racing for at least six weeks. Now (two weeks later), his Yamaha France team had altered the footrest height and the Scots rider tackled Assen, surviving a very low speed tumble on Saturday and scoring points in a painful race.

Randy Mamola was another. He'd torn ligaments in his left hand in Germany, and was finding the high speed flicks of Assen hard work. Gardner was concussed when he fell in the last session, and X-rays revealed that he was still carrying an undiagnosed injury from one of his previous falls this year, in the form of a fractured vertebra. And 125 rider Ueda was another spectator after his Hockenheim crash.

Lucky Strike Suzuki rider Wilco Zeelenberg also returned earlier than had been predicted after breaking his ankle badly four weeks before in Spain. Amid whispers that he'd only come back to stop Wakai getting a second 250 race, he proved barely able to manage six laps at a stretch in practice, but turned the tide of opinion with a heroic finish in the race.

There were other forces which made sure that, once again, the trip to the cathedral was a significant event, among them the fact that drone-clone Honda-style engines for the first time outnumbered the old-style screamers at the front of the field. The newcomers here were Cagiva, who secured pole position as a reward for their efforts back at the Varese race shop.

Long ill favoured, the Italian bikes had suddenly added an amazing turn of speed to their usually good handling, courtesy of the new engine internals. Like the Suzuki, the Cagiva emulates the Honda NSR's firing order, with pistons firing simultaneously in pairs, timed very close. Not only did they also have the droning exhaust note, but also the surge of high torque mid-range acceleration that has so transformed the 500 class. Unlike the Honda, however, the Yamaha-clone Cagiva had no balance shaft; but in spite of the resultant vibration, Lawson was an instant convert. He praised the ease of riding, adding: 'The sound is real misleading. The old engine feels sharp because it sounds sharp, but the lap times show the new one is much faster.'

The other major development concerned the extraordinary sidecar scandal. Pushed from pillar to post, and banned to outside the official IRTA paddock, the cinderella class of GP racing came close to extinction in Holland, with virtually unpaid competitors wondering if this would be their last race. By the end of the weekend the wheel had gone full circle, and IRTA issued a communiqué confirming that sidecars would from henceforth be an official part of the new GP circus.

It had been, admitted IRTA general secretary Mike Trimby, 'a shotgun wedding'. The likeliest explanation was that Ecclestone, tired of this embarrassing blot on the landscape, told IRTA to sort the matter out once and for all. If so, it was ironical that Ecclestone came in for much mockery from the Dutch crowd – a reflection in part on their loyalty to the Dutch-dominated FIM, as well as to the sidecars.

Then there was the unique deal the Assen organisers thrashed out – instead of Ecclestone's $1 million asking fee, they paid less than half, plus a $2 royalty on each race-day ticket sold (worth something more than $250,000). A Bernie effigy was ceremonially burned at the stake, and among a number of banners was one reading: 'BERNIE – TAKE MY TWO DOLLARS AND SHOVE'M.'

But the clearest protest came at the start of the sidecar race, when the packed grandstand took up the 'F*** Ecclestone' refrain in massed song.

500 cc PRACTICE

Rainey's recently injured left hand was weak, his right leg still stiff and he ached all over. He ran eight slow laps in untimed practice, placing 11th, and decided the game wasn't worth the candle. 'I've tried so hard to be ready for this race, but I want to race to win, not just ride around,' he said ruefully before flying home.

How much more rueful the next day when Doohan fell in the first ten minutes of the final session, changing the complexion of the 1992 World Championship. Half a lap later Schwantz also fell, luckily unhurt (the red flag for Doohan conveniently gave him the chance to get back and fetch his spare bike); and over the course of the next 55 minutes they went down with a depressing regularity: Criville (a low-sider, like Schwantz's); Mamola (a split hose spilt brake fluid on his rear wheel); Mackenzie; privateers Arakaki and Pedercini.

And Wayne Gardner, after leaping up the qualifying order from seventh to fifth and then to third. Still charging, he slid into the barrier – and both Rothmans Hondas were out of the Dutch TT.

If the number of crashes was unexpected, even more so was Lawson with Cagiva's first pole. It was a great moment, received in oddly subdued fashion in the Cagiva pit, where a bevy of Italian pressmen had been anxiously gathered round the monitor. The bike's red-letter day was narrowly achieved, by less than two-hundredths over Doohan's Thursday time. The Australian had shaved another half-second off that in the second 'untimed' practice, so who is to know what he would have managed in the afternoon. But that needn't spoil Lawson's achievement, because lots of other people tried to go faster than him and failed.

Doohan and Gardner had been second and third; Kocinski was the next starter to slot in, having been fast throughout, but failing to improve as he butted up against the familiar problem of getting the bike to change direction the way he likes it. 'You can imagine what it's like here

Right: **The battle for the lead was brilliant, but the participants unexpected: Barros, Criville, Kocinski and Garriga jostle for position.**

Briton Simon Buckmaster's garish Padgetts Harris Yamaha was 14th in a strong privateers' battle.

with all the high speed flicks.' In morning warm-up, he gave a graphic demonstration on the fifth-gear right-left onto the back straight, losing the footrests and just making it through, feet flapping behind. That prompted a change back to his first bike, and the avowed intention for the race merely to: 'Stay on.'

The absentees freed up front row positions for both Suzukis. Schwantz was the faster, and widespread favourite for a third successive win – another master of Assen, exploiting his bike's manoeuvrability and his own adaptability to the maximum.

He might have qualified faster, too, but he only had one of the new droner engines reckoned just right for Assen, and that was in the bike he crashed. Thus he finished practice and set his fastest lap using the old engine with its much sharper power curve, in the certain knowledge that whatever changes he made to suspension settings or tyre choices might not be valid at all on the bike he had hoped to race. Overnight, he and his team resolved to stick with the old bike, on the grounds that it was better developed as a package, and had after all won at Mugello.

Schwantz was chasing the front wheel; team-mate Chandler is on the other end of the delicately balanced Suzuki see-saw, and was chasing the rear. Like Kevin, he believed in the droner motor. 'It's the grippiest track all year, and with the extra torque it comes off the corner real good. There are other tracks where I might still prefer the old motor, though.'

In the new order Garriga led the second row, with Criville next, and seeming at first to be rather at sea in his first 500 attempt here. He'd benefited from a guided tour behind Chandler to set his fast time.

Then came Mamola, stripped of his Budweiser sponsorship decals by a local advertising regulation, but enjoying being at a track that favours experience. Still having trouble with the hand he'd hurt in Germany, he was lucky to escape injury when he crashed spectacularly in the last session.

Barros completed row two; Mackenzie took over row three, unhurt by his tumble, which happened at very low speed after he'd taken to the grass. Lucky, for he was riding two weeks after breaking a bone in his right foot, wearing a special boot and finding it difficult but enjoyable.

Then came Corrado Catalano, top privateer and really finding his feet, looking fast and aggressive. He was ahead of Eddie Laycock, and of DuHamel, learning his way round the hardest track of the year.

The hard-charging Arakaki led row four from Rudroff, injury victim Goddard and Kevin Mitchell. There were 31 qualifiers – four non-starters – with Leuthe's VRP last but on the grid for its first-ever GP.

500 cc RACE – 20 LAPS

The opening laps held all the promise of a classic Assen race. Schwantz had seized the lead and seemed to be in control of the fairly slow pace. Lawson challenged continuously and looked much faster, but the Suzuki rider foiled every overtaking move with his late braking, including one well-timed surge that saw the Cagiva clearly ahead at the end of the back straight.

Barros was up with them, challenged by Chandler, putting Schwantz's screamer among a buzz of droners as the quartet quickly pulled away from the field.

The first upset came on lap three, when Chandler suddenly went missing round the first loop. He had lost the front wheel at the right-hand Ossebroeken curve, and slid harmlessly out. 'I worked my front tyre too hard too soon,' he explained. 'I was expecting the other guys to catch up with us, and I wanted to make a break with the leaders. I guess I should have looked over my shoulder.'

Now there were three, and the battle was furious. Among Lawson's repertoire of concerted attacks was a move at the end of the start-finish straight, where he'd come off the kinks faster than Schwantz, then charge up inside under braking. He'd practised it a couple of times, then on lap seven he seemed to have made it stick.

Schwantz would have none of it. With the Cagiva alongside, even a little ahead, he eased off his brakes again to lead into the corner, and flicked the Suzuki to the apex. Trouble was, the Cagiva was heading for the same piece of track.

Lawson's front wheel struck the Suzuki's right-rear quarter. It flicked sideways and spat Schwantz heavily into the barrier. Lawson stayed wheels down but ran onto the grass where he too was thrown, landing unhurt in a dyke.

It is interesting to speculate on why they collided. Schwantz was in front and on line, but Lawson had certainly been ahead or at least alongside as they commenced braking. He may also not have anticipated the braking ability of the Suzuki's special AP carbons. Certainly, Schwantz is justified in expressing his amazement at being T-boned from behind so early in the race, by such an experienced rider. 'I'd probably have accepted second place – but why didn't he leave it until nearer the end of the race?' he said.

Lawson was very firm in the opposite point of view, and had the advantage of being able to speak directly about it afterwards, while Schwantz was still under anaesthetic. 'I was past him, then he got off the brakes for an instant. Then I was already down on maximum lean right next to the paint when he slammed the door on me. I don't know how he thought I would make the corner, or why he found it necessary to do that. I thought that I could ride safely with him right to the last lap.'

This left Barros in a clear lead, but he lived up to his reputation of requiring companions to ride fast and within two laps he'd been caught by another hard race between Criville and Garriga. Shortly afterwards, Kocinski latched on to the group, and they swapped the lead back and forth until Garriga ran wide and lost ground; with his tyres shot he was never able to regain it.

Kocinski had been working his tyres hard catching up from a poor start, and said later: 'I blew it from there.' Barros was looking strong, though, and with Criville leading on the final lap, the young Brazilian put a well-timed pass on Kocinski to pursue the Honda into the final long loop, so as to be in position for an attack on Criville at the chicane.

Instead, he slid wide before he got there, slowing Kocinski behind him before losing second to the American, and at the same time giving

Photos: Malcolm Bryan

Criville the chance to press home his breakaway sprint, and cross the line first by three-quarters of a second. 'I never expected to win a 500 GP in my first season,' the delighted former 125 champion said later. Nor had anybody else.

Kocinski held second from Barros by mere hundredths of a second, to become the grandfather of the rostrum party – he was 24, Criville 22 and Barros just 21.

Garriga was over two seconds adrift at the finish. Way back came Mamola, who'd had a mainly lonely race though under constant pressure from the blue Yamaha France bikes of Mackenzie and DuHamel. The Scotsman had caught up from a poor start and seemed to have defeated Assen first-timer DuHamel, only to lose sixth place on the last lap, unwilling to duke it out because of his injuries.

Only another three seconds back an on-form Catalano finally triumphed in a close dice with Laycock; and the last point went to Briton Kevin Mitchell, his first of the season and the first for a Harris Yamaha since they were introduced at the start of this year.

Then came Rudroff, with Doorakkers 12th. A little way back, Arakaki defeated Buckmaster and Crine in another good dice. At least it had been a good day for the privateers.

250 cc PRACTICE

Max Biaggi turned 21 at Assen, and adulthood brought him his third pole position in succession. 'I don't want to say anything about winning the race, because I'm superstitious,' he said. There was also, of course, the matter of looking over his shoulder and seeing a pair of similar Aprilias within tenths of his time – last year's winner Chili, then top privateer Andy Preining, the Austrian finally showing something of the 1991 form that got him his leased works Aprilia motor. The first Honda only appeared on the far end of the front row – ridden, of course, by Cadalora. But he was more than one-and-a-half seconds down on Biaggi, and it hurt.

It is at circuits like this with high corner speeds that the waspish throttle response of the rotary-valve Aprilia engine matters least, and that fact put the pressure on the title leader. His NSR was clearly outgunned and he was depressed, saying: 'When people pass me in the corners, then I know there is something wrong with my bike. It means that not just the engine but also the handling of the Aprilias is now better. I may be on the front row, but there is a lot of difference between us. I'll have to go out to get as many points as I can.'

He might not even have been on row one if Reggiani hadn't been battling. 'Only the tyres are okay,' he said wryly, with his time almost a second down on Biaggi's though close enough to give Cadalora a headache. Apart from his other troubles, the veteran factory Aprilia rider had tried an electronic quickshift gearchange, but found his habit of snicking at the gear lever to make sure top gear was fully home kept cutting the ignition.

Bradl crashed again in practice, and decided forthwith to abandon his attempts at matching the Aprilias. 'It was like at Hockenheim. The back slipped away, and I have no way of controlling it,' he said. He ended up alongside Loris, with Puig's lease-engine Aprilia and Schmid's works Yamaha alongside.

Torrontegui, steadily improving on the Suzuki, led row three from Ruggia's Gilera, and the Hondas of Romboni (factory RS) and Shimizu (factory NSR) – with Cardus still away injured, his was the last works Honda. Lavado led row four on the Gilera – another seasoned track veteran who loves Assen, he quipped: 'I hope my Gilera enjoys it as much as I do.'

Capirossi was next, then home hero Zeelenberg on the Suzuki. It was a brave effort, and there were many who felt he shouldn't be racing at all. His left ankle injury was less than four weeks old, and he was having trouble not only backshifting for the bends (which meant he was forced to brake early), but also in stringing more than six laps together. Wilco left his decision whether or not to race until the last minute, but most people inside and outside his team thought he would be well advised to give it a miss.

Photos: Malcolm Bryan

250 cc RACE – 18 LAPS

Biaggi made a flier from pole and kept on pushing in an attempt to break away. Chili had also started well, and bit by bit he caught up with his younger team-mate. The contrast in their riding styles was entertaining and revealing: the youngster devastatingly daring, surviving one hair-raising moment after another; Chili only a little smoother as he was forced to live on the ragged edge. They almost collided once, and it hardly seemed as though the battle could last much longer.

It was Biaggi who dropped out – not through any riding error, but with piston failure which struck suddenly as he passed the pits to start the seventh lap, forcing him to slow unexpectedly into the kink with Chili swerving past as he rattled to a stop.

This was a gift to Chili, who'd expected a tough battle with three or four riders, he said, but had instead found himself alone and fully in charge. Cadalora had been chasing the leading pair, and no doubt hoping they would slow each other down, but now Chili was able to keep a watch on the Honda and control the gap.

'Control' was the word also chosen by Luca, after further frustrating proof that an Aprilia can outrun a 1992 Honda. 'If I got close to Chili, he simply went away from me. With five laps to go I decided there was no chance that I'd be able to stop him from winning. In the top three gears, I simply cannot compete on speed any more.' He finished almost seven seconds adrift, his face grim with frustration.

Reggiani had a dismal start, and gradually picked his way through from ninth at the end of lap one to take third off Schmid's Yamaha on lap nine. By then, the leaders were far out of reach, and he went on alone to take third, another seven seconds down.

A slightly smaller distance separated the next group, having a frenzied battle that lasted to the very end. Schmid, complaining of a shortage of power, was gradually swallowed up by Puig and Shimizu. He crossed the line sixth, narrowly ahead of Bradl's Honda, after the latter had survived one big slide and said to himself: 'That's enough. I want to see the chequered flag this time.' Capirossi, having also been active in this brawling group, was eighth, with less than two seconds covering from him to Puig.

Ruggia's Gilera had pitted with electrical problems, but Lavado's ran strongly in a lonely ninth, and the Venezuelan former triple champion opened his World Championship score.

There was another stirring battle behind them, all Dutch, and involving the van den Goorbergh clan and Zeelenberg: two Aprilias against the injured Wilco's works Suzuki. First Patrick vdG dropped out, his Aprilia seized, leaving Jurgen and Wilco to scrap to the finish, with all Wilco's earlier thoughts of retirement forgotten in the heat of battle. It came down, almost inevitably, to a barging match in the final chicane as they each tried to outbrake the other, and arrived simultaneously, aiming firmly for the same piece of track.

They collided, with Jurgen bouncing off on the inside of the first corner to run horribly wide on the exit of the next one, and Wilco standing

Left: **Gianola, Casanova, Gresini and Debbia make an Italian championship round out of the 125 race.**

Bottom: **The Güdel brothers temporarily fend off Ralph Bohnhorst/Bruno Hiller. Note the amount of rubbish in the radiators.**

on the footpegs as he motocrossed across the gravel and the grass. Then both wound the power on for a drag to the line.

A jubilant Jurgen won tenth place and the last point, with less than a tenth in it; but doubtful starter Wilco was still justly proud of finishing – the only Lucky Strike rider to do so all weekend (his 250 team-mate Torrontegui crashed after a second-lap top ten tangle with Shimizu).

There were 24 finishers: notable among retirements was practice crasher Romboni, too sore to continue, and Stefan Prein, who crashed his HB Honda very spectacularly on the kink after the first corner and was lucky to escape unhurt.

Another Aprilia triumph, and another all-Italian rostrum. And again the strongest of them all, Cadalora, increased his points lead.

125 cc RACE – 17 LAPS

The first race got off to a botched start when Luis Alvaro took off from the third row before the green light. It was red-flagged at once and, after some confusion, they all pitted to refuel and the whole race process began again.

For five riders, it was all over by the first bend – Lüthi, Wada, Ricci (on the Yamaha), Patrickson and Sanchez collided at low speed, at least within easy walking distance of the pits.

Meanwhile, pole-starter Gianola's Honda led the pack out into the flat countryside, and stayed in front until the 12th lap. Any early attempt at a breakaway had been foiled by the usual rabble, including Aprilia riders Casanova and Gramigni and Gresini's Honda, soon being joined by Gianola's team-mate Debbia and Waldmann, though the latter was soon to fade to ninth with more niggling engine trouble as his season continued to go downhill.

This left five scrapping to the finish, with the end result a lottery of luck and skill.

Casanova came bottom, crashing after losing the rear late in the final lap.

By then Gianola's very fast Semprucci Honda had gained him enough of a breathing space to secure victory by half a second, with Gresini exerting his authority in the closing stages to make sure of second by a similar distance from Gramigni, with Debbia right on his tail. Four Italians this time, all in a row.

Some 20 seconds back Jorge Martinez climbed steadily from a bad start to attack and ultimately transcend a tough fight for fifth. This had involved fearsome Japanese Honda pilots Wakai, Sakata and Takao Shimizu as well as the Aprilia of rising Spaniard Giro. Wakai dropped out with three laps left when his chain broke, but not before he and his kamikaze countrymen had earned the disfavour of the Europeans for their typically hard riding. The finishing order was Martinez, Sakata, Shimizu, Giro, with Waldmann dropping off the back of the group to ninth and Casanova remounting and finishing tenth, keeping Peter Öttl out of the points.

SIDECAR RACE – 17 LAPS

It was a dreadful weekend for the sidecars, with competitors (especially Webster and Biland) spending more time in meetings than in preparation and practice, emerging from time to time looking bleak and bearing bad news: to many it seemed this really might be their last GP.

By the time the race came – supported by a hugely enthusiastic crowd – accord had been reached with IRTA, and the future was assured (said Biland) 'for the next ten years'.

Sadly, at one track where they are loved, they did not reward the fans with much of a race. Biland and Waltisperg had qualified on pole, and led from start to finish, winning by more than 15 seconds from Webster/Simmons. The Briton had been using an F1 car-type carbon-fibre clutch developed by AP Racing, but he messed up the start and by the time he'd forced his way past Klaus Klaffenböck to take second, at the end of lap one, Biland had broken the tow and was far enough ahead to be able to control the race without much trouble.

Klaffenböck was a distant third, while slow-starting Egbert Streuer came through to claim fourth, leaving Ralph Bohnhorst to fend off the Güdel brothers for fifth.

British hope Darren Dixon retired after one lap with engine trouble.

The race marked a turning point for Biland, as well as for the class, while all left with their share of the second half of the FIM's $100,000 payment at last safely in hand. But subsequent events showed they were not yet out of the woods.

Grote Prijs van Nederland, 27 June/statistics

Circuit van Drenthe, Assen, 3.759-mile/6.049-km circuit

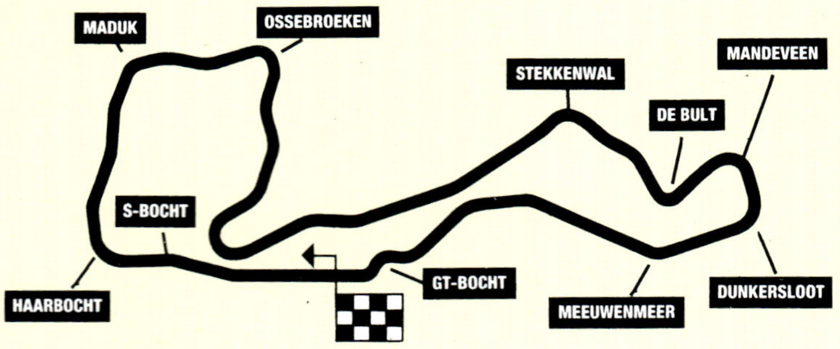

500 cc

20 laps, 75.180 miles/120.980 km

Place	Rider	Nat.	Machine	Laps	Time & speed	Fastest lap	Lap
1	**Alex Criville**	**E**	**Honda**	**20**	**42m 00.424s 107.372 mph/ 172.799 km/h**	**2m 04.893s**	**20**
2	**John Kocinski**	**USA**	**Yamaha**	**20**	**42m 01.186s**	**2m 04.865s**	**11**
3	**Alexandre Barros**	**BR**	**Cagiva**	**20**	**42m 01.217s**	**2m 04.704s**	**6**
4	**Juan Garriga**	**E**	**Yamaha**	**20**	**42m 02.678s**	**2m 04.625s**	**6**
5	**Randy Mamola**	**USA**	**Yamaha**	**20**	**42m 34.430s**	**2m 06.083s**	**5**
6	**Miguel DuHamel**	**CAN**	**Yamaha**	**20**	**42m 40.368s**	**2m 06.419s**	**3**
7	**Niall Mackenzie**	**GB**	**Yamaha**	**20**	**42m 40.839s**	**2m 06.990s**	**13**
8	**Corrado Catalano**	**I**	**Yamaha**	**20**	**42m 44.013s**	**2m 06.770s**	**15**
9	**Eddie Laycock**	**IRL**	**Yamaha**	**20**	**42m 44.472s**	**2m 06.854s**	**15**
10	**Kevin Mitchell**	**GB**	**Yamaha**	**20**	**43m 00.539s**	**2m 07.571s**	**9**
11	Michael Rudroff	D	Yamaha	20	43m 22.209s	2m 08.284s	13
12	Cees Doorakkers	NL	Yamaha	20	43m 28.262s	2m 08.945s	7
13	Toshiyuki Arakaki	J	Yamaha	20	43m 34.188s	2m 09.638s	12
14	Simon Buckmaster	GB	Yamaha	20	43m 34.423s	2m 09.764s	5
15	Thierry Crine	F	Yamaha	20	43m 34.689s	2m 09.694s	12
16	Serge David	CH	Yamaha	20	43m 58.071s	2m 09.395s	14
17	Niggi Schmassman	CH	Yamaha	20	44m 04.377s	2m 10.049s	11
18	Marco Papa	I	Librenti	20	44m 17.574s	2m 10.466s	2
19	Peter Graves	GB	Yamaha	19	42m 23.330s	2m 12.390s	10
20	Lucio Pedercini	I	Paton	19	43m 02.119s	2m 12.949s	10
21	Sepp Doppler	A	Yamaha	15	43m 55.780s	2m 14.817s	11
	Claude Arciero	F	Yamaha	7	DNF	2m 12.825s	2
	Kevin Schwantz	USA	Suzuki	6	DNF	2m 04.675s	6
	Eddie Lawson	USA	Cagiva	6	DNF	2m 04.643s	6
	Dominique Sarron	F	Yamaha	6	DNF	2m 09.163s	2
	Doug Chandler	USA	Suzuki	2	DNF	2m 05.186s	2
	Andreas Leuthe	D	VRP	2	DNF	2m 25.950s	2
	Michael Doohan	AUS	Honda		DNS		
	Wayne Gardner	AUS	Honda		DNS		
	Peter Goddard	AUS	Yamaha		DNS		
	Juan Lopez Mella	E	Yamaha		DNS		

Fastest lap: Garriga, 2m 04.625s, 108.576 mph/174.735 km/h.
Lap record: Kevin Schwantz, USA (Suzuki), 2m 02.443s, 110.519 mph/177.849 km/h (1991).

Practice leaderboard: 1 Lawson, 2m 03.675s; **2** Doohan, 2m 03.692s; **3** Gardner, 2m 03.829s; **4** Kocinski, 2m 03.995s; **5** Schwantz, 2m 04.001s; **6** Chandler, 2m 04.366s; **7** Garriga, 2m 04.688s; **8** Criville, 2m 04.726s; **9** Mamola, 2m 04.964s; **10** Barros, 2m 05.703s; **11** Mackenzie, 2m 06.351s; **12** Catalano, 2m 06.374s; **13** Laycock, 2m 06.515s; **14** DuHamel, 2m 06.595s; **15** Arakaki, 2m 06.956s.

World Championship: 1 Doohan, 130; **2** Schwantz, 77; **3** Rainey, 65; **4** Chandler, 57; **5** Kocinski, 51; **6** Criville, 49; **7** Garriga, 35; **8** Mamola, 29; **9** Mackenzie, 26; **10** Barros, 24; **11** Beattie and Lawson, 18; **13** DuHamel, 16; **14** Gardner, 12; **15** Goddard and Itoh, 10; **17** Ohishi, 6; **18** Catalano, 5; **19** Honma and Laycock, 3; **21** Fujiwara, 2; **22** Mitchell and Tsujimoto, 1.

250 cc

18 laps, 67.662 miles/108.882 km

Place	Rider	Nat.	Machine	Laps	Time & speed	Fastest lap	Lap
1	**Pier Francesco Chili**	**I**	**Aprilia**	**18**	**38m 52.184s 104.435 mph/ 168.072 km/h**	**2m 07.831s**	**2**
2	**Luca Cadalora**	**I**	**Honda**	**18**	**38m 58.858s**	**2m 08.630s**	**2**
3	**Loris Reggiani**	**I**	**Aprilia**	**18**	**39m 06.942s**	**2m 09.114s**	**9**
4	**Alberto Puig**	**E**	**Aprilia**	**18**	**39m 09.736s**	**2m 09.831s**	**16**
5	**Masahiro Shimizu**	**J**	**Honda**	**18**	**39m 10.188s**	**2m 09.537s**	**8**
6	**Jochen Schmid**	**D**	**Yamaha**	**18**	**39m 10.940s**	**2m 09.912s**	**11**
7	**Helmut Bradl**	**D**	**Honda**	**18**	**39m 11.145s**	**2m 09.640s**	**15**
8	**Loris Capirossi**	**I**	**Honda**	**18**	**39m 11.345s**	**2m 09.668s**	**7**
9	**Carlos Lavado**	**YV**	**Gilera**	**18**	**39m 23.388s**	**2m 10.037s**	**8**
10	**Jurgen van den Goorbergh**	**NL**	**Aprilia**	**18**	**39m 38.759s**	**2m 11.067s**	**17**
11	Wilco Zeelenberg	NL	Suzuki	18	39m 38.843s	2m 11.027s	17
12	Bernard Hänggeli	CH	Aprilia	18	39m 44.563s	2m 11.542s	2
13	Bernd Kassner	D	Aprilia	18	39m 44.828s	2m 11.165s	10
14	Harald Eckl	D	Aprilia	18	39m 47.789s	2m 10.538s	10
15	Luis D'Antin	E	Honda	18	40m 02.606s	2m 11.468s	6
16	Yves Briguet	CH	Honda	18	40m 02.879s	2m 12.017s	4
17	Frédéric Protat	F	Aprilia	18	40m 18.103s	2m 12.966s	5
18	Jean-Pierre Jeandat	F	Honda	18	40m 23.459s	2m 13.240s	14
19	Adrian Bosshard	CH	Honda	18	40m 23.468s	2m 12.860s	6
20	Eskil Suter	CH	Aprilia	18	40m 23.832s	2m 13.325s	14
21	Michele Gallina	I	Yamaha	18	40m 32.497s	2m 13.482s	8
22	Erkka Korpiaho	SF	Aprilia	18	40m 34.979s	2m 14.266s	12
23	Renzo Colleoni	I	Yamaha	18	40m 43.274s	2m 13.556s	8
24	Fokko Kuiper	NL	Aprilia	17	39m 44.556s	2m 17.453s	6
	Katsuyoshi Kozono	J	Honda	12	40m 53.045s	2m 16.503s	6
	Paolo Casoli	I	Yamaha	17	DNF	2m 11.246s	11
	Patrick van den Goorbergh	NL	Aprilia	13	DNF	2m 11.168s	9
	Jonnie Boerman	NL	Honda	13	DNF	2m 16.417s	6
	Bernard Cazade	F	Honda	10	DNF	2m 16.397s	8
	Doriano Romboni	I	Honda	9	DNF	2m 09.933s	6
	Jean-Philippe Ruggia	F	Gilera	8	DNF	2m 11.460s	3
	Adi Stadler	D	Honda	7	DNF	2m 14.257s	3
	Massimiliano Biaggi	I	Aprilia	6	DNF	2m 07.876s	2
	Stefan Prein	D	Honda	2	DNF	2m 12.107s	2
	Herri Torrontegui	E	Suzuki	1	DNF	2m 16.893s	1
	Andy Preining	A	Aprilia	0	DNF		

Fastest lap: Chili, 2m 07.831s, 105.852 mph/170.353 km/h (record).
Previous record: Luca Cadalora, I (Honda), 2m 08.178s,105.566 mph/169.892 km/h (1991).

Practice leaderboard: 1 Biaggi, 2m 06.736s; **2** Chili, 2m 06.949s; **3** Preining, 2m 08.346s; **4** Cadalora, 2m 08.489s; **5** Reggiani, 2m 08.575s; **6** Bradl, 2m 09.031s; **7** Puig, 2m 09.055s; **8** Schmid, 2m 09.194s; **9** Torrontegui, 2m 09.296s; **10** Ruggia, 2m 09.363s; **11** Romboni, 2m 09.366s; **12** Shimizu, 2m 09.623s; **13** Lavado, 2m 09.661s; **14** Capirossi, 2m 09.725s; **15** Zeelenberg, 2m 10.326s.

World Championship: 1 Cadalora, 135; **2** Reggiani, 82; **3** Chili, 72; **4** Bradl, 61; **5** Puig, 50; **6** Biaggi, 43; **7** Cardus, 37; **8** Shimizu, 34; **9** Zeelenberg, 26; **10** Schmid, 25; **11** Romboni, 17; **12** Okada, 15; **13** Aoki, 12; **14** Capirossi, 11; **15** Preining, Ruggia and Wakai, 4; **18** Casoli, Nanba and Torrontegui, 3; **21** Lavado and Prein, 2; **23** Jeandat, Kassner and J. van den Goorbergh, 1.

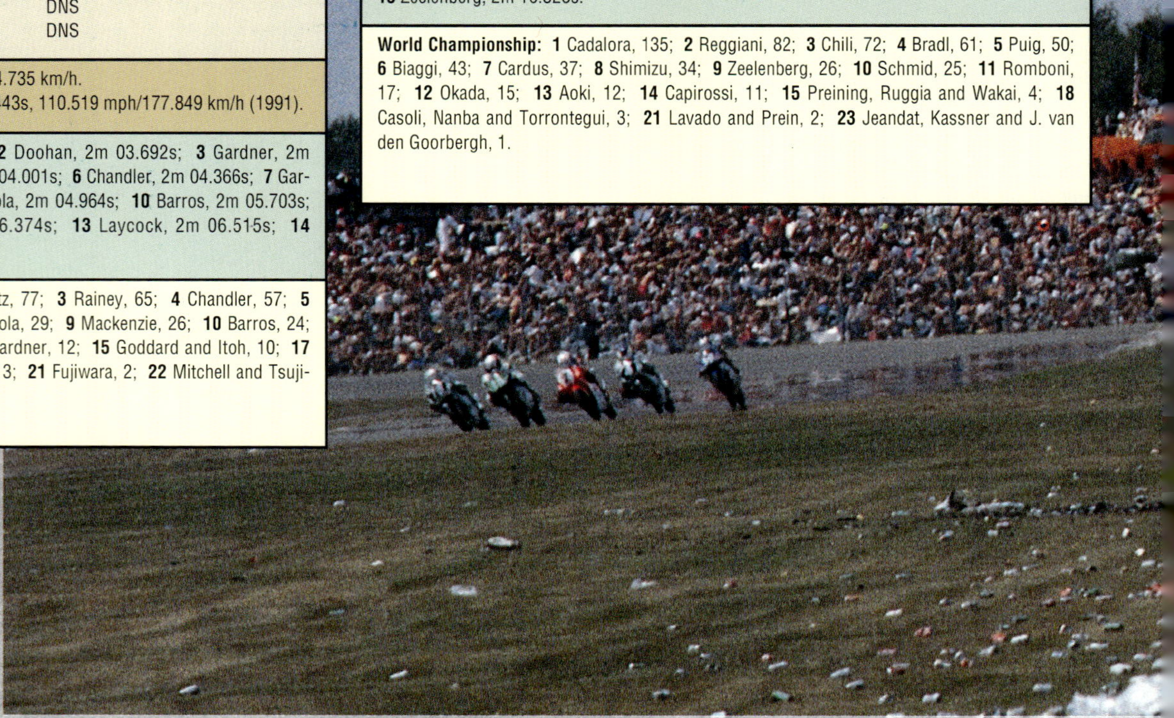

Malcolm Bryan

Assen atmosphere is so strong you could throw a beer can at it. Many people did.

125 cc

17 laps, 63.903 miles/102.833 km

Place	*Rider*	*Nat.*	*Machine*	*Laps*	*Time & speed*	*Fastest lap*	*Lap*
1	**Ezio Gianola**	**I**	**Honda**	**17**	**39m 14.559s 97.696 mph/ 157.226 km/h**	**2m 17.317s**	**6**
2	**Fausto Gresini**	**I**	**Honda**	**17**	**39m 15.236s**	**2m 17.217s**	**5**
3	**Alessandro Gramigni**	**I**	**Aprilia**	**17**	**39m 15.304s**	**2m 17.451s**	**6**
4	**Gabriele Debbia**	**I**	**Honda**	**17**	**39m 15.548s**	**2m 16.851s**	**5**
5	**Jorge Martinez**	**E**	**Honda**	**17**	**39m 40.854s**	**2m 18.056s**	**3**
6	**Kazuto Sakata**	**J**	**Honda**	**17**	**39m 41.616s**	**2m 18.619s**	**11**
7	**Takao Shimizu**	**J**	**Honda**	**17**	**39m 45.382s**	**2m 18.415s**	**5**
8	**Carlos Giro**	**E**	**Aprilia**	**17**	**39m 49.421s**	**2m 18.620s**	**11**
9	**Ralf Waldmann**	**D**	**Honda**	**17**	**39m 56.624s**	**2m 18.553s**	**2**
10	**Bruno Casanova**	**I**	**Aprilia**	**17**	**39m 57.748s**	**2m 17.251s**	**7**
11	Peter Öttl	D	Rotax	17	40m 05.958s	2m 19.002s	6
12	Oliver Petrucciani	CH	Honda	17	40m 07.321s	2m 19.215s	17
13	Loek Bodelier	NL	Honda	17	40m 08.529s	2m 19.949s	4
14	Hisashi Unemoto	J	Honda	17	40m 09.330s	2m 20.079s	5
15	Maik Stief	D	Aprilia	17	40m 09.536s	2m 19.677s	16
16	Arie Molenaar	NL	Aprilia	17	40m 14.630s	2m 20.464s	2
17	Julian Miralles	E	Honda	17	40m 16.523s	2m 20.590s	11
18	Hans Koopman	NL	Honda	17	40m 17.514s	2m 20.497s	11
19	Manuel Hernandez	E	Aprilia	17	40m 27.038s	2m 20.462s	2
20	Hans Spaan	NL	Aprilia	17	40m 45.138s	2m 20.087s	16
21	Alfred Waibel	D	Honda	17	40m 47.470s	2m 22.332s	14
22	Jos van Dongen	NL	Honda	17	40m 47.724s	2m 22.827s	13
23	Giuseppe Fiorillo	I	Yamaha	17	40m 48.396s	2m 22.834s	7
24	Hubert Abold	D	Honda	17	40m 49.294s	2m 22.329s	14
25	Robin Appleyard	GB	Honda	17	40m 49.568s	2m 22.537s	2
26	Luis Alvaro	E	Aprilia	17	41m 23.790s	2m 20.772s	11
	Nobuyuki Wakai	J	Honda	14	DNF	2m 18.327s	10
	Peter Galvin	AUS	Honda	13	DNF	2m 24.930s	7
	Giovanni Palmieri	I	Gazzaniga	5	DNF	2m 25.737s	4
	Garry McCoy	AUS	Honda	4	DNF	2m 20.869s	2
	Maurizio Vitali	I	Gazzaniga	2	DNF	2m 21.555s	2
	Alain Bronec	F	Honda	1	DNF	2m 29.553s	1
	Heinz Lüthi	CH	Honda	0	DNF		
	Kinya Wada	J	Honda	0	DNF		
	Fausto Ricci	I	Yamaha	0	DNF		
	Steve Patrickson	GB	Honda	0	DNF		
	Antonio Sanchez	E	Honda	0	DNF		
	Dirk Raudies	D	Honda		DNS		

Fastest lap: Debbia, 2m 16.851s, 98.876 mph/159.125 km/h (record).
Previous record: Ralf Waldmann, D (Honda), 2m 19.094s, 97.281 mph/156.559 km/h (1991).

Practice leaderboard: **1** Gianola, 2m 17.175s; **2** Gresini, 2m 17.303s; **3** Gramigni, 2m 17.407s; **4** Casanova, 2m 17.557s; **5** Waldmann, 2m 17.980s; **6** Sakata, 2m 17.997s; **7** Debbia, 2m 18.282s; **8** Martinez, 2m 18.399s; **9** Wakai, 2m 18.500s; **10** Giro, 2m 19.023s; **11** Shimizu, 2m 19.130s; **12** Vitali, 2m 19.536s; **13** Bodelier, 2m 19.692s; **14** Alvaro, 2m 19.748s; **15** Petrucciani, 2m 19.797s.

World Championship: **1** Waldmann, 86; **2** Gianola, 81; **3** Gresini, 76; **4** Casanova, 70; **5** Gramigni, 67; **6** Debbia, 50; **7** Raudies, 47; **8** Wakai, 35; **9** Martinez, 33; **10** Giro and Sakata, 22; **12** Ueda, 15; **13** Öttl, 10; **14** Koch and Saitoh, 8; **16** Fujihara and Shimizu, 4; **18** Kurfiss and Wada, 3; **20** Spaan, 2; **21** Lüthi and Petrucciani, 1.

Sidecars

17 laps, 63.903 miles/102.833 km

Place	*Driver & passenger*	*Nat.*	*Machine*	*Laps*	*Time & speed*	*Fastest lap*	*Lap*
1	**Rolf Biland/ Kurt Waltisperg**	**CH CH**	**LCR- Krauser**	**17**	**37m 20.486s 102.669 mph/ 165.231 km/h**	**2m 10.345s**	**4**
2	**Steve Webster/ Gavin Simmons**	**GB GB**	**LCR- ADM**	**17**	**37m 36.173s**	**2m 10.572s**	**8**
3	**Klaus Klaffenböck/ Christian Parzer**	**A A**	**LCR- ADM**	**17**	**37m 55.659s**	**2m 11.024s**	**2**
4	**Egbert Streuer/ Peter Brown**	**NL GB**	**LCR- Stredor**	**17**	**38m 01.287s**	**2m 12.778s**	**7**
5	**Ralph Bohnhorst/ Bruno Hiller**	**D D**	**BRM**	**17**	**38m 22.569s**	**2m 13.635s**	**8**
6	**Paul Güdel/ Charly Güdel**	**CH CH**	**LCR- Yamaha**	**17**	**38m 24.081s**	**2m 13.696s**	**3**
7	**Steve Abbott/ Shaun Smith**	**GB GB**	**LCR- Krauser**	**17**	**38m 28.768s**	**2m 13.763s**	**16**
8	**Markus Egloff/ Urs Egloff**	**CH CH**	**LCR- Yamaha**	**17**	**38m 41.138s**	**2m 14.235s**	**3**
9	**Barry Brindley/ Scott Whiteside**	**GB GB**	**LCR- Yamaha**	**17**	**38m 42.565s**	**2m 14.459s**	**4**
10	**Yoshisada Kumagaya/ Bryan Houghton**	**J GB**	**LCR- Krauser**	**17**	**38m 44.951s**	**2m 13.855s**	**7**
11	Theo van Kempen/ Geral de Haas	NL NL	LCR- Krauser	17	38m 45.401s	2m 15.012s	13
12	Markus Bösiger/ Rinie Bettgens	CH NL	LCR- ADM	17	38m 47.522s	2m 14.001s	3
13	Derek Brindley/ Nick Roche	GB GB	LCR- Krauser	17	38m 59.710s	2m 15.106s	5
14	Tony Wyssen/ Kilian Wyssen	CH CH	LCR- Yamaha	17	39m 16.707s	2m 16.611s	8
15	Billy Gällros/ Peter Berglund	S S	LCR- Streuer	17	39m 28.552s	2m 16.496s	6
16	Tony Baker/ Simon Prior	GB GB	LCR- Krauser	17	39m 34.743s	2m 17.262s	5
17	Robert Fisher/ Trevor Crone	GB GB	LCR- Krauser	17	39m 43.348s	2m 17.835s	4
18	Hans Hügli/ Adolf Hänni	CH CH	LCR- Krauser	16	37m 26.312s	2m 18.359s	2
19	André Bosman/ Dave Kellett	AUS AUS	LCR- Krauser	16	37m 47.391s	2m 18.608s	3
	Jukka Lauslehto/ Jurgen Levinsen	SF DK	LCR- ADM	13	DNF	2m 18.058s	2
	Reiner Koster/ Jurg Egli	CH CH	LCR- Yamaha	9	DNF	2m 19.105s	3
	Peter Lemstra/ Jan Kuyt	NL NL	LCR- Krauser	9	DNF	2m 25.544s	2
	Mark Reddington/ Kim Andreasen	GB DK	LCR- Krauser	6	DNF	2m 19.196s	3
	Darren Dixon/ Andy Hetherington	GB GB	LCR- Krauser	1	DNF	2m 20.786s	1
	Eddie Wright/ Peter Hill	GB GB	LCR- Krauser		DNQ		

Fastest lap: Biland, 2m 10.345s, 103.811 mph/167.067 km/h.
Lap record: Egbert Streuer/Peter Brown, NL/GB (LCR-Yamaha), 2m 10.178s, 103.944 mph/167.282 km/h (1991).

Practice leaderboard: **1** Biland, 2m 09.733s; **2** Webster, 2m 10.274s; **3** Streuer, 2m 10.834s; **4** Dixon, 2m 11.099s; **5** Klaffenböck, 2m 11.782s; **6** Abbott, 2m 12.097s; **7** Güdel, 2m 12.927s; **8** Bohnhorst, 2m 13.428s; **9** Kumagaya, 2m 13.622s; **10** D. Brindley, 2m 13.967s; **11** B. Brindley, 2m 14.182s; **12** Egloff, 2m 14.633s; **13** Wyssen, 2m 15.576s; **14** van Kempen, 2m 16.222s; **15** Bösiger, 2m 16.254s.

World Championship: **1** Webster, 55; **2** Klaffenböck, 42; **3** Biland, 23; **4** Kumagaya, 21; **5** Güdel, 20; **6** Bohnhorst and B. Brindley, 16; **8** Dixon and Streuer, 12; **10** Bösiger, 10; **11** Egloff, 6; **12** Abbott and Wyssen, 4; **14** Baker and D. Brindley, 1.

HUNGARIAN GRAND PRIX

Once every 12 years or so, something will happen in racing that gladdens the heart. Sunday in Hungary was one of those days. There, amid the collapse of the race strategies of the surviving lions of the class, Eddie Lawson claimed the tactical victory of his career to give Cagiva a first-ever 500 class GP win.

Even he admitted afterwards that he'd only won because his tyre gamble had paid off. The difference between zero and hero depended entirely on the caprice of the weather. His defeated rivals were also quick to point out that while Eddie could afford to take a gamble like that, they all had championship positions to defend and were obliged to copy one another. In making the wrong choice.

Photos: Malcolm Bryan

WORLD CHAMPIONSHIP • ROUND 9

500 cc	LAWSON
250 cc	CADALORA
125 cc	GRAMIGNI
SIDECARS	BILAND

Opposite: **Mayhem in the Cagiva pit – after 12 years, victory was a brand new experience. Was it good management or good timing that put Giacomo Agostini (behind Lawson, left of the girl with the plait) in the glory seat?**

Inset: **'Is there someone up there I should thank for this?'**

Right: **Emergency Ward 10 – on wheels. Schwantz was an unexpected arrival three weeks after breaking his left arm (still in a cast) and dislocating his left hip. GP patch-'em-up medic Dr Claudio Costa (blue shirt) seems pleased with his handiwork.**

All the same, the moment when the avenging Eddie, having sliced through from seventh place on the drying track, took the lead from the flummoxed Chandler was one to be savoured. But it wasn't then that he won the race. Nor was it when, after one start had already been aborted by a sweeping shower, Dunlop chief Jeremy Ferguson took an inspired guess that the dark skies were shortly to lift and advised him to go racing on an intermediate front and a cut-slick rear, while all the others were fitting full wets. The true strength of his victory came in the early laps, when his tyres were as wrong as could be and his carbon brakes were terrifyingly treacherous. It took all his experience just to stay wheels down, and all his determination to maintain position so as to be able to attack later on.

Lawson, being Lawson, was entirely nonchalant afterwards. It was his 31st win; he was pretty used to the feeling. But he had the satisfaction of having proved a point, and the knowledge that he'd made another little piece of history. Cagiva's first win in 12 years of trying showed that his presence had transformed the Italian team effort, and this rare 500 class European triumph over the might of Japan was a shot in the arm for bike GP racing as a whole.

And let us not forget Michael Doohan, watching the race on TV in his hospital bed in Bologna, in far worse condition than anyone in Hungary was letting on. He'd heard that Rainey was back and that his Yamaha was also now equipped with a drone-clone motor; and that fellow-Assen victim Kevin Schwantz had turned up in Hungary, amazingly ready to keep going without missing a race. Like Rainey, the Texan saw a small window of opportunity for his own chances, and he was ready to leap through it, broken arm and all. Them getting beaten by Eddie was far more than Doohan could have hoped for.

For almost everyone, it was a relief when the race was over. The meeting had begun under a cloud, most especially because of lingering bad impressions formed during the first visit two years before. The layout and condition of the track had almost resulted in a riders' strike, and caused the race to be struck off the calendar until the track was modified. Aside from being too slow for 500s (an 85 mph lap record) and very much one-line, the surface was patchy and bumpy, the kerbs dangerously high, and there was a bridge abutment by the track, right in the high-side A-zone on the exit of the first looping turn.

Now, a programme of changes had improved safety aspects, if not the overall layout. The kerbs had gone and the bridge support was cut right back. The full lap had been resurfaced, though rather surprisingly it was still very bumpy. Then a weird complaint surfaced – that the track had been overcleaned! There was still so much detergent on the surface that in the first wet practices the bikes were leaving trails of foam.

The biggest surprise at Budapest was the presence of Kevin Schwantz, hardly limping after a lucky quick recovery from his dislocated hip, but wearing a plaster cast on his broken left arm, as well as a bandage on a swollen right elbow where a patch of road rash had become infected. This was now in many ways the most troublesome of all his injuries. He'd been in hospital with Doohan after their Assen accidents, and had seen how his own quick recuperation was mirrored by the Honda rider's deterioration. It was all the encouragement he needed.

Even his team had doubted his ability to get back, and general manager Garry Taylor had already arranged for a replacement rider – Donald Jacks, a young American prominent in WERA endurance racing, if little known elsewhere. Jacks had flown in to Britain to test the Suzuki, even as Schwantz was deciding to have a go, fell twice in appalling conditions at Donington Park, then travelled to the Hungaroring somewhat chastened in the vain hope that Kevin might either change his mind or prove unfit in early practice. Instead, the 22-year-old Florida kid cooled his heels, and absorbed the news that he'd been sacked from the US Suzuki endurance team because his abortive test had been on Michelins and Motul while he was contracted to Dunlop and Valvoline. Meanwhile conspiracy theorists insisted that he had never been anything more than a stalking horse, to prevent Honda and others from realising that Schwantz would be racing after all.

Schwantz was not the only injured rider. As well as convalescents Rainey and Mamola, Gardner was also still stiff and sore, and fresh X-rays diagnosed a broken rib undetected at Assen. The list went on, for 250 riders Zeelenberg and Cardus were not fully recovered, Cardus actually withdrawing after qualifying second fastest, while Adi Stadler had torn ankle ligaments. Hurt 125 riders included Dirk Raudies, who'd broken three bones in his right hand at Assen, and Oliver Koch (broken ankle at Hockenheim).

It made a worrying picture, with the serious danger of one of these semi-cripples not only crashing again, but perhaps involving others as well. Nobody could blame the riders for their bravery, but many people felt it was time for IRTA to introduce stricter medical criteria. Yet attitudes remained muddled, and Peter Goddard's team faced criticism for not letting the Australian ride, on medical advice, when he felt fit enough. He had been thrice concussed in seven crashes this season, the last a fortnight before at Assen, and IRTA neurosurgeon Peter Richards advised him against racing. The disgruntled Australian's place was taken by New Zealander Andrew Stroud, fresh from a Battle of the Twins race at Monza on the home-brewed V-twin Britten.

There was trouble in the ranks, though a threatened riders' boycott of the last two races fizzled out before it had really got under way. A mass meeting of riders' association IMRA was demanding a return to previous rules in a number of matters, including prize money (now paid to teams not riders in the new regime), paddock passes for pals, a return to three timed practice sessions and points to 15th place. Some smooth talking from IRTA calmed a potentially troublesome situation, and everyone got down to business.

Rainey was back and looking serious. Now he too finally had a drone-clone engine, Yamaha being the last of the twin-crankers to adopt Honda-style firing order. Rather frustratingly for the factory, neither Rainey nor Kocinski was terribly enthusiastic, running similar times with old and new types. Rainey also had an electronic kill-shifter, which momentarily cuts the ignition to allow open-throttle clutchless changes. Confusingly for trackside observers, Rainey closed the throttle on the low-gear upshifts anyway, saying later that otherwise there was too much wheelspin.

Cagiva had new electronic rear damping control, operating only on compression damping, which Barros had earlier tested at Mugello. 'It made the bike unstable on the fast corners there,' he said. 'But it works well here.'

In an echo of the ghost rider episode, the Japanese factories had made another attempt to give two of their top riders an outing. Yamaha and Honda had applied for wild card entries for Harada and Okada, and had even packed and started shipping bikes for them. Instead, the Hungarian federation nominated two riders of their own. Neither made the race: one was injured and the other shifted down to the 125 class. But by then the Japanese bikes had been turned back at the airport and the plan was off. This incident provoked a fresh ruling to close the loophole, that wild card entries could only be accepted from the home country of each GP.

And so the race belonged to Eddie Lawson, to Dunlop and to Cagiva, and it made a day to remember. And all played out in front of only 7000 spectators at a genuine Ecclestone TV special GP.

500 cc PRACTICE

Rain on Friday left everyone short of time, with Lawson looking set to dominate. Then it started to dry, and there was a hectic scramble for times just in case it rained on Saturday too. First Rainey led, then Gardner, but in the last gasp Chandler displaced the invalids to take his third provisional pole of the year after pitting right near the end of the session to fit a slick rear tyre (the rest were all still on intermediates front and rear).

He used similar tactics and timing to underline his challenge in the dry on Saturday afternoon, laying both hands on his first pole of his two-year GP career. 'I thought I'd missed it, because I got held up that lap and I was expecting to really go for it next time round. Instead I saw the flag signalling the end of the session and I really cursed,' he said.

He and Schwantz were both using only the new drone engines, and finding the friendlier low-range power worked well on the many slow corners. 'You need the front good here too because of the downhill corner entries.' Doug proved that he is now familiar with the Suzuki, for he'd been able to get on the pace at once; and he also showed how he has improved the bike over the season, excelling at the sort of track with tight unbanked corners that has in the past been bad territory for the delicately balanced RGV.

Rainey was a close second, after testing both old and new Yamaha

Malcolm Bryan

engines. Close to full strength after his sabbatical, he was riding aggressively again, with his eye on the championship. 'They always say anything can happen in racing, and I know it's true,' he said prophetically. 'You never give up hope.'

Kocinski was next, still bitching about his Yamaha chassis. 'I'm doing consistent laps,' he said. 'Consistently slow. I've tried outriding the chassis before, and it doesn't pay.' But he did feel that the new engine gave a reduced risk of high-siding compared with the old one because of its less abrupt power and, like Rainey, he elected to race it.

Gardner completed row one, using some new engine parts that had already been available to Doohan. 'I can't really tell what they're like,' he said. 'The last thing you want here is more power.' He was in pain from the freshly diagnosed broken rib, but planned to try to forget about it in the race.

Schwantz led row two after a remarkable performance for a man with a broken arm – doctors had told him less than a fortnight before that he would still be on crutches now. His hip was only slightly troublesome, making it hard for him to shift his weight, but lack of strength in his arms was more significant, and he was conserving his strength by running only a few laps back to back in practice, and by setting his bike accordingly. 'We've screwed the steering damper up some so I'm fighting the steering less, and chosen gearing to minimise the number of shifts I have to make. I'm sure I can make race distance, but I'm not sure how fast. I hope it rains, because that will make it easier on me,' he said.

Garriga was alongside, just over a second down on pole and three-tenths quicker than Lawson, who found himself 'short of motor' in the dry. Barros was alongside him to complete row two.

Row three was headed by Mamola, with Assen winner Criville unsettled by the bumps and qualifying tenth. Then came Mackenzie, who got a bad fright in the last session when his suspension bottomed out and he had to take to the dirt. He didn't fall, but he was irate: 'That's the third time this thing has tried to kill me.'

Toshiyuki Arakaki was 12th and top privateer, putting his Roc Yamaha ahead of the works bike of Miguel DuHamel, who was struggling round the endless bumps. Then came Catalano, Sarron, Rudroff and Crine, with Goddard's replacement, Andrew Stroud, placing a creditable 18th in his first 500 ride.

There were 29 qualifiers, the last being Simon Buckmaster. But the British privateer was a non-starter after falling and breaking his arm when his drive sprocket came adrift in the last session. The injuries effectively ended a difficult season for him. Venezuelan Larry Moreno, who finally made it to a GP after having been entered all year, failed to qualify.

500 cc RACE – 30 LAPS

The race started dry, but there was a frisson of fear in the paddock as Kocinski led the screaming pack back, directly into a sudden and very localised rainstorm. The red flags came out promptly, but Kocinski still ran off the track at the wet

The second corner of the 500 restart. Schwantz, Chandler and Garriga line up in pursuit of invisible leader Mamola while Rainey looks for a way past on the outside. Lawson, with the wrong tyres and brakes for the wet track, is running wide and doing all he can to stay on board.

penultimate bend, narrowly escaping a crash.

They all lined up on slicks for the restart, but before they got away another heavy shower swept across the wooded hills, and there was frantic activity as everybody switched to full wet tyres.

Well, almost everybody. Ready and able to take the double gamble, Eddie Lawson (and one or two privateers) fitted an intermediate front and a cut-slick rear.

In Lawson's case, this also meant fitting dry weather carbon discs, with their notorious lack of power when cold. Thus his first corner was fraught – and most of the rest of them for the initial part of the race. He'd led off the line, but Mamola piled past him into turn one, 'like he was on slicks in the dry' Lawson said later. Steadily the Cagiva dropped back as what looked like the real race developed up ahead.

Mamola galloped away, with Rainey pushing past Schwantz to take second before the end of the first lap. Chandler was already fourth, and he moved past his teammate on lap four and closed steadily on Rainey, taking second on lap eight. Mamola was at that stage almost six seconds clear, but the Suzuki rider was on the boil and remorselessly closed up to sweep into the lead and start pulling away on lap 12.

By now Kocinski was closing on Schwantz for a battle for fourth, Garriga was a lonely sixth, Lawson back in seventh, while Gardner had already been into the pits after scaring himself in the early laps with no traction. He fitted an intermediate rear and rejoined just behind Chandler, one lap adrift, saying later that he wished he'd fitted an intermediate front too. All the same, it was sound tactics – as became clear when the sun broke through two laps later.

Lawson may even have cracked a small smile inside his helmet, but he had a lot of work to do. With half the race gone he was almost a minute adrift, and had spent most of his time so far resisting a strong attack by Catalano, before the Italian spluttered to a stop.

Now he could set his sights on bigger game, and soon he was making ground as those who had fitted wet tyres were forced to back off in the bends, and weave down the straight seeking puddles to cool their rubber.

Eddie sliced past one after the other, giving Schwantz in particular not an inch as he carved past. All the while the tension was rising in the pits as it became clear that he was cutting the lead by four – five – six – seven seconds a lap. At that rate he could catch Chandler before the finish.

It was almost an anti-climax when he did so with four laps to spare, passing Doug so decisively as to make the earlier race leader look as though he was going backwards.

'That was a gamble that almost didn't pay off,' said Lawson. 'The first couple of laps were really miserable. My brakes didn't stop, and I had no grip.' By the finish, however, the opposite was true, and he charged to a popular victory.

Chandler was safe in second. 'I couldn't stop him, and I'd probably have landed on my head if I'd tried,' he said. 'We needed another five minutes of rain. But we didn't have the choice Lawson did. When Rainey and Kevin both fitted wets, I had to as well. I couldn't afford to gamble. When I saw it was clearing, I tried to get in as many good laps as I could. The race was just a bit too long.'

Mamola was thrilled to be back on the rostrum in the year when he got a reprieve from enforced retirement, and was magnanimous enough to express his pleasure at victory at last for the Cagiva team which had almost ended his GP career. 'I knew what Eddie's situation was with tyres, and when I saw steam coming off the track I knew he'd be coming. I saw the pit signals showing he was 17 seconds behind, and then three seconds. I looked round, and all I could see was his number seven.'

Schwantz had caught and passed Rainey, his major target for second in the championship, and said afterwards: 'There was so much smoke coming off his rear tyre the next thing would have been to see flames.' A fine result for a man in his condition, and another gamble that paid off. 'The rain was the best thing we could have had,' he said. 'It meant I didn't have to muscle the bike around.'

Rainey was in agonies of indecision over whether or not to pit. The longer he left it, the less point there was in doing it but the worse his tyres became. Obliged to settle for fifth, he said later: 'I almost pitted about five times.'

Gardner, with his fresh rubber, pulled through to sixth, finishing strongly and passing the fading Kocinski two laps from the end. Behind them, Garriga was a lone eighth, the last rider not to be lapped.

Barros was ninth and set the fastest lap, after pitting for a tyre change, with Laycock claiming the last championship point. DuHamel was 11th, and GP debutant Andrew Stroud a good 12th, after Mackenzie had lost ninth place in a lengthy tyre-changing pit stop.

There were several sad stories among the privateers. Briton Kevin Mitchell (Harris Yamaha) had taken the same tyre gamble as Lawson and was well placed for a charge into the points when a water-bleed bolt backed out of his cylinder head.

The most extraordinary performance came from Criville. He was out of the points when he was called in by his team and put onto his spare bike, ready warmed up and wearing intermediate tyres. His team manager had misunderstood the rules and thought it was now legal to change bikes. Officials were so bemused that they took a couple of laps before they pulled out the black flag to disqualify him.

250 cc PRACTICE

The 250s copped all the rain on Friday, and the conditions threw up some odd times. Cadalora was strong throughout, however, and ended up taking his first pole position since Jerez – he is usually content to save his best for the race. 'I found it quite easy,' he said demoralisingly, before paying his usual tribute to the speed of the Aprilias. 'That doesn't matter so much here,' he said, adding that he liked the track for its twists and bumps,

Photos: Malcolm Bryan

because of the technical challenge it posed, and doubtless also because such conditions suit his softer reed-valve engine better than the more snappish disc-valve Aprilias.

Another Honda was second fastest, even though Cardus had vowed to take it easy because of his injured shoulder. It was his first race since crashing in Germany, but his practice efforts cost him dear, with torn ligaments giving him hell, and on Sunday morning he decided he'd be better off giving it a miss.

Reggiani was next, and crediting his electronic suspension for the fact that he was the best of the Aprilias. In the same breath, he blamed it for leaving him short of the Hondas. 'The suspension is good over the bumps, but we still don't have the adjustment right yet,' he said.

Lavado was fourth fastest, giving the Gilera its first-ever 250 front row position. He was showing flashes of his old brilliance, but also evoked his mercurial past by crashing twice, lucky to escape unhurt. His team hoped for the best, since they had replaced their troublesome Italian ignition with an Austrian-made Comtek item, and thought that for once they might be able to get off the line cleanly.

Romboni led row two after showing well throughout to qualify his factory-kitted RS narrowly ahead of NSR-equipped Helmut Bradl. Puig was seventh overall, with Chili completing row two, on his first visit to the track.

This put Biaggi on row three, unable to reproduce his recent form after struggling to get the right gearing as well as having difficulties with his suspension. He had Ruggia alongside on the second Gilera, then came Schmid (who had led the first day in the wet on his works Yamaha), with Torrontegui's Suzuki completing the row.

Capirossi led the fourth row on his Spl Honda from the works bikes of Zeelenberg and Shimizu. All 35 entrants qualified.

250 cc RACE – 28 LAPS

The start was delayed once by threatening weather, then with an echo of the 500 race they got away only to run into rain on the first lap, so the red flags came out again.

It was dry once more when they did get going, with Romboni leading the charge from Reggiani, the latter taking the lead on the second lap and making a small break. By now, however, Cadalora had recovered from a slow start and was in second, and he closed up onto the Aprilia's tail as the two old rivals drew gradually ahead.

'I was confident of winning because of my practice time,' said Cadalora; but he was not confident enough to play cat and mouse until the last lap, as he does so often. This time he moved confidently inside Reggiani on the ninth lap, and drew away to win by more than 11 seconds.

Reggiani was similarly unmolested in second, while Puig seemed to be safe in third. Until Chili turned up, on a major charge. Left at the start, he'd finished lap one in 16th, but had been storming through, emerging at the front of a close battle for fourth at two-thirds distance.

He quickly closed up on Puig, and set about him, but the Spaniard fought back and regained the place after Chili's first overtaking move, and they settled into a fierce fight. It ended abruptly on the 25th lap. Chili's ride through the field had used up his tyres, and he was flicked over the high-side and into the bales.

The fight for fourth was excellent, incorporating seven bikes at one stage, before Ruggia retired his Gilera with ignition problems (!) and Biaggi crashed out (one lap after Chili). This left Shimizu, Zeelenberg, Bradl and Romboni scrapping it out, with Schmid losing ground behind by the finish, and they passed the flag in that order.

It was a good result for Zeelenberg, who almost crashed after Shimizu dragged his knee on the inside of one corner and threw grit under the Suzuki's front wheel. He held off Bradl, who had followed Chili through from a poor start of his own, but stopped taking too many risks after a couple of near misses.

Lavado had wasted his front row start and completed lap one in 20th, but he also gradually pulled through on the Gilera to finish ninth, too far behind Schmid to be a threat, but consigning Torrontegui's Suzuki to tenth.

Hänggeli (Aprilia) was 11th, after a race-long battle with Kozono's Honda; Andy Preining took 13th in a close finish with Stefan Prein (Honda) and fellow-Aprilia rider Bernd Kassner.

125 cc RACE – 26 LAPS

Ezio Gianola burst past pole-starter Gramigni in a convincing effort at another breakaway win. He seemed set for a dominant victory, for after only six laps he was almost five seconds clear, with a huge ten-bike brawl losing ground behind.

They were slowing one another up, but Waldmann was picking his way to the front of the grisly gang, and at one-third distance his Honda was pulling away rapidly, with Casanova, Debbia, Gramigni and Wakai all piling up behind Gresini, hanging grimly onto third.

By half-distance, Waldmann was on Gianola's tail, and the Italian was clearly in trouble. 'My bike was jumping around. Something must have broken in my front forks,' he explained. He was consigned to second on lap 15, and then promptly to third by Gramigni, who had found a way past Gresini. Gianola gradually dropped back, eventually finishing 11th and out of the points.

Gresini soon joined the two up front, with Gramigni giving it all he had to take the lead on lap 18; and it looked like a three-man battle to the

***Left:* Doriano Romboni continued to build his formidable reputation. Here he urges his 'double-special' RS Honda through a fast practice lap after blitzing the Yamahas of Michele Gallina and Paolo Casoli (10). He just missed a front-row start.**

Even in the 125 class, the top works teams have whole crews of mechanics devoted to looking at sparking plugs. British privateer Steve Patrickson does it himself.

finish. Then Japanese charger Wakai closed up to turn the last lap into a brawling dash for glory.

Gramigni held them all off, with Waldmann hanging on to second, Gresini third and then Wakai, with just over three-tenths of a second covering the first four across the line.

Debbia won a fierce tussle with Spaan for fifth by a similar margin; Sakata was seventh after succumbing to the Dutch veteran in his best race of a poor year; but he managed to hold off his deadly rival Ueda (Honda) by just over a tenth. Ueda was making his return after breaking his wrist in Germany, and was labouring under the unusual disadvantage of not being able to open the throttle fully in one handful.

Casanova was ninth after losing touch and narrowly escaping falling in an off-track excursion. Takao Shimizu was tenth.

It was a costly race for Gianola, and a fateful one for the championship. Had he not run into trouble, it would have given him the points lead, and probably ultimate victory too. Instead, Waldmann's advantage increased, and both Gresini and Gramigni moved ahead of him.

SIDECAR RACE – 26 LAPS

The last race of a day of variety was also one of the most settled. Rolf Biland's plan had been to grab an early lead and then save his tyres, and that's exactly what he did, winning by almost eight seconds at the finish.

His second successive win was considerably helped by the nature of the track. Narrow and perpetually twisty, it offered few passing opportunities for solos and almost none for the sidecars.

Title leader Webster had no chance to attack after he took 19 laps to get past coming man Klaus Klaffenböck, only succeeding when the Austrian ran into gearchange problems, dropping to third, eight seconds behind the Briton.

Bohnhorst was fourth, hard pressed at the finish by Streuer, who got an appalling start and had a dramatic afternoon charging through. The Dutchman's last victim had been sixth-placed Kumagaya, with Briton Abbott seventh, Darren Dixon eighth and the Egloff brothers ninth, the last outfit not to be lapped out of 15 finishers.

The Güdel brothers were among eight retirements after a strong ride.

Hungarian Grand Prix, 12 July/statistics

Hungaroring, 2.465-mile/3.968-km circuit

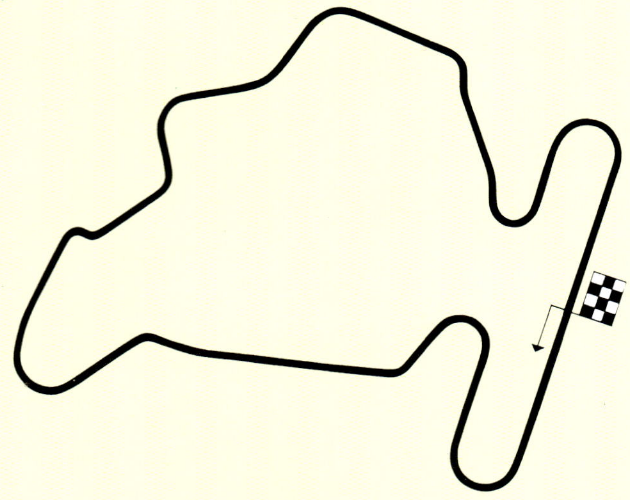

500 cc

30 laps, 73.950 miles/119.040 km

Place	Rider	Nat.	Machine	Laps	Time & speed	Fastest lap	Lap
1	**Eddie Lawson**	**USA**	**Cagiva**	**30**	**58m 21.786s 74.126 mph/ 119.295 km/h**	**1m 48.269s**	27
2	**Doug Chandler**	**USA**	**Suzuki**	**30**	**58m 35.980s**	**1m 54.077s**	24
3	**Randy Mamola**	**USA**	**Yamaha**	**30**	**58m 59.516s**	**1m 55.165s**	24
4	**Kevin Schwantz**	**USA**	**Suzuki**	**30**	**59m 25.394s**	**1m 54.486s**	23
5	**Wayne Rainey**	**USA**	**Yamaha**	**30**	**59m 29.448s**	**1m 55.838s**	28
6	**Wayne Gardner**	**AUS**	**Honda**	**30**	**59m 57.138s**	**1m 51.252s**	29
7	**John Kocinski**	**USA**	**Yamaha**	**30**	**60m 04.510s**	**1m 57.053s**	25
8	**Juan Garriga**	**E**	**Yamaha**	**30**	**60m 06.863s**	**1m 55.649s**	29
9	**Alexandre Barros**	**BR**	**Cagiva**	**29**	**58m 32.708s**	**1m 46.862s**	29
10	**Eddie Laycock**	**IRL**	**Yamaha**	**29**	**58m 38.296s**	**1m 50.628s**	29
11	Miguel DuHamel	CAN	Yamaha	29	58m 55.951s	1m 55.850s	27
12	Andrew Stroud	NZ	Yamaha	29	59m 52.953s	2m 00.176s	23
13	Thierry Crine	F	Yamaha	29	60m 11.020s	1m 59.019s	29
14	Niall Mackenzie	GB	Yamaha	28	58m 31.562s	1m 48.094s	27
15	Dominique Sarron	F	Yamaha	28	59m 31.503s	2m 03.827s	21
16	Michael Rudroff	D	Yamaha	28	60m 03.135s	1m 50.606s	25
17	Cees Doorakkers	NL	Yamaha	27	58m 29.369s	2m 04.504s	23
18	Peter Graves	GB	Yamaha	27	58m 37.838s	2m 02.491s	21
19	Andreas Leuthe	D	VRP	27	60m 04.956s	2m 08.711s	17
20	Serge David	CH	Yamaha	26	59m 30.652s	1m 52.007s	24
21	Sepp Doppler	A	Yamaha	26	59m 56.897s	2m 02.204s	21
	Alex Criville	E	Honda	21	DSQ	1m 48.809s	20
	Toshiyuki Arakaki	J	Yamaha	17	DNF	2m 00.653s	15
	Corrado Catalano	I	Yamaha	12	DNF	2m 01.692s	7
	Niggi Schmassman	CH	Yamaha	12	DNF	2m 25.477s	10
	Kevin Mitchell	GB	Yamaha	6	DNF	2m 06.936s	5
	Lucio Pedercini	I	Paton	4	DNF	2m 06.413s	4
	Claude Arciero	F	Yamaha	0	DNF		
	Simon Buckmaster	GB	Yamaha		DNS		
	Larry Moreno	YV	Yamaha		DNQ		

Fastest lap: Barros, 1m 46.862s, 80.968 mph/130.306 km/h.
Lap record: Michael Doohan (AUS), Honda, 1m 44.390s, 85.029 mph/136.841 km/h (1990).

Practice leaderboard: **1** Chandler, 1m 43.028s; **2** Rainey, 1m 43.147s; **3** Kocinski, 1m 43.477s; **4** Gardner, 1m 43.524s; **5** Schwantz, 1m 44.006s; **6** Garriga, 1m 44.258s; **7** Lawson, 1m 44.589s; **8** Barros, 1m 44.691s; **9** Mamola, 1m 44.802s; **10** Criville, 1m 45.055s; **11** Mackenzie, 1m 45.174s; **12** Arakaki, 1m 45.296s; **13** DuHamel, 1m 45.448s; **14** Catalano, 1m 46.005s; **15** Sarron, 1m 46.206s.

World Championship: **1** Doohan, 130; **2** Schwantz, 87; **3** Rainey, 73; **4** Chandler, 72; **5** Kocinski, 55; **6** Criville, 49; **7** Mamola, 41; **8** Garriga and Lawson, 38; **10** Barros and Mackenzie, 26; **12** Beattie and Gardner, 18; **14** DuHamel, 16; **15** Goddard and Itoh, 10; **17** Ohishi, 6; **18** Catalano, 5; **19** Laycock, 4; **20** Honma, 3; **21** Fujiwara, 2; **22** Mitchell and Tsujimoto, 1.

250 cc

28 laps, 69.020 miles/111.104 km

Place	Rider	Nat.	Machine	Laps	Time & speed	Fastest lap	Lap
1	**Luca Cadalora**	**I**	**Honda**	**28**	**49m 29.109s 81.596 mph/ 131.317 km/h**	**1m 45.012s**	13
2	**Loris Reggiani**	**I**	**Aprilia**	**28**	**49m 40.847s**	**1m 45.623s**	22
3	**Alberto Puig**	**E**	**Aprilia**	**28**	**49m 47.202s**	**1m 45.666s**	21
4	**Masahiro Shimizu**	**J**	**Honda**	**28**	**49m 52.483s**	**1m 45.870s**	26
5	**Wilco Zeelenberg**	**NL**	**Suzuki**	**28**	**49m 52.607s**	**1m 45.772s**	22
6	**Helmut Bradl**	**D**	**Honda**	**28**	**49m 52.820s**	**1m 45.301s**	14
7	**Doriano Romboni**	**I**	**Honda**	**28**	**49m 55.771s**	**1m 45.810s**	20
8	**Jochen Schmid**	**D**	**Yamaha**	**28**	**50m 00.401s**	**1m 46.136s**	20
9	**Carlos Lavado**	**YV**	**Gilera**	**28**	**50m 24.118s**	**1m 46.290s**	23
10	**Herri Torrontegui**	**E**	**Suzuki**	**28**	**50m 27.256s**	**1m 47.004s**	14
11	Bernard Hänggeli	CH	Aprilia	28	50m 30.756s	1m 47.155s	15
12	Katsuyoshi Kozono	J	Honda	28	50m 31.063s	1m 47.194s	11
13	Andy Preining	A	Aprilia	28	50m 45.014s	1m 47.324s	14
14	Stefan Prein	D	Honda	28	50m 45.126s	1m 47.104s	11
15	Bernd Kassner	D	Aprilia	28	50m 45.388s	1m 47.026s	13
16	Frédéric Protat	F	Aprilia	28	51m 08.846s	1m 47.459s	10
17	Renzo Colleoni	I	Yamaha	28	51m 09.769s	1m 47.551s	25
18	Jurgen van den Goorbergh	NL	Aprilia	28	51m 14.363s	1m 48.566s	13
19	Michele Gallina	I	Yamaha	28	51m 18.977s	1m 47.874s	14
20	José Kuhn	F	Honda	27	49m 29.351s	1m 48.387s	14
21	Bernard Cazade	F	Honda	27	49m 30.981s	1m 48.402s	11
22	Patrick van den Goorbergh	NL	Aprilia	27	49m 32.086s	1m 47.145s	26
23	Eskil Suter	CH	Aprilia	27	49m 34.751s	1m 48.461s	8
24	Adi Stadler	D	Honda	27	49m 35.031s	1m 48.506s	12
25	Luis D'Antin	E	Honda	27	49m 40.197s	1m 47.803s	4
	Massimiliano Biaggi	I	Aprilia	26	DNF	1m 45.958s	19
	Pier Francesco Chili	I	Aprilia	25	DNF	1m 44.995s	21
	Jean-Philippe Ruggia	F	Gilera	23	DNF	1m 45.239s	12
	Paolo Casoli	I	Yamaha	23	DNF	1m 46.992s	7
	Loris Capirossi	I	Honda	18	DNF	1m 46.147s	14
	Yves Briguet	CH	Honda	17	DNF	1m 48.164s	13
	Adrian Bosshard	CH	Honda	11	DNF	1m 48.879s	5
	Harald Eckl	D	Aprilia	8	DNF	1m 49.475s	5
	Erkka Korpiaho	SF	Aprilia	2	DNF	2m 06.016s	1
	Carlos Cardus	E	Honda		DNS		

Fastest lap: Chili, 1m 44.995s, 82.408 mph/132.623 km/h.
Lap record: John Kocinski, USA (Yamaha), 1m 46.266s, 83.258 mph/134.425 km/h (1990).

Practice leaderboard: **1** Cadalora, 1m 44.069s; **2** Cardus, 1m 45.047s; **3** Reggiani, 1m 45.079s; **4** Lavado, 1m 45.116s; **5** Romboni, 1m 45.252s; **6** Bradl, 1m 45.279s; **7** Puig, 1m 45.342s; **8** Chili, 1m 45.373s; **9** Biaggi, 1m 45.486s; **10** Ruggia, 1m 45.886s; **11** Schmid, 1m 45.950s; **12** Torrontegui, 1m 46.112s; **13** Capirossi, 1m 46.229s; **14** Zeelenberg, 1m 46.389s; **15** Shimizu, 1m 46.404s.

World Championship: **1** Cadalora, 155; **2** Reggiani, 97; **3** Chili, 72; **4** Bradl, 67; **5** Puig, 62; **6** Shimizu, 44; **7** Biaggi, 43; **8** Cardus, 37; **9** Zeelenberg, 34; **10** Schmid, 28; **11** Romboni, 21; **12** Okada, 15; **13** Aoki, 12; **14** Capirossi, 11; **15** Lavado, Preining, Ruggia, Torrontegui and Wakai, 4; **20** Casoli and Nanba, 3; **22** Prein, 2; **23** Jeandat, Kassner and J. van den Goorbergh, 1.

125 cc

26 laps, 64.090 miles/103.168 km

Place	Rider	Nat.	Machine	Laps	Time & speed	Fastest lap	Lap
1	**Alessandro Gramigni**	**I**	**Aprilia**	**26**	**48m 15.620s 77.691 mph/ 125.032 km/h**	**1m 50.338s**	**8**
2	**Ralf Waldmann**	**D**	**Honda**	**26**	**48m 15.739s**	**1m 49.994s**	**10**
3	**Fausto Gresini**	**I**	**Honda**	**26**	**48m 15.766s**	**1m 49.982s**	**17**
4	**Nobuyuki Wakai**	**J**	**Honda**	**26**	**48m 15.952s**	**1m 50.132s**	**10**
5	**Gabriele Debbia**	**I**	**Honda**	**26**	**48m 22.796s**	**1m 50.294s**	**13**
6	**Hans Spaan**	**NL**	**Aprilia**	**26**	**48m 23.175s**	**1m 50.646s**	**9**
7	**Kazuto Sakata**	**J**	**Honda**	**26**	**48m 24.702s**	**1m 50.650s**	**26**
8	**Noboru Ueda**	**J**	**Honda**	**26**	**48m 24.860s**	**1m 50.085s**	**26**
9	**Bruno Casanova**	**I**	**Aprilia**	**26**	**48m 29.667s**	**1m 50.393s**	**7**
10	**Takao Shimizu**	**J**	**Honda**	**26**	**48m 34.011s**	**1m 50.902s**	**4**
11	Ezio Gianola	I	Honda	26	48m 35.663s	1m 50.581s	6
12	Loek Bodelier	NL	Honda	26	48m 51.101s	1m 51.464s	6
13	Oliver Petrucciani	CH	Honda	26	48m 57.373s	1m 52.172s	16
14	Arie Molenaar	NL	Aprilia	26	48m 57.430s	1m 51.748s	17
15	Dirk Raudies	D	Honda	26	49m 03.977s	1m 52.208s	12
16	Julian Miralles	E	Honda	26	49m 04.308s	1m 52.106s	10
17	Giovanni Palmieri	I	Gazzaniga	26	49m 13.419s	1m 51.765s	12
18	Alain Bronec	F	Honda	26	49m 27.023s	1m 52.465s	14
19	Robin Appleyard	GB	Honda	26	49m 27.124s	1m 52.651s	18
20	Luis Alvaro	E	Aprilia	26	49m 42.547s	1m 52.467s	13
21	Hisashi Unemoto	J	Honda	26	49m 42.792s	1m 52.696s	23
22	Alfred Waibel	D	Honda	26	49m 43.335s	1m 52.656s	24
23	Giuseppe Fiorillo	I	Yamaha	26	49m 44.177s	1m 53.309s	11
24	Hubert Abold	D	Honda	26	49m 52.049s	1m 53.111s	14
25	Steve Patrickson	GB	Honda	26	49m 53.811s	1m 53.958s	7
26	Peter Galvin	AUS	Honda	26	49m 53.955s	1m 53.760s	22
27	Tibor Kis	HU	Honda	25	49m 16.570s	1m 56.945s	24
28	Attila Szabo	HU	Honda	24	49m 02.478s	2m 00.627s	6
	Manuel Hernandez	E	Aprilia	22	DNF	1m 52.478s	5
	Jorge Martinez	E	Honda	17	DNF	1m 51.374s	13
	Maurizio Vitali	I	Gazzaniga	16	DNF	1m 52.194s	4
	Oliver Koch	D	Honda	15	DNF	1m 53.221s	5
	Kinya Wada	J	Honda	13	DNF	1m 54.419s	13
	Peter Öttl	D	Rotax	8	DNF	1m 52.831s	5
	Heinz Lüthi	CH	Honda	8	DNF	1m 53.895s	3
	Fausto Ricci	I	Yamaha	3	DNF	1m 54.832s	2
	Carlos Giro	E	Aprilia	3	DNF	1m 52.564s	3
	Maik Stief	D	Aprilia		DNQ		

Fastest lap: Gresini, 1m 49.982s, 78.672 mph/126.610 km/h (record).
Previous record: Bruno Casanova, I (Honda), 1m 52.866s, 78.643 mph/126.564 km/h (1990).

Practice leaderboard: 1 Gramigni, 1m 50.034s; **2** Gianola, 1m 50.129s; **3** Wakai, 1m 50.177s; **4** Shimizu, 1m 50.247s; **5** Casanova, 1m 50.330s; **6** Debbia, 1m 50.373s; **7** Gresini, 1m 50.564s; **8** Waldmann, 1m 50.687s; **9** Martinez, 1m 50.819s; **10** Petrucciani, 1m 50.935s; **11** Sakata, 1m 50.983s; **12** Spaan, 1m 51.052s; **13** Giro, 1m 51.146s; **14** Ueda, 1m 51.304s; **15** Raudies, 1m 51.452s.

World Championship: 1 Waldmann, 101; **2** Gresini, 88; **3** Gramigni, 87; **4** Gianola, 81; **5** Casanova, 72; **6** Debbia, 58; **7** Raudies, 47; **8** Wakai, 45; **9** Martinez, 33; **10** Sakata, 26; **11** Giro, 22; **12** Ueda, 18; **13** Öttl, 10; **14** Koch, Saitoh and Spaan, 8; **17** Shimizu, 5; **18** Fujihara, 4; **19** Kurfiss and Wada, 3; **21** Lüthi and Petrucciani, 1.

Sidecars

26 laps, 64.090 miles/103.168 km

Place	Driver & passenger	Nat.	Machine	Laps	Time & speed	Fastest lap	Lap
1	**Rolf Biland/ Kurt Waltisperg**	**CH CH**	**LCR- Krauser**	**26**	**46m 24.347s 80.796 mph/ 130.029 km/h**	**1m 45.924s**	**8**
2	**Steve Webster/ Gavin Simmons**	**GB GB**	**LCR- ADM**	**26**	**46m 32.029s**	**1m 45.900s**	**8**
3	**Klaus Klaffenböck/ Christian Parzer**	**A A**	**LCR- ADM**	**26**	**46m 40.102s**	**1m 46.126s**	**6**
4	**Ralph Bohnhorst/ Bruno Hiller**	**D D**	**BRM**	**26**	**46m 54.012s**	**1m 47.146s**	**15**
5	**Egbert Streuer/ Peter Brown**	**NL GB**	**LCR- Stredor**	**26**	**46m 57.029s**	**1m 46.938s**	**15**
6	**Yoshisada Kumagaya/ Bryan Houghton**	**J GB**	**LCR- Krauser**	**26**	**47m 00.066s**	**1m 47.070s**	**10**
7	**Steve Abbott/ Shaun Smith**	**GB GB**	**LCR- Krauser**	**26**	**47m 02.171s**	**1m 47.307s**	**21**
8	**Darren Dixon/ Andy Hetherington**	**GB GB**	**LCR- Krauser**	**26**	**47m 10.420s**	**1m 46.733s**	**10**
9	**Markus Egloff/ Urs Egloff**	**CH CH**	**LCR- Yamaha**	**26**	**48m 07.470s**	**1m 48.594s**	**4**
10	**Jukka Lauslehto/ Jurgen Levinsen**	**SF DK**	**LCR- ADM**	**25**	**46m 34.547s**	**1m 49.567s**	**7**
11	Reiner Koster/ Jurg Egli	CH CH	LCR- Yamaha	25	46m 59.734s	1m 50.819s	8
12	Tony Baker/ Simon Prior	GB GB	LCR- Krauser	25	47m 38.922s	1m 49.788s	13
13	Peter Lemstra/ Jan Kuyt	NL NL	LCR- Krauser	24	48m 06.634s	1m 57.148s	2
14	Hans Hügli/ Adolf Hänni	CH CH	LCR- Krauser	22	48m 33.099s	1m 51.838s	3
15	Mark Reddington/ Kim Andreasen	GB DK	LCR- Krauser	21	48m 10.664s	1m 52.406s	4
	Derek Brindley/ Nick Roche	GB GB	LCR- Krauser	17	DNF	1m 48.651s	11
	Theo van Kempen/ Geral de Haas	NL NL	LCR- Krauser	17	DNF	1m 49.553s	8
	Barry Brindley/ Scott Whiteside	GB GB	LCR- Yamaha	12	DNF	1m 49.274s	6
	Paul Güdel/ Charly Güdel	CH CH	LCR- Yamaha	11	DNF	1m 47.119s	10
	Robert Fisher/ Trevor Crone	GB GB	LCR- Krauser	11	DNF	1m 50.875s	3
	André Bosman/ Dave Kellett	AUS AUS	LCR- Krauser	10	DNF	1m 50.800s	5
	Markus Bösiger/ Beat Leibundgut	CH CH	LCR- ADM	9	DNF	1m 50.171s	7
	Tony Wyssen/ Kilian Wyssen	CH CH	LCR- Yamaha	2	DNF	1m 58.963s	1

Fastest lap: Webster, 1m 45.900s, 81.704 mph/131.490 km/h (record).
Previous record: Paul Güdel/Charly Güdel, CH/CH (LCR-Yamaha), 1m 49.009s, 81.426 mph/131.042 km/h (1990).

Practice leaderboard: 1 Biland, 1m 44.838s; **2** Webster, 1m 45.625s; **3** Klaffenböck, 1m 46.087s; **4** Dixon, 1m 46.322s; **5** Streuer, 1m 46.521s; **6** Bohnhorst, 1m 46.919s; **7** Kumagaya, 1m 47.020s; **8** Güdel, 1m 47.046s; **9** Abbott, 1m 47.135s; **10** Egloff, 1m 47.745s; **11** B. Brindley, 1m 47.789s; **12** D. Brindley, 1m 48.263s; **13** Wyssen, 1m 48.376s; **14** Lauslehto, 1m 48.616s; **15** Bösiger, 1m 48.868s.

World Championship: 1 Webster, 70; **2** Klaffenböck, 54; **3** Biland, 43; **4** Kumagaya, 27; **5** Bohnhorst, 26; **6** Güdel and Streuer, 20; **8** B. Brindley, 16; **9** Dixon, 15; **10** Bösiger, 10; **11** Abbott and Egloff, 8; **13** Wyssen, 4; **14** Baker, D. Brindley and Lauslehto, 1.

Malcolm Bryan

Gresini hangs on grimly from Gramigni, Casanova (obscured), Waldmann (3), Debbia and Wakai (10).

WORLD CHAMPIONSHIP • ROUND 10

500 cc	RAINEY
250 cc	REGGIANI
125 cc	GIANOLA
SIDECARS	BILAND

FRENCH GRAND PRIX

Photos: Malcolm Bryan

The king of Spain is a GP regular, but prime ministers seldom associate themselves with the (increasingly less) raffish world of motor cycle racing. True, we once had Chancellor Helmut Kohl at Hockenheim, but it was election year and his helmetless lap on the pillion of Toni Mang's BMW may even have helped keep him in office.

French prime minister Pierre Bérégovoy's motives in attending his home GP were less clear. Perhaps, having also visited the F1 race, he really was just a fan, as he told a press conference on race morning. Did he, came the question, prefer bikes or cars? I like them both, he replied. It's only trucks I don't like. Laughter all round: a fortnight before, France had been virtually paralysed by a truckers' blockade of the main roads.

Bérégovoy flatly refused to answer any political questions, an unexpected stance by a man in his position. A pity, too, for there was one burning question – and by ignoring it he gave ammunition to those who believed he had only come to the French GP because he knew it would be the last one.

Opposite: **Kocinski steals inches from Rainey and pole man Chandler beyond him, while Gardner (5) is still on the line. Showing good anticipation, third-row starter Arakaki (32) is already down behind the screen.**

Right: **Gianola's fourth win of the season was also to be his last; but it was the first time in the top three for Ueda and Martinez.**

This theory proved again just how much the sport is hostage to tobacco. The threat to the French GP was an impending total ban on cigarette advertising – a far more sweeping restriction than the 'cover-up' rules in Britain and Germany. To the current establishment, this would simply be unthinkable. Would all the top Japanese works teams be obliged to run with plain white fairings? No sir! They would race elsewhere. After 41 years, the French GP would have to die, to be replaced by races in more amenable countries – candidates included Russia, India and Korea, among others, with the whole South American continent besides. And, according to the scaremongers, France would be just the first European country to go. Spain was also in the throes of framing similarly restrictive legislation, and it was only a matter of time before the EC as a whole would follow.

A bleak picture, with racing being squeezed out of its birthplace to face a Third World future, barricaded into hotel rooms against muggers and racing in front of empty grandstands under the cold all-seeing TV cameras.

Well, we will have to see about that. And about the 1993 French GP. The increasingly threatening battle against cigarettes is one which will not go away, but the current top sponsors aren't anxious to leave either, and there is hardly a clamouring of 'clean' sponsors eager to take their place. Racing's future is in thrall to racing's present, so enjoy live action while you may.

The new venue for the French GP – the second virgin circuit of the year – is pleasantly sited in the languid and spacious Loire valley outside medieval Nevers. All facilities are superb, with extensive grandstands and a vast pits-paddock complex that is generously equipped in every respect. Rather too generously when it came to security guards, whose diligence brought them into direct physical confrontation with (as usual) Lawson as well as Gardner and Mamola, whose speed in retreat after striking some telling blows of his own was reckoned to have saved him from a major post-race hiding.

The track itself was another disappointing affirmation of the current malaise in circuit design, with a preponderance of slow corners preceded by second-gear chicanes – fine for acrobatics, but with nowhere for a good 500 rider to let rip. Much of this is done in the name of safety, but the only place where sixth gear was used – an interestingly kinked uphill straight – terminated in an ultra-slow first-gear hairpin, and many riders doubted the safety aspects of having to brake from top speed to walking pace while in close company. Slow ess-bends were liberally placed before and after the U-turns, and Magny-Cours kept the 500 riders jumping around and flipping up and down the gearbox for all the world like stadium motocrossers. Nobody thought much of this addition to the calendar, especially since it had supplanted the well-loved Paul Ricard. 'It's like they made the facilities, then thought they'd better build the track. What a waste of a piece of ground,' said Roberts. Schwantz summed it up: 'Silly slow corners, then a series of drag races to chicanes.'

Two of the corners were really silly. The first was the Adelaide Hairpin at the end of the back straight, so acute that the paving machine hadn't been able to make the radius and the apex was filled in later, making a rough patch right where it should be smooth.

The second was the controversial last corner, whose exit high-side 'A-zone' was bang on the pit wall. This obvious danger spot was the reason for the long delay in homologating the new track for bikes, but the solution was still a stop-gap one. The apex kerb had been extended outwards to make what would have been a second-gear surge into a first-gear stop-and-go dribble. Not only was the corner slow, but it was very definitely one line only, and the interposition of back-markers with front-of-action dicing was to play a significant part in robbing the racing of drama.

The athletic requirements for guiding a 500 cc missile round this sort of course were at least entertaining for the onlookers, with any number of prime spots to study style and technique. The downhill chicanes were very delicate, while the uphill 'straight' was curvy enough to set Schwantz's Suzuki in particular into a fearsome top gear twitch. One of the slow corners caught out Kocinski in practice, with the resultant fire extinguished shortly before it became a conflagration; the same bend also washed away the front wheels of both Suzukis in the race. Chandler fell before Schwantz, after yet again qualifying on pole. There were a number of other crashes, with Barros breaking his collarbone and fast privateer Thierry Crine his hand, both out for the next two races; also Criville (twice without injury) and wild card Bernard Garcia (on a spare Banco Yamaha) who dislocated his hip and broke his pelvis in an unlucky Friday fall.

Tempers were twitching too in the muggy French summer, with several open fracas over and above those between riders and security guards. One involved a boiling over of the row between Schwantz and Lawson, each of whom will forever blame the other for their Assen crash. Schwantz was peeved that Lawson had forced past rather brusquely in Hungary, and now they had another monster mutual carve-up during Thursday's free practice (to learn the new circuit) that had them both up the escape road at Adelaide, shaking fists all the way back home, whereupon Lawson pulled his Cagiva into the Suzuki pit to continue the argument. 'Why are you always doing this to me? Why me?' he shouted. They stopped short of fisticuffs, and Schwantz went to visit Lawson later in his motorhome. 'Eddie admitted he'd over-reacted a bit today, but we still disagree about Assen,' said Schwantz later; and they embarked on an uneasy truce.

More pit lane pugilism came during 125 practice, symptomatic of the increasing desperation of Ralf Waldmann's crew as one niggle after another prevented him from regaining his earlier race-winning form. A difference of opinion over bike setting so incensed a mechanic that he came to blows with team owner Gerd-Heinz Zwafink, and was promptly sacked.

Fisticuffs aside, there was not much new on the track – Rainey had both bikes fitted with the new drone engine, but Kocinski only had one, while lesser 'works riders' Mackenzie and Garriga could only look on with envy. Lawson had more new electronics to go with the new electronic rear suspension – his own kill-shifter (he quipped: 'One day this thing's gonna short out and I'll go up in smoke').

There was a notable 500 class newcomer, too – British four-stroke racer James Whitham, riding the injured Buckmaster's Harris, and with great verve. With his curious cornering style, almost falling off inside the bike, and an immediate willingness to spin the tyre and slide the rear out of the tight bends, he made a good impression, and walked away with points in his first GP.

End-of-season speculation was brewing up nicely and rumours chased one another among the motorhomes. Rainey either had or hadn't signed a letter of intent to go to Cagiva; Cadalora had a 500 offer from Yamaha; Chandler had offers from Yamaha and Honda as well as Suzuki; Marlboro were going to take over from Rothmans with Honda ... and so it went on, some items true, some merely plausible, some downright malicious.

Rather malicious also was the response to the GP debut of Jean-Michel Bayle, who was riding a stock Honda RS in Rothmans

Photos: Malcom Bryan

colours in the 250 class as a wild card. The wonder-man of stadium cross, in his first road race, soon earned the nickname Jean-Michel Snayle, for he was struggling to get anywhere near the limits of slick tyres and the standards of even the back-markers. And all this attended by extreme media hype, every move dogged by at least two video crews, watching him come plumb last in practice and ditto in the race. (Kozono was actually behind him, but the Japanese rider had stopped twice.) The final indignity, when being lapped, was finding himself in the way of Jochen Schmid, who felt this had contributed to his being pipped for third by Cadalora, and denied Yamaha's first 250 rostrum since 1989. 'Perhaps he should stick to motocross,' sneered Schmid.

The meeting ended with a flurry of helicopters and fast cars, as several 500 riders took off for their date with Suzuka. Schwantz's no-score decided him in favour of an attack on the Eight Hour, and he joined Chandler, Gardner, Mackenzie *et al.* in the rush to Japan.

While the new circuit at Magny-Cours lived up to predictions of not providing particularly close racing, the results did serve one purpose, in all four classes, of keeping the championships open for one more race at least. Most especially for Rainey, who moved into second on points with a convincing win in his old dominant manner as Schwantz crashed out, probably because of his residual injuries.

But it wasn't much of a race for the 500s, small consolation for a group of Canary Island VIP guests of Spanish tobacco giant Coronas. A party of 30 had been flown over to France to see the race. But they'd gone to the wrong race track – Paul Ricard, some 350 miles away. They didn't miss much.

500 cc PRACTICE

Gardner, Kocinski and Rainey dominated early practice, and it looked as though Rainey had control of the crucial last timed session too. Until Chandler did his last minute tyre-change trick again, and found a clear track to claim his second successive pole.

The Californian is now clearly well on top of the Suzuki, and able to set the bike up quickly, though he is still working on its frustrating balance problem through the many downhill corner entries. 'It needs more weight on the front,' he said. 'I'm already leaning forward with my head in the screen to cut weight transfer out of the corners.'

The displaced Rainey was looking fit and strong for the first time all year, although he complained that his leg was still not strong enough for him to go running, his favoured training, and that his confidence was low in the bike's capacity to respond to his preferred aggressive corner entries. Difficulties in setting up a revised front fork from Ohlins weren't helping; but he at least found a small advantage in his kill-shift, though he was still declutching and closing the throttle in the lower gears to avoid wheelies. 'It saves a little time in the top three gears,' he said, adding: 'The important thing here is that the bike should be easy to ride.'

Kocinski was alongside him, less than a tenth down after messing around with gearing. He was so much at sea that he was forced to switch back to his spare bike with the old engine in the final session, because his gearing choice for the new one was so far off. He matched times on both engines, but decided to race the new one. John badly needed a good result to bolster his own delicate confidence, and this highly technical circuit represented a good chance. But he crashed unhurt on Friday, and was feeling the pressure.

Gardner completed the first row, on a time from the first session after spending the second day testing tyres to find one that would give him positive steering for the downhill corner entries. That was only part of the puzzle, which had him fiddling with suspension combinations. 'You can also lose the back going into the turns here,' he said.

Lawson led row two, with the Cagiva well on the pace. He had Criville alongside, the Spaniard having fallen unhurt on the first day of practice; then came Schwantz, who had been third in the morning but simply didn't get a clear track in the afternoon. Getting desperate at the end, he'd wasted time failing to find a way past Garriga – there are few passing places and the Spaniard is a demon late braker; then on the last lap he'd been balked by Dominique Sarron. Eventually the pair collided, luckily without serious consequences. Schwantz still had a lightweight cast on his left arm, and admitted that the chicanes were causing him trouble. 'I can get

GP debutant James Whitham showed no inhibitions in his first ride on a 500 GP two-stroke, and proved wrong those who thought that his unusual riding style presaged imminent disaster.

Below: **At 19, Loris Capirossi was the youngest fast man in any class. He did his best not to show it.**

through the right-hand part, but it's painful pulling the bike through the left-hand second parts,' he said.

Garriga completed row two, saying: 'I like it here, because it's a rider's circuit and not a bike circuit.' Which was true, but with the ultra-slow corners not quite true enough.

Mamola's Yamaha was again without the Budweiser logos because of local liquor advertising laws. He headed row three from Barros, but the Brazilian had crashed the Cagiva, breaking his collarbone. Then came Mackenzie, making the best of things in spite of many disagreements with his team. Arakaki was next, the top privateer.

DuHamel led row four, riding more calmly as the season wore on, but still almost sliding into the pit wall, then bowing at the awed mechanics leaning over the railing as he continued.

Next to him, debutant Whitham was showing unexpected and rather worrying aggression, moving up to place second privateer after following Schwantz in the last session. 'It's the best bike I've ever ridden,' he enthused. Serge David's Roc Yamaha was next, with Mitchell completing the row on his Harris. Goddard's replacement, Andrew Stroud, was again impressive, heading row five from Rudroff, Sarron and Catalano, the latter crashing twice in the same practice session but without serious injury.

Eddie Laycock led row six with a sad story of his own – the gearbox mainshaft had broken and destroyed the casings of his '91 YZR Yamaha on both sides. The Irish rider was reduced to begging for major engine parts so he could make the race.

There were 29 qualifiers, but only 26 starters, with Barros, Crine and Garcia already out. Leuthe's VRP and Moreno's Harris didn't make it.

500 cc RACE – 27 LAPS

Kocinski led into the first turn, but Rainey had forced past by the end of the first lap, with Chandler tucked up in third.

As Rainey tried to make a break, Gardner – in bullish mood – came charging into the group to seize second place. Chandler followed him past Kocinski, and the pair set off in pursuit of the fleeing Rainey.

Gardner was really flying, and was too fast for Chandler. On lap five, the Suzuki's front slid away on the entry to one of the second-gear turns, and Doug slid off unhurt, remounting to freewheel back to the pits, his engine full of gravel. As a counterpoint to his growing confidence, it was the second time in three races he had made a similar mistake. 'I seem to be having trouble getting through the early laps,' he said ruefully.

Rainey was riding perfectly under pressure, maintaining a slight but frustrating gap as he resisted all Gardner's efforts. The Australian set fastest lap on the fifth time round, but then: 'The bike seemed to eat the rear tyre up really quickly, and I was getting tired. I thought I'd spent enough time lying on the ground this year and I'd be better off finishing second.'

But he could not relax too much, for Kocinski was now coming back at him, with Garriga hanging on, and even ahead briefly after the American ran wide. 'He never overtook me,' said Kocinski. 'I just made a couple of mistakes that allowed him to get ahead.'

They were closing gradually on Gardner until the Australian managed to get a couple of back-markers between them for one of the first-gear corners, and that opened the gap up again for their positions to be fixed, with fourth-placed Garriga three seconds adrift at the end.

Schwantz had been a solitary fifth until just after half-distance, when he lost the front wheel in exactly the same place as Chandler. 'If I'd been 100 per cent strong I may have saved it, but I just didn't have enough strength in my left arm,' he said.

This left the position to Lawson. Earlier, he had looked vulnerable to Mackenzie, coming through from his usual poor start; but Eddie doesn't give up, and he still had a little in hand when his pursuer was caught up behind lapped riders in the final corner, and lost touch. Niall managed to stay comfortably ahead of team-mate DuHamel, though, who was relieved of the attentions of Mamola when the American faded, to finish a lonely eighth.

Criville had also crashed early in the race, leaving points available for the privateers. They were led by Whitham, who had started well and never did have the crash he seemed to be courting, even though he came under sustained attack from Arakaki until the Japanese charger obligingly ran wide a few laps from the end, recovering to take tenth and the last point some 12 seconds adrift.

Stroud had been up with this scrap until he faded to 11th with his rear Dunlop blistering; David was 12th and Doorakkers 13th. There were 18 finishers, with Papa's Librenti last, two laps behind.

250 cc PRACTICE

There were a number of fallers in this class, too – notably Reggiani and Cadalora. The former broke a rib on Friday, but raced anyway, pumped full of painkillers; the latter crashed during race morning warm-up, and was heavily winded, causing anxious moments for his team as he staggered to the barrier and fought to get his breath.

The Honda man was already up against it as his title bid came towards its climax – starting from the second row of the grid as three Italian rivals and one unexpected German claimed the front row.

Chili was fastest, which was a little surprising, because the low gear stop-go corners should have favoured the reed-valve Hondas over the all-or-nothing rotary disc-valve Aprilias. Pole here was a measure not only of Chili's stylish riding but also Aprilia's progress with electronic control for the Rotax-based engine.

Talking of progress – what was a Yamaha doing second fastest? Schmid's year with the factory's new works bike had seen a steady flow of new engine parts and he was now knocking on the door of the Aprilia stronghold. 'I always felt the bike had the potential to get up there,' he said.

And, talking of potential, Capirossi took advantage of the highly technical nature of the track to put his factory special Honda RS third fastest, ahead of countryman Reggiani, who was trying hard to ignore the pain.

This left Cadalora to lead row two, after taking a bad guess on gearbox settings and sprockets on the second

Right: **Webster's sidecar hugs the road, Simmons hugs the sidecar. Control niggles kept the champion off the rostrum.**

'Perhaps if we punch it it will go faster.' Ralf Waldmann *(below)* discusses his mounting problems that later led to fisticuffs in the Zwafink pit.

day, leaving himself more testing to do on race morning. He had the chance of tying up the title, but he wanted to do it with a race win, and said: 'That will be difficult here.' After recovering from his fall on race morning, he ran back to the pits for his spare bike.

Cardus was back and battling hard, qualifying the Campsa NSR sixth; then came Romboni's Honda RS/Spl, with Biaggi the last man on row two. The young Aprilia rider was as spectacular as ever, but also crashed, without injury.

His '91 Euro-championship rival, Dutchman Jurgen van den Goorbergh, hit top form on his Yokohama-shod Aprilia to lead row three from the NSRs of Shimizu and Bradl. Both works Honda riders had crashed: Shimizu was okay, but Bradl was not, and withdrew from the race with an injured back.

Preining's Aprilia completed the row; Puig's similar lease-motor bike led row four from Zeelenberg's works Suzuki, Ruggia's Gilera and Torrontegui's Suzuki.

There were 38 qualifiers, and lots more hard-luck stories. One came from Jeandat, sacked from his Honda France team two weeks ago but given a reprieve with a lent bike for his home GP. He qualified 21st to lead the sixth row, then crashed and broke his wrist.

Bayle scored what must be the highest profile last place in history, making the qualifying cut comfortably but five seconds off pole and, more significantly, after failing to improve much from the first practice to the last. He was smooth and steady, but simply too slow compared with riders used to taking their bikes and especially their tyres to the maximum week in, week out. The wild card Rothmans rider rode a stock RS in between video appearances and press conferences, and broke down three times on Friday. (He didn't crash, although many papers reported that he had.) But his best efforts still placed him 38th, right at the very back.

250 cc RACE – 26 LAPS

Biaggi had ignition trouble in the warm-up lap and was out before the start. Capirossi was more than ready to fill the vacancy for the role of precocious Italian, and led off the line, only to be overwhelmed by Chili, Reggiani and Romboni on the second lap. Cardus was also in the leading pack, and Shimizu, with Cadalora close behind and Schmid closing up.

The first major shuffle happened at the end of lap three, when Shimizu was high-sided at the pit lane corner. He was lucky to avoid getting hit, and slowed down first Schmid and then Ruggia.

Romboni's charge didn't last long either. He was in second when he slowed dramatically and ran over the kerbs at the same bend, fortunate not to crash. His gearbox had seized. Capirossi stayed with the leaders until lap 15, when he suddenly slowed on the pit straight. His factory RS Honda had also suffered gearbox failure.

By then, Chili and Reggiani were long gone up front, embroiled in a race-long duel. Chili led most of the first half; Reggiani took over from laps 16 to 21, then Chili moved back for the last few laps. But Reggiani, injury or not, was in the mood. He judged his last lap perfectly, outbraking Chili into the hairpin at the end of the back straight. Then he kept on the narrow edge to the flag, to win his second race of the year by a quarter of a second.

As the end drew nigh, Schmid had worked his way through to third, and had a little gap over Cadalora. He thought he had done enough – but then they came up to lap Bayle, who unwittingly helped his temporary Rothmans Honda team-mate just by being there and being slow. Schmid was obliged to follow through the one-line corners and wait his chance, and he lost enough time for Cadalora to close right up and practise his familiar last lap stalk-and-pounce.

By the finish Cardus had faded to a respectable but lonely fifth, with Puig winning a fierce battle for sixth over Zeelenberg and his gradually improving Suzuki team-mate Torrontegui.

Another fierce Aprilia battle for the last points saw Swiss rider Hänggeli take ninth. He was lucky, though, for Jurgen van den Goorbergh had had a storming ride through from near last at the start to tenth, and would probably have had the Aprilia rider too but for a last lap collision with 11th-placed Eskil Suter. The Dutchman had messed up his start after his good qualifying position, otherwise he might have been higher still up the top ten.

Among the retirements, Ruggia failed to finish after a strong start on his Gilera – until 'the bike sud-

denly died just as it did at Budapest.'

Thus Cadalora would have to wait one more race before claiming his second title. He would do so without any further help from Honda.

125 cc RACE – 25 LAPS

Honda held the high ground, with Gianola on pole from Wakai, Ueda (now with water-cooled crankcases) and Gresini, and it was the last-named who led from the start. He was just inches in front of a typical brawling pack, and while it took Gianola only one lap to get ahead, he was left to defend second from a group swapping positions one bend after another.

Gianola held off Gresini until his fellow-countryman fell unhurt on the eighth lap, then romped away to win by more than five seconds. It was his fourth win of a year of solid worth on the well-prepared non-works Honda.

The battle for second behind him was truly hectic, including Casanova's and Gramigni's Aprilias and the Hondas of Debbia and Raudies, with Wakai dropping off the back, Ueda climbing through, and Sakata and Waldmann both catching up fast.

The German's charge carried him through and into the thick of it. Although he was never higher than eighth, he seemed set to improve before his orange Honda faded again with a broken reed-valve, and he dropped back until he was gradually out of touch again.

At the end, Ueda and Martinez drew ahead of the pack in a fierce battle, with Sakata holding fourth, Gramigni unable to close up on him in fifth, and Casanova surviving a major moment to take sixth, narrowly ahead of Raudies. Wakai was out of touch in eighth.

Meanwhile Hans Spaan had been coming through well from a poor start, breaking free from his own group to close up on Waldmann and displacing the German at the end to finish ninth.

SIDECAR RACE – 26 LAPS

Biland rampant secured pole position, led into the first bend and simply galloped away to make sure of his third successive win by 3.4 seconds at the end. His biggest threat came from front row starter Dixon, who displaced Klaffenböck from second on lap ten and set fastest lap as he began to close on Biland. But his charge ended prematurely, with another mechanical failure for the Britons, and they retired after 12 laps.

This left a fine battle for second, with Klaffenböck's yellow outfit leading Streuer, and Webster hanging on behind.

The first two gradually outdistanced the championship leader. 'I had carburation problems, and I had to keep blipping the throttle in the bends,' said Webster later, after finishing fourth.

Streuer, displaying all his old forcefulness, made it past the Austrian with two laps to spare, and pulled away to secure his best finish of the season by a comfortable two seconds. 'I didn't drive any better than at the other GPs,' said Streuer. 'I just got a good start with the right group.'

Japanese rider Kumagaya was fifth, with Abbott and Smith a distant sixth, narrowly ahead of the Güdel brothers. There were just 13 finishers.

Photos: Malcolm Bryan

Grand Prix de France, 19 July/ statistics

Circuit de Nevers Magny-Cours, 2.654-mile/4.271-km circuit

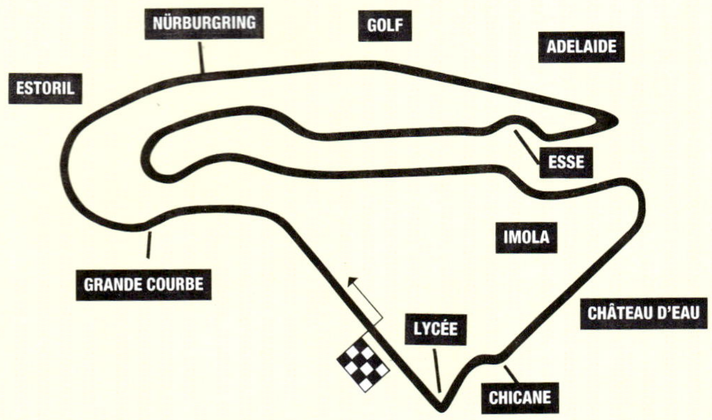

500 cc

27 laps, 71.658 miles/115.317 km

Place	Rider	Nat.	Machine	Laps	Time & speed	Fastest lap	Lap
1	**Wayne Rainey**	**USA**	**Yamaha**	**27**	**45m 05.182s 94.888 mph/ 152.707 km/h**	**1m 39.377s**	**5**
2	**Wayne Gardner**	**AUS**	**Honda**	**27**	**45m 11.864s**	**1m 39.273s**	**5**
3	**John Kocinski**	**USA**	**Yamaha**	**27**	**45m 13.869s**	**1m 39.626s**	**13**
4	**Juan Garriga**	**E**	**Yamaha**	**27**	**45m 16.827s**	**1m 39.469s**	**4**
5	**Eddie Lawson**	**USA**	**Cagiva**	**27**	**45m 39.083s**	**1m 40.580s**	**20**
6	**Niall Mackenzie**	**GB**	**Yamaha**	**27**	**45m 50.888s**	**1m 40.529s**	**4**
7	**Miguel DuHamel**	**CAN**	**Yamaha**	**27**	**45m 56.631s**	**1m 40.975s**	**18**
8	**Randy Mamola**	**USA**	**Yamaha**	**27**	**46m 02.397s**	**1m 40.965s**	**20**
9	**James Whitham**	**GB**	**Yamaha**	**27**	**46m 32.015s**	**1m 41.714s**	**4**
10	**Toshiyuki Arakaki**	**J**	**Yamaha**	**27**	**46m 44.473s**	**1m 41.607s**	**19**
11	Andrew Stroud	NZ	Yamaha	27	46m 49.749s	1m 42.484s	2
12	Serge David	CH	Yamaha	26	45m 18.911s	1m 42.625s	3
13	Cees Doorakkers	NL	Yamaha	26	45m 37.830s	1m 44.098s	23
14	Michael Rudroff	D	Yamaha	26	45m 48.825s	1m 43.157s	20
15	Niggi Schmassman	CH	Yamaha	26	45m 49.214s	1m 44.147s	16
16	Peter Graves	GB	Yamaha	26	45m 49.769s	1m 44.442s	15
17	Sepp Doppler	A	Yamaha	26	46m 51.068s	1m 46.091s	4
18	Marco Papa	I	Librenti	25	45m 45.453s	1m 48.202s	18
	Kevin Schwantz	USA	Suzuki	17	DNF	1m 40.241s	5
	Kevin Mitchell	GB	Yamaha	14	DNF	1m 42.287s	4
	Dominique Sarron	F	Yamaha	11	DNF	1m 42.799s	3
	Doug Chandler	USA	Suzuki	5	DNF	1m 39.736s	3
	Alex Criville	E	Honda	4	DNF	1m 40.303s	3
	Eddie Laycock	IRL	Yamaha	3	DNF	1m 48.281s	2
	Corrado Catalano	I	Yamaha	3	DNF	1m 47.673s	2
	Claude Arciero	F	Yamaha	1	DNF	1m 57.237s	1
	Alex Barros	BR	Cagiva		DNS		
	Thierry Crine	F	Yamaha		DNS		
	Bernard Garcia	F	Yamaha		DNS		
	Andreas Leuthe	D	VRP		DNQ		
	Larry Moreno	YV	Yamaha		DNQ		

Fastest lap: Gardner, 1m 39.273s, 95.766 mph/154.120 km/h (record).
Previous record: none.

Practice leaderboard: 1 Chandler, 1m 38.524s; 2 Rainey, 1m 38.738s; 3 Kocinski, 1m 38.811s; 4 Gardner, 1m 39.055s; 5 Lawson, 1m 39.070s; 6 Criville, 1m 39.167s; 7 Schwantz, 1m 39.416s; 8 Garriga, 1m 39.543s; 9 Mamola, 1m 39.895s; 10 Barros, 1m 39.936s; 11 Mackenzie, 1m 40.580s; 12 Arakaki, 1m 40.667s; 13 DuHamel, 1m 40.841s; 14 Whitham, 1m 40.895s; 15 David, 1m 41.612s.

World Championship: 1 Doohan, 130; 2 Rainey, 93; 3 Schwantz, 87; 4 Chandler, 72; 5 Kocinski, 67; 6 Criville, 49; 7 Garriga, 48; 8 Lawson, 46; 9 Mamola, 44; 10 Gardner, 33; 11 Mackenzie, 32; 12 Barros, 26; 13 DuHamel, 20; 14 Beattie, 18; 15 Goddard and Itoh, 10; 17 Ohishi, 6; 18 Catalano, 5; 19 Laycock, 4; 20 Honma, 3; 21 Fujiwara and Whitham, 2; 23 Arakaki, Mitchell and Tsujimoto, 1.

250 cc

26 laps, 69.004 miles/110.046 km

Place	Rider	Nat.	Machine	Laps	Time & speed	Fastest lap	Lap
1	**Loris Reggiani**	**I**	**Aprilia**	**26**	**44m 37.434s 92.320 mph/ 148.575 km/h**	**1m 41.428s**	**25**
2	**Pier Francesco Chili**	**I**	**Aprilia**	**26**	**44m 37.691s**	**1m 41.506s**	**25**
3	**Luca Cadalora**	**I**	**Honda**	**26**	**44m 47.040s**	**1m 42.136s**	**16**
4	**Jochen Schmid**	**D**	**Yamaha**	**26**	**44m 47.483s**	**1m 42.247s**	**18**
5	**Carlos Cardus**	**E**	**Honda**	**26**	**45m 04.931s**	**1m 43.057s**	**5**
6	**Alberto Puig**	**E**	**Aprilia**	**26**	**45m 13.318s**	**1m 43.220s**	**10**
7	**Wilco Zeelenberg**	**NL**	**Suzuki**	**26**	**45m 13.688s**	**1m 43.296s**	**18**
8	**Herri Torrontegui**	**E**	**Suzuki**	**26**	**45m 15.694s**	**1m 43.534s**	**18**
9	**Bernard Hänggeli**	**CH**	**Aprilia**	**26**	**45m 21.661s**	**1m 43.916s**	**20**
10	**Jurgen van den Goorbergh**	**NL**	**Aprilia**	**26**	**45m 22.026s**	**1m 43.355s**	**15**
11	Eskil Suter	CH	Aprilia	26	45m 23.981s	1m 43.780s	10
12	Frédéric Protat	F	Aprilia	26	45m 24.965s	1m 43.430s	20
13	Paolo Casoli	I	Yamaha	26	45m 25.111s	1m 43.820s	25
14	Adrian Bosshard	CH	Honda	26	45m 29.023s	1m 43.823s	17
15	Luis D'Antin	E	Honda	26	45m 42.552s	1m 43.798s	15
16	Bernd Kassner	D	Aprilia	26	45m 43.623s	1m 44.262s	12
17	Michele Gallina	I	Yamaha	26	45m 56.325s	1m 44.783s	23
18	Adi Stadler	D	Honda	26	45m 56.452s	1m 44.866s	20
19	Bernard Cazade	F	Honda	26	45m 56.675s	1m 44.944s	20
20	Carlos Lavado	YV	Gilera	26	45m 59.036s	1m 44.467s	25
21	Erkka Korpiaho	SF	Aprilia	26	46m 06.471s	1m 45.425s	9
22	Harald Eckl	D	Aprilia	26	46m 12.820s	1m 45.356s	6
23	Renzo Colleoni	I	Yamaha	26	46m 15.844s	1m 45.160s	15
24	Jean-Michel Bayle	F	Honda	25	44m 49.309s	1m 46.428s	7
25	Katsuyoshi Kozono	J	Honda	25	46m 11.606s	1m 44.499s	24
	Patrick van den Goorbergh	NL	Aprilia	21	DNF	1m 43.506s	20
	Loris Capirossi	I	Honda	16	DNF	1m 43.066s	7
	José Kuhn	F	Honda	10	DNF	1m 45.775s	5
	Andy Preining	A	Aprilia	7	DNF	1m 45.059s	2
	Doriano Romboni	I	Honda	7	DNF	1m 43.318s	5
	Jean-Philippe Ruggia	F	Gilera	5	DNF	1m 44.286s	5
	Yves Briguet	CH	Honda	5	DNF	1m 45.976s	2
	Masahiro Shimizu	J	Honda	2	DNF	1m 43.425s	2
	Marc Garcia	F	Yamaha	2	DNF	1m 45.813s	2
	Stefan Prein	D	Honda	0	DNF		
	Massimiliano Biaggi	I	Aprilia		DNS		
	Helmut Bradl	D	Honda		DNS		
	Jean-Pierre Jeandat	F	Aprilia		DNS		

Fastest lap: Reggiani, 1m 41.428s, 93.731 mph/150.846 km/h (record).
Previous record: none.

Practice leaderboard: 1 Chili, 1m 41.215s; 2 Schmid, 1m 41.764s; 3 Capirossi, 1m 41.770s; 4 Reggiani, 1m 41.841s; 5 Cadalora, 1m 41.909s; 6 Cardus, 1m 42.056s; 7 Romboni, 1m 42.090s; 8 Biaggi, 1m 42.119s; 9 J. van den Goorbergh, 1m 42.254s; 10 Shimizu, 1m 42.289s; 11 Bradl, 1m 42.664s; 12 Preining, 1m 42.680s; 13 Puig, 1m 42.744s; 14 Zeelenberg, 1m 42.861s; 15 Ruggia, 1m 43.004s.

World Championship: 1 Cadalora, 167; 2 Reggiani, 117; 3 Chili, 87; 4 Puig, 68; 5 Bradl, 67; 6 Cardus, 45; 7 Shimizu, 44; 8 Biaggi, 43; 9 Schmid and Zeelenberg, 38; 11 Romboni, 21; 12 Okada, 15; 13 Aoki, 12; 14 Capirossi, 11; 15 Torrontegui, 7; 16 Lavado, Preining, Ruggia and Wakai, 4; 20 Casoli and Nanba, 3; 22 Hänggeli, Prein and J. van den Goorbergh, 2; 25 Jeandat and Kassner, 1.

Malcolm Bryan

125 cc

25 laps, 66.350 miles/106.775 km

Place	Rider	Nat.	Machine	Laps	Time & speed	Fastest lap	Lap
1	**Ezio Gianola**	**I**	**Honda**	**25**	**45m 37.526s 86.821 mph/ 139.725 km/h**	**1m 47.674s**	**7**
2	**Noboru Ueda**	**J**	**Honda**	**25**	**45m 42.796s**	**1m 48.949s**	**8**
3	**Jorge Martinez**	**E**	**Honda**	**25**	**45m 42.972s**	**1m 48.637s**	**15**
4	**Kazuto Sakata**	**J**	**Honda**	**25**	**45m 43.454s**	**1m 48.840s**	**9**
5	**Alessandro Gramigni**	**I**	**Aprilia**	**25**	**45m 44.379s**	**1m 49.026s**	**25**
6	**Bruno Casanova**	**I**	**Aprilia**	**25**	**45m 46.128s**	**1m 48.773s**	**5**
7	**Dirk Raudies**	**D**	**Honda**	**25**	**45m 46.635s**	**1m 49.023s**	**25**
8	**Nobuyuki Wakai**	**J**	**Honda**	**25**	**45m 54.057s**	**1m 49.150s**	**20**
9	**Hans Spaan**	**NL**	**Aprilia**	**25**	**45m 57.374s**	**1m 49.492s**	**22**
10	**Ralf Waldmann**	**D**	**Honda**	**25**	**45m 58.765s**	**1m 49.094s**	**8**
11	Takao Shimizu	J	Honda	25	46m 00.008s	1m 49.092s	19
12	Maik Stief	D	Aprilia	25	46m 01.031s	1m 49.449s	4
13	Oliver Koch	D	Honda	25	46m 04.709s	1m 49.581s	14
14	Gabriele Debbia	I	Honda	25	46m 14.837s	1m 48.747s	6
15	Kinya Wada	J	Honda	25	46m 29.929s	1m 49.874s	4
16	Arie Molenaar	NL	Aprilia	25	46m 33.018s	1m 49.642s	22
17	Oliver Petrucciani	CH	Aprilia	25	46m 36.455s	1m 50.766s	15
18	Loek Bodelier	NL	Honda	25	46m 36.709s	1m 50.175s	10
19	Alain Bronec	F	Honda	25	46m 39.627s	1m 50.433s	22
20	Manuel Hernandez	E	Aprilia	25	46m 40.678s	1m 50.968s	24
21	Steve Patrickson	GB	Honda	25	46m 40.824s	1m 50.458s	8
22	Peter Galvin	AUS	Honda	25	46m 49.725s	1m 51.289s	16
23	Noel Ferro	F	Honda	25	47m 14.444s	1m 51.979s	8
24	Hubert Abold	D	Honda	25	47m 14.969s	1m 51.879s	19
25	Hisashi Unemoto	J	Honda	24	46m 33.024s	1m 52.378s	6
26	Regis Laconi	F	Honda	24	46m 38.004s	1m 52.847s	3
	Luis Alvaro	E	Aprilia	10	DNF	1m 51.986s	7
	Fausto Gresini	I	Honda	7	DNF	1m 47.890s	7
	Peter Öttl	D	Rotax	7	DNF	1m 51.732s	5
	Giuseppe Fiorillo	I	Yamaha	6	DNF	1m 54.094s	2
	Alfred Waibel	D	Honda	5	DNF	1m 54.671s	4
	Julian MIralles	E	Honda	5	DNF	1m 52.360s	3
	Robin Appleyard	GB	Honda	4	DNF	1m 50.855s	2
	Heinz Lüthi	CH	Honda	3	DNF	1m 52.340s	2
	Carlos Giro	E	Aprilia	2	DNF	1m 51.880s	2
	Fausto Ricci	I	Yamaha	0	DNF		

Fastest lap: Gianola, 1m 47.674s, 88.294 mph/142.096 km/h (record).
Previous record: none.

Practice leaderboard: 1 Gianola, 1m 47.530s; **2** Wakai, 1m 47.783s; **3** Ueda, 1m 48.105s; **4** Gresini, 1m 48.292s; **5** Debbia, 1m 48.317s; **6** Raudies, 1m 48.546s; **7** Sakata, 1m 48.683s; **8** Martinez, 1m 48.703s; **9** Giro, 1m 48.740s; **10** Spaan, 1m 48.776s; **11** Gramigni, 1m 48.882s; **12** Casanova, 1m 48.942s; **13** Stief, 1m 49.278s; **14** Shimizu, 1m 49.405s; **15** Waldmann, 1m 49.434s.

World Championship: 1 Waldmann, 102; **2** Gianola, 101; **3** Gramigni, 95; **4** Gresini, 88; **5** Casanova, 78; **6** Debbia, 58; **7** Raudies, 51; **8** Wakai, 48; **9** Martinez, 45; **10** Sakata, 36; **11** Ueda, 33; **12** Giro, 22; **13** Öttl and Spaan, 10; **15** Koch and Saitoh, 8; **17** Shimizu, 5; **18** Fuji-hara, 4; **19** Kurfiss and Wada, 3; **21** Lüthi and Petrucciani, 1.

Sidecars

26 laps, 69.004 miles/110.046 km

Place	Driver & passenger	Nat.	Machine	Laps	Time & speed	Fastest lap	Lap
1	**Rolf Biland/ Kurt Waltisperg**	**CH CH**	**LCR-Krauser**	**26**	**45m 58.883s 89.595 mph/ 144.189 km/h**	**1m 45.206s**	**2**
2	**Egbert Streuer/ Peter Brown**	**NL GB**	**LCR-Stredor**	**26**	**46m 02.284s**	**1m 45.213s**	**4**
3	**Klaus Klaffenböck/ Christian Parzer**	**A A**	**LCR-ADM**	**26**	**46m 04.701s**	**1m 45.397s**	**3**
4	**Steve Webster/ Gavin Simmons**	**GB GB**	**LCR-ADM**	**26**	**46m 08.222s**	**1m 45.161s**	**4**
5	**Yoshisada Kumagaya/ Bryan Houghton**	**J GB**	**LCR-Krauser**	**26**	**46m 27.543s**	**1m 45.552s**	**3**
6	**Steve Abbott/ Shaun Smith**	**GB GB**	**LCR-Krauser**	**26**	**46m 29.200s**	**1m 46.019s**	**8**
7	**Paul Güdel/ Charly Güdel**	**CH CH**	**LCR-Yamaha**	**26**	**46m 29.603s**	**1m 45.991s**	**10**
8	**Barry Brindley/ Scott Whiteside**	**GB GB**	**LCR-Yamaha**	**26**	**47m 04.650s**	**1m 46.884s**	**3**
9	**Markus Egloff/ Urs Egloff**	**CH CH**	**LCR-Yamaha**	**26**	**47m 07.330s**	**1m 46.753s**	**4**
10	**Theo van Kempen/ Geral de Haas**	**NL NL**	**LCR-Krauser**	**26**	**47m 39.990s**	**1m 48.531s**	**13**
11	Hans Hügli/ Adolf Hänni	CH CH	LCR-Krauser	25	46m 40.469s	1m 49.059s	5
12	Mark Reddington/ Kim Andreasen	GB DK	LCR-Krauser	25	47m 02.636s	1m 50.463s	4
13	M. Fernand/ M. Charpentier	F F	Krauser	24	46m 37.736s	1m 53.365s	8
	Reiner Koster/ Jurg Egli	CH CH	LCR-Yamaha	24	DNF	1m 48.914s	5
	Darren Dixon/ Andy Hetherington	GB GB	LCR-Krauser	12	DNF	1m 45.008s	11
	Robert Fisher/ Trevor Crone	GB GB	LCR-Krauser	12	DNF	1m 49.222s	5
	Markus Bösiger/ Peter Höss	CH CH	LCR-ADM	11	DNF	1m 46.984s	5
	Tony Wyssen/ Kilian Wyssen	CH CH	LCR-Yamaha	10	DNF	1m 48.808s	9
	Derek Brindley/ Nick Roche	GB GB	LCR-Krauser	9	DNF	1m 46.939s	3
	Ralph Bohnhorst/ Bruno Hiller	D D	BRM	8	DNF	1m 46.836s	5
	Jukka Lauslehto/ Jurgen Levinsen	SF DK	LCR-ADM	6	DNF	1m 50.308s	4
	Tony Baker/ Simon Prior	GB GB	LCR-Krauser	6	DNF	1m 51.218s	2
	Billy Gällros/ Peter Berglund	S S	LCR-Streuer	5	DNF	1m 48.371s	5
	André Bosman/ Dave Kellett	AUS AUS	LCR-Krauser	5	DNF	1m 49.482s	5
	Peter Lemstra/ Jan Kuyt	NL NL	LCR-Krauser		DNQ		

Fastest lap: Dixon, 1m 45.008s, 90.536 mph/145.703 km/h (record).
Previous record: none.

Practice leaderboard: 1 Biland, 1m 42.982s; **2** Webster, 1m 44.157s; **3** Dixon, 1m 44.167s; **4** Klaffenböck, 1m 44.390s; **5** Streuer, 1m 44.490s; **6** Bohnhorst, 1m 44.814s; **7** Kumagaya, 1m 45.274s; **8** Güdel, 1m 45.280s; **9** Egloff, 1m 45.428s; **10** Bösiger, 1m 45.740s; **11** Abbott, 1m 46.217s; **12** Lauslehto, 1m 46.276s; **13** B. Brindley, 1m 46.316s; **14** D. Brindley, 1m 46.949s; **15** Gällros, 1m 47.920s.

World Championship: 1 Webster, 80; **2** Klaffenböck, 66; **3** Biland, 63; **4** Kumagaya and Streuer, 35; **6** Bohnhorst, 26; **7** Güdel, 24; **8** B. Brindley, 19; **9** Dixon, 15; **10** Abbott, 14; **11** Bösiger and Egloff, 10; **13** Wyssen, 4; **14** Baker, D. Brindley, Lauslehto and van Kempen, 1.

500 cc	GARDNER
250 cc	CHILI
125 cc	GRESINI
SIDECARS	BILAND

WORLD CHAMPIONSHIP • ROUND 11

BRITISH GRAND PRIX

British race organisers expect it to be taken as read that their races are run with an efficiency and decorum found nowhere else in the world. They would never do anything so vulgar as to boast about what is, after all, one of those imperial truths. They are less restrained by false modesty when it comes to the British race marshals. Trumpeting the virtues of these volunteers is easier than paying them or even, in these straitened times, feeding and watering them. And they are, of course, the best marshals in the world.

Thus it was a double shock to see these same marshals bemused and befuddled as three of the top 500 riders fell on the same invisible spillage within the space of a lap and a half – and then to see victim Kevin Schwantz remonstrate with them, and eventually seize the oil flag and thrust it under the noses of the surviving riders.

It seems, as a gleeful Italian journalist put it, that the best marshals in the world had an off day.

The Redgate Affair saw action-man Schwantz save the day, leaving marshals looking puzzled and foolish. No trace of spillage was found after the race.

Photos: Paul Kearney

The Redgate Affair remains something of a mystery. Everyone had seen Kocinski's drone Yamaha spit the dummy – it obligingly blew up directly in front of the pits. (Mackenzie's YZR drone suffered an identical blow-up, but more modestly at the very far end of the circuit.) Eye-witnesses spoke of a cloud of vapour as it blew, and clearly something slippery was left behind. But whatever it was that fetched off Chandler, Schwantz and a charging Carl Fogarty was apparently invisible to the marshals, and had certainly gone by the time the track was inspected after the race.

Prompted by the yelling crowd, they were waving a tentative oil flag after Chandler had been the first to tip off, but it was too little and too late – right on top of the spillage, said Schwantz. And in his entirely understandable bate (he had been a candidate for victory, and certain of a rostrum finish) he made the marshals look stupid and feel small as he seized the striped bunting and waved it in the face of riders diving for Redgate's temporarily treacherous apex. Loyally, several riders including top Briton Terry Rymer attributed their own survival directly to this selfless act, but the marshals were left nonplussed in front of a howling mob as Schwantz ostentatiously stalked off to sit on his helmet by the trackside for the remaining few laps.

Since all this had been televised, the organisers and TWP race director Pierpaolo Gardella were anxious for a public damage-control exercise. Schwantz met the marshals to hear their side of the story, and was told that they had complained and been over-ruled about the siting of the post that was too far down the track to provide proper warning. The Texan superstar agreed to go on TV, not to apologise but to make some conciliatory remarks of the 'Your British policemen are wonderful' variety. As it happened, no TV slot became available, and the marshals were left under a cloud that lasted longer than any trace of the spillage.

There is still doubt over what actually caused the trouble. Some suggested it was vapourised petroil mix from the smashed crankcases that settled, only to evaporate by the time the race was over – though it hardly seemed likely that a few crankcases-full would be enough to have such a devastating effect. Others blamed coolant, suggesting that some illegal additive had been mixed with the water, and that this too had evaporated. Then again, Kocinski's gearbox shed plenty of oil into the fairing, but this surely would have left traces. Probably it was a combination of all the above, but we will never know for sure.

What is at least highly probable is that if Schwantz hadn't gone Rainey would have been one place lower. This would have knocked three points off his championship tally. Comfortingly, for the marshals at least, he ended up with a four-point lead over Doohan, but Schwantz's chances were now used up, and his title hopes over.

It is equally obvious that the whole affair was acutely embarrassing for Yamaha, for it showed that their new drone-clone engine had serious flaws. Within minutes two bikes suffered identical catastrophic drive-side crankshaft failures – a wholesale destruction at the very heart of the engine, whereby crankcases, gearbox casings and primary drive gears were smashed. This was entirely consistent with stress fractures induced by torsional or other vibration from the revised firing order; and the failure was indicative of a hastily engineered lash-up.

Major engine blow-ups are regular if not frequent events, but they are generally kept secret; and everybody is at great pains to ensure that they should never actually happen in a race. In the case of the drone-clones, all the factories had discovered the destructive potential of the new vibration pattern – including Honda, although they had the luxury of doing so in pre-season tests rather than in the middle of the season. Suzuki droners also popped their crankshafts, but the stop-gap solution of slashing their scheduled service life in half meant they only did it in practice or while testing.

Yamaha's problems were compounded by outside influences. Their race shop resources were already stretched thin by the introduction of the works-replica Harris and Roc privateer bikes, and they were also hard at work developing a works 250 with Jochen Schmid. Now they also had to rush out a drone-clone motor, initially only for Rainey and Kocinski. But Mackenzie and Garriga were clamouring for drones – the former racing at home, the latter's switch to Michelins now starting to bear fruit. Yamaha obliged them both a day late; but the effort had left them short of spares, and the end result was that both Kocinski and Mackenzie suffered fatigue failures. A worry for Rainey and the other YZR riders thus equipped, since it cast deep doubt over the integrity of the engine.

This was, of course, especially crucial for Rainey in his bid to catch Doohan on points. He now settled his mind (and many weeks of increasingly fevered speculation) by deciding to stay with Marlboro Roberts, while Roberts in turn signed to stay with Yamaha, after floating a red herring that he was contemplating a switch to Honda. Wayne's other problem came after the race. Worried about yobbish pitch invasions, the organisers had already done away with the victory lap, pulling riders up promptly after the finish. The crowd invaded anyway and Rainey, getting his breath back before climbing into the escape bus, was overwhelmed, knocked over and trampled. He was taken away groaning in pain, but luckily there was no permanent damage to his weak right knee, and his championship hopes remained alive.

The rest was up to Doohan, and after a week or so of will-he/won't-he stories it emerged that he would not be fit to race in Britain. The day after the French GP he had undergone eight hours of surgery to graft skin onto the open wound, and he was now back in a plaster cast with both legs sewn together to help the graft take quickly. The title leader's presence was substituted by tapes of a Dorna TV interview in hospital. He looked awful, pumped full of drugs, his face skeletal and his manner vague as he spoke about his hopes of riding in Brazil, and racing strongly at Kyalami, and of his dismay at the treatment he had received after the first operation at Assen. 'What went wrong there is that I didn't ... shoot the doctor.'

Doohan didn't mention the puzzling fact that HRC had not fielded a replacement to keep a few points away from his title rivals – particularly Beattie, a rider of proven ability, although admittedly currently busy winning the Suzuka Eight Hour and trying to stop Magee winning the All-Japan title. But HRC has always been inscrutable to say the least, and now proved it again in the 250 class, where Cadalora had a chance of securing his second successive title for them. Instead of easing his way, they produced a pair of NSRs for two renowned hotheads – Romboni and Capirossi. This was

Malcolm Bryan

not compensation for their joint gearbox failures in France, we were assured, simply a demonstration run for next year's production Honda. Certainly neither had orders to let Cadalora finish ahead of them; to beat him would be a significant boost to their fledgling careers. Thus it was an oblique rap on the knuckles for Cadalora, whose relationship with Rothmans and the factory was getting strained. It told him he'd be better off looking for his planned 500 ride elsewhere – advice he took with enthusiasm, since he was by now negotiating to replace Kocinski at Team Roberts.

There were a number of would-be 500 class GP riders wandering round the paddocks, including former regulars Rob McElnea and Kevin Magee. Three others were actually wearing leathers – James Whitham and Carl Fogarty were getting a one-off chance at an outing via the wild card system, and Terry Rymer was a last-minute (literally) replacement for the still-injured Buckmaster. In fact, he rode a 1993 prototype Harris Yamaha, which matches the '92 Roc in having adjustable engine mounts and swing-arm pivot. Fogarty raced another '93 chassis as nominal team-mate to Kevin Mitchell in MBM colours; Whitham stuck to Buckmaster's bike, which he had raced at Magny-Cours.

It was the acid test for all of them, and for British racing in general. They had been facing criticism at home for failing to get themselves into GP racing while lesser privateers (like Buckmaster and the ever-optimistic Peter Graves) had exploited the new IRTA/TWP financial system to get onto the grids. Whitham had, of course, already proved that British riders are good enough in France; Fogarty had some bad memories to erase of a couple of fruitless Honda NSR outings in 1990. Rymer was a genuine GP virgin, and ran into all sorts of practice problems including an embarrassing first day crash when the throttle stuck open. In the end, he was the only one of the three to prove his worth with a fine sixth place, but all went well, especially Fogarty, running with the leaders early on.

The last European round had an end of term atmosphere: the big teams were to say goodbye to their hospitality suites, and they all teamed up for a paddock party on Friday night. Not invited was Claude Arciero; the ultra-slow French privateer didn't turn up for practice, and he was promptly ruled in breach of contract and out of the game.

Bernie Ecclestone was invited but didn't show, although he was there on race day to watch his first-ever bike GP.

Some details emerged of the sidecar rescue plan, with the FIM promising more money, and IRTA, Dorna and TWP between them promising another $500,000-odd and a place at four or five 1993 GPs, the balance to be run elsewhere. The sidecars said they would miss Brazil this year, but would go to South Africa. Wrong again.

Political manoeuvring at the other end of the scale saw announcement of an important new set of initials – GPMA, standing for GP Manufacturers Association, a powerful but as yet shadowy organisation who promised more information in the future. Members were drawn only from the 500 cc class – Honda, Yamaha, Suzuki and Cagiva – and there was no word whether 250 constructors Gilera and Aprilia would be invited to join. At last the Japanese factories would have a voice other than the Japanese federation.

This was just another footnote in the developing story of motor cycle racing as a promotional business, but for the fans the real memory of the British GP of 1992 will come from the closing chapters of a different kind of motor cycle story – the blood-and-guts saga of gritty Wayne Gardner. World Champion, charger, crasher, fighter and hero, Gardner came to Donington fresh from his fourth victory in the Suzuka Eight Hour, and on a roll. By courtesy of the already dominant NSR, now further developed with Erv Kanemoto, he was riding better than ever, since he no longer needed to venture so far into the accident to run at the front. His race victory was calm and unflurried, he seemed always in control and easily able to take the lead first from Rainey and then to retake it from Schwantz. The oil at Redgate freed him from any threat of a last lap Schwantz attack, and he recorded his 18th and last GP win with great fluency.

Wayne Gardner rode as well as ever in his life to record his last GP win.

His last, because he announced his retirement before the race, at a typically emotional press conference. A man who puts heart and soul into racing, he cries as easily (if not as frequently) as he loses his temper, and the announcement was a two-hankie affair. And why not, for it marked the end of a remarkable up-and-down career.

500 cc PRACTICE

Donington Park is a circuit both revered and reviled for it has a dual character, at once blissful and fatuous. Most of its lap is highly technical, comprising complex corner sets, many with delicate downhill entries or treacherous post-apex crests – a fit canvas for a true GP artist. Then comes the chicane and the much-vilified Melbourne Hairpin, a bumpy first-gear piece of silliness scarcely improved upon by the ensuing and final second-gear U-turn.

Lawson has long criticised what he calls 'the car park section' that finishes the lap, but found the rhythm on the rest of the track to secure his second pole position. It is no coincidence that the other was at that supreme riders' circuit, Assen.

Lawson also uses Dunlops, which have a fine record at the track closest to their Birmingham headquarters, though this is something of a coincidence. Their success has more to do with the grip of their front tyres, so important here, especially at the set of three throttle-on downhillers running down to the Old Hairpin. Eddie was one of only a handful to run faster here this year than last, but he was a second down on Schwantz's 1991 pole. Yet again, at a directly comparable track, the works Yamaha and Suzuki riders who had switched to Michelin appeared to have gone backwards, though it was becoming clear that if individual lap times were generally slower this year, race averages were faster. The new Michelins may not grip as well as Dunlops, but they do so for longer in race conditions.

Lawson set his time on Friday, and fully expected to be deposed on Saturday afternoon. Not so, with Kocinski slotting into second, looking smooth and unhurried as he skated on the edge of tipping off in a front-wheel slide, as he had done at mercifully slow speed on Friday, blaming 'brain fade'.

Rainey was only hundredths slower in third, and might have been ahead but for running into traffic when going for a fast lap at the end of the session. He was muscling the bike in his old aggressive style, marking a continuing improvement in the season-long battle to get it to steer. 'We've got the new forks working, but it took a lot of work and left us behindhand with overall set-up,' he explained. 'I still haven't got my gearing settled – I'll still be testing in free training on race morning.'

Gardner was the last man on a closely spaced front row, also riding with signature aggression and brinkmanship, head down and elbows out, his Honda squirming and quavering out of the bends. Then he had a signature crash in the final session, losing the front into Redgate in full view of the pits. He was puzzled, for he had had three laps on the tyre and it should have been warm. But the jolt somehow freed up a trapped nerve or something in his neck, and if he wasn't able to keep on cutting his lap time as a result of the spill, it did leave him in an even better physical condition.

This was barely plausible, but racers say all sorts of things designed to keep the opposition guessing. Ditto Schwantz, who led row two. His trip (with Chandler) to the Eight Hour had been tiring and disappointing, and his left arm was still bandaged on Friday. 'It's bothering me some,' he said, adding: 'Don't write that – the others don't need to know. My arm feels great.' He was also bothered by the fact that his accustomed superiority here had deserted him, and the usually flickable Suzuki had lost much of the agility that had meant he could push hard without losing the all-important one fast line round the corner combinations. A new chassis offered no instant solutions, and was quietly put on one side until the last race of the year. A fourth win in succession was looking a tall order. 'It's moving around in the fast bends, and the front's vague, so I don't have confidence to chuck it into slow corners,' he said. 'We've been working on the front end, but I think the problem may be coming from somewhere else.'

Garriga was alongside, his form continuing to improve although he was running a temperature and feeling horrible. He was already going well on Friday, and on Saturday Yamaha completed late delivery of the drone engine he'd been awaiting with increasing impatience. The amenable power worked its magic with him as well, and he improved still further. 'I wish I'd been sick all year,' he quipped.

Sixth place, remarkably, went to Fogarty, the TT and Superbike hero's first race on a two-stroke since his troubled two rides on the injured Chili's NSR in 1990. He was conspicuously aggressive, but also smooth and confident, in spite of a spill on Friday. 'I'm just doing the same as always,' he said. 'The Honda was a nightmare, but the Yamaha suits me. I need to prove I can ride a 500. English riders always seem to miss out.'

Mackenzie was thus displaced to become the second-best Briton. He was under a different kind of pressure – the disagreements within his team had been growing, and now a report in a French paper said he would lose his ride at the end of this season. There was also the stress of riding at home, compounded by the switch (like Garriga) to a different engine with practice already half finished. Luckily he loved the engine, the smooth corner exit filling in gaps in his riding style: he's as fast as anyone into the corner and at the mid-point, but has never really mastered the corner exit slide as well as the Americans. Then, just as he was putting it all together for a sizzling fast lap, he ran out of fuel!

Chandler was frustrated, having dropped from pole at the last two races to ninth, heading row three. Like Schwantz, his Suzuki had run into unexpected balance problems. 'We've had a few tracks with downhill corner entries, but this one's worse because you're accelerating all the way, which makes the front lighter.' He was unable to compensate by charging through the car park, and was trying to find gear ratios that could cut the number of gearchanges – seven shifts on the short run from the chicane to the Melbourne Hairpin alone. A kill-shift might save considerable time here, but he didn't have one.

Echoes of Doohan's Assen spill – a high-sider caused unexpectedly late in the corner – were evoked by Criville on Friday morning. He also blamed unexpected wheelspin when the bike was already almost upright, and his bike ended up on the *inside* of the Old Hairpin exit. He finished up 10th; Mamola was alongside in 11th, but only 1.5 seconds down on pole. He was to have a similarly surprising late corner exit high-sider in the race, causing some to wonder about the new Michelins, the common ingredient in these tip-offs.

Whitham was alongside, riding even more spectacularly than at Magny-Cours, treating the 500 two-stroke if not with contempt then with more familiarity than his single previous outing would suggest, and doing rather better than England had expected. He was overshadowed only by Fogarty in their proof that their racing careers had stalled below GP level for reasons other than a shortage of talent.

Goddard was back after missing two races, and took his usual place at the head of the regular privateers, leading row four from Sarron, Laycock and Mitchell. Row five comprised Catalano, Rudroff, DuHamel and Rymer. The Canadian was having trouble sizing up the difficult track in his first visit; the Briton was hampered in his own first top two-stroke race by pre-race uncertainty (his ride was only confirmed by Buckmaster's belated withdrawal 15 minutes before first practice), and his subsequent tip-off with a stuck throttle.

All 30 entrants qualified, and the

GPs are just drag races with corners. Cadalora (1), Chili (7), Biaggi (29) and Romboni (15) fan out from the 250 start. Also prominent are Zeelenberg (4), Puig (16), Cardus (3), Ruggia (9), Patrick van den Goorbergh (36) and Bradl (2). In the middle, Casoli (10) and Jurgen van den Goorbergh (33) have collided, though both continued.

Below: **Carl Fogarty, the fastest of the three one-race Britons, proved plenty at Donington Park. Here he holds off rostrum finisher Garriga.**

closeness of the top times was more redolent of some 250 races than the 500 grids of recent years, with the first 11 riders within 1.5 seconds, and a few more close behind. It would surely be a humdinger of a race.

500 cc RACE – 30 LAPS

And humdinger it was, from the start until the time the pace proved too hot for two of the Yamahas, and one of them took three other bikes out with it.

Kocinski leapt into the lead from the start, but it didn't last beyond the first two corners, with Rainey finding his way past, then Lawson at the Old Hairpin, then Schwantz and then Gardner, dropping the youngster to fifth by the end of a hectic lap.

He continued to lose ground, unable to find either rhythm or grip, and soon succumbed to Fogarty, who was riding brilliantly, to the delight of the crowd. Then came Garriga, having one of his best-ever races, and he relegated the American to seventh, going on to pass Fogarty on lap four and close on the leading quartet.

Rainey was still in front of this battle royal, but Gardner had picked his way smoothly through it into second on lap three. He took the lead for the first time on lap six, outbraking Rainey for the Melbourne Hairpin, then shaking his head vigorously as the American tried to dive back inside him mid-corner before gassing it earlier and surging firmly ahead. Even now, he was clearly riding well within himself, cool and calm, and far short of his full wild-man potential.

Schwantz had already taken third from Lawson and, as he saw Gardner run, he set about Rainey and then took off after the Honda. His overnight chassis guesswork had gone a long way towards giving him the bike he needed, and he knew he had a chance of winning.

Sure enough, he passed Gardner on lap ten, and led for the first time. But he had nothing in hand, and even slowed the pace, so that soon the four up front packed up tight behind him, prompting Gardner to make another escape bid. He powered past on the back straight, fast enough to foil Schwantz's inevitable and immediate outbraking attempt at the chicane, and was never headed again.

After two more laps, Rainey swept inside Schwantz at Redgate, then set fastest lap so far as he hunkered down after Gardner, but while he closed a little the Australian was able to respond to maintain his lead. Then Schwantz came back again, seizing second, still in touch with Gardner, and a brilliant race far from over.

Lawson had been watching all this from close behind, but now he started to drop back, succinctly blaming his 16-in. rear Dunlop. 'It didn't last,' he said. Garriga now passed the American to close up yet again on the leading trio, able to lap with them but seemingly lacking the mental strength to mount a challenge.

Up front, Gardner now forced the pace again and it was enough, it seemed, to establish a finishing order, with Schwantz second, just out of attacking range, and Rainey ditto in third. And that's probably how it would have been but for the Yamaha explosions.

Mackenzie's was the first to go. Until then, he said later, 'It was the best bike I'd ever ridden.' He'd made his usual mediocre start, but gradually climbed from 13th on lap one to sixth on lap 18, ahead of Kocinski and moving up on Lawson. He was climbing the hill out of the sharp right at McLeans when his crankshaft blew. 'At first I didn't know what had happened. It just lost power and I was working the throttle to see if it would pick up.' Not much chance of that, and he coasted over the crest of the hill at Coppice, luckily right on the inside of the track, for his back wheel was shiny with oil.

Kocinski suffered an identical failure as he began his 25th lap, slowing dramatically past the pits, then coasting through Redgate to pull off onto the grass on the inside of the corner. He was also right on the inside of the track, but the apex here is one that riders cut very close with the power off, unlike the power-on Coppice Corner, where the bike is already tending to drift wide.

Ironically, Chandler, lying eighth, was congratulating himself on having managed for once to get his troublesome Suzuki to turn in tight. Right onto the oil. 'I saw something black on the track, then I was down so fast I didn't know what hit me,' he said.

Next time round, Gardner and Schwantz both hit it too. Gardner later said he'd also lost the front, but that he'd managed to save it with his knee. Not so Schwantz, still on the brakes there and down like a skittle. He had hardly got to his feet when Fogarty joined him and Chandler; and with the crowd howling at the marshals, Schwantz saw red. He ran across the track, grabbed the oil flag and embarked on the controversial performance for which many riders were thankful.

Rainey again cut the race best lap time as he chased after Gardner (though he was still more than half a second off the record), but it was a vain pursuit of a genuine hero having one of his best-ever wins. He was able to slacken off on the last lap to wheelie across the line, with Rainey still trying hard but finishing a second behind. Garriga was charging at the finish to take third, his best-ever 500 class result; Lawson was a safe fourth, some 20 seconds behind him.

The depletion of the field was a blessing for the privateers. Goddard took fifth after running steadily and mainly alone for his best result of the year. A long way back and last rider not to be lapped came Rymer, a tremendous result after his slow start in practice, achieved with a steadfast ride that went a long way towards salvaging an unfairly endangered reputation.

He'd stayed clear of a three-bike battle, with DuHamel eventually pulling ahead of Rudroff and Sarron. Arakaki narrowly took tenth and the last point, after a long battle with Serge David and Bruno Bonhuil, who had replaced the injured Crine.

Mamola had crashed out of tenth place on the tenth lap, with a late corner exit high-sider out of the Melbourne Hairpin. Criville was an early retirement, misfiring into the pits after two laps; other retirements included Laycock with generator failure, Mitchell – 'popping and banging from the start', Catalano after a collision with Sarron followed by an off-track excursion, and Whitham with a slipping clutch. He'd cooked it with a practice start on the warm-up lap, and it never recovered. What next for the last of the three promising Britons? 'Back to Cadwell, I suppose.'

Photos: Malcolm Bryan

250 cc PRACTICE

Dunlops clearly held the upper hand in this class as well, with the full front row using the British tyres. All were Italian, and the top three rode Italian motor cycles. The Aprilia excels on the challenging sweeps and swoops of Donington, and also had good enough brakes and acceleration not to lose it all through the car park. It was only a matter of which Aprilia would claim pole.

It was Chili in the end, capping the achievement by insisting he could easily have gone faster still but for traffic in the final session. He needed some reassurance other than the stopwatch, for two-tenths covered his two rivals, with Biaggi second and Reggiani third. Luckless Loris was well below par, again a frequent visitor to Dr Costa's injection parlour, this time suffering from 'flu. 'It's lucky my bike doesn't also feel sick,' he joked.

Cadalora's depression at this vista, at a race where he needed to finish fourth to be sure of the title, was deepened by his own difficulties in balancing the Honda on its Michelins, all the while knowing if he got it dead right he would still only be fourth fastest. The presence of two rogue NSRs also had its effect on him, most especially when Romboni qualified his Dunlop-shod HB bike faster to take the last front row position, narrowly surviving one practice trip onto the grass to fulfil the promise of a year in which he has tamed his high risk technique to show growing potential.

Luca led row two, almost half a second down on Chili, and openly disappointed. 'Things were not too good yesterday, and I'm afraid they are even worse today,' he said.

His grid companion was the other temporary NSR rider Capirossi, just a tenth slower. He was an enthusiastic convert to works bike riding, but fell spectacularly though unhurt in the first session. Next to him was Bradl, still up against it for reasons that were not entirely clear, and narrowly ahead of his countryman Schmid, with yet another consignment of new engine parts from Yamaha.

Puig's Aprilia led row three from his fellow-Spaniard, the troubled Cardus. Ruggia was alongside, ahead of Shimizu on the slowest of the six NSRs. The Suzukis were having trouble finding the pace, with Torrontegui 14th, between the Aprilias of Preining and Patrick van den Goorbergh; Zeelenberg was really struggling, 17th fastest at the head of row five. All 37 entrants qualified, the last being James Haydon, a wild card entry under the Team Great Britain banner. The other wild card, Ian Newton, was 28th.

250 cc RACE – 28 LAPS

Perhaps it was inevitable that so closely matched a front row would clash literally as well as figuratively. Biaggi had seized the lead, and rode with his accustomed zeal to hang on to it for the first four laps. In his wake, Reggiani was sizing the youngster up, and now mounted a challenge.

It ended instead in a minor collision after Biaggi braked unexpectedly early, and while he was unscathed it pushed Reggiani wide, and both Chili and Romboni dived through on the inside.

Now it was Chili's turn to attack, and he waited one lap before taking a quicker run through the fast right-handers to slingshot past onto the back straight. He was able to start working on a cushion immediately, and after 12 laps he was almost four seconds ahead.

At this point, Reggiani was back in second, but he'd lost enough time getting back past his younger countryman to spike any chance of a challenge to Chili, who was now firmly in control on a clear track. Biaggi was tucked in behind Reggiani, with Romboni, unable to match their pace, gradually losing ground.

There was every chance that the old-timer and the young maverick would collide again, before Biaggi made a mistake at the chicane on lap 23. He'd been battling a notchy gearchange all race, and now he found a false neutral on the way into the chicane. He stamped it into gear and declutched, but it was first, and it locked the rear wheel and tipped him off the low-side and out of the race.

Reggiani pushed on again, and was within two seconds of Chili at the flag. But that was more than enough for comfort, for Chili had done

polini
elf
2
Fimi
BIEFFE
alpinestars
TEAM PILERI

LONGINES
uvex
2
design
LONGINES
KARL RUPP AG
BP
HESS
schoeller
HUGO WOLF fiberglass

Left: **Gresini's only win of the year was achieved with impressive assurance.**

Below left: **Biland's fourth win in succession ensured an exciting finish to the championship – whenever and wherever that would be.**

Right: **Wilco's woes worsened with a rare but comprehensive blow-up. The works Suzuki should have been fast, but somehow he didn't seem to mesh with it.**

enough early on, and then set a new record on lap 19, to win at his own pace.

What of Cadalora, who needed to finish fourth to be unassailable in the championship? He'd been holding a cautious fifth early on, then started to close on Romboni by half-distance. But he was also coming under pressure himself, with Schmid and Bradl locked together and closing up on him. For the second half, the quartet fought it out, with Bradl dropping off the back as the pace speeded up in the closing laps.

Cadalora had been back and forth with the inspired Romboni, a risky pastime in his position, but was ahead when he inherited third when Biaggi crashed out. But the Honda-riding youngster forced his way back in front with four laps to go.

Fourth was good enough, but Cadalora was now under attack from Schmid, who outbraked him more than once. But Luca had Honda power on his side – over the Yamaha at least, if not the Aprilias – and once he had led into the final hairpin he was able to stay in front to cross the line less than half a second in front. Fourth place, and his second title in succession.

Bradl was sixth, Capirossi a lonely seventh, blaming a bad choice of tyres. Then came Cardus, equally alone some way back, leading Shimizu by eight seconds.

Another five seconds down, Torrontegui won a fierce scrap for the final point. It was a good ride, after he'd been put on the grass on the first lap when Ruggia and Prein crashed together at the Old Hairpin. The Spaniard finished that lap in 20th place, then charged through to attack on-form Dutch privateer Patrick van den Goorbergh, and finally he passed Lavado. The Venezuelan now lost all hope of points as his Gilera's power mysteriously faded away, and he was also overtaken by Bernd Kassner (Aprilia) in the hectic brawl, with two seconds covering from 10th to 13th.

There were 23 finishers. Notable retirements included Puig, who had engine trouble after running ahead of Shimizu for most of the race. Zeelenberg had a short race. Running 12th after three laps, better than his practice form, his bike suddenly locked up at the end of the back straight. A con rod had snapped – a first for the hitherto almost bullet-proof V-twin Suzuki.

Newton and Jurgen van den Goorbergh collided with the former crashing spectacularly after the Dutchman's Aprilia had seized a big end on the run down the hill.

125 cc RACE – 26 LAPS

As has happened several times this year, the usual brawling pack of the world's best 125 riders did not include the leaders. They were long gone ahead of this sordid but scintillating fracas, engaged in private demonstrations of their own.

Casanova had qualified on pole, but it was Gramigni's factory Aprilia that led away, with Gresini's Honda sandwiching Casanova in third, and they started to stretch away from the pursuit, with Gresini moving smoothly into second on lap four, then lining up to outbrake Gramigni into the chicane on lap six. It was his day, for he continued to draw steadily but inexorably away from the youngster to take his first race win of the year, and to put himself firmly into the title battle.

Gramigni later angrily blamed himself for using his brakes too hard in the warm-up lap, but he had the consolation of personally moving into the championship lead by two points from Gresini.

Casanova was unable to stay with them, gradually falling back into the clutches of the pursuit group, to be overwhelmed on lap 13.

Martinez was leading the group at that point, with Ueda in close company. The Japanese rider moved ahead on the back straight, then across to the outside to brake for the chicane. Martinez was already there, trying to fend off the attack, and they collided. Martinez was forced to run on straight, where he almost fell in the grass, to rejoin six places back, and livid. Ueda also wobbled and dropped five places, but he was still with the group and could get back on terms. The Spaniard's subsequent protest against Ueda's tactics was not upheld.

This incident put Casanova back into third, but Gianola had fought his way up and now he took over for a couple of laps, as Ueda moved back past Waldmann and then Raudies. Then, on lap 20, Gianola high-sided at the Melbourne Hairpin, forcing Casanova wide while Waldmann almost fell as he ran onto the grass, just missing Gianola's legs.

Thus Ueda gained the breathing space he needed, and while Raudies attacked again in the closing laps, the Japanese rider narrowly held him off to claim third. Casanova was fifth, Sakata a close sixth, having kept out of trouble with the fast men for once. Waldmann was now out of touch in seventh, with the fuming Martinez eighth. Some way back, Wada pipped Wakai for ninth in a Japanese Honda battle.

Gianola remounted to finish 12th, behind Maik Stief's private Honda, but ahead of a tight group comprising Giro and Debbia. There was good scrapping all the way down the field, with Robin Appleyard running well at home to prevail over a desperate six-strong group battling for 19th place.

Top ten qualifier Hans Spaan was the first of a number of people to crash, tumbling out of the melee at the hairpin on the first lap.

SIDECAR RACE – 26 LAPS

With two rounds supposedly remaining, Webster needed to win here more to maintain his own confidence than to preserve his shrinking but still defensible points lead. He needed to stop Biland's run of wins and reassert himself, especially at home.

Then in practice he had a heavy thump into the barriers, and the night before the race was busy repairing his LCR chassis while passenger Gavin Simmons dashed through the night to York in a borrowed van to pick up bodywork spares.

Meanwhile, Biland had taken pole position, with Streuer second, and Webbo ready to join the far end of the front row on the 3-2-3 grid.

Biland was right on form, however, and led from start to finish but for a brief moment on lap one, when fourth-fastest qualifier Dixon nosed ahead briefly. It was the Swiss rider's 22nd win, and a significant boost to his championship campaign.

By the end of lap one, Ralph Bohnhorst/Bruno Hiller were in second with Dixon/Hetherington third, while Webster/Simmons were closing up. By lap three, both British crews had overwhelmed Bohnhorst and were battling with each other, with Webster outbraking his rival one lap later to set off in pursuit of Biland.

He never did have much hope of catching him, however, and instead, as the race wore on, his engine with its Honda cylinders on ADM crankcases gradually lost power, and he fell back behind Dixon again with seven laps left. He was lucky not to be caught by Bohnhorst as well, for the German was just two seconds behind in fourth at the finish.

The Egloff brothers were fifth and the Güdel brothers sixth, while Yoshi Kumagaya narrowly won a battle for eighth with Derek Brindley.

The last-named had been involved in one of several first lap collisions – crashing with his elder brother Barry, who was forced to retire.

Egbert Streuer was also involved in a crash with tenth-placed Bösiger, and was forced to pit for a new fairing. He was plumb last when he came out of the pits, and his ride through from the back was one of the highlights of the race. He finished ninth.

British Grand Prix, 2 August/statistics

Donington Park Race Circuit, 2.5-mile/4.023-km circuit

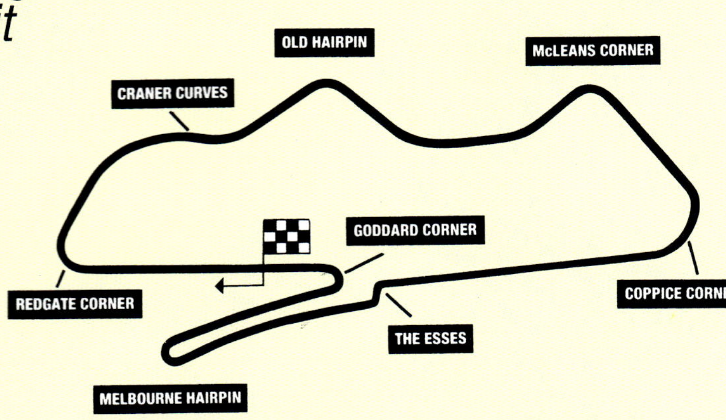

500 cc

30 laps, 75.000 miles/120.690 km

Place	Rider	Nat.	Machine	Laps	Time & speed	Fastest lap	Lap
1	**Wayne Gardner**	AUS	Honda	30	47m 38.373s 94.451 mph/ 152.004 km/h	1m 34.381s	24
2	**Wayne Rainey**	USA	Yamaha	30	47m 39.228s	1m 34.194s	25
3	**Juan Garriga**	E	Yamaha	30	47m 44.228s	1m 34.547s	24
4	**Eddie Lawson**	USA	Cagiva	30	48m 04.452s	1m 34.829s	17
5	**Peter Goddard**	AUS	Yamaha	30	48m 42.464s	1m 36.266s	17
6	**Terry Rymer**	GB	Yamaha	30	49m 00.703s	1m 36.585s	9
7	**Miguel DuHamel**	CAN	Yamaha	29	47m 51.156s	1m 37.899s	2
8	**Michael Rudroff**	D	Yamaha	29	47m 54.582s	1m 37.715s	5
9	**Dominique Sarron**	F	Yamaha	29	48m 12.695s	1m 37.619s	3
10	**Toshiyuki Arakaki**	J	Yamaha	29	48m 24.051s	1m 38.665s	15
11	Serge David	CH	Yamaha	29	48m 24.823s	1m 38.752s	8
12	Bruno Bonhuil	F	Yamaha	29	48m 25.553s	1m 38.751s	4
13	Niggi Schmassman	CH	Yamaha	29	48m 50.684s	1m 39.914s	9
14	Peter Graves	GB	Yamaha	29	48m 52.023s	1m 39.532s	6
15	Cees Doorakkers	NL	Yamaha	28	48m 17.446s	1m 40.167s	3
16	Marco Papa	I	Librenti	22	47m 42.815s	1m 41.343s	3
	Kevin Schwantz	USA	Suzuki	25	DNF	1m 34.419s	17
	Carl Fogarty	GB	Yamaha	25	DNF	1m 35.325s	6
	John Kocinski	USA	Yamaha	24	DNF	1m 35.358s	13
	Doug Chandler	USA	Suzuki	24	DNF	1m 35.712s	8
	Niall Mackenzie	GB	Yamaha	18	DNF	1m 35.031s	15
	Randy Mamola	USA	Yamaha	9	DNF	1m 36.214s	5
	Sepp Doppler	A	Yamaha	9	DNF	1m 42.138s	3
	James Whitham	GB	Yamaha	8	DNF	1m 36.393s	4
	Corrado Catalano	I	Yamaha	7	DNF	1m 37.706s	3
	Eddie Laycock	IRL	Yamaha	6	DNF	1m 38.610s	4
	Kevin Mitchell	GB	Yamaha	5	DNF	1m 37.856s	4
	Lucio Pedercini	I	Paton	5	DNF	1m 41.194s	3
	Andreas Leuthe	D	VRP	3	DNF	1m 44.762s	2
	Alex Criville	E	Honda	1	DNF	1m 45.302s	1

Fastest lap: Rainey, 1m 34.194s, 95.539 mph/153.755 km/h.
Lap record: Kevin Schwantz, USA (Suzuki), 1m 33.569s, 96.106 mph/154.667 km/h (1991).

Practice leaderboard: 1 Lawson, 1m 33.814s; **2** Kocinski, 1m 34.042s; **3** Rainey, 1m 34.080s; **4** Gardner, 1m 34.196s; **5** Schwantz, 1m 34.343s; **6** Garriga, 1m 34.581s; **7** Fogarty, 1m 34.860s; **8** Mackenzie, 1m 35.031s; **9** Chandler, 1m 35.036s; **10** Criville, 1m 35.234s; **11** Mamola, 1m 35.292s; **12** Whitham, 1m 35.725s; **13** Goddard, 1m 35.857s; **14** Sarron, 1m 36.296s; **15** Laycock, 1m 36.472s.

World Championship: 1 Doohan, 130; **2** Rainey, 108; **3** Schwantz, 87; **4** Chandler, 72; **5** Kocinski, 67; **6** Garriga, 60; **7** Lawson, 56; **8** Gardner, 53; **9** Criville, 49; **10** Mamola, 44; **11** Mackenzie, 32; **12** Barros, 26; **13** DuHamel, 24; **14** Beattie and Goddard, 18; **16** Itoh, 10; **17** Ohishi and Rymer, 6; **19** Catalano, 5; **20** Laycock, 4; **21** Honma and Rudroff, 3; **23** Arakaki, Fujiwara, Sarron and Whitham, 2; **27** Mitchell and Tsujimoto, 1.

Malcolm Bryan

Mamola's King of Beers outfit had notable Antipodean Warren Willing (with headset) as crew chief.

250 cc

28 laps, 70.000 miles/112.644 km

Place	Rider	Nat.	Machine	Laps	Time & speed	Fastest lap	Lap
1	**Pier Francesco Chili**	I	Aprilia	28	45m 17.158s 92.736 mph/ 149.244 km/h	1m 35.857s	19
2	**Loris Reggiani**	I	Aprilia	28	45m 19.039s	1m 35.866s	18
3	**Doriano Romboni**	I	Honda	28	45m 31.996s	1m 36.584s	18
4	**Luca Cadalora**	I	Honda	28	45m 32.160s	1m 36.462s	18
5	**Jochen Schmid**	D	Yamaha	28	45m 32.411s	1m 36.534s	18
6	**Helmut Bradl**	D	Honda	28	45m 34.969s	1m 36.516s	11
7	**Loris Capirossi**	I	Honda	28	45m 45.751s	1m 37.160s	11
8	**Carlos Cardus**	E	Honda	28	46m 07.303s	1m 37.248s	11
9	**Masahiro Shimizu**	J	Honda	28	46m 16.082s	1m 37.598s	5
10	**Herri Torrontegui**	E	Suzuki	28	46m 21.479s	1m 38.145s	24
11	Patrick van den Goorbergh	NL	Aprilia	28	46m 22.960s	1m 37.931s	27
12	Bernd Kassner	D	Aprilia	28	46m 23.236s	1m 37.990s	24
13	Carlos Lavado	YV	Gilera	28	46m 23.493s	1m 38.376s	26
14	Andy Preining	A	Aprilia	28	46m 31.226s	1m 38.053s	10
15	Paolo Casoli	I	Yamaha	28	46m 44.126s	1m 38.833s	7
16	Adrian Bosshard	CH	Honda	28	46m 54.393s	1m 39.409s	19
17	Katsuyoshi Kozono	J	Honda	28	46m 55.527s	1m 39.383s	10
18	José Kuhn	F	Honda	27	45m 25.567s	1m 39.638s	15
19	Frédéric Protat	F	Aprilia	27	45m 25.574s	1m 38.370s	27
20	Bernard Cazade	F	Honda	27	45m 27.241s	1m 39.559s	15
21	Erkka Korpiaho	SF	Aprilia	27	45m 30.927s	1m 39.601s	15
22	Yves Briguet	CH	Honda	27	45m 38.124s	1m 39.694s	22
23	Michele Gallina	I	Yamaha	27	45m 49.871s	1m 40.218s	14
	Massimiliano Biaggi	I	Aprilia	22	DNF	1m 35.884s	22
	Alberto Puig	E	Aprilia	22	DNF	1m 37.804s	12
	Harald Eckl	D	Aprilia	21	DNF	1m 38.887s	11
	James Haydon	GB	Yamaha	17	DNF	1m 39.967s	10
	Bernard Hänggeli	CH	Aprilia	13	DNF	1m 39.085s	10
	Adi Stadler	D	Honda	12	DNF	1m 39.369s	9
	Jurgen van den Goorbergh	NL	Aprilia	6	DNF	1m 39.691s	6
	Ian Newton	GB	Aprilia	6	DNF	1m 39.336s	6
	Eskil Suter	CH	Aprilia	6	DNF	1m 39.876s	3
	Wilco Zeelenberg	NL	Suzuki	3	DNF	1m 38.665s	3
	Luis D'Antin	E	Honda	1	DNF	1m 53.380s	1
	Jean-Philippe Ruggia	F	Gilera	0	DNF		
	Stefan Prein	D	Honda	0	DNF		
	Renzo Colleoni	I	Yamaha		DNS		

Fastest lap: Chili, 1m 35.857s, 93.882 mph/151.088 km/h (record).
Previous record: Loris Reggiani, I (Aprilia), 1m 36.200s, 93.477 mph/150.437 km/h (1991).

Practice leaderboard: 1 Chili, 1m 36.259s; **2** Biaggi, 1m 36.281s; **3** Reggiani, 1m 36.399s; **4** Romboni, 1m 36.545s; **5** Cadalora, 1m 36.662s; **6** Capirossi, 1m 36.761s; **7** Bradl, 1m 36.962s; **8** Schmid, 1m 37.106s; **9** Puig, 1m 37.165s; **10** Cardus, 1m 37.188s; **11** Ruggia, 1m 37.618s; **12** Shimizu, 1m 37.812s; **13** Preining, 1m 37.869s; **14** Torrontegui, 1m 37.953s; **15** P. van den Goorbergh, 1m 38.118s.

World Championship: 1 Cadalora, 177; **2** Reggiani, 132; **3** Chili, 107; **4** Bradl, 73; **5** Puig, 68; **6** Cardus, 48; **7** Schmid and Shimizu, 46; **9** Biaggi, 43; **10** Zeelenberg, 38; **11** Romboni, 33; **12** Capirossi and Okada, 15; **14** Aoki, 12; **15** Torrontegui, 8; **16** Lavado, Preining, Ruggia and Wakai, 4; **20** Casoli and Nanba, 3; **22** Hänggeli, Prein and J. van den Goorbergh, 2; **25** Jeandat and Kassner, 1.

125 cc

26 laps, 65.000 miles/104.598 km

Place	Rider	Nat.	Machine	Laps	Time & speed	Fastest lap	Lap
1	**Fausto Gresini**	**I**	**Honda**	**26**	**44m 46.145s 87.106 mph/ 140.183 km/h**	**1m 42.405s**	**14**
2	**Alessandro Gramigni**	**I**	**Aprilia**	**26**	**44m 49.424s**	**1m 42.465s**	**24**
3	**Noboru Ueda**	**J**	**Honda**	**26**	**44m 53.542s**	**1m 42.405s**	**14**
4	**Dirk Raudies**	**D**	**Honda**	**26**	**44m 53.856s**	**1m 42.435s**	**25**
5	**Bruno Casanova**	**I**	**Aprilia**	**26**	**44m 56.976s**	**1m 42.975s**	**24**
6	**Kazuto Sakata**	**J**	**Honda**	**26**	**45m 00.319s**	**1m 42.539s**	**23**
7	**Ralf Waldmann**	**D**	**Honda**	**26**	**45m 01.571s**	**1m 42.725s**	**23**
8	**Jorge Martinez**	**E**	**Honda**	**26**	**45m 13.608s**	**1m 42.589s**	**11**
9	**Kinya Wada**	**J**	**Honda**	**26**	**45m 20.468s**	**1m 42.921s**	**18**
10	**Nobuyuki Wakai**	**J**	**Honda**	**26**	**45m 20.769s**	**1m 43.042s**	**26**
11	Maik Stief	D	Aprilia	26	45m 21.384s	1m 43.460s	17
12	Ezio Gianola	I	Honda	26	45m 30.657s	1m 42.848s	10
13	Carlos Giro	E	Aprilia	26	45m 30.897s	1m 43.440s	17
14	Gabriele Debbia	I	Honda	26	45m 31.162s	1m 43.396s	4
15	Julian Miralles	E	Honda	26	45m 37.346s	1m 44.143s	11
16	Heinz Lüthi	CH	Honda	26	45m 57.991s	1m 44.722s	12
17	Maurizio Vitali	I	Gazzaniga	26	45m 59.057s	1m 44.807s	12
18	Luis Alvaro	E	Aprilia	26	46m 08.999s	1m 44.839s	14
19	Robin Appleyard	GB	Honda	26	46m 12.340s	1m 45.200s	22
20	Arie Molenaar	NL	Aprilia	26	46m 12.490s	1m 45.166s	21
21	Steve Patrickson	GB	Honda	26	46m 12.639s	1m 45.406s	24
22	Giovanni Palmieri	I	Gazzaniga	26	46m 13.138s	1m 44.846s	17
23	Peter Galvin	AUS	Honda	26	46m 13.535s	1m 45.079s	18
24	Johnny Wickström	SF	Honda	26	46m 13.711s	1m 45.249s	23
25	Hubert Abold	D	Honda	26	46m 17.731s	1m 45.552s	23
26	Neill Hodgson	GB	Honda	26	46m 30.174s	1m 45.398s	19
27	Giuseppe Fiorillo	I	Yamaha	25	46m 11.436s	1m 48.641s	6
28	Takao Shimizu	J	Honda	24	45m 41.792s	1m 44.383s	20
	Robert Dunlop	GB	Honda	24	DNF	1m 44.731s	4
	Manuel Hernandez	E	Aprilia	24	DNF	1m 44.724s	22
	Alain Bronec	F	Honda	18	DNF	1m 44.689s	4
	Alfred Waibel	D	Honda	12	DNF	1m 47.113s	4
	Peter Öttl	D	Rotax	10	DNF	1m 45.549s	6
	Oliver Petrucciani	CH	Honda	9	DNF	1m 43.673s	5
	Fausto Ricci	I	Yamaha	6	DNF	1m 48.710s	2
	Hans Spaan	NL	Aprilia	1	DNF	1m 53.105s	1
	Loek Bodelier	NL	Honda	0	DNF		
	Oliver Koch	D	Honda		DNS		

Fastest lap: Ueda, 1m 42.405s, 87.879 mph/141.427 km/h (record).
Previous record: Loris Capirossi, I (Honda), 1m 43.155s, 87.239 mph/140.398 km/h (1991).

Practice leaderboard: **1** Casanova, 1m 42.344s; **2** Sakata, 1m 42.385s; **3** Gianola, 1m 42.421s; **4** Gramigni, 1m 42.521s; **5** Gresini, 1m 42.596s; **6** Raudies, 1m 42.634s; **7** Waldmann, 1m 43.142s; **8** Ueda, 1m 43.229s; **9** Spaan, 1m 43.238s; **10** Martinez, 1m 43.238s; **11** Wada, 1m 43.532s; **12** Petrucciani, 1m 43.523s; **13** Debbia, 1m 43.534s; **14** Koch, 1m 43.554s; **15** Wakai, 1m 43.752s.

World Championship: **1** Gramigni, 110; **2** Gresini, 108; **3** Waldmann, 106; **4** Gianola, 101; **5** Casanova, 86; **6** Raudies, 61; **7** Debbia, 58; **8** Wakai, 49; **9** Martinez, 48; **10** Ueda, 45; **11** Sakata, 42; **12** Giro, 22; **13** Öttl and Spaan, 10; **15** Koch and Saitoh, 8; **17** Shimizu and Wada, 5; **19** Fujihara, 4; **20** Kurfiss, 3; **21** Lüthi and Petrucciani, 1.

Sidecars

26 laps, 65.000 miles/104.598 km

Place	Driver & passenger	Nat.	Machine	Laps	Time & speed	Fastest lap	Lap
1	**Rolf Biland/ Kurt Waltisperg**	**CH CH**	**LCR-Krauser**	**26**	**42m 55.364s 90.853 mph/ 146.213 km/h**	**1m 37.863s**	**2**
2	**Darren Dixon/ Andy Hetherington**	**GB GB**	**LCR-Krauser**	**26**	**43m 15.890s**	**1m 38.635s**	**7**
3	**Steve Webster/ Gavin Simmons**	**GB GB**	**LCR-ADM**	**26**	**43m 20.854s**	**1m 38.340s**	**8**
4	**Ralph Bohnhorst/ Bruno Hiller**	**D D**	**BRM**	**26**	**43m 22.910s**	**1m 39.351s**	**2**
5	**Markus Egloff/ Urs Egloff**	**CH CH**	**LCR-Yamaha**	**26**	**43m 26.079s**	**1m 38.620s**	**5**
6	**Paul Güdel/ Charly Güdel**	**CH CH**	**LCR-Yamaha**	**26**	**43m 54.678s**	**1m 39.639s**	**5**
7	**Yoshisada Kumagaya/ Bryan Houghton**	**J GB**	**LCR-Krauser**	**26**	**43m 57.977s**	**1m 40.158s**	**15**
8	**Derek Brindley/ Nick Roche**	**GB GB**	**LCR-Krauser**	**26**	**43m 58.432s**	**1m 39.852s**	**24**
9	**Egbert Streuer/ Peter Brown**	**NL GB**	**LCR-Stredor**	**26**	**44m 10.558s**	**1m 39.619s**	**12**
10	**Markus Bösiger/ Beat Leibundgut**	**CH CH**	**LCR-ADM**	**26**	**44m 24.571s**	**1m 40.183s**	**6**
11	Tony Wyssen/ Kilian Wyssen	CH CH	LCR-Yamaha	26	44m 26.988s	1m 40.993s	4
12	Billy Gällros/ Peter Berglund	S S	LCR-Streuer	25	43m 03.150s	1m 41.641s	9
13	Reiner Koster/ Jurg Egli	CH CH	LCR-Yamaha	25	43m 27.214s	1m 43.111s	10
14	Eddie Wright/ Peter Hill	GB GB	LCR-Krauser	25	43m 27.879s	1m 42.948s	9
15	Robert Fisher/ Trevor Crone	GB GB	LCR-Krauser	25	43m 48.377s	1m 43.129s	13
16	Jukka Lauslehto/ Jurgen Levinsen	SF DK	LCR-ADM	25	44m 05.090s	1m 40.120s	21
	Steve Abbott/ Shaun Smith	GB GB	LCR-Krauser	25	DNF	1m 39.663s	17
	Theo van Kempen/ Geral de Haas	NL NL	LCR-Krauser	17	DNF	1m 43.304s	13
	Mark Reddington/ Kim Andreasen	GB DK	LCR-Krauser	15	DNF	1m 43.119s	4
	Tony Baker/ Simon Prior	GB GB	LCR-Krauser	13	DNF	1m 42.941s	3
	Barry Brindley/ Scott Whiteside	GB GB	LCR-Yamaha	4	DNF	1m 42.857s	2
	Gary Knight/ Malcolm Jackson	GB GB	LCR-Krauser	3	DNF	1m 46.236s	2
	Klaus Klaffenböck/ Christian Parzer	A A	LCR-ADM		DNS		
	Peter Lemstra/ Jan Kuyt	NL NL	LCR-Krauser		DNQ		

Fastest lap: Biland, 1m 37.863s, 91.957 mph/147.991 km/h (record).
Previous record: Steve Webster/Gavin Simmons, GB/GB (Krauser), 1m 37.954s, 91.803 mph/147.743 km/h (1991).

Practice leaderboard: **1** Biland, 1m 37.358s; **2** Streuer, 1m 37.940s; **3** Webster, 1m 38.224s; **4** Dixon, 1m 38.449s; **5** Bohnhorst, 1m 38.834s; **6** Egloff, 1m 39.169s; **7** Klaffenböck, 1m 39.258s; **8** Bösiger, 1m 39.637s; **9** Lauslehto, 1m 39.823s; **10** Abbott, 1m 39.937s; **11** Kumagaya, 1m 39.939s; **12** B. Brindley, 1m 39.981s; **13** Güdel, 1m 40.030s; **14** D. Brindley, 1m 40.344s; **15** Wyssen, 1m 41.236s.

World Championship: **1** Webster, 92; **2** Biland, 83; **3** Klaffenböck, 66; **4** Kumagaya, 39; **5** Streuer, 37; **6** Bohnhorst, 36; **7** Dixon and Güdel, 30; **9** B. Brindley, 19; **10** Egloff, 18; **11** Abbott, 14; **12** Bösiger, 11; **13** D. Brindley and Wyssen, 4; **15** Baker, Lauslehto and van Kempen, 1.

BRAZILIAN GRAND PRIX

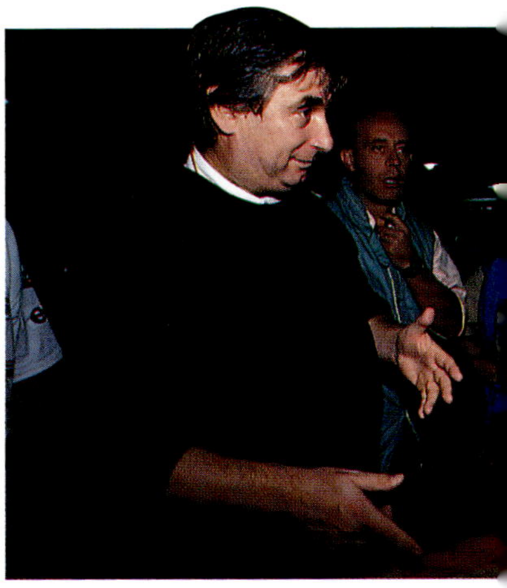

Photos: Malcolm Bryan

The very notion of having a GP at the Interlagos circuit, set in urban squalor on the outskirts of São Paulo in Brazil, has always produced raging controversy, centred on an unsafe track in an unsavoury location.

When, after two years of cancellations and recriminations, the race actually took place, the controversy spilled over into open arguments and threats of boycott.

By now, there were several added complications, over and above the fact that everybody was already in Brazil rather than arguing safely from Europe. And the major one was the World Championship.

WORLD CHAMPIONSHIP • ROUND 12

500 cc	RAINEY
250 cc	CADALORA
125 cc	RAUDIES

Opposite: **Conditions were dreadful in Brazil – and that included the weather.**

Left: **Dr Costa and a gaunt Doohan. If only the race had been two weeks later.**

'Whatever you guys do, I'll do the opposite.' Lawson walks out of the riders' meeting; Barros and Preining watch him leave.

Doohan was back at last, after an absence of eight weeks and four races, desperate to stop the rot that had seen his championship lead drop from 53 points over Schwantz in June to just 22 points over Rainey now. His physical condition was alarmingly bad, and his race performance – finishing 12th and out of the points – proof that he was in no way ready to do serious battle. Doohan, barely ambulatory, would have been more than delighted had the race been called off.

On the other side was Rainey, who needed every chance he could get to make ground on his injured victim, and would probably have been prepared to race on the Isle of Man if that had been an option. The double champion had seen his own position go from hopeless at Assen to suddenly very promising in Brazil. He is a racer first and foremost, and nobody can criticise him for wanting to win the title. But he is also a decent sort of a bloke who was the prime mover in setting up this year's IMRA riders' association, one of whose objects was to give riders a say in track safety. The questions that resurfaced on arrival at São Paulo caused him a lot of agony.

The problem itself was simple enough. The track is another purpose-built (and not very good) F1 car track, and the proximity of solid walls to fast corners simply made it a life-threatening prospect to the motor cycle racers. Opinions were forthright and almost universal. 'I've never raced on a more dangerous circuit,' said Niall Mackenzie. Chandler opined: 'There's no room for error.' Schwantz also: 'A mistake here means injury for sure.'

The first visit to the track had added plenty of detail, but there was nothing new in the substance of the complaints – the Interlagos circuit has been deluged with them ever since it was first mooted as a replacement for Goiania, which was itself no longer homologated. But how had the Brazilian GP slipped through the safety net this time?

Last year Schwantz was sent out, and showed heroic moral courage in telling a pack of angry Brazilian journalists that the track was not good enough. This year, a deputation comprising Paul Butler of IRTA, Hans Bahme of the FIM and newly appointed IMRA riders' rep. Didier de Radiguès had visited São Paulo after the French GP, and had declared the track fit for racing following modifications, provided that air-fencing was installed at one point where a retaining wall could not be moved for fear of draining mud across the track.

What had looked safe from a rentacar to de Radiguès and the others was obviously a different matter when whizzing round on a 500 – though it was hard to understand the leniency in interpretation applied by the pre-race approval party when looking at the scary concrete-lined sixth-gear kink on the front straight and the lack of run-off down the hill out of the first bends. One barely had to leave the control tower area to see the obvious danger there.

But the riders' own system had clearly failed, and Rainey felt they were morally obliged to live with the consequences. 'We needed someone out there inspecting tracks. We found de Radiguès, and we respected him. He came back and showed us pictures of the track and said it was good enough. We came here and found it's pretty close on the exits – but we have nobody to blame but ourselves. We've got to be professional. We've got to go with what the riders' rep. said.'

He was thus determined to race, come what may, even though both team boss Kenny Roberts and sponsors Marlboro had given their sanction if he wished to withdraw. But he had an answer to suggestions that he was only arguing to defend his own championship chances. 'I'm the only guy with anything to lose by not racing,' he said. 'I know what I'm gonna do.'

The riders' meeting revealed the usual rifts, and ended in a somewhat woolly decision that they would race, but reserved the right to withdraw if it was raining. Much of the argument came from Lawson, outraged by what he saw as Rainey's cynical manipulation of the situation in his own championship interests. 'I'm not much for all the politics. I tend to see things in black and white,' he told me later. 'Rainey asked me and the others to get behind him to give IMRA some strength, then we find a dangerous track and he tells us we have to race. When I argued, he told me: "You don't have to ride if you don't want to." I couldn't believe it. I've been in that position myself' (in 1988, when the issue was whether or not to attend the Argentinian GP. Lawson declined to take part in the vote, and went on to win the title from Gardner). 'He should have kept out and left it to the others to decide.'

Rainey, also talking later, shrugged it off. 'I must have been the last friend Eddie had left in the paddock before that. He's argued with everyone. I know what he'd have done in my position. He'd have raced.'

Lawson walked out of the meeting after delivering a classic piece of rhetoric. 'Whatever you guys decide to do, I'll do the opposite,' he said. And, true to his word, when Saturday afternoon practice turned wet, while the others stayed firmly in their pits, Lawson ostentatiously revved his Cagiva down pit lane to be first out for a pair of slow but defiant laps.

In typical Brazilian fashion, things had gone wrong from the start. Elf had shipped out 20,000 litres of fuel two weeks before the race – but the local representative had neglected to fetch the consignment from the docks. Cagiva had brought their own supply, but all the others had empty tanks. Thus Thursday's free training, laid down in the regulations as time for familiarisation with a new track, had to be abandoned while IRTA's freight manager, Paul Gibson, personally went and retrieved the racing gasoline.

But there was none of the Brazilian party spirit that had helped make such inevitabilities tolerable at Goiania. The track was set amid the squalor of the outskirts of scary big city São Paulo, leaving GP folk scurrying between the track and their international hotels, with their rentacar doors locked and their hands on their wallets.

There was also growing unease as contract shuffling reached a new high point. The interest in the 500 class centred on Doug Chandler, who was pondering whether to stay with Suzuki or take a lucrative offer from Cagiva; Kocinski seemed likely to move too, and was a Suzuki candidate to replace Chandler. (He was also mulling over a return to 250 racing, with Suzuki on the menu there as well.) In all cases, it was important to make a good impression in the remaining races, and this made an interesting overlay to the secondary battle in the 500 cc championship, with Schwantz, Chandler and Kocinski all close enough still to take third place overall.

There was some of the same in the 250 class, the kingpin here being Luca Cadalora. The Italian champion had signed a provisional contract to take his number one plate to Aprilia next year, unless a 500 cc ride came his way first (the name of Team Roberts was mentioned). Biaggi had meanwhile signed to replace Luca at Kanemoto's Rothmans Honda.

Meanwhile, poor Carlos Cardus concluded his disastrous season in the worst possible way for a man in danger of losing his sponsorship. In Friday morning's untimed practice, he had a coming together with April-

Right: **Juan Garriga found a safe place to fall off shortly after the start – and spoiled Mamola's race in the process. Note Doohan tucked behind Catalano (33) in the midfield pack.**

A rare chance to race at home was no thrill for Barros *(below left)*, still not fully fit after missing two races.

ia rider Fred Protat, and crashed heavily at high speed. His race was over, and he returned home after lodging an unsuccessful protest against the French privateer's riding.

The sidecar race had finally fallen through, after much to-ing and froing; but they were well out of it, on a nasty track for a nasty GP, with the survival of the race hanging on a tenuous thread of bad weather (and there was plenty of that during the weekend), and Doohan's championship chances hanging there as well. Naturally enough, something had to break.

500 cc PRACTICE

The only topic as eagerly discussed as the track was the condition of championship leader Doohan. Already bony, the usually superfit Australian was especially gaunt, his legs mere spindles, a cast still covering his right calf. He walked haltingly, and the fact that he was able to get onto his motor cycle at all was in itself surprising.

'Moving around on the bike is the biggest trouble,' he admitted, adding with the typically absurd (and often amazingly justified) optimism of a returning race-junkie getting back to his fix: 'But it's getting easier all the time. It's just a matter of getting in as many laps as possible.'

In truth he was battling, his right foot often sliding off the footpeg, prompting a modification both to the footrest and to his plaster cast on Friday night, at which point he lay 14th overall. All this was being made more difficult by a balky gearbox, punishing his weak legs and losing him practice time as his team sorted it out. 'At times I was back-shifting ten times to go down three gears,' he said.

With all eyes on his progress, he came back on Saturday morning with a lighter cast and slimmer boot, and went out on a slightly damp track on intermediates. 'I'm still getting my eye back, but this morning I was braking later than yesterday on slicks,' he said. 'I get frustrated because I feel I can flick the bike in hard, but I have to make sure my foot is in the right place before I do it.' He was clearly getting back in the groove, but was also still a long way short of the mark, and his best hope was to pick up a point or two.

This one-man drama was played out against the highly distracting off-track battles, which combined with the disruptive weather to make qualifying something of a lottery.

The four practice sessions were run in a variety of conditions from clear to full rain, with fog thrown in for good measure. Only the first timed session on Friday afternoon was completely dry, and fastest that hour was Kocinski.

His first pole of the year did not ease his mind, with the bumpy track seeing him more at odds than ever with his bikes. 'I have no confidence in them – they've let me down too much this year. It depends whether the bike's in a good mood or a bad mood how I'll do.' He had a new frame, but raced the old one for its greater predictability in the changing conditions. Typically, he wasn't for complaining about the track. 'To me, the race tracks don't matter. It's getting the bike to do what I want to do. I never complained about a circuit in my life. I came here to race – that's what it said on my calendar.'

Rainey sat alongside, embattled by his decision to take a leadership position among disagreeable riders, but resolute. All that remained was to make his new chassis work and he was well on his way. 'The difference is where everything's bolted on – engine position, footpeg height, seating position. It makes the bike feel better than all year, mostly in directional change and stability.'

Rainey was among the handful who did ride in Saturday's wet timed session, and he said conditions weren't as bad as the track's staunchest opponents had described. 'You can motor round this place. At least if it rains I'll know where the puddles are.'

Donington winner Gardner was third, and his major preoccupation was trying to make his leaping Honda negotiate the ever-present bumps and ripples. 'It's well bumpy,' he said. 'It's a real physical job just to ride over them. You can do so much with the suspension but in the end you just have to hang on. It's like riding motocross.' He looked enviously at the Yamahas with their longer travel computer-controlled suspension. 'They're smoother on the power than the Hondas, and they'll be hard to beat,' he prophesied.

Schwantz's Suzuki perspective had led him to the same conclusions. 'You have to pick your way round to find the smooth way,' he said, adding: 'It's kind of hard to find any suspension that works good. You try to get it halfway decent.' The harder he went, the more he hated the track. 'The barriers get bigger and bigger every lap when you start to push it.' He vowed that this would dictate his race strategy, especially if the weather changed. 'I'll go out and start and see what happens. If there's more at risk than to gain I'll pull in.' He declined to practise in the wet, saying: 'I don't think there's anything to learn out there except how to bust your ass.'

Team-mate Chandler, who led row two, did go out in the wet, and found it very sobering. 'There's already no room for error. You're not seeing any run-off. You look at corners and you look at the wall. In the rain, it's dangerous, really dangerous. On the front straight I'm clicking into fifth in the last bend before the pit with both wheels drifting up to the wall at quarter-throttle. In the dry, you're pegged in sixth and using a quarter of the track.' But in spite of his misgivings he was resolute. 'I'm not one of those guys who'll say he's just going to ride around. If you start the race, you're gonna race.'

Criville was sixth fastest, sitting out the wet practice after getting a handle on dry weather gearing and settings on Saturday morning. He was ahead of the rebellious Lawson, who was still trying to get his rear

Photos: Malcolm Bryan

suspension and rear Dunlop to co-operate. 'The suspension is going to be crucial, because there are some real bumpy corners.' Obviously his Friday night adjustments had been in the right direction, because he was one of only a few riders to move up on Saturday, turning his best time before the rain began about 12 minutes into the session.

Garriga was eighth fastest, just seven-thousandths off Lawson's time, and almost a full second faster than Mamola, who was ninth and leading row three. Alongside him, the blue Yamahas of DuHamel and Mackenzie were tenth and 12th, with the French Canadian for once faster as he enjoyed a new chassis that made his bike the same as the Scotsman's. 'It reminds me a lot of the superbike I raced last year,' he said. Mackenzie, meanwhile, had the advantage of the droner engine, but he just hated the track.

They sandwiched Barros, who was battling his Cagiva in the spotlight of his ever-controversial home GP. His workload was harder to bear because he was still hampered by collarbone and especially right wrist ligament injuries sustained in France.

With the mandatory presence of IRTA's paid privateers, there was a full grid of 30 qualifiers.

500 cc RACE – 28 LAPS

Race day started with a downpour, leaving the track slick and dangerous for morning warm-up. The riders kept a careful eye on the weather to see if they would be obliged to carry out their race boycott threat. Instead the temperature rose and the clouds lifted to a less ominous height. As the 500s came to the grid, the track was still wet in spots but all wore slick tyres.

The race belonged to Rainey from flag to flag. He needed to win and he made no mistakes, setting a blistering pace to record no less than seven fastest laps as his fuel load lightened, spurred on by not being able to see his pit board fully. 'I was going down the front straight so fast all I saw was point eight. I thought Gardner was there the whole time. I pushed for eight laps and the next time I looked I saw the full figure of 10 seconds. That shocked me for a few laps,' he explained.

With the opposition successfully consigned to the caboose, Rainey had time to worry about his engine. After the British GP, a strip-down had revealed that his droner had only narrowly escaped the same primary gear failure that had sidelined Mackenzie and Kocinski. But the nature of the track meant it was fairly easy on tyres and transmission. 'You don't use a lot of throttle because of the bumps,' he said. 'A lot of the corners are quarter-throttle.'

His third win of the year may have been the most important in his career, for it closed him to within two points of Doohan, who rode valiantly and was at one stage in the top ten. But he couldn't hold on to the position, and ended up a bitterly disappointed 12th, and last of the works bikes. 'At least I proved I can ride a 28-lap race, and I should be a lot fitter in two weeks for the South African GP,' he said, before jetting back to Italy to continue intensive physiotherapy.

Rainey made it look easy; the others were struggling.

Schwantz had taken off with Rainey, but noticed early on that his temperature gauge wasn't registering, and that the Suzuki's engine felt sluggish. The symptoms suggested a loss of coolant and imminent seizure – unless, of course, it was only a faulty gauge. Still second on lap four, he was obliged to back off and await developments. 'It just gradually got slower,' he said. 'I was trying to keep myself on the inside of the corners in case it tied up. That way I could get the thing stood up if I had to.' It never did blow, but was virtually dry at the finish – remarkable durability from an engine once considered rather fragile. With his fingers crossed and all lucky charms doing full duty, the Texan gradually dropped back to an eventual seventh. Later, his team diagnosed a leak at the cylinder heads caused by a bad batch of studs.

Second was promptly snatched by Kocinski and Chandler, engaged in battle, each coping with their own problems as they fought every inch of the way. The Suzuki was in front from laps 11 to 14, then Kocinski got past for good.

'My bike wasn't working as well as the Yamahas,' said Chandler. 'I was losing a bit of time into the tighter corners, and I couldn't get off the

Photos: Malcolm Bryan

turn onto the back straight for nuthin'.'

And it was in a straight line that Kocinski finally beat him. 'That's the first time this year it actually ran down the straights,' the disgruntled Yamaha rider said, after his second runner-up finish of the year. As usual, second wasn't nearly good enough, and nor was his bike. 'I knew from the first corner. I was nearly pitched off. I think something broke in the shock – I screwed the handlebar adjuster down and it got a bit better, but when I went faster it started wobbling again.' By then he was clear of Chandler, but way out of touch with Rainey.

The best dice of the race was for fourth: Gardner, DuHamel and Criville swapping places lap after lap, generally under brakes for the first turn. Gardner was frustrated by keeping company with class novices. 'I struggled – the bike was never right,' he said. 'It wouldn't accelerate, though it ran okay off the top.' His team suspected a powervalve problem after he'd told them it felt as though the engine was still on rain settings, adding: 'I tried to run it faster into the corners and nearly high-sided.'

He waited his time in sixth approaching the midway point, then passed both of the youngsters in one sweep to take over fourth on lap 15. DuHamel, having the ride of his life, fought back, earning praise from the veteran who managed to reassert himself to the finish. 'He was a bit desperate at the beginning, but I was impressed,' said Gardner. The French Canadian, for his part, was delighted with his new chassis. 'The Hondas were faster, but I could make up time under braking. The new bike changes direction easier, and it lets me punch it into the corners.' He fell behind Criville again, only to pounce and just pip him over the line in an impressive race-finishing move he has used before.

The sixth-placed Spaniard was glad enough to finish his first GP since winning Assen four races back. 'I had some stability problems towards the end. It was a tough race. It's so bumpy here it really tires you out.'

Schwantz hung on to seventh, with Barros holding eighth from start to finish. Behind the injured Brazilian, an increasingly disillusioned Mackenzie was ninth in front of Mamola, the Scotsman blaming a failed tyre experiment for his poor form. 'I tried a narrower front rim than in practice, and the race tyre didn't work on it. I was pushing the front everywhere. It's not a good feeling at a track like this.'

An early mistake had hurt Mamola, but it wasn't his own. On lap one, Garriga had fallen right in front of the American in the first left-right combination. Mamola was forced to stand his bike right up and was lucky not to crash himself. He dropped to last: 'Once I got going again it was hard to pass,' he said, and he was forced to use daringly late braking to end up where he did.

Lawson was a smouldering 11th, Doohan a bitter 12th, out of luck, off the pace, and finishing the race physically and emotionally drained. He was the last rider not to be lapped.

Dominique Sarron's Roc Yamaha won the privateers' race easily from the impressive Arakaki, who fended off Michi Rudroff and Kevin Mitchell in a tight battle for 14th. Marco Papa was a close 17th after swapping his Librenti for a spare Cagiva. There were 23 finishers, with Buckmaster, Catalano and Goddard not finishing.

Thus they left for the last race of the year with just two points in it for the title and Doohan in a pitiful condition. He could still secure a moral victory, but adding up the points is a pitiless process, and the end result was a cliff-hanger. 'I'm still behind,' said Rainey; while Doohan observed: 'I've said from the start of the year that it's not over until the very end.'

250 cc PRACTICE

The 250 riders were equally critical of the circuit, and had a harder time of it in practice than the 500s. In short, they lost a full session, with Friday's timed practice cancelled because a dense sea-fog rolled in off the south Atlantic.

The best that could be done under the circumstances was to declare both of Saturday's sessions timed, and pole position was determined in the first of them, with the second run in desultory fashion in more heavy rain. ('Why didn't you come in springtime?' asked a dismayed Brazilian official. 'This is our wet season now.')

One of the most vocal critics was Reggiani, who set a sombre tone by saying: 'It's the kind of race track where if you fall down you can die.' All the same, this consummate GP racer was second on the grid by the end of it all, pole being taken for a fourth time this year by Biaggi. Having signed to take Cadalora's place in the victorious Kanemoto Rothmans Honda squad for 1993, he only had two more chances to win on an Aprilia, and in his debut year. 'Time is running out,' he said. 'If it's dry tomorrow and the bike is still going well I'll be going 100 per cent for the win.'

Romboni was back on his double-special RS Honda, and nosed it on to the front row among the Aprilias, third fastest, with Chili's Telkor Aprilia fourth, half a second down on pole.

These were snatched times in the abbreviated qualifying period, but they none the less put the same top six in almost the same order as at Donington Park. This time, however, Cadalora had won the title and certainly had nothing to prove in practice. He led row two from Capirossi (also back on his Spl/Spl), with Carlos Lavado putting his Gilera alongside in a fine display of Latin American verve over the bumps. Schmid completed row two, a whisker slower on the Yamaha.

Bradl led row three from Preining, Ruggia and Puig; Zeelenberg's Suzuki was on the back end of row four; luckless Stefan Prein's RS/Spl was 33rd, on the back row of a grid of 35 qualifiers, with times covering an unusually large spread as a result of the interruptions and abbreviations to practice time.

250 cc RACE – 26 LAPS

Luca may have secured his second championship, but with his future still undecided it didn't hurt to display his talents, and that's just what he did. The race belonged to him, as the 500 had to Rainey, though he took a little longer to claim it.

Cadalora started in third as young blood Biaggi set the early pace, moving into the lead of a close-packed group comprising Biaggi, Chili, Reggiani and Capirossi on the third of the 26 laps, and then pulling away steadily and certainly to win by a sufficient margin of less than four seconds.

Far left: **Victory here brought a third World Championship within reach for Rainey.**

Dirk Raudies proved that lack of size can sometimes be worth more than all the 125 power-up kits in the world.

'It was not the hardest of wins, but it was a difficult race,' he said. 'We didn't get much dry practice, and I was still learning the track to the chequered flag. But my bike worked well – the suspension was excellent and we chose the right tyres.' Even when sure of victory, he kept pressing on, with his fastest lap being his penultimate.

Of course his seventh win was just icing on the cake. The real business concerned who would be runner-up, with Chili desperate to close the gap on Reggiani. On the track, Biaggi held a steady second according to the lap chart – but that was deceptive, because it was by the narrowest of margins. Reggiani was always in his shadow, and Romboni not far behind. They finished in that order, with Reggiani just a quarter of a second behind Biaggi. Later, Loris also blamed a lack of practice time for not having his bike set up good enough to beat the youngster. 'Even if I'd got going earlier, I couldn't have beaten Luca today,' he added.

Chili, meanwhile, had lost touch with the leaders before the halfway point, his gearbox starting to get notchy. It eventually became so bad he retired on the 16th lap.

Schmid and Bradl had been away with Romboni, not far behind the leaders, and the Yamaha rider made his move as Chili retired, passing Capirossi and setting about Bradl to get by on the 20th lap and move ahead to claim a secure fifth, for the fourth time this season. Bradl and Capirossi followed him home in sixth and seventh.

Another five seconds back Puig moved ahead in the closing stages to claim eighth, leaving Patrick van den Goorbergh and Andy Preining to dispute ninth to the line. It went to the delighted Dutchman, his best-ever GP finish, after Preining had nearly run into his back wheel.

Zeelenberg was 11th, out of the points and narrowly the victor in a scrap with Ruggia's Gilera. Shimizu's NSR was 13th, while Carlos Lavado narrowly fought off Torrontegui's Suzuki for 14th. There were 27 finishers.

Chili's non-finish and Reggiani's third place tied up second and third in the championship, with Reggiani now unassailable runner-up. The last remaining battle was for fourth – and Bradl, Puig and Biaggi were all in with a chance...

125 cc RACE – 24 LAPS

Dirk Raudies, diminutive 28-year-old computer programmer turned racer, had been knocking on the door all year, frequently up with the leading pack, on a kitted Honda that had shown an impressive turn of outright speed – whether through engine tuning or merely because he is so tiny (less than five foot four inches and 110 lb) being a question that vexed all his rivals.

In Brazil, circumstances finally came together to give him a first win, and it was a dominant affair, the German rider leading from the fourth lap to pull out an advantage of almost ten seconds at the finish. His major problem, he said later, was keeping the Honda on the surface over the bumps. 'Maybe it was worse for me because of my size,' he said. 'My bike was really jumping around.'

The 125 battlers were hardly restrained by the perils of the track, and the usual tight pack formed up in pursuit. Again, interest was as much on championship positions as race results, with all eyes on Gramigni, Gianola, Gresini and Waldmann.

Gramigni was the only one who made the rostrum, embroiled to the finish in a stirring close race for second with Martinez and Casanova, with the Spaniard on the Honda taking the position for his best finish of a bad year by four-tenths from the works Aprilia rider. Gramigni complained later that he had hoped Casanova (on a factory-favoured private Aprilia) might have helped him rather than fighting him to the finish. He had eventually secured third place by a mere three-thousandths of a second.

More than 15 seconds behind this tooth-and-nail battle Swiss rider Oliver Petrucciani, team-mate to Waldmann, rode by far his best race of the year to pull ahead of another high class group. This comprised Gresini, battling with gearbox problems; Ueda, having a similarly hard time; and Wakai. They finished in that order, within three-quarters of a second.

Another close battle saw Giro push Gianola down to tenth place by just over one-tenth of a second; the Italian's team-mate, Debbia, was a close 11th, and impressive Dutch upstart Loek Bodelier took 12th for his best finish of the year.

Waldmann was 15th and bitterly disappointed after yet more mechanical niggles kept him out of the points and virtually killed the early leader's title chances stone dead.

Now it was up to the Italians, with Gramigni's lead over Gresini having stretched to eight points.

Brazilian Grand Prix, 23 August/statistics

Interlagos, São Paulo, 2.686-mile/ 4.323-km circuit

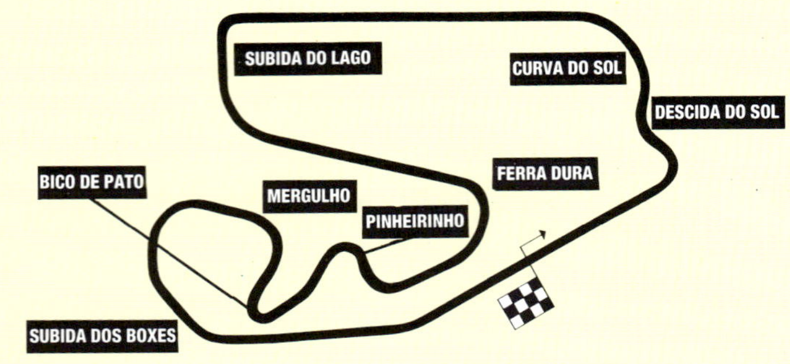

500 cc

28 laps, 75.208 miles/121.044 km

Place	Rider	Nat.	Machine	Laps	Time & speed	Fastest lap	Lap
1	**Wayne Rainey**	**USA**	**Yamaha**	**28**	**48m 33.539s 92.934 mph/ 149.563 km/h**	**1m 42.872s**	**7**
2	**John Kocinski**	**USA**	**Yamaha**	**28**	**48m 46.549s**	**1m 43.318s**	**16**
3	**Doug Chandler**	**USA**	**Suzuki**	**28**	**48m 54.294s**	**1m 43.248s**	**8**
4	**Wayne Gardner**	**AUS**	**Honda**	**28**	**49m 02.432s**	**1m 43.453s**	**27**
5	**Miguel DuHamel**	**CAN**	**Yamaha**	**28**	**49m 04.773s**	**1m 43.874s**	**18**
6	**Alex Criville**	**E**	**Honda**	**28**	**49m 04.793s**	**1m 43.804s**	**24**
7	**Kevin Schwantz**	**USA**	**Suzuki**	**28**	**49m 23.940s**	**1m 44.724s**	**19**
8	**Alexandre Barros**	**BR**	**Cagiva**	**28**	**49m 27.060s**	**1m 44.966s**	**11**
9	**Niall Mackenzie**	**GB**	**Yamaha**	**28**	**49m 35.826s**	**1m 45.084s**	**14**
10	**Randy Mamola**	**USA**	**Yamaha**	**28**	**49m 44.507s**	**1m 44.954s**	**15**
11	Eddie Lawson	USA	Cagiva	28	49m 54.376s	1m 45.142s	18
12	Michael Doohan	AUS	Honda	28	50m 05.114s	1m 45.763s	9
13	Dominique Sarron	F	Yamaha	27	48m 43.900s	1m 46.967s	11
14	Toshiyuki Arakaki	J	Yamaha	27	49m 12.135s	1m 47.338s	25
15	Michael Rudroff	D	Yamaha	27	49m 13.620s	1m 47.861s	20
16	Kevin Mitchell	GB	Yamaha	27	49m 13.628s	1m 47.101s	11
17	Marco Papa	I	Cagiva	27	49m 15.248s	1m 47.733s	10
18	Serge David	CH	Yamaha	27	49m 22.205s	1m 47.673s	22
19	Niggi Schmassman	CH	Yamaha	27	49m 29.436s	1m 48.532s	14
20	Eddie Laycock	IRL	Yamaha	27	49m 44.578s	1m 48.239s	13
21	Andreas Leuthe	D	Yamaha	27	49m 50.894s	1m 48.851s	23
22	Cees Doorakkers	NL	Yamaha	27	49m 53.253s	1m 48.650s	23
23	Peter Graves	GB	Yamaha	26	48m 59.742s	1m 50.791s	7
	Sepp Doppler	A	Yamaha	24	DNF	1m 51.994s	19
	Lucio Pedercini	I	Paton	12	DNF	1m 52.613s	9
	Peter Goddard	AUS	Yamaha	4	DNF	1m 46.063s	3
	Corrado Catalano	I	Yamaha	3	DNF	1m 47.785s	3
	Simon Buckmaster	GB	Yamaha	1	DNF	2m 25.357s	1
	Juan Garriga	E	Yamaha	0	DNF		
	Juan Lopez Mella	E	Yamaha		DNS		

Fastest lap: Rainey, 1m 42.872s, 94.003 mph/151.283 km/h (record).
Previous record: none.

Practice leaderboard: **1** Kocinski, 1m 43.403s; **2** Rainey, 1m 43.910s; **3** Gardner, 1m 44.023s; **4** Schwantz, 1m 44.274s; **5** Chandler, 1m 44.334s; **6** Criville, 1m 44.339s; **7** Lawson, 1m 44.372s; **8** Garriga, 1m 44.379s; **9** Mamola, 1m 45.236s; **10** DuHamel, 1m 45.662s; **11** Barros, 1m 45.712s; **12** Mackenzie, 1m 45.905s; **13** Papa, 1m 46.295s; **14** Doohan, 1m 46.880s; **15** Goddard, 1m 47.091s.

World Championship: **1** Doohan, 130; **2** Rainey, 128; **3** Schwantz, 91; **4** Chandler, 84; **5** Kocinski, 82; **6** Gardner, 63; **7** Garriga, 60; **8** Lawson, 56; **9** Criville, 55; **10** Mamola, 45; **11** Mackenzie, 34; **12** DuHamel, 32; **13** Barros, 29; **14** Beattie and Goddard, 18; **16** Itoh, 10; **17** Ohishi and Rymer, 6; **19** Catalano, 5; **20** Laycock, 4; **21** Honma and Rudroff, 3; **23** Arakaki, Fujiwara, Sarron and Whitham, 2; **27** Mitchell and Tsujimoto, 1.

250 cc

26 laps, 69.836 miles/112.398 km

Place	Rider	Nat.	Machine	Laps	Time & speed	Fastest lap	Lap
1	**Luca Cadalora**	**I**	**Honda**	**26**	**45m 45.808s 91.568 mph/ 147.364 km/h**	**1m 44.800s**	**25**
2	**Massimiliano Biaggi**	**I**	**Aprilia**	**26**	**45m 49.458s**	**1m 44.761s**	**20**
3	**Loris Reggiani**	**I**	**Aprilia**	**26**	**45m 49.730s**	**1m 44.478s**	**24**
4	**Doriano Romboni**	**I**	**Honda**	**26**	**45m 53.368s**	**1m 45.019s**	**7**
5	**Jochen Schmid**	**D**	**Yamaha**	**26**	**46m 02.029s**	**1m 45.501s**	**17**
6	**Helmut Bradl**	**D**	**Honda**	**26**	**46m 07.242s**	**1m 45.264s**	**13**
7	**Loris Capirossi**	**I**	**Honda**	**26**	**46m 16.372s**	**1m 45.457s**	**7**
8	**Alberto Puig**	**E**	**Aprilia**	**26**	**46m 21.887s**	**1m 45.630s**	**19**
9	**Patrick van den Goorbergh**	**NL**	**Aprilia**	**26**	**46m 24.087s**	**1m 46.230s**	**18**
10	**Andy Preining**	**A**	**Aprilia**	**26**	**46m 24.102s**	**1m 45.882s**	**18**
11	Wilco Zeelenberg	NL	Suzuki	26	46m 28.304s	1m 46.145s	25
12	Jean-Philippe Ruggia	F	Gilera	26	46m 28.529s	1m 46.128s	25
13	Masahiro Shimizu	J	Honda	26	46m 30.087s	1m 46.090s	25
14	Carlos Lavado	YV	Gilera	26	46m 43.214s	1m 46.545s	24
15	Herri Torrontegui	E	Suzuki	26	46m 43.954s	1m 46.738s	13
16	Bernd Kassner	D	Aprilia	26	46m 52.600s	1m 46.836s	8
17	Jurgen van den Goorbergh	NL	Aprilia	26	47m 10.636s	1m 47.506s	5
18	Yves Briguet	CH	Honda	26	47m 14.397s	1m 47.562s	10
19	Bernard Hänggeli	CH	Aprilia	26	47m 21.990s	1m 48.105s	12
20	Frédéric Protat	F	Aprilia	26	47m 31.256s	1m 48.252s	11
21	Stefan Prein	D	Honda	26	47m 34.146s	1m 48.418s	8
22	Katsuyoshi Kozono	J	Honda	26	47m 35.436s	1m 48.901s	6
23	Renzo Colleoni	I	Aprilia	25	45m 46.271s	1m 48.543s	14
24	Bernard Cazade	F	Honda	25	45m 58.223s	1m 48.507s	17
25	Luis Lavado	YV	Yamaha	25	46m 02.452s	1m 48.745s	5
26	Adi Stadler	D	Honda	25	46m 13.770s	1m 49.175s	6
27	Michele Gallina	I	Yamaha	25	46m 13.838s	1m 49.711s	15
	Eskil Suter	CH	Aprilia	21	DNF	1m 46.679s	14
	Pier Francesco Chili	I	Aprilia	16	DNF	1m 45.363s	13
	Luis D'Antin	E	Honda	15	DNF	1m 47.476s	14
	Paolo Casoli	I	Yamaha	15	DNF	1m 47.153s	10
	Harald Eckl	D	Aprilia	8	DNF	1m 49.984s	5
	José Kuhn	F	Honda	7	DNF	1m 48.902s	6
	Adrian Bosshard	CH	Honda	2	DNF	1m 49.380s	2
	Walter Catania	ARG	Aprilia		DNS		

Fastest lap: Reggiani, 1m 44.478s, 92.256 mph/148.958 km/h (record).
Previous record: none.

Practice leaderboard: **1** Biaggi, 1m 44.752s; **2** Reggiani, 1m 44.879s; **3** Romboni, 1m 45.019s; **4** Chili, 1m 45.265s; **5** Cadalora, 1m 45.698s; **6** Capirossi, 1m 45.864s; **7** C. Lavado, 1m 45.904s; **8** Schmid, 1m 45.957s; **9** Bradl, 1m 45.963s; **10** Preining, 1m 46.232s; **11** Ruggia, 1m 46.296s; **12** Puig, 1m 46.569s; **13** P. van den Goorbergh, 1m 46.679s; **14** Kassner, 1m 46.835s; **15** D'Antin, 1m 46.852s.

World Championship: **1** Cadalora, 197; **2** Reggiani, 144; **3** Chili, 107; **4** Bradl, 79; **5** Puig, 71; **6** Biaggi, 58; **7** Schmid, 54; **8** Cardus, 48; **9** Shimizu, 46; **10** Romboni, 43; **11** Zeelenberg, 38; **12** Capirossi, 19; **13** Okada, 15; **14** Aoki, 12; **15** Torrontegui, 8; **16** Preining, 5; **17** Lavado, Ruggia and Wakai, 4; **20** Casoli and Nanba, 3; **22** Hänggeli, Prein, J. van den Goorbergh and P. van den Goorbergh, 2; **26** Jeandat and Kassner, 1.

125 cc

24 laps, 64.464 miles/103.752 km

Place	Rider	Nat.	Machine	Laps	Time & speed	Fastest lap	Lap
1	**Dirk Raudies**	**D**	**Honda**	**24**	**44m 37.091s 86.694 mph/ 139.520 km/h**	**1m 50.262s**	**9**
2	**Jorge Martinez**	**E**	**Honda**	**24**	**44m 48.400s**	**1m 50.676s**	**18**
3	**Alessandro Gramigni**	**I**	**Aprilia**	**24**	**44m 48.808s**	**1m 50.983s**	**23**
4	**Bruno Casanova**	**I**	**Aprilia**	**24**	**44m 48.811s**	**1m 50.568s**	**5**
5	**Oliver Petrucciani**	**CH**	**Honda**	**24**	**45m 05.449s**	**1m 51.335s**	**11**
6	**Fausto Gresini**	**I**	**Honda**	**24**	**45m 09.066s**	**1m 51.551s**	**15**
7	**Noboru Ueda**	**J**	**Honda**	**24**	**45m 09.339s**	**1m 51.280s**	**8**
8	**Nobuyuki Wakai**	**J**	**Honda**	**24**	**45m 09.798s**	**1m 51.419s**	**9**
9	**Carlos Giro**	**E**	**Aprilia**	**24**	**45m 13.814s**	**1m 51.172s**	**17**
10	**Ezio Gianola**	**I**	**Honda**	**24**	**45m 13.936s**	**1m 51.550s**	**24**
11	Gabriele Debbia	I	Honda	24	45m 15.281s	1m 51.755s	8
12	Loek Bodelier	NL	Honda	24	45m 18.698s	1m 51.681s	9
13	Maik Stief	D	Aprilia	24	45m 22.391s	1m 52.065s	5
14	Kazuto Sakata	J	Honda	24	45m 32.643s	1m 52.396s	16
15	Ralf Waldmann	D	Honda	24	45m 34.907s	1m 52.388s	7
16	Oliver Koch	D	Honda	24	45m 43.461s	1m 52.827s	9
17	Takao Shimizu	J	Honda	24	45m 46.392s	1m 52.885s	24
18	Manuel Hernandez	E	Aprilia	24	45m 56.349s	1m 53.565s	6
19	Arie Molenaar	NL	Aprilia	24	45m 56.356s	1m 52.916s	6
20	Robin Appleyard	GB	Honda	24	46m 16.092s	1m 54.099s	20
21	Giovanni Palmieri	I	Gazzaniga	24	46m 16.482s	1m 53.998s	11
22	Hubert Abold	D	Honda	24	46m 16.861s	1m 53.991s	20
23	Heinz Lüthi	CH	Honda	24	46m 31.239s	1m 55.102s	16
24	Johnny Wickström	SF	Honda	22	45m 27.974s	1m 56.091s	2
	Steve Patrickson	GB	Honda	17	DNF	1m 54.788s	16
	Peter Öttl	D	Rotax	17	DNF	1m 52.090s	12
	Julian Miralles	E	Honda	15	DNF	1m 55.011s	4
	Kinya Wada	J	Honda	11	DNF	1m 53.298s	8
	Peter Galvin	AUS	Honda	7	DNF	1m 57.973s	4
	Alfred Waibel	D	Honda	6	DNF	1m 56.761s	2
	Alain Bronec	F	Honda	5	DNF	2m 03.889s	4
	Luis Alvaro	E	Aprilia	3	DNF	1m 53.231s	2
	Maurizio Vitali	I	Gazzaniga	2	DNF	1m 55.568s	2
	Hans Spaan	NL	Aprilia	1	DNF	2m 02.146s	1

Fastest lap: Raudies, 1m 50.262s, 87.703 mph/141.144 km/h (record).
Previous record: none.

Practice leaderboard: **1** Sakata, 1m 55.715s; **2** Gresini, 1m 56.229s; **3** Waldmann, 1m 56.463s; **4** Gramigni, 1m 56.473s; **5** Alvaro, 1m 56.772s; **6** Wakai, 1m 57.200s; **7** Raudies, 1m 57.928s; **8** Hernandez, 1m 59.107s; **9** Petrucciani, 1m 59.507s; **10** Bodelier, 1m 59.741s; **11** Ueda, 1m 59.763s; **12** Debbia, 1m 59.837s; **13** Öttl, 1m 59.958s; **14** Gianola, 1m 59.970s; **15** Spaan, 2m 00.389s.

World Championship: **1** Gramigni, 122; **2** Gresini, 114; **3** Waldmann, 106; **4** Gianola, 102; **5** Casanova, 96; **6** Raudies, 81; **7** Martinez, 63; **8** Debbia, 58; **9** Wakai, 52; **10** Ueda, 49; **11** Sakata, 42; **12** Giro, 24; **13** Öttl and Spaan, 10; **15** Petrucciani, 9; **16** Koch and Saitoh, 8; **18** Shimizu and Wada, 5; **20** Fujihara, 4; **21** Kurfiss, 3; **22** Lüthi, 1.

Photos: Malcolm Bryan

500 cc	KOCINSKI
250 cc	BIAGGI
125 cc	MARTINEZ

WORLD CHAMPIONSHIP • ROUND 13

SOUTH AFRICAN GRAND PRIX

The last race of the year started under a cloud. Of black smoke, rather than the highveld thunderheads that are always a threat at Kyalami. In the current state of random violence in that perennially politically troubled country, this was viewed with alarm, for smoke often means a bomb. Not so this time – a stray spark from a barbecue igniting tinder-dry grass beside a VIP car park was blamed for the subsequent blaze that burned out 42 cars.

The impressive Mercedes and BMW bonfire almost cleared a whole terrace of the corporate entertainment suites that lined much of the twice-rebuilt Kyalami circuit. Pampered guests hastily abandoned buffet, braaivleis and bar, for it was their cars that could be seen blazing merrily down the hill by the main gate. It also almost delayed the race, for fear that emergency vehicles would be required from the track. But Bernie's TV schedules are not to be trifled with, and the cars were left to burn while fire tenders came from distant parts so the race could begin on time.

Thus the funereal pall was able to serve another purpose – to mark the end of Michael Doohan's World Championship of 1992. By the time the fire was under control, the race was almost over – and his last hopes of rescuing a title that had earlier seemed his by right had also smouldered to extinction.

The final showdown: Doohan *(far left)* was much fitter than in Brazil, but still wished the race could be two more weeks away. Rainey *(left)* just wanted it to be over.

It was remarkable that he was able to finish sixth, although the improvement in his condition since Brazil was impressive. 'Dr Costa did a year's therapy in nine weeks,' he said. But though he was walking well and looking much fitter, his right leg was too stiff for him to use the rear brake, and bereft of this subtle but vitally important element of bike control (he doesn't use it hard, as did Spencer, to modulate wheelspin, but more as an extra steering aid, to tighten the line or alter the bike's attitude when confronted with unexpected circumstances) he was at a major disadvantage. Amazingly, he was once again able to run with the leaders. But he couldn't fight with them on equal terms, and he couldn't stop Wayne Rainey sweeping to an historic third title in succession, matching the achievement of his team owner, Kenny Roberts, in 1988, '89 and '90.

Rainey's title win came after a safe third place, and was of course only made possible by Doohan's Assen crash. At that point the Australian's points lead had been vast. But the American had himself conquered setbacks, including pain and injury, to match that of his luckless Australian rival. He has nothing to be ashamed of because he beat an injured man.

After the garlanding and post-race TV interviews, Rainey went straight to Doohan's pit to commiserate. Just what had he said? 'That I'd called him when he was hurt to wish him better, but that I'd also told him then I'd be trying to catch him up,' Rainey confided later that night. 'Earlier on, if you'd have told me I was going to be champion again, I'd have thought you were mad. But you know, that's racing.'

This sting in the tail to a strong and ultimately unpredictable season of revived 500 class racing rather overshadowed the actual event. This was, for a second year, rather unfair to the winner of the final race of the season. In Malaysia last year Kocinski's first 500 win had been undermined by the absence of Schwantz and Rainey; here he beat everyone fair and square, but his victory was celebrated less both inside and outside his team than Rainey's title. Along the way he'd defeated Schwantz and Chandler in the fight for third overall, but Kocinski is not the sort of rider who celebrates anything except being champion, and it marked the end of a bitterly frustrating year for him.

The South African GP was back on the calendar after an absence of seven years – dropped as part of the international sporting boycott. Motor cycling had been quick to return, following the lead of the Olympic Committee, for all sorts of reasons including local amenability towards cigarette sponsors, a well-equipped new modern track, an efficent infrastructure that made a welcome contrast to the Latin American alternatives and a strong bike racing tradition.

Those who had been here for the first three South African GPs remembered an epic track with a long kinked straight and some fine fast corners. Now they found a completely different circuit, rebuilt once, then lengthened again. It included four interesting bends from the old track (including the fast looping bowl where Spencer's carbon-fibre rear wheel collapsed in 1984, a pivotal event of that first year of the V4 NSR), but turned left down the hill where the old track had turned right. Most of the lap was made up of corners that at first glance were reminiscent of the worst aspects of Eastern Creek and Magny-Cours, looping back and forth in what had become a relatively confined space. But this impression was deceptive, for the new Kyalami proved that a circuit can comply with modern requirements and still provide interesting racing.

The continual twists dictated the lowest gearing used all year – the 500s were geared for around 245 km/h in sixth, but most only used the first five gears (the 125s less than 200!). But an average lap speed of more than 150 km/h was fairly high for this type of circuit, and riders praised the fact that the individual corners are still of a reasonable speed, emphasising riding technique rather than stop-and-go bends that favour brute power. Another asset is the rising and falling terrain, vertically complicating corner entries and exits, while a number of bends tighten up, forcing the exit line over the paint and onto the concrete.

While all the riders enjoyed the challenge, however, there were serious safety problems, and the track escaped wider censure largely because of the awkward political situation the riders found themselves in after the debacle at Interlagos. It would simply have been too embarrassing to kick up a fuss now.

The pit entry and exit were both dangerously placed, especially the

Photos: Hidenobu Takeuchi

Hidenobu Takeuchi

former, where a blind third-gear corner sent fast runners drifting wide directly where pit visitors were at a slow cruise. The pit exit put slow traffic uncomfortably close to riders at top speed lining up for the thrilling, almost flat-out Turn One, a downhill kink that really sorted the fast from the fearful, and was a favourite spectating spot for off-duty riders. They were alarmed to see Schwantz nearly collect Criville there, after the Spaniard had pulled out of the pits and was indolently readjusting his gloves and visor on the racing line. He earned a punch from the American two corners later, and an official reprimand; and the same observers were amused that afternoon to see him pay so much attention to looking over his shoulder in the same circumstances that he ran off the other side of the track into the gravel pit.

This first corner was also the most menacing of several where concrete walls were uncomfortably close to corner exits. Soberingly, there had been a fatal crash there the weekend before in a national race, and the bales that had been piled up against the wall didn't look very reassuring. In two other places, air-fences were installed, and Mackenzie became the first person to test their impact protection when he flipped over the high-side on Saturday morning. His bike slid half under the inflated barrier, and he followed soon afterwards, to lie momentarily stunned.

Viewers on pit lane monitors were then horrified to see him trussed up in a head-to-toe body-splint and bundled into an ambulance, giving the impression that he was badly hurt. In fact he was mainly winded, and the full emergency treatment earned wide praise as being just the way to treat a fallen rider whose injuries might potentially be serious. And when he emerged from the medical centre, the other riders crowded round to ask just whether the impact with the air-fence had been as luxurious as the makers claimed. Sadly, he couldn't remember.

Kyalami's most unique ingredient is its altitude. At 6000 ft – one mile high – it is by far the highest circuit; the Salzburgring and Járama, off the calendar this year, are the next highest, but they are only half as high. The thin air made life difficult for motors accustomed to richer stuff, and gave engineers unfamiliar tasks as they found ways to compensate for the lack of charge density.

Some used special cylinder base gaskets to increase compression, some had special ignition and exhaust valve chips, and all fitted the smallest jets of the year. Even so, the power loss was inevitably around 15 per cent, approaching 25 bhp on a top 500. This was enough to make them quite different to ride. 'It feels more like a superbike,' said Chandler of his Suzuki. 'It's the first time all year it doesn't stand on its back wheel every time you open the throttle. You can pin it in first even with the low gearing. That means we have to set the handling up better, because we need to carry more speed in the corner to compensate for the lost acceleration.' Everyone agreed that their bikes felt a bit flat, while Rainey, Garriga and Mackenzie all tried the supposedly less user-friendly pre-droner engine because the lack of power made that easier to ride as well. (In Rainey's case, there was also the lingering doubt over the drone's durability.)

The 250 class saw Aprilia finish on as high a note as they could have asked, again taking the top three positions, and with their man of the year, Biaggi, claiming his first win. This was narrowly achieved. Although he won by a comfortable margin, his own exuberance saw him in the dirt and almost off the bike on his last lap. Aprilia also clinched the bitterly fought 125 title, with Alessandro Gramigni finishing a hard-fought third to triumph at last.

Kyalami marked the end of three notable careers.

Eddie Lawson, the dominant racer of the last decade, finished his in uncompromisingly anti-social fashion, ostentatiously snubbing a presentation by all the riders to GP medico Dr Claudio Costa in favour of a personal tribute later ('I don't want anything to do with those jerks'), then pulling out of the race when his Cagiva was embroiled and getting beaten in a battle for seventh – a bit infra dig for a man in his position. He left the track with hardly a backward glance to fly home at once, declining to take part in a massive and raucous end of season party. As he left, an anonymous American voice yelled out from the riders' caravans behind the pits: 'Get the f*** outta here, and don't ever come back!' A sad postscript, but it seemed to be the way he wanted it.

The words 'team orders' weren't in Kocinski's vocabulary – but Rainey didn't need to beat him, and once the younger Yamaha man was ahead he drew away unchallenged.

Wayne Gardner closed his career with a flourish. He might have said that his second place, beating Rainey, was his way of doing the best he could to help Mick, and it would have been true. But those who knew him better were well aware that he was more than happy to retire as the only Australian 500 class World Champion.

Carlos Lavado, cavalier Venezuelan 250 champion in 1983 and 1986, was the third – a hero of the tough privateer years of the class, whose quicksilver talent had given Gilera a few good days in their first year back in racing.

The major gossip concerned those who were staying. On the one hand there was news that Chandler had signed for Cagiva, leaving an interesting vacant slot at Lucky Strike Suzuki; on the other was speculation that Kocinski wanted to switch back to 250s, to dominate and rebuild his confidence. Cadalora was also moving ever closer to replacing him at Marlboro Roberts, while it was at last confirmed that Daryl Beattie was to take over from Gardner at Rothmans Honda.

The old season was followed by the new with barely a pause. Team Roberts were to test Dunlops at Kyalami the next week, and were shortly to be followed by Kanemoto's Honda squad, testing with new Australian star Mat Mladin and (hold your breath) Freddie Spencer – the latter running hard and impressively fast as his Napoleonic return gathered momentum. Suzuki were hot-footing it back to Jerez, where Kocinski smashed all records on their 250.

After all, the season had been dominated by those who were best prepared at the start of this year (though a twist of fate meant Doohan remained uncrowned). And everybody wanted to be as ready as possible for the start of the next one.

500 cc PRACTICE

Doohan's biggest surprise came ten minutes from the end of the final practice session, when he moved to the top of the leaderboard. He'd been fast all along, clearly close to fitness and hardly slowed by his lack of a rear brake. The only sign that he was not yet fully fit could be seen in a somewhat deliberate riding style, shifting his weight carefully and well in advance of the corners. He was here to defend his title lead to the hilt.

His pole position didn't last, though. Kocinski had been fastest more or less throughout, and pushed through to lead again with a blistering time almost half a second ahead of the rest. Gardner nosed narrowly into second, but Doohan stayed third, with his title rival Rainey fourth and right alongside for the drag race into Turn One.

This was remarkable. But could he do it all race long? Well, he was riding with assurance, and looked a hundred times fitter off the bike than he had in Brazil, though a full GP would obviously be a bit of a trial. He was more worried about his lack of a rear brake. 'I didn't realise how much I use it,' he said. 'It's one of those things you don't miss until it's not there.' (You wouldn't, would you?) While it didn't affect his speed, it spoiled his manoeuvrability, which he thought might be a problem when they ran up among the back-markers. 'I'll give it a go tomorrow,' he promised. 'I don't think Rainey would like it if I didn't.'

Rainey's task was two-fold. First, obviously, he had to beat Doohan; second (assuming, as he must, that Doohan was right behind him), he had to be first or second to glean a big enough points gap. Outwardly calm, he looked strong and fast on the circuit, but his weakest point may have been doubt about his machinery, which diverted his full attention from his drone engine race bike in the latest version of the chassis to spend time testing the old well-proven screamer engine. This was not just whimsy, but was due to the fact that Yamaha were again running short of spare parts for the new engine, with its appetite for primary gears, engine cases and other not-so-durables. Then he lost more time in the final session and one chance of a fast lap when a clutch oil seal failed. 'I just can't wait to get the race going,' he said.

Kocinski's second successive pole came after he too had switched to the new chassis that Rainey had used in Brazil. 'For the amount of time I've had with it, I'm happy with what we've done,' he said. 'If only Yamaha, the team and myself could concentrate on making a bike to suit my style, I feel I could race for better than third overall.' He dubbed the latest Michelins 'awesome', but had only faint praise for the frame improvement. 'Now it kind of hints that it wants to think about going round a corner, but for sure it's better than anything else I've had all year.' Another pressure was the fact that he might be obliged to let team-mate Rainey finish ahead. Not so, he asserted firmly. 'The words "team orders" aren't in my vocabulary.'

Gardner was certainly another candidate to beat Rainey, which was about all he could try and do in the interests of his own team-mate. He approached his last GP in typical fighting style, hunkered down over the bars and going for it. He was also following no team orders. 'I spoke to Mick and he said the best thing I can do is to go and do my best. If I can win here, it would be a fairy tale ending,' he said. He was only a tenth ahead of Doohan, and heading a batch of tight-up times that put from second to seventh within one second.

This produced a menacing second row, from Rainey's point of view. It had Schwantz up front, also using a new chassis for the first time since it had arrived for Donington – and it went a long way towards solving his long-standing problems of handling balance. 'With the old chassis, I was always chasing the front, and I could only get it to grip by taking away from the rear. The new one's better, but I'm still chasing the front a little.' The chassis was for him alone, cooked up by his crew chief, Stuart Shenton, and the factory. But he had another problem – a bad engine. He blew a crankshaft on Friday morning, but the replacement motor remained sluggish and obstinate throughout the rest of practice. Why didn't he follow the Yamaha lead set by Rainey, Kocinski, Mackenzie and Garriga by trying an old screamer engine? 'It would be interesting. But we don't have one.'

Mackenzie was alongside, by virtue of a charging time scored in the windy first timed session on Friday, using the old high-pitched engine and in a fast pack. He stuck with that engine ('The new one went well at Donington, but it's never run right since then') and liked the highly technical circuit, high lean angles and high corner speed; but he came to grief with his high-sider at the pair of sharp lefts at the top of the hill. He had nothing worse than a cut arm and a headache, and was declared fit to go out again in final practice, when he was over a second slower than the day before after spending a lot of time readjusting his badly damaged and rebuilt bike.

Next, an off-colour Chandler found his last Suzuki ride frustrating, with traffic spoiling every attempt at a fast lap. He was still aiming high in the final session when his usual late charge on fresh rubber was again thwarted. 'I was already over the paint and onto the concrete passing someone when he straightened up on me. I had to stay out there until we were almost past the corner.'

The last place on the row was taken by Mamola who did, after all, conclude a full season on the Budweiser Yamaha, and who was at last fit and strong in all his limbs. Another rider to enjoy the deceptive nature of the tricky corners, he was less than two-tenths off Chandler, and a similar distance from Criville, leading row three.

Goddard was tenth, after solving a front fork problem that he said had damaged his performance since Assen and had caused his crash in Brazil. A tenth down came Lawson, who was trying hard to make something of his last race but couldn't overcome the Cagiva's lack of mid-range at this circuit of twists and hills. Team-mate Barros was alongside, to conclude row three.

Row four was led by the increasingly impressive Roc rider Arakaki, smoother now but still very lively, and ending up narrowly ahead of

Photos: Hidenobu Takeuchi

Garriga's works bike. The Spaniard tried too hard to move up at the end of the final session, and fell at one of the hairpins. A broken coccyx was suspected, but he too was passed fit to race.

DuHamel alongside was using a droner engine and tumbled on the first day of practice. He was a critic of the circuit's safety problems, but politics left him a lone voice and he said: 'I'll have to put that feeling out of my mind.'

Lopez Mella completed the row, 16th out of 31 qualifiers. South African wild cards Russell Wood (who tested the V-twin Bimota extensively last year) and Mike Wilson were both on row five out of eight, an impressive 18th and 20th. Wilson rode a Roc; Wood the 1992 prototype Harris raced by Terry Rymer at Donington, entered by Mick Grant, who hoped to team him with James Whitham in 1993.

500 cc RACE – 28 LAPS

Just to underline his threat, Schwantz had been fastest in morning warm-up. But when the flag fell, it was the two Yamahas at the head of the field, Rainey leading Kocinski, with Doohan chasing on their tail and Chandler packed up close, the rest of the works bikes tight behind.

The first shuffle to the top ten came when Mamola flipped out in the last turn by the pit wall. He landed safely, but was out.

Doohan's first lap had been his best, however, and he couldn't match the pace of the Yamahas. By the end of lap two he was down to fifth, behind Chandler and Schwantz.

Gardner had got away behind Lawson, but was ahead of him at the end of lap one. He was in fine form, and after half a lap behind Doohan, he dived inside him under braking, consigning him to the sixth place he held from then until the finish. Wayne said later that it had taken him a few laps to build up momentum, and he closed on Schwantz all the time.

Then, on the sixth lap, the Suzuki rider did his bit to help, forced to drop his own pace as a rear tyre with the same number that had given him best time in the morning inexplicably proved to lack grip in the afternoon. 'Perhaps it was the heat,' he said. He dropped to fifth, and also stayed there, to finish almost ten seconds ahead of Doohan.

By now, the lead had changed hands for the only time in the race. For three laps, Kocinski had been either following Rainey dutifully or sizing him up for a chance to overtake. It turned out to be the latter, and on lap four he moved past cleanly and immediately began to draw away. By lap seven, he had almost one-and-a-half seconds on his teammate.

Gardner had quickly left Schwantz behind, and steadily gnawed away at the gap Chandler had built up so that, before half-distance, he was in a position to attack. Typically, he wasted no time doing so. Chandler, the most level-headed of riders, succumbed to the inevitable. 'My bike was a bit down on power, but it was handling really well, so I was able to stay with the Yamahas until the tyres warmed up,' he said. Even so, he rated it his best race of the year. 'What's satisfying is when you get the absolute best out of yourself and your bike. It felt as though I did every corner perfectly. But when Gardner came by, I couldn't stay with him even though he was making a few mistakes.'

Mistakes or not, Gardner had the scent of a possible victory, with Rainey now in sight ahead of him. Again he piled on more pressure, gradually closing up, and then making a big handful of time on him through lapped traffic. With six laps to go, he was closing; with three he was on his tail; and he broke the lap record for the final time as he attacked under braking. At the flag, he was two seconds ahead of Rainey, and only three behind Kocinski, who had been obliged to up his pace again as the blue-and-white tornado closed in.

For Kocinski, his first win of the year was vindication of his long-standing complaints about the lack of direction in the factory's chassis development, as well as proof that he could do it when all the best riders were also in the race. 'It's the first time I've felt really confident all year,' he said. 'It's a shame there aren't any more races left.'

Gardner's hard-earned second was a fitting close to his career – though who knows what Rainey might have done had it been Doohan's Honda and not Gardner's, or if his title rival had been closer behind. But third was more than good enough to take the crown that had been hovering over Doohan's head and put it firmly back where it had been for the previous two years.

Chandler was seven seconds behind Rainey, with Schwantz almost ten seconds behind that, but comfortably clear of the lone Doohan who, by the end of the race, had

Left: **Rainey leads Kocinski, Chandler, Schwantz, Doohan and Gardner (obscured), while in the background Mamola bows out of the last race of the year. Chasing the leaders is fast-starting Peter Goddard (21).**

Max Biaggi *(below)* was always prepared to use more track than his rivals, and often more than the designers had provided. He leads narrowly from Romboni and the hidden Reggiani, with Cadalora doing all he can to try and stay in touch with his countrymen.

become resigned to his fate. There were no tears, only a wry grin, and a promise to be back next year. Like Rainey, the last resort was the serviceable cliché 'That's racing' and the only satisfaction was that 'I've said all year that it's not over until the last race.'

A good battle for seventh saw Lawson overwhelmed and obliged to trade blows with a five-strong pack of middle order works riders. He held off Goddard, but then Mackenzie came through strongly, and though Lawson replied to his first outbraking attempt by passing him straight back on the way out of the corner, Mackenzie was not to be stopped, and got by for good on lap 14, followed directly by Goddard.

Now slow starter Criville was with the group and moving through, with DuHamel on his back wheel and Garriga trying painfully to stay in touch. When he found himself embroiled with this lot, Lawson decided he'd had enough, and pitted; Criville, meanwhile, passed Goddard, who almost immediately succumbed to race-long nausea, was sick in his helmet and promptly crashed.

The young Spaniard had been obliged to change to his spare bike after his race bike gave trouble on the sighting lap, and it was not geared right. But he was able to battle it out with Mackenzie, a fight he won by less than a second, with the Scot complaining about a lack of bottom end from his screamer engine.

DuHamel was short of front-wheel grip throughout, and dropped back to finish ninth, comfortably ahead of the stiff and sore Garriga, who claimed the last point. Arakaki won a good fight with Catalano for 11th, while wild cards Wood and Wilson were back and forth all race, the former slowing with a strange temporary power loss, then getting back past Sarron and ahead of his countryman again for 14th, only five seconds behind Lopez Mella.

Barros had retired after one lap. There were 25 finishers, proving that the new IRTA series was able to sustain its strength of numbers all through the year.

250 cc PRACTICE

The final Aprilia–Honda showdown saw the bikes on more equal terms than at faster circuits, at least on the strength of the ultra-close top practice times. Low gearing, the power-sapping altitude and a lack of a real flat-out gallop seemed to make all the bikes more equal.

Chili had raced here a year before, though the track had been changed since then, but he was confident that he would have dominated practice anyway, having led the first day and saved his best until the end of the final session. 'The bike is fine, though I am having some trouble with my back,' he said (a long-standing tendency to go into painful seizure had been getting worse of late). 'And I didn't realise Bradl was behind me.'

For the German had followed Chili round his fast lap, and no sooner had the Italian's name been flashed at the top of the list on the Olivetti timing monitors than Bradl crossed the line and displaced him to claim his second pole of a disappointing year. 'I had a good soft tyre on at the right time and I rode one really fast, risky lap. That's one thing – doing 26 laps is altogether different,' he said.

The upset was merely the culmination of a last minute scramble that saw the lead change hands four times. Reggiani had been on top, but Jochen Schmid had been showing well all weekend and was now whizzing around, towing Cadalora's Honda, which simply didn't seem able to get by. And then he put the sole works Yamaha on top.

Only minutes remained, but that was enough for Cadalora. The champion backed off, then used the head-down German as a marker to go just two-hundredths faster. But even that wasn't good enough, with Chili also part of the group, and stealing better than a tenth from his Honda-mounted countryman.

All were slipstreaming each other by now, and the final victor of this pre-race battle was Bradl, less than a tenth ahead of Chili, with Cadalora a similar distance behind. He was closely matched by Schmid, whose move to Yamaha seems to have been well timed, with the bike really looking competitive by the end of the year.

Row two saw Biaggi within a whisker of Schmid, followed by Reggiani and the pair of up-and-coming Latins, Romboni and Capirossi, making an all-Italian row two.

Biaggi, leading row two, had also almost matched Cadalora's time,

Alex Gramigni could have played it safe, but he prefers racing for victory. Here he leads eventual winner Jorge Martinez and fellow-Spanish Honda rider Carlos Giro.

Hidenobu Takeuchi

and was only a quarter of a second down on pole. He'd tumbled once on Friday, which meant he had to switch to his second bike and start again in trying to improve fork performance over the bumpy apexes. He did so well enough to topple Reggiani from first to an ultimate sixth on the grid, although still within a half-second of pole. Romboni had almost matched his time in the last session too, with Capirossi close behind, so the two double-special Hondas were in with a fighting chance.

Zeelenberg led row three in what he now knew would be his last Suzuki ride, after a year when his style seemed never to have meshed with the quirkily fast-but-slow V-twin. Better had been expected of both him and the bike than to be starting alongside the Aprilias of Preining and Puig, with Ruggia (another on his last ride) on the far end, on the Gilera.

Shimizu led row four from the retiring Lavado, the blossoming Patrick van den Goorbergh and the Aprilia of Swiss ex-motocrosser Eskil Suter.

A grid of 35 meant nine rows, the ever misfortunate Stefan Prein on the second to last of them.

250 cc RACE – 26 LAPS

There is a school of thought, common among denizens of the rearmost rows of the grid, that since all riders cross the same finishing line, they should really all start from the same startline. In other words, as long as you don't pass the front row before the lights go green, you're not cheating.

Race officials don't necessarily agree, but with attention focused on the front rows those further back often get away with this sort of thing and, while the faster riders soon overhaul them, they gain valuable feet and places in the privateer battle.

It can be taken too far, however, as at Kyalami, where conspiratorial Dutchmen Zeelenberg and Patrick van den Goorbergh exploded through from the fourth row to dispute the lead with Cadalora. The private Aprilia was even in front for a short time, but then the moment of glory was over: officials imposed a one-minute penalty on both of them.

They dropped back in any case. Zeelenberg said the other bikes came past his Suzuki on the straight 'like flies'. Cadalora made the running, with Romboni coming through to second, van den Goorbergh hanging on gamely for two more laps and Capirossi coming up from behind.

All the Aprilias had got away slowly, with Biaggi seventh at the end of lap one, and Chili and Reggiani ninth and tenth. That couldn't last, and Biaggi led the Italian charge in familiar hang-it-out style. He was up among the Hondas of Cadalora and Romboni on lap three, and briefly in front before both Honda riders fought back.

He waited three more laps before making another, more decisive bid for the front, passing both his rivals in short order and managing to hang on until the opposition was broken. By now there was a regular brawl behind him, with Capirossi joined by Reggiani, and Bradl and Chili packing in behind.

The order changed back and forth on every bend, but the trend was clear – the Aprilias were on their way through, with Reggiani in second by lap eight, and Chili in third four laps later. Reggiani attacked Biaggi, but in vain, with the youngster determined this time to hold his advantage and gain at least one debut-season Aprilia victory. The older man was forced to accept second in any case after a few unexpected slides made him suspect that water was leaking onto his back tyre.

Chili meanwhile also emerged from the pack, too far behind the other Aprilias to catch up, but able to take a safe third.

Now the battle was for fourth, and there were still four people locked in combat. Romboni looked semi-wild, as usual, but went too far this time, on lap 15, running wide onto the dirt where he tried his damnedest to save the bike as it sped towards an unprotected concrete wall. He baled out in the nick of time, tumbling and rolling to end up stationary against the wall without actually hitting it.

This incident also spread them out a bit, with Bradl seizing the advantage and fighting off another challenge from Capirossi to make sure of fourth. Fifth was Capirossi's best finish in his first 250 year.

Cadalora faded to a disappointed sixth, complaining of a pain in his neck as well as a shortage of speed compared with the Aprilias.

Schmid was seventh, unable to match his qualifying performance on the sole works Yamaha, but five seconds ahead of the next group, which was led across the line by Herri Torrontegui after a strong ride on the Lucky Strike Suzuki. The young Spaniard had started well and not only stayed ahead of Ruggia's Gilera, but also of team-mate Zeelenberg, who in any case dropped from tenth across the line to 22nd after the application of his one-minute penalty.

The last point went to Preining, after the Austrian privateer had defeated Shimizu's lacklustre NSR Honda.

There were 26 finishers, with Carlos Lavado 15th in the last race of a fine career.

125 cc RACE – 24 LAPS

In contrast to the 250s, Alessandro Gramigni proved that starting technique really isn't that important if you are the fastest rider on the fastest bike. He'd qualified on pole, then stalled on the line. Paddle-starting while the rest were feeding their clutches in, he got away well down in the midfield brawl – and

still ended up World Champion.

The situation was simple. Gramigni had eight points over Gresini, so had to finish at least close to him, though not necessarily in front. Waldmann and Gianola both had a mathematical chance of the title, but only if the others failed to finish.

Gianola led from the line, with Gresini hanging on grimly in second from Casanova and Sakata. On lap three, Casanova was gone – a high-side crash removed one challenger. He was immediately replaced by another: Gramigni had brawled his way through to the front and was in no mood for safe tactics. He'd finished an amazing first lap in tenth place, saying later: 'It's a miracle I didn't crash. I must have had ten collisions.'

It wasn't long before Gianola's lead was dwindling. At the same time, Gresini was falling victim to a persistent rear suspension malaise, and dropped away out of contention, to finish seventh. But still Gramigni declined the soft option of an easy finish.

He was ready for battle, and hit the front shortly before half-distance, only to be displaced at once by Martinez, whose Honda had tagged on to the back. Giro was also on his way on his Aprilia, setting fastest lap as he closed up, and the leading trio embarked on a scrap to the flag.

As Gianola also fell back, to finish eighth, Brazil winner Raudies pushed his Honda into the leading battle as well, and it was high risk and dangerous living all the way.

The race was won by Martinez, with Giro seizing second and third-placed Gramigni fighting to the end – a good way of avoiding thinking about the championship. He beat Raudies over the line by less than half a second.

Ueda was fifth, with Waldmann pushing through to take sixth.

Hans Spaan (Aprilia) was ninth and Oliver Koch took the last point on his Honda. Non-finishers included crashers Wakai and (for the umpteenth time) Sakata.

Thus new boy Gramigni took the title for Aprilia, with Gresini second in the final points table, early leader Waldmann third and Gianola fourth. It had been a year-long battle of outstanding brilliance.

South African Grand Prix, 6 September/statistics

Kyalami Race Circuit, 2.645-mile/4.260-km circuit

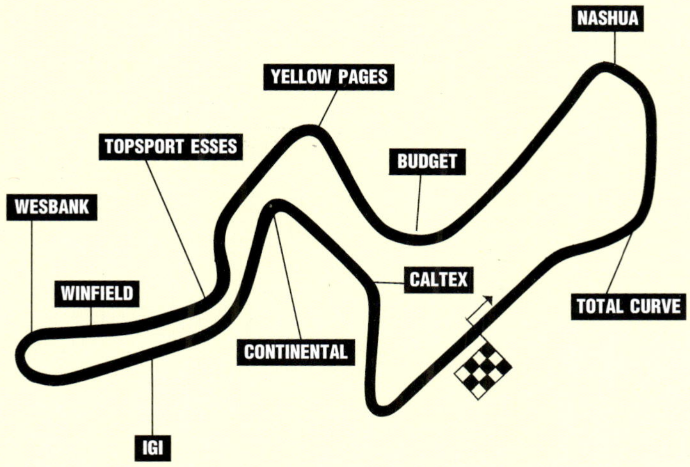

500 cc

28 laps, 74.060 miles/119.280 km

Place	Rider	Nat.	Machine	Laps	Time & speed	Fastest lap	Lap
1	**John Kocinski**	**USA**	**Yamaha**	**28**	**47m 00.729s 94.593 mph/ 152.233 km/h**	**1m 39.979s**	**18**
2	**Wayne Gardner**	**AUS**	**Honda**	**28**	**47m 03.664s**	**1m 39.952s**	**25**
3	**Wayne Rainey**	**USA**	**Yamaha**	**28**	**47m 05.598s**	**1m 40.190s**	**22**
4	**Doug Chandler**	**USA**	**Suzuki**	**28**	**47m 13.306s**	**1m 40.195s**	**19**
5	**Kevin Schwantz**	**USA**	**Suzuki**	**28**	**47m 22.779s**	**1m 40.813s**	**9**
6	**Michael Doohan**	**AUS**	**Honda**	**28**	**47m 31.042s**	**1m 40.937s**	**12**
7	**Alex Criville**	**E**	**Honda**	**28**	**47m 34.599s**	**1m 40.744s**	**27**
8	**Niall Mackenzie**	**GB**	**Yamaha**	**28**	**47m 35.248s**	**1m 40.708s**	**27**
9	**Miguel DuHamel**	**CAN**	**Yamaha**	**28**	**48m 03.852s**	**1m 41.369s**	**7**
10	**Juan Garriga**	**E**	**Yamaha**	**28**	**48m 10.955s**	**1m 41.829s**	**6**
11	Toshiyuki Arakaki	J	Yamaha	28	48m 25.760s	1m 42.526s	12
12	Corrado Catalano	I	Yamaha	28	48m 25.770s	1m 42.532s	14
13	Juan Lopez Mella	E	Yamaha	27	47m 01.999s	1m 43.745s	9
14	Russell Wood	ZA	Yamaha	27	47m 06.665s	1m 43.667s	14
15	Mike Wilson	ZA	Yamaha	27	47m 12.617s	1m 43.520s	9
16	Marco Papa	I	Cagiva	27	47m 19.328s	1m 43.327s	7
17	Dominique Sarron	F	Yamaha	27	47m 32.868s	1m 43.597s	8
18	Eddie Laycock	IRL	Yamaha	27	47m 33.907s	1m 44.462s	12
19	Michael Rudroff	D	Yamaha	27	47m 52.728s	1m 44.791s	8
20	Serge David	CH	Yamaha	27	48m 06.702s	1m 45.117s	7
21	Niggi Schmassman	CH	Yamaha	27	48m 10.649s	1m 45.299s	27
22	Peter Graves	GB	Yamaha	27	48m 10.935s	1m 45.148s	25
23	Andreas Leuthe	D	Yamaha	27	48m 12.104s	1m 45.242s	21
24	Sepp Doppler	A	Yamaha	26	47m 24.585s	1m 47.138s	5
	Peter Goddard	AUS	Yamaha	19	DNF	1m 41.155s	19
	Cees Doorakkers	NL	Yamaha	16	DNF	1m 45.824s	6
	Eddie Lawson	USA	Cagiva	15	DNF	1m 41.632s	10
	Simon Buckmaster	GB	Yamaha	8	DNF	1m 46.943s	6
	Kevin Mitchell	GB	Yamaha	2	DNF	1m 48.322s	2
	Alexandre Barros	BR	Cagiva	1	DNF	1m 50.535s	1
	Randy Mamola	USA	Yamaha	0	DNF		

Fastest lap: Gardner, 1m 39.952s, 95.340 mph/153.434 km/h (record).
Previous circuit record: Freddie Spencer, USA (Honda), 1m 24.91s, 108.11 mph/173.99 km/h (1985).

Practice leaderboard: **1** Kocinski, 1m 39.548s; **2** Gardner, 1m 40.072s; **3** Doohan, 1m 40.180s; **4** Rainey, 1m 40.222s; **5** Schwantz, 1m 40.526s; **6** Mackenzie, 1m 40.945s; **7** Chandler, 1m 40.960s; **8** Mamola, 1m 41.113s; **9** Criville, 1m 41.289s; **10** Goddard, 1m 41.375s; **11** Lawson, 1m 41.472s; **12** Barros, 1m 41.656s; **13** Arakaki, 1m 41.931s; **14** Garriga, 1m 42.025s; **15** DuHamel, 1m 42.544s.

Final 500 cc World Championship points: see page 180.

250 cc

26 laps, 68.770 miles/110.760 km

Place	Rider	Nat.	Machine	Laps	Time & speed	Fastest lap	Lap
1	**Massimiliano Biaggi**	I	Aprilia	26	44m 43.367s 92.332 mph/ 148.595 km/h	1m 42.094s	15
2	**Loris Reggiani**	I	Aprilia	26	44m 47.954s	1m 42.240s	10
3	**Pier Francesco Chili**	I	Aprilia	26	44m 53.116s	1m 42.576s	13
4	**Helmut Bradl**	D	Honda	26	44m 55.758s	1m 42.955s	18
5	**Loris Capirossi**	I	Honda	26	45m 00.611s	1m 42.580s	11
6	**Luca Cadalora**	I	Honda	26	45m 06.255s	1m 42.796s	10
7	**Jochen Schmid**	D	Yamaha	26	45m 13.768s	1m 43.536s	11
8	**Herri Torrontegui**	E	Suzuki	26	45m 18.033s	1m 43.697s	19
9	**Jean-Philippe Ruggia**	F	Gilera	26	45m 18.586s	1m 43.639s	23
10	**Andy Preining**	A	Aprilia	26	45m 38.645s	1m 44.236s	7
11	Masahiro Shimizu	J	Honda	26	45m 44.358s	1m 44.503s	8
12	Eskil Suter	CH	Aprilia	26	45m 47.262s	1m 44.581s	20
13	Bernd Kassner	D	Aprilia	26	45m 47.458s	1m 44.639s	19
14	Katsuyoshi Kozono	J	Honda	26	45m 52.184s	1m 44.807s	21
15	Carlos Lavado	YV	Gilera	26	46m 01.971s	1m 44.730s	13
16	Jurgen van den Goorbergh	NL	Aprilia	26	46m 04.985s	1m 44.969s	15
17	Martin Paetzold	ZA	Yamaha	26	46m 09.211s	1m 45.042s	6
18	Yves Briguet	CH	Honda	26	46m 11.928s	1m 45.549s	8
19	Bernard Hänggeli	CH	Aprilia	26	46m 12.029s	1m 45.602s	10
20	Adrian Bosshard	CH	Honda	26	46m 12.680s	1m 45.333s	18
21	Renzo Colleoni	I	Aprilia	26	46m 12.948s	1m 45.360s	18
22	Wilco Zeelenberg	NL	Suzuki	26	46m 19.452s	1m 43.824s	24
23	Bernard Cazade	F	Honda	26	46m 23.138s	1m 45.859s	7
24	Patrick van den Goorbergh	NL	Aprilia	26	46m 35.768s	1m 44.203s	10
25	Gavin Ramsay	ZA	Yamaha	25	45m 16.933s	1m 47.309s	19
26	José Kuhn	F	Honda	25	45m 23.750s	1m 47.515s	8
	Frédéric Protat	F	Aprilia	24	DNF	1m 44.866s	11
	Michele Gallina	I	Yamaha	23	DNF	1m 46.825s	10
	Luis D'Antin	E	Honda	17	DNF	1m 45.592s	6
	Doriano Romboni	I	Honda	15	DNF	1m 42.965s	14
	Adi Stadler	D	Honda	11	DNF	1m 47.497s	8
	Harald Eckl	D	Aprilia	8	DNF	1m 48.399s	4
	Paolo Casoli	I	Yamaha	3	DNF	1m 46.388s	3
	Alberto Puig	E	Aprilia	2	DNF	1m 48.330s	2
	Stefan Prein	D	Honda	1	DNF	1m 56.987s	1

Fastest lap: Biaggi, 1m 42.094s, 93.340 mph/150.215 km/h (record).
Previous circuit record: Mario Rademeyer, ZA (Yamaha), 1m 28.14s, 104.15 mph/167.61 km/h (1985).

Practice leaderboard: **1** Bradl, 1m 42.056s; **2** Chili, 1m 42.137s; **3** Cadalora, 1m 42.265s; **4** Schmid, 1m 42.284s; **5** Biaggi, 1m 42.306s; **6** Reggiani, 1m 42.545s; **7** Romboni, 1m 42.619s; **8** Capirossi, 1m 42.958s; **9** Zeelenberg, 1m 43.331s; **10** Preining, 1m 43.704s; **11** Puig, 1m 43.712s; **12** Ruggia, 1m 43.850s; **13** Shimizu, 1m 44.235s; **14** Lavado, 1m 44.263s; **15** P. van den Goorbergh, 1m 44.337s.

Final 250 cc World Championship points: see page 180.

125 cc

24 laps, 63.480 miles/102.240 km

Place	Rider	Nat.	Machine	Laps	Time & speed	Fastest lap	Lap
1	**Jorge Martinez**	E	Honda	24	44m 02.803s 86.538 mph/ 139.270 km/h	1m 49.220s	7
2	**Carlos Giro**	E	Aprilia	24	44m 03.056s	1m 48.687s	14
3	**Alessandro Gramigni**	I	Aprilia	24	44m 03.241s	1m 49.126s	6
4	**Dirk Raudies**	D	Honda	24	44m 03.604s	1m 48.932s	14
5	**Noboru Ueda**	J	Honda	24	44m 08.949s	1m 49.209s	14
6	**Ralf Waldmann**	D	Honda	24	44m 18.023s	1m 49.191s	8
7	**Fausto Gresini**	I	Honda	24	44m 18.608s	1m 49.756s	17
8	**Ezio Gianola**	I	Honda	24	44m 21.530s	1m 49.920s	7
9	**Hans Spaan**	NL	Aprilia	24	44m 27.767s	1m 49.845s	13
10	**Oliver Koch**	D	Honda	24	44m 32.578s	1m 49.890s	18
11	Maik Stief	D	Aprilia	24	44m 38.876s	1m 50.216s	12
12	Kinya Wada	J	Honda	24	44m 39.052s	1m 50.435s	15
13	Gabriele Debbia	I	Honda	24	44m 50.187s	1m 50.612s	6
14	Giovanni Palmieri	I	Gazzaniga	24	45m 03.268s	1m 50.796s	7
15	Takao Shimizu	J	Honda	24	45m 16.029s	1m 51.640s	4
16	Robin Appleyard	GB	Honda	24	45m 16.163s	1m 52.306s	21
17	Hubert Abold	D	Honda	24	45m 21.974s	1m 51.334s	19
18	Manuel Hernandez	E	Aprilia	24	45m 32.982s	1m 52.163s	11
19	Manie Maritz	ZA	Aprilia	24	45m 33.358s	1m 52.491s	17
20	Maurizio Vitali	I	Gazzaniga	24	45m 33.523s	1m 52.488s	24
21	Johnny Wickström	SF	Honda	24	45m 38.551s	1m 52.522s	10
22	Brendon Crookes	ZA	Honda	23	45m 53.770s	1m 57.982s	17
	Kazuto Sakata	J	Honda	22	DNF	1m 49.969s	3
	Oliver Petrucciani	CH	Honda	19	DNF	1m 50.292s	13
	Arie Molenaar	NL	Aprilia	18	DNF	1m 52.091s	6
	Peter Galvin	AUS	Honda	15	DNF	1m 53.514s	13
	Steve Patrickson	GB	Honda	13	DNF	1m 53.071s	6
	Alfred Waibel	D	Honda	8	DNF	1m 53.989s	4
	Peter Öttl	D	Rotax	7	DNF	1m 50.218s	7
	Loek Bodelier	NL	Honda	7	DNF	1m 50.628s	5
	Heinz Lüthi	CH	Honda	7	DNF	1m 52.927s	5
	Alain Bronec	F	Honda	7	DNF	1m 56.874s	2
	Nobuyuki Wakai	J	Honda	6	DNF	1m 51.739s	5
	Luis Alvaro	E	Aprilia	4	DNF	1m 52.826s	4
	Bruno Casanova	I	Aprilia	2	DNF	1m 50.841s	2

Fastest lap: Giro, 1m 48.687s, 87.677 mph/141.102 km/h (record).
Previous circuit record: not available.

Practice leaderboard: **1** Gramigni, 1m 48.869s; **2** Raudies, 1m 49.002s; **3** Casanova, 1m 49.015s; **4** Martinez, 1m 49.065s; **5** Gresini, 1m 49.329s; **6** Sakata, 1m 49.371s; **7** Giro, 1m 49.521s; **8** Gianola, 1m 49.595s; **9** Ueda, 1m 49.627s; **10** Waldmann, 1m 49.850s; **11** Koch, 1m 50.082s; **12** Bodelier, 1m 50.208s; **13** Debbia, 1m 50.308s; **14** Stief, 1m 50.317s; **15** Petrucciani, 1m 50.338s.

Final 125 cc World Championship points: see page 181.

Hidenobu Takeuchi

Sidecar World Championship Race, 13 September/statistics

Circuit van Drenthe, Assen, 2.431-mile/3.913-km circuit

Rolf Biland and Kurt Waltisperg, wily veterans both, took their fourth title together in a 14-year partnership, and Biland's fifth.

The sidecars staggered lopsidedly to the eventual conclusion of their abbreviated season, appropriately enough at Assen, a last stronghold of spectator support. After the cancellation of their participation in South Africa and their withdrawal from Brazil, they had flirted with Monza and Brno before settling on just one final round on 13 September, as guests at the World Superbike/European Championship round at Assen.

The final showdown was scheduled for 26 laps of the 3.913-km short circuit, and the situation was tense. Biland had been gaining ground on Webster hand over fist, but the defending Briton still led by the now slender margin of nine points.

Biland had dominated practice, but Webster was comfortably in second; then, on the first bend, Klaffenböck and Biland collided, with the Egloff brothers also involved, and Kumagaya's British passenger, Bryan Houghton, getting unseated in the melee. The Egloffs were out at once, Klaffenböck continued for five laps, then retired with an oil-soaked clutch because of a faulty seal, while the passengerless Kumagaya went on for a while unawares, and was lucky not to flip over on the next left-hander.

Biland was hardly delayed, however, and was soon disputing the lead with Webster and Streuer. Then Webster went missing – he was in the pits, a joint on his gear linkage broken and his championship hopes over. Ironically, he later said, it was a Swiss part that had failed: but he was 'only lending the title' to his victorious Swiss rival.

Biland didn't realise he'd gone, and was going head down in front. He was worried that he was losing pace because, having locked his rear wheel under hard braking, he'd put a flat on the rear tyre. Then he was surprised to be overtaken on the last lap by his Hollywood-sponsored team-mate Egbert Streuer, to claim his first win of a troubled season. Since they had agreed that Streuer wouldn't spoil his title chances, Biland realised that either something had happened to Webster or he'd been double-crossed. It turned out to be the former.

Third went to Dixon, his third rostrum finish and second in succession, pressed to the line by on-form Swiss rider Markus Bösiger, who finished only two-tenths adrift. The pair had outdistanced the Güdel brothers in the process; Ralph Bohnhorst had also been involved, but failed with four laps to go. Derek Brindley was sixth, some way back from this battle.

Thus Biland's late season surge had won him his fifth world title, 14 years after his first one. Webster was second overall, Klaffenböck third, with Streuer moving up to fourth because of his win, and Dixon also promoting himself to take a well-deserved fifth overall. The racing was in good health, even if the class was teetering on the brink.

Photos: Henk Keulemans

The first-lap melee: Klaffenböck (19) has spun, and Bryan Houghton has been knocked out of his chair, to be struck by Barry Brindley/Scott Whiteside (11). He broke his right arm; driver Yoshi Kumagaya continued unawares and almost crashed at the next bend.

Sidecars

26 laps, 63.206 miles/101.738 km

Place	*Driver & passenger*	*Nat.*	*Machine*	*Laps*	*Time & speed*	*Fastest lap*
1	**Egbert Streuer/ Peter Brown**	**NL GB**	**LCR- Stredor**	**26**	**37m 41.18s 100.645 mph/ 161.975 km/h**	**1m 25.73s**
2	**Rolf Biland/ Kurt Waltisperg**	**CH CH**	**LCR- Krauser**	**26**	**37m 41.64s**	**1m 25.55s**
3	**Darren Dixon/ Andy Hetherington**	**GB GB**	**LCR- Krauser**	**26**	**38m 06.04s**	**1m 26.71s**
4	**Markus Bösiger/ Beat Leibundgut**	**CH CH**	**LCR- ADM**	**26**	**38m 06.25s**	**1m 26.83s**
5	**Paul Güdel/ Charly Güdel**	**CH CH**	**LCR- Yamaha**	**26**	**38m 27.18s**	**1m 26.92s**
6	**Derek Brindley/ Paul Hutchinson**	**GB GB**	**LCR- Krauser**	**26**	**38m 39.40s**	**1m 27.37s**
7	**Billy Gällros/ Peter Berglund**	**S S**	**LCR- Streuer**	**26**	**38m 57.54s**	**1m 28.43s**
8	**Theo van Kempen/ Geral de Haas**	**NL NL**	**LCR- Krauser**	**26**	**39m 04.12s**	**1m 28.48s**
9	**Reiner Koster/ Jurg Egli**	**CH CH**	**LCR- Yamaha**	**25**	**37m 44.14s**	**1m 28.47s**
10	**Gary Knight/ Guy Scott**	**GB GB**	**Windle- Krauser**	**25**	**38m 01.38s**	**1m 29.43s**
11	Harry Smit/ Ted de Rijk	NL NL	LCR- Krauser	25	39m 18.45s	1m 31.97s
12	Benny Janssen/ Frans Geurts	NL NL	LCR- Krauser	24	38m 05.13s	1m 33.64s
13	Mark Reddington/ Kim Andreasen	GB DK	LCR- Krauser	24	38m 57.34s	1m 29.69s
14	Tony Baker/ Simon Prior	GB GB	LCR- Krauser	21	38m 00.09s	1m 30.27s
15	Hans Hügli/ Adolf Hänni	CH CH	LCR- Krauser	21	38m 19.19s	1m 30.57s
	Ralph Bohnhorst/ Bruno Hiller	D D	BRM	22	DNF	1m 26.70s
	Robert Fisher/ Trevor Crone	GB GB	LCR- Krauser	21	DNF	1m 29.31s
	Steve Webster/ Gavin Simmons	GB GB	LCR- ADM	20	DNF	1m 25.76s
	Peter Lemstra/ Jan Kuyt	NL NL	LCR- Krauser	10	DNF	1m 34.30s
	Tony Wyssen/ Kilian Wyssen	CH CH	LCR- ADM	8	DNF	1m 28.43s
	Barry Brindley/ Scott Whiteside	GB GB	LCR- Yamaha	7	DNF	1m 27.60s
	Klaus Klaffenböck/ Christian Parzer	A A	LCR- ADM	5	DNF	1m 29.35s
	Markus Egloff/ Urs Egloff	CH CH	LCR- Yamaha	0	DNF	
	Yoshisada Kumagaya/ Bryan Houghton	J GB	LCR- Krauser	0	DNF	
	Jukka Lauslehto/ Jurgen Levinsen	SF DK	LCR- ADM		DNS	

***Fastest lap**:* Biland, 1m 25.55s, 102.316 mph/164.661 km/h (record).
Previous record: Egbert Streuer/Peter Brown, NL/GB (LCR), 1m 26.25s, 101.485 mph/163.325 km/h.

Practice leaderboard: 1 Biland, 1m 24.64s; **2** Webster, 1m 25.36s; **3** Streuer, 1m 25.71s; **4** Bösiger, 1m 26.21s; **5** Egloff, 1m 26.34s; **6** Dixon, 1m 26.34s; **7** Klaffenböck, 1m 26.54s; **8** Güdel, 1m 26.73s; **9** Bohnhorst, 1m 26.77s; **10** Kumagaya, 1m 26.87s; **11** B. Brindley, 1m 27.30s; **12** Lauslehto, 1m 27.55s; **13** Gällros, 1m 28.14s; **14** D. Brindley, 1m 28.21s; **15** Knight, 1m 29.08s.

Final Sidecar World Championship points: see page 181.

WORLD CHAMPIONSHIP RESULTS – 1992

500 cc

Position	Rider	Nationality	Machine	Japan	Australia	Malaysia	Spain	Italy	Europe	Germany	Holland	Hungary	France	Britain	Brazil	South Africa	TOTAL
1	**Wayne Rainey**	USA	Yamaha	–	15	15	15	–	20	–	–	8	20	15	20	12	**140**
2	**Michael Doohan**	AUS	Honda	20	20	20	20	15	15	20	–	–	–	–	–	6	**136**
3	**John Kocinski**	USA	Yamaha	–	–	–	8	12	8	8	15	4	12	–	15	20	**102**
4	**Kevin Schwantz**	USA	Suzuki	12	10	–	10	20	10	15	–	10	–	–	4	8	**99**
5	**Doug Chandler**	USA	Suzuki	15	8	8	1	10	12	3	–	15	–	–	12	10	**94**
6	**Wayne Gardner**	AUS	Honda	–	–	–	–	–	–	12	–	6	15	20	10	15	**78**
7	**Juan Garriga**	E	Yamaha	–	2	10	4	6	1	2	10	3	10	12	–	1	**61**
8	**Alex Criville**	E	Honda	–	4	12	–	3	–	10	20	–	–	–	6	4	**59**
9	**Eddie Lawson**	USA	Cagiva	–	6	–	–	–	6	6	–	20	8	10	–	–	**56**
10	**Randy Mamola**	USA	Yamaha	8	3	4	3	1	2	–	8	12	3	–	1	–	**45**
11	**Niall Mackenzie**	GB	Yamaha	4	–	–	12	2	4	–	4	–	6	–	2	3	**37**
12	**Miguel DuHamel**	CAN	Yamaha	–	1	–	2	4	3	–	6	–	4	4	8	2	**34**
13	**Alexandre Barros**	BR	Cagiva	–	–	–	–	8	–	4	12	2	–	–	3	–	**29**
14=	**Daryl Beattie**	AUS	Honda	–	12	6	–	–	–	–	–	–	–	–	–	–	**18**
14=	**Peter Goddard**	AUS	Yamaha	–	–	3	6	–	–	1	–	–	–	8	–	–	**18**
16	**Shinichi Itoh**	J	Honda	10	–	–	–	–	–	–	–	–	–	–	–	–	**10**
17=	**Keiji Ohishi**	J	Suzuki	6	–	–	–	–	–	–	–	–	–	–	–	–	**6**
17=	**Terry Rymer**	GB	Yamaha	–	–	–	–	–	–	–	–	–	–	6	–	–	**6**
19	**Corrado Catalano**	I	Yamaha	–	–	2	–	–	–	–	3	–	–	–	–	–	**5**
20	**Eddie Laycock**	IRL	Yamaha	–	–	1	–	–	–	–	2	1	–	–	–	–	**4**
21=	**Toshihiko Honma**	J	Yamaha	3	–	–	–	–	–	–	–	–	–	–	–	–	**3**
21=	**Michael Rudroff**	D	Yamaha	–	–	–	–	–	–	–	–	–	–	3	–	–	**3**
23=	**Toshiyuki Arakaki**	J	Yamaha	–	–	–	–	–	–	–	–	–	1	1	–	–	**2**
23=	**Norihiko Fujiwara**	J	Yamaha	2	–	–	–	–	–	–	–	–	–	–	–	–	**2**
23=	**Dominique Sarron**	F	Yamaha	–	–	–	–	–	–	–	–	–	–	2	–	–	**2**
23=	**James Whitham**	GB	Yamaha	–	–	–	–	–	–	–	–	–	2	–	–	–	**2**
27=	**Kevin Mitchell**	GB	Yamaha	–	–	–	–	–	–	–	1	–	–	–	–	–	**1**
27=	**Satoshi Tsujimoto**	J	Honda	1	–	–	–	–	–	–	–	–	–	–	–	–	**1**

250 cc

Position	Rider	Nationality	Machine	Japan	Australia	Malaysia	Spain	Italy	Europe	Germany	Holland	Hungary	France	Britain	Brazil	South Africa	TOTAL
1	**Luca Cadalora**	I	Honda	20	20	20	10	20	20	10	15	20	12	10	20	6	**203**
2	**Loris Reggiani**	I	Aprilia	–	8	–	20	15	15	12	12	15	20	15	12	15	**159**
3	**Pier Francesco Chili**	I	Aprilia	8	–	12	6	–	6	20	20	–	15	20	–	12	**119**
4	**Helmut Bradl**	D	Honda	10	12	–	15	10	10	–	4	6	–	6	6	10	**89**
5	**Massimiliano Biaggi**	I	Aprilia	–	3	–	1	12	12	15	–	–	–	–	15	20	**78**
6	**Alberto Puig**	E	Aprilia	6	–	15	4	6	3	6	10	12	6	–	3	–	**71**
7	**Jochen Schmid**	D	Yamaha	–	–	8	3	–	8	–	6	3	10	8	8	4	**58**
8	**Carlos Cardus**	E	Honda	–	15	10	8	4	–	–	–	–	8	3	–	–	**48**
9	**Masahiro Shimizu**	J	Honda	–	–	3	12	3	–	8	8	10	–	2	–	–	**46**
10	**Doriano Romboni**	I	Honda	–	6	6	–	1	4	–	–	4	–	12	10	–	**43**
11	**Wilco Zeelenberg**	NL	Suzuki	4	10	4	–	8	–	–	–	8	4	–	–	–	**38**
12	**Loris Capirossi**	I	Honda	2	–	2	–	2	–	2	3	–	–	4	4	8	**27**
13	**Tadayuki Okada**	J	Honda	15	–	–	–	–	–	–	–	–	–	–	–	–	**15**
14	**Nobuatsu Aoki**	J	Honda	12	–	–	–	–	–	–	–	–	–	–	–	–	**12**
15	**Herri Torrontegui**	E	Suzuki	–	–	–	–	–	–	3	–	1	3	1	–	3	**11**
16=	**Andy Preining**	A	Aprilia	–	4	–	–	–	–	–	–	–	–	–	1	1	**6**
16=	**Jean-Philippe Ruggia**	F	Gilera	–	2	–	–	–	2	–	–	–	–	–	–	2	**6**
18=	**Carlos Lavado**	YV	Gilera	–	–	–	–	–	–	–	2	2	–	–	–	–	**4**
18=	**Nobuyuki Wakai**	J	Suzuki	–	–	–	–	–	–	4	–	–	–	–	–	–	**4**
20=	**Paolo Casoli**	I	Yamaha	–	1	1	–	–	1	–	–	–	–	–	–	–	**3**
20=	**Kyoji Nanba**	J	Yamaha	3	–	–	–	–	–	–	–	–	–	–	–	–	**3**
22=	**Bernard Hänggeli**	CH	Aprilia	–	–	–	–	–	–	–	–	–	2	–	–	–	**2**
22=	**Stefan Prein**	D	Honda	–	–	–	2	–	–	–	–	–	–	–	–	–	**2**
22=	**Jurgen van den Goorbergh**	NL	Aprilia	–	–	–	–	–	–	–	1	–	1	–	–	–	**2**
22=	**Patrick van den Goorbergh**	NL	Aprilia	–	–	–	–	–	–	–	–	–	–	–	2	–	**2**
26=	**Jean-Pierre Jeandat**	F	Honda	1	–	–	–	–	–	–	–	–	–	–	–	–	**1**
26=	**Bernd Kassner**	D	Aprilia	–	–	–	–	–	–	1	–	–	–	–	–	–	**1**

Malcolm Bryan

125 cc

Position	Rider	Nationality	Machine	Japan	Australia	Malaysia	Spain	Italy	Europe	Germany	Holland	Hungary	France	Britain	Brazil	South Africa	TOTAL
1	**Alessandro Gramigni**	I	Aprilia	6	15	20	–	–	10	4	12	20	8	15	12	12	**134**
2	**Fausto Gresini**	I	Honda	–	8	3	15	8	12	15	15	12	–	20	6	4	**118**
3	**Ralf Waldmann**	D	Honda	20	20	12	20	–	–	12	2	15	1	4	–	6	**112**
4	**Ezio Gianola**	I	Honda	10	2	–	1	20	20	8	20	–	20	–	1	3	**105**
5	**Bruno Casanova**	I	Aprilia	15	12	15	–	3	4	20	1	2	6	8	10	–	**96**
6	**Dirk Raudies**	D	Honda	2	4	8	4	15	8	6	–	–	4	10	20	10	**91**
7	**Jorge Martinez**	E	Honda	–	6	10	2	6	1	–	8	–	12	3	15	20	**83**
8	**Gabriele Debbia**	I	Honda	–	1	4	6	4	15	10	10	8	–	–	–	–	**58**
9	**Noboru Ueda**	J	Honda	–	–	–	–	12	3	–	–	3	15	12	4	8	**57**
10	**Nobuyuki Wakai**	J	Honda	12	10	–	8	1	2	2	–	10	3	1	3	–	**52**
11	**Kazuto Sakata**	J	Honda	–	–	6	10	–	–	–	6	4	10	6	–	–	**42**
12	**Carlos Giro**	E	Aprilia	–	–	–	12	–	6	1	3	–	–	–	2	15	**39**
13	**Hans Spaan**	NL	Aprilia	–	–	2	–	–	–	–	–	6	2	–	–	2	**12**
14	**Peter Öttl**	D	Rotax	–	–	–	–	10	–	–	–	–	–	–	–	–	**10**
15=	**Oliver Koch**	D	Honda	–	3	–	3	2	–	–	–	–	–	–	–	1	**9**
15=	**Oliver Petrucciani**	CH	Honda	1	–	–	–	–	–	–	–	–	–	–	8	–	**9**
17	**Akiro Saitoh**	J	Honda	8	–	–	–	–	–	–	–	–	–	–	–	–	**8**
18=	**Takao Shimizu**	J	Honda	–	–	–	–	–	–	–	4	1	–	–	–	–	**5**
18=	**Kinya Wada**	J	Honda	3	–	–	–	–	–	–	–	–	–	2	–	–	**5**
20	**Yutaka Fujihara**	J	Honda	4	–	–	–	–	–	–	–	–	–	–	–	–	**4**
21	**Stefan Kurfiss**	D	Honda	–	–	–	–	–	–	3	–	–	–	–	–	–	**3**
22	**Heinz Lüthi**	CH	Honda	–	–	1	–	–	–	–	–	–	–	–	–	–	**1**

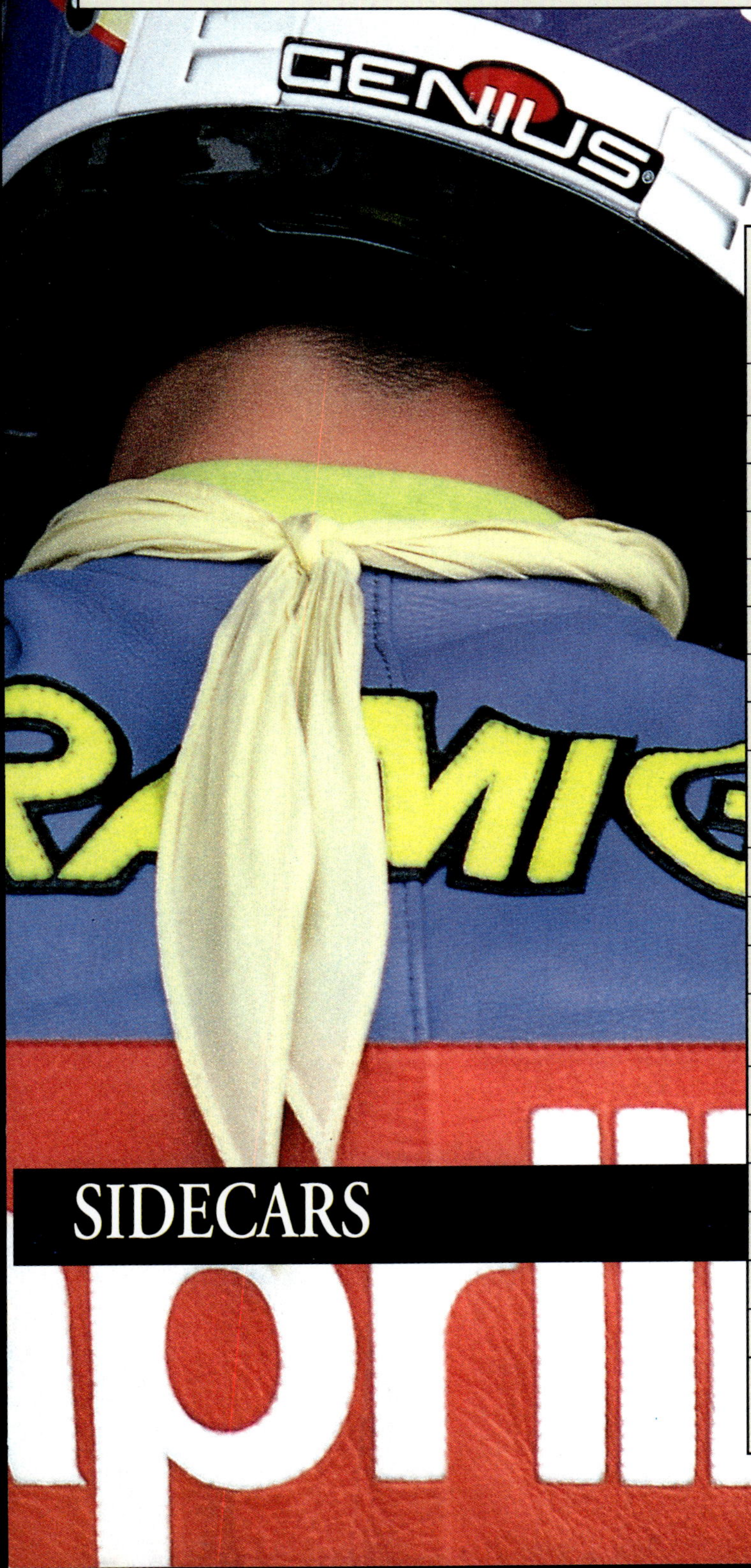

SIDECARS

Position	Driver & Passenger	Nationality	Machine	Spain	Germany	Holland	Hungary	France	Britain	Assen	TOTAL
1	**Rolf Biland/ Kurt Waltisperg**	CH CH	LCR- Krauser	–	3	20	20	20	20	15	**98**
2	**Steve Webster/ Gavin Simmons**	GB GB	LCR- ADM	20	20	15	15	10	12	–	**92**
3	**Klaus Klaffenböck/ Christian Parzer**	A A	LCR- ADM	15	15	12	12	12	–	–	**66**
4	**Egbert Streuer/ Peter Brown**	NL GB	LCR- Stredor	2	–	10	8	15	2	20	**57**
5	**Darren Dixon/ Andy Hetherington**	GB GB	LCR- Krauser	–	12	–	3	–	15	12	**42**
6	**Yoshisada Kumagaya/ Bryan Houghton**	J GB	LCR- Krauser	10	10	1	6	8	4	–	**39**
7	**Paul Güdel/ Charly Güdel**	CH CH	LCR- Yamaha	8	6	6	–	4	6	8	**38**
8	**Ralph Bohnhorst/ Bruno Hiller**	D D	BRM	–	8	8	10	–	10	–	**36**
9	**Markus Bösiger/ Beat Leibundgut Rinie Bettgens Peter Hoss**	CH CH NL CH	LCR- ADM	6	4	–	–	–	1	10	**21**
10	**Barry Brindley/ Scott Whiteside**	GB GB	LCR- Yamaha	12	2	2	–	3	–	–	**19**
11	**Markus Egloff/ Urs Egloff**	CH CH	LCR- Yamaha	3	–	3	2	2	8	–	**18**
12	**Steve Abbott/ Shaun Smith**	GB GB	LCR- Krauser	–	–	4	4	6	–	–	**14**
13	**Derek Brindley/ Nick Roche Paul Hutchinson**	GB GB GB	LCR- Krauser	–	1	–	–	–	3	6	**10**
14=	**Billy Gällros/ Peter Berglund**	S S	LCR- Streuer	–	–	–	–	–	–	4	**4**
14=	**Theo van Kempen/ Geral de Haas**	NL NL	LCR- Krauser	–	–	–	–	1	–	3	**4**
14=	**Tony Wyssen/ Kilian Wyssen**	CH CH	LCR- Yamaha	4	–	–	–	–	–	–	**4**
17	**Reiner Koster/ Jurg Egli**	CH CH	LCR- Yamaha	–	–	–	–	–	–	2	**2**
18=	**Tony Baker/ Simon Prior**	GB GB	LCR- Krauser	1	–	–	–	–	–	–	**1**
18=	**Jukka Lauslehto/ Jurgen Levinsen**	SF DK	LCR- ADM	–	–	–	1	–	–	–	**1**
18=	**Gary Knight/ Guy Scott Malcolm Jackson**	GB GB GB	Windle- Krauser	–	–	–	–	–	–	1	**1**

UNITED STATES ROAD RACING

By PAUL CARRUTHERS

VERY seldom do things turn out as they should, but in 1992 everything went right for Superbike road racing in the United States. Furious battles throughout the field, a host of different winners, four brands of winning motor cycles and the crowning of a worthy champion. Yes, it was a season the AMA can hang its hat on for years to come.

Four men – Scott Russell, Doug Polen, Jamie James and Freddie Spencer – won AMA Superbike Nationals in 1992, riding bikes from Kawasaki, Ducati, Yamaha and Honda. In the end, the fastest of them won the championship – Scott Russell on the Muzzy Kawasaki ZX750R – after a significant season.

It was a year that saw the AMA series take a step forward seriously to distinguish itself as one of the best in the world, and at least reclaim its reputation as the premier series in the US.

There were a few notable occurrences that truly helped the AMA National Championship series reach the next level. The series benefited greatly from a television contract that showed viewers eight of the nine rounds in 16 taped shows. Ironically, the AMA series was also aided by the loss of the United States Grand Prix and the American round of the World Superbike series, which allowed the National Championship to return to two of the country's premier race tracks – Laguna Seca International Raceway and Brainerd International Raceway. It also didn't hurt that World Superbike Champion Doug Polen made a habit of returning home for AMA races that didn't conflict with his World Superbike effort, and that three-times World Champion Freddie Spencer was nearly always a factor in his full season of AMA Superbike racing.

Again, the AMA series attracted the top American teams and riders.

Defending champion Thomas Stevens made an off-season jump to Rob Muzzy's Kawasaki team, joining Russell, and giving Muzzy the top two finishers in the 1991 championship. Polen announced that he would try to win two titles in 1992 on the Fast By Ferracci Ducati – the AMA Superbike National Championship and the World Superbike Championship – and he would be joined on the all-red V-twins by French Canadian Pascal Picotte. Vance & Hines Yamaha had lost their number one plate when Stevens jumped ship, but they held on to Jamie James and elevated young hopeful Larry Schwarzbach to a full-time Superbike ride. Honda's effort was spearheaded by two teams – Martin Adams's Camel-backed squad of former WERA F-USA Champion and Yoshimura Suzuki rider, Mike Smith, and Tom Kipp; and Two Brothers Racing, which boasted the talents of Freddie Spencer and Canadian Steve Crevier. Yoshimura Suzuki, meanwhile, would attempt to salvage one more year out of their archaic GSXR750s with former Daytona 200 winner Dave Sadowski and Supersport standout Britt Turkington. And, unlike years past, the Kawasaki ZX750 was the principal choice of motor cycle for top privateers such as veteran Dale Quarterley.

At season's end it was a deserving Russell who earned his first-ever AMA Superbike National Championship. The Georgian, who now calls Monterey, California, home, won three races, finished second three times, was fifth once and failed to finish two races – one (Mid-Ohio) while leading with only four laps to go. He also sat on pole position for three of the nine races.

The only man who may have been quicker was Polen. The Texan missed two races due to his overseas commitments, but when he was here he was a constant factor: he sat on

Photos: Nigel Kinrade

Left: **Title winner Scott Russell leads Pascal Picotte, Dale Quarterley, James and Smith at Charlotte. James won the race; Quarterley survived this near high-sider to finish fourth.**

World Champion Doug Polen *(below)* contested the US Superbike title when he wasn't busy in Europe, and finished a creditable third in a good year.

pole four times, won three races, finished second twice, placed tenth at Texas World in May (due in part to a wrong tyre choice in wet conditions) and, uncharacteristically, crashed a single time in his seven AMA outings. Despite missing those two races and not scoring in another, he finished the year as the third-ranked rider, missing out on second place in the title chase to Stevens by just two points.

The season-opening 51st running of the Daytona 200 provided a glimpse of things to come: Polen v. Russell; Ducati v. Kawasaki; the fastest qualifier v. the second fastest man; the victor in doubt until the finish.

First blood went to Russell, in the fastest-ever Daytona 200. The Georgian averaged a record 110.669 mph, beating Polen by a scant 0.182 seconds in a race that had it all – except a pace car. Polen looked to have things in hand as the pair exited the second chicane for the 57th and final time, but Russell and the ZX7 were able to draft past the V-twin Ducati, giving Kawasaki its first-ever win in what is still America's most prestigious motor cycle race.

Third place at Daytona went to Mike Smith in his debut ride aboard the Camel Honda RC30. The Georgian wasn't able to match the pace set by Russell and Polen, but he was the best of the rest and the only other rider to stay on the same lap as the lead duo. Remarkably, fourth place was taken by Dave Sadowski, on the dated Yoshimura Suzuki, meaning the first four places were filled by four different brands of motor cycles – Kawasaki, Ducati, Honda and Suzuki. This would be the first but not the only time that four different makes would fill the first four places.

With the demise of the US Grand Prix, the AMA brought their National Championship back to Laguna Seca International Raceway for the first time in four years, and Polen was able to reverse the Daytona decision on Russell. Again, it was close. This time it was Polen who did the stalking, patiently waiting until two laps from the finish to make his move and take the victory. Smith, again, was a surprise, finishing third for a second successive race. Pascal Picotte got the best of Jamie James to finish fourth.

Laguna Seca also marked a first for Freddie Spencer since his return. The former phenomenon not only showed that he could run with the top two until brake fade caused him to run off the track at the infamous Corkscrew, but also that he was prepared to finish races he had no chance of winning. While the Freddie of old may have pulled in and called it a day, the 1992 Spencer model rejoined the race just inside the top twenty and fought his way back up to tenth place.

Charlotte Motor Speedway has been classified by Dunlop tyre technician Jim Allen as the least tyre-friendly race track in the country, and he'd get little argument from Spencer. The Louisianan battled with fellow-Southerner James until Spencer's rear tyre chunked, forcing him out of the race. James, like the majority of the top runners, with the exception of Spencer and privateer Dale Quarterley, was on Dunlops and he and his Yamaha proved both fast and kind to the tyres. James went on to take the victory, his first of the season, ahead of Russell and defending champion Stevens, in his first rostrum position of the year and his first on a Kawasaki. Quarterley was fourth, with Tom Kipp fifth on the second Camel Honda; pole sitter Polen crashed in the makeshift chicane when his front brake lever hit a hay bale.

The last time Spencer had won was in the final race of the 1991 season in Miami. The last time he'd won in the rain was in 1985, at the British Grand Prix at Silverstone. Well, the skies opened up prior to the fourth round of the 1992 AMA series at Texas World Speedway, and Spencer used his rain experi-

Born-again Superbike racer Freddie Spencer *(right)* proved not only that he could still win races, but more importantly that he was prepared to keep trying even when his Two Brothers Honda was outclassed and beaten.

***Below:* Yamaha's best shot came from Jamie James, who won twice and was a close fourth overall.**

Flick of the Wrist

ence and Michelin rain tyres to win his only race of the season. Freddie took control at the drop of the flag and never looked back, ending up some ten seconds clear of Quarterley, who equalled his best-ever National finish by following the three-times World Champion's lead, and riding his Michelin rain-tyre-shod Kawasaki smoothly in the iffy conditions. It is also worth noting that Spencer had qualified on pole – in dry conditions.

Mike Smith looked as though he would catch Spencer, but he crashed on the 14th lap, sliding to a stop in the mud before remounting to finish ninth. Third went to Picotte on the second Ducati, ahead of Kipp and the careful, championship-leading Russell. Polen, with the World Superbike Championship in the back of his mind, and the wrong tyres on his Ducati, rode cautiously to tenth.

Probably the most impressive ride of the season came a race later, and it came from Doug Polen. The Texan blitzed the field at Brainerd International Raceway, beating James by an unheard-of 23.183 seconds in the 60-mile race; third place went to Stevens. Polen had qualified over a second faster than Russell, setting a lap record in the process, and in the race it only got worse for the competition. By the fifth lap Polen was five seconds clear, and he went on to put a second a lap on the field until slowing the pace late in the race. It was fitting that Polen would miss the next two races, due to his World Superbike commitments – he definitely wouldn't be missed by his Stateside rivals!

Attrition played a big role, with points leader Russell and series runner-up Smith failing to score in Minnesota. Russell pitted on the fifth lap with a flat rear tyre, and Smith followed suit two laps later when his Honda RC30 dropped a valve.

Russell turned up the heat in Polen's absence, winning the 100-mile Loudon Classic at New Hampshire International Speedway. Scott won the race – which was split into two legs when riders complained prior to the event that 63 laps around the physically demanding 1.6-mile road course would simply be too much – topping James, Picotte, Spencer and Stevens. As a result, Russell's lead over James grew to 20 points and it appeared that the Georgian was in complete control of the championship that had eluded him by only a handful of points in both 1989 and 1991.

Mike Smith's surprising season came apart at Loudon, the Georgian crashing in the 600 cc Supersport event and breaking his lower leg in two places. He would undergo surgery and not return until the final round of the series.

Thrilling two-rider duels were seen at Daytona and Laguna Seca, and again at the final round of the series in Texas, but at Road America the crowd was entertained by a three- and four-rider battle. Russell, James, Spencer and Stevens raced for nearly the duration at the ultra-fast circuit in central Wisconsin, with James ending up the victor after getting through lapped traffic a little cleaner only laps from the finish. Russell managed to hold off Spencer at the finish line, the pair only 0.516 seconds behind James, with Stevens slowing to fourth after his rear Dunlop suffered a construction failure.

Polen returned for Mid-Ohio, but he was forced to play second fiddle to Russell, who stole pole position away from the World Champion. In the race, Russell looked to have things in hand as he led his rival, but then everything went horribly wrong when the Kawasaki's ignition failed only four laps from the finish. Polen took the win, and Russell's lead over James, who finished fourth, was suddenly only four points with one round remaining. Stevens had his best finish of the season, taking second over third-placed Kipp.

The race, though, was marred by the horrific accident that took the life of 27-year-old Larry Schwarzbach. The Texan was dicing with Crevier for seventh place when he high-sided the Yamaha in the high speed left-hander that leads on to the front straight; Crevier had nowhere to go and Schwarzbach was struck by the fallen Canadian's motor cycle. Crevier was lucky to walk away with only a sore neck; Schwarzbach died two days later from massive head injuries.

Fittingly, the season finale saw another epic Russell v. Polen duel.

Nigel Kinrade

Below: **Colin Edwards II in typical headlong 250 action in the only US class using GP bikes. A novice in 1991, he won the title in 1992 and was the discovery of the year.**

Bottom: **The man who pushed Edwards hardest and most often was Kenny Roberts Jnr, who proved to have talent as well as a famous name.**

Photos: Nigel Kinrade

At the finish, in the series' second visit to Texas World Speedway, only 0.005 seconds separated the two rivals, with Russell taking both the victory and his first-ever AMA Superbike National Championship. Stevens finished third, the Floridian parlaying his consistent finishes into second place in the championship. James, meanwhile, the only real threat to Russell's title going into the final round, suffered a flat front tyre early in the race that dashed his hopes, though he was never really in the thick of the battle up front anyway. Polen's second place gave him third in the title chase, with James earning fourth and Picotte, sixth in Texas, finishing fifth overall.

The young man many feel has the brightest future in AMA road racing is Colin Edwards II. The 18-year-old Texan won five of the nine 250 cc Grand Prix races and captured the championship in the process – not bad considering he was a novice club racer only a season ago. Edwards ended up beating his Southwest Motorsports team-mate Chris D'Aluisio for the title, though it was never really close and he clinched it with a race to spare.

The main competition early in the season came from an 18-year-old with a famous name, Kenny Roberts Jnr, and from former Grand Prix winner Jimmy Filice. Although 'Little Kenny' never won a race, he gave Edwards a tough time at nearly every one. Roberts, though, suffered from too many crashes late in the season and ended his year sitting out the final race after yet another practice crash left him with a fracture in his left hand.

Filice was hindered mostly by his rather slow Camel-backed Honda RS250, while the others had quicker Yamaha TZ250s. Still, the gritty Filice won two races and ended up third in the championship.

Last year WERA's run-what-you-brung Formula USA class had its most successful season, thanks to the presence of Kenny Roberts's Marlboro Yamaha YZR500s in the hands of class champion Rich Oliver and runner-up Robbie Petersen. This season the YZRs were gone, the Marlboro team was disbanded, and Oliver and Petersen headed to the AMA's 250 cc class. Roberts even took his son, Kenny Jnr, to the AMA series and the Wayne Rainey-owned Otsuka Electronics team went with him. Gone, too, was the television package WERA once touted.

What was left was Valvoline Suzuki, and not much else. In the end, the championship was likely to go to Donald Jacks, riding the big-bore Suzuki GSXR. With one round remaining in the series at the time of going to press, Jacks led his team-mate Michael Martin by 18 points. Surprisingly, Chris D'Aluisio was equal fifth in the standings after competing in only a handful of events – on his Yamaha TZ250.

At the end of the season it appeared that Jacks, too, would be another WERA defector, as it looked certain he would join the Yoshimura Suzuki team to contest the 1993 AMA Superbike National Championship.

The F-II series, the counterpart to the AMA's 250 cc Grand Prix series, would certainly be won by F-USA and endurance racing veteran Kurt Hall in his first full season on a Yamaha TZ250. Hall led defending champion Donnie Greene by 14 points heading into the final round.

WORLD SUPERBIKE CHAMPIONSHIP

By JOHAN VANDEKERCKHOVE

Opposite page: **Doug Polen – on target for a second title on the Fast by Ferracci Ducati.**

Many thought Rob Phillis deserved the championship, but after he had lost the points lead things started going downhill for the Australian Kawasaki rider.

STRANGE as it may seem, World Superbike racing was almost more affected by the FIM–IRTA battle for power in Grands Prix than the actual world of two-stroke racers. As the palace revolution hotted up and Bernie Ecclestone and IRTA finally got the better of the FIM, the Italian Flammini Group could only watch and wonder whether the new hierarchy would be favourable to the future development of four-stroke racing.

Things got off to a bad start. When the little man from London finally revealed his Grand Prix calendar to the world, Francis Batta (the man responsible for promoting World Superbikes) had to do his homework all over again. Many previously arranged Superbike dates now clashed with Grand Prix weekends – an unacceptable situation for someone who makes his living out of selling the series to television stations all over the world.

The FIM had also judged it necessary to add a few more events to the original Superbike calendar: Sweden and Czechoslovakia had lost their GPs, and it seemed only a Superbike race could recompense them. Anderstorp was later removed from the calendar for a second time, for reasons of safety and because of the absence of television coverage; and the Most event was cancelled only a few weeks before it should have taken place, after it became apparent during a national German championship meeting that the track did not have adequate drainage during wet races.

Racing has become big business. In these troubled times this fact is often interpreted as 'a product is only as good as its promotion'. In the case of World Superbikes, this is most definitely a wrong assumption, because the racing is intensely exciting (the only equal in Grands Prix this year was the epic 125 contests); the upgraded street bikes sport the most sophisticated racing technology; and the top riders are accessible and approachable, for spectators and journalists alike.

Unfortunately, Flammini Racing has not quite managed to put this message across, working as they do on a shoestring budget and competing for publicity with the all-powerful new Grand Prix formula. Several of the leading teams had had their budgets cut, while many private riders could only finance a limited programme. Even former World Champions did not escape: Raymond Roche survived only because of the 'pocket money' he got from the Castiglione brothers, while Fred Merkel's new Yamaha was remarkably free of sponsor stickers. Riders such as Carl Fogarty and Terry Rymer began their season on private bikes, wondering if they would still be around for the next race, and counting on earning some extra money in World Endurance and national races.

Despite all this, increasing numbers of spectators discovered the joys of World Superbikes, with huge crowds attending the races at Albacete, Donington, Hockenheim, Járama, Zeltweg and Assen. The Flammini Group, however, is still considering changing the format of the races, with some talk about altering the two-heat formula to a single leg (which can be sold more easily to television networks). And now it seems likely that a Superbike weekend might also incorporate a supersport or a singles race in future.

With the politicians industriously searching for a new image to guarantee the World Superbike series its place next to Grands Prix, the 1992 season was also a transitional year from a technical point of view.

Ducati were quite confident that their 888 would come out on top again – especially since the technical regulations remained unchanged, and the new world-beaters from Honda, Kawasaki and Yamaha weren't due to arrive until the end of the year. Pretty soon, however, it became clear that Honda had no Superbike plans for 1993, much to the disappointment of Team Rumi. And, in fact, the Suzuki GSXR750WN was the only really new bike to take part in World Superbike races this year, although unfortunately Suzuki never committed itself to four-stroke racing; it was left to the French, German and British importer teams to keep the flag flying.

This season, though, the bikes were definitely on more equal terms than during the last couple of years. Privateers again had a chance to get on the rostrum, and even to win races. With two rounds left at the time of going to press, no fewer than seven riders have so far claimed a victory, and the championship was led for a few weeks by popular veteran Kawasaki rider Rob Phillis. For a while, it looked as if the FIM had done the right thing in not changing the weight and cylinder capacity rules which had so upset the 'Japanese' teams before. But when the teams congregated Down Under, for the final Australian and New Zealand rounds, it seemed that Ducati was set for an historic one-two-three victory, with only Rob Phillis able to stop the all-conquering red bikes.

Ducati certainly did a fine job when they developed their 888 several seasons ago. At first merely an interesting, although extremely unreliable bike, the Italian twin soon started to dominate World Superbike racing; and with the help of Eraldo Ferracci, it became almost unbeatable in Doug Polen's hands in 1991.

For the technical boys in Bologna, the winter's work became a matter of fine-tuning the winning bike. A new exhaust camshaft was designed, and the stronger clutch now made well-known slow starters like Raymond Roche and Stéphane Mertens forces to be reckoned with when the lights turned green. Throughout the season, the six (!) full factory racers were regularly given new goodies, with test rider Davide Tardozzi the guinea pig. A smaller, lighter fuel pump soon produced problems, but a different exhaust – giving the riders 300 extra revs – gave the desired result.

Basically, this is what Superbike racing is all about: trying to push the envelope, in order to build the experience into the street bikes of the future. And talking about street bikes, Ducati did a fine job with their 30 Corsa-version 888s. These bikes differed from the factory machines mainly in weight (147 kg for the slimmest Corsas as against 142 kg for Polen's Ducati), and proved to be good enough to propel Carl Fogarty to victory at Donington. Nevertheless, it's now becoming clear that the 888 is slowly reaching the end of its racing life: during the course of the season, several factory riders were sidelined with cracked crankcases and broken pistons and connecting rods. Ducati, which already has its next world-beater ready, still wants one more year with the 888, though – in order not to discourage its Japanese rivals?

After 1991's excellent results, however, Kawasaki was not even close to getting discouraged, and victories at Daytona and Albacete seemed to indicate they really did have a chance to take the title. Various sources mentioned an extra 6 or 7 bhp had been found during the winter, but Peter Doyle (manager of the Australian Moving Kawasaki Team) maintained that not too much work had been done on the engine. Different camshafts and exhausts provided more mid-range power, the traditional flaw of the ZXR750R. Chassis-wise, a lot of attention had been paid to making the bike more rigid, with a redesigned (home-made) rear suspension and stiffened steering head. Private bikes, in the hands of Piergiorgio Bontempi, John Reynolds and Terry Rymer, turned out to be very competitive.

Yamaha provided two teams with their A-kit: in the BYRD outfit, Beppe Russo equipped Pirovano's and Merkel's bikes with a dry clutch, special pistons and a modified chassis; and Udo Mark got the same through the German Yamaha importer. Suspension set-up continued to be the biggest headache for the Yamaha riders, but that did not stop them gaining some well-earned rostrum placings and victories.

Honda was a different story altogether. Team Rumi kept their faith with the world's largest motor cycle manufacturer, hoping for better times in 1993. Baldassarre Monti's factory machine was really only a (slightly) updated '91-spec RC30, the bike which had taken Fred Merkel to an unrepresentative eighth place in the point standings. The Italians concentrated on the chassis, bringing the weight down to the 165 kg limit, and on stop-gap solutions in order to cope with the bike's inherent heating problems.

The best Suzuki performances came from Dominique Méliand's SERT team, with Hervé Moineau aboard the new water-cooled GSX-R750WN, though many observers wondered why Suzuki had opted for slingshot carbs instead of the more promising flat-slides. The four-cylinder Suzuki now produces some 136 bhp.

Finally, it became clear in 1992 that Superbike technology is no longer the poor relation of the Grands Prix. At the same time as Aprilia's 250 racers were equipped with what is commonly called a 'semi-automatic' gearchange, identical systems were being used extensively by Doug Polen, Fabrizio Pirovano, Davide Tardozzi and many other teams. Who said that four-stroke racing technology is boring and light-years behind that of the two-strokes?

And then there were the men on

Right: **Roche leads Polen, Mertens and Falappa in a Ducati train. The Italian factory effort was spread to include more riders this year, and their bikes were less dominant as a result.**

Below: **The perennial Italian/Japanese confrontation is a highlight of Superbike racing: Giancarlo Falappa's Ducati holds off New Zealander Aaron Slight's Kawasaki. Each won races during the year.**

Bottom: **One of Carl Fogarty's roles in a busy year was that of race-winning privateer on a Ducati.**

their incredible flying machines. As the season drew to a close, only two riders were really in with a chance of becoming the new World Superbike Champion. Well, new is not really the right word. Both have already proved themselves the world's fastest four-stroke specialists – although that's about the only thing that Doug Polen and Raymond Roche have in common.

Doug Polen is the defending World Champion. Last year he steamrollered the opposition on his way to 17 wins out of 24 starts. This year, things were never going to be that easy. The man from Corinth, Texas, had a disastrous start to the season (by his own high standards), making it to the rostrum only once in the first four races. Doug and Eraldo Ferracci couldn't get the new Ducati really working well, and only when they returned to the set-ups that had proved so successful in 1991 was the Polen roadshow up and rolling.

His first double victory of the year came at Hockenheim but, even so, the championship never seemed to go the way he wanted it to. A clutch problem at Járama caused a first DNF, and there were even races where he did not get to the rostrum because the other guys 'just did not leave enough room on the track to pass them', as Doug said at Zeltweg, after an eventful final battle with Mertens and Falappa. He was still riding his bike as hard and in as masterly a fashion as last year, but this time he wasn't the only rider with the right Dunlop/Ducati package; and Michelin had done an excellent job making up ground lost through their absence in early 1991.

Finally, also, perhaps Ducati had taken too much on their plate – keeping six riders supplied, all year long, with the best technology they had to offer – plus left-overs to the likes of Carl Fogarty and Virginio Ferrari? Whatever the reason, the red rockets from Bologna never seemed as dominant in 1992 as they were the previous year...

With two races to go, the talkative Texan had a slender 16-point lead over Raymond Roche, the 1990 champion. The gritty 35-year-old Frenchman has always been an extreme character. Ebullient after a good race, intractable after a poor result, he had almost as many reasons to grumble as to celebrate this season. He crashed at Francorchamps on cold tyres, at Monza on wet asphalt, and he retired at Zeltweg because of a blown motor – but he claimed victory in five other races along the way. Roche was severely hampered by injury in 1991, but was spared this year. Could he beat Polen when fully fit? Maybe tyres might give him the decisive edge? It certainly became apparent at Monza that Michelins are now very competitive in the wet.

There's one other rider who deserves the title, though – and he's another veteran. Rob Phillis joined World Superbike racing in 1990, and never finished lower than fourth on his factory-supported Kawasaki. For the last couple of years, he has been – with Fabrizio Pirovano – the best man on a Japanese bike in this Ducati-dominated series. This year has been no different, with Rob even leading the championship for a few weeks. But losing the front end dur-

Photos: Kel Edge

ing the first race at Mugello, the 36-year-old Australian not only forfeited the championship lead but also seemed to lose some of his motivation. The season still held some brief moments of glory for Rob – and then he heard, only a few days before the final European round at Monza, that there would probably be no place for him in the official Kawasaki team next year...

This season also marked a real breakthrough for Giancarlo Falappa. The man whose nickname used to be 'Madman' has grown wiser with the years – and after a few big crashes. He is still capable of 'surprising' his fellow-riders with some unconventional racing lines (and they don't really appreciate him for that!), but most were delighted to see the young Italian's double success at Zeltweg – scene of his horrific crash in 1990 – and at Assen, where he won one race.

Fabrizio Pirovano was the only other rider to take at least two victories in 1992. Just like two years ago, he rode his BYRD Yamaha to a double victory on his – wet – home track at Monza. With Falappa a specialist in ultra-fast starts, Piro lined up his usual consistent results, though interrupted more often this year by the troubles of his ageing OW01.

The two remaining European heats were won by Aaron Slight and Carl Fogarty. Slight shook the Superbike establishment by winning the first race of the year at Albacete. (Later on, the gentle New Zealander would spend most of his time behind his team-mate and friend, Rob Phillis.) And Carl Fogarty might be called one of the riders of the year. Aboard his own private Ducati, he showed everybody the way around Donington to take his first World Superbike victory, put in an incredible performance during the British 500 Grand Prix at the same circuit, and won almost everything that is worth winning in the World Endurance Championship. A natural riding talent, the man from Blackburn could prove unbeatable on a really good bike – whatever class of racing he decides to tackle.

Other Superbike riders worth mentioning include Stéphane Mertens, Piergiorgio Bontempi and Scott Russell.

The Belgian has never been out of the top four since the Superbike World Championship began, but he had a terrible year in 1992: he never got his factory Ducati properly dialled in, and he never seemed to display the eagerness that had earned him a victory over Polen in 1991.

Private Kawasaki rider Piergiorgio Bontempi went faster as the season drew to an end. Excellent at Assen, he grabbed the headlines at Monza. Travelling across gravel traps if need be, he rode his ZXR750R to fourth and third places, making the top ten in the points standings, at the expense of Scott Russell.

The lanky Georgian had come to Europe with the firm intention of giving champion Doug Polen another beating – as he had done at Daytona at the beginning of the year. Russell made a big impression on the World Superbike scene, but also made some mistakes on his way to three rostrum places in eight starts. After the Belgian round, he went unwillingly back to the States, where he became AMA Superbike Champion for the first time. Scott is determined to come back to World Superbikes in 1993, though – on the new Kawasaki and ready to take on the Ducatis for a second time.

Arai
MICHELIN
Phillip McCallen
9
MICHELIN

ISLE OF MAN TT RACES

Phillip McCallen, eyes focused way ahead down the road, took his first TT win in the F1, and another later in the week.

SPECTATOR figures are still going up at the TT while racing entries and prize money are still going down. The situation is worrying because there's a distinct lack of new talent coming through the ranks and a lot of the old experts and crowd favourites are thinking of calling it a day. That the last of the great road races will survive is not in doubt – but it desperately needs to attract new blood, and especially some new overseas competitors.

British racing is in a mess anyway. That a rider of the calibre of Carl Fogarty should find himself forced to ride at the TT because the money is at least better than it is on the mainland amounts to a shameful indictment of the national scene.

The stars of the last three years, Fogarty and Steve Hislop, say they won't be back. But they certainly left their mark this year, in a glorious swansong display of high speed, closed roads racing. The fact that there were no works RVFs around and everybody was on fairly equal machinery made it the toughest, hardest TT for years. The 226-mile Senior, in particular, will be remembered as one of the greatest TT races of all time.

While the racers continue to feel the chill of recession – it is horrendously expensive to compete there – the spectators are busy having the time of their lives. Being there, doing it and enjoying the crack are about all the motivation any of them needs.

And the TT continues to attract all kinds of people, too. Veteran Radio 1 DJ, John Peel, is a recent convert and a non-biker but in two visits has become one of the Island's biggest fans. He explained its timeless appeal well. 'Most things in life', he said, 'turn out to be not quite as good as you expect them to be. But the TT is that rare and curious thing, it is much, much better than you could ever reasonably hope for ... and it's *all* free.'

PRACTICE

The whole of practice week was strangely muted. The weather didn't help, but most of the speeds were down as well. The main attractions, Steve Hislop and Carl Fogarty, were setting up new bikes they hadn't ridden before – Hislop was on a leased Norton rotary while Fogarty had switched to a Loctite Yamaha OW01. Other teams were more familiar – Honda still had Joey Dunlop, Phillip McCallen and Nick Jefferies. Norton had Robert Dunlop. Yamaha had recruited Brian Reid and Mark Farmer. And, of course, Suzuki and Kawasaki weren't there.

Even between the shower bursts, practice week lacked atmosphere. There was none of the usual sense of mounting excitement as race week approached. And there was little sign that the miserable weather was about to break. But it did ... race week weather was glorious, the sun shone and the races were all absolute belters.

FORMULA ONE

The Kings of the Mountain Road assembled in the sunny paddock for the first race of the 1992 TT. Conditions were perfect – the roads were dry and 40,000 spectators lined the course, eagerly anticipating the six-lap, 226-mile drama that was about to unfold.

On the first lap it took until Ramsey to separate Fogarty from McCallen on corrected time but, by the Grandstand, Carl had forged a ten-second advantage by piling on the speed over his favourite section – the ascent and descent of Snaefell Mountain. Leading on the road as well as on the clock, he now piled on the coals around the rest of the course.

By the first pit stop he was 23 seconds ahead, with opening laps of 121 and 122 mph. McCallen, Hislop, Joey Dunlop and Nick Jefferies all lapped above 120 mph but couldn't match Fogarty's ferocious pace. This was his game plan – high early stakes and speeds. He was making ten seconds a lap on the field and looking to increase it further. It was a hard, sustained charge.

Robert Dunlop's Norton had already seized at Kirk Michael so, during Hislop's pit stop, the mechanics tore off the front mudguard to allow more air through to the twin rotors. That cost him 40 seconds – and he was losing more time on the course just trying to control Norton's missile. 'Race speed is very different to practice speed,' he explained. 'The Norton has no engine braking. It runs on even when the throttle's shut, so it drags you into corners and you end up running wide.'

Fogarty had the race in the bag. By the end of the fourth lap and the second refuel he was over 40 seconds ahead and in cruise control mode. He'd finally switched off the aggression and quit trying to increase the gap between every signal board; he was content just to see it stay the same. But during what should have been the formality of the fifth-lap climb up the Mountain, the Yamaha's gearbox broke at the Bungalow and that was that. 'I changed down to second and there was this horrible noise and no drive.' He had led for 180 miles.

Fogarty's unlucky departure handed the race to McCallen. The man from Portadown had been consistent and steady, and he fully deserved his first TT victory which he sealed with a big final lap of 122.5 mph. He won the race by 12 seconds but had to get a move on because Hislop was on a roll, rocketing around at the death, making up for lost time hand over clenched fist, and plainly inspired by news of Fogarty's retirement.

Hislop's last lap (the only flying lap of the race) was an almighty 123.30 mph, a mere 1.6 seconds outside his own outright lap record set on Honda's factory bike, the RVF. Not bad for an old Norton conceived in a garage, eh?

Joey Dunlop was third, having held onto his Honda's gas tank with his knees after the mounts had snapped early on. Nick Jefferies was a worthy fourth, with Yamaha's Mark Farmer a fine fifth. It was Honda's 11th consecutive TT Formula One victory.

Sadly, an Austrian competitor, Manfred Stengl, died after a fifth-lap crash at the 33rd Milestone. Competing in his tenth TT, he was lying last in the race at the time.

SUPERSPORT 400

Delayed by half an hour because of drifting fog, Monday morning's 400 race was run concurrently with the 125s and, as a spectacle, rather strangely fell under the shadow of the smaller bikes, albeit for one rather special reason (see below).

Shortly after dawn on the opening day of practice (i.e. 5.15 on Monday morning, when even Manx flies are still dreaming), Carl Fogarty sauntered out on his Yamaha FZR400 for a few exploratory laps around a course he hadn't seen in a year. He promptly sliced 24 seconds off Dave Leach's class lap record. It was a time and speed that were never bettered all week. The top eight riders lapped above 107 mph, though, so all the 400 cc records were sure to be savaged.

Yamaha's very pretty and expensive miniature, the fully acronymed FZR400RR SP was the machine of choice (even Steve Hislop rode one). Honda's VFR400 is a lovely, jewel-like sports roadster but it hasn't quite got the 16,000 rpm top end legs of the Yamaha. There were a handful of 250 cc two-stroke Suzukis and Kawasakis entered, but while they must have been sheer delight to pilot through the twisty, leafy sections of the course, they had no chance on top speed over the Mountain and were effectively a lost cause.

The four-lap race was flagged away in far from ideal conditions. Swirling, fast-moving mists obscured much of the racing line over the Mountain on the first lap and lots of frustrated riders found themselves backing off a bit. Not so the committed course experts, who hurtled head first and flat out into corners they couldn't even see the entrance to, let alone the exit. One of the most experienced TT riders of them all, Brian Reid, led the race from start to finish, piling on the early speed where others feared for their tread.

The 36-year-old Ulsterman, twice a TT winner before and a former Formula Two World Champion, had fully recovered from a horrible crash in the Junior last year, when his Yamaha's rear suspension had collapsed in the middle of Handley's Bends. At the time it was widely thought, even by Reid, that he would never race again. But with recovery came self-knowledge. 'I didn't want to end a 16-year racing career with a bad crash. As soon as I was fit I made a decision to race the TT again and approached Mitsui Yamaha for some bikes. I know all about good luck and bad luck on the Island but to me the TT is still the greatest race.'

Reid gave Yamaha their 100th TT victory in a faultless display, riding like a man reborn, reeling in the years and rolling away from his pursuers. He won by 55 seconds and set

By JOHN CUTTS

Two Plus Two

Giant TT talent, tiny bike – Joey Dunlop took his 14th win on his 125 Honda, equalling Hailwood's record.

a new 112.27 mph record lap.

McCallen followed him home, getting the best out of a Honda motor that had lost its edge and wouldn't pull top gear on the last lap. Fogarty challenged early on but had blown the engine by Hillberry, at the end of the second lap. Hislop was never in the hunt and retired early with front suspension 'wash-out' problems. Steve Linsdell (FZR) had but one signalling board and was a surprised and delighted third, with Nick Jefferies (VFR) fourth.

It's in the nature of TT racing that you always keep an eye and a stopwatch on the leaders. But soon after the crowds had watched the first six or so 400 cc riders comfortably through, all eyes were focused for the first sight of the fast-approaching 125s...

ULTRA LIGHTWEIGHT 125

With the top 12 riders lapping at over 100 mph in practice, the 151-mile race for single-cylinder two-stroke race bikes promised to be a bit special. The machines may be small but, as many a Supersport 400 back-marker discovered, they're not exactly slow, even in a straight line. Mastery of a racing 125 makes for the sternest test of riding ability – you have to squeeze the speed out of them. Maximum momentum is everything. Drop out of the tiny powerband or lift your head above the screen and you've lost.

Every bike entered was a Honda and it was every man for himself, tucked in, moulded flat to the bike and flat out against the clock and the course. (Actually one rather striking Italian lady named Francesca Giordano entered an Aprilia but failed to qualify.) And it was Yer Maun Himself, one Joey Dunlop MBE, 40-year-old Ballymoney publican and people's hero, who everyone wanted to win.

The years are running out for Joey. No matter how prodigious his TT talent, he's always likely to find one or two younger, hungrier riders too good for him on the F1 bikes these days. The 125 race was his best chance of equalling Mike Hailwood's all-time record of 14 TT wins. He'd been in exactly the same position last year but lost the race to his younger brother Robert after a bungled fuel stop.

Robert Dunlop has dominated the class ever since its reintroduction in 1989, winning all three races and setting all the lap records. He topped the leaderboard again this year with 104.2 mph and was due to start some 50 seconds ahead of Joey. Both would be setting off only a minute or so behind the last of the 400s and would soon be in the thick of the stragglers.

On corrected time, Joey led from the off and had accrued a seven-second lead by Glen Helen on the second lap. Robert cut that back to zero by the end of the lap and, as they pitted for the half-distance refuel, there was nothing between them: they were 50 seconds apart on the road but dead level in the race. Time lost in refuelling would be crucial and Robert squandered a handful of seconds when his bike failed to run back into life first time. It had been running a tad rich and took one expensive cough to clear its throat.

There was to be no brotherly surrender over the remaining 75 miles. Way ahead of the field, the brothers in arms raced each other and the clock, pushing harder and at higher speed all the way. Robert had been the quicker on the second lap but Joey used the precious seconds granted him by the pit stop to try and hammer home the advantage. He led by seven seconds at the end of the third lap, not quite enough to be safe, so he gave it everything on the last lap, defying the Mountain's winds to register a record 108.69 mph. Robert ran 108 mph on the last as well but lost by 8.4 seconds *and* saw his race record reduced by well over two minutes. Yer Maun had done it, and in indefatigable style. It was a performance fully worthy of equalling Hailwood's all-time record. The great man himself would've approved.

Mick Lofthouse was a steady third, albeit over two minutes behind the younger Dunlop. He said he regarded it as an honour to be sharing the rostrum with the pair of them. In sixth spot was Dennis McCullough, who averaged 102 mph over the distance with a best lap just short of 105 mph, which was some feat since it was his TT debut. For his gutsy performance he rightly won the Newcomer's Award.

Joey Dunlop revealed afterwards that he'd been fasting for two weeks before the race and had lost over a stone. 'Robert's a lot lighter than me and I needed every possible advantage. It was a hard race. The lap times are higher and closer than I thought possible.'

At the prize-giving, this quiet, unassuming figure who kept insisting that he was very pleased to win but that the record wasn't really that important, received a solid five-minute standing ovation from the 3000-strong crowd. There was barely a dry eye in the house. There were certainly no dry throats.

SIDECARS

Against the odds, sidecar racing is flourishing on the Isle of Man. The two races attracted the highest entry of the week (bar the non-competitive Classic Parade), with 76 heroic crews assembling for what must be the ultimate challenge for driver and passenger alike. That the three-wheelers are more of a thrill for the competitors than the spectators can't detract from the fact that, on the Island at least, the outfits are thriving.

There are still an awful lot of retirements, but standards of machine preparation have come on in leaps and bounds since F2 rules were introduced in 1990, and lap speeds have increased accordingly. The Formula Two specification (for 350 cc two-strokes and 600 cc four-strokes) clearly works and is still developing. The 350s dominate mainland short circuit racing, but their days are numbered around the TT course. Over the bumps and the distance, the four-stroke 600s have firmly come of age.

Roughly half the field, though, still subscribe to the idea that a tiny TZ350 engine is capable of propelling two adults and a necessarily heavy duty chassis around 113 miles of the Mountain Road Course at 100 mph – believing that the TZ is, after all, a lightweight racing engine. The other half are running various 600 cc four-stroke production roadster motors tuned variously for torque or top end according to how fast the driver believes he can lap the circuit. All the sidecar teams work long and hard fettling their outfits, as much in ritual as in thoroughness. But the four-stroke runners save hours in engine preparation time, the idea of 'leaving it well alone if it's running right' being no longer completely foreign to them.

Nine-times TT winner Mick Boddice was one of the first to abandon the two-stroke faith and he won both of last year's races with Honda CBR600 power. Another nine-times

Gently aviating passenger Keith Cornbill, double winner Geoff Bell's 600 Yamaha outfit clocked three laps at more than 100 mph, and won both heats of the sidecar race.

winner, Dave Saville, had been injured last year but was back with his trusty lap-record-holding Yamaha 350 for what promised to be a bit of a showdown. If either driver could secure a tenth victory, he would become the most successful TT sidecar racer of all time. (Siggi Schauzu scored nine outfit wins between 1967 and 1975.)

Three crews managed over 100 mph in practice, with Boddice/Wells and Saville/Roche behind the leading FZR600 outfit of Geoff Bell and Keith Cornbill. They ran at 101.4 mph, unofficially bettering the record.

True to practice form, Bell/Cornbill won both races. They won the first leg by over half a minute from Eddy Wright/Peter Hill (Honda 600) after Saville had retired at Alpine Cottage on the second lap with a wayward ignition and Boddice had to nurse home his overheating Honda from half-distance, just hanging on to third place. Bell said afterwards: 'I rode like an old woman on the first lap and didn't feel safe until we reached Ramsey. On the second lap I went a bit potty.' He did too, raising the lap record to 102.54 mph and the race record to 101.50 mph.

Monday's second leg was easier for Bell/Cornbill who led throughout and dictated from the front with three 101 mph laps. 'My only moment', said Bell, 'was when I clipped Keith's backside on the bank at Ginger Hall and tore his leathers.'

Boddice was second, having cured his overheating problems. He said he'd never ridden so hard and graciously admitted he'd been beaten by a better crew.

In addition to those mentioned above, Dave Molyneaux/Karl Ellison (600 Kawasaki) joined the ton-up club with two laps *en route* to third in the second race; and Terrie Salone, passenger to Neil Smith, became the first lady to lap above 100 mph in an F2 outfit (350 Yamaha), the pairing finishing fourth in both races.

A special mention should go to TT debutants, the Australians Gavin Porteous and Jeff Spencer, who scored two ninths with their Kawasaki 600 and impressed everyone with their enthusiasm. They'd arrived well before practice week as part of their familiarisation campaign, had gone so well in practice that the ACU changed their starting number from 70 (serious traffic problems) to 8 – and they sure knew how to party.

Norton ended years of Japanese domination with their first Senior win since 1961. Steve Hislop's victory on the new Norton Wankel revived happy memories.

JUNIOR TT

The Junior four-lap race for two-stroke twins continues to be the most fascinating of contests – real racing bikes on slicks going for it over a decent distance. It's a shame that not everybody can afford this year's Yamaha TZ or Honda RS but, well ... that's racing! And there are plenty of well-sorted, fairly trusty 250s out there.

A dozen men were capable of lapping above 112 mph, maybe half of them above 115, and, barring retirement, one of them would win. Would it be Ian Lougher, whose 1990 lap record of 117.8 mph was looking freakishly fast since they'd changed the fuel rules? Or one of the Dunlops again? Or Hislop, who headed the leaderboard at 116 mph and who has led and lost this race so many times? Or a pale horse, wily old campaigner like Brian Reid or Johnny Rea – or even Ian Newton on his £30,000 GP-spec Aprilia?

Running a profitable book on the 250 race would be easy since, whoever wins, it's a certainty that the favourite, Hislop, has a Junior jinx and will lose. It happened again this year.

Hislop didn't exactly snatch defeat from the jaws of victory since Brian Reid led throughout. Both Yamaha mounted, the pair staged a thrilling dice. The gap was never more than a dozen seconds and the last two laps were belters, with Hislop remorselessly shaving away the seconds and Reid riding a 250 down the Mountain faster than any 250 rider has ever dared to.

It was Reid's early charge and, again, Hislop's kind of lacklustre (for him) opening lap that set a gap Steve was doomed always to be chasing. Ian Newton's expensive Aprilia had embarrassingly expired by Quarter Bridge on the first lap. Reid set off 2m 20s ahead of Hislop and was 2m 30s ahead on the road at the end of the first lap. Joey was gone with a broken gearshift on lap two but Robert Dunlop was a clear third, lapping at 115.7 mph.

With smooth refuels for the leaders, Reid saw his ten-second advantage nibbled at by Hislop throughout the third lap, and he fought back accordingly. The gap was eight seconds going into the last, a mere four by Glen Helen and nothing by Ramsey. By the final commentary point Hislop was fractionally ahead.

There remained the race over the Mountain and whatever really happened up there, one thing is certain. Reid rode like fury down the Mountain. He got a minus signal at Windy Corner and his sheer speed over the last five miles through Kate's, the Creg, Brandish, Hillberry and Signpost was wondrous to behold. He crossed the line first and had to wait an agonising 2m 20s before learning he'd won by three seconds. Hislop was more than gutted on being told he'd lost it. He was devastated. He'd given it everything, yet he hadn't won.

Both riders flew that final lap at 250 cc speeds the Island hasn't seen for a while – Reid at 117, Hislop quicker still at 117.51 mph. Hislop said afterwards he'd had a big slide at Kepple Gate after going in too hard, too deep and he'd brushed the bank. Maybe that had lost him the race, he said. And in truth, maybe it had.

Robert Dunlop was third, nearly a minute behind the victory battle. Steve Johnson was fourth with an excellent best lap of 115 mph and some good ol' boys like Ian Lougher, Bob Jackson, Bob Heath and Steve Williams filled the places.

SUPERSPORT 600

The most exciting class in motor cycling doesn't often make for the most exciting TT race since there are currently only two machine contenders – Honda's CBR and Yamaha's FZR – and in the manner of all Japanese production roadsters they whistle rather than roar. They do fair whistle along on their street-legal tyres, though.

Before the race, Steve Hislop and Honda were the lap record holders at a fair old 115.6 mph and this time around he raised it to an almighty 117.01 mph or 19m 20.8s for a lap on over-the-counter Metzeler tyres on a pretty highly tuned Magic Wheels CBR. That's an incredible time for a hot street bike on street rubber. And it gives the spectators and roadster owners something they can really identify with, as well as providing a useful yardstick measure of Hislop's outstanding TT ability. That 117 mph lap was but a handful of seconds slower than the Junior 250 runners shod with slicks.

But Hislop didn't win, Phillip McCallen did. For reasons he didn't care to discuss, Hislop didn't get going or dialled in until after the half-distance pit stop. 'I didn't realise how slow I was until I got a board saying I was fifth,' he said.

Over the last two laps, he flew. But he had no chance of catching Phil McCallen who had been flying from the off with two 116 mph laps, putting him 30 seconds ahead of the field by the gas stop.

Having guessed at the suspension settings, McCallen's CBR was all over the place. Out of shape, with the wheels out of line, the deciding factor was that the tyres were only rarely both in contact with the road at the same time because he never shut off. 'After the disappointment of breaking down in the Junior this morning I was very determined and I wasn't gonna lose that race.'

The 14-times Irish Champion sliced 31 seconds off the race record on his way to a TT double. Hislop's many boards around the course told him he'd left his charge too late, though he cut a 42-second deficit to 20 seconds at the flag with his storming 117 mph last lap. McCallen, of course, did the opposite. The cushion was considerable and, having done the hard work early, he could cruise and defend it. 'I knew Hislop would have to do a 120 mph lap to catch me. I enjoy the 600 but it's just a crazy production bike. I was nursing it on the last. I was afraid I'd been too hard on it and it was gonna blow up.'

Hislop, meanwhile, was left to ponder his third runner-up spot of the week. In all three he'd set the fastest lap but that was proving little consolation. 'I don't want to even talk about the 600 race. I'm beginning to think I'm riding too many bikes.'

The leading pair were way ahead of third man Steve Ward who was followed by Nick Jefferies and Bob Jackson (all Honda). And apart from the sheer, dazzling speed of Hislop and McCallen, it was a pretty uneventful and unevocative race.

Perhaps the highest drama came afterwards when McCallen's Honda was found to contain illegal, excessively leaded fuel. A three-man jury allowed the result to stand but not before one of them had resigned in protest. The situation rapidly degen-

Nigel Kinrade

erated into farce when Honda team manager, Neil Tuxworth, appeared brandishing petrol coupons and receipts while claiming that the ACU's official unleaded fuel source had contaminated delivery pipes. All the ACU and race officials declined to discuss the matter further in a bold, tight-lipped 'no comment' display of disunity. The question of whether unleaded has changed its dictionary definition isn't as interesting as the fact that everybody uses Avgas and octane boosters anyway – and everybody knows they use it.

One final point. The likes of Hislop and Fogarty are always saying that the 750s are too fast for the Island and that 600 cc should be the maximum size. Yet it's the 600 roadsters that all the top men moan about and berate as being the most difficult bikes to set up because of their inherent, imperfect handling.

Still, the spectators and the manufacturers like Supersport racing and, for the record, Honda took eight of the ten available silver replicas. The first Yamaha home was Johnny Rea in sixth. No other make of machine finished.

SENIOR TT

The final race was billed as the ultimate showdown between Hislop and Fogarty. And it was. The lap-by-lap details are too numerous and varied to list here, so let's just say it was a prolonged personal vendetta and an epic duel in bright sunshine between the two fastest men the Isle of Man has ever known in the fastest race ever recorded. It was probably the most exciting race since Hailwood's famous dice with Agostini, 25 years ago in 1967.

Hislop wanted to leave his mark. Norton had spent the week modifying the bike to suit him better – and a spectator had pointed out that he was trying too hard early on in each race and was going slower as a result. 'He was right,' said Hislop. 'This time I was determined to relax more and concentrate on getting a smooth, flowing rhythm.'

Fogarty was out for revenge, pure and simple. He needed no race plan or new tactics. He was just going to go as fast as possible and see what developed. 'I'll be bloody hard to beat,' he said.

They both had opening laps of 121 mph (and so did Robert Dunlop on the other Norton). On the second, Hislop ran over 123, Fogarty a mere 122 ... and so it went on, tooth and claw all the way.

They never saw each other on the road, yet they swapped the lead half a dozen times and the gap was never bigger than eight seconds.

Robert Dunlop was always holding third and had two laps at 121 mph. Nick Jefferies did much the same and was a steady fourth. Mark Farmer's second lap put him into the exclusive 120 mph-plus club (of which there are only nine members). He would finish fifth, but Joey Dunlop and Phil McCallen retired. They were all but bit players in the all-action drama that was exploding up ahead of them.

Fogarty had predicted that if it was close going into the sixth and final lap, then the outright lap record might fall. In fact it fell twice. Hislop raised his own outright course record on the Norton but Fogarty went a shade quicker still at a searing 123.61 mph or 18m 18.8s. Hislop and Norton got the win, though, by 4.4 seconds after 226 miles of sizzling spectacle. Norton also scored the distinction of setting the fastest six-lap race average ever, at 121.28 mph.

It was Norton's first TT win since 1973 and their first victory in the Senior since 1961 and a chap called Hailwood. Norton team manager Barry Symmons said the greatest pleasure of all was in beating the mighty Japanese factories with a British machine built on a shoestring. He agreed that those who had witnessed the 1992 Senior TT would probably cherish the memory of it for ever.

WORLD ENDURANCE CHAMPIONSHIP

Kenny P.

TWO underdog Britons and a pair of factory Kawasakis injected much-needed life into the 1992 World Endurance Championship. With the series still struggling to maintain credibility as a full-blown world championship, the world-beating Kawasaki ZXR-7s more than made up for the no-show of HRC's RVF750s in the only remaining international series for factory Formula One-spec four-strokes.

Kawasaki France proved the saviour of the class, scraping together sufficient funds to run two ZXRs in the series – and hire top riders to pilot them. Team boss Christian Bourgeois took unprecedented flak from the partisan French press as he splashed out on a trio of British riders to join world champ Alex Vieira. He teamed TT hero Steve Hislop – robbed of the 1991 world endurance crown by political pressure and lack of interest from Honda – with veteran Vieira. And, as a back-up, he hired endurance debutants Terry Rymer and Carl Fogarty on the number two machine. Determined riding and calculated aggression by relative youngsters Rymer and Fogarty proved the old hands didn't hold any advantage in the oddball world of through-the-night competition.

Nobody doubted the speed of either of the young gun Brits. But Fogarty's unfairly earned reputation as a crasher had critics writing him off before the first race – and with both men used to putting their machinery through punishing, intense, short-circuit scratching races, the reliability of the second Kawasaki team was always suspect.

Luck, good judgement, a professional team and mature riding saw Rymer and Fogarty win all three of the 24-hour races on the six-round calendar. And with each of the 24-hour marathons offering double points for the winner, the pair had cleared off to a virtually insurmountable points lead after only four rounds.

Reeling at the prospect of adding another world title to his existing three world F1 accolades, Fogarty said: 'They all wrote us off. They said we were too inexperienced, too young and too likely to crash. But we did it. We showed them.'

The opening round at Le Mans made headlines throughout the world – for all the wrong reasons. More than 70,000 boozed-up bikers partied their way through the weekend but spoiled the fun by taking to the roads and terrifying the locals. Alcohol-related road accidents and skirmishes with the police left an astounding 11 dead and 54 injured.

As French politicians scratched their heads to establish the reasons for the carnage and to cope with its aftermath, the race teams inside the impressive Le Mans race track rode on, blissfully unaware of events in the outside world. None more so than Fogarty and Rymer, who scorched to a win in their first-ever endurance race, courtesy of a mechanical failure by team-mates Vieira and Hislop.

Vieira, Hislop and third team man, Jean-Louis Battistini, swapped the lead with Fogarty, Rymer and Michel Simul in an exciting battle. Even the added danger of darkness couldn't stop Hislop shattering the lap record as the team eased ahead. 'I need a check-up, from the neck-up,' quipped Hislop. 'We were smokin' 'em, boy.' But their excitement turned to despair as a cam-chain failed and they were suddenly out. Vieira, close to tears at losing, said: 'It's all finished. It's bad for the team, mechanics and riders.'

Fogarty, fresh from a World Superbike win a week earlier, had meanwhile inherited the lead. After being last away when the Blackburn-based rider fluffed the start, the predominantly British team suddenly found themselves with a five-lap buffer in front of the Suzuki team of Christian Lavieille, Hervé Moineau and Michel Graziano. And with carefully timed pit stops, the Anglo-French Kawasaki boys maintained their lead until the predictable track invasion caused an early end to the race after just 23 hours.

Ashen-faced and distant after his first-ever taste of long-distance racing, Rymer said: 'It was hell. I'm glad it's all over.'

After holding an initial lead, Moineau crossed the line runner-up, giving an almost dream debut to their all-new water-cooled Suzuki GSX-R750. Only a loose exhaust, which enforced an extended nine-minute pit stop, robbed them of the win. 'I had to stop as I was scared of breaking the engine,' he said.

By ADAM DUCKWORTH

Adam Duckworth

Left: **Britain's top domestic riders were supported by France, and won the world championship. This is Carl Fogarty *en route* to victory in the Bol d'Or.**

Daryl Beattie *(right)* shared the works Honda at Suzuka with Wayne Gardner for his first classic Eight Hour victory.

Bottom: **Terry Rymer, Jehan d'Orgeix and Carl Fogarty share their golden bowl.**

The Suzuki team were even unluckier when it came to round two, at Spa-Francorchamps in Belgium. Moineau – this time teamed with Lavieille and Patrick Igoa – challenged Fogarty, Rymer and Jehan d'Orgeix for the lead for an astounding 22 hours, with the lead switching no less than eight times. The Brits were clearly faster but were hindered by poor pit stops. In one botched stop, Kawasaki mechanics had to remove the fairing after they knocked the chain off the gearbox sprocket. Another stop saw them splash fuel in Fogarty's eyes, blinding him for almost a minute. Fast refuelling helped the Suzuki remain in contention. But the GSX-R bid ended when Moineau, aiming to reduce a 52-second deficit, crashed at the 150 mph Blanchimont left-hander after his always suspect engine blew up – and the crash almost ended Fogarty's race on the following lap when he came within inches of slamming into the pace car after sliding on the Suzuki's dropped oil.

Fogarty, who also broke the little finger of his right hand when he clipped a ridiculously dangerous, foot-high corner post during the race, said: 'I thought I'd had it when I hit that oil. There were no warning flags and I was sliding towards the pace car, flat out in sixth gear.' Carl survived, though, and even an extra stop to mend a broken gear lever couldn't reduce their margin at the front over battered Kawasaki teammates Vieira, Hislop and Battistini. Rymer crossed the line side by side with Hislop – who was eight full laps back – to claim a perfect win.

Terry said later: 'That was one of the hardest races I've ever had. We were lapping at World Superbike pace for 23 hours.'

Runner-up spot was a dream come true for Hislop, who thought he'd lost it all when he had a frightening 140 mph spill in a sudden rainstorm. Trying to squeeze in an extra lap on slicks before pitting to change to wets, Steve lost the rear end and slammed into the Armco. 'Well scary,' he said, happy to be uninjured.

Yamaha's factory-assisted OW01 came in third after a trouble-free race, courtesy of Philippe Monneret, Bruno Bonhuil and Jean-Michel Mattioli. And the French Suzuki team of Mario DuHamel, Michel Simeon and Michel Graziano – now suddenly runners-up in the series – came home fourth.

The world championship then converged on Suzuka, Japan, for the all-important Eight Hour race – and the European teams failed to score. It's been called the world's most important motor cycle race, as it's where all the top Japanese factories field their newest, most exotic bikes and their top GP and World Superbike riders – and all in their own back yard.

Temperatures soaring into the nineties and 90 per cent humidity wreaked havoc on the few Euro teams that made the journey. 'It feels like your fingers and toes are on fire,' explained Fogarty, in a fraught practice session.

It was the top factory riders that the keen but always reserved Japanese fans had come to see, though, and they weren't disappointed. The European endurance regulars were just downright outclassed.

Fastest of the Euro-regulars were Fogarty and Rymer, mounted on an all-new but ill-handling and portly ZXR. Their race ended after 15 laps when Rymer slipped off. Fogarty said: 'I told him to just leave the bike there if we crashed. There's no way of winning once you've been off here.'

Suzuki men Lavieille and Moineau finished 38th after crashing in the early stages of the race. Vieira had teamed up with d'Orgeix when Hislop withdrew after practice, suffering from heat exhaustion, but the stand-in Frenchman crashed out.

The race saw HRC celebrate as Australians Wayne Gardner and Daryl Beattie blasted to the win as an oil slick decimated their main opposition. Beattie, out to impress his Honda bosses as he aimed for a 1993 GP ride, said: 'The track was greasy and just caught some people out.'

Beattie and Gardner led from the start and were only headed when they stopped for fuel. Japanese HRC men Satoshi Tsujimoto and Shinichi Itoh kept up the pressure after beating off an early race challenge from HRC's Shinya Takeishi and Kenichiro Iwahashi. With only 30 minutes remaining, an untimely pit stop saw Beattie lead Itoh by a couple of seconds. Over-excited, Itoh made his move but went down on an oil slick.

Briton Niall Mackenzie, teamed with Aussie Kevin Magee on a factory Yamaha, inherited runner-up spot after finally winning a race-long dice with Takeishi. Magee said: 'This isn't an endurance race – it's an eight-hour sprint.' Takeishi held third place from comeback hero Freddie Spencer, mounted on a slower but good-handling 1991-model Honda RVF750.

Kenny P.

The Euros came back to reality with the final 24-hour race of the year, the hilltop Bol d'Or at Circuit Paul Ricard in France. Bathed in September sunshine, the race turned into a benefit for world champs-elect Fogarty and Rymer, this time teamed up with fellow-Brit Hislop. They knew they had to win the race to clinch the title.

Moineau's Suzuki went out after an hour with yet another engine failure, at the same time as the factory Yamaha of Bruno Bonhuil crashed out and dumped oil on the circuit. So the race climaxed in a predictable clash between the two factory Kawasakis, with the British team making all the running at the front, easing out a workmanlike five-lap buffer over the French pretenders. 'We just had to make sure we didn't break the bike or do anything silly,' Fogarty said modestly.

As Fogarty and Rymer celebrated what they thought was a sure world title, 'reserve' rider Graziano took a fine fourth place, teamed up with Simeon and DuHamel. With 40 points available from the final two rounds in Malaysia and Australia, it looked as though Rymer and Fogarty's 34-point lead over Graziano was enough to clinch the title.

Graziano had never been scheduled to compete in the final two races, but politics now soured the air. Kawasaki, convinced they were champions, announced they weren't going to race in the final two long-haul events. Suzuki then briefly considered teaming Graziano with Moineau for the final two races as they still had a mathematical, though slim, chance of taking the crown. This still wasn't enough to tempt Kawasaki to enter the races.

Earlier rumours that the Australian round would be cancelled resurfaced when Kawasaki withdrew – and a cancelled event would mean the championship would lose its world status, spelling disaster for the future of endurance racing. To save the series and make sure they remained world champs, Kawasaki finally swallowed their pride, stretched their budgets and decided to fly Fogarty and Rymer to the final expensive rounds.

Fogarty sighed: 'I suppose it's spoiled it a little. I don't think anyone really wants to race there but we have to go. We have to finally make sure we're World Champions!'

EUROPEAN CHAMPIONSHIP

'THE future is looking very bleak for the European Championship,' admitted FIM Road Racing Commission President, Jo Zegwaard, speaking at the Assen World Superbike round in September, which also included a hastily rearranged 125 European Championship race.

'The European Championship has become very expensive for organisers and there is little return for them,' he continued. 'And with the announcement of the new Spanish Ducados Championship offering $1.5 million in prize money and seven out of ten races televised, I think this is where many European riders will be racing in 1993.'

With the balance of Grand Prix power now virtually out of FIM hands, it could be argued that the European Championship, which was inaugurated in 1981 as a feeder class for the Grands Prix, has become redundant.

And that's a pity, because the series has been the platform for some great names to make their mark. If you want evidence, look no further than last year when Massimiliano 'Max' Biaggi stole the 250 cc show on his Team Italia Aprilia, subsequently becoming one of the 'finds' of the 1992 Grand Prix season.

But the championship has been teetering on the brink of extinction for some time. Financially, the European Championship, with no established names to promote, has proved a disaster for many promoters.

This year the series has really lacked any direct input from the sport's governing body. The calendar has been a mess. Scheduled rounds were called off and riders and teams were frustrated by the last-minute cancellation of the 250 round at Monza – and the addition of an extra 125 cc race at Assen.

Many felt that the series could have provided an ideal support show for the Diesel Jeans World Superbikes – especially at the two Spanish rounds, where there were no supporting races at all.

Some organisers, like the British, Belgians and Germans, proved such a package could work but, generally, the two championships went their own ways and there was the ludicrous situation of two separate Austrian meetings, one for Superbikes (at the Öesterreichring – with no support programme) and one for Euros at the Salzburgring, with only three races.

But even if the FIM wanted to continue 'promoting' the European Championship they face a big rival in 1993 in the big money, ten-round Spanish Ducados Championship, catering for international competitors at 125 cc, 250 cc and Supersport 600 cc levels. The series offers two things the Euros have never had – money and television!

The FIM have not given up entirely, however. Instead of the Euros, Jo Zegwaard's vision of the future for up-and-coming riders is an Inter-Continental Championship. He said: 'I hope the CCR will support the idea of having four zones worldwide, maybe two of them in Europe, each with six to eight races and then having one big final round with something like 50 riders trying to qualify in each class.'

He added: 'There would be six to eight classes, but only two of them compulsory so each country could adapt the races to suit their national programmes. The important thing is that I do not want us to push this idea until we have the finances in place to support such a championship.'

With the Ducados series now in place, though, and most nations already promoting well-established competitions, the FIM plan looks decidedly shaky...

As an epitaph, what is likely to be the final year of European Championship racing provided some thrilling action and the usual crop of promising young – and sometimes not so young – talent.

The 125 cc class was won by 22-year-old Spaniard, Juan Borja, after a typically close-fought battle, although after the first three rounds it looked like anything but. Borja, a protégé of Jorge 'Aspar' Martinez, and riding a Coronas-backed Honda in a team set up by the Spanish superstar, won the first three races and looked on course for the title.

At first round Jerez, Borja, in his first season on a pure racing machine after previously racing production bikes in national competition, led a Spanish 1-2-3 with fellow-locals José Luis Cardosa and José Luis Rabadan, both on JJ Cobas machines, on the podium with him.

On to Kirkistown and Borja won again, this time after battling with Honda-mounted 24-year-old Italian Serafino Foti, while Team Italia's prospects, 21-year-old Lucio Cecchinello and 20-year-old Luigi Ancona, took third and fourth respectively on their semi-factory Aprilias. Ancona, into his third season of European Championship racing, had missed the opening round while completing his compulsory military service.

Borja made it three in a row with a runaway victory at Donington, with Foti again second, but the Spaniard's challenge faltered in Germany when he was sidelined with a seizure caused by a water pump failure. His points lead remained intact, however, when Foti also failed to score, having crashed.

It was Ancona's turn to win at Hockenheim, but only just, from Britain's Rob Orme, who had also finished third in the Donington round on his Mobil 1 Honda.

Borja's title hopes could have taken a dive in Belgium when he crashed out while fourth, but Foti again failed to capitalise when he was forced out with a tyre problem. A closely fought race was won by Austrian Manfred Baumann on a Honda from Cecchinello, while experienced 30-year-old German, Stefan Kurfiss, finished third, first podium of the year from the former 80 cc and 125 cc GP campaigner.

Borja bounced back to finish fourth in another nail-biting race, this time at Assen during TT week. Foti retired with handling problems, later traced to a front fork, while Ancona, after breaking a chain in Belgium, won from Cecchinello, Kurfiss and another Spaniard, Emilio Gracia.

Cecchinello was now only seven points behind Borja, but the championship took another turn as the Spaniard scored third place and 15 points in a second Assen round, this time on the short circuit and as support to the World Superbikes, while his Italian rival failed to score.

The race was given to second-placed finisher Baumann after Ireland's Robert Dunlop had crossed the line first, only to be excluded when his bike was found to be underweight. Ancona's second place moved him to second in the standings, 18 points adrift of Borja and only four ahead of team-mate Cecchinello.

Going into the final round at Monza, Borja needed only two points to assure himself of the title – but it would have been so easy to throw the championship away in the most appalling weather conditions. Ancona, though, was the only rider who could possibly prevent him from winning the crown.

Early on, Ancona and Cecchinello were in the middle of a five-way battle for the lead while Borja was down in 12th place. But the championship was decided when Ancona pitted, to retire on the sixth of 13 laps, with water in the electrics.

Cecchinello went on to win the race by 0.349s from Alzamora while Borja threaded his way through the pack to fifth place – and the title.

The 250 cc championship saw two classy performers, Spaniard Luis Carlos Maurel and Briton, Ian Newton, dominate the racing – even if Newton failed to dominate the results!

Newton became a reject of the new GP hierarchy at the end of the 1991 season. He had spent a fortune contesting the 1991 GP series on a standard Yamaha but, come the end of the year, his loyal sponsors put down the cash for a brand new Aprilia only to learn later that Newton's team application for the 1992 World Championship GP2 class had been rejected.

So Newton decided, with the full

By GARY PINCHIN

Photos: Clive Challinor

Opposite page: **Ian Newton did almost everything right in his campaign to score a top three championship place – but his bike had other plans.**

Spaniard Luis Carlos Maurel's Ducados-backed 250 team *(right)* brought an impressive big-budget effort to the championship, and won the title.

Juan Borja *(below right)*, here winning at Donington Park, hung on to his 125 title lead to the end of the season to score a Spanish double.

support of his sponsors, to switch back to European Championship racing with the intention of securing a top three placing in the points, thus earning his place back on the GP scene.

At the start of the year, he had said the Euro 250 cc champ would be the rider whose Aprilia kept going. Sadly it was not his!

And it wasn't that Newton's bike was any less reliable than those of his rivals, just that his failed in races and not during qualifying as his rivals' did. Some riders get the occasional stroke of bad luck in a season. Newton seemed to get everyone's!

Maurel was back in the Euros after a season of Spanish Superbike racing on a Yamaha. He had been a leading contender in the 1990 Euro 250 cc class, riding an ex-Alberto Puig kitted Yamaha sponsored by a Spanish bank, but for 1992 he was riding an Aprilia, sponsored by Ducados.

Maurel started the season well, holding off a stern challenge from fellow-countryman Oscar Sainz at Jerez. Newton, who had taken pole but crashed at over 120 mph in the final session when his bike seized, finished fourth behind Team Italia's Massimo Pennacchioli, after a fairing-bashing last lap with another Spaniard, Enrique de Juan.

At Kirkistown, everyone lined up on slicks, even though the track was still damp in places. Newton started cautiously and was down in 17th at the end of the first lap, but he stormed through the field as the track dried out and stuffed inside leader Pennacchioli in the second to last corner of the last lap to win.

Maurel was third but went ahead in the championship after winning at Donington. The cold track conditions there appeared to affect the Dunlop runners more than those on Michelins. Nigel Bosworth was well in contention but his fast early pace wrecked his tyres. Newton, also on Dunlops, began more conservatively but his tyres went away mid-distance leaving Michelin-shod Maurel unchallenged up front.

At this stage, Maurel had a five-point lead in the championship over Newton but the British rider saw his title hopes fade in Germany when a chain adjuster broke up as he left the start. With him sidelined, Pennacchioli took his only win of the year while Maurel was happy cruising to a distant second but a clear points lead.

Belgian local, Laurent Naveau, gave Yamaha a rare win at Spa, a race which started on a wet track but dried out quickly. His Dunlop intermediates suited the conditions well but those on wets, like Newton and Pennacchioli, struggled down-field. Maurel was happy to finish second again, to consolidate his points lead.

Maurel and Newton went head to head in Austria, but Newton lost fourth gear and Maurel cruised to victory. He then clinched the title at Assen with another win after Newton broke down on the third lap while two seconds clear.

With the final round of the championship at Monza cancelled, Maurel was proclaimed champion, 50 points ahead of runner-up Pennacchioli while Naveau, after claiming second at Assen, moved into third place in the table. Newton missed the cut of an automatic shot at GP selection, finishing fourth overall.

The Supersport 600 cc championship was an all-Honda affair. Lanky German, Stefan Scheschowitsch, clinched the title with one round left, having led the series from the second round.

Spaniard Pere Riba won the first tussle at Jerez from Italian Antonio Calasso and another Spaniard, Ricardo Suarez. Scheschowitsch could only finish fifth in Spain – but that was his worst result all year.

The German then went on to win three races, placed second to experienced Frenchman Rachel Nicotte (third in the 1989 European 500 cc Championship) at Donington and finished third behind Riba and Calasso at Assen. He didn't ride in the final round, which was won by Calasso after a thrilling battle with Riba: the Italian actually rode around Riba in the Parabolica, on a streaming wet track!

Before the end of the year, Scheschowitsch had already lined up some World Superbike outings on Helmut Fath's Kawasaki – Superbike being the only natural progression for Superport 600 riders, perhaps? Unless, of course, the FIM's projected Supersport 600 'world' championship is included as part of the 1993 World Superbike package...

The sidecar class was the domain of the British crews. The series, while offering full grids, only served to underline the limited appeal of three-wheeler racing at anything below World Championship level. Comprising just four rounds, and very little top class foreign competition, the championship bore all the hallmarks of a British national series.

But that's not taking anything away from champions Gary Knight and Malcolm Jackson who won three of the four rounds on their Redline Motorcycles Windle-Krauser and placed third in the other.

Knight, running one of the very stiff, carbon-fibre Windle chassis built in 1990, cleared off to win a very wet opener at Kirkistown by ten seconds from the LCR-Krauser of Tony Baker and Simon Prior.

Hockenheim looked to be shaping up for a classic confrontation between ex-GP regulars Barry Smith/Trevor Hopkinson – who didn't compete in the opening round – and Knight, but Smith's Windle-ADM succumbed to mechanical trouble and Knight again cleared off for an easy victory over Gary Thomas and Dutch passenger Rinie Bettgens.

Smith won at the Salzburgring while Knight fought off a stern challenge from Clive Stirrat/Tony Strevens, passing them on the last lap, two corners from home, for third.

In what turned out to be the final round at Assen, following the cancellation of the scheduled final two races at Most and Hockenheim, Knight quickly built up a 25-second lead over Smith, then relaxed his pace – almost too much. In the closing stages, Smith mounted a last ditch charge but Knight just hung on to clinch victory by four-hundredths of a second!

Roger Body and Andy Peach finished third on the RMC LCR-Krauser to secure second place in the championship, while Smith finished fourth overall in the standings behind Thomas/Bettgens.

With the future of the European Championship in question, the World Championship in turmoil and no place for three-wheelers in the Ducados series, where does that leave the up-and-coming sidecar men?

BRITISH NATIONAL RACING

Painting the track green – John Reynolds was the winningest rider in the MCN Superbike Challenge, and Supercup champion too.

By JOHN BROWN

THE crowds did start to drift back, if not in their droves, for a British national season that produced a number of memorable encounters but did border on the monotonous at times. The reason for this was the parallel running of the televised Supercup series and the near-identical combined MCN Superbike Challenge and the MRPC championships. Both centred on the same major solo classes, with the same two races per meeting format for the 750s; and in fact the only break from the tedium came with the addition of the highly competitive MCN Superteen championship in the MRPC (Motorcycle Race Promoters Committee) presentation.

There was a slight diversion on the sidecar front, with only an Open class in the Supercup but a double bill of Open and Formula Two in the MRPC series.

Seemingly to produce a little confusion and stretch out the racing, not all the championship classes were included in every MRPC event. This, for example, resulted in the last Supersport 400 round being run at the penultimate MRPC fixture at Knockhill and not in the finals weekend at Brands Hatch a week later.

The system also produced such programme contrasts as a full house of eight points-scoring races at Donington Park in August compared to just one each at that same Leicestershire circuit and at Brands Hatch during the May Bank Holiday weekend.

The number of rounds for each class also differed. The MCN TT Superbikes had ten outings of two legs a time, the 125s and 250s had 14 rounds apiece, the Superteens 12, Supersport 600 and both sidecar categories 11 and, for the Supersport 400s, just ten. All this was inclined to bewilder spectators and leave the general media uninterested.

The Supercup British Championship, run over six rounds for six classes, was again regarded as the premier British series – but, just the same, it failed to attract a major new sponsor when Shell finally did what was feared and withdrew their support. The oil company, who had pioneered the event from the beginning, in 1989, had warned of an impending withdrawal but little real effort had been made by the ACU to find a replacement. When the gravity of the situation finally sank in and efforts to find another sponsor were renewed it was far too late. Budgets had been finalised and the coffers were empty.

Even when the BBC confirmed its continued mix of live and recorded coverage – and Supercup seemed to be an exceptionally saleable package for an asking price of around £100,000 – there had still been no takers. At the eleventh hour *Motor Cycle News* stepped in with an offer that, although not really what was being sought, did help to relieve pressure on the organisers and promoters of the series, which still boasted an overall prize fund of £90,000. The season ahead will see several major changes and a general tidying up of the British national scene.

The six-round Supercup is to be upgraded to international status, a move aimed at creating a world class series based in Britain. The prospect of a return of foreign riders, taking on the best of British on their home ground, is an exciting one and could be just the incentive required to lure a big-time sponsor to the series that will again be captured by the BBC's cameramen.

The MRPC championships are being dropped and replaced by a more streamlined eight-round British championship, and a UK Riders' Cup, also over eight rounds, will be introduced. (The purpose of the latter is to make the rider's transition from clubman racing to national level easier and at the same time more competitive.)

On the track the 1992 season will be remembered as the year of Team Green Kawasaki. Their four-cylinder ZXR 750R became the dominant machine, notably in the hands of Nottinghamshire rider John Reynolds. The 'King' at Donington and Cadwell, Snetterton's 'Ace' and winner of the Mallory Park Race of the Year, the 29-year-old former motocross rider clinched the MCN Superbike Challenge with two rounds still remaining and secured the Supercup in the final dramatic round at Brands Hatch.

Reynolds went into that final holding third place in the championship to Terry Rymer, who was away in France on World Endurance race duty, and his own Scottish teammate from Dalbeattie, Brian Morrison, who started as favourite. But it was not to be the Scotsman's day: he crashed at Clark Curve early in the first race and was brought off at exactly the same place in the second by Mick Grant's Suzuki rider, James Whitham, who also put himself out of action with a left leg injury. Reynolds added two more victories to his previous total of seven in that series and took the title by a clear 32 points from defeated champion Rob McElnea.

Reynolds's reason for having to come from behind in the Supercup was that he'd failed to score in three races. At Donington, in the series opener, he crashed in the first race and pulled out of the second because of brake fade, a decision that did not please team manager Colin Wright, who agreed that victory was out of the question but felt that at least some points were there for the taking. Reynolds's only other no-score came in the second race at Cadwell in August, when a faulty battery forced him out of the action.

Even before the final round at Brands in October Reynolds had notched up 14 wins in the Superbike Challenge. Again, he had to battle back from a first round setback, this time at a very wet Thruxton in March. After his team-mate Morrison crashed in practice and suffered a badly broken right elbow, Wright decided that conditions were unsafe and withdrew Reynolds from the first race. It went ahead anyway and ended with victory for Whitham. As conditions had improved for the second race Reynolds was back on the track, content to settle for third place.

Morrison was back for the fourth round at Knockhill where he shared victory on his home ground with his Team Green partner, whose only other non-winning ride came at Cadwell in August. After making an uncharacteristically bad start he was beaten fair and square by Robert Dunlop on a JPS Norton in a four-rider fight-out that also featured third-placed Whitham and Terry Rymer, who crashed the second JPS Norton on the last lap.

Morrison's mishaps almost certainly robbed him not only of Supercup success but also of the chance to take on Reynolds in the Superbike chase. The Thruxton incident kept him out for three rounds, or six races, and left him racing for the rest of the year with pins and wires in his elbow that restricted its movement.

It was an eventful year for the JPS Norton team, to put it mildly. They ended the year facing a bleak future when the tobacco manufacturers announced a withdrawal of sponsorship. And the Superbike championship was only three meetings old when team leader Ron Haslam crashed at Snetterton and broke his left leg, an injury that was to keep him out of racing for over six months. The blow of this setback was partly offset a week later at Donington, when replacement Rymer slipped in a victory double during his first-ever rides on a rotary-engined machine.

This put the rider from South London firmly into a Supercup lead, a position he maintained right up to the final round. But the lead he'd established was not enough to keep him at the top during his absence from Brands to race at the Bol d'Or 24 Hours and he ended the championship in fourth place, 33 points behind winner Reynolds.

Ulsterman Robert Dunlop, until now regarded as a 125 cc rider, quickly mastered the vastly different JPS Norton and, as the only rider to score in all 12 Supercup races, took joint second place on points with Rob McElnea. He also gave the team its only Superbike victory, in the four-way fight-out at Cadwell, but third place in that championship was in jeopardy when he injured himself while contesting a European Championship 125 cc race at Monza, two weeks before the final round at Brands in October.

Haslam was back in the team on that occasion, having been second in a non-title race at Snetterton earlier in the month. The rider who beat him by just seven-tenths of a second on that occasion was Crawley-based Ulsterman Mark Farmer, on a rival 'Crighton' Norton. Ironically, as the JPS support was nearing its end, the Midland development engineer who'd produced the original rotary racing engine, Brian Crighton, was at last getting some financial backing for his own breakaway project.

Through a sports management organisation headed by former top sidecar driver, Colin Seeley (who in fact produced machines based on the famous 500 cc G50 and 350 cc 7R singles that featured his own name

Kawasaki
ABUS
Silkolene
DUNLOP
NGK
D.I.D
GOODRIDGE

Right: **Robert Dunlop, better known as a 125 jockey, soon mastered the JPS Norton Wankel Rotary, scored in every Supercup round and gave the British bike its only Superbike victory at Cadwell Park.**

Below: **Style and substance: defending champion Rob McElnea (Yamaha, on left) and the contortionist Jamie Whitham (Suzuki) had many duels, but were out of luck for the championships.**

in the Seventies), Duckhams now head a formidable list of sponsors. Although Crighton is back as senior development engineer at the Norton factory, his team will continue to run independently of the official one managed by Barry Symmons.

Crighton's original 'Roton' machine name was dropped in favour of the new title in time for the Supercup final. On this occasion Farmer, who only joined the team in July, clinched an impressive second place to Reynolds in the first race and was leading the second until the rotary suffered a power loss. The well-deserved cash injection made it possible for Crighton to add a second bike in the end-of-season Duckhams Powerbike International at Brands Hatch, which was raced by nine-times TT winner, Steve Hislop.

Although a double runner-up in the championships, Rob McElnea insisted that his Loctite Yamaha was no longer a speed match for the Kawasakis or the Norton – a view shared about his machine by lone Suzuki campaigner, James Whitham.

New Zealander Simon Crafar found himself caught up in the red tape of officialdom when he arrived to take his place in the Castrol Honda Britain Team (based in Louth, Lincolnshire). The team had set its sights on contesting all the major home meetings, but it was ruled that, although Crafar would be allowed to contest Superbike, he would not be permitted to take part in the – more beneficial to the team – Supercup, because it incorporated a British national championship. To add to his confusion, it is an all-change situation for 1993 when he will be allowed into the Supercup but not into Superbike, which will be run as the domestic championship! Despite all this, Crafar showed style and ability to take a less than competitive RC30 to fourth place in the MCN Superbike Challenge.

Paul Brown literally threw away his opportunity to retain the 250 cc Supercup title in the final round at Brands. It was a race that turned out to be arguably the most dramatic of the season.

Nigel Bosworth was just about home and dry as the race got under way. All he wanted was a downfield scoring finish – but while in the lead on the second lap, the engine of his Yamaha seized. Brown, in a leading pack that included Honda's Alan Carter, Team Great Britain rider James Haydon, and Niall Mackenzie guesting on a Loctite Yamaha, only needed to finish fourth and the title was his. For some unknown reason, and one that left team manager McElnea aghast, Brown took on a determined Carter in a victory fight-out and then slid off at Westfield bend.

Bosworth's tears of dismay turned to smiles of joy – but not for long,

Phil Masters

Mark Wernham

Phil Masters

Left: **Steve Sawford (Yamaha), came from behind to seize the 250 Supercup title at the last gasp, at the expense of (among others) Paul Brown *(below left)*, who crashed his Loctite Yamaha. Brown took the MRPC 250 title instead.**

Below: **Supercup 125 champion Neil Hodgson was reckoned the find of the year.**

James Wright

Clive Challinor

because the drama was far from over. Outsider Steve Sawford got the signal that fifth place would give him the championship. He was in sixth at the time, but with an all-out effort the Bedfordshire rider forced his Yamaha past Woolsey Coulter to snatch glory on the final lap.

There was some sort of consolation for Brown two weeks later when he was presented with the MRPC championship: the only remaining challenger, Alan Carter, crashed and injured his ankle.

Nineteen-year-old Neil Hodgson from Burnley wrapped up the 125 cc Supercup series in confident style and set himself up for the 'find of the year' accolade.

Sixth place was all he needed in the final round and that's what he got on his Honda. He then set off with a vengeance, using his winning ways in a bid to add the MRPC title to his tally. He faced a fight-out with former South African champion Fernando Mendes and experienced Derbyshire rider Barry Stanley.

Mike Edwards won a last-round decider with Mark Farmer to take the Supercup 400 Supersport title by just one point. By contrast, Phil Borley overcame a serious early season arm injury to hammer home three wins and two second places to take the Supersport 600 title by 26 points from motor cycle journalist Sean Emmett.

Farmer, banned from the Supercup 600 for using illegal fuel, won the corresponding MRPC championship and the MRPC 400 Supersport championship as well.

Steve Webster and Gavin Simmons went some way towards making up for losing their world crown with success in the Supercup sidecar series. They took four victories from five rides. Sidecar driver brothers Derek and Barry Brindley went into the final round tying for the runner-up spot: it went to Derek and passenger Paul Hutchinson, by just two points.

In its second year the Superteen championship grew in stature and, by giving up-and-coming young riders a chance to show their potential in front of the people who matter at major events, not just in the backwoods of club racing, filled a need that was becoming acute. Richard Wynn from Burnley, Sam Harrison from Penshurst in Kent and Scot Callum Ramsey were never more than a few points apart throughout a series that saw Roki Read, the 19-year-old son of eight-times World Champion Phil Read, come through to claim the novice award.

OTHER MAJOR 1992 RESULTS

Isle of Man Tourist Trophy Races

ISLE OF MAN TOURIST TROPHY COURSE, 1-12 June. 37.73-mile/60.72-km course.

TT Formula 1 (6 laps, 226.38 miles/364.32 km)
1 Phillip McCallen, GB (750 Honda), 1h 53m 22.4s, 119.80 mph/192.79 km/h.
2 Steve Hislop, GB (588 Norton), 1h 53m 34.4s; **3** Joey Dunlop, GB (750 Honda), 1h 55m 13.0s; **4** Nick Jefferies, GB (750 Honda), 1h 55m 25.0s; **5** Mark Farmer, GB (750 Yamaha), 1h 55m 45.6s; **6** Steve Ward, GB (750 Honda), 1h 56m 45.4s; **7** Bob Jackson, GB (750 Honda), 1h 57m 02.6s; **8** Trevor Nation, GB (888 Ducati), 1h 58m 10.8s; **9** Iain Duffus, GB (750 Kawasaki), 1h 58m 31.2s; **10** Jason Griffiths, GB (750 Honda), 1h 58m 37.0s; **11** Tom Knight, GB (750 Honda), 1h 58m 57.2s; **12** Ian Lougher, GB (750 ITL), 1h 59m 07.0s; **13** Simon Beck, GB (750 Honda), 1h 59m 40.4s; **14** Gary Radcliffe, GB (750 Honda), 1h 59m 49.0s; **15** Colin Gable, GB (750 Honda), 1h 59m 53.2s; **16** Shaun Harris, NZ (750 Suzuki), 2h 00m 31.6s; **17** Derek Young, GB (750 Honda), 2h 01m 49.6s.
Fastest lap: Hislop, 18m 21.6s, 123.30 mph/198.43 km/h.

Supersport 400 (4 laps, 150.92 miles/242.88 km)
1 Brian Reid, GB (400 Yamaha), 1h 21m 56.6s, 110.50 mph/177.83 km/h.
2 Phillip McCallen, GB (400 Honda), 1h 22m 51.4s; **3** Steve Linsdell, GB (400 Yamaha), 1h 23m 09.8s; **4** Nick Jefferies, GB (400 Honda), 1h 23m 47.4s; **5** Iain Duffus, GB (400 Yamaha), 1h 24m 33.6s; **6** Mark Farmer, GB (400 Yamaha), 1h 25m 46.0s; **7** David Morris, GB (400 Yamaha), 1h 25m 59.4s; **8** Rob Haynes, GB (400 Yamaha), 1h 26m 10.8s; **9** Mark Langton, GB (400 Yamaha), 1h 26m 56.4s; **10** Chris Petty, GB (400 Yamaha), 1h 27m 14.6s; **11** Robert Grant, GB (400 Yamaha), 1h 28m 04.2s; **12** Grant Goodings, GB (400 Yamaha), 1h 28m 24.0s.
Fastest lap: Reid, 20m 09.8s, 112.27 mph/180.68 km/h (record).

Supersport 600 (4 laps, 150.92 miles/242.88 km)
1 Phillip McCallen, GB (600 Honda), 1h 18m 42.8s, 115.04 mph/185.14 km/h.
2 Steve Hislop, GB (600 Honda), 1h 19m 05.6s; **3** Steve Ward, GB (600 Honda), 1h 19m 30.2s; **4** Nick Jefferies, GB (600 Honda), 1h 19m 40.8s; **5** Bob Jackson, GB (600 Honda), 1h 19m 47.0s; **6** Johnny Rea, GB (600 Yamaha), 1h 20m 25.0s; **7** Robert Holden, NZ (600 Yamaha), 1h 20m 27.0s; **8** Derek Young, GB (600 Honda), 1h 20m 35.4s; **9** Joey Dunlop, GB (600 Honda), 1h 20m 53.8s; **10** Iain Duffus, GB (600 Honda), 1h 20m 57.0s; **11** Colin Gable, GB (600 Yamaha), 1h 21m 01.2s; **12** Alan Batson, GB (600 Honda), 1h 21m 30.2s; **13** Mark Farmer, GB (600 Yamaha), 1h 21m 48.6s; **14** Ian Lougher, GB (600 Yamaha), 1h 22m 18.6s; **15** Grant Goodings, GB (600 Yamaha), 1h 22m 19.0s; **16** Chris Petty, GB (600 Yamaha), 1h 22m 33.2s; **17** Stan Rea, GB (600 Yamaha), 1h 23m 59.0s.
Fastest lap: Hislop, 19m 20.8s, 117.01 mph/188.31 km/h.

Ultra Lightweight 125 (4 laps, 150.92 miles/242.88 km)
1 Joey Dunlop, GB (125 Honda), 1h 25m 01.6s, 106.49 mph/171.38 km/h.
2 Robert Dunlop, GB (125 Honda), 1h 25m 10.0s; **3** Mick Lofthouse, GB (125 Honda), 1h 27m 30.2s; **4** Stan Rea, GB (125 Honda), 1h 27m 57.8s; **5** Stephen Johnson, GB (125 Honda), 1h 28m 08.2s; **6** Dennis McCullough, GB (125 Honda), 1h 28m 10.8s; **7** Ian Lougher, GB (125 Honda), 1h 28m 13.8s; **8** Mark Westmorland, GB (125 Honda), 1h 29m 57.6s; **9** Noel Clegg, GB (125 Honda), 1h 30m 06.8s; **10** Alan Caughey, GB (125 Honda), 1h 30m 36.8s; **11** Lee Pullan, GB (125 Honda), 1h 30m 41.2s; **12** Michael O'Connor, GB (125 Honda), 1h 30m 54.0s; **13** Bob Jackson, GB (125 Honda), 1h 31m 19.4s; **14** Peter Wakefield, GB (125 Honda), 1h 31m 43.6s; **15** Richard Mortimer, GB (125 Honda), 1h 31m 59.0s; **16** Phil Armes, GB, (125 Honda), 1h 32m 08.6s; **17** Ted Roebuck, GB (125 Honda), 1h 32m 09.8s.
Fastest lap: J. Dunlop, 20m 49.6s, 108.69 mph/174.92 km/h.

Junior TT (4 laps, 150.92 miles/242.88 km)
1 Brian Reid, GB (250 Yamaha), 1h 18m 38.8s, 115.13 mph/185.28 km/h.
2 Steve Hislop, GB (250 Yamaha), 1h 18m 42.0s; **3** Robert Dunlop, GB (250 Yamaha), 1h 19m 30.2s; **4** Stephen Johnson, GB (250 Yamaha), 1h 19m 49.8s; **5** Ian Lougher, GB (250 T.C.R.), 1h 19m 54.4s; **6** Bob Jackson, GB (250 Yamaha), 1h 21m 16.2s; **7** Bob Heath, GB (250 Honda), 1h 21m 22.2s; **8** Steve Williams, GB (250 Yamaha), 1h 21m 37.4s; **9** Jason Griffiths, GB (250 Yamaha), 1h 22m 03.2s; **10** Lee Pullan, GB (250 Yamaha), 1h 22m 32.8s; **11** Gavin Lee, GB (250 Yamaha), 1h 23m 03.8s; **12** Gary Radcliffe, GB (250 Yamaha), 1h 23m 21.8s; **13** Denis McCullough, GB (350 Yamaha), 1h 23m 52.0s; **14** Marek Nofer, GB (250 Yamaha), 1h 24m 46.4s; **15** Tony Anderson, GB (250 Yamaha), 1h 25m 26.8s; **16** Martin Ayles, GB (250 Yamaha), 1h 25m 32.6s.
Fastest lap: Hislop, 19m 15.8s, 117.51 mph/189.11 km/h.

Senior TT (6 laps, 226.38 miles/364.32 km)
1 Steve Hislop, GB (588 Norton), 1h 51m 59.6s, 121.28 mph/195.18 km/h.
2 Carl Fogarty, GB (750 Yamaha), 1h 52m 04.0s; **3** Robert Dunlop, GB (588 Norton), 1h 54m 02.6s; **4** Nick Jefferies, GB (750 Honda), 1h 54m 33.2s; **5** Mark Farmer, GB (750 Yamaha), 1h 54m 47.6s; **6** Robert Holden, NZ (750 Yamaha), 1h 57m 03.6s; **7** Iain Duffus, GB (750 Kawasaki), 1h 58m 05.6s; **8** Colin Gable, GB (750 Honda), 1h 58m 24.2s; **9** Derek Young, GB (750 Honda), 1h 59m 48.2s; **10** Johnny Rea, GB (750 Honda), 1h 59m 53.4s; **11** Gary Radcliffe, GB (750 Honda), 2h 00m 08.8s; **12** John Barton, GB (750 Honda), 2h 00m 20.8s; **13** Tom Knight, GB (750 Honda), 2h 00m 27.8s; **14** David Goodley, GB (750 Honda), 2h 00m 55.0s; **15** Ian Lougher, GB (750 ITL), 2h 01m 51.0s; **16** Allan McDonald, GB (750 Honda), 2h 01m 59.8s.
Fastest lap: Fogarty, 18m 18.8s, 123.61 mph/198.93 km/h (record).

Sidecar TT: Race A (3 laps, 113.19 miles/182.16 km)
1 Geoff Bell/Keith Cornbill, GB/GB (600 Yamaha), 1h 06m 54.4s, 101.50 mph/163.35 km/h.
2 Eddy Wright/Peter Hill, GB/GB (600 Honda), 1h 07m 29.6s; **3** Mick Boddice/Dave Wells, GB/GB (600 Honda), 1h 08m 04.0s; **4=** Roy Hanks/Tom Hanks, GB/GB (350 Ireson), 1h 08m 07.2s; **4=** Neil Smith/Terrie Salone, GB/GB (350 Shellbourne), 1h 08m 07.2s; **6** Dave Molyneux/Karl Ellison, GB/GB (600 Kawasaki), 1h 08m 28.4s; **7** Richard Crossley/Ken Waller, GB/GB (600 Yamaha), 1h 09m 49.6s; **8** Dick Hawes/Eddy Kiff, GB/GB (600 Kawasaki), 1h 10m 48.2s; **9** Gavin Porteous/Jeff Spencer, AUS/AUS (600 Kawasaki),1h 11m 12.8s; **10** Pete Nuttall/Raymond Burns, GB/GB (600 Honda), 1h 11m 16.8s; **11** Mick Hamblin/Robert Smith, GB/GB (350 Shellbourne), 1h 11m 22.4s; **12** David Wallis/Tim Kirkham, GB/GB (350 Yamaha), 1h 11m 56.4s; **13** John Booth/Peter Smethurst, GB/GB (600 Honda),1h 12m 45.2s.
Fastest lap: Bell/Cornbill, 22m 04.6s, 102.54 mph/165.02 km/h (record).

Sidecar TT: Race B (3 laps, 113.19 miles/182.16 km)
1 Geoff Bell/Keith Cornbill, GB/GB (600 Yamaha), 1h 06m 55.0s, 101.49 mph/163.33 km/h.
2 Mick Boddice/Dave Wells, GB/GB (600 Honda), 1h 07m 28.0s; **3** Dave Molyneux/Karl Ellison, GB/GB (600 Kawasaki), 1h 07m 54.2s; **4** Neil Smith/Terrie Salone, GB/GB (350 Shellbourne), 1h 08m 05.8s; **5** Peter Krukowski/Chris McGahan, GB/GB (350 Ireson), 1h 08m 18.8s; **6** Dave Saville/Nick Roche, GB/GB (350 Sabre), 1h 08m 35.0s; **7** Vince Biggs/Jamie Biggs, GB/GB (350 Yamaha), 1h 09m 23.6s; **8** Richard Crossley/Ken Waller, GB/GB (600 Yamaha), 1h 09m 47.0s; **9** Gavin Porteous/Jeff Spencer, AUS/AUS (600 Kawasaki), 1h 09m 53.8s; **10** Dick Hawes/Eddy Kiff, GB/GB (600 Kawasaki), 1h 09m 59.6s; **11** Mick Hamblin/Robert Smith, GB/GB (350 Shellbourne), 1h 10m 30.6s; **12** David Wallis/Tim Kirkham, GB/GB (350 Yamaha), 1h 10m 38.6s; **13** Derek Plummer/Chris Plant, GB/GB (600 Kawasaki), 1h 10m 51.4s.
Fastest lap: Bell/Cornbill, 22m 16.0s, 101.66 mph/163.61 km/h.

Diesel Jeans World Superbike Championship

CIRCUITO DE ALBACETE, Spain, 5 April. 2.199-mile/3.539-km circuit.
Diesel Jeans World Superbike Championship, round 1 (2 x 28 laps, 61.572 miles/99.092 km)
Leg 1
1 Aaron Slight, NZ (Kawasaki), 48m 45.07s, 75.779 mph/121.956 km/h.
2 Doug Polen, USA (Ducati); **3** Fabrizio Pirovano, I (Yamaha); **4** Giancarlo Falappa, I (Ducati); **5** Daniel Amatriain, E (Ducati); **6** Baldassarre Monti, I (Honda); **7** Raymond Roche, F (Ducati); **8** Takahiro Sohwa, J (Kawasaki); **9** Rob Phillis, AUS (Kawasaki); **10** Juan Lopez Mella, E (Honda); **11** Stéphane Mertens, B (Ducati); **12** Carl Fogarty, GB (Ducati); **13** Christer Lindholm, S (Yamaha); **14** Terry Rymer, GB (Kawasaki); **15** Jean-Yves Mounier, F (Yamaha).
Fastest lap: Slight, 1m 42.95s, 76.897 mph/123.753 km/h.
Leg 2
1 Raymond Roche, F (Ducati), 46m 17.74s, 79.799 mph/128.425 km/h.
2 Rob Phillis, AUS (Kawasaki); **3** Daniel Amatriain, E (Ducati); **4** Fabrizio Pirovano, I (Yamaha); **5** Giancarlo Falappa, I (Ducati); **6** Doug Polen, USA (Ducati); **7** Scott Russell, USA (Kawasaki); **8** John Reynolds, GB (Kawasaki); **9** Terry Rymer, GB (Kawasaki); **10** Carl Fogarty, GB (Ducati); **11** Virginio Ferrari, I (Ducati); **12** Stéphane Mertens, B (Ducati); **13** Fabrizio Furlan, I (Ducati); **14** Juan Lopez Mella, E (Honda); **15** Christer Lindholm, S (Yamaha).
Fastest lap: Amatriain, 1m 36.44s, 82.087 mph/132.107 km/h.
Championship points: **1** Roche, 29; **2** Pirovano, 28; **3** Polen, 27; **4** Amatriain, 26; **5** Falappa and Phillis, 24.

DONINGTON PARK CIRCUIT, England, 19 April. 2.5-mile/4.023-km circuit.
Diesel Jeans World Superbike Championship, round 2 (2 x 25 laps, 62.5 miles/100.575 km)
Leg 1
1 Raymond Roche, F (Ducati), 40m 57.60s, 91.55 mph/147.33 km/h.
2 Fabrizio Pirovano, I (Yamaha); **3** Scott Russell, USA (Kawasaki); **4** Rob Phillis, AUS (Kawasaki); **5** Aaron Slight, NZ (Kawasaki); **6** Doug Polen, USA (Ducati); **7** Stéphane Mertens, B (Ducati); **8** Jean-Yves Mounier, F (Yamaha); **9** Ray Stringer, GB (Kawasaki); **10** Baldassarre Monti, I (Honda); **11** James Whitham, GB (Suzuki); **12** Daniel Amatriain, E (Ducati); **13** John Reynolds, GB (Kawasaki); **14** Jeffry de Vries, NL (Yamaha); **15** Christer Lindholm, S (Yamaha).
Fastest lap: Carl Fogarty, GB (Ducati), 1m 36.91s, 92.86 mph/149.45 km/h.
Leg 2
1 Carl Fogarty, GB (Ducati), 40m 48.92s, 91.87 mph/147.86 km/h.
2 Raymond Roche, F (Ducati); **3** Scott Russell, USA (Kawasaki); **4** Doug Polen, USA (Ducati); **5** Fabrizio Pirovano, I (Yamaha); **6** Aaron Slight, NZ (Kawasaki); **7** Rob Phillis, AUS (Kawasaki); **8** Giancarlo Falappa, I (Ducati); **9** John Reynolds, GB (Kawasaki); **10** Daniel Amatriain, E (Ducati); **11** Takahiro Sohwa, J (Kawasaki); **12** Rob McElnea, GB (Yamaha); **13** Baldassarre Monti, I (Honda); **14** James Whitham, GB (Suzuki); **15** Christer Lindholm, S (Yamaha).
Fastest lap: Fogarty, 1m 37.00s, 92.78 mph/149.32 km/h.
Championship points: **1** Roche, 66; **2** Pirovano, 56; **3** Polen, 50; **4** Phillis, 46; **5** Slight, 41; **6** Russell, 39.

HOCKENHEIMRING, Germany, 10 May. 4.220-mile/6.792-km circuit.
Diesel Jeans World Superbike Championship, round 3 (2 x 14 laps, 59.08 miles/95.088 km)
Leg 1
1 Doug Polen, USA (Ducati), 29m 52.33s, 118.675 mph/190.989 km/h.
2 Rob Phillis, AUS (Kawasaki); **3** Aaron Slight, NZ (Kawasaki); **4** Scott Russell, USA (Kawasaki); **5** Raymond Roche, F (Ducati); **6** Stéphane Mertens, B (Ducati); **7** Hervé Moineau, F (Suzuki); **8** Andreas Hofmann, D (Kawasaki); **9** Daniel Amatriain, E (Ducati); **10** Piergiorgio Bontempi, I (Kawasaki); **11** Virginio Ferrari, I (Ducati); **12** Klaus Liegibel, D (Yamaha); **13** Andreas Meklau, A (Ducati); **14** Jean-Yves Mounier, F (Yamaha); **15** Sven Seidel, D (Suzuki).
Fastest lap: Fabrizio Pirovano, I (Yamaha), 2m 06.67s, 119.943 mph/193.030 km/h.
Leg 2
1 Doug Polen, USA (Ducati), 29m 51.83s, 118.709 mph/191.043 km/h.
2 Rob Phillis, AUS (Kawasaki); **3** Giancarlo Falappa, I (Ducati); **4** Raymond Roche, F (Ducati); **5** Aaron Slight, NZ (Kawasaki); **6** Fabrizio Pirovano, I (Yamaha); **7** Scott Russell, USA (Kawasaki); **8** John Reynolds, GB (Kawasaki); **9** Andreas Hofmann, D (Kawasaki); **10** Hervé Moineau, F (Suzuki); **11** Carl Fogarty, GB (Ducati); **12** Edwin Weibel, D (Ducati); **13** Stéphane Mertens, B (Ducati); **14** Massimo Broccoli, I (Kawasaki); **15** Virginio Ferrari, I (Ducati).
Fastest lap: Phillis, 2m 06.92s, 119.707 mph/192.650 km/h.
Championship points: **1** Polen and Roche, 90; **3** Phillis, 80; **4** Slight, 67; **5** Pirovano, 66; **6** Russell, 61.

SPA-FRANCORCHAMPS CIRCUIT, Belgium, 24 May. 4.312-mile/6.940-km circuit.
Diesel Jeans World Superbike Championship, round 4 (2 x 14 laps, 60.368 miles/97.160 km)
Leg 1
1 Rob Phillis, AUS (Kawasaki), 35m 21.99s, 102.422 mph/164.833 km/h.
2 Stéphane Mertens, B (Ducati); **3** Scott Russell, USA (Kawasaki); **4** Giancarlo Falappa, I (Ducati); **5** Doug Polen, USA (Ducati); **6** Aaron Slight, NZ (Kawasaki); **7** Daniel Amatriain, E (Ducati); **8** Andreas Hofmann, D (Ducati); **9** Baldassarre Monti, I (Honda); **10** Virginio Ferrari, I (Ducati); **11** Jeffry de Vries, NL (Yamaha); **12** Christer Lindholm, S (Yamaha); **13** Richard Arnaiz, USA (Honda); **14** Piergiorgio Bontempi, I (Kawasaki); **15** Simon Crafar, NZ (Honda).
Fastest lap: Polen, 2m 30.37s, 103.241 mph/166.150 km/h.
Leg 2
1 Doug Polen, USA (Ducati), 35m 22.22s, 102.412 mph/164.816 km/h.
2 Giancarlo Falappa, I (Ducati); **3** Fabrizio Pirovano, I (Yamaha); **4** Raymond Roche, F (Ducati); **5** Rob Phillis, AUS (Kawasaki); **6** Stéphane Mertens, B (Ducati); **7** Aaron Slight, NZ (Kawasaki); **8** Carl Fogarty, GB (Ducati); **9** Scott Russell, USA (Kawasaki); **10** Hervé Moineau, F (Suzuki); **11** Daniel Amatriain, E (Ducati); **12** Davide Tardozzi, I (Ducati); **13** Piergiorgio Bontempi, I (Kawasaki); **14** Jeffry de Vries, NL (Yamaha); **15** Christer Lindholm, S (Yamaha).
Fastest lap: Polen, 2m 29.89s, 103.571 mph/166.682 km/h.
Championship points: **1** Polen, 121; **2** Phillis, 111; **3** Roche, 103; **4** Slight, 86; **5** Russell, 83; **6** Pirovano, 81.

CIRCUITO DEL JARAMA, Spain, 21 June. 2.393-mile/3.850-km circuit.
Diesel Jeans World Superbike Championship, round 5 (2 x 24 laps, 57.432 miles/92.400 km)
Leg 1
1 Rob Phillis, AUS (Kawasaki), 39m 16.216s, 87.905 mph/141.469 km/h.
2 Raymond Roche, F (Ducati); **3** Giancarlo Falappa, I (Ducati); **4** Daniel Amatriain, E (Ducati); **5** Carl Fogarty, GB (Ducati); **6** Aaron Slight, NZ (Kawasaki); **7** Christer Lindholm, S (Yamaha); **8** Davide Tardozzi, I (Ducati); **9** Baldassarre Monti, I (Honda); **10** Piergiorgio Bontempi, I (Kawasaki); **11** Jehan d'Orgeix, F (Kawasaki); **12** Richard Arnaiz, USA (Honda); **13** Jari Suhonen, SF (Yamaha); **14** Fabrizio Furlan, I (Ducati); **15** Jeffry de Vries, NL (Yamaha).
Fastest lap: Fabrizio Pirovano, I (Yamaha), 1m 37.127s, 88.854 mph/142.996 km/h.
Leg 2
1 Doug Polen, USA (Ducati), 39m 10.739s, 88.109 mph/141.798 km/h.
2 Rob Phillis, AUS (Kawasaki); **3** Fabrizio Pirovano, I (Yamaha); **4** Stéphane Mertens, B (Ducati); **5** Aaron Slight, NZ (Kawasaki); **6** Raymond Roche, F (Ducati); **7** Giancarlo Falappa, I (Ducati); **8** Fabrizio Furlan, I (Ducati); **9** Christer Lindholm, S (Yamaha); **10** Baldassarre Monti, I (Honda); **11** Piergiorgio Bontempi, I (Kawasaki); **12** Richard Arnaiz, USA (Honda); **13** Jehan d'Orgeix, F (Kawasaki); **14** Jari Suhonen, SF (Yamaha); **15** Antonio Moreno, E (Yamaha).
Fastest lap: Polen, 1m 36.955s, 89.011 mph/143.250 km/h.
Championship points: **1** Phillis, 148; **2** Polen, 141; **3** Roche, 130; **4** Slight, 107; **5** Falappa, 101; **6** Pirovano, 96.

ÖSTERREICHRING, Zeltweg, Austria, 28 June. 3.636-mile/5.853-km circuit.
Diesel Jeans World Superbike Championship, round 6 (2 x 18 laps, 65.448 miles/105.350 km)
Leg 1
1 Giancarlo Falappa, I (Ducati), 33m 56.202s, 115.712 mph/186.228 km/h.
2 Rob Phillis, AUS (Kawasaki); **3** Doug Polen, USA (Ducati); **4** Fabrizio Pirovano, I (Yamaha); **5** Davide Tardozzi, I (Ducati); **6** Carl Fogarty, GB (Ducati); **7** Aaron Slight, NZ (Kawasaki); **8** Daniel Amatriain, E (Ducati); **9** Fred Merkel, USA (Yamaha); **10** Simon Crafar, NZ (Honda); **11** Ernst Gschwender, D (Kawasaki); **12** Andreas Meklau, A (Ducati); **13** Jeffry de Vries, NL (Yamaha); **14** Piergiorgio Bontempi, I (Kawasaki); **15** Virginio Ferrari, I (Ducati).
Fastest lap: Falappa, 1m 51.552s, 117.349 mph/188.854 km/h.
Leg 2
1 Giancarlo Falappa, I (Ducati), 33m 51.061s, 116.018 mph/186.713 km/h.
2 Stéphane Mertens, B (Ducati); **3** Raymond Roche, F (Ducati); **4** Rob Phillis, AUS (Kawasaki); **5** Doug Polen, USA (Ducati); **6** Fabrizio Pirovano, I (Yamaha); **7** Carl Fogarty, GB (Ducati); **8** Davide Tardozzi, I (Ducati); **9** Daniel Amatriain, E (Ducati); **10** Fred Merkel, USA (Yamaha); **11** Simon Crafar, NZ (Honda); **12** Jeffry de Vries, NL (Yamaha); **13** Andreas Meklau, A (Ducati); **14** Jari Suhonen, SF (Yamaha); **15** Udo Mark, D (Yamaha).
Fastest lap: Phillis, 1m 50.707s, 118.244 mph/190.295 km/h.
Championship points: **1** Phillis, 178; **2** Polen, 167; **3** Roche, 145; **4** Falappa, 141; **5** Pirovano, 119; **6** Slight, 116.

AUTODROMO INTERNAZIONALE DEL MUGELLO, Italy, 19 July. 3.259-mile/5.245-km circuit.
Diesel Jeans World Superbike Championship, round 7 (2 x 18 laps, 58.662 miles/94.410 km)
Leg 1
1 Raymond Roche, F (Ducati), 36m 02.346s, 97.667 mph/157.179 km/h.
2 Doug Polen, USA (Ducati); **3** Giancarlo Falappa, I (Ducati); **4** Stéphane Mertens, B (Ducati); **5** Fabrizio Pirovano, I (Yamaha); **6** Adrien Morillas, F (Yamaha); **7** Carl Fogarty, GB (Ducati); **8** Daniel Amatriain, E (Ducati); **9** Richard Arnaiz, USA (Honda); **10** Christer Lindholm, S (Yamaha); **11** Piergiorgio Bontempi, I (Kawasaki); **12** Virginio Ferrari, I (Ducati); **13** Andreas Hofmann, D (Kawasaki); **14** Jeffry de Vries, NL (Yamaha); **15** Baldassarre Monti, I (Honda).
Fastest lap: Roche, 1m 58.330s, 99.152 mph/159.570 km/h.
Leg 2
1 Raymond Roche, F (Ducati), 35m 58.846s, 97.825 mph/157.434 km/h.
2 Giancarlo Falappa, I (Ducati); **3** Doug Polen, USA (Ducati); **4** Carl Fogarty, GB (Ducati); **5** Rob Phillis, AUS (Kawasaki); **6** Adrien Morillas, F (Yamaha); **7** Daniel Amatriain, E (Ducati); **8** Christer Lindholm, S (Yamaha); **9** Piergiorgio Bontempi, I (Kawasaki); **10** Jeffry de Vries, NL (Yamaha); **11** Andreas Hofmann, D (Kawasaki); **12** Richard Arnaiz, USA (Honda); **13** Karl Truchsess, A

Compiled by KAY EDGE

(Kawasaki); **14** Fabrizio Furlan, I (Ducati); **15** Massimo Broccoli, I (Kawasaki).
Fastest lap: Roche, 1m 58.504s, 99.007 mph/159.336 km/h.
Championship points: 1 Polen, 199; **2** Phillis, 189; **3** Roche, 185; **4** Falappa, 173; **5** Pirovano, 130; **6** Slight, 116.

JOHOR CIRCUIT, Malaysia, 23 August. 2.398-mile/3.860-km circuit. Diesel Jeans World Superbike Championship, round 8 (2 x 25 laps, 59.950 miles/96.500 km)
Leg 1
1 Raymond Roche, F (Ducati), 38m 47.26s, 92.752 mph/149.270 km/h.
2 Fabrizio Pirovano, I (Yamaha); **3** Rob Phillis, AUS (Kawasaki); **4** Aaron Slight, NZ (Kawasaki); **5** Stéphane Mertens, B (Ducati); **6** Giancarlo Falappa, I (Ducati); **7** Christopher Haldane, NZ (Yamaha); **8** Doug Polen, USA (Ducati); **9** Piergiorgio Bontempi, I (Kawasaki); **10** Adrien Morillas, F (Yamaha); **11** Fred Merkel, USA (Yamaha); **12** Steve Hislop, GB (Kawasaki); **13** Davide Tardozzi, I (Ducati); **14** Trevor Jordan, AUS (Kawasaki); **15** Andrew Stroud, NZ (Kawasaki).
Fastest lap: Jordan, 1m 31.90s, 93.951 mph/151.200 km/h.
Leg 2
1 Doug Polen, USA (Ducati), 38m 25.14s, 93.641 mph/150.700 km/h.
2 Raymond Roche, F (Ducati); **3** Aaron Slight, NZ (Kawasaki); **4** Giancarlo Falappa, I (Ducati); **5** Fred Merkel, USA (Yamaha); **6** Fabrizio Pirovano, I (Yamaha); **7** Daniel Amatriain, E (Ducati); **8** Rob Phillis, AUS (Kawasaki); **9** Trevor Jordan, AUS (Kawasaki); **10** Piergiorgio Bontempi, I (Kawasaki); **11** Andrew Stroud, NZ (Kawasaki); **12** Christopher Haldane, NZ (Yamaha); **13** Adrien Morillas, F (Yamaha); **14** Virginio Ferrari, I (Ducati); **15** Jeffry de Vries, NL (Yamaha).
Fastest lap: Roche, 1m 31.30s, 94.573 mph/152.200 km/h.
Championship points: 1 Polen, 227; **2** Roche, 222; **3** Phillis, 212; **4** Falappa, 196; **5** Pirovano, 157; **6** Slight, 144.

SUGO CIRCUIT, Japan, 30 August. 2.335-mile/3.737-km circuit. Diesel Jeans World Superbike Championship, round 9 (2 x 25 laps, 58.375 miles/93.425 km)
Leg 1
1 Doug Polen, USA (Ducati), 39m 11.247s, 88.895 mph/143.062 km/h.
2 Kevin Magee, AUS (Yamaha); **3** Fabrizio Pirovano, I (Yamaha); **4** Syouichi Tsukamoto, J (Kawasaki); **5** Raymond Roche, F (Ducati); **6** Aaron Slight, NZ (Kawasaki); **7** Keiichi Kitagawa, J (Kawasaki); **8** Stéphane Mertens, B (Ducati); **9** Piergiorgio Bontempi, I (Kawasaki); **10** Mat Mladin, AUS (Kawasaki); **11** Rob Phillis, AUS (Kawasaki); **12** Shinichiro Imai, J (Kawasaki); **13** Davide Tardozzi, I (Ducati); **14** Adrien Morillas, F (Yamaha); **15** Tetsuya Shirai, J (Honda).
Fastest lap: Pirovano, 1m 33.232s, 89.674 mph/144.317 km/h.
Leg 2
1 Doug Polen, USA (Ducati), 39m 07.205s, 89.048 mph/143.309 km/h.
2 Kevin Magee, AUS (Yamaha); **3** Fabrizio Pirovano, I (Yamaha); **4** Aaron Slight, NZ (Kawasaki); **5** Syouichi Tsukamoto, J (Kawasaki); **6** Giancarlo Falappa, I (Ducati); **7** Keiichi Kitagawa, J (Kawasaki); **8** Raymond Roche, F (Ducati); **9** Davide Tardozzi, I (Ducati); **10** Rob Phillis, AUS (Kawasaki); **11** Piergiorgio Bontempi, I (Kawasaki); **12** Mat Mladin, AUS (Kawasaki); **13** Fred Merkel, USA (Yamaha); **14** Wataru Yoshikawa, J (Yamaha); **15** Baldassarre Monti, I (Honda).
Fastest lap: Magee, 1m 32.938s, 89.959 mph/144.774 km/h.
Championship points: 1 Polen, 267; **2** Roche, 241; **3** Phillis, 223; **4** Falappa, 206; **5** Pirovano, 187; **6** Slight, 167.

CIRCUIT VAN DRENTHE, Assen, Holland, 13 September. 2.431-mile/3.913-km circuit. Diesel Jeans World Superbike Championship, round 10 (2 x 24 laps, 58.344 miles/93.912 km)
Leg 1
1 Doug Polen, USA (Ducati), 33m 51.05s, 103.431 mph/166.457 km/h.
2 Stéphane Mertens, B (Ducati); **3** Raymond Roche, F (Ducati); **4** Carl Fogarty, GB (Ducati); **5** Rob Phillis, AUS (Kawasaki); **6** Piergiorgio Bontempi, I (Kawasaki); **7** Aaron Slight, NZ (Kawasaki); **8** Giancarlo Falappa, I (Ducati); **9** Fabrizio Pirovano, I (Yamaha); **10** Adrien Morillas, F (Yamaha); **11** Terry Rymer, GB (Ducati); **12** Christer Lindholm, S (Yamaha); **13** Fred Merkel, USA (Yamaha); **14** Daniel Amatriain, E (Ducati); **15** Roger Kellenberger, CH (Yamaha).
Fastest lap: Roche, 1m 23.58s, 104.727 mph/168.542 km/h.
Leg 2
1 Giancarlo Falappa, I (Ducati), 34m 03.34s, 102.809 mph/165.456 km/h.
2 Carl Fogarty, GB (Ducati); **3** Raymond Roche, F (Ducati); **4** Aaron Slight, NZ (Kawasaki); **5** Daniel Amatriain, E (Ducati); **6** Fabrizio Furlan, I (Ducati); **7** Adrien Morillas, F (Yamaha); **8** Fabrizio Pirovano, I (Yamaha); **9** Roger Kellenberger, CH (Yamaha); **10** Jean-Yves Mounier, F (Yamaha); **11** Mile Pajic, NL (Kawasaki); **12** Johnny Verwijst, NL (Kawasaki); **13** Andreas Meklau, A (Ducati); **14** Jehan d'Orgeix, F (Kawasaki); **15** Florian Ferracci, F (Ducati).
Fastest lap: Roche, 1m 23.11s, 105.319 mph/169.495 km/h.
Championship points: 1 Polen, 287; **2** Roche, 271; **3** Falappa and Phillis, 234; **5** Pirovano, 202; **6** Slight, 189.

AUTODROMO NAZIONALE DI MONZA, Italy, 4 October. 3.6039-mile/5.800-km circuit. Diesel Jeans World Superbike Championship, round 11 (2 x 16 laps, 57.662 miles/92.800 km)
Leg 1
1 Fabrizio Pirovano, I (Yamaha), 35m 06.230s, 98.559 mph/158.615 km/h.
2 Stéphane Mertens, B (Ducati); **3** Rob Phillis, AUS (Kawasaki); **4** Piergiorgio Bontempi, I (Kawasaki); **5** Valerio Destefanis, I (Ducati); **6** Daniel Amatriain, E (Ducati); **7** Jehan d'Orgeix, F (Kawasaki); **8** Mauro Lucchiari, I (Ducati); **9** Jari Suhonen, SF (Yamaha); **10** Doug Polen, USA (Ducati); **11** Virginio Ferrari, I (Ducati); **12** Giancarlo Falappa, I (Ducati); **13** Udo Mark, D (Yamaha); **14** Patrick Igoa, F (Suzuki); **15** Vittorio Scatola, I (Kawasaki).
Fastest lap: Pirovano, 2m 08.355s, 101.080 mph/162.673 km/h.
Leg 2
1 Fabrizio Pirovano, I (Yamaha), 34m 35.065s, 100.039 mph/160.997 km/h.
2 Raymond Roche, F (Ducati); **3** Piergiorgio Bontempi, I (Kawasaki); **4** Stéphane Mertens, B (Ducati); **5** Doug Polen, USA (Ducati); **6** Giancarlo Falappa, I (Ducati); **7** Jehan d'Orgeix, F (Kawasaki); **8** Daniel Amatriain, E (Ducati); **9** Virginio Ferrari, I (Ducati); **10** Jari Suhonen, SF (Yamaha); **11** Gastone Grassetti, I (Ducati); **12** Mauro Lucchiari, I (Ducati); **13** Patrick Igoa, F (Suzuki); **14** Michel Amalric, F (Yamaha); **15** Rob Phillis, AUS (Kawasaki).
Fastest lap: Pirovano, 2m 06.858s, 102.273 mph.164.593 km/h.
Championship points: 1 Polen, 304; **2** Roche, 288; **3** Phillis, 250; **4** Falappa, 248; **5** Pirovano, 242; **6** Slight, 189.

PHILLIP ISLAND, Australia, 18 October. 2.764-mile/4.448-km circuit. Diesel Jeans World Superbike Championship, round 12
Leg 1 (22 laps, 60.808 miles/97.856 km)
1 Kevin Magee, AUS (Yamaha), 36m 25.23s.
2 Doug Polen, USA (Ducati); **3** Stéphane Mertens, B (Ducati); **4** Aaron Slight, NZ (Kawasaki); **5** Giancarlo Falappa, I (Ducati); **6** Rob Phillis, AUS (Kawasaki); **7** Carl Fogarty, GB (Kawasaki); **8** Piergiorgio Bontempi, I (Kawasaki); **9** Malcolm Campbell, AUS (Honda); **10** Fred Merkel, USA (Yamaha); **11** Michael O'Connor, AUS (Honda); **12** Fabrizio Pirovano, I (Yamaha); **13** Martin Craggill, AUS (Kawasaki); **14** Jeffry de Vries, NL (Yamaha); **15** Peter Guest, AUS (Yamaha).
Fastest lap: Slight, 1m 38.29s.
Leg 2 (21 laps, 58.044 miles/93.408 km)
1 Raymond Roche, F (Ducati), 34m 59.57s.
2 Kevin Magee, AUS (Yamaha); **3** Aaron Slight, NZ (Kawasaki); **4** Doug Polen, USA (Ducati); **5** Mat Mladin, AUS (Kawasaki); **6** Fabrizio Pirovano, I (Yamaha); **7** Piergiorgio Bontempi, I (Kawasaki); **8** Michael O'Connor, AUS (Honda); **9** Rob Phillis, AUS (Kawasaki); **10** Scott Doohan, AUS (Yamaha); **11** Martin Craggill, AUS (Kawasaki); **12** Fred Merkel, USA (Yamaha); **13** Jeffry de Vries, NL (Yamaha); **14** Troy Corser, AUS (Yamaha); **15** Kirk McCarthy, AUS (Suzuki).
Fastest lap: Polen, 1m 38.03s.
Championship points: 1 Polen, 334; **2** Roche, 308; **3** Phillis, 267; **4** Falappa, 259; **5** Pirovano, 256; **6** Slight, 217.

MANFEILD, New Zealand, 25 October. 1.94-mile/3.122-km circuit. Diesel Jeans World Superbike Championship, round 13 (2 x 33 laps, 64.02 miles/103.026 km)
Leg 1
1 Doug Polen, USA (Ducati), 36m 18.88s.
2 Aaron Slight, NZ (Kawasaki); **3** Raymond Roche, F (Ducati); **4** Rob Phillis, AUS (Kawasaki); **5** Fabrizio Pirovano, I (Yamaha); **6** Fred Merkel, USA (Yamaha); **7** Piergiorgio Bontempi, I (Kawasaki); **8** Scott Doohan, AUS (Yamaha); **9** Daniel Amatriain, E (Ducati); **10** Troy Corser, AUS (Yamaha); **11** Tony Rees, NZ (Yamaha); **12** Russell Josiah, NZ (Kawasaki); **13** Paul McQuilkin, NZ (Suzuki); **14** Mike King, NZ (Ducati); **15** Scott Buckley, NZ (Yamaha).
Fastest lap: Slight, 1m 07.38s, 100.693 mph/162.05 km/h.
Leg 2
1 Giancarlo Falappa, I (Ducati), 37m 15.17s.
2 Doug Polen, USA (Ducati); **3** Aaron Slight, NZ (Kawasaki); **4** Raymond Roche, F (Ducati); **5** Fabrizio Pirovano, I (Yamaha); **6** Fred Merkel, USA (Yamaha); **7** Rob Phillis, AUS (Kawasaki); **8** Scott Doohan, AUS (Yamaha); **9** Daniel Amatriain, E (Ducati); **10** Troy Corser, AUS (Yamaha); **11** Christer Lindholm, S (Yamaha); **12** Tony Rees, NZ (Yamaha); **13** Paul McQuilkin, NZ (Suzuki); **14** Russell Josiah, NZ (Kawasaki); **15** Scott Buckley, NZ (Yamaha).
Fastest lap: Polen, 1m 06.97s, 101.308 mph/163.04 km/h.

Final Championship points

1	Doug Polen, USA	371
2	Raymond Roche, F	336
3	Rob Phillis, AUS	289
4	Giancarlo Falappa, I	279
5	Fabrizio Pirovano, I	278
6	Aaron Slight, NZ	249

7 Stéphane Mertens, B, 182; **8** Daniel Amatriain, E, 156; **9** Carl Fogarty, GB, 134; **10** Piergiorgio Bontempi, I, 125; **11** Scott Russell, USA, 83; **12** Kevin Magee, AUS, 71; **13** Fred Merkel, USA, 65; **14** Christer Lindholm, S, 50; **15** Adrien Morillas, F, 46.

World Endurance Championship

24 HEURES DU MANS, Bugatti Circuit, Le Mans, France. 25-6 April. World Endurance Championship, round 1. 741 laps of the 2.753-mile/4.430-km circuit, 2039.973 miles/3282.63 km
1 Carl Fogarty/Terry Rymer/Michel Simul, GB/GB/B (750 Kawasaki), 23h 28m 52.57s, 86.866 mph/139.798 km/h.
2 Hervé Moineau/Christian Lavieille/Michel Graziano, F/F/F (750 Suzuki), 737 laps; **3** Guy Bertin/Adrien Morillas/Arnaud de Puniet, F/F/F (750 Honda), 728; **4** Serge David/G. Furling/Jean-Jacques Niklaus, CH/F/CH (750 Honda), 705; **5** Mario DuHamel/Michel Simeon/P. Perrin, CAN/B/F (750 Suzuki), 702; **6** Bruno Langlois/Rachel Nicotte/Jean-Jacques Lovichi, F/F/F (750 Honda), 700; **7** André Lussiana/Peter Linden/Doug Toland, F/S/USA (750 Honda), 695; **8** E. Delarbre/Bruno Soulon/Charles Artigu, F/F/F (750 Honda), 688; **9** Eric Barret/E. Cot/Gilles Fersler, F/F/F (750 Honda), 681; **10** Yannick Legaudu/François Ciciliani/Bernard Darie, F/F/F (750 Suzuki), 680; **11** Simon Watson/Iain Duffus/Dave Hill, GB/GB/GB (750 Kawasaki), 679; **12** Eric Kermarec/O. Morandas/Renaud Dernoncourt, F/F/F (750 Suzuki), 674; **13** Alexandre Jeannin/Patrick Beltzung/Jean-Pierre Schneider, F/F/F (750 Suzuki), 673; **14** Emmanuel Lentaigne/Thierry Autissier/D. Marzloff, F/F/F (750 Suzuki), 664; **15** Russell Benney/Steve Bateman/Steve Manley, GB/GB/GB (750 Kawasaki), 664.
Fastest lap: Fogarty, 1m 46.90s, 92.699 mph/149.186 km/h.
Championship points: 1 Fogarty, Rymer and Simul, 40; **4** Graziano, Lavieille and Moineau, 34; **7** Bertin, Morillas and de Puniet, 30.

24 HEURES DE LIEGE, Spa-Francorchamps, Belgium, 4-5 July. World Endurance Championship, round 2. 531 laps of the 4.340-mile/6.985-km circuit, 2304.688 miles/3709.035 km
1 Terry Rymer/Carl Fogarty/Jehan d'Orgeix, GB/GB/F (750 Kawasaki), 24h 02m 13.94s, 95.880 mph/154.304 km/h.
2 Alex Vieira/Steve Hislop/Jean-Louis Battistini, F/GB/F (750 Kawasaki), 523 laps; **3** Philippe Monneret/Bruno Bonhuil/Jean-Michel Mattioli, F/F/F (750 Yamaha), 509; **4** Michel Simeon/Mario DuHamel/Michel Graziano, B/CAN/F (750 Suzuki), 505; **5** Bruno Soulon/M. Amalric/Simon Buckmaster, F/F/GB (750 Honda), 501; **6** Bernard Millet/Alfred Colet/Léon Planken, F/NL/NL (750 Yamaha), 495; **7** Kurt Gasser/Ruedi Breitenstein/Remy Chaffard, CH/CH/F (750 Yamaha), 489; **8** Thierry Micha/J. Jaquier/R. Emonts, B/CH/B (750 Honda), 487; **9** Hermann Perren/St Ambord/Herbert Graf, CH/CH/CH (750 Kawasaki), 484; **10** Volker Urbanski/Hartmut Rieckmann/Gerard van der Wal, D/D/NL (750 Yamaha), 482; **11** Jean-Jacques Niklaus/J.-P. Verkenne/D. Heinen, CH/B/D (750 Honda), 476; **12** K. Schmidt/Rüdiger Seefeldt/M. Mogendorf, D/D/D (750 Suzuki), 474; **13** H. Fischer/P. Doppenberg/D. Euwens, NL/NL/NL (750 Kawasaki), 474; **14** B. Weynand/B. Scheiff/M. Deville, B/B/B (750 Honda), 473; **15** H. Vandenbroek/J. Bosh/J. Damen, NL/NL/NL (750 Kawasaki), 461.
Fastest lap: not available.
Championship points: 1 Fogarty and Rymer, 80; **3** Graziano, 60; **4** DuHamel and Simeon, 48; **6** d'Orgeix, 40.

SUZUKA EIGHT HOURS, Suzuka International Racing Course, Japan, 26 July. World Endurance Championship, round 3. 208 laps of the 3.662-mile/5.859-km circuit, 761.696 miles/1218.672 km
1 Wayne Gardner/Daryl Beattie, AUS/AUS (750 Honda), 8h 00m 07.117s, 94.709 mph/152.42 km/h.
2 Kevin Magee/Niall Mackenzie, AUS/GB (750 Yamaha), 208 laps; **3** S. Takeishi/Kenichiro Iwahashi, J/J (750 Honda), 206; **4** Freddie Spencer/Ryuji Tsuruta, USA/J (750 Honda), 204; **5** Masano Aoki/K. Ohsaka, J/J (750 Suzuki), 204; **6** Rob Phillis/Aaron Slight, AUS/NZ (750 Kawasaki), 204; **7** A. Yanagawa/N. Numata, J/J (750 Suzuki), 204; **8** Keiichi Kitagawa/T. Crookes, J/ZA (750 Kawasaki), 204; **9** N. Aoki/T. Aoki, J/J (750 Honda), 203; **10** Scott Russell/Thomas Stevens, USA/USA (750 Kawasaki), 202; **11** Norihiko Fujiwara/Yasutomo Nagai, J/J (750 Yamaha), 201; **12** Shunji Yatsushiro/Malcolm Campbell, J/AUS (750 Moriwaki), 201; **13** Takahiro Sohwa/Syouichi Tsukamoto, J/J (750 Kawasaki), 200; **14** W. Yoshikawa/M. Hanawa, J/J (750 Yamaha), 199; **15** Y. Sugai/T. Kaneyasu, J/J (750 Honda), 198.
Fastest lap: not available.
Championship points: 1 Fogarty and Rymer, 80; **3** Graziano, 60; **4** DuHamel and Simeon, 48; **6** d'Orgeix, 40.

56e BOL D'OR, Circuit Paul Ricard, France, 19-20 September. World Endurance Championship, round 4. 635 laps of the 3.610-mile/5.810-km circuit, 2292.35 miles/3689.35 km
1 Terry Rymer/Carl Fogarty/Steve Hislop, GB/GB/GB (750 Kawasaki), 23h 08m 27.78s, 99.457 mph/160.060 km/h.
2 Alex Vieira/Jean-Louis Battistini/Jehan d'Orgeix, F/F/F (750 Kawasaki), 630 laps; **3** Guy Bertin/Adrien Morillas/Arnaud de Puniet, F/F/F (750 Honda), 621; **4** Michel Simeon/Mario DuHamel/Michel Graziano, B/CAN/F (750 Suzuki), 618; **5** Bruno Langlois/Yves Briguet/Bernard Cazade, F/F/F (750 Honda), 617; **6** Mark Linscott/Steve Bateman/Steve Manley, GB/GB/GB (750 Kawasaki), 608; **7** Serge David/Jean-Luc Romanens/D. Heinen, CH/CH/D (750 Honda), 605; **8** Rachel Nicotte/Jean-Jacques Lovichi/Philippe Mouchet, F/F/F (750 Honda), 604; **9** Bruno Soulon/Alain Bronec/Simon Buckmaster, F/F/GB (750 Honda), 601; **10** Bernard Millet/Alfred Colet/Léon Planken, F/NL/NL (750 Yamaha), 600; **11** Bernard Dujardin/Krummenacher/Tercier, B/B/B (750 Honda), 590; **12** Pascal Barthod/Yves Besson/Bruno Germain, F/F/F (750 Honda), 588; **13** Maurice Coq/Bernard Fourcadet/Thierry Pelletant, F/F/F (750 Honda), 585; **14** Joël Petit/Patrick Lelan/Alexandre Serves, F/F/F (750 Honda), 582; **15** Eric Barret/Bernard Darie/Gilles Fersler, F/F/F (750 Honda), 580.
Fastest lap: Fogarty, 2m 01.22s, 107.639 mph/173.229 km/h.
Championship points: 1 Fogarty and Rymer, 120; **3** Graziano, 86; **4** d'Orgeix, DuHamel, Hislop and Simeon, 74.

6 HOUR DAY-NIGHT ENDURANCE, Phillip Island, Australia, 17 October. World Endurance Championship, round 5. 176 laps of the 2.764-mile/4.448-km circuit, 486.464 miles/782.848 km
1 Terry Rymer/Carl Fogarty, GB/GB (750 Kawasaki), 5h 59m 21.15s.
2 Jehan d'Orgeix/Trevor Jordan, F/AUS (750 Kawasaki), 173 laps; **3** Steve Manley/Mark Linscott, GB/GB (750 Kawasaki), 169; **4** Michel Graziano/Steve Martin, F/AUS (750 Suzuki), 169; **5** Ed Miller/Stephen Tozer, AUS/AUS (750 Honda), 169; **6** Tony Yates/Michael Bubb, AUS/AUS (750 Suzuki), 169; **7** Doug Pitman/Ben Archibald, AUS/AUS (750 Yamaha), 161; **8** Paul Mead/Derek Aboltins, AUS/AUS (750 Yamaha), 159; **9** Darren Lewis/Michael Milligan, AUS/AUS (600 Honda), 159; **10** John Chiodo/Geoff Winzer, AUS/AUS (600 Honda), 158; **11** Jim Raskatos/Scott Webster, AUS/AUS (750 Honda), 155; **12** Darryl Mallam/Graeme Wilshaw, AUS/AUS (750 Suzuki), 155; **13** Kym Grosser/Graeme Snaith, AUS/AUS (600 Honda), 155; **14** Paul Gibson/Graeme McDonough, AUS/AUS (600 Yamaha), 153; **15** Paul Caridi/Rebecca Belbin, AUS/AUS (600 Yamaha), 152.
Fastest lap: Fogarty, 1m 52.55s.
Championship points: 1 Fogarty and Rymer, 140; **3** Graziano, 99; **4** d'Orgeix, 91; **5** DuHamel, Hislop and Simeon, 74.

JOHOR 6 HOURS, Johor Racing Circuit, Malaysia, 25 October. World Endurance Championship, round 6. 227 laps of the 2.39-mile/3.846-km circuit, 542.53 miles/873.042 km
1 Terry Rymer/Carl Fogarty, GB/GB (750 Kawasaki), 6h 1m 24.35s.
2 Chris Haldane/Michael Dowson, NZ/AUS (750 Yamaha), 223 laps; **3** Michel Graziano/Michel Simeon, F/B (750 Suzuki), 217; **4** M. Watanabe/K. Kaminao, J/J (750 Honda), 210; **5** N. Miura/S. Ohisuka, J/J (750 Honda), 209; **6** P. Smolik/Sepp Doppler, A/A (750 Honda), 207; **7** T. Yamamoto/M. Hyuga, J/J (750 Honda), 207; **8** D. Buckmaster/J. Hafey, AUS/AUS (750 Honda), 205; **9** Y. Shinjo/S. Noguchi, J/J (750 Honda), 204; **10** K. Iamura/H. Hiyagi, J/J (750 Honda), 200; **11** F. Beliermann/Tony Carey, D/IRL (750 Suzuki), 195; **12** M. Grein/Hermann Perren, D/D (750 Suzuki), 193; **13** Dave Hill/Dennis Winterbottom, GB/GB (750 Yamaha), 190; **14** T. Hauser/Karl-Heinz Lemberg, D/D (750 Suzuki), 189.
Fastest lap: Fogarty, 1m 31.73s, 94.13 mph/151.488 km/h.

Final Championship points

1=	Carl Fogarty, GB	160
1=	Terry Rymer, GB	160
3	Michel Graziano, F	114
4	Jehan d'Orgeix, F	91
5	Michel Simeon, B	89
6=	Mario DuHamel, CAN	74
6=	Steve Hislop, GB	74

8 Jean-Louis Battistini, F and Alex Vieira, F, 68; **10** Guy Bertin, F, Adrien Morillas, F and Arnaud de Puniet, F, 60; **13** Bruno Soulon, F, 52; **14** Bruno Langlois, F, 42; **15** Michel Simul, B, 40.

European Championship

CIRCUITO DE JEREZ, Spain, 8 March. 2.621-mile/4.218-km circuit. European Championship, 125 cc, round 1 (17 laps, 44.557 miles/71.706 km)
1 Juan Borja, E (Honda), 33m 11.62s, 80.548 mph/129.614 km/h.
2 José Luis Cardoso, E (Cobas); **3** José Luis Rabadan, E (Cobas); **4** Serafino Foti, I (Honda); **5** Jos van Dongen, NL (Honda); **6** Lucio Cecchinello, I (Aprilia); **7** Robert Dunlop, GB (Honda); **8** Manfred Baumann, A (Honda); **9** Eugenio Moncayo, E (Cobas); **10** Emilio Alzamora, E (Honda); **11** Kristian Kaas, SF (Honda); **12** Robert Duss, CH (Honda); **13** Paolo Capriolo, I (Honda); **14** Emilio Gracia, E (Honda); **15** Stefan Kurfiss, D (Honda).
Fastest lap: Cardoso, 1m 55.95s, 81.375 mph/130.960 km/h.
Championship points: 1 Borja, 20; **2** Cardoso, 17; **3** Rabadan, 15; **4** Foti, 13; **5** van Dongen, 11; **6** Cecchinello, 10.

250 cc, round 1 (18 laps, 47.178 miles/75.924 km)
1 Luis Maurel, E (Aprilia), 34m 00.55s, 83.231 mph/133.947 km/h.
2 Oscar Sainz, E (Aprilia); **3** Massimo Pennacchioli, I (Aprilia); **4** Ian Newton, GB (Aprilia); **5** Enrique de Juan, E (Yamaha); **6** Alex Sirera, E (Yamaha); **7** Francesco Bastianini, I (Aprilia); **8** Christian Boudinot, F (Aprilia); **9** Jean Foray, F (Yamaha); **10** Woolsey Coulter, GB (Honda); **11** Paul Brown, GB (Yamaha); **12** Bernard Garcia, F (Yamaha); **13** Nigel Bosworth, GB (Yamaha); **14** Volker Bähr, D (Honda); **15** Jorg Seel, D (Yamaha).
Fastest lap: Maurel, 1m 52.09s, 84.177 mph/135.470 km/h.
Championship points: 1 Maurel, 20; **2** Sainz, 17; **3** Pennacchioli, 15; **4** Newton, 13; **5** de Juan, 11; **6** Sirera, 10.

Supersport 600, round 1 (22 laps, 57.662 miles/92.796 km)
1 Pere Riba, E (Honda), 43m 21.66s, 79.787 mph/128.405 km/h.
2 Antonio Calasso, I (Honda); **3** Ricardo Suarez, E (Honda); **4** Ernesto Gomez, E (Yamaha); **5** Stefan Scheschowitsch, D (Honda); **6** Josep Volta, E (Honda); **7** Rafael Rodriguez,

E (Yamaha); **8** Rodrigo Mut, E (Honda); **9** Alfred Grossauer, A (Honda); **10** Vicens Santolaya, E (Honda); **11** Lars Bosson, S (Honda); **12** José Ferrara, E (Honda); **13** Gilles Riva, F (Honda); **14** Massimiliano Degiovanni, I (Honda); **15** Jorge Calabuig, E (Honda).
Fastest lap: Calasso, 1m 56.88s, 80.727 mph/128.405 km/h.
Championship points: **1** Riba, 20; **2** Calasso, 17; **3** Suarez, 15; **4** Gomez, 13; **5** Scheschowitsch, 11; **6** Volta, 10.

KIRKISTOWN, Co. Down, Northern Ireland, 11 April. 1.5-mile/2.414-km circuit.
European Championship, 125 cc, round 2 (30 laps, 45 miles/72.42 km)
1 Juan Borja, E (Honda), 32m 04.24s, 83.96 mph/135.121 km/h.
2 Serafino Foti, I (Honda); **3** Lucio Cecchinello, I (Aprilia); **4** Luigi Ancona, I (Aprilia); **5** Paolo Capriolo, I (Honda); **6** Stefan Kurfiss, D (Honda); **7** Carlos Checa, E (Honda); **8** Rafael Roses, E (Honda); **9** Emilio Alzamora, E (Honda); **10** Jeremy McWilliams, GB (Honda); **11** Ron Reniers, NL (Honda); **12** Marc Fissette, B (Honda); **13** Luciano Fabiani, I (Honda); **14** Roberto Sassone, I (Honda); **15** Alain Kempener, B (Honda).
Fastest lap: Borja, 85.98 mph/138.371 km/h.
Championship points: **1** Borja, 40; **2** Foti, 30; **3** Cecchinello, 25; **4** Cardoso, 17; **5** Rabadan, 15; **6** Capriolo, 14.

250 cc, round 2 (32 laps, 48 miles/77.248 km)
1 Ian Newton, GB (Aprilia), 40m 57.32s, 90.68 mph/145.935 km/h.
2 Massimo Pennacchioli, I (Aprilia); **3** Luis Maurel, E (Aprilia); **4** Jean Foray, F (Yamaha); **5** Marc Garcia, F (Yamaha); **6** Jeremy McWilliams, GB (Yamaha); **7** Michele Gallina, I (Aprilia); **8** Laurent Naveau, B (Yamaha); **9** Evren Bischoff, D (Aprilia); **10** José Kuhn, F (Honda); **11** Steve Sawford, GB (Yamaha); **12** Beni Metzger, CH (Yamaha); **13** William Costes, F (Yamaha); **14** Miguel Castilla, E (Honda); **15** Hori Yoshinari, B (Honda).
Fastest lap: Newton and Sawford, 92.50 mph/148.864 km/h.
Championship points: **1** Maurel, 35; **2** Newton, 33; **3** Pennacchioli, 32; **4** Foray, 20; **5** Sainz, 17; **6** de Juan and M. Garcia, 11.

Supersport 600, round 2 (38 laps, 57 miles/91.732 km)
1 Stefan Scheschowitsch, D (Honda), 42m 24.93s, 80.42 mph/129.423 km/h.
2 Derek Young, GB (Honda); **3** Ian King, GB (Honda); **4** Joaquin Escoda, E (Honda); **5** Christian Zwedorn, A (Honda); **6** F.P. Baro, E (Honda); **7** Antonio Calasso, I (Honda); **8** Josep Volta, E (Honda); **9** Rodrigo Mut, E (Honda); **10** Lars Bosson, S (Honda); **11** Vincenzo de Marco, I (Bimota); **12** Michel Eberle, D (Honda); **13** Jurg Kappeli, CH (Honda); **14** Mario Liverani, I (Honda); **15** Thomas Schwing, D (Honda).
Fastest lap: Scheschowitsch, 82.61 mph/132.937 km/h.
Championship points: **1** Scheschowitsch, 31; **2** Calasso, 26; **3** Riba, 20; **4** Volta, 18; **5** Mut and Suarez, 15.

Sidecars, round 1 (32 laps, 48 miles/77.248 km)
1 Gary Knight/Malcolm Jackson, GB/GB (Windle-Krauser), 36m 50.54s, 77.96 mph/125.464 km/h.
2 Tony Baker/Simon Prior, GB/GB (LCR-Krauser); **3** Eddy Wright/Andy Hetherington, GB/GB (LCR-Krauser); **4** Kenny Howles/Phil Coombes, GB/GB (Ireson-Krauser); **5** Clive Stirrat/Tony Stevens, GB/GB (LCR-JDK); **6** Harry Smit/Ted de Rijk, NL/NL (LCR-Krauser); **7** Barry Laidlow/Kevin Morgan, GB/GB (LCR); **8** Albert Giesemann/Lohmann, D/D (LCR-Krauser); **9** Eric Cornes/Graham Wellington, GB/GB (Ireson-Krauser); **10** Roger Body/Andy Peach, GB/GB (LCR-Krauser); **11** Brian Gray/Ruth Clements, GB/GB (ADM); **12** Lutz Herdram/Holser, D/D (Windle-ADM); **13** David Lee/Richard Lee, GB/GB (Windle-ADM).
Fastest lap: Knight/Jackson, 79.47 mph/127.895 km/h.
Championship points: **1** Knight, 20; **2** Baker, 17; **3** Wright, 15; **4** Howles, 13; **5** Stirrat, 11; **6** Smit, 10.

DONINGTON PARK CIRCUIT, England, 19 April. 2.5-mile/4.023-km circuit.
European Championship, 125 cc, round 3 (24 laps, 60 miles/96.552 km)
1 Juan Borja, E (Honda), 42m 19.68s, 85.05 mph/136.87 km/h.
2 Serafino Foti, I (Honda); **3** Rob Orme, GB (Honda); **4** Robert Dunlop, GB (Honda); **5** Carlos Checa, E (Honda); **6** Neil Hodgson, GB (Honda); **7** Gérard Rolland-Piegue, B (Honda); **8** Jos van Dongen, NL (Honda); **9** Manfred Baumann, A (Honda); **10** Ivan Tschudin, CH (Honda); **11** Alan Patterson, IRL (Honda); **12** Paolo Capriolo, I (Honda); **13** Ron Renier, NL (Honda); **14** Paolo Aicardi, I (Honda); **15** Barry Stanley, GB (Honda).
Fastest lap: Foti, 1m 44.63s, 86.01 mph/138.43 km/h.
Championship points: **1** Borja, 60; **2** Foti, 47; **3** Cecchinello, 25; **4** Dunlop, 22; **5** Checa, 20; **6** van Dongen, 19.

250 cc, round 3 (24 laps, 60 miles/95.552 km)
1 Luis Maurel, E (Aprilia), 40m 01.05s, 89.96 mph/144.77 km/h.
2 Ian Newton, GB (Aprilia); **3** Jeremy McWilliams, GB (Yamaha); **4** Christian Boudinot, F (Aprilia); **5** Laurent Naveau, B (Yamaha); **6** Massimo Pennacchioli, I (Aprilia); **7** Bernard Garcia, F (Yamaha); **8** Nigel Bosworth, GB (Yamaha); **9** Enrique de Juan, E (Yamaha); **10** Marc Garcia, F (Yamaha); **11** David Heal, GB (Yamaha); **12** Beni Metzger, CH (Yamaha); **13** Woolsey Coulter, GB (Honda); **14** Alex Sirera, E (Yamaha); **15** José Kuhn, F (Honda).
Fastest lap: Maurel, 1m 39.05s, 90.86 mph/146.23 km/h.
Championship points: **1** Maurel, 55; **2** Newton, 50; **3** Pennacchioli, 42; **4** Boudinot, 21; **5** Foray, 20; **6** de Juan, 18.

Supersport 600, round 3 (25 laps, 62.5 miles/100.575 km)
1 Rachel Nicotte, F (Honda), 43m 21.75s, 86.48 mph/139.17 km/h.
2 Stefan Scheschowitsch, D (Honda); **3** Ricardo Suarez, E (Honda); **4** Rodrigo Mut, E (Honda); **5** Antonio Calasso, I (Honda); **6** Lars Bosson, S (Honda); **7** Antonio Palizzi, I (Honda); **8** Mario Liverani, I (Honda); **9** Gilles Riva, F (Honda); **10** Lars de Jorge, E (Honda); **11** Martin Johansson, S (Honda); **12** Vincens Santolaya, E (Honda); **13** Alfred Grossauer, A (Honda); **14** Thomas Schwing, D (Honda); **15** Joaquin Escoda, E (Honda).
Fastest lap: Pere Riba, E (Honda), 1m 42.87s, 87.48 mph/140.80 km/h.
Championship points: **1** Scheschowitsch, 48; **2** Calasso, 37; **3** Suarez, 30; **4** Mut, 28; **5** Bosson, 21; **6** Riba, 20.

HOCKENHEIMRING, Germany, 10 May. 4.220-mile/6.792-km circuit.
European Championship, 125 cc, round 4 (11 laps, 46.420 miles/74.712 km)
1 Luigi Ancona, I (Aprilia), 26m 59.45s, 103.199 mph/166.083 km/h.
2 Rob Orme, GB (Honda); **3** Manolo Omarini, I (Honda); **4** Stefan Kurfiss, D (Honda); **5** Alessandro de Carli, I (Honda); **6** Hans Koopman, NL (Honda); **7** Hakan Olsson, S (Rotax); **8** Roberto Sassone, I (Honda); **9** Lucio Cecchinello, I (Aprilia); **10** Carlos Checa, E (Honda); **11** Henrik Rasmussen, DK (Yamaha); **12** Emilio Alzamora, E (Honda); **13** Armin Fischer, D (Cobas); **14** Jos van Dongen, NL (Honda); **15** Oliver Kohlinger, D (Honda).
Fastest lap: Ancona, 2m 25.57s, 104.370 mph/167.968 km/h.
Championship points: **1** Borja, 60; **2** Foti, 47; **3** Ancona, 33; **4** Cecchinello and Orme, 32; **6** Checa, 26.

250 cc, round 4 (12 laps, 50.640 miles/81.504 km)
1 Massimo Pennacchioli, I (Aprilia), 26m 56.74s, 112.769 mph/181.485 km/h.
2 Luis Maurel, E (Aprilia); **3** Bernard Garcia, F (Yamaha); **4** Christian Boudinot, F (Aprilia); **5** Volker Bähr, D (Honda); **6** Riccardo Ascone, I (Aprilia); **7** Laurent Naveau, B (Yamaha); **8** Oscar Sainz, E (Aprilia); **9** Jorg Seel, D (Yamaha); **10** Jean Foray, F (Yamaha); **11** Rolf Ammann, CH (Yamaha); **12** Pierre-André Fontannaz, CH (Aprilia); **13** Peter Koller, D (Honda); **14** Miguel Castilla, E (Yamaha); **15** Marc Garcia, F (Yamaha).
Fastest lap: B. Garcia, 2m 13.46s, 113.841 mph/183.209 km/h.
Championship points: **1** Maurel, 72; **2** Pennacchioli, 62; **3** Newton, 50; **4** Boudinot, 34; **5** B. Garcia and Naveau, 28.

Sidecars, round 2 (11 laps, 46.420 miles/74.712 km)
1 Gary Knight/Malcolm Jackson, GB/GB (Windle-Krauser), 26m 00.21s, 107.118 mph/172.389 km/h.
2 Gary Thomas/Rinie Bettgens, GB/NL (LCR-Krauser); **3** Roger Body/Andy Peach, GB/GB (LCR-Krauser); **4** Harry Smit/Ted de Rijk, NL/NL (LCR-Krauser); **5** Michel Ferrand/Martial Charpentier, F/F (LCR); **6** Markus Schlosser/B. Hänni, CH/CH (LCR); **7** Barry Laidlow/Kevin Morgan, GB/GB (LCR-JPX); **8** Ingemar Eriksson/Peter Linden, S/S (LCR); **9** Kenny Howles/Phil Coombes, GB/GB (Ireson); **10** Benny Janssen/Frans van Kessel, NL/NL (LCR-Krauser); **11** Eric Cornes/Graham Wellington, GB/GB (Reson-Krauser); **12** Ward Scarth/Lin Scarth, GB/GB (Windle-JPX); **13** Thomas Reuter/Ulla Harms, D/D (LCR-ADM); **14** Janez Remse/Borut Krajnc, SLO/SLO (Busch-Honda); **15** Gianpaolo Arlati/Oscar Combi, I/I (LCR).
Fastest lap: Knight, 2m 20.36s, 108.245 mph/174.203 km/h.
Championship points: **1** Knight, 40; **2** Smit, 23; **3** Body, 21; **4** Howles, 20; **5** Laidlow, 18; **6** Baker and Thomas, 17.

SPA-FRANCORCHAMPS CIRCUIT, Belgium, 24 May. 4.312-mile/6.940-km circuit.
European Championship, 125 cc, round 5 (11 laps, 47.432 miles/76.340 km)
1 Manfred Baumann, A (Honda), 30m 18.49s, 93.906 mph/151.127 km/h.
2 Lucio Cecchinello, I (Aprilia); **3** Stefan Kurfiss, D (Honda); **4** Carlos Checa, E (Honda); **5** Hans Koopman, NL (Honda); **6** Alain Kempener, B (Honda); **7** Sven Dolenc, D (Gazzaniga); **8** Emilio Alzamora, E (Honda); **9** Ivan Tschudin, CH (Honda); **10** Alessandro de Carli, I (Honda); **11** Robert Zeyen, D (Honda); **12** Paolo Aicardi, I (Honda); **13** Livio Bellone, I (Aprilia); **14** Manolo Omarini, I (Honda); **15** Serge Julin, B (Honda).
Fastest lap: Baumann, 2m 43.20s, 95.124 mph/153.088 km/h.
Championship points: **1** Borja, 60; **2** Cecchinello, 49; **3** Foti, 47; **4** Checa and Kurfiss, 39; **6** Baumann, 35.

250 cc, round 5 (12 laps, 51.744 miles/83.290 km)
1 Laurent Naveau, B (Yamaha), 34m 22.03s, 90.345 mph/145.394 km/h.
2 Luis Maurel, E (Aprilia); **3** Oscar Sainz, E (Aprilia); **4** José Kuhn, F (Honda); **5** Siegfried Minich, A (Yamaha); **6** Jorg Seel, D (Yamaha); **7** Michael Schulten, D (Rotax); **8** Marc Garcia, F (Yamaha); **9** Beni Metzger, CH (Yamaha); **10** Miguel Castilla, E (Yamaha); **11** Ian Newton, GB (Aprilia); **12** Jean Foray, F (Yamaha); **13** Rainer Braunweiler, D (Yamaha); **14** Stefan Steiner, CH (Yamaha); **15** Volker Bähr, D (Honda).
Fastest lap: Beat Muff, CH (Yamaha), 2m 42.71s, 95.411 mph/153.549 km/h.
Championship points: **1** Maurel, 89; **2** Pennacchioli, 62; **3** Newton, 55; **4** Naveau, 48; **5** Sainz, 40; **6** Boudinot, 34.

Supersport 600, round 4 (13 laps, 56.056 miles/90.220 km)
1 Stefan Scheschowitsch, D (Honda), 34m 48.16s, 96.647 mph/155.539 km/h.
2 Rachel Nicotte, F (Honda); **3** Pere Riba, E (Honda); **4** Rodrigo Mut, E (Honda); **5** Joaquin Escoda, E (Honda); **6** Peter Haug, CH (Honda); **7** Michael Eberle, D (Honda); **8** Alfred Grossauer, A (Honda); **9** Lars Bosson, S (Honda); **10** Mario Liverani, I (Honda); **11** Michael Paquay, B (Honda); **12** Josep Volta, E (Honda); **13** Hugues Blanc, CH (Honda); **14** Antonio Calasso, I (Honda); **15** Massimiliano Degiovanni, I (Honda).
Fastest lap: Nicotte, 2m 38.83s, 97.742 mph/157.300 km/h.
Championship points: **1** Scheschowitsch, 68; **2** Mut, 41; **3** Calasso, 39; **4** Nicotte, 37; **5** Riba, 35; **6** Suarez, 30.

SALZBURGRING, Austria, 31 May. 2.636-mile/4.243-km circuit.
European Championship, 250 cc, round 6 (18 laps, 47.448 miles/76.374 km)
1 Luis Maurel, E (Aprilia), 26m 06.413s, 109.067 mph/175.527 km/h.
2 Massimo Pennacchioli, I (Aprilia); **3** Maxwald Hannes, A (Yamaha); **4** Enrique de Juan, E (Yamaha); **5** Marc Garcia, F (Yamaha); **6** Laurent Naveau, B (Yamaha); **7** Jean Foray, F (Yamaha); **8** David Vasquez, E (Aprilia); **9** William Costes, F (Yamaha); **10** Miguel Castilla, E (Yamaha); **11** José Kuhn, F (Honda); **12** Alex Sirera, E (Yamaha); **13** Francesco Bastianini, I (Aprilia); **14** Manuel Gibernau, E (Yamaha); **15** Angelo Teta, CH (Yamaha).
Fastest lap: Maurel, 1m 25.509s.
Championship points: **1** Maurel, 109; **2** Pennacchioli, 79; **3** Naveau, 58; **4** Newton, 55; **5** Sainz, 40; **6** Foray, 39.

Supersport 600, round 5 (22 laps, 57.992 miles/93.346 km)
1 Stefan Scheschowitsch, D (Honda), 32m 41.039s, 106.479 mph/171.361 km/h.
2 Christian Zwedorn, A (Honda); **3** Pere Riba, E (Honda); **4** Antonio Calasso, I (Honda); **5** Mario Liverani, I (Honda); **6** Joaquin Escoda, E (Honda); **7** Antonio Palizzi, I (Honda); **8** Massimiliano Degiovanni, I (Honda); **9** Rodrigo Mut, E (Honda); **10** Alfred Grossauer, A (Honda); **11** Mauro Mastrelli, I (Honda); **12** Lars de Jorge, E (Honda); **13** Josep Volta, E (Honda); **14** Ricardo Suarez, E (Honda); **15** Karl Lindinger, A (Honda).
Fastest lap: Escoda, 1m 27.938s.
Championship points: **1** Scheschowitsch, 88; **2** Calasso, 52; **3** Riba, 50; **4** Mut, 48; **5** Nicotte, 37; **6** Escoda, 35.

Sidecars, round 3 (17 laps, 44.812 miles/72.131 km)
1 Barry Smith/Trevor Hopkinson, GB/GB (Windle-ADM), 25m 34.994s, 107.006 mph/172.209 km/h.
2 Brian Gray/Steve Pointer, GB/GB (LCR); **3** Gary Knight/Malcolm Jackson, GB/GB (Windle-Krauser); **4** Clive Stirrat/Tony Stevens, GB/GB (LCR); **5** Roger Body/Andy Peach, GB/GB (LCR-Krauser); **6** Gary Thomas/Rinie Bettgens, GB/NL (LCR-Krauser); **7** Gianpaolo Arlati/Oscar Combi, I/I (LCR); **8** Eric Cornes/Horne, GB/GB (Reson-Krauser); **9** Barry Laidlow/Ruth Clements, GB/GB (LCR-JPX); **10** Benny Janssen/Frans van Kessel, NL/NL (LCR-Krauser); **11** Baptist Kohlmann/Ernst Theuer, D/D (LCR-ADM); **12** Hans Peters/Van de Kamp, NL/NL (LCR-Krauser); **13** Chris Baert/Willem van Dis, B/B (ADM); **14** Janez Remse/Borut Krajnc, SLO/SLO (Busch-Honda).
Fastest lap: Smith, 1m 28.669s.
Championship points: **1** Knight, 55; **2** Body, 32; **3** Thomas, 27; **4** Laidlow, 25; **5** Stirrat, 24; **6** Smit, 23.

CIRCUIT VAN DRENTHE, Assen, Holland, 23 June. 3.759-mile/6.049-km circuit.
European Championship, 125 cc, round 6 (12 laps, 45.108 miles/72.588 km)
1 Luigi Ancona, I (Aprilia), 28m 32.34s, 94.826 mph/152.608 km/h.
2 Lucio Cecchinello, I (Aprilia); **3** Stefan Kurfiss, D (Honda); **4** Juan Borja, E (Honda); **5** Emilio Gracia, E (Honda); **6** Adrie Nijenhuis, NL (Honda); **7** Manfred Baumann, A (Honda); **8** Bert Smit, NL (Honda); **9** Henri Sala, NL (Aprilia); **10** Carlos Checa, E (Honda); **11** Henrik Rasmussen, DK (Yamaha); **12** Emilio Alzamora, E (Honda); **13** Hakan Olsson, S (Rotax); **14** Livio Bellone, I (Aprilia); **15** Sven Dolenc, D (Gazzaniga).
Fastest lap: Kurfiss, 2m 21.36s, 95.722 mph/154.049 km/h.
Championship points: **1** Borja, 73; **2** Cecchinello, 66; **3** Kurfiss, 54; **4** Ancona, 53; **5** Foti, 47; **6** Checa, 45.

250 cc, round 7 (52.626 miles/84.686 km)
1 Luis Maurel, E (Aprilia), 31m 03.53s, 101.654 mph/163.597 km/h.
2 Laurent Naveau, B (Yamaha); **3** Marc Garcia, F (Yamaha); **4** Bernard Garcia, F (Yamaha); **5** Evren Bischoff, D (Aprilia); **6** Alex Sirera, E (Yamaha); **7** William Costes, F (Yamaha); **8** Volker Bähr, D (Honda); **9** Jeremy McWilliams, GB (Yamaha); **10** Francesco Bastianini, I (Aprilia); **11** Riccardo Ascone, I (Aprilia); **12** Jean Foray, F (Yamaha); **13** Miguel Castilla, E (Yamaha); **14** Enrique de Juan, E (Yamaha); **15** Christian Boudinot, F (Aprilia).
Fastest lap: Maurel, 2m 11.44s, 102.946 mph/165.675 km/h.

Supersport 600, round 6 (16 laps, 60.144 miles/96.784 km)
1 Pere Riba, E (Honda), 36m 42.46s, 98.298 mph/158.196 km/h.
2 Antonio Calasso, I (Honda); **3** Stefan Scheschowitsch, D (Honda); **4** Phil Borley, GB (Honda); **5** Christian Zwedorn, A (Honda); **6** Antonio Palizzi, I (Honda); **7** Rodrigo Mut, E (Honda); **8** Josep Volta, E (Honda); **9** Mario Liverani, I (Honda); **10** Lars Bosson, S (Honda); **11** Ricardo Suarez, E (Honda); **12** Jorge Calabuig, E (Honda); **13** Johnny Nordberg, S (Yamaha); **14** Gilles Riva, F (Honda); **15** Roger Karlsson, S (Honda).
Fastest lap: Riba, 2m 16.31s, 99.268 mph/159.756 km/h.
Championship points: **1** Scheschowitsch, 103; **2** Riba, 70; **3** Calasso, 69; **4** Mut, 57; **5** Zwedorn, 39; **6** Nicotte and Suarez, 37.

Sidecars, round 4 (12 laps, 45.108 miles/72.588 km)
1 Gary Knight/Malcolm Jackson, GB/GB (Windle-Krauser), 28m 00.59s, 96.618 mph/155.491 km/h.
2 Barry Smith/Trevor Hopkinson, GB/GB (Windle-ADM); **3** Roger Body/Andy Peach, GB/GB (LCR-Krauser); **4** Gary Thomas/Rinie Bettgens, GB/NL (LCR-Krauser); **5** Albert Giesemann/Eckhart Rösinger, D/D (LCR-ADM-Krauser); **6** Kenny Howles/Phil Coombes, GB/GB (Ireson); **7** Benny Janssen/Frans van Kessel, NL/NL (LCR-Krauser); **8** Kurt Hock/Kuno Hock, D/D (Hock-Eigenbau); **9** Ingemar Eriksson/Peter Linden, S/S (LCR); **10** Barry Laidlow/Ruth Clements, GB/GB (LCR-JPX); **11** Markus Schlosser/Daniel Locher, CH/CH (LCR); **12** Baptist Kohlmann/Ernst Theuer, D/D (LCR-ADM); **13** Hans Blaauw/Harry Hofsteenge, NL/NL (LCR-Krauser); **14** Gianpaolo Arlati/Oscar Combi, I/I (LCR); **15** Michel Ferrand/Martial Charpentier, F/F (LCR).
Fastest lap: Knight, 2m 17.28s, 98.566 mph/158.627 km/h.

CIRCUIT VAN DRENTHE, Assen, Holland, 13 September. 2.431-mile/3.913-km circuit.
European Championship, 125 cc, round 7 (18 laps, 43.758 miles/70.434 km)
1 Manfred Baumann, A (Honda), 27m 57.07s, 93.947 mph/151.193 km/h.
2 Luigi Ancona, I (Aprilia); **3** Juan Borja, E (Honda); **4** Emilio Alzamora, E (Honda); **5** Adrie Nijenhuis, NL (Honda); **6** Ajo Aki, SF (Honda); **7** Serafino Foti, I (Honda); **8** Oliver Kohlinger, D (Honda); **9** Hermann Scherpen, NL (Honda); **10** Paolo Aicardi, I (Honda); **11** Jos van Dongen, NL (Honda); **12** José Luis Rabadan, E (Cobas); **13** Stuart Nicholls, GB (Honda); **14** Ron Reniers, NL (Honda); **15** Henrik Rasmussen, DK (Yamaha).
Fastest lap: Baumann, 1m 31.92s, 95.225 mph/153.250 km/h.
Championship points: **1** Borja, 88; **2** Ancona, 70; **3** Cecchinello, 66; **4** Baumann, 64; **5** Foti, 56; **6** Kurfiss, 54.

AUTODROMO NAZIONALE DI MONZA, Italy, 4 October. 3.6039-mile/5.800-km circuit.
European Championship, 125 cc, round 8 (13 laps, 46.851 miles/75.400 km)
1 Lucio Cecchinello, I (Aprilia), 31m 09.815s, 90.204 mph/145.169 km/h.
2 Emilio Alzamora, E (Honda); **3** Simone Giannecchini, I (Honda); **4** Aldo Brenna, I (Honda); **5** Juan Borja, E (Honda); **6** Manfred Baumann, A (Honda); **7** Hans Koopman, NL (Honda); **8** Stefan Kurfiss, D (Aprilia); **9** Fabio Colombo, I (Aprilia); **10** Serafino Foti, I (Honda); **11** Manolo Omarini, I (Honda); **12** Gregor Gorek, SLO (Honda); **13** Fabrizio degli Esposti, I (Honda); **14** Maurizio Chucciarini, I (Honda); **15** Massimo Pennacchioli, I (Aprilia).
Fastest lap: Cecchinello, 2m 21.089s, 91.957 mph/147.991 km/h.

Supersport 600, round 7 (16 laps, 57.662 miles/92.800 km)
1 Antonio Calasso, I (Honda), 38m 07.135s, 90.763 mph/146.069 km/h.
2 Pere Riba, E (Honda); **3** Massimiliano Degiovanni, I (Honda); **4** Viscardo Zanella, I (Honda); **5** Rachel Nicotte, F (Honda); **6** Joaquin Escoda, E (Honda); **7** Peter Haug, CH (Honda); **8** Francesco Baro, E (Honda); **9** Ramon Criado, E (Honda); **10** Eric Maillard, CH (Honda); **11** Gilberto Gambelli, I (Honda); **12** Gerhard Lindener, D (Honda); **13** Jorge Calabuig, E (Honda); **14** Roger Karlsson, S (Honda); **15** Alain Schorderet, CH (Honda).
Fastest lap: Calasso, 2m 19.843s, 92.777 mph/149.310 km/h.

Final Championship points (125 cc)

1	Juan Borja, E	99
2	Lucio Cecchinello, I	86
3	Manfred Baumann, A	74
4	Luigi Ancona, I	70
5=	Serafino Foti, I	62
5=	Stefan Kurfiss, D	62

7 Emilio Alzamora, E, 59; **8** Carlos Checa, E, 45; **9** Rob Orme, GB, 32; **10** Hans Koopman, NL, 30; **11** Jos van Dongen, NL, 26; **12** Robert Dunlop, GB and Manolo Omarini, I, 22; **14** Adrie Nijenhuis, NL, 21; **15** José Luis Rabadan, E, 19.

Final Championship points (250 cc)

1	Luis Maurel, E	129
2	Massimo Pennacchioli, I	79
3	Laurent Naveau, B	75
4	Ian Newton, GB	55
5	Marc Garcia, F	52
6	Jean Foray, F	43

7 Bernard Garcia, F, 41; **8** Oscar Sainz, E, 40; **9** Christian Boudinot, F, 35; **10** Enrique de Juan, E, 33; **11** Jeremy McWilliams, GB, 32; **12** Alex Sirera, E, 26; **13** José Kuhn, F, 25; **14** Volker Bähr, D, 22; **15** Miguel Castilla, E and William Costes, F, 19.

Final Championship points (Supersport 600)

1	Stefan Scheschowitsch, D	103
2	Antonio Calasso, I	89
3	Pere Riba, E	87
4	Rodrigo Mut, E	57
5	Rachel Nicotte, F	48
6	Joaquin Escoda, E	45

7 Christian Zwedorn, A, 39; **8** Ricardo Suarez, E, 37; **9** Lars Bosson, S and Mario Liverani, I, 34; **11** Josep Volta, E, 33; **12** Antonio Palizzi, I, 28; **13**

Massimiliano Degiovanni, I, 26; **14** Alfred Grossauer, A, 24; **15** Peter Haug, CH, 19.

Final Championship points (Sidecars)

1	Gary Knight, GB	75
2	Roger Body, GB	47
3	Gary Thomas, GB	40
4	Barry Smith, GB	37
5	Barry Laidlow, GB	31
6	Kenny Howles, GB	30

7 Clive Stirrat, GB, 24; **8** Harry Smit, NL, 23; **9** Brian Gray, GB, 22; **10** Benny Janssen, NL, 21; **11** Eric Cornes, GB, 20; **12** Albert Giesemann, D, 19; **13** Tony Baker, GB, 17; **14** Ingemar Eriksson, S, Markus Schlosser, CH and Eddy Wright, GB, 15.

AMA National Championship Road Race Series (Superbike)

DAYTONA INTERNATIONAL SPEEDWAY, Daytona Beach, Florida, 8 March 1992. 203 miles/326.69 km
1 Scott Russell (Kawasaki); **2** Doug Polen (Ducati); **3** Mike Smith (Honda); **4** David Sadowski (Suzuki); **5** Steve Crevier (Honda); **6** Shoichi Tsukamoto (Kawasaki); **7** James Adamo (Ducati); **8** Thomas Stevens (Kawasaki); **9** Larry Schwarzbach (Yamaha); **10** Scott Zampach (Yamaha).

LAGUNA SECA INTERNATIONAL RACEWAY, Monterey, California, 26 April 1992. 60 miles/96 km
1 Doug Polen (Ducati); **2** Scott Russell (Kawasaki); **3** Mike Smith (Honda); **4** Pascal Picotte (Ducati); **5** Jamie James (Yamaha); **6** Thomas Stevens (Kawasaki); **7** Tom Kipp (Honda); **8** David Sadowski (Suzuki); **9** Steve Crevier (Honda); **10** Freddie Spencer (Honda).

CHARLOTTE MOTOR SPEEDWAY, Concord, North Carolina, 3 May 1992. 49.5 miles/79.2 km
1 Jamie James (Yamaha); **2** Scott Russell (Kawasaki); **3** Thomas Stevens (Kawasaki); **4** Dale Quarterley (Kawasaki); **5** Tom Kipp (Honda); **6** Mike Smith (Honda); **7** Scott Zampach (Yamaha); **8** Pascal Picotte (Ducati); **9** Michael Taylor (Kawasaki); **10** John Ashmead (Kawasaki).

TEXAS WORLD SPEEDWAY, College Station, Texas, 31 May 1992. 36 miles/57.6 km
1 Freddie Spencer (Honda); **2** Dale Quarterley (Kawasaki); **3** Pascal Picotte (Ducati); **4** Tom Kipp (Honda); **5** Scott Russell (Kawasaki); **6** Britt Turkington (Suzuki); **7** James Adamo (Ducati); **8** Phil Kress (Kawasaki); **9** Mike Smith (Honda); **10** Doug Polen (Ducati).

BRAINERD INTERNATIONAL RACEWAY, Brainerd, Minnesota, 14 June 1992. 60 miles/96 km
1 Doug Polen (Ducati); **2** Jamie James (Yamaha); **3** Thomas Stevens (Kawasaki); **4** Larry Schwarzbach (Yamaha); **5** Pascal Picotte (Ducati); **6** Dave Sadowski (Suzuki); **7** Freddie Spencer (Honda); **8** Christian Gardner (Yamaha); **9** Britt Turkington (Suzuki); **10** Tom Kipp (Honda).

NEW HAMPSHIRE INTERNATIONAL SPEEDWAY, Loudon, New Hampshire, 21 June 1992. 100.8 miles/161.28 km
1 Scott Russell (Kawasaki); **2** Jamie James (Yamaha); **3** Pascal Picotte (Ducati); **4** Freddie Spencer (Honda); **5** Thomas Stevens (Kawasaki); **6** Tom Kipp (Honda); **7** Larry Schwarzbach (Yamaha); **8** Dale Quarterley (Kawasaki); **9** Michael Taylor (Kawasaki); **10** Steve Crevier (Honda).

ROAD AMERICA, Elkhart Lake, Wisconsin, 28 June 1992. 60 miles/96 km
1 Jamie James (Yamaha); **2** Scott Russell (Kawasaki); **3** Freddie Spencer (Honda); **4** Larry Schwarzbach (Yamaha); **5** Thomas Stevens (Kawasaki); **6** Randy Renfrow (Honda); **7** Dale Quarterley (Kawasaki); **8** Pascal Picotte (Ducati); **9** Steve Crevier (Honda); **10** Tom Kipp (Honda).

MID-OHIO SPORTS CAR COURSE, Lexington, Ohio, 2 August 1992. 60 miles/96 km
1 Doug Polen (Ducati); **2** Thomas Stevens (Kawasaki); **3** Tom Kipp (Honda); **4** Jamie James (Yamaha); **5** Dale Quarterley (Kawasaki); **6** Scott Gray (Kawasaki); **7** Pascal Picotte (Ducati); **8** Michael Taylor (Kawasaki); **9** Christian Gardner (Yamaha); **10** Linnley Clarke (Yamaha).

TEXAS WORLD SPEEDWAY, College Station, Texas, 11 October 1992. 60 miles/96 km
1 Scott Russell (Kawasaki); **2** Doug Polen (Ducati); **3** Thomas Stevens (Kawasaki); **4** Mike Smith (Honda); **5** Freddie Spencer (Honda); **6** Pascal Picotte (Ducati); **7** Dale Quarterley (Kawasaki); **8** Tom Kipp (Honda); **9** Christian Gardner (Yamaha); **10** Craig Gleason (Suzuki).

Final Championship points

1	Scott Russell	122
2	Thomas Stevens	102
3	Doug Polen	100
4	Jamie James	98
5	Pascal Picotte	89

6 Tom Kipp, 78; **7** Freddie Spencer, 74; **8** Dale Quarterley, 69; **9** Mike Smith, 60; **10** Larry Schwarzbach, 45.

WERA Formula USA Series

WILLOW SPRINGS INTERNATIONAL RACEWAY, Rosamond, California, 5 April 1992. 60 miles/96 km
1 Chuck Graves (Suzuki); **2** Lee Shierts (Suzuki); **3** Robert Miller (Suzuki); **4** Mike Harth (Suzuki); **5** Bruce Tebo (Suzuki); **6** Thomas Stevens (Kawasaki); **7** Chris D'Aluisio (Yamaha); **8** Donald Jacks (Suzuki); **9** Don Greene (Yamaha); **10** Michael Martin (Suzuki).

ROAD ATLANTA, Braselton, Georgia, 17 May 1992. 60 miles/96 km
1 Donald Jacks (Suzuki); **2** Michael Martin (Suzuki); **3** Lee Shierts (Suzuki); **4** Chuck Graves (Suzuki); **5** Stephen Mathews (Ducati); **6** Joe Pittman (Yamaha); **7** Mark Chin (Yamaha); **8** Bill Himmelsbach (Yamaha); **9** Mat Macheca (Suzuki); **10** Jim Bonner (Yamaha).

SHANNONVILLE MOTORSPORTS PARK, Shannonville, Ontario, Canada, 31 May 1992. 50 miles/80.5 km
1 Steve Crevier (Kawasaki); **2** Chuck Graves (Suzuki); **3** Benoit Pilon (Yamaha); **4** Steve Wykes (Yamaha); **5** Joe Pittman (Yamaha); **6** Kurt Hall (Yamaha); **7** Al Salaverria (Aprilia); **8** Sean Smythe (Honda); **9** Linnley Clarke (Yamaha); **10** Keith Code (Yamaha).

SEATTLE INTERNATIONAL RACEWAY, Kent, Washington, 14 June 1992. 60 miles/96 km
1 Donald Jacks (Suzuki); **2** Michael Martin (Suzuki); **3** Lee Shierts (Suzuki); **4** Doug Renfrow (Yamaha); **5** Keith Pinkstaff (Yamaha); **6** Chris Callan (Suzuki); **7** Michael Graves (Yamaha); **8** Robert Marsh (Suzuki); **9** Jay Bartlow (Yamaha); **10** Mike Sullivan (Yamaha).

INDIANAPOLIS RACEWAY PARK, Indianapolis, Indiana, 9 August 1992. 60 miles/96 km
1 Fritz Kling (Yamaha); **2** Michael Martin (Suzuki); **3** Donald Jacks (Suzuki); **4** Chris D'Aluisio (Yamaha); **5** Robbie Petersen (Yamaha); **6** Chuck Graves (Suzuki); **7** Andrew Stroud (Suzuki); **8** Scott Zampach (Yamaha); **9** Danny Walker (Yamaha); **10** Lee Shierts (Suzuki).

POCONO INTERNATIONAL RACEWAY, Pocono, Pennsylvania, 23 August 1992. 60 miles/96 km
1 Chuck Graves (Suzuki); **2** Donald Jacks (Suzuki); **3** Michael Martin (Suzuki); **4** Michael Taylor (Kawasaki); **5** Chris D'Aluisio (Yamaha); **6** David Sadowski (Suzuki); **7** James Adamo (Ducati); **8** Lee Shierts (Suzuki); **9** Rich Oliver (Yamaha); **10** Don Greene (Yamaha).

MOROSO MOTORSPORTS PARK, West Palm Beach, Florida, 21 September 1992. 60 miles/96 km
1 Donald Jacks (Suzuki); **2** Michael Martin (Suzuki); **3** Fritz Kling (Suzuki); **4** Jacques Guenette (Yamaha); **5** Michael Barnes (Honda); **6** Danny Walker (Yamaha); **7** Rich Oliver (Yamaha); **8** Doug Carmichael (Yamaha); **9** Lee Shierts (Suzuki); **10** Bruce Baldus (Yamaha).

Championship points (prior to final round at Braselton in November)

1	Donald Jacks	107
2	Michael Martin	89
3	Chuck Graves	86
4	Lee Shierts	70
5=	Fritz Kling	33
5=	Chris D'Aluisio	33

7 Joe Pittman, 27; **8** Rich Oliver, 22; **9** Steve Crevier and Joe Brett Williams, 20.

Motor Cycle News Supercup/ACU British Championship

DONINGTON PARK CIRCUIT, 24 May. 2.5-mile/4.023-km circuit. Motor Cycle News Supercup/ACU British Championship, round 1
125 cc Supercup (12 laps, 30 miles/48.276 km)
1 Rob Orme (Honda), 21m 44.74s, 82.77 mph/133.21 km/h.
2 Jimmy Brown (Honda); **3** Mick Lofthouse (Honda); **4** Stuart Nicholls (Honda); **5** Barry Stanley (Honda); **6** Julian Perry (Cobas); **7** Mark Taylor (Honda); **8** Alan Patterson (Cotoni); **9** Jeremy McWilliams (Honda); **10** Nicholas Lang (Honda); **11** Andy Hatton (Honda); **12** Chris Palmer (Honda); **13** Ian Emberton (Honda); **14** Martin Johnson (Honda); **15** Darran Gawley (Honda).
Fastest lap: Orme, 1m 47.40s, 83.79 mph/134.86 km/h.
Championship points: **1** Orme, 20; **2** Brown, 17; **3** Lofthouse, 15; **4** Nicholls, 13; **5** Stanley, 11; **6** Perry, 10.

250 cc Supercup (16 laps, 40 miles/64.368 km)
1 Nigel Bosworth (Yamaha), 27m 06.77s, 88.51 mph/142.45 km/h.
2 Adrian Clarke (Yamaha); **3** Steve Sawford (Yamaha); **4** David Heal (Yamaha); **5** Steve Johnson (Yamaha); **6** Adrian Butcher (Yamaha); **7** Mark Barker (Yamaha); **8** Darren Mitchell (Yamaha); **9** Lee Pullan (Yamaha); **10** Paul Booler (Honda); **11** Graeme Thompson (Yamaha); **12** Mark Snell (Yamaha); **13** Tim Couzens (Yamaha); **14** Eugene McManus (Honda); **15** Lyndon Powell (Yamaha).
Fastest lap: Ian McConnachie (MAC), 1m 40.02s, 89.98 mph/144.81 km/h.
Championship points: **1** Bosworth, 20; **2** Clarke, 17; **3** Sawford, 15; **4** Heal, 13; **5** Johnson, 11; **6** Butcher, 10.

Supersport 400 Supercup (12 laps, 30 miles/48.276 km)
1 Ian Simpson (Yamaha), 21m 21.15s, 84.29 mph/135.66 km/h.
2 Steve Ives (Honda); **3** Jason Vincent (Suzuki); **4** Howard Selby (Yamaha); **5** Mark Farmer (Yamaha); **6** Sean Emmett (Yamaha); **7** Steve Reape (Suzuki); **8** John McGuinness (Yamaha); **9** Steve Tomes (Yamaha); **10** Ian Smith (Suzuki); **11** Alan Green (Suzuki); **12** Ian Campbell (Yamaha); **13** Ian McConnachie (Kawasaki); **14** Kevin Wholey (Kawasaki); **15** Frank Swain (Suzuki).
Fastest lap: Ives, 1m 45.65s, 85.18 mph/137.09 km/h.
Championship points: **1** Simpson, 20; **2** Ives, 17; **3** Vincent, 15; **4** Selby, 13; **5** Farmer, 11; **6** Emmett, 10.

Supersport 600 Supercup (12 laps, 30 miles/48.276 km)
1 Ian Simpson (Honda), 20m 37.48s, 87.27 mph/140.45 km/h.
2 Jim Moodie (Honda); **3** Mark Farmer (Yamaha); **4** Sean Emmett (Yamaha); **5** Howard Selby (Honda); **6** Steve Ives (Honda); **7** Andrew Corbett (Yamaha); **8** Andrew Pallot (Yamaha); **9** Steve Tomes (Yamaha); **10** Dave Martin (Yamaha); **11** Roger Milne (Honda); **12** Rob Simm (Honda); **13** Jamie Patterson (Yamaha); **14** Bob Grant (Yamaha); **15** Kevin Leach (Honda).
Fastest lap: Simpson, 1m 42.10s, 88.14 mph/141.86 km/h.
Championship points: **1** Simpson, 20; **2** Moodie, 17; **3** Farmer, 15; **4** Emmett, 13; **5** Selby, 11; **6** Ives, 10.

750 cc Supercup (2 x 16 laps, 40 miles/64.368 km)
Leg 1
1 Terry Rymer (Norton), 26m 29.71s, 90.58 mph/145.77 km/h.
2 Rob McElnea (Yamaha); **3** Robert Dunlop (Norton); **4** Trevor Nation (Ducati); **5** Roger Bennett (Ducati); **6** David Jefferies (Yamaha); **7** Simon Watson (Yamaha); **8** Nigel Nottingham (Yamaha); **9** Alex Buckingham (Yamaha); **10** Gary Bull (Yamaha); **11** Michael Rutter (Ducati); **12** Robin Milton (Kawasaki); **13** Nick Jefferies (Yamaha); **14** Peter Boast (Yamaha); **15** Richard Defago (Honda).
Fastest lap: John Reynolds (Kawasaki), 1m 37.91s, 91.92 mph/147.93 km/h.
Leg 2
1 Terry Rymer (Norton), 26m 22.93s, 90.97 mph/146.40 km/h.
2 James Whitham (Suzuki); **3** Brian Morrison (Kawasaki); **4** Rob McElnea (Yamaha); **5** Robert Dunlop (Norton); **6** Ian Simpson (Kawasaki); **7** David Jefferies (Yamaha); **8** Roger Bennett (Ducati); **9** Andy Ward (Kawasaki); **10** Nigel Nottingham (Yamaha); **11** Alex Buckingham (Yamaha); **12** Simon Watson (Yamaha); **13** Michael Rutter (Ducati); **14** Gary Bull (Yamaha); **15** Peter Boast (Yamaha).
Fastest lap: Rymer, 1m 37.72s, 92.09 mph/148.22 km/h.
Championship points: **1** Rymer, 40; **2** McElnea, 30; **3** Dunlop, 26; **4** Bennett and D. Jefferies, 19; **6** Whitham, 17.

Open Sidecars Supercup (12 laps, 30 miles/48.276 km)
1 Darren Dixon/Andy Hetherington (Padgett), 19m 57.43s, 90.19 mph/145.15 km/h.
2 Steve Abbott/Shaun Smith (LCR-Krauser); **3** Steve Webster/Gavin Simmons (LCR); **4** Derek Brindley/Nick Roche (Yamaha); **5** Barry Brindley/Scott Whiteside (Yamaha); **6** Barry Smith/Trevor Hopkinson (Windle-ADM); **7** Brian Gray/Steve Pointer (ADM); **8** Vince Butler/Tony Darby (Windle-ADM); **9** Mark Reddington/Horne (Krauser); **10** Gary Knight/Woodhead (Windle); **11** Robinson/Graham (Suzuki); **12** Kevin Webster/Julian Tailford (LCR-Krauser); **13** Robert Fisher/Trevor Crone (LCR-Krauser); **14** Gordon Shand/Hennigan (Shand); **15** Clive Stirrat/Tony Stevens (LCR-JPX).
Fastest lap: Dixon, 1m 38.22s, 91.63 mph/147.46 km/h.
Championship points: **1** Dixon, 20; **2** Abbott, 17; **3** S. Webster, 15; **4** D. Brindley, 13; **5** B. Brindley, 11; **6** Smith, 10.

MALLORY PARK CIRCUIT, 28 June. 1.370-mile/2.025-km circuit. Motor Cycle News Supercup/ACU British Championship, round 2
125 cc Supercup (20 laps, 27.4 miles/40.5 km)
1 Mick Lofthouse (Honda), 17m 58.79s, 91.43 mph/147.15 km/h.
2 Barry Stanley (Honda); **3** Neil Hodgson (Honda); **4** Patrick Corrigan (Honda); **5** Andy Hatton (Honda); **6** Jamie Robinson (Honda); **7** Darran Gawley (Honda); **8** Ian Lougher (Honda); **9** Darren Martin (Honda); **10** Phelim Owens (Honda); **11** Chris Palmer (Honda); **12** Mark Westmorland (Honda); **13** Jimmy Brown (Honda); **14** Julian Perry (Cobas); **15** Andy Godber (Honda).
Fastest lap: Fernando Mendes (Honda), 52.75s, 93.49 mph/150.46 km/h.
Championship points: **1** Lofthouse, 35; **2** Stanley, 28; **3** Brown and Orme, 20; **5** Hatton, 16; **6** Hodgson, 15.

250 cc Supercup (20 laps, 27.4 miles/40.5 km)
1 Alan Carter (Honda), 17m 02.82s, 96.43 mph/155.20 km/h.
2 Paul Brown (Yamaha); **3** Woolsey Coulter (Honda); **4** Steve Sawford (Yamaha); **5** James Haydon (Yamaha); **6** Ian McConnachie (MAC); **7** Ian Newton (Aprilia); **8** David Heal (Yamaha); **9** Mick Otter (Yamaha); **10** Adrian Butcher (Yamaha); **11** David Rawlins (Yamaha); **12** Lee Pullan (Yamaha); **13** Mark Snell (Yamaha); **14** Adrian Clarke (Yamaha); **15** Tony Goldstraw (Yamaha).
Fastest lap: Nigel Bosworth (Yamaha), 50.27s, 98.11 mph/157.89 km/h.
Championship points: **1** Sawford, 28; **2** Heal, 21; **3** Bosworth and Carter, 20; **5** Clarke, 19; **6** Brown, 17.

Supersport 400 Supercup (20 laps, 27.4 miles/40.5 km)
1 Mike Edwards (Honda), 18m 01.81s, 91.18 mph/146.74 km/h.
2 Mark Farmer (Yamaha); **3** Howard Selby (Yamaha); **4** Ian Simpson (Yamaha); **5** Francis Williamson (Yamaha); **6** Steve Tomes (Yamaha); **7** Jim Moodie (Yamaha); **8** Jason Vincent (Kawasaki); **9** Mark Norman (Kawasaki); **10** Phil Borley (Kawasaki); **11** Steve Reape (Suzuki); **12** Barry Rudd (Suzuki); **13** Ian Smith (Suzuki); **14** Frank Swain (Suzuki); **15** Kevin Wholey (Kawasaki).
Fastest lap: Edwards, 52.63s, 93.71 mph/150.81 km/h.
Championship points: **1** Simpson, 33; **2** Farmer and Selby, 28; **4** Vincent, 23; **5** Edwards, 20; **6** Ives and Tomes, 17.

Supersport 600 Supercup (20 laps, 27.4 miles/40.5 km)
1 Ian Simpson (Honda), 17m 34.60s, 93.53 mph/150.52 km/h.
2 Phil Borley (Honda); **3** Mike Edwards (Honda); **4** Jim Moodie (Honda); **5** Colin Gable (Honda); **6** Sean Emmett (Yamaha); **7** Howard Selby (Honda); **8** Mark Farmer (Yamaha); **9** Dave Martin (Yamaha); **10** Roger Milne (Honda); **11** Iain Macpherson (Honda); **12** Steve Tomes (Yamaha); **13** Dave Redgate (Honda); **14** John Paul Snr (Honda); **15** Andrew Corbett (Yamaha).
Fastest lap: Farmer, 51.69s, 95.41 mph/153.55 km/h.
Championship points: **1** Simpson, 40; **2** Moodie, 30; **3** Emmett and Farmer, 23; **5** Selby, 20; **6** Borley, 17.

750 cc Supercup (2 x 20 laps, 27.4 miles/40.5 km)
Leg 1
1 John Reynolds (Kawasaki), 16m 43.50s, 98.29 mph/158.19 km/h.
2 James Whitham (Suzuki); **3** Terry Rymer (Norton); **4** Robert Dunlop (Norton); **5** Brian Morrison (Kawasaki); **6** Rob McElnea (Yamaha); **7** Sean Emmett (Yamaha); **8** David Jefferies (Yamaha); **9** Trevor Nation (Ducati); **10** Alex Buckingham (Yamaha); **11** Michael Rutter (Ducati); **12** Andrew Corbett (Kawasaki); **13** Tim Bourne (Roton); **14** Nigel Nottingham (Yamaha); **15** Andy Ward (Kawasaki).
Fastest lap: Whitham, 49.50s, 99.63 mph/160.34 km/h.
Leg 2
1 John Reynolds (Kawasaki), 16m 43.62s, 98.28 mph/158.17 km/h.
2 Brian Morrison (Kawasaki); **3** Terry Rymer (Norton); **4** James Whitham (Suzuki); **5** Robert Dunlop (Norton); **6** Rob McElnea (Yamaha); **7** Sean Emmett (Yamaha); **8** Trevor Nation (Ducati); **9** David Jefferies (Yamaha); **10** Alex Buckingham (Yamaha); **11** Tim Bourne (Roton); **12** Andrew Corbett (Kawasaki); **13** Andy Ward (Kawasaki); **14** Graham Ward (Kawasaki); **15** Brett Simpson (Kawasaki).
Fastest lap: Morrison, 49.18s, 100.28 mph/161.39 km/h.
Championship points: **1** Rymer, 70; **2** Dunlop and McElnea, 50; **4** Whitham, 47; **5** Morrison, 43; **6** Reynolds, 40.

Open Sidecars Supercup (20 laps, 27.4 miles/40.5 km)
1 Steve Webster/Gavin Simmons (LCR), 16m 50.15s, 97.64 mph/157.15 km/h.
2 Barry Brindley/Scott Whiteside (Yamaha); **3** Derek Brindley/Nick Roche (Yamaha); **4** Gary Knight/Malcolm Jackson (Krauser); **5** Robert Fisher/Trevor Crone (Krauser); **6** Kevin Webster/Julian Tailford (Krauser); **7** Eddy Wright/Peter Hill (Krauser); **8** Brian Gray/Steve Pointer (ADM); **9** Skidmore/Allen (Krauser); **10** Peter Tubby/Steve Goodey (Suzuki); **11** Roberts/Jones (Yamaha); **12** Barry Fleury/Jane Fleury (JPX).
Fastest lap: Darren Dixon/Andy Hetherington (Padgett), 49.59s, 99.45 mph/160.05 km/h.
Championship points: **1** S. Webster, 35; **2** B. Brindley and D. Brindley, 28; **4** Dixon, 20; **5** Knight, 19; **6** Abbott and Gray, 17.

SNETTERTON CIRCUIT, 12 July. 1.952-mile/3.141-km circuit. Motor Cycle News Supercup/ACU British Championship, round 3
125 cc Supercup (14 laps, 27.328 miles/43.974 km)
1 Neil Hodgson (Honda), 18m 45.52s, 87.40 mph/140.67 km/h.
2 Jamie Robinson (Honda); **3** Stuart Nicholls (Honda); **4** Barry Stanley (Honda); **5** Mark Bingham (Honda); **6** Ian McConnachie (Honda); **7** Greig Ramsey (Honda); **8** Andy Hatton (Honda); **9** Mick Lofthouse (Honda); **10** Ian Lougher (Honda); **11** Andy Bradford (Kenimoto); **12** Darran Gawley (Honda); **13** Chris Palmer (Honda); **14** Ian Emberton (Honda); **15** Andy Godber (Honda).
Fastest lap: Nicholls, 1m 19.17s, 88.76 mph/142.84 km/h.
Championship points: **1** Lofthouse, 42; **2** Stanley, 41; **3** Hodgson, 35; **4** Nicholls, 28; **5** Robinson, 27; **6** Hatton, 24.

250 cc Supercup (15 laps, 29.28 miles/47.115 km)
1 Adrian Butcher (Yamaha), 18m 37.04s, 94.36 mph/151.86 km/h.
2 Nigel Bosworth (Yamaha); **3** Alan Carter (Honda); **4** Paul Brown (Yamaha); **5** Steve Sawford (Yamaha); **6** Mark Barker (Yamaha); **7** Jeremy McWilliams (Yamaha); **8** David Heal (Yamaha); **9** Graeme Mitchell (Aprilia); **10** Woolsey Coulter (Honda); **11** Ian McConnachie (MAC); **12** Adrian Clarke (Yamaha); **13** Mick Otter (Yamaha); **14** Darren Mitchell (Yamaha); **15** Mark Snell (Yamaha).
Fastest lap: Butcher, 1m 13.42s, 95.71 mph/154.03 km/h.
Championship points: **1** Sawford, 39; **2** Bosworth, 37; **3** Butcher, 36; **4** Carter, 35; **5** Brown, 30; **6** Heal, 29.

Supersport 400 Supercup (14 laps, 27.328 miles/43.974 km)
1 Mike Edwards (Honda), 18m 27.52s, 88.82 mph/142.95 km/h.
2 Francis Williamson (Yamaha); **3** Mark Farmer (Yamaha); **4** Ian Simpson (Yamaha); **5** Barry Rudd (Suzuki);

6 Steve Reape (Suzuki); **7** Ian Campbell (Yamaha); **8** Steve Tomes (Yamaha); **9** John McGuinness (Yamaha); **10** Drew Hogg (Yamaha); **11** Callum Ramsey (Suzuki); **12** Frank Swain (Suzuki); **13** Ian Smith (Suzuki); **14** Matthew Godley (Suzuki); **15** Kevin Wholey (Kawasaki).
Fastest lap: Edwards, 1m 17.72s, 90.41 mph/145.51 km/h.
Championship points: **1** Simpson, 46; **2** Farmer, 43; **3** Edwards, 40; **4** Selby and Williamson, 28; **6** Tomes, 25.

Supersport 600 Supercup (14 laps, 27.328 miles/43.974 km)
1 Phil Borley (Honda), 17m 47.98s, 92.11 mph/148.25 km/h.
2 Ian Simpson (Honda); **3** Sean Emmett (Yamaha); **4** Steve Tomes (Yamaha); **5** Colin Gable (Honda); **6** Iain Duffus (Honda); **7** Andrew Pallot (Yamaha); **8** Dave Redgate (Honda); **9** Kevin Leach (Honda); **10** Dave Martin (Yamaha); **11** Chris White (Yamaha); **12** Paul Mackley (Honda); **13** John Laker (Yamaha); **14** Alan Batson (Honda); **15** Mark Ditchfield (Honda).
Fastest lap: Borley, 1m 15.22s, 93.42 mph/150.34 km/h.
Championship points: **1** Simpson, 57; **2** Emmett, 38; **3** Borley, 37; **4** Moodie, 30; **5** Tomes, 24; **6** Farmer, 23.

750 cc Supercup (2 x 18 laps, 35.136 miles/56.538 km)
Leg 1
1 John Reynolds (Kawasaki), 21m 28.67s, 98.15 mph/157.96 km/h.
2 Brian Morrison (Kawasaki); **3** Terry Rymer (Norton); **4** Robert Dunlop (Norton); **5** James Whitham (Suzuki); **6** Carl Fogarty (Ducati); **7** David Jefferies (Yamaha); **8** Alex Buckingham (Yamaha); **9** Brett Sampson (Kawasaki); **10** Michael Rutter (Ducati); **11** Andy Ward (Yamaha); **12** Sean Emmett (Yamaha); **13** Tim Bourne (Roton); **14** Roger Bennett (Ducati); **15** Simon Watson (Kawasaki).
Fastest lap: Morrison, 1m 10.90s, 99.11 mph/159.50 km/h.
Leg 2
1 John Reynolds (Kawasaki), 21m 25.61s, 98.38 mph/158.34 km/h.
2 Brian Morrison (Kawasaki); **3** Terry Rymer (Norton); **4** Robert Dunlop (Norton); **5** James Whitham (Suzuki); **6** Rob McElnea (Yamaha); **7** Tim Bourne (Roton); **8** Michael Rutter (Ducati); **9** Sean Emmett (Yamaha); **10** David Jefferies (Yamaha); **11** Brett Sampson (Kawasaki); **12** Andy Ward (Yamaha); **13** Alex Buckingham (Yamaha); **14** Robin Milton (Kawasaki); **15** Graham Ward (Kawasaki).
Fastest lap: Reynolds, 1m 10.55s, 99.60 mph/160.30 km/h.
Championship points: **1** Rymer, 100; **2** Reynolds, 80; **3** Morrison, 77; **4** Dunlop, 76; **5** Whitham, 69; **6** McElnea, 60.

Open Sidecars Supercup (14 laps, 27.328 miles/43.974 km)
1 Gary Knight/Malcolm Jackson (Krauser), 17m 54.04s, 91.68 mph/147.55 km/h.
2 Brian Gray/Steve Pointer (ADM); **3** David Hoskin/David James (LCR-ADM); **4** Roger Body/Andy Peach (LCR-Krauser); **5** Barry Smith/Trevor Hopkinson (Windle-ADM); **6** Kevin Webster/Julian Tailford (LCR-Krauser); **7** Peter Tubby/Steve Goodey (Suzuki); **8** Kieron Kavanagh/Stephen Campbell (LCR-Krauser); **9** Hall/Eastall (Yamaha); **10** Barry Fleury/Jane Fleury (LCR-JPX); **11** Neil Hodges/Gary Broadley (LCR-Krauser); **12** Eric Cornes/Chris Hibberd (Krauser); **13** Pearce/Pearce (Suzuki); **14** Bryan Aslett/Richard Streeter (Suzuki); **15** David Lee/Richard Lee (Windle-ADM).
Fastest lap: Knight, 1m 15.09s, 93.58 mph/150.60 km/h.
Championship points: **1** Knight, 39; **2** S. Webster, 35; **3** Gray, 34; **4** B. Brindley and D. Brindley, 28; **6** K. Webster, 24.

CADWELL PARK CIRCUIT, 16 August. 2.17-mile/3.472-km circuit. Motor Cycle News Supercup/ACU British Championship, round 4
125 cc Supercup (10 laps, 21.7 miles/34.72 km)
1 Neil Hodgson (Honda), 16m 16.26s, 80.01 mph/128.77 km/h.
2 Mick Lofthouse (Honda); **3** Fernando Mendes (Honda); **4** Chris Palmer (Honda); **5** Stuart Nicholls (Honda); **6** Jimmy Brown (Honda); **7** Phelim Owens (Honda); **8** Jamie Robinson (Honda); **9** Barry Stanley (Honda); **10** Kevin Mawdsley (Honda); **11** Mark Westmorland (Honda); **12** Michael Wilcox (Honda); **13** Ian Lougher (Honda); **14** Mark Coates (Honda); **15** Mick Crick (Honda).
Fastest lap: Lofthouse, 1m 36.10s, 81.29 mph/130.82 km/h.
Championship points: **1** Lofthouse, 59; **2** Hodgson, 55; **3** Stanley, 48; **4** Nicholls, 39; **5** Robinson, 35; **6** Brown, 30.

250 cc Supercup (10 laps, 21.7 miles/34.72 km)
1 Ian Newton (Aprilia), 15m 26.07s, 84.35 mph/135.75 km/h.
2 Nigel Bosworth (Yamaha); **3** Paul Brown (Yamaha); **4** Jeremy McWilliams (Yamaha); **5** Woolsey Coulter (Honda); **6** David Heal (Yamaha); **7** Steve Sawford (Yamaha); **8** Graeme Mitchell (Aprilia); **9** Mark Barker (Yamaha); **10** Ian McConnachie (MAC); **11** Adrian Clarke (Yamaha); **12** Lee Pullan (Yamaha); **13** Mark Snell (Yamaha); **14** Michael Rutter (Yamaha); **15** Tim Couzens (Yamaha).
Fastest lap: McWilliams, 1m 30.87s, 85.96 mph/138.35 km/h.
Championship points: **1** Bosworth, 54; **2** Sawford, 48; **3** Brown, 45; **4** Heal, 39; **5** Butcher, 36; **6** Carter, 35.

Supersport 400 Supercup (12 laps, 26.04 miles/41.664 km)
1 Jim Moodie (Kawasaki), 19m 28.60s, 80.21 mph/129.10 km/h.
2 Mike Edwards (Honda); **3** Mark Farmer (Yamaha); **4** Sean Emmett (Yamaha); **5** Steve Reape (Suzuki); **6** Steve Tomes (Yamaha); **7** Colin Gable (Yamaha); **8** Iain Duffus (Yamaha); **9** Howard Selby (Yamaha); **10** Mark Langton (Yamaha); **11** William Sykes (Kawasaki); **12** Andrew Murphy (Suzuki); **13** Frank Swain (Suzuki); **14** Ian Smith (Suzuki); **15** Callum Ramsey (Suzuki).
Fastest lap: Moodie, 1m 36.19s, 81.21 mph/130.70 km/h.
Championship points: **1** Farmer, 58; **2** Edwards, 57; **3** Simpson, 46; **4** Reape, Selby and Tomes, 35.

Supersport 600 Supercup (12 laps, 26.04 miles/41.664 km)
1 Jim Moodie (Honda), 19m 07.76s, 81.67 mph/131.44 km/h.
2 Phil Borley (Honda); **3** Mike Edwards (Honda); **4** Colin Gable (Honda); **5** Howard Selby (Honda); **6** Phillip McCallen (Honda); **7** Howard Whitby (Honda); **8** Dave Martin (Yamaha); **9** Steve Tomes (Yamaha); **10** Iain Duffus (Honda); **11** Dave Redgate (Honda); **12** Andrew Pallot (Yamaha); **13** Adam Lewis (Honda); **14** Tim Poole (Yamaha); **15** Kevin Leach (Honda).
Fastest lap: Moodie, 1m 34.39s, 82.76 mph/133.19 km/h.
Championship points: **1** Simpson, 57; **2** Borley, 54; **3** Moodie, 50; **4** Emmett, 38; **5** Gable, 35; **6** Selby and Tomes, 31.

750 cc Supercup (2 x 15 laps, 32.55 miles/52.08 km)
Leg 1
1 John Reynolds (Kawasaki), 22m 44.47s, 85.87 mph/138.20 km/h.
2 Brian Morrison (Kawasaki); **3** Rob McElnea (Yamaha); **4** Terry Rymer (Norton); **5** Mark Farmer (Roton); **6** Robert Dunlop (Norton); **7** David Jefferies (Yamaha); **8** Sean Emmett (Yamaha); **9** Jeremy McWilliams (Ducati); **10** Matt Llewellyn (Yamaha); **11** Michael Rutter (Ducati); **12** Peter Boast (Yamaha); **13** Andy Ward (Kawasaki); **14** Graham Ward (Kawasaki); **15** Charlie Corner (Kawasaki).
Fastest lap: Reynolds, 1m 29.04s, 87.73 mph/141.19 km/h.
Leg 2
1 Brian Morrison (Kawasaki), 22m 40.59s, 86.12 mph/138.60 km/h.
2 Terry Rymer (Norton); **3** Rob McElnea (Yamaha); **4** Mark Farmer (Roton); **5** Robert Dunlop (Norton); **6** James Whitham (Suzuki); **7** Jeremy McWilliams (Ducati); **8** Sean Emmett (Yamaha); **9** Andy Ward (Kawasaki); **10** Alex Buckingham (Yamaha); **11** Peter Boast (Yamaha); **12** Graham Ward (Kawasaki); **13** Robin Milton (Kawasaki); **14** Richard Defago (Honda); **15** Tom Knight (Honda).
Fastest lap: John Reynolds (Kawasaki), 1m 28.54s, 88.23 mph/141.99 km/h.
Championship points: **1** Rymer, 130; **2** Morrison, 114; **3** Reynolds, 100; **4** Dunlop, 97; **5** McElnea, 90; **6** Whitham, 79.

Open Sidecars Supercup (12 laps, 26.04 miles/41.664 km)
1 Steve Webster/Gavin Simmons (LCR), 18m 16.73s, 85.47 mph/137.56 km/h.
2 Derek Brindley/Bryan Houghton (Yamaha); **3** Barry Brindley/Scott Whiteside (Yamaha); **4** Robert Fisher/Trevor Crone (LCR-Krauser); **5** Gary Knight/Malcolm Jackson (Krauser); **6** Eddy Wright/Peter Hill (LCR-Krauser); **7** Brian Gray/Steve Pointer (ADM); **8** Mark Reddington/Robert Parker (Krauser); **9** Kevin Webster/Julian Tailford (LCR-Krauser); **10** Roger Body/Andy Peach (LCR-Krauser); **11** Barry Laidlow/Ruth Clements (LCR-JPX); **12** Neil Hodges/Gary Broadley (LCR-Krauser).
Fastest lap: S. Webster, 1m 30.28s, 86.53 mph/139.25 km/h.
Championship points: **1** S. Webster, 55; **2** Knight, 50; **3** D. Brindley, 45; **4** B. Brindley and Gray, 43; **6** K. Webster, 31.

OULTON PARK CIRCUIT, 6 September. 2.77-mile/4.458-km circuit. Motor Cycle News Supercup/ACU British Championship, round 5
125 cc Supercup (10 laps, 27.7 miles/44.58 km)
1 Kevin Mawdsley (Honda), 18m 01.91s, 92.13 mph/148.28 km/h.
2 Jimmy Brown (Honda); **3** Fernando Mendes (Honda); **4** Greig Ramsey (Honda); **5** Chris Palmer (Honda); **6** Neil Hodgson (Honda); **7** Phelim Owens (Honda); **8** Ian Lougher (ITL); **9** Jamie Robinson (Honda); **10** Rob Orme (Honda); **11** Ian Emberton (Honda); **12** Julian Perry (Cobas); **13** Stuart Nicholls (Honda); **14** Barry Stanley (Honda); **15** Mark Westmorland (Honda).
Fastest lap: Mawdsley, 1m 46.45s, 93.64 mph/150.70 km/h.
Championship points: **1** Hodgson, 65; **2** Lofthouse, 59; **3** Stanley, 50; **4** Brown, 47; **5** Nicholls and Robinson, 42.

250 cc Supercup (12 laps, 33.24 miles/53.496 km)
1 Ian Newton (Aprilia), 19m 57.53s, 99.88 mph/160.75 km/h.
2 James Haydon (Yamaha); **3** Paul Brown (Yamaha); **4** Nigel Bosworth (Yamaha); **5** Mark Barker (Yamaha); **6** Alan Carter (Honda); **7** Steve Sawford (Yamaha); **8** David Heal (Yamaha); **9** Iain Challinor (Yamaha); **10** Adrian Clarke (Yamaha); **11** Mike Pomfrey (Yamaha); **12** David Rawlins (Yamaha); **13** Jason Griffiths (Yamaha); **14** Graeme Thompson (Yamaha); **15** Tim Couzens (Yamaha).
Fastest lap: Newton, 1m 38.44s, 101.26 mph/162.96 km/h.
Championship points: **1** Bosworth, 67; **2** Brown, 60; **3** Sawford, 57; **4** Newton, 49; **5** Heal, 47; **6** Carter, 45.

Supersport 400 Supercup (12 laps, 33.24 miles/53.496 km)
1 Colin Gable (Yamaha), 21m 16.00s, 93.74 mph/150.87 km/h.
2 Mike Edwards (Honda); **3** Mark Farmer (Yamaha); **4** Sean Emmett (Yamaha); **5** Iain Duffus (Yamaha); **6** Barry Rudd (Suzuki); **7** Frank Swain (Suzuki); **8** Callum Ramsey (Suzuki); **9** Max Vincent (Suzuki); **10** Steve Linsdell (Yamaha); **11** Matthew Godley (Suzuki); **12** Kevin Wholey (Kawasaki); **13** Simon Gates (Kawasaki); **14** Sean Adams (Suzuki); **15** Stuart Wickens (Suzuki).
Fastest lap: Edwards, 1m 44.45s, 95.43 mph/153.59 km/h.
Championship points: **1** Edwards, 74; **2** Farmer, 73; **3** Simpson, 46; **4** Emmett, 36; **5** Reape, Selby and Tomes, 35.

Supersport 600 Supercup (12 laps, 33.24 miles/53.496 km)
1 Phil Borley (Honda), 20m 49.05s, 95.76 mph/154.12 km/h.
2 Mike Edwards (Honda); **3** Jim Moodie (Honda); **4** Sean Emmett (Yamaha); **5** Howard Whitby (Honda); **6** Phillip McCallen (Honda); **7** Tim Poole (Yamaha); **8** Iain Duffus (Honda); **9** Colin Gable (Honda); **10** Dave Martin (Yamaha); **11** Dave Redgate (Honda); **12** Steve Tomes (Yamaha); **13** Kevin Leach (Honda); **14** Adam Lewis (Honda); **15** Steve Marks (Honda).
Fastest lap: Borley, 1m 41.81s, 97.91 mph/157.57 km/h.
Championship points: **1** Borley, 74; **2** Moodie, 65; **3** Simpson, 57; **4** Emmett, 51; **5** Edwards, 47; **6** Gable, 42.

750 cc Supercup (2 x 14 laps, 38.78 miles/62.412 km)
Leg 1
1 John Reynolds (Kawasaki), 22m 46.53s, 102.12 mph/164.35 km/h.
2 Brian Morrison (Kawasaki); **3** James Whitham (Suzuki); **4** Rob McElnea (Yamaha); **5** Robert Dunlop (Norton); **6** Mark Farmer (Roton); **7** David Jefferies (Yamaha); **8** Michael Rutter (Ducati); **9** Graham Ward (Kawasaki); **10** Alex Buckingham (Yamaha); **11** Iain Challinor (Yamaha); **12** John Barton (Kawasaki); **13** Steve Ives (Honda); **14** Tom Cuddy (Yamaha); **15** Neil Dove (Yamaha).
Fastest lap: Reynolds, 1m 36.57s, 103.22 mph/166.12 km/h.
Leg 2
1 John Reynolds (Kawasaki), 22m 35.39s, 102.96 mph/165.70 km/h.
2 Terry Rymer (Norton); **3** Rob McElnea (Yamaha); **4** Brian Morrison (Kawasaki); **5** Mark Farmer (Roton); **6** Robert Dunlop (Norton); **7** James Whitham (Suzuki); **8** David Jefferies (Yamaha); **9** Alex Buckingham (Yamaha); **10** Michael Rutter (Ducati); **11** Graham Ward (Kawasaki); **12** Iain Challinor (Yamaha); **13** Steve Ives (Honda).
Fastest lap: Rymer, 1m 35.98s, 103.85 mph/167.14 km/h.
Championship points: **1** Rymer, 147; **2** Morrison, 144; **3** Reynolds, 140; **4** Dunlop and McElnea, 118; **6** Whitham, 103.

Open Sidecars Supercup (12 laps, 33.24 miles/53.496 km)
1 Steve Webster/Gavin Simmons (ADM), 20m 20.11s, 98.04 mph/157.78 km/h.
2 Barry Brindley/Scott Whiteside (Yamaha); **3** Derek Brindley/Paul Hutchinson (Yamaha); **4** Gary Knight/Malcolm Jackson (Windle-ADM); **5** Robert Fisher/Trevor Crone (LCR-Krauser); **6** Brian Gray/Steve Pointer (ADM); **7** Roger Body/Andy Peach (LCR-Krauser); **8** Clive Stirrat/Tony Strevens (LCR); **9** Eddy Wright/Peter Hill (LCR-Krauser); **10** Cookson/Hibberd (LCR); **11** Kieron Kavanagh/Tony Darby (LCR-Krauser); **12** Geoff Thomas/Ian Gaunt (LCR-JPX); **13** Eric Cornes/Graham Wellington (Ireson); **14** David Lee/Richard Lee (Windle-ADM).
Fastest lap: Webster, 1m 39.34s, 100.34 mph/161.49 km/h.
Championship points: **1** S. Webster, 75; **2** Knight, 63; **3** B. Brindley and D. Brindley, 60; **5** Gray, 53; **6** Fisher, 38.

BRANDS HATCH GRAND PRIX CIRCUIT, 20 September. 2.6002-mile/4.185-km circuit. Motor Cycle News Supercup/ACU British Championship, round 6
125 cc Supercup (12 laps, 31.202 miles/50.22 km)
1 Steve Patrickson (Honda), 19m 41.42s, 95.07 mph/153.01 km/h.
2 Fernando Mendes (Honda); **3** Chris Palmer (Honda); **4** Robin Appleyard (Honda); **5** Kevin Mawdsley (Honda); **6** Neil Hodgson (Honda); **7** Jimmy Brown (Honda); **8** Rob Orme (Honda); **9** Stuart Nicholls (Honda); **10** Mark Westmorland (Honda); **11** Barry Stanley (Honda); **12** Patrick Corrigan (Honda); **13** Andy Godber (Honda); **14** Martin Cox (Honda); **15** Mark Bingham (Honda).
Fastest lap: Patrickson, 1m 37.30s, 96.20 mph/154.82 km/h.

250 cc Supercup (12 laps, 31.202 miles/50.22 km)
1 Alan Carter (Honda), 18m 38.23s, 100.45 mph/161.66 km/h.
2 Niall Mackenzie (Yamaha); **3** James Haydon (Yamaha); **4** David Heal (Yamaha); **5** Steve Sawford (Yamaha); **6** Woolsey Coulter (Honda); **7** Mark Barker (Yamaha); **8** Iain Challinor (Yamaha); **9** Kevin Mitchell (Yamaha); **10** Mark Whiting (Yamaha); **11** Graeme Mitchell (Aprilia); **12** Darren Mitchell (Yamaha); **13** Adrian Clarke (Yamaha); **14** Adrian Butcher (Yamaha); **15** Paul Booler (Honda).
Fastest lap: Mackenzie, 1m 32.22s, 101.50 mph/163.35 km/h.

Supersport 400 Supercup (12 laps, 31.202 miles/50.22 km)
1 Jim Moodie (Yamaha), 19m 40.73s, 95.13 mph/153.10 km/h.
2 Sean Emmett (Yamaha); **3** Mike Edwards (Honda); **4** Mark Farmer (Yamaha); **5** Colin Gable (Yamaha); **6** Michael Rutter (Ducati); **7** Steve Tomes (Yamaha); **8** Barry Rudd (Suzuki); **9** William Sykes (Kawasaki); **10** Alan Green (Suzuki); **11** Steve Reape (Suzuki); **12** Bob Grant (Yamaha); **13** Phillip McCallen (Honda); **14** Jimmy Brown (Yamaha); **15** Ian Smith (Suzuki).
Fastest lap: Moodie, 1m 37.20s, 96.30 mph/154.98 km/h.

Supersport 600 Supercup (12 laps, 31.202 miles/50.22 km)
1 Phil Borley (Honda), 19m 06.25s, 97.99 mph/157.71 km/h.
2 Mike Edwards (Honda); **3** Sean Emmett (Yamaha); **4** Iain Macpherson (Honda); **5** Phillip McCallen (Honda); **6** Dave Redgate (Honda); **7** Andrew Pallot (Yamaha); **8** Colin Gable (Honda); **9** Steve Tomes (Honda); **10** Paul Mackley (Honda); **11** Steve Marks (Honda); **12** Steven Cunningham (Honda); **13** Mark Hill (Yamaha); **14** Jim McAuley (Yamaha); **15** Mark Coleing (Honda).
Fastest lap: Borley, 1m 34.88s, 98.65 mph/158.77 km/h.

750 cc Supercup (2 x 15 laps, 39.003 miles/62.775 km)
Leg 1
1 John Reynolds (Kawasaki), 22m 39.67s, 103.26 mph/166.19 km/h.
2 Mark Farmer (Yamaha); **3** Rob McElnea (Yamaha); **4** Robert Dunlop (Norton); **5** James Whitham (Suzuki); **6** Ray Stringer (Kawasaki); **7** Sean Emmett (Yamaha); **8** Matt Llewellyn (Yamaha); **9** Alex Buckingham (Yamaha); **10** Steve Ives (Honda); **11** Robin Milton (Kawasaki); **12** Colin Gable (Yamaha); **13** Brett Sampson (Kawasaki); **14** John Barton (Kawasaki); **15** Richard Defago (Honda).
Fastest lap: Reynolds, 1m 29.77s, 104.27 mph/167.81 km/h.
Leg 2
1 John Reynolds (Kawasaki), 22m 45.19s, 102.85 mph/165.52 km/h.
2 Robert Dunlop (Norton); **3** Rob McElnea (Yamaha); **4** Mark Farmer (Yamaha); **5** Sean Emmett (Yamaha); **6** Ray Stringer (Kawasaki); **7** Matt Llewellyn (Yamaha); **8** Michael Rutter (Ducati); **9** David Jefferies (Yamaha); **10** Steve Ives (Honda); **11** Alex Buckingham (Yamaha); **12** Robin Milton (Kawasaki); **13** Richard Defago (Honda); **14** Brett Sampson (Kawasaki); **15** Andy Ward (Kawasaki).
Fastest lap: Reynolds, 1m 30.07s, 103.92 mph/167.25 km/h.

Open Sidecars Supercup (12 laps, 31.202 miles/50.22 km)
1 Steve Webster/Gavin Simmons (ADM), 18m 43.96s, 99.94 mph/160.83 km/h.
2 Derek Brindley/Paul Hutchinson (Yamaha); **3** Barry Brindley/Scott Whiteside (Yamaha); **4** Brian Gray/Steve Pointer (ADM); **5** Steve Abbott/Shaun Smith (Yamaha); **6** Roger Body/Andy Peach (LCR-Krauser); **7** Clive Stirrat/Tony Strevens (LCR-JPX); **8** Mark Reddington/Simon Prior (Krauser); **9** Kieron Kavanagh/Jones (LCR-Krauser); **10** Perry Francis/Tony Darby (LCR); **11** Peter Tubby/Steve Goodey (Suzuki); **12** Colin Nicholson/Eddie Mills (RCN); **13** Barry Fleury/Jane Fleury (LCR-JPX); **14** Brian Reeves/Tim Reeves (LCR); **15** Geoff Thomas/Guy Scott (LCR-JPX).
Fastest lap: Webster, 1m 31.76s, 102.01 mph/164.17 km/h.

Final Championship points (125 cc)

1	Neil Hodgson	75
2	Mick Lofthouse	59
3	Jimmy Brown	56
4	Barry Stanley	55
5	Chris Palmer	51
6	Stuart Nicholls	49

7 Fernando Mendes, 47; **8** Jamie Robinson, 42; **9** Kevin Mawdsley, 37; **10** Rob Orme, 34; **11** Ian Lougher, 25; **12** Andy Hatton and Phelim Owens, 24; **14** Greig Ramsey, 22; **15** Steve Patrickson, 20.

Final Championship points (250 cc)

1	Steve Sawford	68
2	Nigel Bosworth	67
3	Alan Carter	65
4=	Paul Brown	60
4=	David Heal	60
6	Ian Newton	49

7 Mark Barker, 46; **8** James Haydon, 43; **9** Woolsey Coulter, 42; **10** Adrian Butcher, 38; **11** Adrian Clarke, 37; **12** Jeremy McWilliams, 22; **13** Ian McConnachie, 21; **14** Graeme Mitchell, 20; **15** Niall Mackenzie, 17.

Final Championship points (Supersport 400)

1	Mike Edwards	89
2	Mark Farmer	86
3	Sean Emmett	53
4	Jim Moodie	49
5	Ian Simpson	46
6	Steve Tomes	44

7 Colin Gable and Steve Reape, 40; **9** Howard Selby, 35; **10** Barry Rudd, 33; **11** Francis Williamson, 28; **12** Jason Vincent, 23; **13** Iain Duffus and Frank Swain, 19; **15** Steve Ives, 17.

Final Championship points (Supersport 600)

1	Phil Borley	94
2	Sean Emmett	66
3	Jim Moodie	65
4	Mike Edwards	64
5	Ian Simpson	57
6	Colin Gable	50

7 Steve Tomes, 42; **8** Dave Martin, 33; **9** Phillip McCallen, Dave Redgate and Howard Selby, 31; **12** Andrew Pallot, 30; **13** Iain Duffus, 24; **14** Mark Farmer, 23; **15** Howard Whitby, 20.

Final Championship points (750 cc)

1	John Reynolds	180
2=	Robert Dunlop	148
2=	Rob McElnea	148
4	Terry Rymer	147
5	Brian Morrison	144
6	James Whitham	114

7 David Jefferies, 82; **8** Mark Farmer, 75; **9** Alex Buckingham, 66; **10** Sean Emmett, 65; **11** Michael Rutter, 54; **12** Andy Ward, 31; **13** Trevor Nation, 28; **14** Matt Llewellyn, 23; **15** Roger Bennett and Graham Ward, 21.

Final Championship points (Open Sidecars)

1	Steve Webster	95
2	Derek Brindley	77
3	Barry Brindley	75
4	Brian Gray	66
5	Gary Knight	63
6=	Roger Body	38
6=	Robert Fisher	38

8 Kevin Webster, 31; **9** Steve Abbott, 28; **10** Eddy Wright, 26; **11** Mark Reddington, 23; **12** Darren Dixon, Kieron Kavanagh and Peter Tubby, 20; **15** Clive Stirrat, 18.